Atkinson & Hilgard's Introduction to Psychology

Psych 2 Dr. Veronica Benet-Martinez

14th Edition

Edward E. Smith
University of Michigan

Susan Nolen-Hoeksema
University of Michigan

Barbara L. Fredrickson
University of Michigan

Geoffrey R. Loftus
University of Washington

Daryl J. Bern, Contributor
Cornell University

Stephen Maren, Contributor
University of Michigan

THOMSON

* TM

WADSWORTH

Australia · Canada · Mexico · Singapore · Spain · United Kingdom · United States

Atkinson & Hilgard's Introduction to Psychology
Smith/Nolen-Hoeksema/ Fredrickson/ Loftus

Executive Editors:
Michele Baird, Maureen Staudt &
Michael Stranz

Project Development Manager:
Linda de Stefano

Marketing Coordinators:
Lindsay Annett and Sara Mercurio

Production/Manufacturing Supervisor:
Donna M. Brown

Pre-Media Services Supervisor:
Dan Plofchan

Rights and Permissions Specialists:
Kalina Hintz and Bahman Naraghi

Cover Image
Getty Images*

The Adaptable Courseware Program consists of products and additions to existing Thomson products that are produced from camera-ready copy. Peer review, class testing, and accuracy are primarily the responsibility of the author(s).

Atkinson & Hilgard's Introduction to Psychology / Smith/Nolen-Hoeksema/ Fredrickson/ Loftus – 14th Edition
ISBN 0-495-19916-8

International Divisions List

Asia (Including India):
Thomson Learning
(a division of Thomson Asia Pte Ltd)
5 Shenton Way #01-01
UIC Building
Singapore 068808
Tel: (65) 6410-1200
Fax: (65) 6410-1208

Australia/New Zealand:
Thomson Learning Australia
102 Dodds Street
Southbank, Victoria 3006
Australia

Latin America:
Thomson Learning
Seneca 53
Colonia Polano
11560 Mexico, D.F., Mexico
Tel (525) 281-2906
Fax (525) 281-2656

Canada:
Thomson Nelson
1120 Birchmount Road
Toronto, Ontario
Canada M1K 5G4
Tel (416) 752-9100
Fax (416) 752-8102

UK/Europe/Middle East/Africa:
Thomson Learning
High Holborn House
50-51 Bedford Row
London, WC1R 4L$
United Kingdom
Tel 44 (020) 7067-2500
Fax 44 (020) 7067-2600

Spain (Includes Portugal):
Thomson Paraninfo
Calle Magallanes 25
28015 Madrid
España
Tel 34 (0)91 446-3350
Fax 34 (0)91 445-6218

Contents

Artville/Getty Images

THE NATURE OF PSYCHOLOGY

1

Reading opens the door to education and advancement. What's the best way to encourage kids to read? One national chain of pizza restaurants believes it has the answer: Reward kids for reading. Kids' teachers set monthly reading goals—in terms of books or pages read—and give them Pizza Award Certificates when they reach the goals. The kid who brings a certificate to a local participating restaurant gets a free pizza. Parents and teachers say the program works—it gets their kids to read more. Through this program, for nearly 20 years kids have been earning pizza for reading across the United States. Perhaps you or one of your siblings got a free meal this way.

But is this program PC? Is it "psychologically correct"? Let's see what the research says. You might already be aware of one of the fundamental tenets of learning theory: When a reward follows a behavior, that behavior is strength-ened. In Chapter 7 you'll see that this powerful influence of rewards is termed the **law of effect.**[1] When kids are rewarded with pizzas for reading, they read more. Seems like a great success, right?

Consider other outcomes—like how kids feel about reading and whether they continue to read once the pizza program ends. Dozens of psychology experiments, many conducted in school classrooms, have addressed these questions. In one classic experiment (Greene, Sternberg, & Lepper, 1976),[2] psychologists had teachers introduce several new math games to their students and then for 2 weeks simply observe how much time kids spent playing them. In the 3rd week, kids in some classrooms were rewarded for playing these same math games, and kids in other classrooms were not. As expected, the rewards increased the amount of time kids played the math games; the law of effect held. But what happened several weeks later, when the rewards were discontinued? The kids who had received rewards suddenly lost interest in the math games and spent hardly any time on them. By contrast, those who were never rewarded continued to play the math games regularly.

This experiment demonstrates how rewards sometimes backfire and undermine kids' intrinsic interest in activities like reading and math. When people see that their behavior is caused by some external, situational factor—like a free pizza—they discount any internal, personal factors—like their own enjoyment of the activity. So when kids ask themselves why they read, they'll say it's for the pizza. And when there's no more pizza to be had, they'll see no particular reason to read. Even though they enjoyed reading, the rewards loomed larger. This undermining influence of rewards is the **overjustification effect**—going overboard and explaining one's own behavior with too much emphasis on salient situational causes and not enough emphasis on personal causes.

---

[1]Throughout this book you will find core concepts printed in **bold type** and their definitions provided nearby in blue type. A list of these core concepts is also provided at the end of each chapter as a study aid.

[2]Throughout this book you will also find references, cited by author and date, that document or expand the statements made here. Detailed publishing information on these studies appears in the reference list at the end of the book.

© Laura Dwight

Getting kids to read for external reasons—like for free pizzas—can lead them to discount the contribution of any internal reasons for reading—like their own interest. This overjustification effect explains why rewarding desired behaviors sometimes backfires.

You might be thinking that grades in college are also rewards for learning. Do they backfire in the same way as receiving pizza for reading? Not exactly. One important difference is that the grade you get in a college course depends on how well you perform. Research has shown that performance-contingent rewards are less likely to undermine interest—and at times can even increase interest—because they tell you that you are good at an activity (Tang & Hall, 1995). Even so, a focus on grades can sometimes overshadow the sheer interest you might have in a subject. It's useful to remind yourself that two reasons to study course work can exist side by side: to get a good grade and to enjoy the material. It can be "both-and," not "either-or."

Luckily, most students find psychology fascinating. We do, too, and we do our best to convey this fascination to you in the pages of this book. Psychology interests people because it asks questions that touch virtually every aspect of our lives: How does the way your parents raised you affect the way you'll raise your own children? What is the best treatment for drug dependency? Can a man care for an infant as capably as a woman can? Can you remember a traumatic experience in more detail under hypnosis? How should a nuclear power plant be designed to minimize human error? What effects does prolonged stress have on the immune system? Is psy-

chotherapy more effective than drugs in treating depression? Psychologists are conducting research to find answers to these and many other questions.

Psychology also affects our lives through its influence on laws and public policy. Psychological theories and research have influenced laws dealing with discrimination, capital punishment, courtroom practices, pornography, sexual behavior, and personal responsibility for actions. For example, so-called lie-detector tests are not admissible evidence in U.S. courts because psychological research has shown them to be unacceptably inaccurate.

Because psychology affects so many aspects of our lives, even people who do not intend to specialize in it need to know something about this dynamic field. An introductory course in psychology should give you a better understanding of why people think, feel, and act as they do, as well as insights into your own attitudes and reactions.

This course will also help you evaluate the many claims made in the name of psychology. Everyone has seen newspaper headlines like these:

- New Form of Psychotherapy Facilitates Recovery of Repressed Memories
- Anxiety Controlled by Self-Regulation of Brain Waves
- Proof of Mental Telepathy Found
- Babies Learn Speech Sounds While Snoozing
- Emotional Stability Closely Related to Family Size
- Sweet Drink May Boost Exam Performance
- Transcendental Meditation Extends Life Expectancy
- Appearance Concerns Take Mental Toll

How can we decide whether to believe these claims? You need to know two things to evaluate the validity of psychological claims. First, you need to know what psychological facts are already firmly established. If the new claim is not compatible with those facts, you should be cautious. Second, you need to have the knowledge to determine whether the arguments that support the new claim meet the standards of scientific evidence. If they do not, again you have reason for skepticism. This book aims to meet both needs. First, it reviews the current state of knowledge in psychology. It presents the most important findings in the field so that you know the established facts. Second, it examines the nature of research—how a psychologist designs a research program that can provide strong evidence for or against a hypothesis—so that you know the kind of evidence needed to back up a new claim.

In this chapter, we begin by considering the kinds of topics that are studied in psychology. After a brief review of psychology's historical origins, we discuss the perspectives that psychologists adopt in investigating these topics. Then we describe the research methods of psychological investigation, including the ethical guidelines that have been proposed for such research.

THE SCOPE OF PSYCHOLOGY

Psychology can be defined as the scientific study of behavior and mental processes. An astonishing variety of topics fit this definition, as can be seen in the brief examples presented next. (All of these topics are discussed in more detail at various points in this book.)

BRAIN DAMAGE AND FACE RECOGNITION It is no surprise that when people suffer brain damage, their behavior is affected. What is surprising is that damage in a specific part of the brain may change a person's behavior in one way but not in any other ways. In some cases, for example, people are unable to recognize familiar faces as a result of damage to a particular region on the right side of the brain—yet they can do just about everything else normally, a condition called **prosopagnosia**. A famous example of this condition was described by neurologist Oliver Sacks (1985) in his book *The Man Who Mistook His Wife for a Hat*. In another case, a man with prosopagnosia complained to a waiter that someone was staring at him, only to be informed that he was looking in a mirror! Such cases tell us a lot about the way the normal brain works. They indicate that some psychological functions—like face recognition—are localized in particular parts of the brain.

ATTRIBUTING TRAITS TO PEOPLE Suppose that in a crowded department store a person soliciting for a charity approaches a customer and implores her to make a contribution. The woman writes a $50 check to the charity. Would you think the woman was generous, or would you think she had been pressured into making the donation because so many people were watching her? Experiments designed to study situations like this have shown that most people consider the woman generous, even though the situational pressures were so great that just about everybody would behave similarly. When explaining the behavior of others, people tend to overestimate the causal effect of personality traits and underestimate those of situational factors—a mistake social psychologists call the **fundamental attribution error** (see Figure 1-1). If we contrast the fundamental attribution error with the overjustification effect (discussed in the context of earning pizzas for reading), we begin to see some important distinctions between how we judge others and how we judge ourselves. When making sense of our own behavior, we often overestimate—not underestimate—situational causes.

CHILDHOOD AMNESIA Most adults can recall events from their early years, but only back to a certain point. Almost no one can accurately recall events from the first 3 years of life, a phenomenon called **childhood amnesia**.

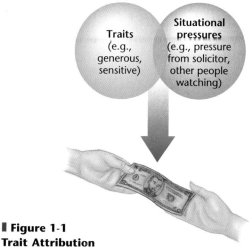

Figure 1-1
Trait Attribution
In deciding whether another person's substantial donation to charity is caused by the giver's traits or by the situation, we are biased toward believing that a trait was the critical factor. This illustrates the fundamental attribution error.

Consider a significant event like the birth of a sibling. If the birth occurred after you were 3 years old, you may have some memory of it. But if the birth occurred before age 3, you probably remember very little about it, if anything at all (see Figure 1-2). Childhood amnesia is partic-

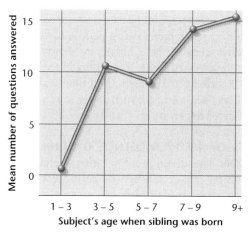

Figure 1-2
Recall of an Early Memory
In an experiment on childhood amnesia, college-age participants were asked 20 questions about the events surrounding the birth of a younger sibling. The average number of questions answered is plotted as a function of the participant's age when the sibling was born. If the birth occurred before the participant's 4th year of life, no participant could recall a thing about it; if the birth occurred after that, recall increased with the participant's age at the time of the event. (K. Sheingold and Y. J. Tenney (1982) "Recall of An Early Memory adapted from "Memory for a Salient Childhood Event" from U. Neisser (ed.) *Memory Observed: Remembering in Natural Context*, copyright © 1982 by W. H. Freeman & Company. Adapted by permission of the publisher.)

Psychologists are interested in what causes people to eat too much. Among the possible causes they have studied are genetic factors and environmental influences, such as a tendency to overeat in the presence of certain stimuli.

ularly striking because our first 3 years are so rich in experience: We develop from helpless newborns to crawling, babbling infants to walking, talking children. But these remarkable transitions leave few traces in our memories.

OBESITY More than a quarter of U.S. adults are **obese;** their weight is 30% or more above the level that would be appropriate for their body structure and height. Obesity is dangerous. It increases vulnerability to diabetes, high blood pressure, and heart disease. Psychologists are interested in what factors lead people to eat too much. One factor seems to be a history of deprivation. If rats are first deprived of food, then allowed to eat until they return to their normal weight, and finally allowed to eat as much as they want, they eat more than rats that have no history of deprivation.

EFFECTS OF MEDIA VIOLENCE ON CHILDREN'S AGGRESSION The question of whether watching violence on television causes children to be more aggressive has long been controversial. Although many observers believe that televised violence affects children's behavior, others suggest that watching violence has a **cathartic effect.** It may actually reduce aggression by allowing children to express it vicariously and "get it out of their system." But research evidence does not support the cathartic effect view. In one experiment, one group of children watched violent cartoons while another group watched nonviolent cartoons for the same amount of time. Children who watched violent cartoons became more aggressive in their interactions with peers, but the children who viewed nonviolent cartoons showed no change in aggressive behavior. These effects can persist over time: The more violent programs a boy watches at age 9, the more aggressive he is likely to be at age 19 (see Figure 1-3).

Psychological studies provide evidence that violent television programming may have harmful effects on young viewers.

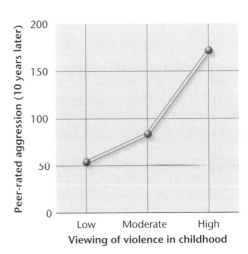

▌Figure 1-3
The Relationship Between Childhood Viewing of Violent Television and Adult Aggression
A classic study shows that preference for viewing violent TV programs by boys at age 9 is related to aggressive behavior as rated by peers at age 19. (L. Eron, et al. (1972) "Does Television Violence Cause Aggression?" *American Psychologist, 27*:253-262. Copyright © 1972 by The American Psychological Association. Adapted by permission.)

- Psychology touches on many aspects of our lives and influences laws and public policy.
- To evaluate new claims made about psychology, you need to know (1) what psychological facts are already firmly established and (2) the standards for scientific evidence.
- Psychology is the scientific study of behavior and mental processes.
- The scope of psychology is broad, covering topics such as face recognition, social judgments, memory, obesity, violence, and many more.

◆ **Critical Thinking Questions**

1. Review the newspaper headlines about psychology printed on page 2. Find an article in the newspaper or on the Internet that covers psychological findings. Do you believe what the news account claims? Why or why not?

2. How do you know when to trust a news article? What more would you need to know to accept as fact the psychological claim you located?

The ancient Greek philosopher Socrates posed fundamental questions about mental life. Many of these questions are as important today as they were in Socrates' time.

THE HISTORICAL ORIGINS OF PSYCHOLOGY

The roots of psychology can be traced to the great philosophers of ancient Greece. The most famous of them, Socrates, Plato, and Aristotle, posed fundamental questions about mental life: What is consciousness? Are people inherently rational or irrational? Is there really such a thing as free choice? These questions, and many similar ones, are as important today as they were thousands of years ago. They deal with the nature of the mind and mental processes, which are the key elements of the cognitive perspective in psychology.

Other psychological questions deal with the nature of the body and human behavior, and they have an equally long history. Hippocrates, often called the "father of medicine," lived around the same time as Socrates. He was deeply interested in **physiology,** the study of the functions of the living organism and its parts. He made many important observations about how the brain controls various organs of the body. These observations set the stage for what became the biological perspective in psychology.

NATURE–NURTURE DEBATE

One of the earliest debates about human psychology is still raging today. This **nature-nurture debate** centers on the question of whether human capabilities are inborn or acquired through experience. The **nature view** holds that human beings enter the world with an inborn store of knowledge and understanding of reality. Early philosophers believed that this knowledge and understanding could be accessed through careful reasoning and introspection. In the 17th century, Descartes supported the nature view by arguing that some ideas (such as God, the self, geometric axioms, perfection, and infinity) are innate. Descartes is also notable for his conception of the body as a machine that can be studied much as other machines are studied. This is the root of modern information-processing perspectives on the mind, discussed later in this chapter.

The **nurture view** holds that knowledge is acquired through experiences and interactions with the world. Although some of the early Greek philosophers had this opinion, it is most strongly associated with the 17th-century English philosopher John Locke. According to Locke, at birth the human mind is a **tabula rasa,** a blank slate on which experience "writes" knowledge and understanding as the individual matures. This perspective gave birth to **associationist psychology.** Associationists denied that there were inborn ideas or capabilities. Instead, they argued that the mind is filled with ideas that enter by way of the senses and then become associated through principles such as similarity and contrast. Current research on memory and learning is related to early association theory.

The classic nature-nurture debate has become much more nuanced in recent decades. Although some psychologists still argue that human thought and behavior result primarily from biology or primarily from experience, most psychologists take a more integrated approach. They acknowledge that biological processes (such as heredity or processes in the brain) affect thoughts, feelings, and behavior, but say that experience leaves its mark, too. So the current question is not whether nature *or* nurture shapes human psychology but rather how nature *and* nurture combine to do so. The nature-nurture issue comes up at numerous points in later chapters.

THE BEGINNINGS OF SCIENTIFIC PSYCHOLOGY

Although philosophers and scholars continued to be interested in the functioning of both the mind and the body through the centuries, scientific psychology is usually considered to have begun in the late 19th century, when Wilhelm Wundt established the first psychological laboratory at the University of Leipzig in Germany in 1879. The impetus for the establishment of Wundt's lab was the belief that mind and behavior, like planets or chemicals or human organs, could be the subject of scientific analysis. Wundt's own research was concerned primarily with the senses, especially vision, but he and his coworkers also studied attention, emotion, and memory.

Wundt relied on introspection to study mental processes. **Introspection refers to observing and recording the nature of one's own perceptions, thoughts, and feelings.** Examples of introspections include people's reports of how heavy they perceive an object to be and how bright a flash of light seems to be. The introspective method was inherited from philosophy, but Wundt added a new dimension to the concept. Pure self-observation was not sufficient; it had to be supplemented by experiments. Wundt's experiments systematically varied some physical dimension of a stimulus, such as its intensity, and used the introspective method to determine how these physical changes modified the participant's conscious experience of the stimulus.

The reliance on introspection, particularly for very rapid mental events, proved unworkable. Even after extensive training, different people produced very different introspections about simple sensory experiences, and

Wilhelm Wundt established the first psychological laboratory at the University of Leipzig. Here he is shown (third from left) in the laboratory with his associates.

few conclusions could be drawn from these differences. As a result, introspection is not a central part of the current cognitive perspective. And, as we will see, some psychologists' reactions to introspection played a role in the development of other modern perspectives.

STRUCTURALISM AND FUNCTIONALISM

During the 19th century, chemistry and physics made great advances by analyzing complex compounds (molecules) into their elements (atoms). These successes encouraged psychologists to look for the mental elements that combined to create more complex experiences. Just as chemists analyzed water into hydrogen and oxygen, perhaps psychologists could analyze the taste of lemonade (perception) into elements such as sweet, bitter, and cold (sensations). The leading proponent of this approach in the United States was E. B. Titchener, a Cornell University psychologist who had been trained by Wundt. Titchener introduced the term **structuralism—the analysis of mental structures—**to describe this branch of psychology.

But some psychologists opposed the purely analytic nature of structuralism. William James, a distinguished psychologist at Harvard University, felt that analyzing the elements of consciousness was less important than understanding its fluid, personal nature. His approach was named **functionalism, studying how the mind works to enable an organism to adapt to and function in its environment.**

Nineteenth-century psychologists' interest in adaptation stemmed from the publication of Charles Darwin's theory of evolution. Some argued that consciousness had evolved only because it served some purpose in guiding the individual's activities. To find out how an organism adapts to its environment, functionalists said that psychologists must observe actual behavior. However, both structuralists and functionalists still regarded psychology as the science of conscious experience.

BEHAVIORISM

Structuralism and functionalism played important roles in the early development of 20th-century psychology. Because each viewpoint provided a systematic approach to the field, they were considered competing schools of psychology. By 1920, however, both were being displaced by three newer schools: behaviorism, Gestalt psychology, and psychoanalysis.

Of the three, behaviorism had the greatest influence on scientific psychology in North America. Its founder, John B. Watson, reacted against the view that conscious experience was the province of psychology. Watson made no assertions about consciousness when he studied the behavior of animals and infants. He decided not only that animal psychology and child psychology could stand on their own as sciences but also that they set a pattern that adult psychology might follow.

For psychology to be a science, Watson believed, psychological data must be open to public inspection like the data of any other science. Behavior is public;

consciousness is private. Science should deal only with public facts. Because psychologists were growing impatient with introspection, the new behaviorism caught on rapidly, and many younger psychologists in the United States called themselves "behaviorists." (The Russian physiologist Ivan Pavlov's research on the conditioned response was regarded as an important area of behavioral research, but it was Watson who was responsible for behaviorism's widespread influence.)

Watson, and others ascribing to **behaviorism,** argued that nearly all behavior is a result of conditioning and the environment shapes behavior by reinforcing specific habits. For example, giving children cookies to stop them from whining reinforces (rewards) the habit of whining. The conditioned response was viewed as the smallest unit of behavior, from which more complicated behaviors could be created. All types of complex behavior patterns coming from special training or education were regarded as nothing more than an interlinked fabric of conditioned responses.

Behaviorists tended to discuss psychological phenomena in terms of stimuli and responses, giving rise to the term *stimulus-response (S-R) psychology*. Note, however, that S-R psychology itself is not a theory or perspective but a set of terms that can be used to communicate psychological information. S-R terminology is still sometimes used in psychology today.

William James, John B. Watson, and Sigmund Freud were key figures in the early history of psychology. James developed the approach known as functionalism, Watson was the founder of behaviorism, and Freud originated the theory and method of psychoanalysis.

❚ Figure 1-4
A Gestalt Image
When we look at the three angles of an equilateral triangle, we see a single large triangle rather than three small angles.

GESTALT PSYCHOLOGY

About 1912, at the same time that behaviorism was catching on in the United States, Gestalt psychology was appearing in Germany. **Gestalt** is a German word meaning "form" or "configuration," which referred to the approach taken by Max Wertheimer and his colleagues Kurt Koffka and Wolfgang Köhler, all of whom eventually emigrated to the United States.

The Gestalt psychologists' primary interest was perception, and they believed that perceptual experiences depend on the patterns formed by stimuli and on the organization of experience. What we actually see is related to the background against which an object appears, as well as to other aspects of the overall pattern of stimulation (see Chapter 5). The whole is different from the sum of its parts, because the whole depends on the relationships among the parts. For example, when we look at Figure 1-4, we see it as a single large triangle—as a single form or Gestalt—rather than as three small angles.

Among the key interests of Gestalt psychologists were the perception of motion, how people judge size, and the appearance of colors under changes in illumination. These interests led them to a number of perception-centered interpretations of learning, memory, and problem solving that helped lay the groundwork for current research in cognitive psychology.

The Gestalt psychologists also influenced key founders of modern social psychology—including Kurt Lewin, Solomon Asch, and Fritz Heider—who expanded on Gestalt principles to understand interpersonal phenomena (Jones, 1998). For instance, Asch (1946) extended the Gestalt notion that people see wholes rather than isolated parts from the simple case of object perception to the more complex case of person perception

(Taylor, 1998). Plus, they saw the process of imposing meaning and structure on incoming stimuli as automatic and outside conscious awareness, a Gestalt view that continues to infuse contemporary research on social cognition to this day (see Chapter 18; Moskowitz, Skurnik, & Galinsky, 1999).

PSYCHOANALYSIS

Psychoanalysis is both a theory of personality and a method of psychotherapy originated by Sigmund Freud around the turn of the 20th century.

At the center of Freud's theory is the concept of the **unconscious**—the thoughts, attitudes, impulses, wishes, motivations, and emotions of which we are unaware. Freud believed that childhood's unacceptable (forbidden or punished) wishes are driven out of conscious awareness and become part of the unconscious, where they continue to influence our thoughts, feelings, and actions. Unconscious thoughts are expressed in dreams, slips of the tongue, and physical mannerisms. During therapy with patients, Freud used the method of **free association,** in which the patient was instructed to say whatever comes to mind as a way of bringing unconscious wishes into awareness. The analysis of dreams served the same purpose.

In classical Freudian theory, the motivations behind unconscious wishes almost always involved sex or aggression. For this reason, Freud's theory was not widely accepted when it was first proposed. Contemporary psychologists do not accept Freud's theory in its entirety, but they tend to agree that people's ideas, goals, and motives can at times operate outside conscious awareness.

LATER DEVELOPMENTS IN 20TH-CENTURY PSYCHOLOGY

Despite the important contributions of Gestalt psychology and psychoanalysis, until World War II psychology was dominated by behaviorism, particularly in the United States. After the war, interest in psychology increased. Sophisticated instruments and electronic equipment became available, and a wider range of problems could be examined. It became evident that earlier theoretical approaches were too restrictive.

This viewpoint was strengthened by the development of computers in the 1950s. Computers were able to perform tasks—such as playing chess and proving mathematical theorems—that previously could be done only by human beings. They offered psychologists a powerful tool for theorizing about psychological processes. In a series of papers published in the late 1950s, Herbert Simon (who was later awarded a Nobel prize) and his colleagues described how psychological phenomena could be simulated with a computer. Many psychological issues were recast in terms of **information-processing models,** which viewed human beings as processors of information and provided a more dynamic approach to psychology than behaviorism. Similarly, the information-processing approach made it possible to formulate some of the ideas of Gestalt psychology and psychoanalysis more precisely. Earlier ideas about the nature of the mind could be expressed in concrete terms and checked against actual data. For example, we can think of the operation of memory as analogous to the way a computer stores and retrieves information. Just as a computer can transfer information from temporary storage in its internal memory chips (RAM) to more permanent storage on the hard drive, so, too, our working memory can act as a way station to long-term memory (Atkinson & Shiffrin, 1971a; Raaijmakers & Shiffrin, 1992).

Another important influence on psychology in the 1950s was the development of modern linguistics. Linguists began to theorize about the mental structures required to comprehend and speak a language. A pioneer in this area was Noam Chomsky, whose book *Syntactic Structures,* published in 1957, stimulated the first significant psychological analyses of language and the emergence of the field of psycholinguistics.

At the same time, important advances were occurring in neuropsychology. Discoveries about the brain and nervous system revealed clear relationships between neurological events and mental processes. In recent decades, advances in biomedical technology have enabled rapid progress in research on these relationships. In 1981 Roger Sperry was awarded a Nobel prize for demonstrating the links between specific regions of the brain and particular thought and behavioral processes, which we discuss in Chapter 2.

The development of information-processing models, psycholinguistics, and neuropsychology has produced an approach to psychology that is highly cognitive in orientation. Although its principal concern is the scientific analysis of mental processes and structures, cognitive psychology is not exclusively concerned with thought and knowledge. As illustrated throughout this book, this approach has been expanded to many other areas of psychology, including perception, motivation, emotion, clinical psychology, personality, and social psychology.

In sum, during the 20th century the focus of psychology came full circle. After rejecting conscious experience as ill-suited to scientific investigation and turning to the study of overt, observable behavior, psychologists are once again theorizing about covert aspects of the mind, this time with new and more powerful tools.

◆ Interim Summary

- The roots of psychology can be traced to the 4th and 5th centuries B.C. One of the earliest debates about human psychology focused on the question of whether human capabilities are inborn or acquired through experience (the nature-nurture debate).

- Scientific psychology was born in the late 19th century with the idea that mind and behavior could be the subject of scientific analysis. The first experimental laboratory in psychology was established by Wilhelm Wundt at the University of Leipzig in 1879.

- Among the early "schools" of psychology in the 20th century were structuralism, functionalism, behaviorism, Gestalt psychology, and psychoanalysis.

- Later developments in 20th-century psychology included information-processing theory, psycholinguistics, and neuropsychology.

◆ Critical Thinking Questions

1. What assumptions about human nature underlie the various historical approaches to psychology?

2. Considering these underlying assumptions, which of the historical approaches are compatible with one another? Which are incompatible?

CONTEMPORARY PSYCHOLOGICAL PERSPECTIVES

What is a **psychological perspective**? Basically, it is an approach, a way of looking at topics within psychology. Any topic in psychology can be approached from different perspectives. Indeed, this is true of any action a person takes. Suppose that, following an insult, you punch someone in the face. From a biological perspective, we can describe this act as involving certain brain areas and as the firing of nerves that activate the muscles that move your arm. From a behavioral perspective, we can describe the act without reference to anything within your body; rather, the insult is a stimulus to which you respond by punching, a learned response that has been rewarded in the past. A cognitive perspective on this action would focus on the mental processes involved in producing the behavior, and we might explain your punch in terms of your goals and plans: Your goal is to defend your honor, and aggressive

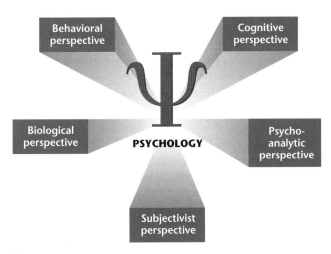

▌ Figure 1-5
Perspectives in Psychology

The analysis of psychological phenomena can be approached from several perspectives. Each offers a somewhat different account of why individuals act as they do, and each can make a contribution to our conception of the total person. The Greek letter *psi* (*ψ*) is sometimes used as an abbreviation for *psychology*.

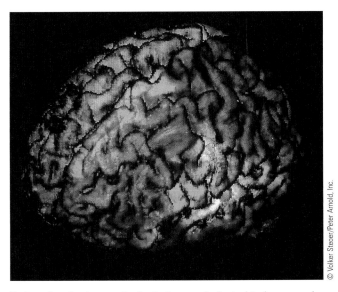

By imaging the human brain during psychological tasks, researchers learn which brain structures underlie the targeted phenomena. Here we see a 3-dimensional representation of the human brain while listening to speech obtained through functional MRI (magnetic resonance imaging). Red indicates the greatest areas of activation, whereas yellow indicates areas of moderate activation. The neural activity is located in Wernicke's area of the brain. This approach illustrates a biological perspective on psychology.

behavior is part of your plan for achieving that goal. From a psychoanalytic perspective, your action could be described as an expression of an unconscious aggressive instinct. And finally, from a subjectivist perspective, your aggressive act can be understood as a reaction to interpreting the person's utterance as a personal insult.

Despite the many possible ways to describe any psychological act, these five perspectives represent the major approaches to the contemporary study of psychology (see Figure 1-5). Because these five perspectives are discussed throughout the book, here we provide only a brief description of some main points for each of them. Keep in mind that these approaches need not be mutually exclusive; rather, they may focus on different aspects of the same complex phenomenon. In fact, understanding many psychological topics requires an **eclectic approach** that spans multiple perspectives.

The Neural Basis of Behavior

THE BIOLOGICAL PERSPECTIVE

The human brain contains well over 10 billion nerve cells and an almost infinite number of interconnections between them. It may be the most complex structure in the universe. In principle, all psychological events can be related to the activity of the brain and nervous system. The biological approach to the study of human beings and other species attempts to relate overt behavior

to electrical and chemical events taking place inside the body. Research from the **biological perspective** seeks to specify the neurobiological processes that underlie behavior and mental processes. The biological approach to depression, for example, tries to understand this disorder in terms of abnormal changes in levels of neurotransmitters, which are chemicals produced in the brain that make communication between nerve cells possible.

We can use one of the problems described earlier to illustrate this perspective. The study of face recognition in patients with brain damage indicates that particular regions of the brain are specialized for face recognition. The human brain is divided into right and left hemispheres, and the regions devoted to face recognition seem to be located mainly in the right hemisphere. There is considerable hemispheric specialization in humans. In most right-handed people, for example, the left hemisphere is specialized for understanding language, and the right hemisphere is specialized for interpreting spatial relations.

The biological perspective has also assisted in the study of memory. It emphasizes the importance of certain brain structures, including the hippocampus, which is involved in consolidating memories. Childhood amnesia may be partly due to an immature hippocampus, a structure that is not fully developed until a year or two after birth. ▌

THE BEHAVIORAL PERSPECTIVE

As described in our brief review of the history of psychology, the **behavioral perspective** focuses on observable stimuli and responses and regards nearly all behavior as a result of conditioning and reinforcement. For example, a behavioral analysis of your social life might focus on which people you interact with (the social stimuli), the kinds of responses you make to them (rewarding, punishing, or neutral), the kinds of responses they in turn make to you (rewarding, punishing, or neutral), and how the responses sustain or disrupt the interaction.

We can use our sample problems to further illustrate this approach. With regard to obesity, some people may overeat (a specific response) only in the presence of specific stimuli (such as watching television), and learning to avoid these stimuli is part of many weight-control programs. With regard to aggression, children are more likely to express aggressive responses, such as hitting another child, when such responses are rewarded (the other child withdraws) than when their responses are punished (the other child counterattacks).

Historically, the strict behavioral approach did not consider the individual's mental processes at all, and even contemporary behaviorists usually do not conjecture about the mental processes that intervene between the stimulus and the response. Nevertheless, psychologists other than strict behaviorists often record what people say about their conscious experiences (a verbal self-report) and draw inferences about their mental activity

from these subjective data. Although few psychologists today would define themselves as strict behaviorists, many modern developments in psychology have evolved from the work of the earlier behaviorists (Skinner, 1981).

THE COGNITIVE PERSPECTIVE

The contemporary cognitive perspective is in part a return to the cognitive roots of psychology and in part a reaction to the narrowness of behaviorism, which tended to neglect complex human activities like reasoning, planning, decision making, and communication. Like the 19th-century version, the contemporary **cognitive perspective** is concerned with mental processes such as perceiving, remembering, reasoning, deciding, and problem solving. Unlike the 19th-century version, however, the contemporary cognitive approach is not based on introspection. Instead, it assumes that (1) only by studying

Events that happen early in childhood usually are not remembered. This little boy probably will not remember the events surrounding the birth of his baby brother. An explanation that illustrates the cognitive perspective on psychology emphasizes the important role that language plays in organizing memories.

If the aggressive child has her way and the other child yields the swing, the aggressive behavior will be rewarded and the child will be more likely to behave aggressively in the future. This exemplifies a behavioral perspective on psychology.

mental processes can we fully understand what organisms do, and (2) we can study mental processes in an objective fashion by focusing on specific behaviors (just as behaviorists do) but interpreting them in terms of underlying mental processes. In making these interpretations, cognitive psychologists have often relied on an analogy between the mind and a computer. Incoming information is processed in various ways: It is selected, compared and combined with other information already in memory, transformed, rearranged, and so on.

Consider the phenomenon of childhood amnesia described at the beginning of the chapter. Perhaps we cannot remember events from the first few years of life because of a major developmental change in the way we organize our experience in memory. Such changes may be particularly pronounced at about age 3, when our language abilities increase immensely, and language offers us a new way of organizing our memories.

THE PSYCHOANALYTIC PERSPECTIVE

Sigmund Freud developed the psychoanalytic conception of human behavior in Europe at about the same time behaviorism was evolving in the United States. In some respects, psychoanalysis was a blend of the 19th-century versions of cognition and physiology. In particular, Freud combined cognitive notions of consciousness, perception, and memory with ideas about biologically based instincts to forge a bold new theory of human behavior.

The basic assumption of the **psychoanalytic perspective** is that behavior stems from unconscious processes, meaning beliefs, fears, and desires that a person is unaware of but that nonetheless influence behavior. Freud believed that many of the impulses that are forbidden or punished by parents and society during childhood are derived from innate instincts. Because each of us is born with these impulses, they exert a pervasive influence that must be dealt with in some manner. Forbidding them merely forces them

Kactus Fotos/SuperStock

In this painting by M. Morales, a dream conveys unconscious desires. This illustrates the psychoanalytic perspective on psychology.

out of awareness into the unconscious. They do not disappear, however. They may manifest themselves as emotional problems and symptoms of mental illness or as socially approved behavior such as artistic and literary activity. For example, if you feel a lot of anger toward your father but you cannot afford to alienate him, your anger may become unconscious, perhaps expressed in a dream about him being hurt in an atrocious accident.

Freud believed that we are driven by the same basic instincts as animals (primarily sex and aggression) and that we are continually struggling against a society that stresses the control of these impulses. The psychoanalytic perspective suggests new ways of looking at some of the problems described at the beginning of the chapter. For example, Freud claimed that aggressive behavior stems from an innate instinct. Although this proposal is not widely accepted in human psychology, it is in agreement with the views of some biologists and psychologists who study aggression in animals.

The Subjectivist Perspective

The **subjectivist perspective** contends that human behavior is a function of the perceived world, not the objective world. Like the cognitive approach, the subjectivist perspective drew from the Gestalt tradition and reacted against the narrowness of behaviorism. Although allied with cognitive psychology, subjectivism has been most pervasive within social and personality psychology. To understand human social behavior, this view holds, we must grasp the person's own "definition of the situation," which is expected to vary by culture, personal history, and current motivational state. This perspective, then, is the most open to cultural and individual differences and to the effects of motivation and emotion.

In one sense, the idea that people actively construct their own subjective realities calls for introspective methods. Even so, subjectivists do not rely exclusively on subjective self-reports because they also assume that people fail to see their subjective realities as personal constructions. This **naïve realism** refers to people's tendency to take their constructed, subjective realities to be faithful renderings of an objective world. Therefore, a subjectivist approach also involves systematic observation of judgments and behaviors. A subjectivist perspective is illustrated by a classic early study that found that people reliably overestimate the physical size of valuable coins, more so than for coins of lower value. This tendency is exaggerated among poor children (Bruner & Goodman, 1947; note that coins in general probably seemed much more valuable in the 1940s!).

Consider again the problem of trait attribution. The study of how people make sense of other people's actions—

Is this woman generous? Westerners have a strong tendency to say, "Yes, she is," making a trait attribution for her behavior. An emphasis on how people perceive and interpret their social world characterizes the subjectivist perspective.

in the example mentioned earlier, donating $50 to charity—emerged from a subjectivist emphasis on how situations are defined by the people in them (Heider, 1958). One contemporary explanation for the pervasive tendency to attribute other people's actions to their personality traits suggests that, because Western cultures have long emphasized personal agency, Westerners often fail to see the influence of situations (Nisbett, Peng, Choi, & Norenzayan, 2001; see Chapter 18). Likewise, a subjectivist view of the link between media violence and aggression suggests that habitual consumption of violent media instills and strengthens aggressive schemas and scripts, which are later used to define subsequent interpersonal encounters (Anderson & Bushman, 2001).

Concept Review Table
Five Perspectives Within Psychology

Biological Perspective	An orientation toward understanding the neurobiological processes that underlie behavior and mental processes.
Behavioral Perspective	An orientation toward understanding observable behavior in terms of conditioning and reinforcement.
Cognitive Perspective	An orientation toward understanding mental processes such as perceiving, remembering, reasoning, deciding, and problem solving and their relationship to behavior.
Psychoanalytic Perspective	An orientation toward understanding behavior in terms of unconscious motives stemming from sexual and aggressive impulses.
Subjectivist Perspective	An orientation toward understanding behavior and mental processes in terms of the subjective realities people actively construct.

The Neural Basis of Behavior

RELATIONSHIPS BETWEEN PSYCHOLOGICAL AND BIOLOGICAL PERSPECTIVES

The behaviorist, cognitive, psychoanalytic, and subjectivist perspectives all rely on concepts that are purely psychological (such as perception, the unconscious, and attributions). Although these perspectives sometimes offer different explanations for the same phenomenon, those explanations are always psychological in nature. The biological perspective is different. In addition to using psychological concepts, it employs concepts (such as neurotransmitters and hormones) drawn from physiology and other branches of biology.

There is a way, though, in which the biological perspective makes direct contact with the psychological perspectives. Biologically oriented researchers attempt to explain psychological concepts and principles in terms of their biological counterparts. For example, researchers might attempt to explain the normal ability to recognize faces solely in terms of neurons and their interconnections in a certain region of the brain. Such attempts are termed **reductionism** because they involve reducing psychological notions to biological ones. Throughout this book, we present examples of successful reductionism—situations in which what was once understood at only the psychological level is now understood at least in part at the biological level.

If reductionism can be successful, why bother with psychological explanations at all? Is psychology just something to do until the biologists figure everything out? The answer is clearly no.

First, psychological findings, concepts, and principles direct biological researchers in their work. Given that the brain contains billions of brain cells and countless interconnections between these cells, biological researchers cannot hope to find something of interest by arbitrarily selecting some brain cells to study. Rather, they must have a way of directing their efforts to relevant groups of brain cells. Psychological findings can supply this direction. For example, psychological research indicates that our ability to discriminate among spoken words and our ability to discriminate among spatial positions obey different principles. So, biological psychologists might look in different regions of the brain for the neural basis of these two kinds of discrimination capacities (the left hemisphere for word discrimination and the right hemisphere for spatial-position discrimination). As another example, if psychological research indicates that learning a motor skill is a slow process that is hard to undo, biological psychologists can direct their attention to brain processes that are relatively slow but permanently alter connections between neurons (Churchland & Sejnowski, 1988).

Second, our biology always acts in concert with our past circumstances and current environment. For example, obesity can be the result of (1) a genetic predisposition to gain weight (a biological factor), (2) learning bad eating habits (a psychological factor), or (3) a reaction to cultural pressures toward extreme thinness (a sociocultural factor). The biologist can seek to understand the first factor, but it is still up to the psychologist to explore and explain the past experiences and current circumstances that influence a person's eating habits.

Nevertheless, the push for reductionism goes on at an ever-increasing rate. For many topics in psychology, we now have both psychological explanations and knowledge about how the relevant psychological concepts are implemented or executed in the brain (for example, what particular parts of the brain are involved and how they are interconnected). This kind of biological knowledge typically falls short of total reductionism, but it is still very important. Memory researchers, for example, have long distinguished between working memory and long-term memory (which are psychological notions), but now they also know something about how these two kinds of memory are actually coded differently in the brain. So, for many of the topics discussed in this book, we review what is known at the biological level as well as at the psychological level.

Indeed, a central theme of this book—and of contemporary psychology in general—is that psychological phenomena can be understood at both the psychological and biological levels. The biological analysis shows us how the psychological notions can be implemented in the brain. Both levels of analysis are clearly needed (although for some topics, including many dealing with social interactions, biological analyses have only just begun).

MAJOR SUBFIELDS OF PSYCHOLOGY

So far, we have gained a general understanding of the nature of psychology by looking at its topics and perspectives. We can further our understanding by looking at what different kinds of psychologists do and at emerging fields of emphasis in 21st-century psychology (see the Cutting Edge Research feature).

About half the people who have advanced degrees in psychology work in colleges and universities. In addition to teaching, they may devote much of their time to research or counseling. Other psychologists work in schools, hospitals or clinics, research institutes, government agencies, or business and industry. Still others are in private practice and offer their services to the public for a fee. We now turn to a brief description of some of the subfields of psychology.

BIOLOGICAL PSYCHOLOGY Biological psychologists (also referred to as physiological psychologists) look for the relationship between biological processes and behavior.

EXPERIMENTAL PSYCHOLOGY Experimental psychologists usually conduct research from a behaviorist or cognitive perspective and use experimental methods to study how people (and other animals) react to sensory stimuli, perceive the world, learn and remember, reason, and respond emotionally.

DEVELOPMENTAL PSYCHOLOGY Developmental psychologists are concerned with human development and the factors that shape behavior from birth to old age. They might study a specific ability, such as how language develops in children, or a particular period of life, such as infancy.

SOCIAL AND PERSONALITY PSYCHOLOGY These two subfields overlap. **Social psychologists** are interested in how people perceive and interpret their social world and how their beliefs, emotions, and behaviors are influenced by the real or imagined presence of others. They are also concerned with the behavior of groups and with social relationships between and among people. **Personality psychologists** study the thoughts, emotions, and behaviors that define an individual's personal style of interacting with the world. Accordingly, they are interested in differences between individuals, and they also attempt to synthesize all the psychological processes into an integrated account of the total person.

CLINICAL AND COUNSELING PSYCHOLOGY Clinical **psychologists** are the largest group of psychologists. They apply psychological principles to the diagnosis and treatment of emotional and behavioral problems, including mental illness, drug addiction, and marital and family conflict. **Counseling psychologists** perform many of the same functions as clinical psychologists, although they often deal with less serious problems. They frequently work with high school or university students.

SCHOOL AND EDUCATIONAL PSYCHOLOGY Because serious emotional problems often make their first appearance in the early grades, many elementary schools employ psychologists whose training combines courses in child development, education, and clinical psychology. These **school psychologists** work with children to evaluate learning and emotional problems. In contrast, **educational psychologists** are specialists in learning and teaching. They may work in schools, but more often they

work in a university's school of education, where they do research on teaching methods and help train teachers.

ORGANIZATIONAL AND ENGINEERING PSYCHOLOGY **Organizational psychologists** (sometimes called *industrial psychologists*) typically work for a company. They are concerned with selecting people who are most suitable for particular jobs or designing structures that facilitate collaboration and teamwork. **Engineering psychologists** (sometimes called human factors engineers) try to improve the relationship between people and machines. For instance, they improve human-machine interaction by designing machines with the most efficient placement of gauges and controls, which leads to better performance, safety, and comfort.

◆ Interim Summary

- The study of psychology can be approached from several perspectives. Five contemporary perspectives are the biological perspective, the behavioral perspective, the cognitive perspective, the psychoanalytic perspective, and the subjectivist perspective.

- The biological perspective differs from the other perspectives in that its principles are partly drawn from biology. Biological researchers often attempt to explain psychological principles in terms of biological ones; this is known as reductionism.

- Among the major subfields of psychology are biological psychology, experimental psychology, developmental psychology, social and personality psychology, clinical and counseling psychology, school and educational psychology, and organizational and engineering psychology.

- Many new areas of inquiry, including cognitive neuroscience (as well as affective neuroscience and social cognitive neuroscience), evolutionary psychology, cultural psychology, and positive psychology, span traditional subfields and disciplines.

◆ Critical Thinking Questions

1. Consider the question, "What are the determinants of an individual's sexual orientation?" How would the different perspectives outlined in this chapter approach this question?

2. Many of the new approaches to 21st-century psychology (described in the Cutting-Edge Research box) integrate divergent perspectives or fill prior gaps in the field. What other new advances might be on the horizon in 21st-century psychology? That is, what other opportunities for integrating perspectives and filling gaps do you predict?

Increasingly, psychologists span multiple subfields in their research and also stretch beyond psychology to forge collaborations with researchers in other disciplines. These cross-area and interdisciplinary approaches have gained considerable momentum at the start of the 21st century and promise to be very important in the next few decades. Of particular interest are cognitive neuroscience, evolutionary psychology, cultural psychology, and positive psychology. Here we briefly describe each of these approaches, with examples of the kinds of research being done in each field.

COGNITIVE NEUROSCIENCE

Cognitive neuroscience focuses on cognitive processes and relies heavily on the methods and findings of neuroscience (the branch of biology that deals with the brain and nervous system). In essence, **cognitive neuroscience** attempts to learn how mental activities are executed in the brain. The key idea is that cognitive psychology provides hypotheses about specific cognitive capacities—such as recognizing faces—and neuroscience supplies proposals about how these specific functions might be executed in the brain.

What is particularly distinctive about cognitive neuroscience is its reliance on new techniques for studying the brains of normal participants (as opposed to brain-damaged ones) while they are performing a cognitive task. These neuroimaging or brain-scanning techniques create visual images of a brain in action, with an indication of which regions of the brain show the most neural activity during a particular task. An example is the study of how people remember information for brief or long periods. When people are asked to remember information for a few seconds, neuroimaging results show increases in neural activity in regions in the front of the brain. When they are asked to remember information for a long period, there is increased activity in an entirely different region, one closer to the middle of the brain. Thus, different mechanisms seem to be used for the short-term and long-term storage of information (Smith & Jonides, 1994; Squire, Knowlton, & Musen, 1993).

The connection between psychology and neuroscience is not limited to cognitive psychology. Psychologists have also initiated **affective neuroscience** (Panksepp, 1998) to discover how emotional phenomena are executed in the brain, as well as **social cognitive neuroscience** (Ochsner & Lieberman, 2001) to discover how stereotyping, attitudes, person perception, and self-knowledge are executed in the brain.

EVOLUTIONARY PSYCHOLOGY

Evolutionary psychology is concerned with the biological origins of psychological mechanisms. In addition to psychology and biology, the other disciplines involved in this approach include anthropology and psychiatry. The key idea behind evolutionary psychology is that, like biological mechanisms, psychological mechanisms must have evolved over millions of years through a process of natural selection. As such, **evolutionary psychology** holds that psychological mechanisms have a genetic basis and in the past increased our ancestors' chances of surviving and reproducing. To illustrate, consider a liking for sweets. Such a preference can be thought of as a psychological mechanism, and it has a genetic basis. Moreover, we have this preference because it increased our ancestors' chances of survival: The fruit that tasted the sweetest had the highest nutritional value, so by eating it they increased the chances of continued survival of the relevant genes (Symons, 1992).

An evolutionary perspective can affect the study of psychological issues in several ways. Certain topics are of particular importance because of their link to survival or successful reproduction. Such topics include how we select our mates and how we think and behave when experiencing particular emotions (Buss, 1991). An evolutionary perspective can also provide new insights into familiar topics. Concerning obesity, we noted earlier that a history of deprivation can lead to overeating in the future. Evolutionary psychology provides an interpretation of this puzzling phenomenon. Until comparatively recently in human history, people experienced deprivation only when food was scarce. An adaptive mechanism for dealing with scarcity is overeating when food is available. So, evolution may have favored individuals with a tendency to overeat following deprivation.

HOW PSYCHOLOGICAL RESEARCH IS DONE

Now that we have some idea of the topics psychologists study and their perspectives, we can consider the research strategies they use to investigate them. In general, doing research involves two steps: (1) generating a scientific hypothesis and (2) testing that hypothesis.

GENERATING HYPOTHESES

The first step in any research project is to generate a **hypothesis**—a statement that can be tested—about the topic of interest. Regarding childhood amnesia, for example, we might generate the hypothesis that people can retrieve more memories of their early life if they are back in the same place where the incidents originally occurred. How does a researcher arrive at such a hypothe-

CULTURAL PSYCHOLOGY

Scientific psychology in the West has often assumed that people in all cultures have exactly the same psychological processes. Increasingly, this assumption is being challenged by proponents of cultural psychology, an interdisciplinary movement of psychologists, anthropologists, sociologists, and other social scientists. **Cultural psychology** is concerned with how the culture in which an individual lives—its traditions, language, and worldview—influences that person's mental representations and psychological processes.

Here is an example. In the West—North America and much of western and northern Europe—we think of ourselves as separate and autonomous agents with unique abilities and traits. In contrast, many cultures in the East—including those of India, China, and Japan—emphasize the interrelationships among people rather than their individuality. Moreover, Easterners tend to pay more attention to social situations than Westerners do. These differences lead Easterners to explain the behavior of another person differently than do Westerners. Rather than explaining a piece of behavior solely in terms of a person's traits, Easterners also explain it in terms of the social situation in which it occurred (Nisbett et al., 2001). This has profound implications for trait attribution, one of the sample problems discussed at the beginning of the chapter. These differences between East and West in explaining behavior can also have educational implications. Because of their emphasis on collectivism rather than individualism, Asian students tend to study together more

than American students. Such group study may be a useful technique, and it may be part of the reason why Asian students outperform their American counterparts in math. In addition, when an American student is having difficulty in math, both the student and the teacher tend to attribute the difficulty to the student's individual abilities. When a comparable case arises in a Japanese school, student and teacher are more likely to look to the situation—the student-teacher interaction in the instructional context—for an explanation of the poor performance (Stevenson, Lee, & Graham, 1993).

POSITIVE PSYCHOLOGY

After World War II, psychology—especially clinical psychology—became a science devoted to healing. It adopted a disease model of human functioning from the medical sciences and aimed to cure pathologies. Although this focus produced tremendous advances in the field's understanding and treatment of mental illness (see Chapters 15 and 16), it had little to say about what makes life worth living. **Positive psychology** emerged to balance the field's sophisticated scientific understanding of mental illness with an equally sophisticated scientific understanding of human flourishing (Seligman, 2002). Although positive psychology shares with the earlier humanistic psychology a concern with people's development toward their full potential, it departs from humanistic psychology by relying heavily on empirical methods.

Positive psychology targets psychological phenomena at levels ranging from the study of positive subjective experiences, such as happiness and opti-

mism, to the study of positive personality traits, such as courage and wisdom, and the study of positive institutions—social structures that might cultivate civility and responsible citizenship (Seligman & Csikszentmihalyi, 2000). An example that combines the first two levels of analysis comes from current research on positive emotions (see Chapter 11). Unlike negative emotions, which narrow people's ideas about action (e.g., fight or flight), positive emotions have been found to broaden people's mindsets, encouraging them to discover novel lines of thought or action. Joy, for instance, creates the urge to play, and interest creates the urge to explore. A key incidental outcome of these broadened mindsets is an increase in personal resources: As individuals discover new ideas and actions, they build physical, intellectual, social, and psychological resources. Empirical studies support this new broaden-and-build theory of positive emotions, showing that—through their effects on broadened thinking—positive emotions fuel growth-positive personality traits such as resilience and optimism (Fredrickson, 2001). The take-home message for positive psychology is that positive emotions are worth cultivating, not just as end states in themselves but also as a means of triggering upward spirals toward psychological growth and flourishing.

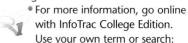 For more information, go online with InfoTrac College Edition. Use your own term or search:

- Affective neuroscience
- Positive psychology

sis? There is no single answer. An astute observer of naturally occurring situations may have an advantage in coming up with hypotheses. For example, you might have noticed that you can remember more about your high school years when you are back home, which could generate such a hypothesis. It also helps to be very familiar with the relevant scientific literature—previously published books and articles about the topic of interest.

The most important source for scientific hypotheses, however, is often a scientific **theory,** an interrelated set of propositions about a particular phenomenon. For example, one theory of sexual motivation (discussed in Chapter 10) proposes a genetic predisposition toward heterosexuality or homosexuality. This leads to the testable scientific hypothesis that pairs of identical twins—who have identical genes—should be more likely to have the same sexual orientation than pairs of fraternal twins, who share only about half their genes. A competing theory emphasizes childhood events as the source of an individual's sexual orientation and generates a competing set of hypotheses that can also be tested. As we will see throughout this book, testing hypotheses derived from competing theories is one of the most powerful ways of advancing scientific knowledge.

The term **scientific** means that the research methods used to collect the data are (1) unbiased (do not favor one hypothesis over another) and (2) reliable (other qualified people can repeat the observations and obtain the same results). The methods considered in this section have these two characteristics. Although some are better suited to certain perspectives than to others, each method can be used with each perspective.

EXPERIMENTS

The most powerful scientific method is the experiment. **Experiments** provide the strongest tests of hypotheses about cause and effect. The investigator carefully controls conditions—often in a laboratory—and takes measurements in order to discover the causal relationships among variables. A **variable** is something that can occur with different values (see Concept Review Table). For example, an experiment might explore whether amount of sleep causes memory changes (does recall of childhood events decrease with lack of sleep?). If an experiment shows that memory performance changes systematically with hours of sleep, an orderly causal relationship between these two variables has been found.

The ability to exercise precise control over a variable distinguishes the experimental method from other methods of scientific observation. For example, if the hypothesis is that individuals will perform better on a math problem if they are offered more money for a good performance, the experimenter might randomly assign participants to one of three conditions: One group is told that they will be paid $10 if they perform well, the second group is promised $5, and the third group is not offered any money. The experimenter then measures and compares the performance of all three groups to see if, in fact, more money (the hypothesized cause) produces better performance (the hypothesized effect).

In this experiment, the amount of money offered is the independent variable because it is a variable that is independent of what the participant does. In fact, the **independent variable** is under the complete control of the experimenter, who creates it and controls its variation. In an experiment, the independent variable represents the hypothesized "cause." The hypothesized "effect" in an experiment is the **dependent variable** because it is hypothesized to depend on the value of the independent variable. In this experiment, the dependent variable is performance on the math problems. The experimenter manipulates the independent variable and observes the dependent variable to learn the outcome of the experiment. The dependent variable is almost always some measure of the participants' behavior. The phrase "is a function of" is often used to express the dependence of one variable on another. For this experiment, we could say that the participants' performance on the math problems is a function of the amount of money offered. The groups that are paid money would be the **experimental groups**, or groups in which the hypothesized cause is present. The group that was not paid would be the **control group**, the group in which the hypothesized cause is absent. In general, a control group serves as a baseline against which experimental groups can be compared.

One important feature of the experiment just described is random assignment of participants to groups or conditions. **Random assignment** means that each participant has an equal probability of being placed in any group. Without random assignment, the experimenter cannot be certain that something other than the independent variable might have produced the results. For example, an experimenter should never let participants choose which group they would like to be in. Although most participants might choose to be in the highest-paid group, those who are made nervous by pressure might choose to be in a "casual" group that was not paid. In any case, the problem is that the groups would now contain different kinds of people, and the differences in their personalities, rather than the amount of money offered, might cause one group to do better than another. Or suppose that an experimenter runs all the paid groups first and runs the no-payment control group afterward. This introduces a host of potential problems. Perhaps performance varies as a function of the time of day (morning, afternoon, or evening); maybe those who participate later in the experiment are closer in time to their final exams than earlier participants. In addition to these uncontrolled variables, many others of which the experimenter is unaware might bias the results. All such problems are resolved by randomly assigning participants to conditions. Only with random assignment can we be certain that all extraneous variables—such as participant personality, time of day, or time of semester—are evenly represented across conditions and therefore unlikely to introduce bias. Random assignment is one of the most important ingredients of an experiment.

The experimental method can be used outside the laboratory as well. For example, in research on obesity, the effects of different methods of weight control can be investigated by trying these methods on separate but similar groups of obese individuals. The experimental method is a matter of logic, not location. Still, most experiments take place in laboratories, chiefly because a laboratory setting allows measuring behavior more precisely and controlling the variables more completely. And again, it is often random assignment that is at issue: If two obesity clinics use different methods and achieve different results, we cannot conclude with confidence that the different methods are responsible because the clinics might attract different kinds of people to their programs or have different staff cultures and expectations.

The experiments described so far examine the effect of one independent variable on one dependent variable. Limiting an investigation to only one independent variable, however, is too restrictive for some problems. **Multivariate experiments**—experiments manipulating several independent variables at once—are common in psychological research. In the hypothetical study in which participants were offered different amounts of money for solving math problems, the experimenter might also vary the level of difficulty of the problems. Now there would be six groups of participants, each combining one of three different amounts of money with one of two levels of difficulty (easy versus difficult).

MEASUREMENT Psychologists using the experimental method often have to make statements about amounts or quantities. Sometimes variables can be measured by physical means, such as hours of sleep deprivation or dosage of a drug. At other times, variables have to be scaled in a manner that places them in some sort of order. In rating a patient's feelings of aggression, for example, a psychotherapist might use a 5-point scale ranging from *never* through *rarely*, *sometimes*, and *often* to *always*. For purposes of precise communication, experiments require some form of **measurement, a system for assigning numbers to variables.**

Experiments usually involve making measurements on many participants, not just one. The results therefore are data in the form of a set of numbers that can be summarized and interpreted. To accomplish this task, the experimenter needs to use **statistics,** the discipline that deals with sampling data from a population of individuals and then drawing inferences about the population from those data. Statistics plays an important role not only in experimental research but in other methods as well.[3] The most common statistic is the **mean,** which is simply the technical term for **an arithmetic average, the sum of a set of scores divided by the number of scores in the set.** In studies with one experimental group and one control group, there are two means to be compared: a mean for the scores of the participants in the experimental group and a mean for the scores of the participants in the control group. The difference between these two means is, of course, what interests the experimenters. If the difference between the means is large, it can be accepted at face value. But what if the difference is small?

CONCEPT REVIEW TABLE
Terminology of Experimental Research

Hypothesis	A statement about cause and effect that can be tested.
Experiment	A well-controlled test of a hypothesis about cause and effect.
Variable	Something that can occur with different values and can be measured.
Independent variable	A variable that represents the hypothesized "cause" that is precisely controlled by the experimenter and independent of what the participant does.
Dependent variable	A variable that represents the hypothesized "effect" whose values ultimately depend on the value of the independent variable.
Experimental group	A group in which the hypothesized cause is present.
Control group	A group in which the hypothesized cause is absent.
Random assignment	A system for assigning participants to experimental and control groups so that each participant has an equal chance of being assigned to any group.
Measurement	A system for assigning numbers to different values of variables.
Statistics	Mathematical techniques for determining the certainty with which a sample of data can be used to draw generalizations or inferences.

What if the measures used are subject to error? What if a few extreme cases are producing the difference? Statisticians have solved these problems by developing tests for determining the significance of a difference. A psychologist who says that the difference between the experimental group and the control group is **statistically significant** means that a statistical test has been applied to the data and the observed difference is unlikely to have arisen by chance or because of a few extreme cases.

CORRELATION

Not all problems can be easily studied by using the experimental method. In many situations the investigator has no control over which participants go in which conditions. For example, if we want to test the hypothesis that anorexic people are more sensitive to changes in taste than normal-weight people, we cannot select a group of normal-weight participants and require half of

[3]This discussion is designed to introduce the experimental tools of measurement and statistics. A more thorough discussion is provided in the Appendix.

them to become anorexic! Rather, we select people who are already anorexic or already of normal weight and see if they also differ in taste sensitivity. More generally, we can use the correlational method to determine whether some variable that is not under our control is associated—or correlated—with another variable of interest.

In the example just given, there were only two values of the weight variable: anorexic and normal. It is more common to have many values of each variable and to determine the degree to which values on one variable are related to values on another. This is done by using a descriptive statistic called the **correlation coefficient,** an estimate of the degree to which two variables are related. The correlation coefficient, symbolized by *r*, is expressed as a number between −1.00 and +1.00. A perfect relationship—which is rare—is indicated by 1.00 (+1.00 if the relationship is positive and −1.00 if the relationship is negative). No relationship at all is indicated by a correlation close to zero. As *r* goes from 0 to +1.00 (or from 0 to −1.00), the strength of the relationship increases.

A correlation can be either + or −. The sign of the correlation indicates whether the two variables are **positively correlated,** meaning that the values of the two variables either increase together or decrease together, or **negatively correlated,** meaning that as the value of one variable increases, the value of the other decreases. Suppose that the number of times a student is absent from class correlates −.40 with the final course grade (the more absences, the lower the grade). On the other hand, the correlation between the number of classes attended and the course grade would be + .40. The strength of the relationship is the same, but the sign indicates whether we are looking at classes missed or classes attended.[4]

To get a clearer picture of a correlation coefficient, consider the hypothetical study presented in Figure 1-6. As shown in Figure 1-6a, the study involves patients with brain damage leading to problems in face recognition (prosopagnosia). What is of interest is whether the degree of deficit, or error, in face recognition increases with the amount of brain tissue that is damaged. Each point on the graph in Figure 1-6a represents the percentage of errors made by one patient on a test of face recognition. For example, a patient who had only 10% brain damage made 15% errors on the face-recognition test, but a patient who had 55% brain damage made 75% errors. If errors in face recognition *always* increased along with the amount of brain damage, the points in the graph would consistently increase in moving from left to right; if the points had all fallen on the diagonal line in the figure, the correlation would have been *r* = 1.0—a perfect correlation. A couple of points fall on either side of the line,

though, so the correlation is about .90. Such a high correlation indicates a very strong relationship between amount of the brain damage and errors in face recognition. In Figure 1-6a, the correlation is positive because more errors are associated with more brain damage.

If, instead of focusing on errors, we plot the percentage of correct responses on the face recognition test, we end up with the diagram in Figure 1-6b. Now the correlation is negative—about −.90—because *fewer* correct responses are associated with *more* brain damage. The diagonal line in Figure 1-6b is simply the inverse of the one in Figure 1-6a.

Finally, consider the diagram in Figure 1-6c. Here we have graphed errors on the face recognition test as a function of the patients' height. Of course, there is no reason to expect a relationship between height and face recognition, and the graph shows that there is none. The points neither consistently increase nor consistently decrease in moving from left to right but rather bounce around a horizontal line. The correlation is 0.

In psychological research, a correlation coefficient of .60 or more is considered quite high. Correlations in the range from .20 to .60 are of practical and theoretical value and are useful in making predictions. Correlations between 0 and .20 must be judged with caution and are only minimally useful in making predictions.

TESTS The familiar use of the correlational method involves tests that measure aptitudes, achievement, or other psychological traits, such as the test of face recognition just discussed. A **test** presents a uniform situation to a group of people who vary in a particular trait (such as brain damage, math ability, manual dexterity, or aggression). The variation in scores on the test can be correlated with variations on another variable. For example, people's scores on a test of math ability can be correlated with their subsequent grades in a college math course. If the correlation is high, then the test score may be used to determine which of a new group of students should be placed in advanced sections of the course.

CORRELATION AND CAUSATION There is an important distinction between experimental and correlational studies. In a typical experimental study, one variable (the independent variable) is systematically manipulated to determine its causal effect on some other variable (the dependent variable). Such cause-and-effect relationships cannot be inferred from correlational studies.

For instance, studies have shown that the more TV violence a young boy watches, the more aggressive he is. But does watching violent TV cause the aggression, or do more aggressive boys choose to watch more violent TV? If all we have is a correlation, we cannot say which variable is cause and which is effect. (As noted earlier in

[4]The numerical method for calculating a correlation coefficient is described in the Appendix.

a) Positive correlation

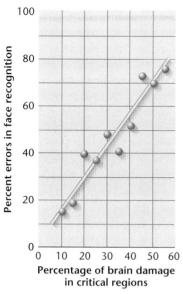

The patients are ordered along the horizontal axis with respect to the amount of brain damage, with the patient represented by the leftmost point having the least brain damage (10%) and the patient represented by the rightmost point having the most brain damage (55%). Each point on the graph represents a single patient's score on a test of face recognition. The correlation is a positive .90.

b) Negative correlation

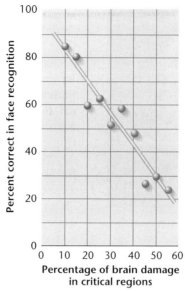

The same data are depicted, but we now focus on the percentage of correct responses (rather than errors). Now the correlation is a negative .90.

c) Zero correlation

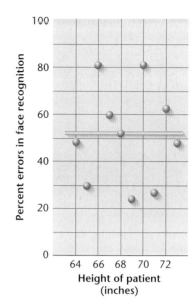

The patients' performance on the face recognition test is graphed as a function of their height. Now the correlation is 0.

❙ **Figure 1-6**
Scatter Diagrams Illustrating Correlations
These hypothesized data are based on 10 patients, all of whom have some damage in regions of the brain known to be involved in face recognition.

the chapter, however, other studies do demonstrate a causal relationship between watching violent TV and behaving aggressively. Experimenters had control over the independent variable and used random assignment of participants to conditions.)

Two variables can also be correlated when neither is the cause of the other. For example, many years before careful medical experiments demonstrated that cigarette smoking causes cancer, a correlation between smoking and lung cancer was shown. That is, it was already known that people who smoked were more likely to contract cancer. But—as the tobacco companies rushed to point out—this correlation left open the possibility that some third cause was responsible. For example, if people who live in smoggy urban areas are more likely to smoke than people who live in rural areas with cleaner air, then air pollution rather than smoking could cause higher cancer rates in smokers.

In short, when two variables are correlated, variation in one of them may possibly be the cause of varia-

tion in the other. Indeed, correlation is a prerequisite for causation. But, without further experiments, no such conclusion is justified from correlational studies, because correlation does not necessarily imply causation.

OBSERVATION

DIRECT OBSERVATION In the early stages of research, the most efficient way of making progress toward an explanation may be **direct observation**—to simply observe the phenomenon under study as it occurs naturally. Careful observation of animal and human behavior is the starting point for a great deal of research in psychology. For example, observation of primates in their native environment may tell us things about their social organization that will help in later laboratory investigations. Video recordings of newborn babies reveal details of their activity shortly after birth and the types of stimuli to which they respond. However, investigators observing

Field studies can often tell us more about social behavior than experimental studies can. Professor Shirley Strum has been observing the same troop of baboons in Kenya for more than 20 years, identifying individual animals, and making daily recordings of their behaviors and social interactions. Her data have provided remarkable information about the mental abilities of baboons and the role of friendships in their social system.

naturally occurring behavior must be trained to observe and record events accurately so that their own biases do not influence what they report.

Observational methods may be used in a laboratory if the problem being studied is partly biological. For example, in their classic study of the physiological aspects of human sexuality, William Masters and Virginia Johnson (1966) developed techniques for directly observing sexual responses in the laboratory. The data included (1) observations of behavior, (2) recordings of physiological changes, and (3) responses to questions about the participants' sensations before, during, and after sexual stimulation. Although the researchers agreed that human sexuality has many dimensions besides the biological one, their observations of the anatomical and physiological aspects of sexual response have been very helpful in understanding the nature of human sexuality, as well as in solving sexual problems.

THE SURVEY METHOD Some problems that are difficult to study by direct observation may be studied by indirect observation through the use of questionnaires or interviews. Rather than observe people engaging in a particular behavior, such as exercising regularly, researchers using the **survey method** simply ask people if they engage in the behavior of interest. The survey method is more open to bias than direct observation, however. Of particular concern are **social desirability effects,** which occur when some people try to present themselves in a favorable light (for example, by saying that they exercise more than they actually do). Still, the survey method has produced many impor-

tant results. For example, before Masters and Johnson conducted their research on the human sexual response, most of the available information on how people behave sexually (as opposed to how laws, religion, or society said they should behave) came from extensive surveys conducted by Alfred Kinsey and his associates 20 years earlier. Information from thousands of interviews was analyzed, resulting in the publication of two pioneering works: *Sexual Behavior in the Human Male* (Kinsey, Pomeroy, & Martin, 1948) and *Sexual Behavior in the Human Female* (Kinsey, Pomeroy, Martin, & Gebhard, 1953).

Surveys have also been used to discover people's political opinions, product preferences, health care needs, and so on. The Gallup poll and the U.S. census are probably the most familiar surveys. An adequate survey requires presenting a carefully pretested questionnaire to a sample of people who have been selected by methods designed to ensure that they are representative of the larger population being studied.

CASE HISTORIES Still another form of indirect observation is to obtain a **case history,** which is a partial biography of a particular individual. This involves asking people to recall relevant experiences from their past. For example, if the research is concerned with the childhood antecedents of adult depression, the researcher might begin by asking questions about earlier life events. These case histories are biographies designed for scientific use, and they are important sources of data for psychologists who are studying individuals.

A major limitation of case histories is that they rely on a person's memories and reconstructions of earlier events, which are frequently distorted or incomplete. Sometimes other data can be used to corroborate information obtained in a case history. For example, written records, such as death certificates, can be used to check on specific dates, or relatives of the person being interviewed can be asked to report their own memories of the relevant events. Even so, their limitations make case histories less useful for testing a theory or hypothesis than for suggesting hypotheses that can then be tested in more rigorous ways or checked with a larger sample of participants. In this way, scientists use the case history in much the same way that a therapist or physician might when trying to formulate a diagnosis and treatment for a particular individual.

LITERATURE REVIEWS

One final way in which psychological research is done is by conducting literature reviews. A **literature review** is a scholarly summary of the existing body of research on a given topic. Because the field of psychology grows at a fast pace, an up-to-date literature review is an indispensable tool for assessing patterns within the accumulating scientific evidence for a particular psychological hypothesis or theory.

Literature reviews come in two forms. One form is a **narrative review,** in which authors use words to describe studies previously conducted and discuss the strength of the available psychological evidence. College students enrolled in upper-level psychology courses often write narrative reviews of a chosen topic for term papers. Another type of review, which has become increasingly popular, is a **meta-analysis,** in which authors use statistical techniques to combine and draw conclusions about studies previously conducted. In any given experiment, as we have seen, participants are treated as "cases," with each participant contributing his or her own unique data, which are then summarized statistically. In a meta-analysis, by contrast, individual studies are treated as "cases," with each study contributing its own unique summary data, which are then further summarized at a higher—or *meta*—level of analysis. As you might imagine, meta-analyses have the potential to be more systematic and evenhanded than narrative reviews. Throughout this book, we often rely on meta-analyses to describe the state of the evidence for psychological theories and hypotheses.

ETHICS OF PSYCHOLOGICAL RESEARCH

Because psychologists study living beings, they need to be sensitive to ethical issues that can arise in the conduct of research. Accordingly, the American Psychological Association (APA) and its counterparts in Canada and Great Britain have established guidelines for the treatment of both human participants and animal subjects (American Psychological Association, 1990). In the United States, federal regulations require any institution that conducts federally funded research to establish an internal review board, which reviews proposed studies to ensure that participants will be treated properly.

RESEARCH WITH HUMANS The first principle governing the ethical treatment of human participants is **minimal risk.** In most cases, the risks anticipated in the research should be no greater than those ordinarily encountered in daily life. Obviously, a person should not be exposed to physical harm or injury, but deciding how much psychological stress is ethically justified in a research project is not always so clear-cut. In everyday life, of course, people may be impolite, lie, or make other people anxious. Under what circumstances is it ethically justifiable for a researcher to treat a participant in such ways to meet the goals of a research project? These are the kinds of questions that review boards consider on a case-by-case basis.

The second principle governing the ethical treatment of human participants is **informed consent.** Par-

Survey researchers ask individuals or, as in this case, a mother and son about their attitudes and behavior. For survey results to be valid, the respondents must be representative of the larger population being studied.

ticipants must be told ahead of time about any aspects of the study that could influence their willingness to cooperate and, after this disclosure, they must enter the study voluntarily and be permitted to withdraw from it at any time they desire without penalty. Like the principle of minimal risk, informed consent is not always easy to implement. In particular, informed consent is sometimes at odds with another common requirement of research: that participants be unaware of the hypotheses being tested in a study. If a researcher plans to compare participants who learn lists of familiar words with participants who learn lists of unfamiliar words, no ethical problem arises by simply telling participants ahead of time that they will be learning lists of words: They do not need to know how the words vary from one participant to another. Nor are any serious ethical issues raised if participants are given a surprise quiz they did not expect. But what if the researcher wants to compare participants who learn words while in a neutral mood with participants who learn words while they are angry or embarrassed? Clearly the research would not yield valid conclusions if participants had to be told ahead of time that they would be intentionally angered (by being treated rudely) or embarrassed (by being led to believe that they had accidentally broken a piece of equipment). Accordingly, the guidelines specify that if such a study is permitted to proceed at all, participants must be debriefed about it as soon as possible afterwards. During **debriefing,** the reasons for keeping them in ignorance—or deceiving them—about the procedures must be explained, and any residual emotional reactions must be dealt with so that participants leave with their dignity intact and their appreciation for the research enhanced. The review board must be convinced that the debriefing procedures are adequate to this task.

Are We Naturally Selfish?

WE ARE NATURALLY SELFISH

George C. Williams, State University of New York, Stony Brook

Yes we are selfish, in a special biological sense, but an important one that should be borne in mind in discussing human affairs, ethical philosophy, and related topics (Williams, 1996: Chs. 3 & 9). We are selfish in the special way that our genes demand. They are maximally selfish because, if they were not, they would not exist. The genes that get passed on through many generations are those that are best at getting themselves passed on. To do this they must be better than any alternatives at making bodies, human or otherwise, that transmit genes more profusely than other members of their population. Individuals can win this genetic contest mainly by surviving to maturity and then competing successfully for the resources (food, nest sites, mates, etc.) needed for their own reproduction.

In this sense we are necessarily selfish, but this need not imply that we are never expected to be unselfish in the sense in which this term is normally understood. Individuals can and often do assist others in gaining resources and avoiding losses or dangers. For a biological understanding of such behavior, the important observations lie in the circumstances in which the apparent benevolence occurs. The most obvious example of helpful behavior is that performed by parents for their own offspring. Its obvious explanation is that parents would not successfully transmit their genes if they did not help their own young in special ways: mammalian mothers must nurse their babies; birds must bring food to their nestlings; a plant must pack an optimum quantity of nutrients into each

of its seeds. Yet this kind of provisioning is never a generalized helpfulness of adults toward young. There are always mechanisms at work by which parents can usually identify their own offspring and confine their helpfulness to them alone.

If all reproduction is sexual and mates are seldom closely related to each other, each offspring has half of each parent's genes. From a parent's perspective, a son or daughter is genetically half as important as itself, and an offspring's reproduction is half as important as its own, for getting genes transmitted. Yet the same kind of partial genetic identity is true of all relatives, not just offspring. It may serve the genetic selfishness of an individual to behave helpfully toward relatives in general, not merely offspring. Such behavior arises from what is termed kin selection, natural selection for the adaptive use of cues that indicate degrees and probabilities of relationship. To whatever extent there is evidence of genealogical connections, an individual is expected to favor relatives over nonrelatives and close relatives (parents, offspring, siblings) over more distant ones.

A male bird whose mate laid eggs in his nest can be favored in evolution if he incubates the eggs and feeds the later hatchlings. But what about possible cuckoldry? Can he really be sure that his mate was not inseminated by a neighboring male so that one or more of those eggs are not actually his own offspring? Extra-pair mating by female birds, with or without consent, does happen in many species. Males in such

species are especially watchful of their mates' behavior and diligent in chasing rival males from their territories. It is expected that males, in species in which an average of 10% of the eggs are fertilized by rivals, will be less conscientious toward their nestlings than in species in which cuckoldry never happens.

Kin selection is one factor that causes what looks like unselfish behavior. Reciprocation between unrelated individuals, with immediate or likely future profit to each participant, is another. So is that which is caused by the selfish deception or manipulation of another's kin-selected or other altruistic or cooperative instincts. Female birds, like males, cannot be certain that nestlings are their own, because egg dumping (Sayler, 1992), the laying of an egg in another bird's nest while its owner is briefly away feeding, happens in many species. One female gains genetically by exploiting the parental instincts of another. The species in which deception and manipulation are most extensively developed is our own, by virtue of our language capability. Henry V, according to Shakespeare, addressed his army as "We band of brothers." Feminist leaders speak of the "sisterhood." Deception and manipulation of others' emotions can, of course, be for either a worthy or an unworthy cause.

George C. Williams

Are We Naturally Selfish?

WE ARE NOT NATURALLY SELFISH
Frans B. M. de Waal, Emory University

"How selfish soever man may be supposed, there are evidently some principles in his nature, which interest him in the fortune of others, and render their happiness necessary to him, though he derives nothing from it, except the pleasure of seeing it."
Adam Smith, 1759

When Lenny Skutnik dove into the icy Potomac in Washington, DC, in 1982, to rescue a plane-crash victim, or when Dutch civilians sheltered Jewish families during World War II, life-threatening risks were taken on behalf of complete strangers. Similarly, Binti Jua, a lowland gorilla at Chicago's Brookfield Zoo, rescued an unconscious boy who had fallen into her enclosure, following a chain of actions no one had taught her.

Such examples make a deep impression mainly because they benefit members of our own species. But in my work on the evolution of empathy and morality, I have found evidence so rich of animals caring for one another and respond-

An adult male chimpanzee, defeated in a fight with a rival, screams while being comforted by a juvenile with an embrace. Such "consolations" have as yet not been reported for other animals. The behavior seems a form of empathy without tangible benefit to the performer.

ing to each other's distress that I am convinced that survival depends not only on strength in combat but also at times on cooperation and kindness (de Waal, 1996). For example, it is common among chimpanzees that a bystander approaches the victim of an attack to gently wrap an arm around his or her shoulder.

Despite these caring tendencies, humans and other animals are routinely depicted by biologists as complete egoists. The reason is theoretical: all behavior is supposed to have evolved to serve the actor's own interests. It is logical to assume that genes that fail to benefit their carrier are at a disadvantage in the process of natural selection. But is it correct to call an animal selfish simply because its behavior evolved for its own good?

The process by which a behavior came to exist over millions of years of evolution is irrelevant when considering why an animal here and now acts in a particular way. Animals only see the immediate consequences of their actions, and even those are not always clear to them. We may think that a spider builds a web to catch flies, but this is true only at the functional level. There is no evidence that spiders have any idea what webs are for. In other words, a behavior's purpose says nothing about its underlying motives.

Only recently has the concept of "selfishness" been robbed of its vernacular meaning and applied outside the psychological domain. Even though the term is now seen by some as synonymous with self-serving, selfishness implies the intention to serve oneself, hence knowledge of what one stands to gain from a particular behavior. A vine may serve its own interests by overgrowing a tree, but since

plants lack intentions and knowledge, they cannot be selfish except in a meaningless, metaphorical sense. For the same reason, it is impossible for genes to be selfish.

Charles Darwin never confused adaptation with individual goals, and endorsed altruistic motives. In this he was inspired by Adam Smith, the moral philosopher and father of economics. It says a great deal about the distinction between self-serving actions and selfish motives that Smith, known for his emphasis on self-interest as the guiding principle of economics, also wrote about the universal human capacity of sympathy.

The origins of this inclination are no mystery. All species that rely on cooperation show group loyalty and helping tendencies. These tendencies evolved in the context of a close-knit social life in which they benefited relatives and companions able to repay the favor. The impulse to help was, therefore, never totally without survival value to the ones showing the impulse. But the impulse became divorced from the consequences that shaped its evolution, permitting its expression even when payoffs were unlikely, such as when strangers were the beneficiaries.

To call all behavior selfish is like describing all life on earth as converted sun energy. Both statements have some general value but offer little help in explaining the diversity we see around us. Some animals survive through ruthless competition, others through mutual aid. A framework that fails to distinguish the contrasting mind-sets involved may be of use to the evolutionary biologist: It has no place in psychology.

A third principle of ethical research is the **right to privacy.** Information about a person acquired during a study must be kept confidential and not made available to others without the research participant's consent. A common practice is to separate the names and other information used to identify participants from the data collected in the study. The data are then identified only by code or case numbers. In that way, no one other than the experimenter has access to how any particular participant responded. Another common practice is to report only aggregated data—for example, data averaged across all participants in the same group or condition. This further protects the privacy of individual research participants.

Even if all of these ethical conditions are met, the researcher must still weigh the costs of the study—not the economic costs but the costs in human terms—against the potential benefits. Is it really necessary to conduct a study in which participants will be deceived or embarrassed? Only if the researcher and the review board are reasonably certain that the study can uncover worthwhile information—either practical or theoretical—can the research proceed.

RESEARCH WITH ANIMALS Another area in which ethical standards must be observed is research with animals. About 7% of psychological studies employ animals, 95% of which are rats, mice, and birds. Psychologists conduct research with animals for two main reasons. One is that animal behavior can itself be interesting and worthy of study. A second is that animal systems can provide models of human systems, and so research on animals can produce knowledge that might be impossible or unethical to obtain from humans. Animal research has in fact played a pivotal role in understanding and treating psychological problems such as anxiety, stress, aggression, depression, drug abuse, eating disorders, hypertension, and Alzheimer's disease (Carroll & Overmier, 2001). Although debate continues about whether and what kind of research with animals is ethical, in the United States most psychologists (80%) and most psychology majors (72%) support the use of animals in research (Plous, 1996a, 1996b). Amid this wide support, concerns remain about the small subset of animal studies that involve painful or harmful procedures. To address these concerns, both federal and APA guidelines require that any painful or harmful procedures imposed on animals must be thoroughly justified in terms of the knowledge to be gained from the study. APA guidelines also underscore that researchers have a moral obligation to treat animals humanely and to minimize their pain and suffering. Specific rules about the living conditions and maintenance of laboratory animals govern how this moral obligation is to be met.

Aside from these specific guidelines, a central principle of research ethics is that those who participate in psychology studies should be considered full partners in the research enterprise. Some of the research discussed in this text was conducted before the ethical guidelines just described were formulated and would not be permitted by most review boards today.

◆ Interim Summary

- Doing psychological research involves generating a hypothesis and then testing it by using a scientific method. Core concepts necessary for understanding psychology experiments include independent and dependent variables, experimental and control groups, random assignment, and measurement and statistics.

- When experiments are not feasible, the correlational method may be used to determine whether one naturally occurring variable is associated with another. The degree of association between two variables is measured by the correlation coefficient, r, which can be positive (up to $+1.00$) or negative (down to -1.00), depending on whether one variable increases with another $(+)$ or one variable decreases as the other increases $(-)$.

- Another way of conducting research is to use the observational method, either through direct observation, indirect survey methods, or case histories.

- A final way of conducting research is by literature review, either narrative reviews or statistical meta-analyses.

- The basic ethical principles governing the ethical treatment of human participants are minimal risk, informed consent, and the right to privacy. Any painful or harmful procedures imposed upon animals must be thoroughly justified in terms of the knowledge to be gained from the study.

◆ Critical Thinking Questions

1. Figure 1-3 displays the results of a classic study showing that preference for viewing violent TV programs by boys at age 9 is related to aggressive behavior at age 19. Why does this study fail to demonstrate that watching violence on TV makes boys more aggressive? What kind of evidence would be needed to make such an argument?

2. Suppose a researcher finds a correlation of $+.50$ between symptoms of disordered eating and a preoccupation with physical appearance. What can the researcher conclude? What might explain the observed relationship? Can you formulate a hypothesis about cause and effect? How could you test that hypothesis?

CHAPTER SUMMARY

1. Psychology is the scientific study of behavior and mental processes.

2. The roots of psychology can be traced to the 4th and 5th centuries B.C. The Greek philosophers Socrates, Plato, and Aristotle posed fundamental questions about the mind, and Hippocrates, the "father of medicine," made many important observations about how the brain controlled other organs. One of the earliest debates about human psychology focused on the question of whether human capabilities are inborn (the nature view) or acquired through experience (the nurture view).

3. Scientific psychology was born in the late 19th century with the idea that mind and behavior could be the subject of scientific analysis. The first experimental laboratory in psychology was established by Wilhelm Wundt at the University of Leipzig in 1879.

4. Among the early "schools" of psychology in the 20th century were structuralism (the analysis of mental structures), functionalism (studying how the mind works so that an organism can adapt to and function in its environment), behaviorism (the study of behavior without reference to consciousness), Gestalt psychology (which focuses on the patterns formed by stimuli and on the organization of experience), and psychoanalysis (which emphasizes the role of unconscious processes in personality development and motivation).

5. Later developments in 20th-century psychology included information-processing theory, psycholinguistics, and neuropsychology.

6. The study of psychology can be approached from several perspectives. The biological perspective relates actions to events taking place inside the body, particularly the brain and nervous system. The behavioral perspective considers only external activities that can be observed and measured. The cognitive perspective is concerned with mental processes, such as perceiving, remembering, reasoning, deciding, and problem solving, and with relating these processes to behavior. The psychoanalytic perspective emphasizes unconscious motives stemming from sexual and aggressive impulses. The subjectivist perspective focuses on how people actively construct and interpret their social worlds, which is expected to vary by culture, personal history, and current motivational state. A particular topic often can be analyzed from more than one of these perspectives.

7. The biological perspective differs from the other viewpoints in that its principles are partly drawn from biology. Often, biological researchers attempt to explain psychological principles in terms of biological ones; this is known as reductionism. Behavioral phe-nomena are increasingly being understood at both the biological and psychological levels.

8. Among the major subfields of psychology are biological psychology, experimental psychology, developmental psychology, social and personality psychology, clinical and counseling psychology, school and educational psychology, and industrial and engineering psychology. Many new areas of inquiry gaining momentum in 21st-century psychology span traditional subfields and disciplines. These new areas include cognitive neuroscience (as well as affective and social cognitive neuroscience), evolutionary psychology, cultural psychology, and positive psychology.

9. Doing psychological research involves generating a hypothesis and then testing it by using a scientific method. When applicable, the experimental method is preferred because it seeks to control all variables except the ones being studied and can thus test hypotheses about cause and effect. The independent variable is the one that is manipulated by the experimenter; the dependent variable (usually some measure of the participant's behavior) is the one being studied to determine whether it is affected by changes in the independent variable. In a simple experimental design, the experimenter manipulates one independent variable and observes its effect on one dependent variable. An essential element of experimental design is the random assignment of participants to experimental and control groups.

10. In many experiments the independent variable is something that is either present or absent. The simplest experimental design includes an experimental group (with the hypothesized cause present for one group of participants) and a control group (with the hypothesized cause absent for another group of participants). If the manipulation of the independent variable results in a statistically significant difference in the dependent variable between the experimental and control groups, we know that the experimental condition had a reliable effect, and the difference is not due to chance factors or a few extreme cases.

11. In situations in which experiments are not feasible, the correlational method may be used. This method determines whether a naturally occurring difference is associated with another difference of interest. The degree of correlation between two variables is measured by the correlation coefficient, r, a number between -1.00 and $+1.00$. The absence of any relationship is indicated by 0; a perfect relationship is indicated by 1. As r goes from 0 to 1, the strength of the relationship increases. The correlation coefficient can be positive or negative,

depending on whether one variable increases with another (+) or one variable decreases as the other increases (−).

12. Another way of conducting research is to use the observational method, in which one observes the phenomenon of interest. Researchers must be trained to observe and record behavior accurately. Phenomena that are difficult to observe directly may be observed indirectly by means of surveys (questionnaires and interviews) or by reconstructing a case history.

13. The basic ethical principles governing the ethical treatment of human participants are minimal risk, informed consent, and the right to privacy. Any painful or harmful procedures imposed upon animals must be thoroughly justified in terms of the knowledge to be gained from the study.

CORE CONCEPTS

law of effect
overjustification effect
psychology
prosopagnosia
fundamental attribution error
childhood amnesia
obese
cathartic effect
physiology
nature-nurture debate
nature view
nurture view
tabula rasa
associationist psychology
introspection
structuralism
functionalism
behaviorism
Gestalt
psychoanalysis
unconscious
free association
information-processing model
psychological perspective
eclectic approach
biological perspective
behavioral perspective

cognitive perspective
psychoanalytic perspective
subjectivist perspective
naïve realism
reductionism
biological psychologists
experimental psychologists
developmental psychologists
social psychologists
personality psychologists
clinical psychologists
counseling psychologists
school psychologists
educational psychologists
organizational psychologists
engineering psychologists
cognitive neuroscience
affective neuroscience
social cognitive neuroscience
evolutionary psychology
cultural psychology
positive psychology
hypothesis
theory
scientific
experiments
variable

independent variable
dependent variable
experimental group
control group
random assignment
multivariate experiments
measurement
statistics
mean
statistically significant
correlation coefficient
positively correlated
negatively correlated
test
direct observation
survey method
social desirability effects
case history
literature review
narrative review
meta-analysis
minimal risk
informed consent
debriefing
right to privacy

WEB RESOURCES

**http://psychology.wadsworth.com/
atkinson14e**

Take a quiz, try the activities and exercises, and explore web links.

http://elvers.stjoe.udayton.edu/history/welcome.htm

This History of Psychology website gives you access to information about important psychologists throughout history, provides a host of web links, and even has a trivia section. Do you know who left human bone dust in the drill presses in the mechanical workshops of the Hungarian Post Office while doing research on the inner ear? Find out here!

http://www.apa.org/science/infostu.html

This site—provided by the American Psychological Association—offers you access to the wide variety of opportunities available for psychology students.

http://www.apa.org/ethics/code.html

If you are concerned about the ethics of psychology, search through this detailed site to learn more about the principles of psychologists and their code of conduct.

InfoTrac Online Library
**http://www.infotrac-college.com/
wadsworth**

Use InfoTrac College Edition to find popular and scientific articles using the search terms below or your own relevant terms.

- Cognitive Psychology
- Ethnopsychology
- Genetic Psychology
- History of Psychology
- Positive Psychology
- Psychoanalysis

CD-ROM LINKS

Psych Odyssey

Check out CD Chapter 1, What Is Psychology?
A. Psychological Perspectives: The 1850s and Beyond
B. Fields Within Psychology
See also CD Chapter 2, Research Methods
A. Research Methods in Psychology

Psyk.trek 2.0

Check out CD Unit 1, History and Methods
1a Psychology's Timeline
1b The Experimental Method
1d Statistics: Correlation
1e How To Do Library Research

PSYCHOLOGICAL DEVELOPMENT

CHAPTER OUTLINE

3

It is parents' night at the beginning of the school year at Lincoln Elementary School. Mrs. Vohland, the kindergarten teacher, has given the parents of her new class a short presentation of the kinds of activities they will be doing over the academic year. The parents are milling around the room, looking at their children's artwork, and getting to know each other. A few parents approach Mrs. Vohland to introduce themselves or thank her for her presentation. One intense-looking father named Philip walks up to Mrs. Vohland and begins to ask her a series of pointed questions about her goals for the children. When will they learn to read? Will they have mastered addition and subtraction by the end of the year? Will his son be able to write short paragraphs by first grade? Mrs. Vohland tries to explain that kindergarten is for developing the building blocks of reading, arithmetic, and writing. Some children will be very advanced by the end of the year, and some will not, because children develop at different paces. Philip is not satisfied with her answer, though, and informs Mrs. Vohland that his son has tested as "bright" and he expects him to have accomplished all these goals by the end of kindergarten.

When Philip finally lets her go, Mrs. Vohland takes a deep breath and begins to tidy her desk. Another father, Sam, approaches. He also looks a bit intense, and Mrs. Vohland braces herself for another onslaught of questions. Sam begins by saying that he is concerned about his son, who apparently has also been labeled as "bright" by some early intelligence tests. Sam's concerns, however, are quite different from Philip's. "I just want him to have a normal childhood. He's only 5, and the hard work will come later. I want him to have fun and to enjoy school. I'm worried you might push him too hard because he's supposedly smart."

Parents, obviously, can have very different expectations for their children. Particularly with a first child, these expectations are often based on their own personal experiences as a child, or what they've read in the media or heard from friends. In addition, children vary greatly in their pace of development. In this chapter, we describe the progress of "normal" development, but keep in mind the variations from this norm across children, families, and cultures.

Of all mammals, human beings require the longest period of maturation and learning before they are self-sufficient. In general, the more complex an organism's nervous system, the longer the organism takes to reach maturity. A lemur (a primitive primate) can move about on its own shortly after birth and is soon able to fend for itself. An infant monkey is dependent on its mother for several months, a chimpanzee for several years. But even a chimpanzee—one of our closest relatives—will be a functioning adult member of its species long before a human of the same age.

Developmental psychologists are concerned with how and why different aspects of human functioning develop and change across the life span. They focus on physical development, such as changes in height and weight and the acquisition of motor skills; cognitive development, such as changes in thought processes, memory, and language abilities; and personality and social development, such as changes in self-concept and interpersonal relationships. The development of particular psychological abilities and functions is treated in more detail in later chapters. In this chapter we provide a general overview of psychological development across the life span and consider two central questions: (1) How do biological factors interact with events in the child's environment to determine the course of development (often called the *nature-nurture question*)? and (2) Is development best understood as a gradual, continuous process of change or as a series of abrupt, qualitatively distinct stages?

NATURE AND NURTURE

The question of whether heredity ("nature") or environment ("nurture") is more important in determining the course of human development has been debated for centuries. The 17th-century British philosopher John Locke rejected the prevailing notion that babies were miniature adults who arrived in the world fully equipped with abilities and knowledge and simply had to grow for these inherited characteristics to appear. On the contrary, Locke believed that the mind of a newborn infant is a tabula rasa (Latin for "blank slate"). What gets written on this slate is what the baby experiences—what he or she sees, hears, tastes, smells, and feels. According to Locke, all knowledge comes to us through our senses. It is provided entirely by experience; there is no built-in knowledge.

Charles Darwin's theory of evolution (1859), which emphasizes the biological basis of human development, led many theorists to emphasize heredity. With the rise of behaviorism in the 20th century, however, the environmentalist position once again dominated. Behaviorists like John B. Watson and B. F. Skinner argued that human nature is completely malleable: Early training can turn a child into any kind of adult, regardless of his or her heredity. Watson stated this argument in its most extreme form:

> Give me a dozen healthy infants, well-formed, and my own specified world to bring them up in, and I'll guarantee to take any one at random and train him to be any type of specialist I might select—doctor, lawyer, artist, merchant-chief, and, yes, even beggar-man and thief, regardless of his talents, penchants, tendencies, abilities, vocations, and race of his ancestors. (1930, p. 104)

Today most psychologists agree not only that both nature and nurture play important roles but also that they interact continuously to guide development. The newborn infant has an estimated 100 billion neurons in his or her brain but relatively few connections between them. The connections between neurons develop rapidly after birth, and the infant brain triples in weight in the first 3 years after birth (DiPietro, 2001). Brain development is heavily influenced both by genetic factors and by the stimulation or deprivation a child receives from the environment in the early years.

Even forms of development that seem to be determined by innate biological timetables can be affected by environmental events. At the moment of conception, a re-

Both John Locke and Charles Darwin influenced the nature-nurture debate, but in different ways. Locke emphasized the role of the senses in the acquisition of knowledge, arguing that knowledge is provided only by experience. Darwin emphasized the biological basis of human development, leading to renewed interest in the role of heredity.

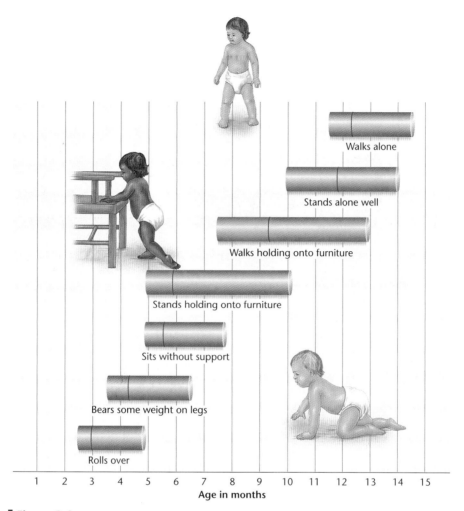

▌ Figure 3-1
Motor Development
The bars indicate the age range in which most infants develop the behavior indicated.

Walks alone

Stands alone well

Walks holding onto furniture

Stands holding onto furniture

Sits without support

Bears some weight on legs

Rolls over

1 2 3 4 5 6 7 8 9 10 11 12 13 14 15
Age in months

markable number of personal characteristics are already determined by the genetic structure of the fertilized ovum. Our genes program our growing cells so that we develop into a person rather than a fish or a chimpanzee. They determine our sex, the color of our skin, eyes, and hair, and our overall body size, among other things. These genetically determined characteristics are expressed through the process of **maturation**—an innately determined sequence of growth and change that is relatively independent of external events. The human fetus develops according to a fairly fixed schedule, and fetal behavior, such as turning and kicking, also follows an orderly sequence that depends on the stage of growth. However, if the uterine environment is seriously abnormal in some way, maturational processes can be disrupted. For example, if the mother contracts rubella during the first 3 months of pregnancy (when the fetus's basic organ systems are developing according to the genetically programmed schedule), the infant may be born deaf, blind, or brain-damaged, depending on which organ system was in a critical stage of development at the time of infection. Maternal malnutrition, smoking, and consumption of alcohol and drugs are other environmental factors that can affect the normal maturation of the fetus.

Motor development after birth also illustrates the interaction between genetically programmed maturation and environmental influences. Virtually all children go through the same sequence of motor behaviors in the same order: rolling over, sitting without support, standing while holding onto furniture, crawling, and then walking (see Figure 3-1). But they go through the sequence at different rates, and developmental psychologists have long wondered about the importance of learning and experience in such differences. Although early studies suggested that the answer was no (Dennis & Dennis, 1940; Gesell & Thompson, 1929; McGraw, 1935/1975), later studies indicate that practice or extra stimulation can accelerate the appearance of motor behaviors to some extent. For

© Laura Dwight

Virtually all children go through the same sequence of motor behaviors in the same order, but they go through the sequence at different rates.

example, newborn infants have a stepping reflex. If they are held in an upright position with their feet touching a solid surface, their legs make stepping movements that are similar to walking. In some cultures, such as the Kipsigis people of rural Kenya, parents actively teach their infants how to sit up, stand, and walk, and these babies reach these developmental milestones 3 to 5 weeks before American babies (Cole & Cole, 2001). In contrast, among the Ache, a nomadic people from eastern Paraguay, children get little experience with locomotion on their own because the forest they live in is so dense. These children begin walking almost a full year later than children in the United States (although they catch up to, and probably surpass, them in motor skills by mid-childhood).

The development of speech provides another example of the interaction between genetically determined characteristics and experience. In the course of normal development, all human infants learn to speak, but not until they have attained a certain level of neurological development. With rare exceptions, infants less than a year old cannot speak in sentences. But children reared in an environment where people talk to them and reward them for making speechlike sounds talk earlier than children who do not receive such attention. For example, children in middle-class American homes begin to talk at about 1 year of age. Children reared in San Marcos, a remote village in Guatemala, have little verbal interaction with adults and do not utter their first words until they are more than 2 years old (Kagan, 1979). Note that the environment affects the *rate* at which children acquire the skills, not the ultimate skill level.

STAGES OF DEVELOPMENT

In explaining the sequence of development, several psychologists have proposed discrete, qualitatively distinct steps or stages of development. Many of us use this concept informally. We think of the life span as being divided into the stages of infancy, childhood, adolescence, and adulthood. Parents might say that their adolescent is going through a "rebellious stage." Developmental psychologists, however, have a more precise concept in mind: The concept of **stages** implies that behaviors at a given stage are organized around a dominant theme or a coherent set of characteristics, behaviors at one stage are qualitatively different from behaviors at earlier or later stages, and all children go through the same stages in the same order. Environmental factors may speed up or slow down development, but the order of the stages does not vary. A child cannot enter a later stage without going through an earlier one first. As we will see later in the chapter, however, not all psychologists agree that development proceeds according to a fixed sequence of qualitatively distinct stages.

Closely related to the concept of stages is the idea of **critical periods** in human development—crucial time periods in a person's life when specific events occur if development is to proceed normally. Critical periods have been identified for some aspects of physical development in the human fetus. For example, the period 6 to 7 weeks after conception is critical for normal development of the sex organs. Whether the primitive sex organ develops into a male or female sexual structure depends on the presence of male hormones, regardless of the XX or XY arrangement of chromosomes. The absence of male hormones means that female sex organs will develop in either case. If male hormones are injected later in development, they cannot reverse the changes that have already taken place.

During postnatal development there is a critical period for the development of vision. If children who are born with cataracts have them removed before age 7, their vision develops fairly normally. But if a child goes through the first 7 years without adequate vision, extensive permanent disability results (DeHart, Sroufe, & Cooper, 2000).

The existence of critical periods for *psychological* development is less well established. It is probably more accurate to say that there are **sensitive periods**—periods that are optimal for a particular kind of development. If a certain behavior is not well established during this sensitive period, it may not develop to its full potential. For example, the first year of life appears to be a sensitive period for the formation of close interpersonal attachments (Rutter, Quinton, & Hill, 1990). The preschool years may be especially significant for intellectual development and language acquisition (DeHart et al., 2000). Children who have not had enough exposure to language before age 6 or 7 may fail to acquire it altogether (Goldin-Meadow, 1982). The experiences of children during such sensitive periods may shape their future course of development in a manner that will be difficult to change later.

◆ Interim Summary

- Two central questions in developmental psychology are (1) How do biological factors ("nature") interact with environmental experiences ("nurture") to determine the course of development? and (2) Is development best understood as a continuous process of change or as a series of qualitatively distinct stages?

- Some developmental psychologists believe that development occurs in a sequence of periods in which (1) behaviors at a given stage are organized around a dominant theme or a coherent set of characteristics, (2) behaviors at one stage are qualitatively different from behaviors at earlier or later stages, and (3) all children go through the same stages in the same order.

- An individual's genetic heritage is expressed through the process of maturation: innately determined sequences of growth or other changes in the body that are relatively independent of the environment.

- Critical or sensitive periods are times during development when specific experiences must occur for psychological development to proceed normally.

◆ Critical Thinking Questions

1. Why do you think some parents are very concerned that their children develop basic skills faster than other children the same age? What effect do you think this has on the child's development?

2. Some theorists have claimed that there are sensitive periods for the development of attachments between an infant and his or her caregiver. What would the implications of such sensitive periods be, if they do exist?

CAPACITIES OF THE NEWBORN

At the end of the 19th century, psychologist William James suggested that the newborn child experiences the world as a "buzzing, blooming confusion," an idea that was still prevalent as late as the 1960s. We now know that newborn infants enter the world with all of their sensory systems functioning and are well prepared to learn about their new environment.

Because babies cannot explain what they are doing or tell us what they are thinking, developmental psychologists have had to design some ingenious procedures to study the capacities of infants. The basic method is to change the baby's environment in some way and observe the responses. For example, an investigator might present a tone or a flashing light and see if there is a change in heart rate or if the baby turns its head or sucks more vigorously on a nipple. In some instances, the researcher presents two stimuli at the same time to determine whether infants look longer at one than at the other. If they do, it indicates that they can tell the stimuli apart and perhaps that they prefer one over the other. In this section we describe some research findings on infant capacities, beginning with studies of infants' vision.

VISION

Newborns have poor visual acuity, their ability to change focus is limited, and they are very nearsighted. The computer-manipulated picture in Figure 3-2 (left) shows how a mother's face may look to an infant. By 7 or 8 months of age, infants' visual acuity is close to that of adults (Cole & Cole, 2001). Newborns spend a lot of time actively looking about. They scan the world in an organized way and pause when their eyes encounter an object or some change in their **visual field,** which is the

❚ Figure 3-2
Visual Acuity
The newborn's poor visual acuity makes the mother's face look fuzzy (left) rather than clear (right), even when viewed from close up.

full scope of what they can see. They are particularly attracted to areas of high contrast, such as the edges of an object. Instead of scanning the entire object, as an adult would, they keep looking at areas that have the most edges. They also prefer complex patterns over plain ones and patterns with curved lines over patterns with straight lines.

The possibility that there is **facial preference**—an inborn, unlearned preference for faces—initially aroused great interest. Newborns do tend to track a moving face-like pattern farther than a scrambled or blank face, but this preference declines sharply between 4 and 6 weeks of age. Later research showed that infants are not attracted to faces per se but to stimulus characteristics such as curved lines, high contrast, edges, movement, and complexity—all of which faces possess (Aslin, 1987; Banks & Salapatek, 1983). Newborns look mostly at the outside contour of a face, but by 2 months they focus on the inside of the face—the eyes, nose, and mouth. By 3 months, infants can recognize photographs of their mothers and prefer pictures of them to pictures of strangers. By 5 months, infants can remember the faces of strangers.

HEARING

Even fetuses 26 to 28 weeks old move in response to a sharp sound. Newborn infants turn their heads toward the source of a sound. Interestingly, the head-turning response disappears at about 6 weeks and does not reemerge until 3 or 4 months, at which time the infants also search with their eyes for the source of the sound. The temporary disappearance of the head-turning response probably represents a maturational transition from a reflexive response controlled by subcortical areas of the brain to a voluntary attempt to locate the source of the sound. By 4 months, infants reach toward the source of a sound in the dark. By 6 months, they show a marked increase in their responsiveness to sounds that are accompanied by visual stimuli and are able to pinpoint the location of a sound more precisely, an ability that continues to improve into their second year (Ashmead, Davis, Whalen, & Odom, 1991; Field, 1987; Hillier, Hewitt, & Morrongiello, 1992).

Newborn infants can also detect the difference between very similar sounds, such as two tones that are only one note apart on the musical scale (Olsho et al., 1982), and they can distinguish between the human voice and other kinds of sounds. They can also differentiate various characteristics of human speech. For example, 1-month-old infants can tell the difference between similar sounds such as "pa" and "ba." Interestingly, infants can distinguish between some speech sounds better than adults can. These are sounds that adults "hear" as identical because there is no distinction between them in their native language (Aslin, Pisoni, & Jusczyk, 1983). For example, "ra" and "la" are separate sounds in English but not in Japanese. Japanese infants can distinguish between them, but Japanese adults cannot.

By 6 months the child has picked up enough information about the language to begin to "screen out" sounds that it does not use (Kuhl, Williams, Lacerda, Stevens, & Lindblom, 1992). Thus, human infants appear to be born with perceptual mechanisms that are already tuned to the properties of human speech that will help them learn language (Eimas, 1975).

TASTE AND SMELL

Infants can discriminate between tastes shortly after birth. They prefer sweet-tasting liquids over liquids that are salty, bitter, sour, or bland. The characteristic response of the newborn to a sweet liquid is a relaxed expression resembling a slight smile, sometimes accompanied by lip-licking. A sour solution produces pursed lips and a wrinkled nose. In response to a bitter solution, the baby opens its mouth with the corners turned down and sticks out its tongue in what appears to be an expression of disgust.

Newborns can also discriminate among odors. They turn their heads toward a sweet smell, and heart rate and respiration slow down; these are indicators of attention. Noxious odors, such as those of ammonia or rotten eggs, cause them to turn their heads away; their heart rate and respiration accelerate, indicating distress. Infants are able to discriminate among even subtle differences in smells. After nursing for only a few days, an infant will consistently turn its head toward a pad saturated with its mother's milk in preference to one saturated with another mother's milk (Russell, 1976). Only breast-fed babies show this ability to recognize the mother's odor (Cernoch & Porter, 1985). When bottle-fed babies are given a choice between the smell of their familiar formula and that of a lactating breast, they choose the breast (Porter, Makin, Davis, & Christensen, 1992). There seems to be an innate preference for the odor of breast milk. In general, the ability to distinguish among smells has a clear adaptive value: It helps infants avoid noxious substances and thereby increase their chances of survival.

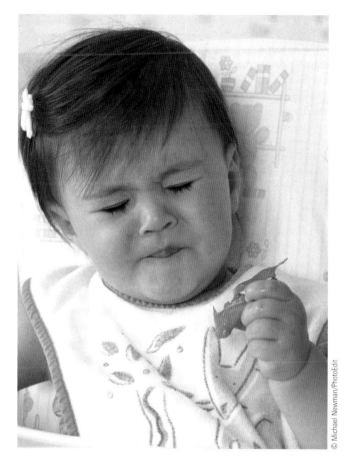

Infants show their likes and dislikes for certain tastes at a very young age using universal facial expressions, such as the expression for disgust.

LEARNING AND MEMORY

It was once thought that infants could neither learn nor remember, but this is not the case. Evidence for early learning and remembering comes from several classic studies. In one, infants only a few hours old learned to turn their heads right or left, depending on whether they heard a buzzer or a tone. To taste a sweet liquid, the baby had to turn to the right when a tone sounded and to the left when a buzzer sounded. After only a few trials, the babies were performing without error—turning to the right when the tone sounded and to the left when the buzzer sounded. The experimenter then reversed the situation so that the infant had to turn the opposite way when either the buzzer or the tone sounded. The babies mastered this new task quickly (Siqueland & Lipsitt, 1966).

By the time they are 3 months old, infants have good memories. When a mobile over an infant's crib was attached to one of the baby's limbs by a ribbon,

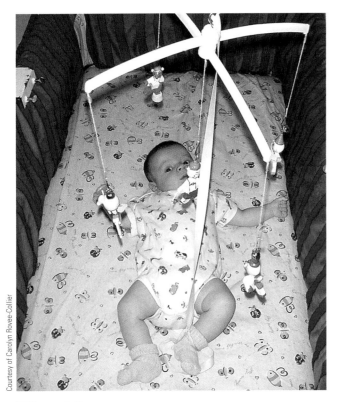

▌Figure 3-3
A Study of Infant Memory
A study showed that 3-month-old infants could easily learn to move a mobile by pulling on a ribbon attached to their leg; the infants remembered this new behavior when tested in the same situation eight days later. (From Rovee-Collier, C. (1999). The development of infant memory. *Current Directions in Psychological Science, 8,* 80–85.)

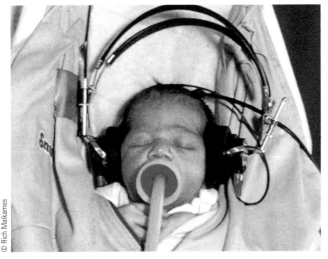

▌Figure 3-4
Preference for Sounds
A newborn can indicate a preference for certain sounds—such as the mother's voice—by sucking more vigorously on a nipple when it causes the preferred sounds to be played through the earphones.

3-month-old infants quickly discovered which arm or leg would move the mobile. When the infants were placed in the same situation 8 days later, they remembered which arm or leg to move (Rovee-Collier, 1999) (see Figure 3-3).

More startling is evidence that infants remember sensations they experienced before birth, while still in the mother's uterus. We noted earlier that newborn infants can distinguish the sound of the human voice from other sounds. They also prefer the human voice over other sounds. A few days after birth, infants can learn to suck on an artificial nipple in order to turn on recorded speech or vocal music, and they suck more vigorously to hear speech sounds than to hear nonspeech sounds or instrumental music (Butterfield & Siperstein, 1972). They also prefer heartbeat sounds and female voices over male voices, and they prefer their mother's voice to other women's voices. But they do not prefer their father's voice to other men's voices (Brazelton, 1978; DeCasper & Fifer, 1980; DeCasper & Prescott, 1984) (see Figure 3-4).

These preferences appear to stem from the infant's prenatal experience with sounds. For example, the mother's voice can also be heard in the uterus, which would appear to explain why a newborn infant prefers her voice over others. Perhaps most surprising is evidence that the fetus may actually be learning to discriminate among some of the sounds of individual words. In an extraordinary experiment, pregnant women read aloud passages from children's stories each day during the last 6 weeks of pregnancy. For example, some women read the first 28 paragraphs of the Dr. Seuss book *The Cat in the Hat*. Others read the last 28 paragraphs of the same story, but with the main nouns changed so that it was about the "dog in the fog" instead of the "cat in the hat." By the time the infants were born, they had heard one of the selected stories for a total of about 3½ hours.

Two or 3 days after the infants were born, they were permitted to suck on a special pacifier wired to record sucking rates (like the apparatus shown in Figure 3-4). Sucking on the pacifier turned on a tape recording of either their mother's voice or an unfamiliar woman's voice reading aloud either the story the infants had heard before birth or the story they had not heard previously. As in previous experiments, the infants showed by their sucking rates that they preferred their mother's voice to the stranger's. The startling finding, however, was that they also preferred the familiar story over the unfamiliar one—even when the two stories were read by the stranger (DeCasper & Spence, 1986).

In sum, the research we have described challenges the view of the newborn as experiencing the world as "buzzing, blooming confusion," as well as the view that the child enters the world as a "blank slate." Clearly, the infant enters the world well prepared to perceive and learn.

CUTTING-EDGE RESEARCH
Massage Therapy for At-Risk Babies

Massage therapy is one of the oldest forms of medical treatment. It was first described in China during the 2nd century B.C. and became popular around the same time in India and Egypt (Field, 1998). In modern times, techniques like massage therapy have been replaced with pharmaceuticals. Still, among proponents of "alternative medicine," massage is still commonly used to treat a variety of ailments, including anxiety.

Is massage therapy useful? Tiffany Field and her colleagues at the Touch Research Institute at the University of Miami School of Medicine have embarked on a program of research to scientifically test the efficacy of massage in the treatment of young children with a variety of medical and emotional problems. They define massage as the manipulation of deep tissue with the presumed stimulation of pressure receptors. They have focused on disorders or conditions that they theorized could be positively affected by such techniques, by facilitating physical growth, reducing pain, increasing alertness, enhancing immune function, and diminishing stress, anxiety, and depression (Field, 1998, 2001).

Many studies of massage therapy have focused on children who have failed to grow normally because of prematurity, exposure to cocaine or HIV, or other conditions. In these studies, children are randomly assigned to receive regular massages from their parents or to be in a control group that receives attention but no massage. In one study of preterm infants in a neonatal intensive care unit, infants given 15-minute massages three times a day for 10 days gained 47% more weight than control infants (see the figure; Field et al., 1986; Scafidi et al., 1990). The infants receiving massage were also hospitalized for 6 days less at a hospital cost savings of $10,000 per infant. Measures of norepinephrine and epinephrine revealed more normal developmental increases over the period of the study in the massaged infants than in the control infants, and the massaged infants had better scores on measure of neonatal behavior. At 1 year of age, the massaged infants still weighed more than the control infants and performed better on measures of mental, motor, and behavioral development (Scafidi et al., 1990). Similar results have been obtained for infants exposed to cocaine or HIV in the womb (Scafidi & Field, 1996; Wheeden et al., 1993)

Full-term infants also seem to benefit from massage. In one study of full-term 1- to 3-month-old infants born to adolescent mothers, infants were given 15 minutes a day of either massage or rocking for a total of 12 days over a 6-week period. During the massage sessions, the massaged infants spent more time in active alert states, cried less, and had lower salivary cortisol levels, suggesting lower stress levels. At the end of the 6-week treatment, the massaged infants had gained more weight, improved more on emotionality, sociability, and soothability, showed better face-to-face interactions, had lower urinary stress hormones, and had higher serotonin levels than the control infants (Field, Grizzle, Scafidi, Abrams, & Richardson, 1996).

Children with juvenile rheumatoid arthritis often suffer chronic pain. Anti-inflammatory agents can relieve the pain but only so much, and some drugs are addictive. One study that had parents provide their arthritic children with daily massages found that these children experienced less anxiety, showed lower stress hormones, and reported less pain over a 1-month period than children who received only training in muscle relaxation (Field, Hernandez-Reif, Seligman et al., 1997). Positive results of massage therapy have also been found with children with asthma by reducing stress hormones and subjective states of anxiety that can trigger asthma attacks (Field et al., 1998).

What is the mechanism for the effects of massage therapy, particularly across such a wide variety of conditions? The

(continued)

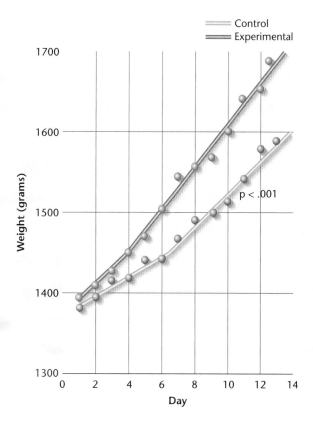

Mean daily weight gain in preterm infants who received massage therapy and control infants who did not. (From T. Field, "Massage Therapy Facilitates Weight Gain in Preterm Infants," *Current Directions in Psychological Science, 10,* pp. 51–53. © 1986 Blackwell Publishers.)

answer is not known yet, but it seems likely that reductions in stress-related hormones and in subjective states of anxiety and depression play an important role. The old notion that massage increases blood flow has not been consistently supported in recent studies (Field, 1998). Some of the positive effects of massage for children probably come from improvements in the rela-tionship between the children and their parents, who are delivering the massage. Parents who provide massages to their children in these studies report that their own anxiety and depression levels de-crease, and they feel they are having a more positive role in their child's illness than before (Field, Hernandez-Reif, Shaw et al., 1997). This may lead to a general improvement in the home environment and family life that has widespread ef-fects on children's well-being.

Whatever the mechanisms, if mas-sage therapy continues to be shown to reliably improve children's function-ing across certain conditions, it repre-sents an inexpensive and safe form of intervention.

 For more information, go online with InfoTrac. Use your own term or search:

- Infant massage
- Massage and pain

◆ Interim Summary

- Early theorists believed that all sensory preferences and abilities had to be learned, but research over the last several decades has established that infants are born with their sensory systems intact and prepared to learn about the world.

- Newborns have poor vision and cannot see as well as an adult until about age 2.

- Some theorists thought infants were born with a preference for faces, but research suggests infants are not attracted to faces per se but to stimulus characteristics such as curved lines, high contrast, edges, movement, and complexity—all of which faces possess.

- Even newborns pay attention to sounds, and they seem to be born with perceptual mechanisms that are already tuned to the properties of human speech that will help them learn language.

- Infants can discriminate between different tastes and odors shortly after birth. They seem to show a prefer-ence for the taste and odor of breast milk.

- Infants can learn from the moment they are born and show good memories by 3 months of age.

◆ Critical Thinking Questions

1. What do you think the evidence regarding infants' memories says about claims that adults can re-member events from their first year of life?

2. Can an infant's environment be too stimulating? What might be the effects of an overly stimulating environment?

COGNITIVE DEVELOPMENT IN CHILDHOOD

Although most parents are aware of the intellectual changes that accompany their children's physical growth, they would have difficulty describing the nature of these changes. How contemporary psychologists describe these changes has been profoundly influenced by the Swiss psychologist Jean Piaget (1896–1980). Prior to Piaget, psy-chological thinking about children's cognitive develop-ment was dominated by two perspectives, the biological-maturation, which emphasized the "nature" component of development, and the environmental-learning perspective, which emphasized "nurture." In contrast, Piaget focused on the interaction between the child's naturally maturing abilities and his or her interactions with the environment. In this section we outline Piaget's stage theory of develop-ment and then turn to a critique of that theory and to some more recent approaches. We also discuss the work of Lev Vygotsky, a Russian psychologist whose ideas about cog-nitive development, originally published in the 1930s, have attracted renewed interest in recent years.

PIAGET'S STAGE THEORY

Partly as a result of his observations of his own children, Piaget became interested in the relationship between the child's naturally maturing abilities and his or her interac-tions with the environment. He saw the child as an active participant in this process, rather than as a passive recipi-ent of biological development or external stimuli. He viewed children as "inquiring scientists" who experiment with objects and events in their environment to see what

Piaget argued that children learn about the world by doing "experiments" with unknown objects or concepts.

CONCEPT REVIEW TABLE
Piaget's Stages of Cognitive Development

The ages given are averages. They may vary considerably depending on intelligence, cultural background, and socioeconomic factors, but the order of the progression is assumed to be the same for all children. Piaget has described more detailed phases within each stage; only a general characterization of each stage is given here.

Stage	Characterization
1. Sensorimotor (birth–2 years)	Differentiates self from objects
	Recognizes self as agent of action and begins to act intentionally; for example, pulls a string to set a mobile in motion or shakes a rattle to make a noise
2. Preoperational (2–7 years)	Learns to use language and to represent objects by images and words
	Thinking is still egocentric: has difficulty taking the viewpoint of others
	Classifies objects by a single feature; for example, groups together all the red blocks regardless of shape or all the square blocks regardless of color
3. Concrete operational (7–11 years)	Can think logically about objects and events
	Achieves conservation of number (age 6), mass (age 7), and weight (age 9)
	Classifies objects according to several features and can order them in series along a single dimension, such as size
4. Formal operational (11 years and up)	Can think logically about abstract propositions and test hypotheses systematically
	Becomes concerned with the hypothetical, the future, and ideological problems

will happen. ("What does it feel like to suck on the teddy bear's ear?" "What happens if I push my dish off the edge of the table?") The results of these "experiments" are used to construct **schemas**—theories about how the physical and social worlds operate. Upon encountering a novel object or event, the child attempts to **assimilate** it—understand it in terms of a preexisting schema. Piaget argued that if the new experience does not fit the existing schema, the child—like any good scientist—will engage in **accommodation**—modifying a schema to fit new information, thereby extending the child's theory of the world (Piaget & Inhelder, 1969). For example, if a boy's schema for firefighter is a male adult who wears a big, bulky uniform, but he sees a picture of a woman in a firefighter's uniform, he may first refuse to believe that women can be firefighters. He may argue that the woman in the picture must be playing "dress-up." Upon further evidence of women firefighters, however, the boy may engage in accommodation of his schema for firefighters, accepting that firefighters can be women, too.

Piaget's first job as a postgraduate student in psychology was as an intelligence tester for Alfred Binet, the inventor of the IQ test (see Chapter 12). In the course of this work, he began wondering why children made the kinds of errors they did. What distinguished their reasoning from that of adults? He observed his own children closely as they played, presenting them with simple scientific and moral problems and asking them to explain how they arrived at their answers. Piaget's observations convinced him that children's ability to think and reason progresses through a series of qualitatively distinct stages. He divided cognitive development into four major stages, each of which has a number of substages. The major stages are the sensorimotor stage, the preoperational stage, the stage of concrete operations, and the stage of formal operations (see Concept Review Table).

Figure 3-5
Object Permanence
When the toy is hidden by a screen, the infant acts as if the toy no longer exists. From this observation, Piaget concluded that the infant had not yet acquired the concept of object permanence.

THE SENSORIMOTOR STAGE Piaget designated the first 2 years of life as the **sensorimotor stage,** when infants are busy discovering the relationships between their actions and the consequences of those actions. They discover, for example, how far they have to reach to grasp an object and what happens when they push their dish over the edge of the table. In this way they begin to develop a concept of themselves as separate from the external world.

An important discovery during this stage is the concept of **object permanence,** the awareness that an object continues to exist even when it is not present. If a cloth is placed over a toy that an 8-month-old is reaching for, the infant immediately stops reaching and appears to lose interest in the toy. The baby seems neither surprised nor upset, makes no attempt to search for the toy, and acts as if the toy had ceased to exist (see Figure 3-5). In contrast, a 10-month-old will actively search for an object that has been hidden under a cloth or behind a screen. The older baby, having attained the concept of object permanence, seems to realize that the object exists, even though it is out of sight. But even at this age, search is limited. The infant who has had repeated success in retrieving a toy hidden in a particular place will continue to look for it in that spot even after watching an adult conceal it in a new location. Not until about 1 year of age will a child consistently look for an object where it was last seen, regardless of what happened on previous trials.

THE PREOPERATIONAL STAGE By about $1\frac{1}{2}$ to 2 years of age, children have begun to use symbols. Words can represent things or groups of things, and one object can represent another. A 3-year-old may treat a stick as a horse and ride it around the room, a block of wood can become a car, and one doll can become a father and another a baby. But although 3- and 4-year-olds can think in symbolic terms, their words and images are not yet organized in a logical manner. During this **preoperational stage** of cognitive development, the child does not yet comprehend certain rules or operations. An **operation** is a mental routine for separating, combining, and otherwise transforming information in a logical manner. For example, if water is poured from a tall, narrow glass into a short, wide one, adults know that the amount of water has not changed because they can reverse the transformation in their minds. They can imagine pouring the water from the short glass back into the tall glass, thereby arriving back at the original state. In the preoperational stage of cognitive development, a child's understanding of reversibility and other mental operations is absent or weak. As a result, according to Piaget, preoperational children have not yet attained **conservation**—the understanding that the amount of a substance remains the same even when its form is changed. They fail to understand that the amount of water is conserved—remains the same—when it is poured from the tall glass into the short one (see Figure 3-6).

Piaget believed that preoperational thinking is dominated by visual impressions. A change in the visual appearance of the clay influences the child more than less obvious but more essential qualities, such as mass or weight. This reliance on visual impressions is illustrated by an experiment on the conservation of number. If two

▌ Figure 3-6
The Concept of Conservation
A 4-year-old acknowledges that the two short, wide glasses contain the same amount of liquid. However, when the contents of one glass is poured into a tall, thin glass, she says that it contains more liquid. Not until she is several years older will she state that the two different-shaped glasses contain the same amount of liquid.

rows of checkers are matched one for one against each other, young children will say, correctly, that the rows have the same number of checkers (see Figure 3-7). If the checkers in one row are brought closer together to form a cluster, 5-year-olds say that there are now more checkers in the straight row—even though no checkers have been removed. The visual impression of a long row of checkers overrides the numerical equality that was obvious when the checkers appeared in matching rows. In contrast, 7-year-olds assume that if the number of objects was equal before, it must remain equal. At this age,

numerical equality has become more significant than visual impression.

Another key characteristic of preoperational children, according to Piaget, is **egocentrism.** Preoperational children are unaware of perspectives other than their own—they believe that everyone else perceives the environment the same way they do (Piaget, 1950a). To demonstrate this, Piaget created the "three-mountain problem." A child is allowed to walk around a table on which are arranged three mountains of different heights. Then the child stands on one side of the table while a

▌ Figure 3-7
Conservation of Number
When the two rows of ten checkers are evenly spaced, most children report that they contain the same amount. When one row is then spread out into a larger space, children under age 6 or 7 say that the original row contains fewer checkers.

doll is placed on the table at various locations (and therefore has a different view of the three mountains than the child). The child is asked to choose a photograph that shows what the doll is seeing. Before the age of 6 or 7, most children choose the photograph that illustrates their own perspective on the three mountains (Piaget & Inhelder, 1948/1956).

Piaget believed that egocentrism explains the rigidity of preoperational thought. Because young children cannot appreciate points of view other than their own, they cannot revise their schemas to take into account changes in the environment. This is why they are unable to reverse operations or conserve quantity.

OPERATIONAL STAGES Between the ages of 7 and 12, children master the various conservation concepts and begin to perform other logical manipulations. They can place objects in order on the basis of a dimension such as height or weight. They can also form a mental representation of a series of actions. Five-year-olds can find their way to a friend's house but cannot direct you there or trace the route with paper and pencil. They can find their own way because they know that they have to turn at certain places, but they have no overall picture of the route. In contrast, 8-year-olds can readily draw a map of the route. Piaget calls this period the **concrete operational stage:** Although children are using abstract terms, they are doing so only in relation to concrete objects—objects to which they have direct sensory access.

At about the age of 11 or 12, children arrive at adult modes of thinking. In the **formal operational stage,** the person is able to reason in purely symbolic terms. In one test for formal operational thinking, the child tries to discover what determines how long a pendulum will swing back and forth (its period of oscillation). Given a length of string suspended from a hook and several weights that can be attached to the lower end, the child can vary the length of the string, change the attached weight, and alter the height from which the bob is released. Children who are still in the concrete operational stage experiment by changing some of the variables but not in a systematic way. Average adolescents, however, set up a series of hypotheses and test them systematically. They reason that if a particular variable (weight) affects the period of oscillation, the effect will appear only if they change one variable and hold all others constant. If this variable seems to have no effect on how long the pendulum swings, they rule it out and try another. Considering all the possibilities—working out the consequences for each hypothesis and confirming or denying these consequences—is the essence of formal operational thought.

A Critique of Piaget's Theory

Piaget's theory was a major intellectual achievement that revolutionized the way we think about children's cognitive development. However, new, more sophisticated methods of testing the intellectual functioning of infants and preschool children reveal that Piaget underestimated their abilities. Many of the tasks designed to test stage theories actually require several skills, such as attention, memory, and specific factual knowledge. Children may have the ability being tested but be unable to perform the task because they lack one of the other required skills.

Take the example of object permanence. As we saw earlier, when infants younger than 8 months are shown a toy that is then hidden or covered while they watch, they act as if the toy no longer exists and do not attempt to search for it. Note, however, that successful performance on this test requires children not only to understand that the object still exists but also to remember where the object was hidden and to show through some physical action that they are searching for it. Because Piaget believed that early cognitive development depends on sensorimotor activities, he did not consider the possibility that the infant might know that the object still exists but be unable to show this knowledge through searching behavior.

In a study designed to test this possibility, children were not required to actively search for the hidden object. As shown in the far left section of Figure 3-8, the apparatus was a screen hinged at one edge to the top of a table. At first the screen lay flat on the table. As the infant watched, the screen was slowly rotated away from the infant through a complete 180-degree arc until it was again flat on the table. The screen was then rotated in the opposite direction, toward the infant.

When the infants were first shown the rotating screen, they looked at it for almost a full minute, but after repeated trials they lost interest and turned their attention elsewhere. At that point a brightly painted box appeared on the table beyond the hinge, where it would be hidden as the screen moved into its upright position. (The infant was actually seeing a reflected image of a box, not the actual box.) As shown in Figure 3-8, the infants were then shown either a possible event or an impossible event. One group of infants saw the screen rotate from its starting position until it reached the point where it should bump against the box. At that point the screen stopped and then moved back to its starting position. The other group saw the screen rotate to the upright position but then continue to rotate all the way to the other side of the 180-degree arc, just as though no box was in the way. The investigators reasoned that if the infants thought the

Possible event

Impossible event

a) Habituation event
   Infants are shown a rotating screen until they no longer attend to it.

b) Test events
   In these test events, a box is placed where it can be hidden by the screen. The infants then see either a possible event (the screen rotates until it would hit the box and then returns to its starting position) or an impossible event (the screen appears to pass right through the box). Infants attend more to the impossible event, indicating that they realize that the hidden box still exists.

▌**Figure 3-8**
Testing Object Permanence

(Adapted from Baillargeon, R., "Object Performance in 3½ and 4½-Month-Old Infants," from *Developmental Psychology, 23*:655–664. Copyright © 1987. Reprinted by permission of the Academic Press.)

box still existed even when the screen hid it, they would be surprised when it seemed to pass through the box—an impossible event. The infants would then look at the screen longer than they would when the screen seemed to bump into the box before returning to its starting point. This is exactly what happened. Even though the impossible event was perceptually identical to an event that they had seen repeatedly and lost interest in, the infants found it more interesting than a physically possible event that they had never seen before—the screen stopping halfway through the arc and then reversing direction (Baillargeon, Spelke, & Wasserman, 1985).

Because the infants in this experiment were only 4½ months old, they displayed object permanence 4 to 5 months earlier than Piaget's theory predicts. Replications of this study have found that some infants as young as 3½ months display object permanence (Baillargeon, 1987; Baillargeon & DeVos, 1991).

More recent experiments using Piaget's conservation tasks have also yielded evidence that children's mental capacities develop earlier than he thought. In one study of number conservation, two sets of toys were lined up in one-to-one correspondence (as in Figure 3-6). The experimenter then said, "These are your soldiers and these are my soldiers. What's more, my soldiers, your soldiers, or are they both the same?" After the child answered this question correctly, the experimenter spread out one of the rows of toys and repeated the question. As Piaget and others had previously reported, 5-year-old children failed to conserve, stating that the spread-out row contained more soldiers. But then the investigator introduced a second set of conditions. Instead of describing

the toys as individual soldiers, she said, "This is my army and this is your army. What's more, my army, your army, or are they both the same?" With this simple change of wording, most of the children were able to conserve, judging the two "armies" to be the same size, even when one of them was spread out. When children are prompted to interpret the display as an aggregate or collection rather than as a set of individual items, their judgments of equality are less likely to be influenced by irrelevant perceptual transformations (Markman, 1979).

Other research has identified more factors that can influence the development of concrete operational thought. For example, the experience of going to school seems to promote mastery of Piagetian tasks (Artman & Cahan, 1993). This and other evidence suggest that concrete operational reasoning may not be a universal stage of development that emerges during middle childhood but, instead, a product of the cultural setting, schooling, and the specific wording of questions and instructions.

ALTERNATIVES TO PIAGET'S THEORY

Developmental psychologists generally agree that these kinds of findings show that Piaget underestimated children's abilities, and his theory has been challenged on many grounds. However, there is no consensus on the best alternative to pursue. Some psychologists favor information-processing approaches, and others have pursued knowledge-acquisition and sociocultural approaches.

INFORMATION-PROCESSING APPROACHES We have already noted that many of the experiments challenging

Piaget's views were inspired by investigators who view cognitive development as the acquisition of several separate **information-processing skills—** specific skills at gathering and analyzing information from the environment. Accordingly, they think that the standard Piagetian tasks fail to separate these skills from the skill that the task is supposed to assess. But they disagree among themselves about exactly how their views challenge Piaget's theory. For example, they disagree on the important question of whether development is best understood as a series of qualitatively distinct stages or as a continuous process of change. Some think that the entire notion of stages should be abandoned (Klahr, 1982). In their view, the separate skills develop smoothly and continuously rather than in a series of discrete stages. But other information-processing theorists think that gradual changes in information-processing skills do in fact lead to discontinuous, stagelike changes in children's thinking (Case & Okamoto, 1996). These theorists are sometimes referred to as neo-Piagetians. Other neo-Piagetians agree that there are genuine stages but only within more narrow domains of knowledge. For example, a child's language skills, mathematical understanding, social reasoning, and so forth may all develop in a stagelike fashion, but each domain proceeds at its own pace relatively independently of the others (Mandler, 1983).

KNOWLEDGE-ACQUISITION APPROACHES Some developmental psychologists think that after infancy, children and adults have essentially the same cognitive processes and capacities and that the primary difference between them is the adult's more extensive knowledge base. By **knowledge** they mean not just a larger collection of facts but a deeper understanding of how facts in a particular domain are organized.

The distinction between facts and the organization of facts is shown in a study that compared a group of 10-year-old chess experts competing in a tournament with a group of college students who were chess amateurs. When asked to memorize and recall lists of random numbers, the college students easily outperformed the 10-year-olds. But when tested on their ability to recall actual positions of the chess pieces on the board, the 10-year-old chess experts did better than the 18-year-old chess amateurs (Chi, 1978). The relevant difference between the two groups is not different stages of cognitive development or different information-processing abilities, but domain-specific knowledge. Because the 10-year-olds had a deeper grasp of the underlying structure of chess, they could organize and reconstruct the arrangements from memory by "chunking" the separate

Studies of young chess experts suggest their greater store of knowledge about chess allows them to process information about appropriate moves more efficiently, giving them the upper hand in competitions with older but less expert chess players.

pieces of information into larger meaningful units (for example, a king-side attack by white) and eliminating from consideration implausible placements of the pieces. (We discuss experts versus amateur problem solvers in Chapter 9.)

Increasing knowledge of the world, rather than a qualitative shift in cognitive development, may also account for children's increasing ability to solve Piaget's conservation tasks as they grow older. For example, a child who does not know that mass or number is the critical feature that defines "more clay" or "more checkers" is likely to judge that the quantity has changed when only its visual appearance has changed. An older child may simply have learned the essential defining feature of "more." If this hypothesis is correct, children who fail to show conservation in one domain may show conservation in another, depending on their understanding of the domain. For example, in a study kindergarten children were told about a series of "operations" that doctors or scientists had performed. Some operations altered an animal so that it looked like a different animal; other operations altered an animal so that it looked like a plant (see Figure 3-9). Children were told that

the doctors took a horse [shows child picture of horse] and did an operation that put black and white stripes all over its body. They cut off its mane and braided its tail. They trained it to stop neighing like a horse, and they trained it to eat wild grass instead of oats and hay. They also trained

▌Figure 3-9
Early Testing of Conservation
Children are told that doctors or scientists operated on an animal until it looked like a different animal (horse to zebra) or until it looked like a plant (porcupine to cactus). Children who say that the animal is "really" the new animal or plant are failing to show conservation; children who say that the animal is still "really" the original animal are showing conservation.

it to live in the wilds in Africa instead of in a stable. When they were all done, the animal looked just like this [shows picture of zebra]. When they were finished, was this animal a horse or a zebra? (Keil, 1989, p. 307)

When asked about operations that transformed one kind of animal into another, a majority of the children failed to conserve. About 65% agreed that the horse had been genuinely changed into a zebra. But when faced with the transformation of an animal into a plant, only about 25% agreed that a porcupine had been genuinely changed into a cactus (Keil, 1989). Studies like these demonstrate that in some domains preoperational children can ignore dramatic changes in visual appearance because they have learned that an invisible but essential defining feature of the object has remained unchanged.

SOCIOCULTURAL APPROACHES Although Piaget emphasized the child's interactions with the environment, the environment he had in mind was the immediate physical environment. The social and cultural context plays virtually no role in Piaget's theory. Yet much of what children must learn is the particular ways their culture views reality, what roles different people—and different sexes—are expected to play, and what rules and norms govern social relationships in their particular culture. In these areas there are no universally valid facts or correct views of reality. According to those who take a **sociocultural approach to development,** the child should be seen not as a physical scientist seeking "true" knowledge but as a newcomer to a culture who seeks to become a native by learning how to look at social reality through the lens of that culture (Rogoff, 2000).

Culture can influence children's development in several ways (Cole & Cole, 2001):

1. By providing the opportunity for specific activities: Children learn by observation, experience, or at least hearing about an activity. For example, because water is scarce in the desert, children of the Kung of the Kalahari Desert are unlikely to learn about conservation by pouring water from one glass to another, but children growing up in Seattle or Paris are unlikely to learn how to find water-bearing roots in the desert.

2. By determining the frequency of certain activities: For example, traditional dancing is important in Balinese culture, so children growing up in Bali become skilled dancers, but Norwegian children become expert skiers or skaters.

3. By how they relate different activities: For example, in cultures in which making pottery is important, children associate molding clay with interaction with their parents and perhaps with selling pots in the market. In cultures where making pottery is not important, children may view molding clay only as a nursery school pastime.

4. By controlling the child's role in the activity: In many cultures, meat is obtained in a supermarket, and children (and their parents) play no role in trapping, killing, and preparing the animal from which the meat comes. In other cultures, children learn from a young age how to hunt, kill, and prepare animals for family meals.

The origins of this view of cognitive development can be seen in the work of the Russian scholar Lev Vygotsky (1934/1986). Vygotsky believed that we develop understanding and expertise primarily through what might be described as apprenticeship—we are guided by more knowledgeable individuals, who help us understand more and more about our world and develop new skills. He also distinguished between two levels of cognitive development: the child's actual level of development, as expressed in problem-solving ability, and the child's level of potential development, which is determined by the kind of problem solving the child can do when guided by an adult or a more knowledgeable peer. According to Vygotsky, we need to know both the actual and potential levels of development in a particular child to fully understand that child's level of cognitive development and provide appropriate instruction.

Because language is the primary means by which humans exchange social meanings, Vygotsky viewed language development as central to cognitive development. In fact, he regarded language acquisition as the most important aspect of children's development (Blanck, 1990). Language plays an important role in developing new skills and knowledge. As adults and peers help children master new tasks, the communication between them becomes part of the children's thinking. The children then use their language ability to guide their own actions as they practice the new skill. What Piaget referred to as egocentric speech Vygotsky considered an essential component of cognitive development: Children speak to themselves to give themselves guidance and direction. This kind of self-instruction is termed *private speech.* You can observe this process in a child who gives herself instructions about how to perform a task, such as tying her shoes, that she previously heard from an adult (Berk, 1997).

THEORY OF MIND

As adults, we behave and think in ways that reflect our understanding that other people have minds—they think, they have expectations and beliefs, they have their own assumptions, and so on. Much of our behavior toward other people is based on our understanding of what they are thinking. For example, we have a date to meet a friend for coffee at 2 P.M. but realize that the meeting we are in is not going to be finished until 2:30 P.M. Knowing the friend expects us to be at the coffee house at 2 P.M., we take a break from the meeting to call our friend and tell her we are going to be late. We also occasionally reflect on our own thinking process by, for example, evaluating what we think about a situation or wondering how we could have been mistaken in a belief. This thinking about thinking is referred to as **metacognition.**

In recent years, psychologists have become interested in how metacognition, or more generally an individual's **theory of mind,** develops. These researchers have studied children's knowledge about basic mental states, such as desires, percepts, beliefs, knowledge, thoughts, intentions, and feelings (Flavell, 1999). The following study is typical in research on theory of mind and illustrates the basic developmental finding (Flavell, 1999).

> An experimenter shows a 5-year-old child a candy box with pictures of candy on it and asks her what she thinks is in it. "Candy," she replies. Then the child gets to look inside and discovers to her surprise that it actually contains crayons, not candy. The experimenter then asks her what another child who had not yet seen inside the box would think it contained. "Candy," the child answers, amused at the deception. The experimenter then tries the same procedure with a 3-year-old. The response to the initial question is the expected "Candy," but the response to the second is surprising—an unamused "Crayons." Even more surprising is that in response to further questioning, the 3-year-old claims that she had initially thought that there were crayons in the box and had even said that there were.

The basic interpretation of this finding is that preschoolers do not yet have a theory of mind, a conception that other people have minds and thoughts different from their own, and therefore do not understand that people can have beliefs different from their own or different from reality.

How does a child's theory of mind develop? Bartsch and Wellman (1995) argue that the developmental sequence has three steps. First, about age 2, children have an elementary conception of simple desires, emotions, and perceptual experiences. They understand that people can have wants and fears, and can see and feel things, but they do not understand that people mentally represent both objects and their own desires and beliefs. Second, at about age 3, children begin to talk about beliefs and thoughts as well as desires, and they seem to understand that beliefs can be false as well as true and can differ from one person to another. Yet, they still continue to explain their own actions and others' actions by appealing to desires rather than beliefs. Finally, at about age 4, children begin to understand that people's thoughts and beliefs affect their behaviors and that people can have beliefs that simply do not reflect reality.

One of the most interesting applications of research on theory of mind is the study of **autism**, a serious disorder in which children can seem unresponsive to others and tend to have significant problems in communicating with others. Henry Wellman (1994) has suggested that autistic children lack a fundamental theory of mind, which robs them of the ability to understand others' feelings, desires, and beliefs. As a result, people can seem like any other object to an autistic child. This contributes to the autistic child's apparent lack of interest in others and retreat into an inner world. Author Temple Grandin,

Theory of mind studies suggest that very young children tend to think that everyone else has the same perspective on the world—including what is in a closed box—as they do.

who has autism but has still achieved much in her life, describes it this way:

> Social interactions that come naturally to most people can be daunting for people with autism. As a child, I was like an animal that had no instincts to guide me; I just had to learn by trial and error. I was always observing, trying to work out the best way to behave, but I never fit in. I had to think about every social interaction. When other students swooned over the Beatles, I called their reaction an ISP—interesting sociological phenomenon. I was a scientist trying to figure out the ways of the natives. I wanted to participate, but did not know how. . . .
>
> All my life I have been an observer, and I have always felt like someone who watches from the outside. I could not participate in the social interactions of high school life. . . . My peers spent hours standing around talking about jewelry or some other topic with no real substance. What did they get out of this? I just did not fit in. I never fit in with the crowd, but I had a few friends who were interested in the same things, such as skiing and riding horses. Friendship always revolved around what I did rather than who I was. (Grandin, 1995, p. 132).

The Development of Moral Judgment

In addition to studying the development of children's thought, Piaget was interested in how children develop **moral judgment,** children's understanding of moral rules and social conventions. He believed that children's overall level of cognitive development determined their moral judgment. On the basis of observations he made of children of different ages playing games with rules, such as marbles, he proposed that children's understanding of rules develops in a series of four stages (Piaget, 1932/1965). The first stage emerges at the beginning of the preoperational period. Children at this stage engage in "parallel play," in which each child follows a private set of idiosyncratic rules. For example, a child might sort marbles of different colors into groups or roll all the big ones across the room, followed by all the small ones. These "rules" give the child's play some regularity, but they are frequently changed and serve no collective purpose such as cooperation or competition.

Beginning about age 5, the child develops a sense of obligation to follow rules, treating them as absolute moral imperatives handed down by some authority such as God or the child's parents. Rules are permanent, sacred, and not subject to modification. Obeying them to the letter is more important than any human reason for changing them. For example, children at this stage reject the suggestion that the position of the starting line in the marble game might be changed to accommodate younger children who might want to play.

At this stage, children judge an act more by its consequences than by the intentions behind it. Piaget told children several pairs of stories. In one pair, a boy broke a teacup while trying to steal some jam when his mother was not home; another boy, who was doing nothing wrong, accidentally broke a whole trayful of teacups. "Which boy is naughtier?" Piaget asked. Preoperational children tended to judge as naughtier the person in the stories who did the most damage, regardless of the intentions or motivation behind the act.

In Piaget's third stage of moral development, the child begins to appreciate that some rules are social conventions—cooperative agreements that can be arbitrarily changed if everyone agrees. Children's moral realism also declines: When making moral judgments, children in this stage give weight to subjective considerations such as a person's intentions, and they see punishment as a human choice rather than as inevitable, divine retribution.

The beginning of the formal operational stage coincides with the fourth and final stage in children's understanding of moral rules. Youngsters show an interest in generating rules to deal even with situations they have never encountered. This stage is marked by an ideological mode of moral reasoning, which addresses wider social issues rather than just personal and interpersonal situations.

The American psychologist Lawrence Kohlberg extended Piaget's work on moral reasoning to adolescence and adulthood (Kohlberg, 1969, 1976). He looked for universal stages in the development of moral judgments by presenting research participants with moral dilemmas in the form of stories. In one story, a man whose dying wife needs a drug he cannot afford pleads with a pharmacist to let him buy the drug at a cheaper price. When the pharmacist refuses, the man decides to steal the drug. Participants are asked to discuss the man's action.

By analyzing answers to several such dilemmas, Kohlberg arrived at six developmental stages of moral

Although young children participate in parallel play with one another, only when they become older do they begin to understand the rules that govern social interaction.

CONCEPT REVIEW TABLE
Stages of Moral Reasoning

Kohlberg believed that moral judgment develops with age according to these stages. (Kohlberg, L. (1969), "Stages of Moral Reasoning," from "Stage and Sequence: The Cognitive Development Approach to Socialization," in *Handbook of Socialization Theory and Research*, D. A. Goslin (ed.). Reprinted by permission of Rand McNally.)

Level I:	Preconventional Morality
Stage 1	Punishment orientation (Obeys rules to avoid punishment)
Stage 2	Reward orientation (Conforms to obtain rewards, to have favors returned)

Level II:	Conventional Morality
Stage 3	Good-boy/good-girl orientation (Conforms to avoid disapproval of others)
Stage 4	Authority orientation (Upholds laws and social rules to avoid censure of authorities and feelings of guilt about not "doing one's duty")

Level III:	Postconventional Morality
Stage 5	Social-contract orientation (Actions guided by principles commonly agreed on as essential to the public welfare; principles upheld to retain respect of peers and, thus, self-respect)
Stage 6	Ethical principle orientation (Actions guided by self-chosen ethical principles, which usually value justice, dignity, and equality; principles upheld to avoid self-condemnation)

judgment, which he grouped into three levels: preconventional, conventional, and postconventional (see Concept Review Table). The answers are scored on the basis of the reasons given for the decision, not on the basis of whether the action is judged to be right or wrong. For example, agreeing that the man should have stolen the drug because "If you let your wife die, you'll get in trouble" or disagreeing because "If you steal the drug, you'll be caught and sent to jail" are both scored at Level I, or **preconventional.** In both instances, the man's actions are evaluated as right or wrong on the basis of anticipated punishment.

Kohlberg believed that all children are at Level I until about age 10, when they begin to evaluate actions in terms of other people's opinions, which characterizes the **conventional** level. Most youngsters can reason at this level by age 13. Following Piaget, Kohlberg argued that only individuals who have achieved formal operational thought are capable of the abstract thinking that is necessary for Level III, **postconventional** morality, in which actions are evaluated in terms of higher-order ethical principles. The highest stage, Stage 6, requires the ability to formulate abstract ethical principles and uphold them in order to avoid self-condemnation.

Kohlberg reported that fewer than 10% of his adult participants showed the kind of "clear-principled" Stage 6 thinking that is exemplified by the following response of a 16-year-old to the story described earlier: "By the

law of society [the man] was wrong. But by the law of nature or of God the druggist was wrong and the husband was justified. Human life is above financial gain. Regardless of who was dying, if it was a total stranger, man has a duty to save him from dying" (Kohlberg, 1969, p. 244). Before he died, Kohlberg eliminated Stage 6 from his theory; Level III is now sometimes simply referred to as high-stage principled reasoning.

Kohlberg presented evidence for this sequence of stages in children from several cultures, including the United States, Mexico, Taiwan, and Turkey (Colby, Kohlberg, Gibbs, & Lieberman, 1983; Nisan & Kohlberg, 1982). On the other hand, there is evidence that people use different rules for different situations and that the stages are not sequential (Kurtines & Greif, 1974). The theory has also been criticized as "male centered" because it places a "masculine" style of abstract reasoning based on justice and rights higher on the moral scale than a "feminine" style of reasoning based on caring and concern for the integrity and continuation of relationships (Gilligan, 1982).

Piaget's assertion that young children cannot distinguish between social conventions (rules) and moral prescriptions has also been challenged. In one study, 7-year-old children were given a list of actions and asked to indicate which ones would be wrong even if there were no rules against them. There was widespread agreement among these children that lying, stealing, hitting, and selfishness would be wrong even if there were no rules against them. In contrast, they thought that there was nothing wrong with chewing gum in class, addressing a teacher by his or her first name, boys entering the girls' bathroom, or eating lunch with one's fingers—as long as there were no rules against these acts (Nuccli, 1981).

◆ Interim Summary

- Piaget's theory describes stages in cognitive development. They proceed from the sensorimotor stage (in which an important discovery is object permanence), through the preoperational stage (when symbols begin to be used) and the concrete operational stage (when conservation concepts develop), to the formal operational stage (when hypotheses are tested systematically in problem solving).

- New methods of testing reveal that Piaget's theory underestimates children's abilities, and several alternative approaches have been proposed.

- Information-processing approaches view cognitive development as reflecting the gradual development of processes such as attention and memory.

- Other theorists emphasize increases in domain-specific knowledge.

- Still others, including Vygotsky, focus on the influence of the social and cultural context.

- Much of the newest research in children's cognitive development focuses on children's theory of mind, or understanding that other people have beliefs and expectations that can be different from their own and different from reality.

- Piaget believed that children's understanding of moral rules and judgments develops along with their cognitive abilities. Kohlberg extended Piaget's work to include adolescence and adulthood. He proposed three levels of moral judgment: preconventional, conventional, and postconventional.

◆ Critical Thinking Questions

1. What does Piaget's theory suggest about the likely success of academic programs for elementary school children that attempt to "accelerate" children's cognitive development? What do newer theories of cognitive development suggest about these programs?

2. What level of moral reasoning seems to be implied by campaigns designed to discourage young people from using drugs or being sexually active? Can you think of campaign themes that would appeal to a higher stage of moral reasoning?

PERSONALITY AND SOCIAL DEVELOPMENT

Soon after Christine brought baby Mike home from the hospital, she noticed that he seemed different from her first child, Maggie, at the same age. Maggie had been an easy baby to deal with—Christine's mother and sisters had been amazed at how quickly she fell into a regular sleeping and eating schedule, and how easily she adapted to changes. It seemed she could fall asleep anywhere, and she didn't seem to mind being passed around from relative to relative at the family's large, noisy holiday gatherings. Mike wasn't really difficult to deal with, but it took a bit more time and patience to get him on a regular schedule. Every new experience, from his first bath to his first taste of strained peas, met with mild but clear protest from Mike. But Christine soon discovered that if she soothed him, kept trying, and gave him a little time, he eventually adjusted to each new thing. (Adapted from DeHart et al., 2000, p. 213)

Like Christine, parents are often surprised that their second child has a very different personality from their first. As early as the first weeks of life, infants show individual differences in activity level, responsiveness to changes in their environment, and irritability. One infant cries a lot; another cries very little. One endures diapering or bathing without much fuss; another kicks and thrashes. One is responsive to every sound; another is oblivious to all but the loudest noises. Infants even differ in "cuddliness": Some seem to enjoy being cuddled and mold themselves to the person holding them; others stiffen and squirm (Rothbart & Bates, 1998). The term **temperament** is used to refer to such mood-related personality characteristics.

TEMPERAMENT

The observation that temperamental differences arise early in life challenges the traditional view that all of an infant's behaviors are shaped by its environment. Parents of a fussy baby, for example, tend to blame themselves for their infant's difficulties. But research with newborns has shown that many temperamental differences are inborn and that the relationship between parent and infant is reciprocal—in other words, the infant's behavior also shapes the parent's response. An infant who is easily soothed, who snuggles and stops crying when picked up, increases the parent's feelings of competence and attachment. An infant who stiffens and continues to cry, despite efforts to comfort it, makes the parent feel inadequate and rejected. The more responsive a baby is to the stimulation provided by the parent (snuggling and quieting when held, attending alertly when talked to or played with), the easier it is for parent and child to establish a loving bond.

Some infants are more readily soothed than others. Such differences are due to differences in temperament.

A pioneering study of temperament began in the 1950s with a group of 140 middle- and upper-class infants. The initial data were gathered through interviews with parents and were later supplemented by interviews with teachers and by scores on tests administered to the children. The infants were scored on nine traits, which were later combined to define three broad temperament types. Infants who were playful, were regular in their sleeping and eating patterns, and adapted readily to new situations were classified as having an **easy temperament** (about 40% of the sample). Infants who were irritable, had irregular sleeping and eating patterns, and responded intensely and negatively to new situations were classified as having a **difficult temperament** (about 10% of the sample). Infants who were relatively inactive, tended to withdraw from new situations in a mild way, and required more time than easy infants to adapt to new situations were classified as having a **slow to warm up temperament** (about 15% of the sample). The re-

maining 35% of the infants were not rated high or low on any of the defining dimensions (Thomas, Chess, Birch, Hertzig, & Korn, 1963)

Of the original sample, 133 individuals were followed into adult life and again assessed on temperament and psychological adjustment. The results provide mixed evidence for the continuity of temperament. On the one hand, temperament scores across the first 5 years of these children's lives showed significant correlations: Children with "difficult" temperaments were more likely than "easy" children to have school problems later on. Adult measures of both temperament and adjustment were also significantly correlated with measures of childhood temperament obtained at ages 3, 4, and 5. On the other hand, all the correlations were low (about .3), and when considered separately, most of the nine traits measured showed little or no continuity across time (Chess & Thomas, 1984; Thomas & Chess, 1986, 1977).

This early research on the stability of temperament was criticized on several methodological grounds. It relied heavily on parents' reports of their infants' temperaments, and there is reason to believe that parents can be biased in their judgments, either rating their baby more positively or negatively than observers rate the baby. Later research, using both parents' reports and direct observation of children's behavior, suggests that the stability of temperamental characteristics shown in the early infant years is low. That is, a child's temperament at 2 months of age doesn't resemble very closely that child's temperament at age 5 years. But assessments of temperament made once a child is at least in the toddler years do predict the child's emotional and behavioral characteristics later in life (Rothbart & Bates, 1998). In one study, 79 children were categorized at 21 months as either extremely inhibited or uninhibited. At age 13, those who had been categorized as inhibited at 21 months of age scored significantly lower on a test of externalizing, delinquent behavior and aggressive behavior (Schwartz, Snidman, & Kagan, 1996). Other research has found that the tendency to approach or avoid unfamiliar events, which is an aspect of temperament, remains moderately stable over time (Kagan & Snidman, 1991). There is evidence that temperament is at least somewhat influenced by heredity. Several studies show more similarity in temperament between identical twins than between fraternal twins (Rothbart & Bates, 1998). This greater similarity between identical twins than fraternal twins suggests that genes play a role in temperament, because identical twins share the same genetic makeup, but fraternal twins are no more alike genetically than any other two siblings.

Researchers emphasize that continuity or discontinuity of temperament is a function of the interaction between the child's genotype (inherited characteristics) and the environment. In particular, they believe that the key to healthy development is a good fit between the child's temperament and the home environment. When parents of a difficult child provide a happy, stable home life, the child's negative, difficult behaviors decline with age (Belsky, Fish, & Isabella, 1991). Thomas and Chess cite the case of Carl, who displayed a very difficult temperament from the first few months of life through age 5. Because Carl's father took delight in his son's "lusty" temperament and allowed for his initial negative reactions to new situations, Carl flourished and became increasingly "easy." At age 23 he was clearly classified into the "easy" temperament group. Nevertheless, Carl's original temperament often emerged briefly when his life circumstances changed. For example, when he started piano lessons in late childhood, he showed an intense negative response, followed by slow adaptability and eventual positive, zestful involvement. A similar pattern emerged when he entered college (Thomas & Chess, 1986).

Strong evidence for an interaction between genes and environment in producing a child's temperament comes from a study of twins raised apart since early in life (Plomin, 1994). Identical twins raised apart showed some similarity in their tendencies to be inhibited and to show negative emotions, which could be considered aspects of temperament. Yet, the similarity of these twins raised apart was significantly less than the similarity of identical twins raised together, suggesting that environment does play a role.

EARLY SOCIAL BEHAVIOR

By 2 months of age, the average child smiles at the sight of its mother's or father's face. Delighted with this response, parents go to great lengths to encourage it. Indeed, the infant's ability to smile at such an early age may have evolved precisely because it strengthened the parent-child bond. Parents interpret these smiles to mean that the infant recognizes and loves them, and this encourages them to be even more affectionate and stimulating in response. A mutually reinforcing system of social interaction is thus established and maintained.

Infants all over the world begin to smile at about the same age, suggesting that maturation plays an important role in determining the onset of smiling. Blind babies also smile at about the same age as sighted infants, indicating that smiling is an innate response (Eibl-Eibesfeldt, 1970).

By their 3rd or 4th month, infants show that they recognize and prefer familiar members of the household by smiling or cooing more when seeing these familiar faces or hearing their voices, but they are still fairly receptive to strangers. At about 7 or 8 months, however, many infants begin to show wariness or distress at the

The infant's ability to smile may contribute to a mutually reinforcing system of social interaction with its primary caregivers.

approach of a stranger and protest strongly when left in an unfamiliar setting or with an unfamiliar person. Parents are often disconcerted when their formerly gregarious infant, who had always happily welcomed the attentions of a babysitter, now cries inconsolably when they prepare to leave—and continues to cry for some time after they have left. Although not all infants show this stranger anxiety, the number of infants who do increases dramatically from about 8 months of age until the end of the first year. Similarly, distress over separation from the parent reaches a peak between 14 and 18 months and then gradually declines. By the time they are 3 years old, most children are secure enough in their parents' absence to interact comfortably with other children and adults.

The waxing and waning of these two fears appears to be only slightly influenced by conditions of child rearing. The same general pattern has been observed among American children reared entirely at home and among those attending a day care center. Figure 3-10 shows that although the percentage of children who cry when their

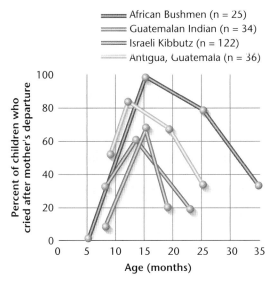

Figure 3-10

Children's Stress at Mother's Departure

Even though the percentages of children who cry when their mothers leave the room varies from one culture to another, the age-related pattern of onset and decline of such distress is similar across cultures. (Reprinted by permission of the publisher from *Infancy: Its Place in Human Development* by Jerome Kagan, R. B. Kearsley and P. R. Zelazo, p. 107, Cambridge, Mass.: Harvard University Press, Copyright © 1978 by the President and Fellows of Harvard College.)

mother leaves the room varies in different cultures, the age-related pattern of onset and decline is very similar (Kagan, Kearsley, & Zelazo, 1978).

How do we explain the systematic timing of these fears? Two factors seem to be important in both their onset and their decline. One is the growth of memory capacity. During the second half of the first year, infants become better able to remember past events and to compare past and present. This makes it possible for the baby to detect, and sometimes fear, unusual or unpredictable events. The emergence of stranger anxiety coincides with the emergence of fear of a variety of stimuli that are unusual or unexpected. A weird-looking mask or a jack-in-the-box that brings smiles to a 4-month-old often causes an 8-month-old to look apprehensive and distressed. As children learn that strangers and unusual objects are not generally harmful, such fears gradually diminish.

Memory development is probably also involved in **separation anxiety,** the child's distress when a caretaker is not nearby. The infant cannot "miss" the parent unless he or she can recall that parent's presence a minute earlier and compare it with the parent's absence now. When the parent leaves the room, the infant is aware that something is amiss, and this can lead to distress. As the child's memory of past instances of separation improves, the child becomes better able to anticipate the return of the absent parent, and anxiety declines.

The second factor is the growth of **autonomy,** the child's independence from caretakers. One-year-olds are still highly dependent on the care of adults, but children 2 or 3 years old can head for the snack plate or toy shelf on their own. They can also use language to communicate their wants and feelings. Dependence on caregivers in general and on familiar caregivers in particular decreases, and the parent's presence becomes less critical for the child.

ATTACHMENT

The term **attachment** is used to describe an infant's tendency to seek closeness to particular people and to feel more secure in their presence. Psychologists at first theorized that attachment to the mother developed because she was the source of food, one of the infant's most basic needs. But some facts did not fit. For example, ducklings and baby chicks feed themselves from birth, yet they still follow their mothers about and spend a great deal of time with them. The comfort they derive from the mother's presence cannot come from her role in feeding. A well-known series of experiments with monkeys also showed that there is more to mother-infant attachment than nutritional needs (Harlow & Harlow, 1969).

Infant monkeys were separated from their mothers shortly after birth and placed with two artificial "mothers" constructed of wire mesh with wooden heads. The torso of one mother was bare wire; the other was covered with foam rubber and terry cloth, making it cuddly and easy to cling to (see Figure 3-11). Either mother could be equipped to provide milk by means of a bottle attached to its chest.

The experiment sought to determine whether the young monkey would cling to the mother that was always the source of food. The results were clear-cut: No matter which mother provided food, the infant monkey spent its time clinging to the terry-cloth mother. This purely passive but soft-contact mother was a source of security. For example, the obvious fear of the infant monkey placed in a strange environment was allayed if the infant could make contact with the cloth mother. While holding on to the cloth mother with one hand or foot, the monkey was willing to explore objects that were otherwise too terrifying to approach.

Although contact with a cuddly, artificial mother provides an important aspect of "mothering," it is not enough for satisfactory development. Infant monkeys raised with artificial mothers and isolated from other monkeys during the first 6 months of life showed bizarre behavior in adulthood. They rarely engaged in normal interaction with other monkeys later on (either cowering in fear or showing abnormally aggressive behavior), and their sexual responses were inappropriate. When female

❙ Figure 3-11
A Monkey's Response to an Artificial Mother
Although it is fed via a wire mother, the infant spends more time with the terry-cloth mother. The terry-cloth mother provides a safe base from which to explore strange objects.

● **Table 3-1**
Episodes in the Strange Situation Procedure

1. A mother and her child enter the room. The mother places the baby on the floor, surrounded by toys, and goes to sit at the opposite end of the room.

2. A female stranger enters the room, sits quietly for a minute, converses with the mother for a minute, and then attempts to engage the baby in play with a toy.

3. The mother leaves the room unobtrusively. If the baby is not upset, the stranger returns to sitting quietly. If the baby is upset, the stranger tries to soothe him or her.

4. The mother returns and engages the baby in play while the stranger slips out of the room.

5. The mother leaves again, this time leaving the baby alone in the room.

6. The stranger returns. If the baby is upset, the stranger tries to comfort him or her.

7. The mother returns and the stranger slips out of the room.

monkeys that had been deprived of early social contact were successfully mated (after considerable effort), they made poor mothers, tending to neglect or abuse their first-born infants—although they became better mothers with their later children. Note, however, that these monkeys were deprived of all social contact. Monkeys with artificial mothers do fine as adults if they are allowed to interact with their peers during the first 6 months.

Although generalizing from research on monkeys to human development requires care, there is evidence that the human infant's attachment to the primary caregiver serves the same functions. Most of the work on attachment in human infants originated with the psychoanalyst John Bowlby in the 1950s and 1960s. Bowlby became interested in attachment while watching the behaviors of infants and young children who were in residential nurseries and hospital wards and therefore separated from their mothers. His research convinced him that a child's failure to form a secure attachment to one or more persons in the early years is related to an inability to develop close personal relationships in adulthood (Bowlby, 1973).

Mary Ainsworth, one of Bowlby's associates, made extensive observations of children and their mothers in Uganda and the United States and then developed a laboratory procedure for assessing the security of a child's attachments from about 12 to 18 months of age (Ainsworth, Blehar, Waters, & Wall, 1978). This procedure, called *the strange situation*, is a series of episodes in which a child is observed as the primary caregiver leaves and returns to the room (see Table 3-1). Throughout this sequence, the baby is observed through a one-way mirror and several observations are recorded: the baby's activity level and play involvement, crying and other distress signs, proximity to and attempts to gain the attention of the mother, proximity to and willingness to interact with the stranger, and so on. On the basis of their behaviors, babies are categorized into one of the following three groups:

Securely attached. Regardless of whether they are upset at the mother's departures (episodes 3 and 5), babies who are classified as securely attached seek to interact with her when she returns. Some are content simply to acknowledge her return from a distance while continuing to play with the toys. Others seek physical contact with her. Still others are completely preoccupied with the mother throughout the entire session, showing intense distress when she leaves. In all, 60% to 65% of American babies fall into this category.

Insecurely attached: avoidant. These babies avoid interacting with the mother during the reunion episodes. Some ignore her almost entirely; others display mixed attempts to interact and avoid interacting. Avoidant babies may pay little attention to the mother when she is in the room and often do not seem distressed when she leaves. If they are distressed, they are as easily comforted by the stranger as by the mother. About 20% of American babies fall into this category.

Insecurely attached: ambivalent. Babies are classified as ambivalent if they show resistance to the mother during the reunion episodes. They simultaneously seek and resist physical contact. For example, they may cry to be picked up and then squirm angrily to get down. Some act very passive, crying for the mother when she returns but not crawling toward her, and then showing resistance when she approaches. About 10% of American babies fall into this category.

PARENTING STYLES

Because some babies did not seem to fit any of these categories, more recent studies have included a fourth category, **disorganized** (Main & Solomon, 1986). Babies in this category often show contradictory behaviors. For example, they may approach the mother while taking care not to look at her, approach her and then show dazed avoidance, or suddenly cry out after having settled down. Some seem disoriented, appear emotionless, or look depressed. About 10% to 15% of American babies fall into this category, with the percentages much higher among babies who are maltreated or whose parents are being treated for mental disorders.

In attempting to account for differences in attachment among babies, researchers have directed most of their attention to the behavior of the primary caregiver, usually the mother. The main finding is that a caregiver's **sensitive responsiveness** to the baby's needs produces secure attachment. Mothers of securely attached babies usually respond promptly when the baby cries and behave affectionately when they pick up the baby. They also tailor their responses to the baby's needs (Clarke-Stewart, 1973). In feeding, for example, they use an infant's signals to determine when to begin and end feeding, and they attend to the baby's food preferences. In contrast, mothers of babies who are insecurely attached respond according to their own needs or moods rather than according to signals from the baby. For example, they respond to the baby's cries for attention when they feel like cuddling the baby but ignore such cries at other times (Stayton, 1973).

Studies of attachment have focused on children's responses to their caregivers after the caregiver has been away for some period of time.

Not all developmental psychologists agree that the caregiver's responsiveness is the major cause of an infant's attachment behaviors. They call attention to the baby's own inborn temperament (Campos, Barrett, Lamb, Goldsmith, & Stenberg, 1983; Kagan, 1984). Perhaps the temperaments that make some babies "easy" also make them more securely attached than do the temperaments of "difficult" babies. And, as noted earlier, a parent's response to a child is often itself a function of the child's own behavior. For example, mothers of difficult babies tend to spend less time playing with them (Green, Fox, & Lewis, 1983). Attachment patterns may reflect this interaction between a baby's temperament and the parents' responsiveness.

In reply, attachment theorists point to evidence that supports the "sensitive responsiveness" hypothesis. For example, in the first year of life, an infant's crying changes much more than the mother's responsiveness to the crying does. Moreover, the mother's responsiveness over a 3-month period predicts the infant's crying over the next 3 months significantly better than the infant's crying predicts the mother's subsequent responsiveness to crying. In short, the mother appears to influence the infant's crying more than the infant influences the mother's responsiveness to crying (Bell & Ainsworth, 1972). In general, the mother's behavior appears to be the most important factor in establishing a secure or insecure attachment (Isabella & Belsky, 1991).

Other research may resolve this debate. Recall that the attachment classification is based not on the baby's distress when the mother leaves but on how the baby reacts when she returns. It appears that an infant's temperament predicts the former but not the latter (Frodi & Thompson, 1985; Vaughn, Lefever, Seifer, & Barglow, 1989). Babies with easy temperaments typically are not distressed when the mother leaves. When she returns, they tend to greet her happily—showing secure attachment—or show the avoidant type of insecure attachment. Babies with difficult temperaments typically are distressed when the mother leaves. When she returns, they tend to seek her out and cling to her—showing secure attachment—or show the ambivalent type of insecure attachment (Belsky & Rovine, 1987). Children's overall reaction to the departure and return of their primary caregiver is a function of both the caregiver's responsiveness to the child and the child's temperament.

LATER DEVELOPMENT

A baby's attachment classification remains quite stable when retested several years later—unless the family experiences major changes in life circumstances (Main & Cassidy, 1988; Thompson, Lamb, & Estes, 1982). Stressful life changes are likely to affect parental responsiveness to the baby, which, in turn, affects the baby's feelings of security.

Early attachment patterns also appear to be related to how children cope with new experiences. In one study, 2-year-olds were given a series of problems requiring the use of tools. Some of the problems were within the child's capacity; others were quite difficult. Children who had been rated as securely attached at 12 months approached the problems with enthusiasm and persistence. When they encountered difficulties, they seldom cried or became angry. Rather, they sought help from adults. Children who had earlier been rated as insecurely attached behaved quite differently. They easily became frustrated and angry, seldom asked for help, tended to ignore or reject directions from adults, and quickly gave up trying to solve the problems (Matas, Arend, & Sroufe, 1978).

These and similar studies suggest that children who are securely attached by the time they enter their second year are better equipped to cope with new experiences. However, we cannot be certain that the quality of children's early attachments is directly responsible for their later competence in problem solving. Parents who are responsive to their children's needs in infancy probably continue to provide effective parenting during early childhood—encouraging autonomy and efforts to cope with new experiences, yet ready with help when needed. A child's competence may therefore reflect the current state of the parent-child relationship rather than the relationship that existed 2 years earlier. Moreover, children's temperament—which, as we saw earlier, affects their behavior in the strange situation procedure—might also influence their competence as preschoolers.

EFFECTS OF DAY CARE

Research on the importance of early attachment experiences in children's development has raised questions about the impact of day care on children's long-term well-being. Day care is a controversial subject in the United States because many people have doubts about its effects on very young children and many Americans believe that children should be cared for at home by one of their parents, usually their mothers. But in a society with most mothers in the labor force, day care is a reality; in fact, more 3- and 4-year-olds (43%) attend day care than are cared for in either their own home or another home (35%).

A prominent critic of day care, developmental psychologist Jay Belsky, has published research suggesting that day care has negative effects on children's development (Belsky, 1986; Belsky, Woodworth, & Crnic, 1996). He has found that infants who receive more than 20 hours of nonmaternal care per week are more likely to be classified as insecurely attached to their mothers in the strange situation task, less compliant in meeting adults' demands, and more aggressive in interactions with peers.

In response to such evidence, the U.S. government initiated a massive study of the influence of various types of day care during infancy and childhood (NICHD Early Child Care Research Network, 1996, 1997). Researchers in 10 locations around the United States collected data on the characteristics of the children's families and the quality of care they received. Overall, the results of this research showed that children who spend 30 or more hours in day care per week are not distinguishable from those who spend less than 10 hours in comparable circumstances.

The quality of the day care facilities did have a major impact on children's well-being and development, however. In low-quality facilities, one caregiver cares for a large number of children, caregivers are inadequately

The quality of day care plays a more important role on its impact on children's development than the amount of time children spend in daycare.

GENDER IDENTITY AND SEX TYPING

Most children acquire a **gender identity,** a firm sense of themselves as either male or female. But most cultures elaborate the biological distinction between male and female into a sprawling network of beliefs and practices that permeate virtually every domain of human activity. Different cultures may define the socially correct behaviors, roles, and personality characteristics differently, and these expectations may change over time within a culture. But whatever its current definition, each culture still strives to transform male and female infants into "masculine" and "feminine" adults.

The term **sex typing** refers to the acquisition of behaviors and characteristics that a culture considers appropriate to one's sex. Note that gender identity and sex typing are not the same thing. A girl may have a firm acceptance of herself as female yet not avoid all behaviors that are labeled masculine.

But are gender identity and sex typing simply the product of cultural prescriptions and expectations, or are they partly a product of "natural" development? In this section we will examine four theories that attempt to answer this question.

PSYCHOANALYTIC THEORY The first psychologist to attempt a comprehensive account of gender identity and sex typing was Sigmund Freud (1933/1964). Psychoanalytic theory and its limitations are discussed in more detail in Chapter 13, but here we present a brief overview of aspects of the theory that are relevant to gender identity and sex typing.

According to Freud, children begin to focus on the genitals at about age 3. He called this the beginning of the phallic stage of psychosexual development. Specifically, both sexes become aware that boys have a penis and that girls do not. During this same stage, they also begin to have sexual feelings toward their opposite-sex parent and feel jealous and resentful of their same-sex parent; Freud called this the *Oedipal conflict* (after the ancient Greek legend of Oedipus, who killed his father and married his mother). As they mature further, both sexes eventually resolve this conflict by identifying with their same-sex parent and modeling their behaviors, attitudes, and personality attributes on that parent in an attempt to be like him or her—sex typing (Freud, 1925/1961). Psychoanalytic theory has always been controversial, and many critics have pointed out that there is no empirical evidence to support the conclusion that a child's discovery of genital sex differences or identification with the same-sex parent determines gender identity

trained, and there is a high turnover of caregivers. Children who spent more time in such facilities fared worse on a number of cognitive and emotional tasks than children who spent less time there or who were in high-quality facilities. Unfortunately, almost half the facilities studied were found to have low-quality caregiving. Low-quality day care was an especially great risk factor for cognitive and social difficulties when it was paired with problems in the child's home life, such as having an insensitive mother or being poor.

Other research on day care has confirmed that the quality of day care plays a major role in determining its impact on children. Children who receive high-quality day care from an early age have been found to be more socially competent in elementary school (Andersson, 1992; Field, 1991; Howes, 1990) and more assertive (Scarr & Eisenberg, 1993) than children who enter day care later. Good-quality day care can reduce the effects of growing up in a highly stressed home life (Phillips, Voran, Kisker, Howes, & Whitebrook, 1994).

In sum, children are not significantly affected by nonmaternal care. Any negative effects tend to be emotional, and positive effects are more likely to be social. Cognitive development is usually affected either positively or not at all. However, these findings apply to day care of reasonable quality. Poor-quality care can have negative effects on children, regardless of their home environment. Day care centers that are well equipped and have a high ratio of caregivers to children have positive effects on children's development.

Psychoanalytic and social learning theories have very different explanations for why children imitate their same-sex parents.

and sex typing (Kohlberg, 1966; Maccoby & Jacklin, 1974; McConaghy, 1979).

SOCIAL LEARNING THEORY In contrast to psychoanalytic theory, social learning theory has a much more straightforward account of sex typing. It emphasizes the rewards and punishments that children receive for sex-appropriate and sex-inappropriate behaviors, respectively, and the ways children learn sex-typed behavior by observing adults (Bandura, 1986; Mischel, 1966; Perry & Bussey, 1984). Observational learning also enables children to imitate same-sex adults and thereby acquire sex-typed behaviors.

Two broader points about social learning theory are worth noting. Unlike psychoanalytic theory, social learning theory treats sex-typed behaviors as any other learned behaviors. No special psychological principles or processes must be proposed to explain how children become sex typed. Second, if there is nothing special about sex-typed behaviors, then sex typing itself is neither inevitable nor unmodifiable. Children become sex typed because sex happens to be the basis on which their culture chooses to base reward and punishment. If a culture becomes less sex typed in its ideology, children become less sex typed in their behavior.

Considerable evidence supports the social learning account of sex typing. Parents do differentially reward and punish sex-appropriate and sex-inappropriate behaviors, as well as serve as the child's first models of masculine and feminine behavior. From infancy on, most parents dress boys and girls differently and provide them with different toys. Observations in the homes of preschool children have found that parents reward their daughters for dressing up, dancing, playing with dolls, and simply following them around but criticize them for manipulating objects, running, jumping, and climbing. In contrast, parents reward their sons for playing with blocks but criticize them for playing with dolls, asking for help, or even volunteering to be helpful (Fagot, 1978). Parents demand more independence of boys and have higher expectations of them. They also respond less quickly to boys' requests for help and focus less on the

Some theorists argue that parents impose sex-roles on their children by insisting they behave in sex-stereotyped behaviors, such as girls competing in beauty contests.

interpersonal aspects of a task. And finally, parents punish boys both verbally and physically more often than they punish girls (Maccoby & Jacklin, 1974).

In reacting differently to boys and girls, some researchers suggest, parents may not be imposing their own stereotypes on them but simply reacting to innate differences between the behaviors of the two sexes (Maccoby, 1998). Even as infants, boys demand more attention than girls do, and research suggests that human males are innately more physically aggressive than human females (Maccoby & Jacklin, 1974), which could be why parents punish boys more often. There may be some truth to this, but it is also clear that adults approach children with stereotyped expectations that lead them to treat boys and girls differently. For example, adults viewing newborn infants through the window of a hospital nursery believe that they can detect sex differences. Infants thought to be boys are described as robust, strong, and large featured; identical-looking infants thought to be girls are described as delicate, fine featured, and "soft" (Luria & Rubin, 1974).

Fathers appear to be more concerned with sex-typed behavior than mothers are, particularly with their sons. They react more negatively than mothers by interfering with the child's play or expressing disapproval when their sons play with "feminine" toys. Fathers are less concerned when their daughters engage in "masculine" play, but they still show more disapproval than mothers do (Langlois & Downs, 1980). But if parents and other adults treat children in sex-stereotyped ways, children themselves are the real "sexists." Peers enforce sex stereotyping

much more severely than parents. Boys, in particular, criticize other boys when they see them engaged in "girls'" activities. They are quick to call another boy a sissy if he plays with dolls, cries when he is hurt, or shows concern toward another child in distress. In contrast, girls seem not to object to other girls who play with "boys'" toys or engage in masculine activities (Langlois & Downs, 1980).

Although social learning theory plausibly explains many phenomena of sex typing, there are some observations that the theory cannot easily explain. First, it treats the child as a passive recipient of environmental forces: Society, parents, peers, and the media all "do it" to the child. This view of the child is inconsistent with the observation that children themselves construct and enforce their own exaggerated version of society's gender rules more insistently than most of the adults in their world. Second, there is an interesting developmental pattern to the child's view of gender rules. For example, a majority of 4-year-olds and 9-year-olds believe that there should be no sex-based restrictions on one's choice of occupation: Let women be doctors and men be nurses if they wish. Between these ages, however, children hold more rigid opinions. Most 6- and 7-year-olds believe that there *should* be sex-based restrictions on occupations.

Do these observations sound familiar? If you think these children sound like Piaget's preoperational moral realists, you are right. That is why Kohlberg (1966) developed a cognitive-developmental theory of sex typing based directly on Piaget's theory of cognitive development.

COGNITIVE-DEVELOPMENTAL THEORY Although 2-year-olds can identify their own sex in a photograph of themselves and are usually able to identify the sex of a stereotypically dressed man or woman in a photograph, they cannot accurately sort photographs into "boys" and "girls" or predict another child's toy preferences on the basis of sex (Thompson, 1975). At about 2½ years, however, a more conceptual awareness of sex and gender begins to emerge, and at this point cognitive-developmental theory becomes relevant. In particular, the theory proposes that gender identity plays a critical role in sex typing. The sequence is "I am a girl [boy]; therefore I want to do girl [boy] things" (Kohlberg, 1966). In other words, it is the motive to behave consistently with one's gender identity—not to obtain external rewards—that prompts children to behave in sex-appropriate ways. As a result, they willingly take on the task of sex typing themselves— and their peers.

According to cognitive-developmental theory, gender identity itself develops slowly over the years from 2 to 7, in accordance with the principles of the preoperational stage of cognitive development. In particular, preoperational children's overreliance on visual impressions and their resulting inability to conserve an object's identity when its appearance changes become relevant to their concept of sex. Thus, 3-year-olds can separate pictures of boys and girls, but many of them cannot say whether they themselves will be a mommy or a daddy when they grow up (Thompson, 1975). The understanding that a person's sex remains the same despite changes in age and appearance is called *gender constancy* and is analogous to conservation of quantity with water, clay, and checkers.

Substantial evidence supports Kohlberg's general sequence of sex-role identity development (Szkrybalo & Ruble, 1999). The notion that sex-role identity becomes stable only after gender constancy is in place has not been supported. Children have strong and clear preferences for activities deemed appropriate for their sex long before they attain gender constancy (Maccoby, 1998). In addition, Kohlberg's theory, as well as social learning theory, fails to address the fundamental question of why children should organize their self-concepts around their maleness or femaleness in the first place. Why should sex have priority over other potential categories of self-definition? It is this question that the next theory, gender schema theory, was designed to answer (Bem, 1985).

GENDER SCHEMA THEORY Both social learning theory and cognitive-developmental theory provide reasonable explanations for how children might acquire information about their culture's rules and norms for sex-appropriate behaviors, roles, and personality characteristics. But the culture is also teaching the child a much deeper lesson—that the distinction between male and female is so important that it should be used as a lens through which all other aspects of culture are viewed. Consider, for example, the child who first enters a day care center offering a variety of new toys and activities. The child could use many potential criteria in deciding which toys and activities to try. Should she consider indoor or outdoor activities? Does he prefer a toy that involves artistic production or one that requires mechanical manipulation? How about an activity that can be done with other children or one that can be done in solitude? But of all the potential criteria, the culture emphasizes one above all others: "Be sure to consider first and foremost whether the toy or activity is appropriate for your sex." At every turn, the child is encouraged to look at the world through the lens of gender—in other words, in terms of the **gender schema,** or set of beliefs about gender (Bem, 1993, 1985, 1981).

Parents and teachers do not directly teach children about the gender schema. Instead, the lesson is embedded in the daily practices of the culture. Consider, for example, a teacher who wishes to treat children of both sexes equally. She lines them up at the drinking fountain by alternating boys and girls. If a boy is selected to be hall monitor on Monday, a girl will be hall monitor on Tuesday. Equal numbers of boys and girls must be selected for the class play. This teacher believes that she is teaching her students the importance of gender equality. She is right, but she is also unwittingly teaching them the importance of gender. The students learn that no matter how unrelated to gender an activity might seem, one cannot engage in it without paying attention to the distinction between boys and girls.

Children also learn to apply the gender schema to themselves, to organize their self-concepts around their maleness or femaleness, and to judge their self-worth in terms of their answer to the question, Am I masculine or feminine enough? For these reasons, gender schema theory is a theory of gender identity as well as of sex typing.

Gender schema theory, then, is one possible answer to the question of why children organize their self-concepts around their maleness or femaleness. Like cognitive-developmental theory, gender schema theory views the developing child as an active agent in his or her own socialization. But like social learning theory, gender schema theory implies that sex typing is neither inevitable nor unmodifiable. According to this theory, children become sex typed because sex happens to be a major focus around which their culture chooses to organize its view of reality. The theory implies that if the culture becomes less sex typed, children will become less sex typed in their behaviors and self-concepts.

◆ Interim Summary

- Some early social behaviors, such as smiling, reflect innate responses that appear at about the same time in all infants, including blind infants. The emergence of many later social behaviors—including wariness of strangers and distress over separation from primary caregivers—appears to depend on the child's developing cognitive skills.

- An infant's tendency to seek closeness to particular people and to feel more secure in their presence is called *attachment.* Attachment can be assessed in a procedure called *the strange situation,* a series of episodes in which a child is observed as the primary caregiver leaves and returns to the room.

- Securely attached infants seek to interact with a caretaker who returns from an absence.

- Insecurely attached: avoidant infants avoid a caretaker returning from an absence.

- Insecurely attached: ambivalent infants show resistance to a caretaker returning from an absence.

- Disorganized infants show contradictory behaviors (sometimes avoidant, sometimes approaching) to a caretaker returning from an absence.

- Research on the effects of day care on children's well-being and attachments suggests that low-quality day care may be detrimental but high-quality day care is not and may counteract the effects of poor home environments.
- Gender identity is the degree to which one regards oneself as male or female. It is distinct from sex typing, the acquisition of characteristics and behaviors that society considers appropriate for one's sex.
- Freud's psychoanalytic theory holds that gender identity and sex typing develop from children's early discovery of the genital differences between the sexes and children's eventual identification with the same-sex parent.
- Social learning theory emphasizes the rewards and punishments that children receive for sex-appropriate and sex-inappropriate behaviors, as well as a process of identification with same-sex adults that is based on observational learning.
- A cognitive-developmental theory of gender identity and sex typing holds that once children can identify themselves as male or female, they are motivated to acquire sex-typed behaviors. Their understanding of sex and gender corresponds to Piaget's stages of cognitive development, especially their understanding of gender constancy—the realization that a person's sex remains constant despite changes of age and appearance.
- Gender schema theory seeks to explain why children base their self-concept on the male-female distinction in the first place. It emphasizes the role of culture in teaching children to view the world through the lens of gender.

◆ Critical Thinking Questions

1. Some psychologists have suggested that our childhood attachment styles can influence the kinds of romantic relationships we form as adults. What forms might the attachment styles discussed in this chapter assume in an adult romantic relationship? Can you relate your own adult "attachment styles" to your childhood attachment style or to features of your childhood environment?

2. Would your parents have characterized your infant personality as easy, difficult, or slow to warm up? Which aspects of your current personality seem to be primarily a reflection of your inborn temperament, which aspects seem to reflect the way you were raised, and which aspects seem to reflect a blend or interaction between nature and nurture?

ADOLESCENT DEVELOPMENT

Adolescence refers to the period of transition from childhood to adulthood. It extends roughly from age 12 to the late teens, when physical growth is nearly complete. During this period, the young person becomes sexually mature and establishes an identity as an individual apart from the family.

SEXUAL DEVELOPMENT Puberty, the period of sexual maturation that transforms a child into a biologically mature adult capable of sexual reproduction, takes place over a period of 3 or 4 years. It starts with a period of very rapid physical growth (the so-called adolescent growth spurt) accompanied by gradual development of the reproductive organs and secondary sex characteristics (breast development in girls, beard growth in boys, and the appearance of pubic hair in both sexes).

Menarche, the first menstrual period, occurs relatively late in puberty—about 18 months after a girl's growth spurt has reached its peak. The first menstrual periods tend to be irregular, and ovulation (the release of a mature egg) does not usually begin until a year or so after menarche. A boy's first ejaculation typically occurs about 2 years after the growth spurt begins. The first seminal fluid does not contain sperm; the number of sperm and their fertility gradually increase.

There is wide variation in the age at which puberty begins and the rate at which it progresses. Some girls attain menarche before age 11, others as late as 17, and the average age is about 12 years. Boys, on the average, experience their growth spurt and mature about 2 years later than girls. They begin to ejaculate semen with live sperm sometime between the ages of 12 and 16; the average age is 14½. The wide variation in the timing of puberty is strikingly apparent in 7th- and 8th-grade classrooms. Some of the girls look like mature women with fully developed breasts and rounded hips; others still have the size and shape of little girls. Some of the boys are gangly adolescents; others look much as they did at the age of 9 or 10. (See the discussion of hormonal changes at puberty in Chapter 10.)

PSYCHOLOGICAL EFFECTS OF PUBERTY Conventional wisdom holds that adolescence is a period of "storm and stress," characterized by moodiness, inner turmoil, and rebellion. Modern research has largely not supported this view (Steinberg & Morris, 2001). Many adolescents do experiment with worrisome behavior, but experimentation leads to enduring problems in only a small subset of adolescents. Many adolescents experiment with alcohol during high school or do something that is against

There is wide variation in the age at which puberty begins and the rate at which it progresses. As a result, some adolescents may be much taller and more physically mature than others of the same age.

the law, but most of them do not develop an alcohol problem or a criminal career (Farrington, 1995). In addition, those adolescents who do show serious behavioral or emotional problems tend to have a history of similar problems during childhood. For example, most adolescent delinquents had recurrent problems with the law from an early age (Moffitt, 1993). Similarly, most adolescents who become seriously depressed suffered from anxiety or other types of psychological distress as children (Zahn-Waxler et al., 2000).

Some of the upsurge in problems in adolescence may be linked directly to the hormonal changes of puberty (Buchanan, Eccles, & Becker, 1992), but most are related to the personal and social effects of physical changes and, most important, the timing of those changes. Being an early or late maturer (1 year earlier or later than average) affects adolescents' satisfaction with their appearance and their body image. In general, 7th- and 8th-grade boys who have reached puberty report positive moods more often than their prepubertal male classmates, and they tend to be more satisfied with their weight and their overall appearance than later-maturing

boys—a reflection of the importance of strength and physical prowess for males in our society. But early-maturing boys also tend to have less self-control and emotional stability than later-maturing boys. They are more likely to smoke, drink, use drugs, and get into trouble with the law (Williams & Dunlop, 1999). In contrast, late-maturing boys feel worst about themselves in 7th grade but typically end up as the healthiest group by their senior year in high school (Petersen, 1989).

Early maturation has the opposite effect on the self esteem of girls. Compared with later maturers, earlier maturers experience more depression and anxiety, have lower self-esteem, and are generally less satisfied with their weight and appearance (Caspi & Moffit, 1991; Ge et al., 1996). They tend to be embarrassed that their bodies are more womanly than those of their female classmates—particularly because current standards for female attractiveness emphasize a lean look. Although early maturers also achieve early popularity, this is partly because they are seen as sexually precocious. They are also more likely to have conflicts with their parents, to drop out of school, and to have both emotional and behavioral problems (Caspi & Moffitt, 1991; Stattin & Magnusson, 1990). Nevertheless, early adolescence is relatively trouble-free for most males and females.

Parents often report a lot of storm and stress in their relationships with their adolescents, and here the research largely backs up the common lore (Steinberg & Morris, 2001). Bickering and squabbling between parents and their offspring increase in adolescence, and there is a decline in how close parents and adolescents feel to each other (Larson & Richards, 1991). Adolescents typically pull away from their parents in an attempt to forge their own individual identities, and many parents are distressed by this withdrawal (Silverberg & Steinberg, 1990). In most families, however, the period of increased conflict in early adolescence is followed by the establishment of a new parent-adolescent relationship that is less volatile and more egalitarian. Parents who remain authoritative—warm and supportive but firm and clear about rules and their enforcement—tend to have adolescents who come through the adolescent years with the least enduring problems (Steinberg & Morris, 2001). In contrast, adolescents whose parents are authoritarian (with rigid rules and little obvious warmth in their dealings with their children) or overly permissive tend to encounter more emotional and behavioral problems (Baumrind, 1980).

IDENTITY DEVELOPMENT The psychoanalyst Erik Erikson believed that the major task confronting the adolescent is to develop a sense of identity, to find answers to the questions "Who am I?" and "Where am I going?" Although Erikson coined the term **identity crisis** to refer to this active process of self-definition, he believed that it is an integral part of healthy psychosocial development. Similarly, most developmental psychologists believe that adolescence should be a period of role experimentation for young people to explore various behaviors, interests, and ideologies. Many beliefs, roles, and ways of behaving may be tried on, modified, or discarded in an attempt to shape an integrated concept of the self.

Adolescents try to synthesize these values and appraisals into a consistent picture. If parents, teachers, and peers project consistent values, the search for identity is easier. In a simple society in which adult models are few and social roles are limited, the task of forming an identity is relatively easy. In a society as complex as ours, it is a difficult task for many adolescents. They are faced with an almost infinite array of possibilities regarding how to behave and what to do in life. As a result, there are large differences among adolescents in how the development of their identity proceeds. Moreover, any particular adolescent's identity may be at different stages of development in different areas of life (for example, sexual, occupational, and ideological).

In most families, conflict between teens and parents is short-lived.

© Ariel Shelley/CORBIS

Ideally, the identity crisis should be resolved by the early or mid-twenties so that the individual can move on to other life tasks. When the process is successful, the individual is said to have achieved an identity—a coherent sense of sexual identity, vocational direction, and ideological worldview. Until the identity crisis is resolved, the individual has no consistent sense of self or set of internal standards for evaluating his or her self-worth in major areas of life. Erikson called this unsuccessful outcome **identity confusion.**

Erikson's theory about adolescent identity development has been tested and extended by other researchers (see Steinberg & Morris, 2001). On the basis of open-ended interviews, James Marcia (1966, 1980) arrived at four identity statuses or positions, based on whether the person perceives an identity issue and whether a resolution has been reached:

Identity achievement. Individuals in this status have passed through an identity crisis, a period of active questioning and self-definition. They are committed
Text continued p. 102

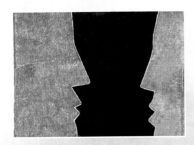

SEEING BOTH SIDES

How Instrumental Are Parents in the Development of Their Children?

PARENTS HAVE NO LASTING INFLUENCE ON THE PERSONALITY OR INTELLIGENCE OF THEIR CHILDREN

Judith Rich Harris, award-winning psychologist and author *(The Nurture Assumption)*

Your parents took good care of you when you were little. They taught you many things. They are leading players in your memories of childhood. All these things could be true, and yet your parents may have left no lasting impression on your personality or intelligence or on the way you behave when they're not around.

Hard to believe? Try, for a moment, to put aside your preconceptions and consider the evidence. Consider, for example, the studies (discussed in Chapter 12) designed to separate the effects of genes from those of the home environment. These studies show that if you eliminate the similarities due to genes, two people who grew up in the same home are not noticeably more alike in personality or intelligence than two people picked at random from the same population. Almost all the similarities between brothers or sisters reared together are due to the genes they have in common. If they are adoptive siblings, they are no more alike than adopted people reared in different homes. On average, an adopted child reared by agreeable parents is no nicer than one reared by grouches, and one reared by parents who love books is no smarter than one reared by parents who love soap operas.

Because these results don't fit the popular theories of child development, many psychologists ignore them or try to explain them away. But results that don't fit the theories have been piling up (Harris, 1995, 1998). A recent study showed that children who spent most of their first three years in day-care centers do not differ in behavior or adjustment from children who spent that time at home (NICHD Early Child Care Research Network, 1998). Children who must vie with their siblings for their parents' attention do not differ in personality from only children (Falbo & Polit, 1986). Boys and girls behave as differently today as they did a generation ago, even though today's parents try hard to treat their sons and daughters alike (Serbin, Powlishta, & Gulko, 1993). Children who speak Korean or Polish at home but English with their peers end up as English speakers. The language learned outside the home takes precedence over the one their parents taught them, and they speak it without an accent (Harris, 1998).

But what about the evidence that dysfunctional parents tend to have dysfunctional offspring and that children who are treated with affection tend to turn out better than children who are treated harshly? The trouble with this evidence is that it comes from studies that provide no way to distinguish genetic from environmental influences or causes from effects. Are the offspring's problems due to the unfavorable environment provided by the dysfunctional parents or to personality characteristics inherited from them? Did the hugs cause the child to develop a pleasant personality, or did her pleasant personality make her parents want to hug her? Judging from studies that use more advanced techniques, it appears that the problems were at least partly inherited and that the child's pleasant personality evoked the hugs (Plomin, Owen, & McGuffin, 1994; Reiss, 1997).

There is no question that parents influence the way their children behave at home, and this is another source of confusion. Is the way children behave at home a good indication of how they'll behave in the classroom or the playground? When researchers discover that children behave differently in different social contexts, they usually assume that the way they behave with their parents is somehow more important or long-lasting than the way they behave elsewhere. But the children who speak Korean or Spanish at home and English outside the home use English as their primary language in adulthood. A boy whose cries evoke sympathy when he hurts himself at home learns not to cry when he hurts himself on the playground, and as an adult he seldom cries. A child who is dominated by her older sibling at home is no more likely than a firstborn to allow herself to be dominated by her peers. Children learn separately how to behave at home and outside the home, and it's their outside-the-home behavior they bring with them to adulthood—which makes sense, since they are not going to spend their adult lives in their parents' house.

The notion that children are in a great hurry to grow up and that they see their own world as a pale imitation of the adult world is an adult-o-centric one. A child's goal is not to be like her mother or his father— it's to be a successful child. Children have to learn how to get along in the world outside the home, and out there the rules are different. Children are not putty in their parents' hands.

Judith Rich Harris

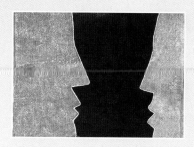

How Instrumental Are Parents in the Development of Their Children?

PARENTS ARE INSTRUMENTAL IN THE DEVELOPMENT OF THEIR CHILDREN

Jerome Kagan, Harvard University

The development of the skills, values, and social behaviors that maximize adaptation to the society in which a particular child grows requires the orchestration of many relatively independent forces. The most important of these include the temperamental biases that the child inherits; the class, ethnic, and religious affiliations of the child's family; relationships with siblings; the historical era in which childhood is spent; and always the behaviors and personality of the parents.

Parental influences on the child assume two different forms. Parental actions with the child are the most obvious. Parents who regularly talk and read to their children usually produce children with the largest vocabularies, the highest intelligence scores, and the best academic grades (Gottfried, Fleming, & Gottfried, 1998; Ninio, 1980). Parents who reason with their children while making requests for obedience usually end up with more civil children (Baumrind, 1967). The power of the family is seen in the results of a study of over 1,000 children from 10 different cities in the United States who were studied extensively by a team of scientists. Some of these children were raised at home, and some attended daycare centers for varied amounts of time. The main result

Jerome Kagan

was that the family had the most important influence on the three-year-old child's personality and character (NICHD Early Child Care Research Network, 1998). One of the most important illustrations of the power of parental behavior is the fact that some children who were orphaned and made homeless by war were able to regain intellectual and social skills they failed to develop during their early privation if they were adopted by nurturant families (Rathbun, DiVirglio, & Waldfogel, 1958).

Parents also influence their children through their own characteristics. Children come to conclusions about themselves, often incorrect, because they assume that since they are the biological offspring of their mother and father, they possess some of the qualities that belong to their parents. This emotionally tinged belief is called *identification,* and it is the basis for national pride and loyalty to ethnic and religious groups. Thus, if a parent is perceived by her child as affectionate, just, and talented, the child assumes that she, too, probably possesses one or more of these desirable traits and, as a result, feels more confident than she has a right to, given the evidence. By contrast, the child who perceives a parent who is rejecting, unfair in doling out punishment, and without talent feels shame because he assumes that he probably is in possession of some of these undesirable characteristics (Kagan, 1998).

Support for this last claim is fact that all children become upset if someone criticizes their family. The anxiety or anger that follows such criticism is strong because children assume, unconsciously, that any criticism of their parents is also a criticism of them.

The provocative suggestion in Harris's "The Nurture Assumption" that parents have minimal influences on their children's personality and character, while peers have a major influence, is undermined by two sets of facts. First, peers are of little influence until the child is five or six years of age, but six-year-olds from varied cultures or children living in different historical eras are very different in their behavior and personality. Puritan children living in New England in the 17th century were more obedient than contemporary Boston children because of parental behaviors toward them.

Second, children select friends who share their values and interests. A child who values schoolwork will choose friends with similar interests. If such a child becomes an academically successful adult, it is not logical to assume that this outcome is due to the influence of friends because the child chose that type of friend in the first place.

It is rare to find a belief that all societies, ancient and modern, share. I know of no society that claimed that the family's influence on the child's mind was without much significance. This degree of consensus implies that it might be a universal truth. To declare that parents have little influence on children, in light of the scientific evidence and every parent's daily experiences, is a little like declaring on a foggy September morning that all the trees have disappeared because you cannot see them.

to ideological positions that they have worked out for themselves, and they have decided on an occupation. They have begun to think of themselves as a future doctor, not just a pre-med chemistry major. They have reexamined their family's religious and political beliefs and discarded those that don't seem to fit their identity.

Foreclosure. Those in this status are also committed to occupational and ideological positions, but they show no signs of having gone through an identity crisis. They have accepted their family's religion without question. When asked about politics, they often say that they have never given it much thought. Some of them seem committed and cooperative; others seem rigid, dogmatic, and conforming. They give the impression that they would be lost if a major event challenged their unexamined rules and values.

Moratorium. These young people are in the midst of an identity crisis. They are actively seeking answers but have not resolved the conflicts between their parents' plans for them and their own interests. They may express a set of political or religious beliefs with great intensity for a while, only to abandon them after a period of reconsideration. At best, they seem sensitive, ethical, and open-minded; at worst, they appear anxiety-ridden, self-righteous, and vacillating (Scarr, Weinberg, & Levine, 1986).

Identity diffusion. This is Marcia's term for what Erikson calls identity confusion. Some individuals in this category have had an identity crisis; others have not. In either case, they still have no integrated sense of themselves. They say that it might be "interesting" to go to law school or start a business, but they are not taking steps in either direction. They say that they are not interested in religion or politics. Some seem cynical, and others shallow and confused. Some, of course, are still too young to have reached the identity development of adolescence.

As expected, the percentage of adolescents who have attained identity achievement increases steadily from before high school to the late college years, as the percentage remaining in identity diffusion steadily decreases (Waterman, 1985).

More contemporary research has focused on the development of self-concept from the perspective of cognitive theories (see Chapter 1), rather than based on Erikson's stages of identity development. As adolescents mature cognitively, they develop more abstract characterizations of themselves. They begin to view themselves more in terms of personal beliefs and standards and less according to social comparisons (Harter, 1998). Adolescents' self-concepts vary across different situations, so that they see themselves differently when they are with parents than when they are with peers (Harter, 1998). They often engage in behaviors that do not represent how they really see themselves, especially among classmates or in romantic relationships.

In early adolescence, self-esteem is somewhat unstable but becomes more stable during later adolescence (Harter, 1998). African American adolescents tend to have higher self-esteem than white adolescents (Gray-Little & Hafdahl, 2000), and males have higher self-esteem than females (Kling et al., 1999). Not surprisingly, however, across both genders and most ethnic groups, higher self-esteem is related to parental approval, peer support, adjustment, and success in school (DuBois et al., 1998).

During adolescence and early adulthood, many minority youth struggle with their ethnic identity, and their resolution of this struggle can come in many forms (Phinney & Alipuria, 1990; Sellers et al., 1998). Some minority youth assimilate into the majority culture by rejecting their own culture. Some live in the majority culture but feel estranged. Some reject the majority culture and focus only on their own culture. And some try to find a balance between the majority culture and their own culture, a resolution sometimes referred to as biculturalism.

◆ Interim Summary

- Puberty has significant effects on an adolescent's body image, self-esteem, moods, and relationships; but most adolescents make it through this period without major turmoil.

- According to Erikson's theory, forming a personal sense of identity is the major task of the adolescent period.

- Identity crisis is the phrase coined by Erikson to describe the active period of self-definition characteristic of adolescence.

- Identity confusion is the unsuccessful outcome of identity crisis. The adolescent has no consistent sense of self or set of internal standards for evaluating his or her self-worth in major areas of life.

◆ Critical Thinking Questions

1. Using the categories of identity achievement, foreclosure, moratorium, and identity diffusion, can you identify how and when your religious, sexual, occupational, and political identities have developed and changed over time?

2. What experiences might influence the development of a minority youth's ethnic identity? For example, what experiences might lead a youth to develop a bicultural identity, and what experiences might lead a youth to reject majority culture?

1. Two central questions in developmental psychology are: (a) How do biological factors ("nature") interact with environmental experiences ("nurture") to determine the course of development? and (b) Is development best understood as a continuous process of change or as a series of qualitatively distinct stages?

2. Some developmental psychologists believe that development occurs in a sequence of periods in which (a) behaviors at a given stage are organized around a dominant theme or a coherent set of characteristics, (b) behaviors at one stage are qualitatively different from behaviors at earlier or later stages, and (c) all children go through the same stages in the same order. Critical or sensitive periods are times during development when specific experiences must occur for psychological development to proceed normally.

3. Early theorists believed that all sensory preferences and abilities had to be learned, but research over the last several decades has established that infants are born with their sensory systems intact and prepared to learn about the world.

4. Newborns have poor vision and cannot see as well as an adult until about age 2. Some theorists thought infants were born with a preference for faces, but research suggests infants are not attracted to faces per se but to stimulus characteristics such as curved lines, high contrast, edges, movement, and complexity—all of which faces possess. Even newborns pay attention to sounds. They seem to be born with perceptual mechanisms that are already tuned to the properties of human speech that will help them learn language. Infants can discriminate between different tastes and odors shortly after birth. They seem to prefer the taste and odor of breast milk. Infants can learn from the moment they are born and show good memories by 3 months of age.

5. Piaget's theory describes stages in cognitive development. These proceed from the sensorimotor stage (in which an important discovery is object permanence), through the preoperational stage (when symbols begin to be used) and the concrete operational stage (when conservation concepts develop), to the formal operational stage (when hypotheses are tested systematically in problem solving). New methods of testing reveal that Piaget's theory underestimates children's abilities, and several alternative approaches have been proposed.

6. Information-processing approaches view cognitive development as reflecting the gradual development of processes such as attention and memory. Other theorists emphasize increases in domain-specific knowledge. Still others, including Vygotsky, focus on the influence of the social and cultural context. Much of the newest research in children's cognitive development focuses on children's theory of mind, or understanding that other people have beliefs and expectations that can be different from their own and different from reality.

7. Piaget believed that children's understanding of moral rules and judgments develops along with their cognitive abilities. Kohlberg extended Piaget's work to include adolescence and adulthood. He proposed three levels of moral judgment: preconventional, conventional, and postconventional.

8. An infant's tendency to seek closeness to particular people and to feel more secure in their presence is called *attachment*. Attachment can be assessed in a procedure called *the strange situation*, a series of episodes in which a child is observed as the primary caregiver leaves and returns to the room. Securely attached infants seek to interact with a caretaker who returns from an absence. Insecurely attached: avoidant infants avoid a caretaker who returns from an absence. Insecurely attached: ambivalent infants show resistance to a caretaker who returns from an absence. Disorganized infants show contradictory behaviors (sometimes avoidant, sometimes approaching) to a caretaker who returns from an absence.

9. Research on the effects of day care on children's well-being and attachments suggests that low-quality day care may be detrimental, but high quality day care is not and may counteract the effects of poor home environments.

10. Gender identity is the degree to which one regards oneself as male or female. It is distinct from sex typing, the acquisition of characteristics and behaviors that society considers appropriate for one's sex. Freud's psychoanalytic theory holds that gender identity and sex typing develop from the children's early discovery of the genital differences between the sexes and children's eventual identification with the same-sex parent. Social learning theory emphasizes the rewards and punishments that children receive for sex-appropriate and sex-inappropriate behaviors, as well as a process of identification with same-sex adults that is based on observational learning. A cognitive-developmental theory of gender identity and sex typing holds that once children can identify themselves as male or female, they are motivated to acquire sex-typed behaviors. Their understanding of sex and gender corresponds to Piaget's stages of cognitive development, especially their understanding of gender constancy—the realization that a person's sex remains constant despite changes of age

and appearance. Gender schema theory seeks to explain why children base their self-concepts on the male-female distinction in the first place. It emphasizes the role of culture in teaching children to view the world through the lens of gender.

11. Puberty has significant effects on an adolescent's body image, self-esteem, moods, and relationships, but most adolescents make it through this period without major turmoil.

12. According to Erikson's theory, forming a personal sense of identity is the major task of the adolescent period. Identity crisis is Erikson's phrase to describe the active period of self-definition characteristic of adolescence. Identity confusion is the unsuccessful outcome of identity crisis in which the adolescent has no consistent sense of self or set of internal standards for evaluating his or her self-worth in major areas of life.

CORE CONCEPTS

maturation
stages
critical period
sensitive periods
visual field
facial preference
schemas
assimilate
accommodation
sensorimotor stage
object permanence
preoperational stage
operation
conservation
egocentrism
concrete operational stage
formal operational stage
information-processing skills

knowledge
sociocultural approach to
   development
metacognition
theory of mind
autism
moral judgment
preconventional level of moral
   development
conventional level of moral
   development
postconventional level of moral
   development
temperament
easy temperament
difficult temperament
slow to warm up temperament
separation anxiety

autonomy
attachment
securely attached
insecurely attached: avoidant
insecurely attached: ambivalent
disorganized
sensitive responsiveness
gender identity
sex typing
gender schema
adolescence
puberty
menarche
identity crisis
identity confusion

WEB RESOURCES

http://psychology.wadsworth.com/ atkinson14e

Take a quiz, try the activities and exercises, and explore web links.

http://home.att.net/xchar/tna/

This site is maintained by Seeing Both Sides author Judith Rich Harris and further explains her controversial book that highlights her belief in the importance of peers and the relative unimportance of parenting styles.

http://www.personal.psu.edu/faculty/n/x/nxd10/ adolesce.htm

Find out more about adolescence here. You can search from a multitude of topics, including cognitive and social transitions, identity, and sexuality, or explore the case studies.

InfoTrac Online Library
http://www.infotrac-college.com/ wadsworth

Use InfoTrac College Edition to find popular and scientific articles by using the search terms below or your own relevant terms.

- Cognitive development
- Developmental psychology
- Gender roles
- Moral development
- Psychosocial development
- Temperament

CD-ROM LINKS

Psych Odyssey

Check out CD Chapter 10, Cognitive Development

A. Theories of Cognitive Development
B. Cognitive Development During Infancy
C. Cognitive Development During Childhood
D. Cognitive Development During Adolescence
See also CD Chapter 11, Social Development
A. Personality Development
B. A Developing Sense of Self
C. Moral Development

Psyk.trek 2.0

Check out CD Unit 9, Human Development
9a Prenatal Development
9b Erikson's Theory of Personality Development
9c Piaget's Theory of Cognitive Development
9d Kohlberg's Theory of Moral Development

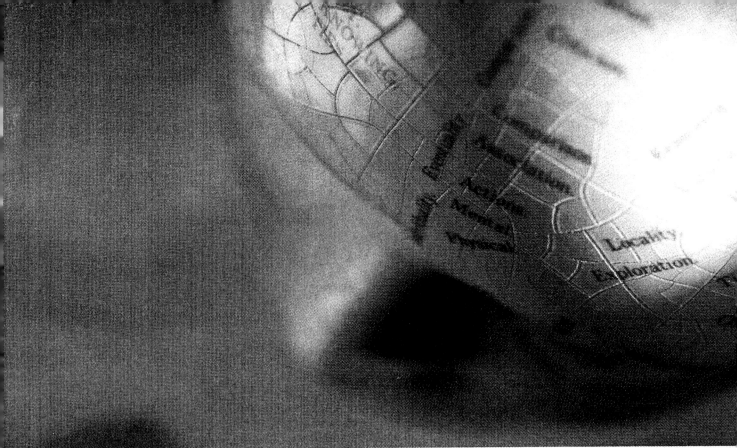

INTELLIGENCE

12

Tommy was born in December 1856 to Janet Woodrow, the daughter of a Presbyterian minister, and Joseph Ruggles Wilson, himself a Presbyterian minister who became a leader of the Presbyterian Church in the American South. Tommy's parents were educated people who highly valued learning. As a schoolboy, however, Tommy had great difficulty reading. Despite attending special schools, he still was not able to read until late childhood, around age 10 or 11. With a great deal of hard work, he was eventually able to qualify for admission to the College of New Jersey, which later became Princeton University. Even in college, however, Tommy did not excel at coursework.

To this point, you might predict that Tommy's chances for success in life were only moderate. We might say today that "he didn't look good on paper." Our modest predictions for

Tommy's future would be proven wrong, however. Tommy was Thomas Woodrow Wilson. After graduating from Princeton, he earned a law degree from the University of Virginia and a doctorate in political science from Johns Hopkins University.

During periods as a professor at Bryn Mawr College, Wesleyan University, and Princeton University, Wilson wrote nine books and became a respected essayist. He was named president of Princeton in 1902 and then won the race for governor of New Jersey in a landslide election in 1910. In 1912, he ran for president of the United States against the incumbent, President William Howard Taft, and won, becoming the 28th U.S. president. During his 8 years in office, Wilson led the United States through World War I and worked tirelessly to establish a lasting and meaningful peace in Europe. In 1919, he won the Nobel Peace prize for his efforts in establishing the League of Nations.

Based on his accomplishments across the course of his life, most people would say that Thomas Woodrow

Wilson was an intelligent man. If he had taken an intelligence test or some other kind of aptitude test as a boy, however, he might not have scored in the "intelligent" range. Wilson's life story raises important questions about what we mean by intelligence.

The concept of intelligence has been one of the most contentious across the history of psychology and continues to be so today. Even defining **intelligence** can be difficult because your definition reflects your theory of what it means to be intelligent, and theories of intelligence differ widely, as we will discuss later. Some theorists have argued that intelligence doesn't exist as a real entity, but simply is a label for what intelligence tests measure. Other theorists suggest that intelligence should be considered more broadly and that it involves the ability to learn from experience, think in abstract terms, and deal effectively with one's environment. We will consider various conceptualizations and theories of intelligence in this chapter. First, however, we discuss how intelligence is measured.

427

ASSESSMENT OF INTELLECTUAL ABILITIES

Many industrialized societies rely heavily on objective assessment of cognitive or intellectual abilities. School-children are often placed in instructional groups on the basis of their performances on such tests. Aptitude or ability tests are part of the admissions procedure in many colleges and most professional and graduate schools. In addition, many industries and government agencies select job applicants and place or promote employees on the basis of test scores. Beyond these practical concerns, methods of assessment are essential to theory and research on intelligence.

Because tests and other assessment instruments play important practical and scientific roles, it is essential that they measure accurately what they are intended to measure. Specifically, they must have reliability and validity. They also must be standardized, meaning that the conditions for taking the test are the same for all test-takers. For example, the instructions accompanying the test must be the same for everyone.

RELIABILITY

If a test or method of assessment has good **reliability, it will yield reproducible and consistent results.** If a test yielded different results when it was administered on different occasions or scored by different people, it would be unreliable. A simple analogy is a rubber yardstick. If we did not know how much it stretched each time we took a measurement, the results would be unreliable no matter how carefully we made each measurement.

Reliability is typically assessed by correlating two sets of scores. For example, the same test might be given to the same group of people on two occasions. If the test is reliable, their scores on the first occasion should correlate highly with their scores on the second. If they do, the test is said to have test-retest reliability or temporal stability.

In practice, of course, we would not usually want to give the same test to the same people twice. But there are many situations in which we would want to give equivalent forms of the same test—for example, when college-bound high school seniors want to take the Scholastic Assessment Test (SAT) more than once. To ensure that two forms of the same test yield equivalent scores, both forms are administered to the same population and the two forms are correlated. The test is said to have **alternative form reliability** if the two forms of the test correlate highly. Some of the questions on the SAT do not actually count toward the student's score but are being statistically evaluated so they can be used on future equivalent forms of the test.

Another common measure of reliability is **internal consistency, the degree to which the separate questions or items on a test measure the same thing.** This can be assessed by correlating the scores obtained by a group of individuals on each item with their total scores. Any item that does not correlate with the total score is an unreliable item that is failing to contribute to what the test is measuring. Discarding unreliable items "purifies" a test by increasing its internal consistency. As the number of reliable items on a test increases, the reliability of the test's total score also increases.

Most tests and assessment instruments are scored objectively, often by computer. But sometimes intellectual performance or social behavior must be subjectively evaluated. An essay examination is a familiar example. To assess the reliability of such subjective judgments, two or more sets of ratings by independent judges are correlated. For example, two observers might independently rate a group of nursery school children for aggression, or two or more judges might be asked to read past U.S. presidential inaugural addresses and rate them for optimism or count the number of negative references to Iraq. If the correlation between raters or judges is high, the method is said to possess **interrater agreement** or **interjudge reliability.**

In general, a well-constructed, objectively scored test of ability should have a reliability coefficient of .90 or greater. For subjective judgments, reliability coefficients of .70 can sometimes be satisfactory for research purposes, but inferences about particular individuals must be

Psychological tests are often used to evaluate job applicants.

made with great caution. But as noted earlier, the reliability of a test's total score increases as the number of reliable items on the test increases. We can apply the same reasoning to subjective judgments and increase the reliability of the method by adding more judges, raters, or observers. For example, if ratings by two observers correlate only .50, the researcher can add a third, comparable observer and thereby raise the interjudge reliability of their summed ratings to .75; adding a fourth rater would raise the reliability to .80.

VALIDITY

Reliability assesses the degree to which a test is measuring something, but high reliability does not guarantee that the test has good **validity**—that is, that it measures what it is intended to measure. For example, if the final examination in your psychology course contained especially difficult vocabulary words or trick questions, it might be a test of your verbal ability or test sophistication rather than of the material learned in the course. Such an examination might be reliable—students would achieve about the same scores on a retest, and the separate items might all be measuring the same thing—but it would not be a valid test of achievement for the course.

In some instances, the validity of a test can be assessed by correlating the test score with some external criterion. This correlation is called a *validity coefficient*, and this kind of validity is called **criterion or empirical validity.** For example, the relatively strong positive correlation between scores on the SAT and freshman grades in college is one indication of the test's validity. Because of sensitivity to race and sex discrimination, the courts are increasingly requiring companies and government agencies that use tests for personnel selection to provide evidence that those tests correlate with on-the-job performance—in other words, that they have criterion or empirical validity.

There may be aspects of intelligence for which it is not clear what the external criterion should be. How, for example, should a researcher assess the validity of a test for achievement motivation? One can think of a number of possibilities. The test could be given to business executives to see if it correlates with their salaries. Perhaps the test will correlate with teachers' ratings of their students' ambition. The problem is that there is no single criterion that the researcher is willing to accept as the ultimate "true" answer. It would be reassuring if the test correlated with executive salaries, but if it did not, the researcher would not be willing to judge the test to be invalid. This is known as the **criterion problem in assessment:** There is no measure of "truth" against which to validate the test. Accordingly, the researcher attempts instead to establish its **construct validity**—to show that scores on the test correlate with outcomes that the theory says it should predict.

This is done through the research process itself. The researcher uses his or her theory both to construct the test and to generate predictions from the theory. Studies using the test are then conducted to test those predictions. To the extent that the results of several converging studies confirm the theory's predictions, both the theory and the test are validated simultaneously. Most often, mixed results suggest ways in which both the theory and the test need to be modified. For example, McClelland (1987) proposed a theory of achievement motivation that was supposed to identify and explain ambitious, high-achieving individuals in any area of activity. A test for assessing achievement motivation was designed and used to test predictions from the theory. Results from several studies indicated that the predictions were confirmed for men involved in entrepreneurial activities but not for women or for individuals involved in other kinds of activities, such as academic research. Accordingly, the theory was modified to apply primarily to entrepreneurial achievement, and the test was modified so that it was more valid for women.

EARLY INTELLIGENCE TESTS

The first attempt to develop tests of intellectual ability was made a century ago by Sir Francis Galton. A naturalist and mathematician, Galton developed an interest in individual differences after considering the evolutionary theory proposed by his cousin, Charles Darwin. Galton believed that certain families are biologically superior to others—that some people are innately stronger or smarter than others. Intelligence, he reasoned, is a question of exceptional sensory and perceptual skills, which are passed from one generation to the next. Because all information is acquired through the senses, the more sensitive and accurate an individual's perceptual apparatus, the more intelligent the person. (Galton's belief in the heritability of intelligence led him to propose that the human race's mental capacities could be enhanced through eugenics, or selective breeding. Fortunately, he is remembered more for his application of statistics to the study of intelligence than for his espousal of eugenics.)

In 1884, Galton administered a battery of tests (measuring variables such as head size, reaction time, visual acuity, auditory thresholds, and memory for visual forms) to more than 9,000 visitors at the London Exhibition. To his disappointment, he discovered that eminent British scientists could not be distinguished from ordinary citizens on the basis of their head size and that measurements such as reaction time were not related to other measures of intelligence. Although his test did not prove very useful, Galton did invent the correlation coefficient, which—as we have already seen—plays an important role in psychology.

The first tests resembling modern intelligence tests were devised by the French psychologist Alfred Binet in the late 19th century. In 1881, the French government passed a law making school attendance compulsory for all children. Previously, slow learners had usually been kept at home, but now teachers had to cope with a wide range of individual differences. The government asked Binet to create a test that would detect children who were too slow intellectually to benefit from a regular school curriculum.

Binet assumed that intelligence should be measured by tasks that required reasoning and problem-solving abilities rather than perceptual-motor skills. In collaboration with another French psychologist, Théophile Simon, Binet published such a test in 1905 and revised it in 1908 and again in 1911.

Binet reasoned that a slow or dull child was like a normal child whose mental growth was retarded. On tests, the slow child would perform like a younger normal child, whereas the mental abilities of a bright child were characteristic of older children. Binet devised a scale of test items of increasing difficulty that measured the kinds of changes in intelligence ordinarily associated with growing older. The higher a child could go on the scale in answering items correctly, the higher his or her mental age (MA). The concept of mental age was critical to Binet's method. Using this method, the MA of a child could be compared with his or her chronological age (CA) as determined by date of birth.

THE STANFORD–BINET INTELLIGENCE SCALE

The test items originally developed by Binet were adapted for American schoolchildren by Lewis Terman at Stanford University. Terman standardized the administration of the test and developed age-level norms by giving the test to thousands of children of various ages. In 1916, he published the Stanford revision of the Binet tests, now referred to as the **Stanford-Binet Intelligence Scale.** It was revised in 1937, 1960, 1972, and most recently in 1986. Despite its age, the Stanford-Binet is still one of the most frequently used psychological tests.

Terman retained Binet's concept of mental age. Each test item was age-graded at the level at which a substantial majority of the children pass it. A child's mental age could be obtained by summing the number of items passed at each level. In addition, Terman adopted a convenient index of intelligence suggested by the German psychologist William Stern. This index is the **intelligence**

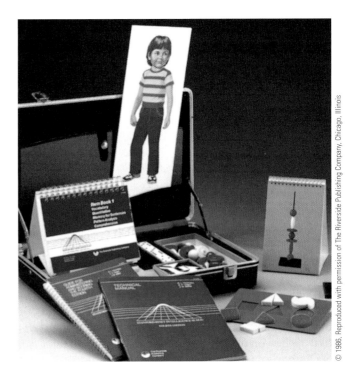

Test materials from the Stanford-Binet Intelligence Scale.

quotient (IQ), which expresses intelligence as a ratio of mental age to chronological age:

$$IQ = MA/CA \times 100$$

The number 100 is used as a multiplier so that the IQ will have a value of 100 when MA is equal to CA. If MA is lower than CA, the IQ will be less than 100; if MA is higher than CA, the IQ will be more than 100.

The most recent revision of the Stanford-Binet uses standard age scores instead of IQ scores. These can be interpreted in terms of percentiles, which show the percentage of individuals in the standardization group falling above or below a given score (Thorndike, Hagen, & Sattler, 1986). And although the concept of IQ is still used in intelligence testing, it is no longer actually calculated by using this equation. Instead, tables are used to convert raw scores on the test into standard scores that are adjusted so that the mean at each age equals 100.

IQ scores tend to fall in the form of a bell-shaped curve, with most people's scores hovering around 100, but some people's scores much higher or lower than 100. Figure 12-1 provides the percentages of the population who will fall in various ranges of IQ scores.

In line with the current view of intelligence as a composite of different abilities, the 1986 revision of the Stanford-Binet groups its tests into four broad areas: verbal reasoning, abstract/visual reasoning, quantitative reasoning, and short-term memory (Sattler, 1988). A separate score is obtained for each area. Table 12-1 gives some examples of items, grouped by area.

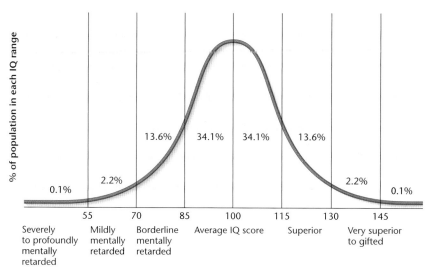

▌Figure 12-1
Frequency Distribution of IQ Scores
IQ scores fall into a normal distribution, with few scores at either the high or low extremes, and most scores falling around 100. (From A. Anastasia and S. Urbina, *Psychological Testing, 7/e,* © 1997 Prentice-Hall.)

● **Table 12-1**
Items From the Stanford-Binet Intelligence Scale

Typical examples of items from the 1986 Stanford-Binet Intelligence Scale for a 6- to 8-year-old.

Test	Description
Verbal Reasoning	
Vocabulary	Defines words, such as "dollar" and "envelope."
Comprehension	Answers questions, such as "Where do people buy food?" and "Why do people comb their hair?"
Absurdities	Identifies the "funny" aspect of a picture, such as a girl riding a bicycle on a lake or a bald man combing his hair.
Verbal Relations	Tells how the first three items in a sequence are alike and how they differ from the fourth: scarf, tie, muffler, shirt.
Quantitative Reasoning	
Quantitative	Performs simple arithmetic tasks, such as selecting a die with six spots because the number of spots equals the combination of a two-spot die and a four-spot die.
Number Series	Gives the next two numbers in a series, such as 20 16 12 8 ___ ___.
Equation Building	Builds an equation from the following array: 2 3 5 + = . One correct response would be $2 + 3 = 5$.
Abstract/Visual Reasoning	
Pattern Analysis	Copies a simple design with blocks.
Copying	Copies a geometrical drawing demonstrated by the examiner, such as a rectangle intersected by two diagonals.
Short-Term Memory	
Bead Memory	Shown a picture of different-shaped beads stacked on a stick. Reproduces the sequence from memory by placing real beads on a stick.
Memory for Sentences	Repeats after the examiner sentences such as "It is time to go to sleep" and "Ken painted a picture for his mother's birthday."
Memory for Digits	Repeats after examiner a series of digits, such as 5-7-8-3, forward and backward.
Memory for Objects	Shown pictures of individual objects, such as a clock and an elephant, one at a time. Identifies the objects in the correct order of their appearance in a picture that also includes extraneous objects; for example, a bus, a clown, an *elephant,* eggs, and a *clock.*

THE WECHSLER INTELLIGENCE SCALES

In 1939, David Wechsler developed a new test because he thought the Stanford-Binet depended too heavily on language ability and was not appropriate for adults. The **Wechsler Adult Intelligence Scale**, or WAIS (1939, 1955, 1981), is divided into two parts—a verbal scale and a performance scale—that yield separate scores as well as a full-scale IQ. The test items are described in Table 12-2. Wechsler later developed a similar test for children, the Wechsler Intelligence Scale for Children (WISC) (1958, 1974, 1991).

Items on the performance scale require the manipulation or arrangement of blocks, pictures, or other materials. The Wechsler scales also provide scores for each subtest, so the examiner has a clearer picture of the individual's intellectual strengths and weaknesses. For example, a discrepancy between verbal and performance scores prompts the examiner to look for specific learning problems such as reading disabilities or language handicaps.

Both the Stanford-Binet and the Wechsler scales show good reliability and validity. They have test-retest reliabilities of about .90, and both are fairly valid predictors of achievement in school, with validity coefficients of about .50 (Sattler, 1988).

GROUP ABILITY TESTS

The Stanford-Binet and the Wechsler scales are individual ability tests. They are administered to a single individual by a specially trained tester. Group ability tests, in contrast, can be administered to a large number of people by a single examiner and are usually in pencil-and-paper form.

● Table 12-2
Tests Composing the Wechsler Adult Intelligence Scale

The tests of the Wechsler Intelligence Scale for Children are similar to those of the adult scale, with some modifications.

Test	Description
Verbal Scale	
Information	Questions tap a general range of information, for example, "What is the capital of Italy?"
Comprehension	Tests practical information and ability to evaluate past experience, for example, "Why do we put stamps on a letter to be mailed?"
Arithmetic	Verbal problems testing arithmetic reasoning.
Similarities	Asks in what way two objects or concepts (for example, *recipe* and *map*) are similar; assesses abstract thinking.
Digit Span	A series of digits presented auditorily (for example, 7-5-6-3-8) is repeated in a forward or backward direction; tests attention and rote memory.
Vocabulary	Assesses word knowledge.
Letter Number Sequencing	Orally presented letters and numbers in a mixed-up order must be reordered and repeated, first with the numbers in ascending order and then with the letters in alphabetical order; assesses working memory.
Performance Scale	
Digit Symbol	A timed coding task in which numbers must be associated with marks of various shapes; assesses speed of learning and writing.
Picture Completion	The missing part of an incompletely drawn picture must be discovered and named; assesses visual alertness, visual memory, and perceptual organization.
Block Design	Pictured designs must be copied with blocks; assesses ability to perceive and analyze patterns.
Picture Arrangement	A series of comic-strip pictures must be arranged in the right sequence to tell a story; assesses understanding of social situations.
Matrix Reasoning	A geometric shape that is similar in some way to a sample shape must be selected from a set of possible alternatives; assesses perceptual organization.
Object Assembly	Puzzle pieces must be assembled to form a complete object; assesses ability to deal with part-whole relationships.
Symbol Search	A series of paired groups of symbols are presented, a target group of two symbols and a search group. Examinee must determine if either target symbol appears in the search group; assesses processing speed.

The **Scholastic Assessment Test (SAT)** and the **American College Test (ACT)** are examples of group-administered general-ability tests that are familiar to most college students in the United States. Virtually all 4-year colleges require applicants to take one of these tests as a way of setting a common standard for students from high schools with different curricula and grading standards. The SAT has been undergoing major revisions in response to criticism, and there are plans to include essay components, among other changes, in upcoming versions. These changes were made in response to recent high school curriculum trends that place a premium on more sophisticated reading, writing, and mathematics skills.

Correlations between SAT scores and freshman grade point averages vary across studies, with a median correlation of about .38 for the verbal section of the SAT and .34 for the mathematics section (Linn, 1982). When these correlations are corrected for the fact that many students with very low scores do not end up attending college (and hence cannot be included in the calculation of the validity correlation), the resulting correlations are about .50. This means that about 44% of students in the top fifth of the distribution of SAT scores will also be in the top fifth of the distribution of freshman grade point averages, compared with only 4% of students in the bottom fifth of the SAT score distribution. SAT scores improve prediction considerably, but it is clear that the freshman grades of students with identical SAT scores will vary widely.

THE FACTORIAL APPROACH

Some psychologists view intelligence as a general capacity for comprehension and reasoning that manifests itself in various ways. This was Binet's assumption. Although his test contained many kinds of items, Binet observed that a bright child tended to score higher than dull children on all of them. He assumed, therefore, that the different tasks sampled a basic underlying ability. Similarly, despite the diverse subscales included the WAIS, Wechsler also believed that "intelligence is the aggregate or global capacity of the individual to act purposefully, to think rationally, and to deal effectively with his environment" (Wechsler, 1958).

Other psychologists, however, question whether there is such a thing as "general intelligence." They believe that intelligence tests sample a number of mental abilities that are relatively independent of one another. One method of obtaining more precise information about the kinds of abilities that determine performance on intelligence tests is **factor analysis,** a statistical technique that examines the intercorrelations among a number of tests and, by grouping those that are most highly correlated, reduces them to a smaller number of independent dimensions, called factors. The basic idea is that two tests that correlate very highly with each other are probably measuring the same underlying ability. The goal is to discover the minimum number of factors, or abilities, required to explain the observed pattern of correlations among an array of different tests.

It was the originator of factor analysis, Charles Spearman (1904), who first proposed that all individuals possess a general intelligence factor (called *g*) in varying amounts. A person could be described as generally bright or generally dull, depending on the amount of *g* he or she possessed. According to Spearman, the *g* factor is the major determinant of performance on intelligence tests. In addition, special factors, each called *s*, are specific to particular abilities or tests. For example, tests of arithmetic or spatial relationships would each tap a separate *s*. An individual's tested intelligence would reflect the amount of *g* plus the magnitude of the various *s* factors possessed by that individual. Performance in mathematics, for example, would be a function of a person's general intelligence and mathematical aptitude.

A later investigator, Louis Thurstone (1938), objected to Spearman's emphasis on general intelligence, suggesting instead that intelligence can be broken down into a number of primary abilities by using factor analysis. After many rounds of administering tests, factor-analyzing the results, purifying the scales, and retesting, Thurstone identified seven factors, which he used to construct his Test of Primary Mental Abilities.

Revised versions of this test are still widely used, but its predictive power is no greater than that of general intelligence tests such as the Wechsler scales. Thurstone's hope of discovering the basic elements of intelligence through factor analysis was not fully realized, for several reasons. For one, his primary abilities are not completely independent. Indeed, the significant intercorrelations among them provide support for the concept of a general intelligence factor underlying the specific abilities. For another, the number of basic abilities identified by factor analysis depends on the nature of the test items. Other investigators, using different test items and alternative methods of factor analysis, have identified from 20 to 150 factors representing the range of intellectual abilities (Ekstrom, French, & Harman, 1979; Ekstrom, French, Harman, & Derman, 1976; Guilford, 1982).

This lack of consistency in number and kinds of factors raises doubts about the value of the factorial approach. Nevertheless, factor analysis remains an important technique for studying intellectual performance (Lubinski, 2000), and we will encounter it again when we discuss personality traits in Chapter 13.

CULTURAL CONSIDERATIONS

Intelligence tests have come under fire in recent years for being biased in favor of middle- and upper-class European Americans and against members of cultural minorities (Helms, 1992). Educated European Americans may be more comfortable in taking intelligence tests because they are more familiar with the kinds of reasoning assessed on intelligence tests and because testers are often also European Americans. In contrast, different cultures within the United States and in other countries may emphasize other forms of reasoning over those assessed on intelligence tests and may not be comfortable with the testing situations of intelligence tests.

A classic example involves the interpretation of syllogisms, logical problems often used in intelligence tests. A typical syllogism runs like this: "All bears in the North are white. My friend saw a bear in the North. What color was that bear?" According to intelligence tests, the "right" answer is that the bear is white. A subject's ability to infer that the bear is white is taken as an indication of his or her deductive reasoning skills.

When researchers asked farmers in Central Asia to solve these syllogisms, however, they discovered that this form of reasoning violated a social norm that you never state something you do not know from firsthand experience (Luria, 1976, pp. 108–109):

> Experimenter: In the Far North, where there is snow, all bears are white. Novaya Zemlya is in the Far North and there is always snow there. What color are the bears there?
>
> Respondent: . . . We always speak only of what we see; we don't talk about what we haven't seen.
>
> E: But what do my words imply? (The syllogism is repeated.)
>
> R: Well, it's like this: our tsar isn't like yours, and yours isn't like ours. Your words can be answered only by someone who was there and if a person wasn't there, he can't say anything on the basis of your words.
>
> E: . . . But on the basis of my words—in the North, where there is always snow, the bears are white, can you gather what kind of bears there are in Novaya Zemlya?

Scores on the Scholastic Assessment Test are used to predict academic achievement in college. The correlation between SAT scores and freshman grad point averages is about .50.

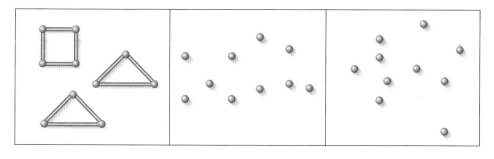

■ Figure 12-2
**Task From the Learning
Potential Assessment Device
(LPAD)**
The Learning Potential Assessment
Device (LPAD) is one test designed
to be culture-fair. The task on the
item shown is to outline the square
and two triangles embedded in
patterns of dots, using each dot
only once.

R: If a man was 60 or 80 and had seen a white bear and had told about it, he could be believed, but I've never seen one and hence I can't say. That's my last word.

This may have been interpreted as unintelligent by the rules of the test, but he was only following a social convention of his culture in his answer to the experimenter. Critics of intelligence tests argue that similar cultural clashes happen in subtler ways whenever persons not of the dominant, educated culture that created intelligence tests are asked to take these tests. A "culture-fair" test would have to include items that are equally applicable to all groups or items that are different for each culture but are psychologically equivalent for the groups being tested. An example of one such test is given in Figure 12-2. In general, attempts at culture-fair tests have proven disappointing.

◆ Interim Summary

- There are many different definitions of intelligence. Some theorists view it as simply what intelligence tests measure. Others view it as a set of general abilities, including the ability to learn from experience, think in abstract terms, and deal effectively with one's environment.

- A good test of intelligence must be reliable—it yields reproducible and consistent results. Alternate form reliability is shown when two forms of a test correlate highly with each other. A test has good internal consistency when various items on the test are correlated highly with each other. When more subjective assessments are used, judges rate the answers of respondents, and the researcher hopes to see interjudge reliability or interrater reliability.

- A test has good validity if it measures what it is intended to measure. Criterion or empirical validity is shown when the test is highly correlated with another test of the same construct. Construct validity is shown when the scores on the test predict outcomes that the researcher's theory suggests it should predict.

- The first successful intelligence tests were developed by the French psychologist Alfred Binet, who pro-

posed the concept of mental age. A bright child's mental age is above his or her chronological age; a slow child's mental age is below his or her chronological age. The concept of the intelligence quotient (IQ), the ratio of mental age to chronological age (multiplied by 100), was introduced when the Binet scales were revised to create the Stanford-Binet. Many intelligence test scores are still expressed as IQ scores, but they are no longer actually calculated according to this formula.

- Both Binet and Wechsler, the developer of the Wechsler Adult Intelligence Scale (WAIS), assumed that intelligence is a general capacity for reasoning.

- Similarly, Spearman proposed that a general factor (*g*) underlies performance on different kinds of test items. Factor analysis is a method for determining the kinds of abilities that underlie performance on intelligence tests.

◆ Critical Thinking Questions

1. Many colleges are now ceasing to use standardized tests such as the SAT or ACT to evaluate students seeking admission, arguing they are poor predictors of the students' overall success in college or in life. What do you think are the advantages and disadvantages of not using standardized tests in admissions procedures?

2. Do you think it is possible to create a culture-fair test of intelligence?

CONTEMPORARY THEORIES OF INTELLIGENCE

Until the 1960s, research on intelligence was dominated by the factorial approach. However, with the development of cognitive psychology and its emphasis on information-processing models (see Chapter 9), a new approach emerged. This approach is defined somewhat differently by different investigators, but the basic idea is to try to understand intelligence in terms of the cognitive processes that operate when we engage in intellectual activities (Stermberg & Kaufman, 1998). The information-processing approach asks:

1. What mental processes are involved in the various tests of intelligence?
2. How rapidly and accurately are these processes carried out?
3. What types of mental representations of information do these processes act upon?

Rather than trying to explain intelligence in terms of factors, this approach attempts to identify the mental processes that underlie intelligent behavior. It assumes that individual differences on a given task depend on the specific processes that different individuals bring into play and the speed and accuracy of those processes. The goal is to use an information-processing model of a particular task to identify appropriate measures of the processes used in performing the task. These measures may be as simple as the response to a multiple-choice item, or they may include response speed or the eye movements associated with the response. The idea is to use whatever information is needed to estimate the efficiency of each component process.

GARDNER'S THEORY OF MULTIPLE INTELLIGENCES

Howard Gardner (1993a) developed his theory of multiple intelligences as a direct challenge to what he calls the "classical" view of intelligence as a capacity for logical reasoning. Gardner was struck by the variety of adult roles in different cultures—roles that depend on a variety of skills and abilities yet are equally important to successful functioning in those cultures. His observations led him to conclude that there is not just one underlying mental capacity or g, but a variety of intelligences that work in combination. He defines an intelligence as the "ability to solve problems or fashion products that are of consequence in a particular cultural setting or community" (1993b, p. 15). It is these multiple intelligences that enable human beings to take on such diverse roles as physicist, farmer, shaman, and dancer (Gardner, 1993a).

Gardner is quick to point out that an intelligence is not a "thing," some sort of commodity inside the head, but "a potential, the presence of which allows an individual access to forms of thinking appropriate to specific kinds of content" (Kornhaber & Gardner, 1991, p. 155). According to **Gardner's theory of multiple intelligences,** there are seven distinct kinds of intelligence that are independent of one another, each operating as a separate system (or module) in the brain according to its own rules. These are (1) linguistic, (2) musical, (3) logical-mathematical, (4) spatial, (5) bodily-kinesthetic, (6) intrapersonal, and (7) interpersonal. These are described more fully in Table 12-3.

Gardner analyzes each kind of intelligence from several viewpoints: the cognitive operations involved, the appearance of prodigies and other exceptional individuals, evidence from cases of brain damage, manifestations in different cultures, and the possible course of evolutionary development. For example, certain kinds of brain damage can impair one type of intelligence and have no effect on the others. He notes that the capacities of adults in different cultures represent different combinations of the various intelligences. Although all normal people can apply all of the intelligences to some extent, each individual is characterized by a unique combination of relatively stronger and weaker intelligences (Walters & Gardner, 1985), which help account for individual differences.

As noted earlier, conventional IQ tests are good predictors of college grades, but they are less valid for predicting later job success or career advancement. Measures of other abilities, such as interpersonal intelligence, may help explain why some people with brilliant college records fail miserably in later life while lesser students become charismatic leaders (Kornhaber, Krechevsky, & Gardner, 1990). Gardner and colleagues therefore call for "intelligence-fair" assessments in schools that would allow children to demonstrate their abilities by other means besides paper-and-pencil tests, such as putting together gears to demonstrate spatial skills.

ANDERSON'S THEORY OF INTELLIGENCE AND COGNITIVE DEVELOPMENT

One criticism of Gardner's theory is that high levels of ability in any of the various intelligences is usually correlated with high ability in the others; that is, no specific intellectual capacity is wholly distinct from the others (Messick, 1992; Scarr, 1985). In addition, psychologist Mike Anderson points out that Gardner's multiple intelligences are ill-defined—they are "sometimes a behavior, sometimes a cognitive process, and sometimes a structure in the brain" (1992, p. 67). Anderson therefore has sought to develop a theory based on the idea of general intelligence proposed by Thurstone and others.

● Table 12-3

Gardner's Seven Intelligences

(Adapted from Gardner, Kornhaber, & Wake, 1996)

Type of Intelligence	Description
1. Linguistic Intelligence	The capacity for speech, along with mechanisms dedicated to phonology (speech sounds), syntax (grammar), semantics (meaning), and pragmatics (implications and uses of language in various settings).
2. Musical Intelligence	The ability to create, communicate, and understand meanings made of sound, along with mechanisms dedicated to pitch, rhythm, and timbre (sound quality).
3. Logical-Mathematical Intelligence	The ability to use and appreciate relationships in the absence of action or objects—that is, to engage in abstract thought.
4. Spatial Intelligence	The ability to perceive visual or spatial information, modify it, and re-create visual images without reference to the original stimulus. Includes the capacity to construct images in three dimensions and to move and rotate those images.
5. Bodily-Kinesthetic Intelligence	The ability to use all or part of the body to solve problems or fashion products; includes control over fine and gross motor actions and the ability to manipulate external objects.
6. Intrapersonal Intelligence	The ability to distinguish among one's own feelings, intentions, and motivations.
7. Interpersonal Intelligence	The ability to recognize and make distinctions among other people's feelings, beliefs, and intentions.

© Bob Daemmrich/Stock Boston

© Jeff Greenberg/Rainbow

© Jack Grove/PhotoEdit

According to Gardner's theory of multiple intelligences, these three individuals are displaying different kinds of intelligence: logical-mathematical, musical, and spatial.

Anderson's theory of intelligence holds that individual differences in intelligence and developmental changes in intellectual competence are explained by different mechanisms. Differences in intelligence result from differences in the "basic processing mechanism" that implements thinking, which in turn yields knowledge. Individuals vary in the speed at which basic processing occurs. A person with a slower basic processing mechanism is likely to have more difficulty acquiring knowledge than a person with a faster processing mechanism. This is equivalent to saying that a low-speed processing mechanism produces low general intelligence.

Anderson notes, however, that there are some cognitive mechanisms that show no individual differences. For example, people with Down syndrome may not be able to add 2 plus 2 yet can recognize that other people hold beliefs and may act on those beliefs (Anderson, 1992). The mechanisms that provide these universal capacities are "modules." Each module functions independently, performing complex computations. Modules are not af-

Emotional Intelligence

New York Times writer Daniel Goleman popularized the term *emotional intelligence* in his 1995 book. He argued that understanding and control of your emotions is one of the most important keys to health and success in life. Goleman's book was based on important new work by psychologists such as Peter Salovey, John Mayer, and Reuven Bar-On showing that, indeed, people who are emotionally astute have a leg up on those of us who are not.

Mayer and Salovey (1997; Mayer, Salovey, & Caruso, 2000) suggest there are four critical components to emotional intelligence. The first is *accurate perception and expression* of emotions. Being able to read the emotions of others enables you to anticipate possible threats they might pose. For example, imagine you are in an argument with a coworker who is known to have a volatile temper. If you can accurately perceive that your coworker is getting extremely agitated, you will know that it may be time to back off and live to fight another day. If you don't accurately perceive your coworker's level of anger, you might end up with a bloody nose. Accurately perceiving and expressing others' emotions also helps you empathize with their position. In turn, you can modify your responses to other people, either to be more persuasive in arguing your point or to make them feel that you understand them well. This can make you an effective negotiator and a trusted friend to others.

Accurately perceiving and expressing your own emotions is the first step to responding appropriately to those emotions. People who don't realize they are anxious can have chronic physiological arousal that costs them physical wear and tear and impairs their health (see Chapter 14). People who don't realize they are sad may not take the necessary actions to change the sources of their sadness. People who don't realize they are angry may suddenly and impulsively lash out at others, feeling out of control.

The second component of emotional intelligence is the ability to *access and generate emotions* in the service of thinking and problem solving. We often ask ourselves, "How do I feel about this?" in trying to make an important decision, such as what college to attend or what major to pursue. Being able to access our current feelings about an issue or to anticipate our future feelings, should we make a particular decision, gives us important information that should go into many decisions.

The third component of emotional intelligence is *understanding emotions and emotional meanings*. We may accurately perceive we are anxious, but if we don't understand why we are anxious, we can't do much about it. We often make incorrect attributions for our emotions, which can lead us to take unwise steps. For example, imagine you have been staying up late each night for many weeks to complete your school assignments and then getting up for early morning classes. Eventually, you begin to feel sad, lethargic, and unmotivated. You might conclude that you are feeling sad and unmotivated because you are pursuing the wrong major, or even that college is not for you. The true reason for your sadness, however, may well be sleep deprivation, which can cause depression-like symptoms (see Chapter 6). Attributing your sadness incorrectly to your college major rather than correctly to your lack of sleep could cause you to make some very bad decisions.

The final component of emotional intelligence is *emotional regulation*—being able to manage and regulate your emotions appropriately. This does not mean completely controlling the emotions you feel or express. Indeed, such emotional overcontrol is unhealthy. But letting your emotions rage unabated can also be unhealthy. The most obvious example is with anger. We all feel angry at times, but most of us know we can't express our anger at any time and in any way we wish (at least we can't get away with it). How we channel our anger is critical to our relationships to others and to our own health. People who completely suppress their anger can be exploited by others, and people who chronically express their anger in a hostile manner lose friends quickly. In contrast, people who can express the reasons for their anger in ways that others can hear and accept are more likely to both maintain their friendships and avoid being exploited. In addition, research we will review in Chapter 14 clearly shows that people who do not channel their anger appropriately experience more heart disease, probably because their cardiovascular system is chronically overaroused and overreactive.

Can you learn emotional intelligence? Many schools now have programs to teach young people how to recognize and better manage their anger, in hopes of reducing school violence, and some evaluations of these programs suggest they can be effective in teaching young people anger control (Graczyk et al., 2000; Topping, Holmes, & Bremner, 2000). Many a crusty corporate executive has also undergone emotional schooling to learn how to better empathize with employees and manage with a bigger heart, and it appears these programs can be successful (Cherniss, 2000). Much of what psychotherapy focuses on is helping people recognize, accurately label, and manage their emotions better, and many studies show psychotherapy to be effective in relieving a variety of psychological disorders (see Chapter 16). These same techniques are sometimes used to help cardiac patients better control anger and stress so as to improve their health (see Chapter 14). Thus, there is increasing evidence that emotional intelligence truly is important to success and well-being, and fortunately, those of us born emotionally challenged can become more intelligent. The empirical research specifically examining emotional intelligence is in its infancy, however, and we are sure to learn much more in years to come (Mayer et al., 2000).

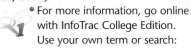 For more information, go online with InfoTrac College Edition. Use your own term or search:

- Emotional intelligence
- Emotional regulation

fected by the basic processing mechanism; they are virtually automatic. According to Anderson, it is the maturation of new modules that explains the increase of cognitive abilities in the course of development. For example, the maturation of a module devoted to language would explain the development of the ability to speak in complete sentences.

In addition to modules, according to Anderson, intelligence includes two "specific abilities." One of these deals with propositional thought (language mathematical expression) and the other with visual and spatial functioning. Anderson suggests that the tasks associated with these abilities are carried out by "specific processors." Unlike modules, which carry out very particular functions, each of the specific processors handles a broad class of problems or knowledge. Also unlike modules, specific processors are affected by the basic processing mechanism. A high-speed processing mechanism enables a person to make more effective use of the specific processors to score higher on tests and accomplish more in the real world.

Anderson's theory of intelligence thus suggests two different "routes" to knowledge. The first involves using the basic processing mechanism, which operates through the specific processors, to acquire knowledge. In Anderson's view, this is what we mean by "thinking," and it accounts for individual differences in intelligence (which, in his view, are equivalent to differences in knowledge). The second route involves the use of modules to acquire knowledge. Module-based knowledge, such as perception of three-dimensional space, comes automatically if the module has matured sufficiently, and this accounts for the development of intelligence.

Anderson's theory can be illustrated by the case of a 21-year-old man known as MA who suffered convulsions as a child and was diagnosed as autistic. As an adult, he could not talk and achieved very low scores on psychometric tests. However, he was found to have an IQ of 128 and had an extraordinary ability to detect prime numbers, doing so more accurately than a scientist with a degree in mathematics (Anderson, 1992). Anderson concludes that MA had an intact basic processing mechanism, which allowed him to think about abstract symbols, but had suffered damage to his linguistic modules, which hindered acquisition of everyday knowledge and communication.

STERNBERG'S TRIARCHIC THEORY

In contrast to Anderson's theory, Robert **Sternberg's triarchic theory** addresses experience and context as well as basic information-processing mechanisms (Sternberg,

1996). His theory has three parts or subtheories: the componential subtheory, which deals with thought processes; the experiential subtheory, which deals with the effects of experience on intelligence; and the contextual subtheory, which considers the effects of the individual's environment and culture. The most highly developed of these subtheories is the componential subtheory.

The componential theory considers the components of thought. Sternberg has identified three types of components:

1. Metacomponents are used to plan, control, monitor, and evaluate processing during problem solving. Sternberg (1996) has relabeled these as analytical abilities. For example, if you were going to cook Thanksgiving dinner, you would have to plan the menu and then monitor your progress toward getting all the ingredients, cooking each dish, and making sure everything was ready to serve at the same time.
2. Performance components carry out problem-solving strategies. Sternberg (1996) now calls these creative abilities. A skilled mechanic can use his creative abilities to devise a way to fix parts of a car that are not working.
3. Knowledge-acquisition components encode, combine, and compare information during the course of problem solving. Sternberg (1996) now calls these practical abilities. You are using your knowledge-acquisition or practical abilities as you read through this chapter and decide to commit certain pieces of information to memory.

These components are intertwined. Each comes into play during the problem-solving process, and none of them can operate independently. Sternberg illustrates the functioning of these components with analogy problems of the following kind:

> lawyer is to client as doctor is to _____
> (a) medicine   (b) patient

A series of experiments with such problems led Sternberg to conclude that the critical components were the encoding process and the comparison process. The participant encodes each of the words in the analogy by forming a mental representation of the word—in this case, a list of attributes of the word that are retrieved from long-term memory. For example, a mental representation of the word *lawyer* might include the following attributes: college-educated, versed in legal procedures, represents clients in court, and so on. Once the participant has formed a mental representation for each word in the analogy, the comparison process scans the representations looking for matching attributes that solve the analogy.

Other processes are involved in analogy problems, but Sternberg has shown that individual differences on this task are determined primarily by the efficiency of the encoding and comparison processes. The experimental evidence shows that individuals who score high on analogy problems (skilled performers) spend more time encoding and form more accurate mental representations than do individuals who score low on such problems (less-skilled performers). In contrast, during the comparison stage, the skilled performers are faster than the less-skilled performers in matching attributes, but both are equally accurate. So, the better test scores for skilled performers are based on the increased accuracy of their encoding process, but the time they require to solve the problem is a complicated mix of slow encoding speeds and fast comparisons (Galotti, 1989; Pellegrino, 1985).

The componential subtheory by itself does not provide a complete explanation of individual differences in intelligence. The experiential subtheory is needed to account for the role of experience in intelligent performance. According to Sternberg, differences in experience affect the ability to solve a given problem. A person who has not previously encountered a particular concept, such as a mathematical formula or an analogy problem, will have more difficulty applying that concept than someone who is experienced in the use of that concept. An individual's experience with a task or problem thus falls somewhere along a continuum that extends from totally novel to completely automatic (that is, totally familiar as a result of long experience).

Of course, a person's exposure to particular concepts depends to a large extent on the environment. This is where the contextual subtheory comes in. This subtheory is concerned with the cognitive activity needed to fit into particular environmental contexts (Sternberg, 1985; Sternberg, Castejon, Prieto, Hautamaeki, & Grigorenko, 2001). It focuses on three mental processes: adaptation, selection, and shaping of real-world environments. According to Sternberg, the individual first looks for ways to adapt, or fit into, the environment. If it is not possible to adapt, the individual tries to select a different environment or to shape the existing environment in order to fit into it better. A spouse who is unhappy in a marriage may not be able to adapt to the current circumstances. He or she may therefore select a different environment (for example, through separation or divorce) or try to shape the existing environment (for example, through counseling) (Sternberg, 1985).

CECI'S BIOECOLOGICAL THEORY

Some critics claim that Sternberg's theory has so many parts that it is not coherent (Richardson, 1986). Others note that it does not show how problem solving occurs in everyday contexts. Still others point out that it largely ignores the biological aspects of intelligence. Stephen Ceci (1990, 1996) has attempted to address these issues by building on Sternberg's theory while placing much more emphasis on context and its impact on problem solving.

Ceci's bioecological theory proposes that there are "multiple cognitive potentials," rather than a single underlying general intelligence or *g*. These multiple abilities, or intelligences, are biologically based and place limits on mental processes. Their emergence, however, is shaped by the challenges and opportunities in the individual's environment, or context.

In Ceci's view, context is essential to the demonstration of cognitive abilities. By "context," he means domains of knowledge as well as factors such as personality, motivation, and education. Contexts can be mental, social, or physical (Ceci & Roazzi, 1994). A particular individual or population may appear to lack certain mental abilities, but if given a more interesting and motivating context, the same individual or population can demonstrate a higher level of performance. To take just one example, in a famous longitudinal study of high-IQ children studied by Lewis Terman (Terman & Oden, 1959), high IQ was thought to be correlated with high achievement. But a closer look at the results revealed that children from upper-income families went on to become more successful adults than children from lower-income families. In addition, those who became adults during the Great Depression ended up less successful than those who became adults later, when there were more job opportunities. In Ceci's words, "The bottom line . . . is that the ecological niche one occupies, including individual and historical development, is a far more potent determinant of one's professional and economic success than is IQ" (1990, p. 62).

Ceci also argues against the traditional view that intelligence is related to a capacity for abstract thinking, regardless of the subject area. He believes that the ability to engage in complex thought is tied to knowledge gained in particular contexts or domains. Rather than being endowed with a greater capacity for abstract reasoning, intelligent people have enough knowledge in a particular domain to enable them to think in a complex way about problems in that area of knowledge (Ceci, 1990). In the course of working in a particular domain—for example, computer programming—the individual's knowledge base grows and becomes better organized. Over time, this

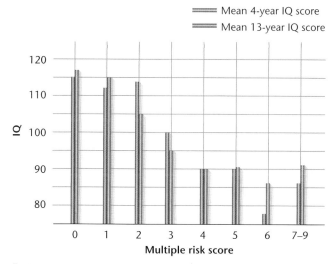

Figure 12-3
The Impact of the Environment on IQ
Research indicates that the more risk factors children are exposed to, the lower their IQs tend to be. (After Sameroff)

Learning environments enriched by technology are important ingredients to eventual success.

makes possible more intelligent performances—for example, more efficient programs.

In sum, according to Ceci, everyday or real-world intellectual performance cannot be explained by IQ alone or by some biological notion of general intelligence. Instead, it depends on the interaction between multiple cognitive potentials with a rich, well-organized knowledge base. For example, a child could be born with strong cognitive potentials, but if she was raised in an extremely impoverished intellectual environment, she might never develop these potentials. One longitudinal study provided evidence of the impact of environment on IQ. Sameroff and colleagues (1993) examined the relationship between the environment children were exposed to in early childhood and their IQs at ages 4 and 13. The more environmental risk factors a child was exposed to—such as lack of education or mental illness in his or her mother, minority status (which is associated with low standard of living and inferior schools), and large family size—the lower the child's IQ was (see Figure 12-3).

COMPARING THEORIES OF INTELLIGENCE

The four theories of intelligence discussed in this section differ in several ways (see the Concept Review Table on the next page). Gardner attempts to explain the wide variety of adult roles found in different cultures. He believes that this diversity cannot be explained by a single underlying intelligence and instead proposes that there are at least seven different intelligences, which are present in different combinations in each individual. To Gardner, an intelligence is an ability to solve problems or create products that are of value in a particular culture. In this view, the Polynesian mariner who is skilled at navigating by the stars, the figure skater who can successfully execute a triple axel, and the charismatic leader who can motivate throngs of followers are as "intelligent" as a scientist, mathematician, or engineer.

Anderson's theory attempts to explain several aspects of intelligence—not only individual differences but also the increase of cognitive abilities with development, the existence of specific abilities, and the existence of universal abilities that do not vary from one individual to another, such as the ability to see objects in three di-

CONCEPT REVIEW TABLE
Comparing Theories of Intelligence

The four theories of intelligence reviewed conceptualize intelligence quite differently.

Theory	Description
Gardner's Theory	Intelligence is an ability to solve problems or create products that are of value in a particular culture.
Anderson's Theory	Intelligence is a basic processing mechanism, along with specific processors that deal with propositional thought and visual and spatial functioning.
Sternberg's Triarchic Theory	It consists of three subtheories: the componential theory, which looks at internal information-processing mechanisms; the experiential subtheory, which takes into account the individual's experience with a task or situation; and the contextual subtheory, which explores the relationship between the external environment and the individual's intelligence.
Ceci's Bioecological Theory	Intelligence involves multiple cognitive potentials that are biologically based, but their expression depends on the knowledge an individual has amassed in a particular domain.

mensions. To explain these aspects, he proposes the existence of a basic processing mechanism, equivalent to Spearman's general intelligence or *g*, along with specific processors that deal with propositional thought and visual and spatial functioning. The existence of universal abilities is explained by the notion of "modules" whose functioning depends on maturation.

Sternberg's triarchic theory stems from the belief that earlier theories are not wrong but merely incomplete. It consists of three subtheories: the componential subtheory, which looks at internal information-processing mechanisms; the experiential subtheory, which takes into account the individual's experience with a task or situation; and the contextual subtheory, which explores the relationship between the external environment and the individual's intelligence.

Ceci's bioecological theory extends Sternberg's theory by examining the role of context in greater depth. Rejecting the idea of a single general capacity for abstract problem solving, Ceci proposes that intelligence rests on multiple cognitive potentials. These potentials

are biologically based, but their expression depends on the knowledge an individual has amassed in a particular domain. Knowledge is crucial to intelligence, in Ceci's view.

Despite their differences, these theories have some aspects in common. They all attempt to take into account the biological basis of intelligence, be it a basic processing mechanism or a set of multiple intelligences, modules, or cognitive potentials. In addition, three of the theories place a strong emphasis on the contexts within which individuals operate—environmental factors that influence intelligence. Thus, the study of intelligence continues to explore the complex interaction between biological and environmental factors that is a central focus of psychological research today.

CROSS-CULTURAL PERSPECTIVES ON INTELLIGENCE

The theories of intelligence discussed thus far have reflected the views largely of Northern American and European cultures. These views are not shared by all cultures. Many cultures put more emphasis on social intelligence (Sternberg & Kaufman, 2001). For example, several African cultures emphasize responsible participation in the family, cooperativeness, and obedience as important to intelligence. In Zimbabwe, the word for "intelligence," *ngware*, actually means to be prudent and cautious, especially in social relationships (Sternberg, 2000). Similarly, some studies of China and Taiwan find that social competence and self-knowledge are important components of intelligence, according to citizens of these cultures (Yang & Sternberg, 1997). It is important to note that African and Asian cultures do not exclusively emphasize social intelligence but also recognize the importance of the cognitive skills.

◆ Interim Summary

- Gardner's theory of multiple intelligences suggests that there are seven distinct kinds of intelligence that are independent of one another, each operating as a separate system (or module) in the brain according to its own rules. These are (1) linguistic, (2) musical, (3) logical-mathematical, (4) spatial, (5) bodily-kinesthetic, (6) intrapersonal, and (7) interpersonal.

- Anderson's theory of intelligence suggests that differences in intelligence result from differences in the "basic processing mechanism" that implements thinking, which in turn yields knowledge.

- Sternberg's triarchic theory has three parts or subtheories: the componential subtheory, which deals with thought processes; the experiential subtheory, which deals with the effects of experience on intelligence; and the contextual subtheory, which considers the effects of the individual's environment and culture. According to his componential subtheory, three components of thought are critical in intelligence: metacomponents or analytical abilities, performance components or creative abilities, and knowledge-acquisition components or practical abilities.

• According to Ceci's bioecological theory of intelligence, everyday or real-world intellectual performance cannot be explained by IQ alone or by some biological notion of general intelligence. Instead, it depends on the interaction between multiple cognitive potentials with a rich, well-organized knowledge base.

• Other cultures tend to emphasize social intelligence more than Europe and North America do.

◆ Critical Thinking Questions

1. From your observations, what skills or abilities do you think are the most important components of intelligence?

2. Do you think there ever can be any theory of intelligence that applies universally, or is intelligence defined by the demands of particular cultures?

GENETICS AND INTELLIGENCE

Some of the fiercest debates over intelligence have focused on the contribution of genetics to determining the level of intelligence in individuals or groups. Advocates of particular political positions and social policies frequently argue either for or against the idea that intelligence is inherited (for example, Herrnstein & Murray, 1994). Because these debates reveal widespread public misunderstanding about the empirical issues involved, we will describe in some detail the reasoning and methods that behavioral scientists use to assess how genetic and environmental factors contribute to individual differences, including differences in intelligence.

We begin with Table 12-4, which lists (in descending order) the scores of a hypothetical examination taken by two groups of six students each. As shown in the last row, the average (mean) score of the students within each group is 82.0. But we can also see that the scores from Class A are much more spread out—that is, more variable—than the scores from Class B. In other words, the students in Class A are more different from one an-

● **Table 12-4**
Hypothetical Examination Scores of Two Groups of Students

	Group A		Group B
Alice	100	Greta	89
Bob	95	Harold	88
Carol	89	Ilene	83
Dan	83	John	80
Emily	67	Karen	77
Fred	58	Leon	75
Average	82.0	Average	82.0

other than the students in Class B. As explained in the Appendix, the degree to which the scores in a set differ from one another can be expressed mathematically by a quantity called their *variance*.

Now consider the scores for Class A. Why are they different from one another? Why do some students do better than others? What accounts for the variance we observe? One obvious possibility is that some students studied for the exam longer than other students did. To find out whether and to what extent this is true, we could conduct a hypothetical experiment in which we "controlled for" the variable of study time by requiring all students to study exactly 3 hours for the exam, no more and no less. If study time really does affect students' scores, what would happen to the variance of those scores?

First, some of the students who would have studied longer than 3 hours and done quite well will now do less well. For example, if Alice—who might have studied for 6 hours to achieve her perfect score of 100—had been permitted to study for only 3 hours, her score might have been more like Greta's score of 89. Second, some of the students who would have studied less than 3 hours and not done very well will now do better. Fred—who had time to only skim the reading for the exam—might have obtained a score higher than 58 if he had studied for 3 hours. Like Leon, he might at least have obtained a score of 75. In other words, if we controlled the study time of Class A, the students' scores would bunch closer together, looking more like Class B's scores—the variance of their scores would decrease. If we actually did this experiment and observed that the variance in Class A's scores decreased by, say, 60%, we could claim that study time had accounted for 60% of the variance in the original scores for this class. In this hypothetical example, then, a major reason the exam scores differed so much from one another in Class A is that students differed in the amount of time they spent studying.

Theoretically, we could test for other potential sources of variance in the same way. If we think that having a good breakfast might affect students' scores, we could feed all the students the same breakfast (or deny breakfast to all the students) and observe whether the variance of their scores is reduced as a result. In general, holding constant any variable that "makes a difference" will reduce the variance of the scores. In the extreme case, if we held all the relevant variables constant, the variance would diminish to zero: Every student would obtain the same score.

However, we cannot say what will happen to the mean of the scores when we hold a variable constant. For example, if the students in Class A had originally studied for the exam for only 2 hours on the average, by requiring them all to study for 3 hours we will raise the class average. If, however, the students had studied for 4 hours on the average, we will lower the class average by limiting everybody to only 3 hours of study time.

HERITABILITY

We are now prepared to ask the "genetics" question: To what extent do some students do better than others on the exam because they are genetically more capable? To put it another way, what percentage of the variance in exam scores is accounted for by genetic differences among the students? In general, the percentage of the variance in any trait that is accounted for by genetic differences among the individuals in a population is the trait's **heritability.** The more individual differences on a trait are due to genetic differences, the closer the heritability is to 100%. For example, height is heavily influenced by genetics: Its heritability ranges from about 85% to 95% across different studies.

Several studies of twins suggest IQ is partly heritable.

Now, however, we face a practical difficulty. We cannot experimentally determine how much of the variance in exam scores is accounted for by genetic differences the way we did for study time because that would require holding the genetic variable constant—that is, turning all the students into genetic clones. But we can take advantage of the fact that nature sometimes produces genetic clones in the form of identical twins. To the extent that identical twins are more alike on a trait than fraternal twins, we can infer that the trait has a genetic or heritable component (assuming that other factors, such as differential parental treatment, can be ruled out).

Across many twin studies the heritability of intelligence (as measured by intelligence tests) has been estimated to be between 60% and 80% (Lubinski, 2000). One difficulty in interpreting the results of twin studies is that identical twin pairs may be treated more alike than fraternal twin pairs, which may account for the greater similarity of their personalities. This is one reason that researchers at the University of Minnesota decided to study sets of twins who had been reared apart (Bouchard, 1994).

The participants in the Minnesota Study of Twins Reared Apart were assessed on a number of ability and personality measures. In addition, they participated in lengthy interviews, during which they were asked questions about such topics as childhood experiences, fears, hobbies, musical tastes, social attitudes, and sexual interests. These studies reveal that twins reared apart are just as similar to each other across a wide range of abilities as twins reared together (see Figure 12-4), permitting us to conclude with greater confidence that identical twins are more similar to each other on personality characteristics than fraternal twins because they are more similar genetically (Bouchard, Lykken, McGue, Segal, & Tellegen, 1990; Lykken, 1982; Tellegen et al., 1988).

MISUNDERSTANDINGS ABOUT HERITABILITY The recurring public debate over nature-nurture questions reveals widespread misunderstanding about the concept of heritability. Therefore, it is important to be clear about the following points:

- Heritability refers to a population, not to individuals. The heritability of a trait refers to differences among individuals within a population, not to percentages of a trait within an individual. To say that height has a heritability of 90% does not mean that 90% of your height came from your genes and 10% came from the environment. It means that 90% of the differences in height among individuals observed in a particular population is due to genetic differences among those individuals.

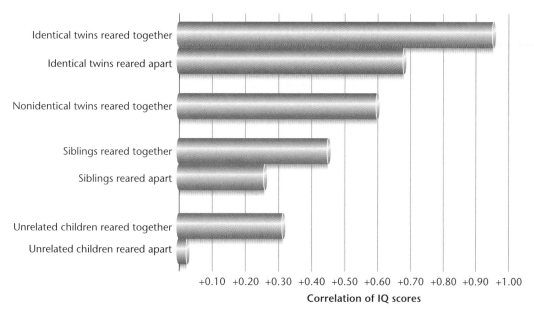

▌ Figure 12-4
IQ Data From Twin Studies
Identical twins tend to have more similar IQs than nonidentical twins or other siblings, even when they were reared apart. (From "Familiar Studies of Intelligence: A Review," T. Bouchard, et al., *Science*, Vol. 212, #4498, p 1055–9, 29 May 1981. Copyright © 1981 American Association for the Advancement of Science. Used by permission of Thomas Bouchard.)

- The heritability of a trait is not a single, fixed number. Heritability refers to an attribute of a trait in a particular population at a particular point in time. If something happens to change the variance of a trait in a population, the heritability of the trait will also change. For example, if everyone in our society were suddenly given equal educational opportunities, the variance of intellectual performance in the society would decrease, and scores on standardized measures of intellectual ability would be more similar. (This is what happened in our hypothetical experiment in which everyone had to study the same length of time for the exam.) And because heritability is the percentage of variance that is due to inherited differences among individuals, the heritability would actually increase because the percentage of the variance due to an important environmental factor, education, would have decreased.

- Heritability does not tell us about the source of mean differences between groups. One of the most contentious and recurring debates in American society is over the question of whether average differences in the intelligence test scores of different ethnic groups are due to genetic differences between the groups. In the early 20th century the debate concerned the relatively low intelligence scores obtained by Hungarian, Italian, and Jewish immigrants when

they were tested upon arrival in the United States. The test scores of these immigrants led some researchers to conclude that the majority were "feebleminded" (Kamin, 1974). Today the debate concerns the lower scores obtained by African Americans and Hispanic Americans compared with white Americans (Herrnstein & Murray, 1994). In these debates, the heritability of intelligence is often used to support the genetic argument. But this claim is based on a logical fallacy, as illustrated by the following "thought experiment":

> We fill a white sack and a black sack with a mixture of different genetic varieties of corn seed. We make certain that the proportions of each variety of seed are identical in each sack. We then plant the seed from the white sack in fertile Field A, while the seed from the black sack is planted in barren Field B. We will observe that within Field A, as within Field B, there is considerable variation in the height of individual corn plants. This variation will be due largely to genetic factors (differences in the seed). We will also observe, however, that the average height of plants in Field A is greater than that of plants in Field B. That difference will be entirely due to environmental factors (the soil). The same is true of IQs: Differences in the average IQ of various human populations could be entirely due to environmental differences, even if within each population all variation were due to genetic differences (Eysenck & Kamin, 1981, p. 97).

Text continued on p. 448

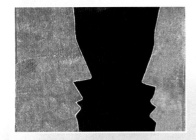

Do Intelligence Tests Accurately Reflect Aptitude?

SATS AND GRES ARE ACCURATE MEASURES OF INTELLIGENCE
Douglas K. Detterman, Case Western Reserve University

How do you know if two measures are really the same thing? You compute a statistic called a *correlation* (ranging from 0 to 1.0) and the higher the correlation, the more similar two measures are. Mental tests called *aptitude, achievement, intelligence,* and *cognitive ability* tests are correlated so highly with one another that many experts believe they are really all the same. What any test of mental ability is called probably has more to do with social acceptability than what the test really measures. It is not surprising that these tests are highly correlated since, from Binet to the most recent computer-administered GRE, they were all designed to predict academic achievement.

A test is nothing more than a sample of behavior hopefully predictive of future behaviors. The easiest thing tests should predict is later behavior on the same test, known as the reliability of a test. Intelligence, aptitude, and achievement tests are the most highly reliable of all psychological tests. Individually administered intelligence tests correlate above .90 with a later administration of the same test. In 1932, a group-administered test was given to every Scottish school child. Recently, the same test was given to some that had taken the original test. The correlation of the two administrations over the 66-year span was .74 (Deary et al.). Compare this with the average reliability of .6 for height, weight, and blood pressure taken in a doctor's office. Most psychological tests of personality, psychopathology, or motivation are lucky to have test-retest reliabilities between .4 and .8.

Do tests predict anything useful? You bet! Anghoff and Johnson correlated the performance of over 20,000 students who had taken the SAT and then later taken the GRE. The correlation was .86. While the addition of gender and major raised the correlation to .93 or higher, college quality mattered little. Paying big bucks for a college education won't help to get you into graduate school, at least as far as test scores are concerned. Other academic criteria like grades or class rank are also predicted by these tests, but less well, because grades and class rank are less reliable themselves. Mental ability tests are highly predictive of many real-world criteria, from flying a jet fighter to becoming a good lawyer or musician. Occupations that have the highest average IQ are also the most socially desirable. Most importantly, mental tests predict academic achievement, the usual doorway to life achievement.

Then why do these tests get so much bad press? First, they are often used improperly. Although nearly all colleges require tests for admission, perhaps 80% of colleges admit nearly everyone who applies. Why do they require tests? I think they want to appear selective. Even for the 20% of colleges that are selective, many other factors than test scores weigh in the decision. Given two students with the same test scores, the one with the best chance of getting in a selective school will have the following characteristics: minority, athlete, attended selective private high school, family income over $70,000 per year and one parent had college education, legacy (a parent attended the college), parent is large donor to college (Bowen & Bok, 1998). Before tests, these sorts of factors were the only thing used for college admission. I think admissions would be fairer at selective schools if only test scores were used.

A second reason that people often get a bad impression of tests is that there are situations in which they cannot predict performance. When applicants are heavily selected for IQ, they will all be very similar in IQ, so IQ cannot contribute to performance. Our educational system selects for intelligence, and each step requires higher levels of academic achievement. You have probably noticed that things are harder in college than they were in high school. Here is the reason. The average IQ of a college graduate is over 110 while the average IQ of those who finish professional or graduate school is over 120. Intelligence will be only a small contributor to performance in medical or graduate school. Other things like hard work and personality will determine differences in success because everyone is smart. You have to be tall to play basketball. The NBA selects players for height and NBA players are much taller than the average person. But the correlation between height and points scored in the NBA is near zero. It is as silly to say that intelligence has nothing to do with performance in medical or graduate school as it is to say height has nothing to do with basketball.

Tests like the SAT and GRE are essentially tests of intelligence. They are highly reliable and predict real-world behaviors better than anything else we know about. Tests have often been misused and are not the measure of the basic worth of a human being. But when used properly, they can make selection decisions fairer and more accurate and can help students in designing their educational future.

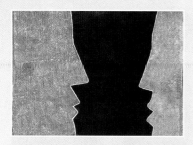

Do Intelligence Tests Accurately Reflect Aptitude?

IQS, SATS, AND GRES ARE NOT MEASURES OF *GENERAL* INTELLIGENCE

Stephen J. Ceci, Cornell University

There is a funny anecdote about a man waiting for a bus. When a woman arrives pushing a pram with her baby in it, the man peers into the pram:

Man: My, what a lovely baby you have!

Woman: Oh don't go by that—you should see her photographs!

We all know individuals who seem more interested in photographs than in reality. For such persons, intelligence test scores (the photos) are more important than the attainments they are supposed to predict (the baby).

Thousands of "validity" studies show that tests of general intelligence predict a wide range of behaviors, imperfectly, but better than anything else we can measure: IQ scores predict freshman grades somewhat better than high-school grades and letters of reference do, and they also predict first-year graduate school grades better than do undergraduate grades and letters. But the prediction from IQ (or SATs or GREs) is modest, and many applicants' grades will differ from expectations based on such scores. Test makers argue that even modest predictability can help admissions officers make better de-

Stephen J. Ceci

cisions than they would by not using the tests (Hunt, 1996).

For many years I chaired a graduate admissions committee. One of the saddest experiences is discovering the tremendous weight given to test scores

such as the GRE. Granted, there are other considerations to distinguish among applicants who are similar in GRE scores and grades; however, at most universities applicants with very low scores won't get admitted unless the school needs to fill seats for financial reasons.

All who serve on admission committees can tell tales—about the applicant with great scores who turned out to be a loser, unable to think creatively and manage work effectively. Or about the occasional applicant with low scores who somehow manages to gain entrance and goes on to disprove the prediction by emerging as the top student. I am not claiming that measures of general intelligence such as the GREs, IQ scores, and SATs are worthless. But they are not perfect, and applicants who excel at them represent but one type of individual who could do well. Other types of applicants (e.g., those with well-honed real-world skills, interpersonal strengths, highly creative) are systematically excluded.

But my most serious complaint about tests of general intelligence is that they do not strike me as measures of general intelligence any more than a math or history achievement test strikes me as one. Like all achievement tests, the SATs, IQs, and GREs are susceptible to external influences, including coaching, quality of school attended, and parental educational level and income. It should come as no surprise to find that the number of math classes taken in school is a predictor of math scores on the SATs and GREs, *even after controlling for initial math aptitude.* This implies that although math scores add to the prediction of college or graduate-school grades, they may not measure inherent math ability

any more than a score on a test of Russian proficiency would for someone who attended a school where Russian was not taught. Thus, I view tests of "general intelligence" as often little more than achievement tests, indexing how much knowledge one has gained. They tell us little about actual ability under different circumstances, particularly those situations that require thinking unlike the type required to answer test questions correctly. And such tests tell us little about potentially valuable talents that are not measured, such as creativity, practical intelligence, and the ability to organize, motivate, and manage oneself and others—skills that appear to be somewhat independent of so-called intelligence tests, and which have been demonstrated to predict important educational outcomes.

Recently, there has been a spate of studies about the predictive validity of SATs and GREs, and while such measures may predict first-year grades, their predictiveness wanes over the years. One recent study even reported that the GREs did not predict at all after the first year of graduate school—not second-, third-, or fourth-year grades, not creativity or quality of the doctoral research (Sternberg & Williams, 1997), although it's possible there will be a "sleeper effect," and intelligence scores could end up predicting later career achievements and earnings. These de facto achievement tests have many valid uses; however, it is unwise to refer to them as tests of "general intelligence" until they can be shown to tap a far wider array of abilities and achievements than they do. And until their predictiveness gets better, we should not confuse the baby with her photographs.

Environmental factors such as parental encouragement can influence intellectual ability—even though these abilities have high heritabilities.

- Heritability does not tell us about the effects of environmental changes on the average level of a trait. Another incorrect claim about heritability is that a trait with high heritability cannot be changed by a change in the environment. For example, it has been argued that it is futile to use preschool intervention programs to help disadvantaged children enhance their intellectual abilities because those abilities have high levels of heritability. But between 1946 and 1982 the height of young adult males in Japan increased by 3.3 inches, mainly owing to improved nutrition (Angoff, 1988). And yet height is one of the most heritable traits we possess. Then, as now, taller Japanese parents have taller children than do shorter Japanese parents. Similarly, IQ test scores have risen significantly over the last century in many cultures (Flynn, 1999). In sum, heritability is about variances, not average levels.

◆ Interim Summary

- Behavioral scientists typically quantify the extent to which a group of people differ from one another on some measure of a trait or ability by computing the variance of the scores obtained. The more the individuals in the group differ from one another, the higher the variance. Researchers can then seek to determine how much of that variance is due to different causes. The proportion of variance in a trait that is accounted for (caused by) genetic differences among the individuals is called the *heritability* of the trait.

- Heritabilities can be estimated by comparing correlations obtained on pairs of identical twins (who share all their genes) and correlations obtained on pairs of fraternal twins (who, on the average, share about half of their genes). If identical twin pairs are more alike on the trait than fraternal twin pairs, the trait probably has a genetic component. Heritabilities can also be estimated from the correlation between identical twin pairs who have been separated and raised in different environments. Any correlation between such pairs must be due to their genetic similarities.

- Heritability refers to differences among individuals; it does not indicate how much of a trait in an individual is due to genetic factors. It is not a fixed attribute of a trait: If something happens to change the variability of a trait in a group, the heritability will also change. Heritability indicates the variance within a group, not the source of differences between groups. Heritability does, however, indicate how much possible environmental changes might change the mean level of a trait in a population.

◆ Critical Thinking Questions

1. What are the political and social policy implications of claims that intelligence is largely due to genetic factors?

2. How might an individual's belief that his or her own level of intelligence is due to genetic factors influence his or her decisions about school or careers?

CHAPTER SUMMARY

1. There are many different definitions of intelligence. Some theorists view it as simply what intelligence tests measure. Others view it as a set of general abilities, including the ability to learn from experience, think in abstract terms, and deal effectively with one's environment.

2. A good test of intelligence must be reliable—it must yield reproducible and consistent results. Alternate form reliability is shown when two forms of a test correlate highly with each other. A test has good internal consistency when various items on the test are correlated highly with each other. When more subjective assessments are used, judges rate the answers of respondents, and the researcher hopes to see interjudge reliability or interrater reliability.

3. A test has good validity if it measures what it is intended to measure. Criterion or empirical validity is shown when the test is highly correlated with another test of the same construct. Construct validity is shown when the scores on the test predict outcomes that the researcher's theory suggests it should predict.

4. The first successful intelligence tests were developed by the French psychologist Alfred Binet, who proposed the concept of mental age. A bright child's mental age is above his or her chronological age; a slow child's mental age is below his or her chronological age. The concept of the intelligence quotient (IQ), the ratio of mental age to chronological age (multiplied by 100), was introduced when the Binet scales were revised to create the Stanford-Binet. Many intelligence test scores are still expressed as IQ scores, but they are no longer actually calculated according to this formula.

5. Both Binet and Wechsler, the developer of the Wechsler Adult Intelligence Scale (WAIS), assumed that intelligence is a general capacity for reasoning.

6. Similarly, Spearman proposed that a general factor (g) underlies performance on different kinds of test items. Factor analysis is a method for determining the kinds of abilities that underlie performance on intelligence tests.

7. Gardner's theory of multiple intelligences suggests that there are seven distinct kinds of intelligence that are independent of one another, each operating as a separate system (or module) in the brain according to its own rules. These are (1) linguistic, (2) musical, (3) logical-mathematical, (4) spatial, (5) bodily-kinesthetic, (6) intrapersonal, and (7) interpersonal.

8. Anderson's theory of intelligence suggests that differences in intelligence result from differences in the "basic processing mechanism" that implements thinking, which in turn yields knowledge.

9. Sternberg's triarchic theory has three parts or subtheories: the componential subtheory, which deals with thought processes; the experiential subtheory, which deals with the effects of experience on intelligence; and the contextual subtheory, which considers the effects of the individual's environment and culture. According to his componential subtheory, three components of thought are critical in intelligence: metacomponents or analytical abilities, performance components or creative abilities, and knowledge-acquisition components or practical abilities.

10. According to Ceci's bioecological theory of intelligence, everyday or real-world intellectual performance cannot be explained by IQ alone or by some biological notion of general intelligence. Instead, it depends on the interaction between multiple cognitive potentials with a rich, well-organized knowledge base.

11. Other cultures tend to emphasize social intelligence more than Europe and North America do.

12. Behavioral scientists typically quantify the extent to which a group of people differ from one another on some measure of a trait or ability by computing the variance of the scores obtained. The more the individuals in the group differ, the higher the variance. Researchers can then seek to determine how much of that variance is due to different causes. The proportion of

variance in a trait that is accounted for (caused by) genetic differences among the individuals is called the *heritability* of the trait.

13. Heritabilities can be estimated by comparing correlations obtained on pairs of identical twins (who share all their genes) and correlations obtained on pairs of fraternal twins (who, on the average, share about half of their genes). If identical twin pairs are more alike on the trait than fraternal twin pairs, the trait probably has a genetic component. Heritabilities can also be estimated from the correlation between identical twin pairs who have been separated and raised in different environments. Any correlation between such pairs must be due to their genetic similarities.

14. Heritability refers to differences among individuals; it does not indicate how much of a trait in an individual is due to genetic factors. It is not a fixed attribute of a trait: If something happens to change the variability of a trait in a group, the heritability will also change. Heritability indicates the variance within a group, not the source of differences between groups. Heritability does, however, indicate how much possible environmental changes might change the mean level of a trait in a population.

CORE CONCEPTS

intelligence
reliability
alternative form reliability
internal consistency
interrater agreement
interjudge reliability
validity
criterion or empirical validity

criterion problem in assessment
construct validity
Stanford-Binet Intelligence Scale
intelligence quotient (IQ)
Wechsler Adult Intelligence Scale
Scholastic Assessment Test (SAT)
American College Test (ACT)
Factor analysis

g
Gardner's theory of multiple intelligences
Anderson's theory of intelligence
Sternberg's triarchic theory
Ceci's bioecological theory
heritability

WEB RESOURCES

http://psychology.wadsworth.com/
atkinson14e

Take a quiz, try the activities and exercises, and explore web links.

http://www.geocities.com/CapitolHill/1641/
iqown.html

Think you're a smart cookie? Put it to the test on this site.

http://www.mugu.com/cgi-bin/Upstream/Issues/
psychology/IQ/index.html

This site contains an interesting mix of links about intelligence.

 InfoTrac Online Library

http://www.infotrac-college.com/
wadsworth

Use InfoTrac to find popular and scientific articles by using the search terms below or your own relevant terms.

- Intelligence
- Intelligence tests

CD-ROM LINKS

 Psych Odyssey

Check out CD Chapter 9, Intelligence
A. The Nature of Intelligence
B. Context & Intelligence
C. Gender & Intelligence

 Psyk.trek 2.0

Check out CD Unit 7, Testing and Intelligence
7a Types of Psychological Tests
7b Key Concepts in Testing
7c Understanding IQ Scores
7d Heritability, Environment, and Intelligence

PERSONALITY

These twins, separated at birth, showed remarkable similarities in interests and habits when they first met at age 31.

13

Oskar Stohr and Jack Yufe are identical twins who were born in Trinidad and separated shortly after birth. Their mother took Oskar to Germany, where he was raised by his grandmother as a Catholic and a Nazi. Jack remained in Trinidad with his Jewish father, was raised as a Jew, and spent part of his youth on an Israeli kibbutz. The two families never corresponded.

When they were in their late forties, Oskar and Jack were brought together by researchers at the University of Minnesota who were studying sets of twins who had been raised apart. Although Oskar and Jack had met only once before, they showed some remarkable similarities. Both showed up for the study wearing mustaches, wire-rimmed glasses, and blue double-breasted suits. Their mannerisms and temperaments were similar, and they shared certain idiosyncrasies: Both liked spicy foods and sweet liqueurs,

were absentminded, flushed the toilet before using it, like to dip buttered toast in their coffee, and enjoyed surprising people by sneezing in elevators.

Many other sets of identical twins studied by the Minnesota researchers also displayed similarities. For example, the twins shown in the accompanying photo were separated at birth and not reunited until they were 31 years old, by which time both had become firefighters. What causes such similarities? Surely there aren't firefighting genes or genes for dipping toast or surprising people in elevators. Such similarities reflect the inherited components of more basic personality characteristics. Indeed, both similarities and differences among individuals provide challenges for psychology.

In many ways, every person is like every other person. The biological and psychological processes discussed in this book—development, consciousness, perception, learning, remembering, thinking, motivation, and emotion—are basically the same for all of us. But in other ways every person is different from every other person. Each of us has a distinctive pattern of abilities, beliefs, attitudes, motivations, emotions, and personality traits that makes each of us unique.

In this chapter we look at four theoretical approaches that dominated personality psychology in the 20th century: the psychoanalytic, behaviorist, humanistic, and cognitive approaches. We will also discuss evolutionary approaches, which have been applied to understand personality only in the last couple of decades. In reviewing these theories, we raise a question that has never been satisfactorily answered: To what degree are our beliefs, emotions, and actions free and in what ways are they determined by causes beyond our control? Are we basically good, neutral, or evil? Fixed or

modifiable? Active or passive in controlling our destinies? What constitutes psychological health or lack of health? These are not empirical questions, and theories of personality do not attempt to answer them explicitly. But each theoretical approach contains implicit answers—a set of distinctive underlying assumptions about human nature. Historically, these more philosophical factors have been as important as the empirical data in provoking controversies and in winning converts for the competing accounts of personality.

We also return to a major theme that we introduced in Chapter 3: the interaction between nature and nurture. In Chapter 3 we discussed how innate biological factors interact with events in an individual's environment to determine the course of development, focusing particularly on factors that make us all alike. We considered, for example, how innately determined sequences of maturation cause all children to go through the same stages of development in the same sequence, regardless of differences in their environments. In this chapter we focus on the biological and environmental factors that make us different from one another—in other words, the factors that create individuality. First, however, we discuss how we measure personality.

ASSESSMENT OF PERSONALITY

Personality can be defined as the distinctive and characteristic patterns of thought, emotion, and behavior that make up an individual's personal style of interacting with the physical and social environment. When we are asked to describe an individual's personality, we are likely to use terms referring to personality traits—adjectives such as extraverted and conscientious. Personality psychologists have attempted to devise formal methods for describing and measuring personality, which go beyond our everyday use of trait terms in three ways. First, they seek to reduce the potential set of trait terms to a manageable set that will still encompass the diversity of human personality. Second, they attempt to ensure that their instruments for measuring personality traits are reliable and valid. Finally, they do empirical research to discover the relationships among traits and between traits and specific behaviors.

One way to begin the task of deriving a comprehensive but manageable number of traits is to consult a dictionary. It is assumed that through the process of linguistic evolution a language will encode most, if not all, of the important distinctions among individuals that make a difference in everyday life. Language embodies the accumulated experience of the culture, and the dictionary is the written record of that experience. In the 1930s two personality psychologists actually undertook this task. They found approximately 18,000 words that refer to characteristics of behavior—nearly 5% of all the words in the dictionary! Next, they reduced the list to about 4,500 terms by eliminating obscure words and synonyms. Finally, they organized the list into psychologically meaningful subsets (Allport & Odbert, 1936).

Subsequent researchers have used such trait terms to obtain personality ratings of individuals. Peers who know an individual well are asked to rate him or her on a scale for each trait. For example, a rater might be asked to rate the person on the trait of friendliness, using a seven-point scale ranging from "not at all friendly" to "very friendly." Often such scales are labeled at the two ends with opposite traits—for example, "domineering-submissive" or "conscientious-unreliable." Individuals can also be asked to rate themselves on the scales.

Raymond Cattell (1957, 1966) condensed the Allport-Odbert list to fewer than 200 traits and obtained both peer and self-ratings for each trait. He then used factor analysis to determine how many underlying personality factors could account for the pattern of correlations among the trait ratings. His analysis yielded 16 factors. A similar procedure was used by the British psychologist Hans Eysenck to arrive at two personality factors: introversion-extraversion and emotional instability-stability, which he calls neuroticism (Eysenck, 1953); he has since added a

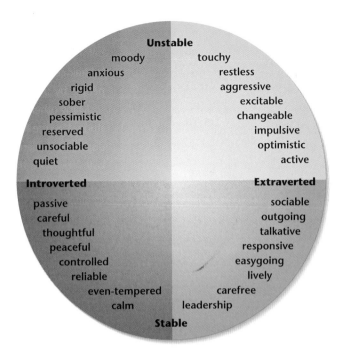

▌ Figure 13-1
Eysenck's Personality Factors
This figure shows the two major factors that emerge from factor-analytic studies of the intercorrelations between traits by Eysenck and others. The Stable-Unstable axis defines the neuroticism factor; the Introverted-Extraverted axis defines the extraversion factor. The other terms around the circle indicate where other traits are placed with respect to these two factors.
(From H. J. Eysenck & S. Rachman (1965), *The Causes and Cures of Neurosis*, by H. J. Eysenck. Copyright © 1965 by H. J. Eysenck and S. Rachman. Reprinted by permission of EdiTS.)

third. **Introversion-extraversion** refers to the degree to which a person's basic orientation is turned inward toward the self or outward toward the external world. At the introversion end of the scale are individuals who are shy and prefer to work alone. They tend to withdraw into themselves, particularly in times of emotional stress or conflict. At the extraversion end are individuals who are sociable and prefer occupations that permit them to work directly with other people. In times of stress, they seek company. **Neuroticism** (instability-stability) is a dimension of emotionality, with moody, anxious, temperamental, and maladjusted individuals at the neurotic or unstable end, and calm, well-adjusted individuals at the other. Figure 13-1 shows how these two dimensions combine to organize a number of subtraits that are correlated with the factors.

How many basic personality factors are there? Even with a rigorous analytic procedure like factor analysis, there is no definitive answer. Cattell arrived at 16 factors, but Eysenck arrived at only 2 (or, now, 3). Other investigators have come up with different numbers. In our discussion of intelligence in Chapter 12, we encountered a similar situation when we noted that the number of factors

Extraverted people are not afraid to be the center of attention.

Despite these disagreements, a consensus is emerging among many trait researchers that five trait dimensions capture most of what we mean by personality—referred to as the "Big Five" (Ozer & Reise, 1994). Although the five factors were originally identified through a factor analysis of the Allport-Odbert trait list (Norman, 1963), the same five have emerged from a wide variety of personality tests (McCrae & Costa, 1999). There is still disagreement about how best to name and interpret the factors, but one reasonable way to summarize them is with the acronym OCEAN: Openness to experience, Conscientiousness, Extraversion, Agreeableness, and Neuroticism. The Concept Review Table displays some representative examples of the trait scales that characterize each of the five factors. Many personality psychologists consider the discovery and validation of the Big Five to be one of the major breakthroughs of contemporary personality psychology. Proponents of the Big Five argue that these core personality traits organize the myriad of more narrowly focused personality characteristics that have been discussed by other researchers (McCrae & Costa, 1999). In other words, they argue that all aspects of personality are subsumed under the Big Five.

CONCEPT REVIEW TABLE
Five Trait Factors

This table presents five trait factors that reliably emerge when a wide variety of assessment instruments are factor-analyzed. The adjective pairs are examples of trait scales that characterize each of the factors. (After McCrae & Costa, 1987)

Trait Factor	Representative Trait Scales
Openness	Conventional-Original
	Unadventurous-Daring
	Conservative-Liberal
Conscientiousness	Careless-Careful
	Undependable-Reliable
	Negligent-Conscientious
Extraversion	Retiring-Sociable
	Quiet-Talkative
	Inhibited-Spontaneous
Agreeableness	Irritable-Good natured
	Ruthless-Soft hearted
	Selfish-Selfless
Neuroticism	Calm-Worrying
	Hardy-Vulnerable
	Secure-Insecure

defining the concept of intelligence could be 1 (Spearman's general intelligence factor, g), 7 (Thurstone's primary mental abilities), or as many as 150 (Guilford, 1982).

Some of the discrepancy occurs because different traits are initially put into the analysis, some occurs because different types of data are being analyzed (for example, peer ratings versus self-ratings), and some occurs because different factor analytic methods are employed. But much of the disagreement is a matter of taste. A researcher who prefers a more differentiated or fine-grained description of personality will set a lower criterion for a factor and thus accept more factors, arguing that important distinctions would be lost if the factors were further merged. Another researcher, like Eysenck, will prefer to merge several lower-level factors into more general ones, arguing that the resulting factors will be more stable (that is, more likely to reemerge in other analyses). For example, when Cattell's 16 factors are factor analyzed, Eysenck's 2 factors emerge as superfactors. We can therefore think of a hierarchy of traits in which each broad general trait is composed of several subordinate, narrower traits.

PERSONALITY INVENTORIES

Most personality tests do not actually ask individuals to directly rate themselves on personality trait dimensions. Instead, individuals are asked a set of questions about how they react in certain situations. For example, they might be asked to indicate how much they agree or disagree with the statement "I often try new and foreign foods" or "I really like most people I meet." Questionnaires that assess personality—called **personality inventories**—ask the same questions of each person, and the answers are usually given in a form that can be easily scored, often by computer. Each item on a personality inventory is composed to exemplify a particular personality trait, and subsets of similar items are summed to give the individual a score on each trait scale. For example, the item "I often try new and foreign foods" is on the Openness to Experience scale of one inventory designed to measure the Big Five; the item "I really like most people I meet" is on the Extraversion scale.

Items on most personality inventories are initially composed according to the developer's theory of each trait and then retained or discarded from the final inventory, depending on whether they correlate or fail to correlate with other items on the same scale. Often a large number of trial items are placed on a preliminary form of the inventory, which is administered to a large number of people. Their responses are then factor-analyzed to determine which subsets of items intercorrelate and whether these subsets actually belong to the trait scale for which they were originally devised.

MINNESOTA MULTIPHASIC PERSONALITY INVENTORY (MMPI) A very different method of test construction, called the *criterion-keyed method* or *empirical construction*, was used to develop one of the most popular of all personality inventories, the **Minnesota Multiphasic Personality Inventory (MMPI)**. The original MMPI was developed to provide a pencil-and-paper version of a psychiatric interview (Hathaway & McKinley, 1943). It has more than 550 statements concerning attitudes, emotional reactions, physical and psychological symptoms, and experiences. The test taker responds to each statement by answering "true," "false," or "cannot say."

Here are four representative items:

I have never done anything dangerous for the thrill of it.

I daydream very little.

My mother or father often made me obey, even when I thought it was unreasonable.

At times my thoughts have raced ahead faster than I could speak them.

Instead of formulating items on the basis of a theory, designers of the MMPI gave hundreds of test items like these to groups of individuals. Each group was known to differ from the norm on a particular criterion. For example, to develop a scale of items that distinguish between paranoid and normal individuals, the same questions were given to two groups. The criterion group was individuals who had been hospitalized with the diagnosis of paranoid disorder; the control group was people who were similar to the criterion group in age, sex, socioeconomic status, and other important variables but had never been diagnosed as having psychiatric problems. Only the questions that discriminated between the psychiatric group and the control group were retained on the inventory. Questions that at face value might seem to distinguish normal from paranoid individuals (for instance, "I think that most people would lie to get ahead") may or may not do so when put to an empirical test. In fact, patients diagnosed as paranoid were significantly less likely to respond "true" to this statement than were normal individuals. On the final test, the responses to each item are scored according to the extent to which they correspond to answers given by the different criterion groups.

The MMPI was the first major inventory to incorporate a number of validity scales within it. These scales attempt to determine whether the person has answered the test items carefully and honestly. If an individual's score on any of these scales is too high, his or her scores on the content scales must be interpreted with particular caution or disregarded altogether. These scales have been helpful but not completely successful at detecting invalid scores. Table 13-1 lists the 3 validity and 10 content scales usually scored on the MMPI.

Because the MMPI is derived from differences between criterion and control groups, it does not really matter whether what the person says is true. What is important is the fact that he or she says it. If people with schizophrenia answer "true" and control participants answer "false" to the statement "My mother never loved me," their answers distinguish the two groups regardless of how their mothers actually behaved. This is an advantage of a test based on the criterion-keyed method over one based on a test constructor's assumption that certain answers indicate specific personality traits. The disadvantage is that one does not really have a theoretical understanding of the connection between the test responses and the personality characteristics they identify.

The MMPI, published in 1943, is based on research that began in 1939. There are now more than 8,000 published studies on the MMPI, and it has been translated into at least 150 languages. There are even several private companies that provide computer-based scoring and interpretation of the inventory.

Over the years, the MMPI has been criticized for the weak reliability and validity of some of its scales. It also

● Table 13-1
MMPI Scales

The first three scales are "validity" scales, which help determine whether the person has answered the test items carefully and honestly. For example, the F (Frequency) scale measures the degree to which infrequent or atypical answers are given. A high score on this scale usually indicates that the individual was careless or confused in responding. (However, high F scores often accompany high scores on the Schizophrenia scale, which measures bizarre thinking.) The remaining "clinical" scales were originally named for categories of psychiatric disorders, but interpretation now emphasizes personality attributes rather than diagnostic categories.

Scale Name	Scale Abbreviation	Interpretation of High Scores
Lie	L	Denial of common frailties
Frequency	F	Invalidity of profile
Correction	K	Defensive, evasive
Hypochondriasis	Hs	Emphasis on physical complaints
Depression	D	Unhappy, depressed
Hysteria	Hy	Reacts to stress by denying problems
Psychopathic Deviancy	Pd	Lack of social conformity; often in trouble with the law
Masculinity-Femininity	Mf	Feminine orientation (males); masculine orientation (females)
Paranoia	Pa	Suspicious
Psychoasthenia	Pt	Worried, anxious
Schizophrenia	Sc	Withdrawn, bizarre thinking
Hypomania	Ma	Impulsive, excitable
Social Introversion-Extraversion	Si	Introverted, shy

became evident that the original inventory was getting out of date and should be revised. But the enormous amount of existing data on the original version discouraged most researchers from undertaking such a daunting task. Nevertheless, it has been done. The MMPI-2, published in 1989, incorporates a number of significant revisions while maintaining the basic features of the original, including most of the original items.

The MMPI has been most valuable in distinguishing in a general way between abnormal and normal populations and can be used to evaluate the overall severity of a particular individual's disturbance (Meehl & Dahlstrom, 1960). It is less successful, however, in making finer distinctions among various forms of psychopathology.

Many criticisms have been raised about the use of the MMPI in culturally diverse samples, however (Dana, 1998). The norms for the original MMPI—the scores that were considered "healthy" scores—were based on samples of people in the United States that were not representative of people from a wide range of ethnic and racial backgrounds, age groups, and social classes. In response to this problem, the publishers of the MMPI established new norms based on more representative samples of communities across the United States. Still, there are concerns that the MMPI norms do not reflect variations across cul-

tures in what is considered normal or abnormal. In addition, the linguistic accuracy of the translated versions of the MMPI and the comparability of these versions to the English version have been questioned (Dana, 1998).

Although the MMPI was originally designed to identify people with serious personality disorders, it has been widely used to study normal populations. But because it does not adequately sample some of the traits that are useful in describing the normal personality, the California Psychological Inventory (CPI) was devised. The CPI uses many of the same items as the MMPI. Its scales measure such traits as dominance, sociability, self-acceptance, responsibility, and socialization. The comparison groups for some of the scales were obtained by asking high school and college students to identify classmates whom they would rate high or low on the trait in question. For the dominance scale, for example, the criterion group consisted of students who were described by their peers as high in dominance (aggressive, confident, self-reliant), and the control group consisted of students who were described by their peers as low in dominance (retiring, lacking in self-confidence, inhibited). Items that revealed a statistically significant difference between the criterion group and the control group formed the dominance scale. The CPI is still one of the most widely validated personality inventories available for use with normal populations (Megargee, 1972).

THE Q-SORT A special method for measuring personality traits is called the **Q-sort** (The Q was chosen arbitrarily and has no particular meaning). In this method, a rater or sorter describes an individual's personality by sorting a set of approximately 100 cards into piles. Each card contains a personality statement (for example, "Has a wide range of interests" and "Is self-defeating"). The rater sorts the cards into nine piles, placing the cards that are least descriptive of the individual in pile 1 on the left and those that are most descriptive in pile 9 on the right. The other cards are distributed in the intermediate piles, with those that seem neither characteristic nor uncharacteristic of the individual going into the middle pile (pile 5). Each Q item receives a score ranging from 1 to 9, with higher numbers indicating that the item is more characteristic of the person. (Some Q-sorts use fewer or more than nine piles, but the technique is the same.)

At first glance, this would seem no different from asking raters to rate an individual on a set of traits, using a 9-point rating scale. And in fact, the item scores can be used in this way if the researcher wishes. But there is an important difference. When filling out rating scales, the rater is implicitly comparing the individual with others (for example, a rating of "very friendly" implies that the individual is very friendly compared with other individuals). When performing a Q-sort, however, the rater is explicitly comparing each trait with other traits within the same individual (for example, placing the item "friendly" in pile 9 implies that, compared with other traits, friendliness stands out as particularly descriptive of the individual).

Researchers can compare two Q-sorts by computing the correlation between them, thereby assessing the degree to which two individuals are similar in their overall personality configurations. If the two Q-sorts are descriptions of the same individual at two different times, the correlation assesses the test-retest reliability of the Q-sort, or the continuity of the individual's overall personality profile over time. If two Q-sorts are descriptions of a single individual made by two raters, the correlation assesses the interjudge reliability of the Q-sort, or the degree to which two people perceive the individual in the same way. (For example, in marital counseling, it could be helpful to assess the degree to which two spouses agree or disagree in their perceptions of each other.) Finally, if one of the Q-sorts is a description of a hypothetical personality type, the correlation between an individual's Q-sort and the hypothetical sort assesses the degree to which the person is similar to that personality type. For example, one researcher asked clinical psychologists to construct Q-sorts of the hypothetical "optimally adjusted personality." The correlation between a person's Q-sort and this hypothetical sort can be directly interpreted as an adjustment score (Block 1961/1978).

By itself, the trait approach is not a theory of personality but a general orientation and set of methods for assessing stable characteristics of individuals. By themselves, personality traits do not tell us anything about the dynamic processes of personality functioning, and trait psychologists who have sought to develop theories of personality have had to look to other approaches to address the second major task of personality psychology: synthesizing the many processes that influence an individual's interactions with the physical and social environments—biology, development, learning, thinking, emotion, motivation, and social interaction—into an integrated account of the total person.

◆ Interim Summary

- To arrive at a comprehensive but manageable number of personality traits on which individuals can be assessed, investigators first collected all the trait terms found in a dictionary (about 18,000) and then reduced them to a smaller number. Ratings of individuals on these terms were factor-analyzed to determine how many underlying dimensions were needed to account for the correlations among the scales.

- Although different investigators arrive at different numbers of factors, most now believe that five factors provide the best compromise. These have been labeled the "Big Five" and form the acronym OCEAN: Openness to experience, Conscientiousness, Extraversion, Agreeableness, and Neuroticism.

- Personality inventories are questionnaires on which individuals report their reactions or feelings in certain situations. Responses to subsets of items are summed to yield scores on separate scales or factors within the inventory.

- Although items on most inventories are composed or selected on the basis of a theory, they can also be selected on the basis of their correlation with an external criterion—the criterion-keyed method of test construction. The best-known example is the Minnesota Multiphasic Personality Inventory (MMPI), which is designed to identify individuals with psychological disorders.

- The Q-sort is a method of assessing personality in which raters sort cards with personality adjectives into nine piles, placing the cards that are least descriptive of the individual in pile 1 on the left and those that are most descriptive in pile 9 on the right.

◆ Critical Thinking Questions

1. There are consistent differences between women and men in scores on some of the Big 5 personality traits. On which traits would you expect to find gender differences, and in what direction?

2. How would you rate yourself on the "Big Five" personality traits? Do you think your personality can be accurately described in this way? What important aspect of your personality seems to be left out of such a description? If you and a close friend (or a family member) were to describe your personality, on which characteristics would you be likely to disagree? Why? Are there traits on which you think this other person might actually be more accurate than you in describing your personality? If so, why?

THE PSYCHOANALYTIC APPROACH

Sigmund Freud, the creator of psychoanalytic theory, is one of the towering intellectual figures of the 20th century. The basic premise of **psychoanalytic theory** is that much of what we think and do is driven by unconscious processes. Despite its shortcomings as a scientific theory, the psychoanalytic account of personality remains the most comprehensive and influential theory of personality ever created. Its impact extends well beyond psychology, influencing the social sciences, the humanities, the arts, and society generally. Even though psychoanalytic theory plays a less central role in psychology today than it did 50 or 60 years ago, many of its ideas have been absorbed into the mainstream of psychological thinking. Even parents who have done nothing more than raise their children with the occasional guidance of psychiatrist Benjamin Spock's best-selling *Baby and Child Care* are more like Freudian psychologists than they realize.

Freud began his scientific career as a neurologist, using conventional medical procedures to treat patients suffering from various "nervous" disorders. Because those procedures often failed, he turned to the technique of hypnosis but soon abandoned it. Eventually he discovered the method of **free association**, in which a patient is instructed to say everything that comes to mind, regardless of how trivial or embarrassing it may seem. By listening carefully to these verbal associations, Freud detected consistent themes that he believed were manifestations of unconscious wishes and fears. He found similar themes in the recall of dreams and early childhood memories.

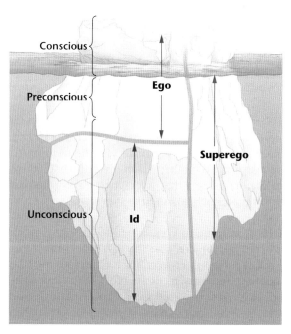

❚ Figure 13-2
Freud's Structural Model of the Mind
In Freud's "iceberg" model of the mind, all of the id and most of the ego and superego are submerged in the unconscious. Small parts of the ego and superego are either in the conscious or in the preconscious.

Freud compared the human mind to an iceberg (see Figure 13-2). The small part that shows above the surface of the water consists of the **conscious**—our current awareness—and the **preconscious**, all the information that is not currently "on our mind" but that we could bring into consciousness if called upon to do so (for example, the name of the president of the United States). The much larger mass of the iceberg below the water represents the **unconscious**, a storehouse of impulses, wishes, and inaccessible memories that affect our thoughts and behavior. Freud was not the first to discover unconscious mental influences—even Shakespeare includes them in his plays—but he gave them primary importance in the everyday functioning of the normal personality.

Closely allied with Freud's focus on unconscious processes was his belief in the determinism of human behavior. **Psychological determinism** is the doctrine that all thoughts, emotions, and actions have causes. Freud maintained not only that all psychological events are caused but also that most of them are caused by unsatisfied drives and unconscious wishes. In one of his earliest publications, *The Psychopathology of Everyday Life* (1901), he argued that dreams, humor, forgetting, and slips of the tongue ("Freudian slips") all serve to relieve psychological tension by gratifying forbidden impulses or unfulfilled wishes.

Freud's writings fill 24 volumes. *The Interpretation of Dreams* was published in 1900, and his final treatise, *An Outline of Psychoanalysis*, was published in 1940, a year after his death. We can present only the barest outline of Freud's theory of personality here.

PERSONALITY STRUCTURE

Freud discovered that his iceberg model was too simple to describe the human personality, so he went on to develop a structural model, which divided personality into three major systems that interact to govern human behavior: the id, the ego, and the superego.

THE ID According to Freud, the **id** is the most primitive part of the personality and the part from which the ego and the superego later develop. It is present in the newborn infant and consists of the most basic biological impulses or drives: the need to eat, to drink, to eliminate wastes, to avoid pain, and to gain sexual (sensual) pleasure. Freud believed that aggression is also a basic biological drive. In fact, he believed that the sexual and aggressive drives were the most important instinctual determinants of personality throughout life. The id seeks immediate gratification of these impulses. Like a young child, it operates on the pleasure principle: It continually strives to obtain pleasure and to avoid pain, regardless of the external circumstances.

THE EGO Children soon learn that their impulses cannot always be gratified immediately. Hunger will not be alleviated until someone provides food. Relief of bladder or bowel pressure must be delayed until the bathroom is reached. Certain impulses—playing with one's genitals or hitting someone—may be punished. A new part of the personality, the ego, develops as the young child learns to consider the demands of reality. The **ego** obeys the reality principle: The gratification of impulses must be delayed until the situation is appropriate. The ego thus is essentially the executive of the personality: It decides which id impulses will be satisfied and in what manner. The ego mediates among the demands of the id, the realities of the world, and the demands of the superego.

THE SUPEREGO The third part of the personality is the **superego,** which judges whether actions are right or wrong. More generally, the superego is the internalized representation of the values and morals of society. It is the individual's conscience, as well as his or her image of the morally ideal person (called the *ego ideal*).

The superego develops in response to parental rewards and punishments. Initially, parents control chil-

"VERY WELL, I'LL INTRODUCE YOU. EGO MEET ID. NOW GET BACK TO WORK."

dren's behavior directly through reward and punishment. By incorporating parental standards into the superego, children bring behavior under their own control. Children no longer need anyone to tell them it is wrong to steal; their superego tells them. Violating the superego's standards, or even the impulse to do so, produces anxiety—beginning with anxiety over loss of parental love. According to Freud, this anxiety is largely unconscious but may be experienced as guilt. If parental standards are overly rigid, the individual may be guilt-ridden and inhibit all aggressive or sexual impulses. In contrast, an individual who fails to incorporate any standards for acceptable social behavior will feel few behavioral constraints and may engage in excessively self-indulgent or criminal behavior. Such a person is said to have a weak superego.

The three components of personality are often in conflict: The ego postpones the gratification that the id wants immediately, and the superego battles with both the id and the ego because behavior often falls short of the moral code it represents. In the well-integrated personality, the ego remains in firm but flexible control; the reality principle governs. In terms of his earlier iceberg model, Freud proposed that all of the id and most of the ego and superego are submerged in the unconscious and that small parts of the ego and superego are in either the conscious or the preconscious (see Figure 13-2).

PERSONALITY DYNAMICS

CONSERVATION OF ENERGY Freud was greatly influenced by the German physicist Hermann von Helmholtz, who argued that physiological events could be explained by the same principles that had been so successful in physics. Freud was particularly impressed by the principle of conservation of energy, which states that energy may be changed into different forms but is neither created nor destroyed. He proposed that humans are also closed energy systems. There is a constant amount of psychic energy for any given individual, which Freud called **libido** (Latin for "lust"), reflecting his view that the sexual drive was primary.

One corollary of the principle of conservation of energy is that if a forbidden act or impulse is suppressed, its energy will seek an outlet somewhere else in the system, possibly appearing in a disguised form. The desires of the id contain psychic energy that must be expressed in some way, and preventing the expression of those desires does not eliminate them. Aggressive impulses, for example, may be expressed in disguised form by racing sports cars, playing chess, or making sarcastic remarks. Dreams and neurotic symptoms are also manifestations of psychic energy that cannot be expressed directly.

ANXIETY AND DEFENSE Individuals with an urge to do something forbidden experience anxiety. One way of reducing this anxiety is to express the impulse in a disguised form that will avoid punishment either by society or by its internal representative, the superego. Freud and his daughter Anna Freud described several additional **defense mechanisms,** or strategies for preventing or reducing anxiety, and several are listed in the Concept Review Table.

CONCEPT REVIEW TABLE
Major Defense Mechanisms

Repression	Excluding from conscious awareness impulses or memories that are too frightening or painful.
Rationalization	Assigning logical or socially desirable motives to what we do so that we seem to have acted rationally.
Reaction formation	Concealing a motive from ourselves by giving strong expression to the opposite motive.
Projection	Assigning our own undesirable qualities to others in exaggerated amounts.
Intellectualization	Attempting to gain detachment from a stressful situation by dealing with it in abstract, intellectual terms.
Denial	Denying that an unpleasant reality exists.
Displacement	Directing a motive that cannot be gratified in one form into another channel.

We all use defense mechanisms at times. They help us over the rough spots until we can deal with stressful situations more directly. Defense mechanisms are maladaptive only when they become the dominant mode of responding to problems. We will discuss a few of the most common defense mechanisms here.

REPRESSION Freud considered repression to be the basic, and most important, defense mechanism. In **repression,** impulses or memories that are too frightening or painful are excluded from conscious awareness. Memories that evoke shame, guilt, or self-deprecation are often repressed. Freud believed that repression of certain childhood impulses is universal. In later life, individuals may repress feelings and memories that could cause anxiety because they are inconsistent with their self-concepts. Feelings of hostility toward a loved one and experiences of failure may be banished from conscious memory.

Repression is different from suppression. Suppression is the process of deliberate self-control, keeping impulses and desires in check (perhaps holding them in privately while denying them publicly) or temporarily pushing aside painful memories. Individuals are aware of suppressed thoughts but are largely unaware of repressed impulses or memories.

Freud believed that repression is seldom completely successful. The repressed impulses threaten to break through into consciousness; the individual becomes anxious (though unaware of the reason) and employs other defense mechanisms to keep the partially repressed impulses from awareness.

RATIONALIZATION When the fox in Aesop's fable rejected the grapes that he could not reach because they were sour, he illustrated a defense mechanism known as **rationalization.** Rationalization does not mean "to act rationally," as we might assume; it refers to the assignment of logical or socially desirable motives to what we do so that we seem to have acted rationally. Rationalization serves two purposes: It eases our disappointment when we fail to reach a goal ("I didn't want it anyway"), and it gives us acceptable motives for our behavior. If we act impulsively or on the basis of motives that we do not wish to acknowledge even to ourselves, we rationalize what we have done in order to place our behavior in a more favorable light.

In searching for the good reason rather than the true reason, individuals make a number of excuses. These excuses are usually plausible; they simply do not tell the whole story. For example, "My roommate failed to wake me" or "I had too many other things to do" may be true, but they may not be the real reasons for the individual's failure to perform the behavior in question. Individuals who are really concerned set an alarm clock or find the time to do what they are expected to do.

A classic experiment involving posthypnotic suggestion (see Chapter 6) demonstrates the process of rationalization. A hypnotist instructs a participant under hypnosis that when he wakes from the trance he will watch the hypnotist. Then, when the hypnotist takes off her glasses, the participant will raise the window but will not remember that the hypnotist told him to do this. Aroused from the trance, the participant feels a little drowsy but soon circulates among the people in the room and carries on a normal conversation, furtively watching the hypnotist. When the hypnotist casually removes her glasses, the participant feels an impulse to open the window. He takes a step in that direction but hesitates. Unconsciously, he mobilizes his desire to be a reasonable person. Seeking a reason for his impulse to open the window, he says, "Isn't it a little stuffy in here?" Having found the needed excuse, he opens the window and feels more comfortable (Hilgard, 1965).

REACTION FORMATION Sometimes individuals can conceal a motive from themselves by giving strong expression to the opposite motive. This tendency is called **reaction formation.** A mother who feels guilty about not wanting her child may become overindulgent and overprotective in order to assure the child of her love and assure herself that she is a good mother. In one case, a mother who wished to do everything for her daughter could not understand why the child was so unappreciative. At great sacrifice, she arranged for the daughter take expensive piano lessons and assisted her in the daily practice sessions. Although the mother thought she was being extremely kind, she was actually being very demanding—in fact, hostile. She was unaware of her own hostility, but when confronted with it, she admitted that she had hated piano lessons as a child. Under the conscious guise of being kind, she was unconsciously being cruel to her daughter. The daughter sensed what was going on and developed symptoms that required psychological treatment.

PROJECTION All of us have undesirable traits that we do not acknowledge, even to ourselves. A defense mechanism known as **projection** protects us from recognizing our own undesirable qualities by assigning them to other people in exaggerated amounts. Suppose that you have a tendency to be critical of or unkind to other people, but you would dislike yourself if you admitted this tendency. If you are convinced that the people around you are cruel or unkind, your harsh treatment of them is not based on your bad qualities—you are simply "giving them

what they deserve." If you can assure yourself that everybody else cheats on college examinations, your unacknowledged tendency to take some academic shortcuts seems not so bad. Projection is really a form of rationalization, but it is so pervasive that it merits discussion in its own right.

INTELLECTUALIZATION Intellectualization is an attempt to gain detachment from a stressful situation by dealing with it in abstract, intellectual terms. This kind of defense may be a necessity for people who must deal with life-and-death matters in their jobs. A doctor who is continually confronted with human suffering cannot afford to become emotionally involved with each patient. In fact, a certain amount of detachment may be essential for the doctor to function competently. This kind of intellectualization is a problem only when it becomes so pervasive that individuals cut themselves off from all emotional experiences.

DENIAL When an external reality is too unpleasant to face, an individual may engage in **denial,** refusing to acknowledge that the undesired reality exists. The parents of a terminally ill child may refuse to admit that anything is seriously wrong, even though they are fully informed of the diagnosis and the expected outcome. Because they cannot tolerate the pain that acknowledging reality would produce, they resort to denial. Less extreme forms of denial may be seen in individuals who consistently ignore criticism, fail to perceive that others are angry with them, or disregard all kinds of clues suggesting that their spouse is having an affair.

Sometimes, denying facts may be better than facing them. In a severe crisis, denial may give the person time

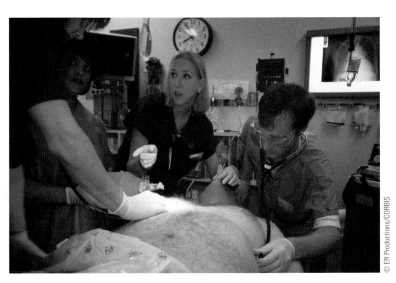

Emergency room physicians may need to develop many defenses to handle their high stress jobs.

to face the grim facts at a more gradual pace. For example, victims of a stroke or a spinal cord injury might give up altogether if they were fully aware of the seriousness of their condition. Hope gives them an incentive to keep trying. Soldiers who have faced combat or imprisonment report that denying the possibility of death helped them function. In such situations, denial clearly has an adaptive value. On the other hand, the negative aspects of denial are evident when people postpone seeking medical help. For example, a woman may deny that a lump in her breast may be cancerous and delay going to a physician until the condition has become life-threatening.

DISPLACEMENT Through the mechanism of **displacement,** a motive that cannot be gratified in one form is directed into a new channel. An example of displacement was provided in our discussion of anger that could not be expressed toward the source of frustration and was redirected toward a less threatening object. Freud felt that displacement was the most satisfactory way of handling aggressive and sexual impulses. The basic drives cannot be changed, but we can change the object toward which a drive is directed. Erotic impulses that cannot be expressed directly may be expressed indirectly in creative activities such as art, poetry, and music. Hostile impulses may find socially acceptable expression through participation in contact sports.

It seems unlikely that displacement actually eliminates the frustrated impulses, but substitute activities do help reduce tension when a basic drive is thwarted. For example, the activities of taking care of others or seeking companionship may help reduce the tension associated with unsatisfied sexual needs.

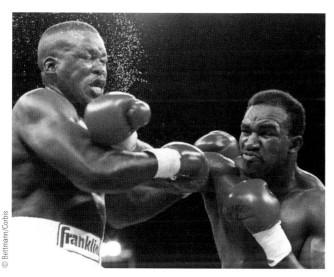

Some people may displace their aggressive impulses by engaging in aggressive sports.

PERSONALITY DEVELOPMENT

Freud believed that during the first 5 years of life, the individual progresses through several developmental stages that affect his or her personality. Applying a broad definition of sexuality, he called these periods **psychosexual stages.** During each stage, the pleasure-seeking impulses of the id focus on a particular area of the body and on activities connected with that area.

Freud called the first year of life the **oral stage** of psychosexual development. During this period, infants derive pleasure from nursing and sucking and begin to put anything they can reach into their mouths. Freud called the second year of life the beginning of the **anal stage** and believed that during this period children find pleasure both in withholding and in expelling feces. These pleasures come into conflict with parents who are attempting toilet training, the child's first experience with imposed control. In the **phallic stage,** from about age 3 to age 6, children begin to derive pleasure from fondling their genitals. They observe the differences between males and females and begin to direct their awakening sexual impulses toward the parent of the opposite sex.

Around the age of 5 or 6, according to Freud, a boy's sexual impulses are directed toward his mother. This leads him to perceive his father as a rival for his mother's affection. Freud called this situation the **Oedipal conflict,** after the ancient Greek myth in which Oedipus unwittingly kills his father and marries his mother. Freud also believed that the boy fears that his father will retaliate against these sexual impulses by castrating him. He labeled this fear castration anxiety and considered it to be the prototype for later anxieties provoked by forbidden internal desires. In a normal case of development, the boy simultaneously reduces this anxiety and vicariously gratifies his feelings toward his mother by identifying with his father—that is, by internalizing an idealized perception of his father's attitudes and values. The same process in a girl—resulting in her identifying with her mother—is analogous but more complicated.

Resolution of the Oedipal conflict ends the phallic stage, which is followed by the **latency period.** During this sexually quiescent time, which lasts from about age 7 to age 12, children become less concerned with their bodies and turn their attention to the skills needed for coping with their environment. Finally, adolescence and puberty usher in the **genital stage,** the mature phase of adult sexuality and functioning.

Freud believed that special problems at any stage could arrest, or fixate, development and have a lasting effect on personality. The individual's libido would remain attached to the activities appropriate for that stage. A person who was weaned very early and did not have enough sucking pleasure might become fixated at the oral stage. As an adult, he or she might be excessively de-

© Tony Freeman/PhotoEdit

According to psychoanalytic theory, a child resolves the Oedipal conflict by identifying with the same-sex parent.

pendent on others and overly fond of oral pleasures such as eating, drinking, and smoking. Such a person is said to have an oral personality. A person fixated at the anal stage of psychosexual development may be abnormally concerned with cleanliness, orderliness, and saving and may tend to resist external pressure. Such a person is said to have an anal personality. Inadequate resolution of the Oedipal conflict can lead to a weak sense of morality, difficulties with authority figures, and many other problems.

MODIFICATIONS OF FREUD'S THEORIES

Freud modified his theories throughout his life. Like a good scientist, he remained open to new data, revising his earlier positions as new observations accumulated that could not be accommodated by the original theory. For example, quite late in his career he completely revised his theory of anxiety. Freud's theory has been further extended by his daughter Anna, who played a particularly important role in clarifying the defense mechanisms (1946/1967) and applying psychoanalytic theory to the practice of child psychiatry (1958).

Although Freud was open to new data, he was not open to dissenting opinions. He was particularly adamant that his colleagues and followers not question the libido theory and the centrality of sexual motivation in the functioning of personality. This dogmatism forced a break between Freud and many of his most brilliant associates, some of whom went on to develop rival theories that placed more emphasis on motivational processes other than sexuality. These former associates included Carl Jung and Alfred Adler, as well as later theorists such as Karen Horney, Harry Stack Sullivan, and Erich Fromm.

Of those who broke with Freud, perhaps the most famous was Carl Jung. Originally one of Freud's most dedicated followers, Jung eventually came to disagree profoundly with some aspects of Freud's theory and founded his own school of psychology, which he called *analytic psychology.* Jung believed that in addition to the personal unconscious described by Freud, there is a **collective unconscious,** a part of the mind that is common to all humans. The collective unconscious consists of primordial images or archetypes inherited from our ancestors. Among those archetypes are the mother, the father, the sun, the hero, God, and death. To gather evidence for the presence of these archetypes, Jung examined dreams, myths, and other cultural products, noting that certain images, such as that of a vulture, often appear in dreams and also in religious writings and ancient mythologies with which the dreamer is not familiar. Although Jung agreed with Freud on the existence of the unconscious, he believed that Freud's theory failed to explain the presence of common images or archetypes in the unconscious minds of all humans.

Another well-known "neo-Freudian" was the American psychologist Harry Stack Sullivan. Sullivan developed his own theory of personality on the basis of his experience with psychoanalysis. He placed primary emphasis on interpersonal relations, arguing that a personality "can never be isolated from the complex of interpersonal relations in which the person lives and has his being" (Sullivan, 1953, p. 10). In his view, people's responses to interpersonal experiences cause them to develop personifications—mental images of themselves and others. Images of the self fall into three categories: the good-me personification, the bad-me personification, and the not-me. The last category contains aspects of the self that are so threatening that the individual dissociates them from the self-system and maintains them in the unconscious. This concept is similar to Freud's concept of repression in that it requires a constant effort to keep these aspects of the self in the unconscious.

Like Freud, Sullivan believed that early childhood experiences play an important role in the development of personality. He believed, however, that the personality continues to develop after childhood. He identified seven

© Laura Dwight

Children must develop ways of handling their sometimes mixed feelings about their parents.

stages of personality development—infancy, childhood, the juvenile era, preadolescence, early adolescence, late adolescence, and adulthood—and maintained that each stage is largely socially determined. Although a person may go through a stage in a particular way because of certain biological factors, the primary influence is the typical situations he or she experiences at that age. Sullivan's view of development therefore differs considerably from Freud's biologically based theory.

These dissidents and more recent psychoanalytic theorists all place greater emphasis on the role of the ego. They believe that the ego is present at birth, develops independently of the id, and performs functions other than finding realistic ways of satisfying id impulses, including learning how to cope with the environment and making sense of experience. Ego satisfactions include exploration, manipulation, and competence in performing tasks. This approach ties the concept of the ego more closely to cognitive processes.

An important part of this new direction is **object relations theory,** which deals with a person's attachments and relationships to other people throughout life. Object relations theorists have not rejected the concept of the id or the importance of biological drives in motivating behavior, but they have an equal interest in such questions as degree of psychological separateness from parents, degree of attachment to and involvement with other people versus preoccupation with self, and the strength of the individual's feelings of self-esteem and competence.

Although we did not identify it as such, Erik Erikson's stage theory of development (discussed in Chapter 3) is an example of a revised psychoanalytic theory. Erikson himself was trained as a psychoanalyst by Anna Freud, and he perceived his own views as expanding rather than altering Freudian theory. Instead of viewing developmental stages in terms of their psychosexual functions, Erikson saw them as psychosocial stages involving primarily ego processes. For Erikson, the important feature of the first year of life is not that it focuses on oral gratification but that the child is learning to trust (or mistrust) the environment as a satisfier of needs. The important feature of the second year of life is not that it focuses on anal concerns such as toilet training but that the child is learning autonomy. Toilet training just happens to be a frequent arena of conflict in which the child's striving for autonomy clashes with new demands by parents. Erikson's theory also adds more stages in order to encompass the entire life span.

PROJECTIVE TESTS

Personality psychologists who follow in Freud's psychoanalytic tradition are particularly interested in assessing unconscious wishes, motivations, and conflicts. Accordingly, they prefer tests that resemble Freud's technique of free association, in which the individual is free to say whatever comes to mind. For this reason, they developed projective tests. A **projective test** presents an ambiguous stimulus to which the person may respond as he or she wishes. Because the stimulus is ambiguous and does not demand a specific response, it is assumed that the individual projects his or her personality onto the stimulus and thus reveals something about himself or herself. Projective tests have also been useful in areas of personality other than psychoanalytic theory. Two of the most widely used projective techniques are the Rorschach Test and the Thematic Apperception Test (TAT).

THE RORSCHACH TEST The **Rorschach Test,** developed by the Swiss psychiatrist Hermann Rorschach in the 1920s, is a series of 10 cards, each of which displays a rather complex inkblot like the one shown in Figure 13-3. Some of the blots are in color; some are black and white.

Figure 13-3
A Rorschach Inkblot
The person is asked to tell what he or she sees in the blot. It may be viewed from any angle.

The person is instructed to look at one card at a time and report everything the inkblot resembles. After the person has finished the 10 cards, the examiner usually goes over each response, asking the person to clarify some responses and indicate which features of the blot gave a particular impression.

The individual's responses may be scored in various ways. Three main categories are location (whether the response involves the entire inkblot or a part of it), determinants (whether the individual responds to the shape of the blot, its color, or differences in texture and shading), and content (what the response represents). Most testers also score responses according to frequency of occurrence; for example, a response is "popular" if many people assign it to the same inkblot.

Several elaborate scoring systems have been devised on the basis of these categories, but most of them have proved to be of limited predictive value. Consequently, many psychologists base their interpretations on an impressionistic evaluation of the response record, as well as on the individual's general reaction to the test situation (for example, whether the person is defensive, open, competitive, cooperative, and so on).

In 1974, a system was introduced that attempted to extract and combine the validated portions of all the scoring systems into one complete system. It has undergone extensive revision and is now supplemented by a computer scoring service and software for microcomputers (Exner & Weiner, 1995). This system is now widely used in clinical and forensic settings (Lillienfield, Wood, & Garb, 2000).

THE THEMATIC APPERCEPTION TEST Another popular projective test, the **Thematic Apperception Test** (TAT), was developed at Harvard University by Henry Murray in the 1930s. The participant is shown as many as 20 ambiguous pictures of persons and scenes, similar to the one in Figure 13-4, and asked to make up a story about each picture. The individual is encouraged to give free rein to his or her imagination and to tell whatever story comes to mind. The test is intended to reveal basic themes that recur in a person's imaginings. (Apperception is a readiness to perceive in certain ways, based on prior experiences.) People interpret ambiguous pictures according to their apperceptions and elaborate stories in terms of preferred plots or themes that reflect personal fantasies. If particular problems are bothering them, those problems may become evident in a number of the stories or in striking deviations from the usual theme in one or two stories. For example, when shown a picture similar to the one in Figure 13-4, a 21-year-old male told the following story:

> She has prepared this room for someone's arrival and is opening the door for a last general look over the room. She is probably expecting her son home. She tries to place

Figure 13-4
The Thematic Apperception Test
This picture is similar to the pictures used on the Thematic Apperception Test. The pictures usually have elements of ambiguity so that the individual can "read into" them something from personal experience or fantasy.

everything as it was when he left. She seems like a very tyrannical character. She led her son's life for him and is going to take over again as soon as he gets back. This is merely the beginning of her rule, and the son is definitely cowed by this overbearing attitude of hers and will slip back into her well-ordered way of life. He will go through life plodding down the tracks she has laid down for him. All this represents her complete domination of his life until she dies. (Arnold, 1949, p. 100)

Although the original picture shows only a woman standing in an open doorway looking into a room, the young man's readiness to talk about his relationship with his mother led to this story of a woman's domination of her son. Facts obtained later confirmed the clinician's interpretation that the story reflected the man's own problems.

In analyzing responses to TAT cards, the psychologist looks for recurrent themes that may reveal the individual's needs, motives, or characteristic way of handling interpersonal relationships.

PROBLEMS WITH PROJECTIVE TESTS

Since the widespread adoption of Exner's scoring system for the Rorschach, hundreds of studies have been done to test the validity and reliability of results of the Rorschach based on this system (see Lillienfield et al., 2000). Unfortunately, the Exner system appears to have done little to make the Rorschach a psychometrically sound test. The system too often misclassifies normal individuals as pathological, particularly individuals who are members of ethnic minority groups in the United States or from other cultures. The reliability of results from the Rorschach has generally been poor, in large part because the same responses may be evaluated quite differently by two trained examiners. And attempts to demonstrate the Rorschach's ability to predict behavior or discriminate between groups have met with limited success.

The TAT has fared somewhat better (Lillienfield et al., 2000). When specific scoring systems are used (for example, to measure achievement motives or aggressive themes), interscorer reliability is fairly good (Winter, 1973). TAT measures have also proven useful in predicting some specific behaviors. For example, the need for power, as assessed by TAT responses, significantly predicted important life outcomes, such as the choice of a career that gave one influence over others, in two long-term studies of female college students (Winter, John, Stewart, Klohnen, & Duncan, 1998).

Many other projective tests have been devised. Some ask the individual to draw pictures of people, houses, trees, and so on. Others involve completing sentences that start with "I often wish . . . ," "My mother . . . ," or "I feel like quitting when they . . . ." In fact, any stimulus to which a person can respond in an individualistic way could be considered the basis for a projective test. But many projective tests have not been subjected to enough research to establish their usefulness in assessing personality, and those that have been researched have not proven to have consistently strong reliability or validity (Lillienfield et al., 2000).

A PSYCHOANALYTIC PORTRAIT OF HUMAN NATURE

At the beginning of the chapter, we noted that each approach to personality carries with it a distinctive philosophy of human nature. To what extent are our actions free or determined? Good, neutral, or evil? Fixed or modifiable? Active or passive? What constitutes psychological health? Our description of Freud's theory has hinted at many of his views on these matters. Freud is often compared with Copernicus and Darwin. Like them, he was accused of undermining the stature and dignity of humanity. The astronomer Copernicus demoted the earth from its position as the center of the universe to one of several planets moving around a minor star; Darwin demoted the human species to one of numerous animal species. Freud took the next step by emphasizing that human behavior is determined by forces beyond our control, thereby depriving us of free will and psychological freedom. By emphasizing the unconscious status of our motivations, he deprived us of rationality; by stressing the sexual and aggressive nature of those motivations, he dealt the final blow to our dignity.

Freud saw the rise of the Nazis and the outbreak of World War II as natural consequences of the human aggressive drive when it is not held in check.

Psychoanalytic theory also paints a portrait of human nature as basically evil. Without the restraining forces of society and its internalized representative, the superego, humans would destroy themselves. Freud was a deeply pessimistic man. He was forced to flee from Vienna when the Nazis invaded in 1938, and he died in September 1939 just as World War II began. He saw these events as natural consequences of the human aggressive drive when it is not held in check.

According to psychoanalytic theory, our personalities are basically determined by inborn drives and by events in our environment during the first 5 years of life. Only extensive psychoanalysis can undo some of the negative consequences of early experiences, and it can do so only in limited ways. We also emerge from psychoanalytic theory as relatively passive creatures. Although the ego is engaged in an active struggle with the id and superego, we are passive pawns of this drama being played out in our unconscious. Finally, for Freud, psychological health consisted of firm but flexible ego control over the impulses of the id. As he noted, the goal of psychoanalysis was to ensure that "Where id is, there ego shall be" (1933).

An Evaluation of the Psychoanalytic Approach

Psychoanalytic theory is so broad in scope that it cannot simply be pronounced true or false. However, there can be no doubt of its impact on our culture, or of the value of some of its scientific contributions. For example, Freud's method of free association opened up an entirely new database of observations that had never before been explored systematically. In addition, the recognition that our behavior often reflects a compromise between our wishes and our fears accounts for many of the apparent contradictions in human behavior better than any other theory of personality. And Freud's recognition that unconscious processes play an important role in much of our behavior is almost universally accepted—although these processes are often reinterpreted in learning-theory or information-processing terms (Funder, 2001).

Nevertheless, as a scientific theory, the psychoanalytic account has been persistently criticized (Grünbaum, 1984). One of the main criticisms is that many of its concepts are ambiguous and difficult to define or measure objectively. Also, psychoanalytic theory assumes that very different behaviors may reflect the same underlying motive. For example, a man who had a hostile and uncaring father may become a hostile parent to his own children or overly protective of them. When opposite behaviors are claimed to result from the same underlying motive, it is difficult to confirm the presence or absence of the motive or to make predictions that can be empirically verified.

A more serious criticism concerns the validity of the observations that Freud obtained through his psychoanalytic procedure. Critics have pointed out that it often is not clear what Freud's patients told him spontaneously about past events in their lives, what he may have "planted" in their minds, and what he simply inferred. For example, Freud reported that many of his patients recalled being seduced or sexually molested as children. At first he believed them, but then he decided that these reports were not literally true but, rather, reflected the patients' own early sexual fantasies. He regarded this realization as one of his major theoretical insights. But one writer argued that Freud's original assumption about the reality of the seductions was probably more accurate, an argument that seems more reasonable in light of our increased awareness of child sexual abuse (Masson, 1984).

Other critics have gone further and suggested that Freud may have questioned his patients so persistently with leading questions and suggestions that they were led to reconstruct memories of seductions that never occurred—a hypothesis that Freud considered but rejected (Powell & Boer, 1994). Others charge that in many cases Freud simply inferred that seduction had occurred, even though the patient never reported such an incident; he actually substituted his theoretical expectations for data (Esterson, 1993; Scharnberg, 1993).

When Freud's theories have been empirically tested, the results have been mixed (Westen, 1998). Efforts to link adult personality characteristics to psychosexually relevant events in childhood have generally met with negative outcomes (Sears, Maccoby, & Levin, 1957; Sewell & Mussen, 1952). When relevant character traits are identified, they appear to be related to similar character traits in the parents (Beloff, 1957; Hetherington & Brackbill, 1963). Thus, even if a relationship were to be found between toilet-training practices and adult personality traits, it could have arisen because both are linked to parental emphasis on cleanliness and order. In such a case, a simple learning-theory explanation—parental reinforcement and the child's imitation of the parents' behavior—would be a more economical explanation of the adult traits than the psychoanalytic hypothesis.

This outcome should also remind us that Freud based his theory on observations of a very narrow range of people—primarily upper-middle-class men and women in Victorian Vienna who suffered from neurotic symptoms. In hindsight, many of Freud's cultural biases are obvious, particularly in his theories about women. For example, his theory that female psychosexual development is shaped largely by "penis envy"—a girl's feelings of inadequacy because she doesn't have a penis—is almost universally rejected as reflecting the sex bias of Freud and the historical period in which he lived. A little girl's personality development during the Victorian era was surely shaped more decisively by her awareness that she lacked the greater independence, power, and social status of her brother than by her envy of his penis.

Despite these criticisms, the remarkable feature of Freud's theory is how well it managed to transcend its narrow observational base. For example, many experimental studies of the defense mechanisms and reactions to conflict have supported the theory in contexts quite different from those in which Freud developed the theory (Blum, 1953; Erdelyi, 1985; Holmes, 1974; Sears, 1943, 1944). The structural theory (ego, id, and superego), the psychosexual theory, and the energy concept have not fared well over the years. Even some psychoanalytic writers are prepared to abandon them or to modify them substantially (Kline, 1972; Schafer, 1976). On the other hand, Freud's dynamic theory—his theory of anxiety and the mechanisms of defense—has withstood the test of time, research, and observation. A survey of psychoanalytically oriented psychologists and psychiatrists found widespread agreement with a number of ideas that were controversial when Freud first introduced them, including the importance of early childhood experiences in shaping adult personality and the centrality of both conflict and the unconscious in human mental life (Westen, 1998).

◆ Interim Summary

- Freud's psychoanalytic theory holds that many behaviors are caused by unconscious motivations. Personality is determined primarily by the biological drives of sex and aggression and by experiences that occur during the first 5 years of life.

- Freud's theory of personality structure views personality as composed of the id, the ego, and the superego. The id operates on the pleasure principle, seeking immediate gratification of biological impulses. The ego obeys the reality principle, postponing gratification until it can be achieved in socially acceptable ways. The superego (conscience) imposes moral standards on the individual. In a well-integrated personality, the ego remains in firm but flexible control over the id and superego, and the reality principle governs.

- Freud's theory of personality dynamics proposes that there is a constant amount of psychic energy (libido) for each individual. If a forbidden act or impulse is suppressed, its energy will seek an outlet in some other form, such as dreams or neurotic symptoms. The theory assumes that unacceptable id impulses cause anxiety, which can be reduced by defense mechanisms.

- Freud's theory of personality development proposes that individuals pass through psychosexual stages and must resolve the Oedipal conflict, in which the young child sees the same-sex parent as a rival for the affection of the opposite-sex parent. Over the years, Freud's theory of anxiety and defense mechanisms has fared better than his structural and developmental theories have.

- Psychoanalytic theory has been modified by later psychologists, notably Carl Jung and Harry Stack Sullivan. Jung proposed that, in addition to the personal unconscious described by Freud, there is a collective unconscious, a part of the mind that is common to all humans. Sullivan suggested that people's responses to interpersonal experiences cause them to develop personifications—mental images of themselves and others.

- Psychologists who take the psychoanalytic approach sometimes use projective tests, such as the Rorschach Test and the Thematic Apperception Test (TAT). Because the test stimuli are ambiguous, it is assumed that the individual projects his or her personality onto the stimulus, thereby revealing unconscious wishes and motives.

◆ Critical Thinking Questions

1. As this section makes clear, the value of Sigmund Freud's impact on psychology is hotly debated. What is your opinion on the value of Freud's legacy?

2. Can you identify some of your own assumptions about other people that are rooted in Freudian theory, whether you previously realized they were or not?

THE BEHAVIORIST APPROACH

In contrast to the psychodynamic approach to personality, the **behaviorist approach** emphasizes the importance of environmental, or situational, determinants of behavior. In this view, behavior is the result of a continuous interaction between personal and environmental variables. Environmental conditions shape behavior through learning; a person's behavior, in turn, shapes the environment. Persons and situations influence each other. To predict behavior, we need to know how the characteristics of the individual interact with those of the situation (Bandura, 1986, 2001).

SOCIAL LEARNING AND CONDITIONING

OPERANT CONDITIONING The effects of other people's actions—the rewards and punishments they provide—

are an important influence on an individual's behavior. Accordingly, one of the most basic principles of behavioral theory is **operant conditioning**—the type of learning that occurs when we learn the association between our behaviors and certain outcomes. The basic tenet of behaviorist theory is that people behave in ways that are likely to produce reinforcement and that individual differences in behavior result primarily from differences in the kinds of learning experiences a person encounters in the course of growing up.

Although individuals learn many behavior patterns through direct experience—that is, by being rewarded or punished for behaving in a certain manner—they also acquire many responses through **observational learning.** People can learn by observing the actions of others and noting the consequences of those actions. It would be a slow and inefficient process, indeed, if all of our behavior had to be learned through direct reinforcement of our responses. Similarly, the reinforcement that controls the expression of learned behaviors may be direct (tangible rewards, social approval or disapproval, or alleviation of aversive conditions), vicarious (observation of someone receiving reward or punishment for behavior similar to one's own), or self-administered (evaluation of one's own performance with self-praise or self-reproach).

Because most social behaviors are not uniformly rewarded in all settings, the individual learns to identify the contexts in which certain behavior is appropriate and those in which it is not. To the extent that a person is rewarded for the same response in many different situations, generalization takes place, ensuring that the same behavior will occur in a variety of settings. A boy who is reinforced for physical aggression at home, as well as at school and at play, is likely to develop an aggressive personality. More often, aggressive responses are differentially rewarded, and the individual learns to distinguish between situations in which aggression is appropriate and situations in which it is not (for example, aggression is acceptable on the football field but not in the classroom). For this reason, behaviorists challenge the usefulness of characterizing individuals with trait terms like *aggressive,* arguing that such terms obscure the cross-situational variability of behavior.

CLASSICAL CONDITIONING To account for emotion or affect, behaviorists add **classical conditioning**—the type of learning that occurs when specific situations become associated with specific outcomes—to their account of personality (see Chapter 7). For example, when a child is punished by a parent for engaging in some forbidden activity, the punishment elicits the physiological responses that we associate with guilt or anxiety. Subsequently, the child's behavior may itself elicit those responses, and the child will feel guilty when engaging in the forbidden be-

"Time-outs" are based on behaviorist principles.

havior. In the terminology of classical conditioning, we would say that the behavior becomes a conditioned stimulus by being paired with the unconditioned stimulus of punishment; the anxiety becomes the conditioned response. For the behaviorist, it is classical conditioning that produces the internalized source of anxiety that Freud labeled the superego.

INDIVIDUAL DIFFERENCES We noted earlier that personality psychology seeks to specify both the variables on which individuals differ from one another and the general processes of personality functioning. Trait approaches have focused on the first task, describing personality differences in detail while saying virtually nothing about personality functioning. Psychoanalytic theory has attempted to do both. In contrast, the behaviorist approach has focused primarily on process, devoting little attention to individual differences. Because this approach sees personality as the product of the individual's unique reinforcement history and emphasizes the degree to which behavior varies across situations, it has not attempted to classify individuals into types or to rate them on traits.

A BEHAVIORIST PORTRAIT OF HUMAN BEHAVIOR

Like the psychoanalytic approach, the behaviorist approach to personality is deterministic. In contrast to the psychoanalytic approach, however, it pays little attention to biological determinants of behavior and focuses on environmental determinants. People are not inherently good or evil but are readily modified by events and situations in their environment. As we noted in Chapter 3, John Watson, the founder of the behaviorist movement in the United States, claimed that he could raise an infant to be anything, regardless of the infant's "talents, penchants, tendencies, abilities, vocations, and race of his [or her] ancestors." Few behaviorists would take such an extreme view today. Nevertheless, behaviorists hold a strong optimism about our ability to change human behavior by changing the environment.

The human personality as described by behavioral theorists may be highly modifiable, but it still has a passive quality. We still seem to be shaped primarily by forces beyond our control. This view changed, however, as social-learning approaches (described later in this chapter) replaced traditional behaviorist theories, increasingly emphasize the individual's active role in selecting and modifying the environment, thereby permitting the person to become a causal force in his or her own life. As we will see, however, this role is not active enough for humanistic theorists. In particular, they do not believe that it is sufficient to define psychological health as merely optimal adaptation to the environment.

AN EVALUATION OF THE BEHAVIORIST APPROACH

Through its emphasis on specifying the environmental variables that evoke particular behaviors, behavioral theory has made a major contribution to both clinical psychology and personality theory. It has led us to see human actions as reactions to specific environments, and it has helped us focus on how environments control our behavior and how they can be changed to modify behavior. As we will see in Chapter 16, the systematic application of learning principles has proved successful in changing many maladaptive behaviors.

Behavioral theorists have been criticized for overemphasizing situational influences on behavior (Carlson, 1971). But the learning theorists' findings on the cross-situational consistency of personality have forced other

personality psychologists to reexamine their assumptions. The result has been a clearer understanding of the interactions between people and situations and an enhanced appreciation of each person's individuality. As we see in the next section, the cognitive theorists built on the work of behavioral theorists to introduce quite a different way of viewing personality.

◆ Interim Summary

- According to behaviorist theory, individual differences in behavior result primarily from differences in the kinds of learning experiences a person encounters in the course of growing up.

- Through operant conditioning, people learn to associate specific behaviors with punishment or reward. They can also learn these associations through observational learning.

- Through classical conditioning, people learn to associate specific situations with certain outcomes, such as anxiety.

◆ Critical Thinking Questions

1. Think about your own tendency to be friendly or unfriendly. To what extent is the situation important in determining your level of friendliness? What are some of the reinforcements and punishments you've had in your life that might have contributed to your tendency to be friendly or unfriendly?

2. Behavioral theorists view all types of human behavior as modifiable. Do you think there are any types of behavior that are not modifiable? Why or why not?

THE COGNITIVE APPROACH

Today most personality psychologists would not identify themselves as "pure" adherents to any one of the three approaches described so far, and the differences among the approaches are no longer as sharp as they once were. This is because most contemporary personality theorists have joined psychologists in other subfields in becoming more "cognitive." In fact, most contemporary experimental work in personality psychology begins from a cognitive base. The **cognitive approach** is not actually a "philosophy" of human nature in the way that the other approaches are. Rather, it is a general empirical approach and a set of topics related to how people process information about themselves and the world.

For the cognitive theorist, differences in personality stem from differences in the way individuals mentally represent information.

SOCIAL LEARNING THEORY

Social-learning theory has its roots in early behavioral theory but was considered a radical departure from behaviorism when it was first introduced. The social-learning perspective is aptly summarized in the following comment by Albert Bandura: "The prospects for survival would be slim indeed if one could learn only from the consequences of trial and error. One does not teach children to swim, adolescents to drive automobiles, and novice medical students to perform surgery by having them discover the requisite behavior from the consequences of their successes and failures" (1986, p. 20). According to **social-learning theorists,** internal cognitive processes influence behavior, as well as observation of the behaviors of others and the environment in which behavior occurs.

As early as 1954, Julian Rotter was introducing cognitive variables into the behaviorist approach (1954, 1982). Rotter proposed the concept of behavior potential, meaning the likelihood of a particular behavior occurring in a particular situation—for example, staying up all night to study for an exam. The strength of the behavior potential is determined by two variables: expectancy and reinforcement value. In the case of pulling an all-nighter, the likelihood of engaging in that behavior is greater if the student expects to receive a higher grade as a result. This expectation will depend on what happened the last time the student was in a similar situation. If studying all night resulted in a higher grade the last time, the student will expect the same result this time. In other words, the more often the student is reinforced for studying all night, the stronger his or her expectancy that the behavior will be reinforced in the future. As for reinforcement value, it depends on the degree to which we prefer one reinforcer over another. If a student prefers sleeping over receiving a higher grade, the likelihood of pulling an all-nighter decreases.

Bandura, one of the leading contemporary theorists in this area, has taken this approach even further, developing what he calls **social-cognitive theory** (1986, 2000). His theory emphasizes reciprocal determinism, in which external determinants of behavior (such as rewards and punishments) and internal determinants (such as beliefs, thoughts, and expectations) are part of a system of interacting influences that affect both behavior and other parts of the system (Bandura, 1986). In Bandura's model, not only can the environment affect behavior but also behavior can affect the environment. In fact, the relationship between environment and behavior is a reciprocal one: The environment influences our behavior, which then affects the kind of environment we find ourselves in, which may in turn influence our behavior, and so on.

Bandura notes that people use symbols and forethought in deciding how to act. When they encounter a new problem, they imagine possible outcomes and consider the probability of each. Then they set goals and develop strategies for achieving them. This is quite different from the notion of conditioning through rewards and punishments. Of course, the individual's past experiences with rewards and punishments will influence his or her decisions about future behavior.

Bandura also points out that most behavior occurs in the absence of external rewards or punishments. Most behavior stems from internal processes of self-regulation. As he expresses it, "Anyone who attempted to change a pacifist into an aggressor or a devout religionist into an atheist would quickly come to appreciate the existence of personal sources of behavioral control" (1977, pp. 128–129).

How do these internal, personal sources of control develop? According to Bandura and other social-learning theorists, we learn how to behave by observing the behavior of others or by reading or hearing about it. We do not have to actually perform the behaviors we observe; instead, we can note whether those behaviors were rewarded or punished and store that information in mem-

Albert Bandura developed social cognitive theory.

ory. When new situations arise, we can behave according to the expectations we have accumulated on the basis of our observation of models.

Bandura's social-cognitive theory thus goes beyond classical behaviorism. Rather than focusing only on how environment affects behavior, it examines the interactions among environment, behavior, and the individual's cognitions. In addition to considering external influences such as rewards and punishments, it considers internal factors such as expectations. And instead of explaining behavior simply in terms of conditioning, it emphasizes the role of observational learning.

Another prominent social-learning theorist, Walter Mischel, has attempted to incorporate individual differences into social learning theory by introducing the following set of cognitive variables:

1. Competencies: What can you do? Competencies include intellectual abilities, social and physical skills, and other special abilities.
2. Encoding strategies: How do you see it? People differ in the way they selectively attend to information, encode (represent) events, and group the information into meaningful categories. An event that is perceived by one person as threatening may be seen by another as challenging.
3. Expectancies: What will happen? Expectations about the consequences of different behaviors will guide the individual's choice of behavior. If you cheat on an examination and are caught, what do you expect the consequences to be? If you tell your friend what you really think of him or her, what will happen to your relationship? Expectations about our own abilities will also influence behavior: We may anticipate the consequences of a certain behavior but fail to act because we are uncertain of our ability to execute the behavior.
4. Subjective values: What is it worth? Individuals who have similar expectancies may choose to behave differently because they assign different values to the outcomes. Two students may expect a certain behavior to please their professor. However, this outcome is important to one student but not to the other.
5. Self-regulatory systems and plans: How can you achieve it? People differ in the standards and rules they use to regulate their behavior (including self-imposed rewards for success or punishments for failure), as well as in their ability to make realistic plans for reaching a goal. (After Mischel, 1973, 1993)

All of these person variables (sometimes referred to as cognitive social-learning person variables) interact with the conditions of a particular situation to determine what an individual will do in that situation.

KELLY'S PERSONAL CONSTRUCT THEORY

George Kelly (1905–1966) was another of the personality psychologists to first suggest that cognitive processes play a central role in an individual's functioning. Kelly noted that personality psychologists typically characterized an individual on dimensions that they themselves had constructed. He proposed instead that the goal should be to discover **personal constructs,** the dimensions that individuals themselves use to interpret themselves and their social worlds. These dimensions constitute the basic units of analysis in Kelly's personal construct theory (1955).

More generally, Kelly believed that individuals should be viewed as intuitive scientists. Like formal scientists, they observe the world, formulate and test hypotheses about it, and make up theories about it. They also categorize, interpret, label, and judge themselves and their world. And, like scientists, individuals can entertain invalid theories, beliefs that hinder them in their daily lives and lead to biased interpretations of events and persons, including themselves.

Like scientists trying to make predictions about events, people want to understand the world so that they can predict what will happen to them. Kelly argued that each individual uses a unique set of personal constructs in interpreting and predicting events. Those constructs tend to take an either-or form: A new acquaintance is either friendly or unfriendly, intelligent or unintelligent, fun or boring, and so on. But two people meeting the same individual may use different constructs in evaluating that individual—someone who seems friendly and intelligent to one person may seem unfriendly and unintelligent to another. These differences lead to differences in behavior—one person will respond positively to the new acquaintance while an-

According to Kelly, personal constructs take an either-or form. A new acquaintance is either friendly or unfriendly, intelligent or unintelligent, fun or boring.

other may avoid him or her. These differences in behavior produce differences in personality.

Because typical trait tests of personality do not meet Kelly's basic criterion that individuals must be assessed in terms of their personal constructs, he devised his own test for eliciting a person's personal constructs, the Role Construct Repertory Test or "Rep Test." On this test, clients fill in a matrix or grid like the one shown in Figure 13-5. Along the top of the grid is a list of people who are important to the individual. These might be supplied by the assessor or by the client, but they usually include "myself" and sometimes include "my ideal self." On each line of the grid, the assessor circles three of the cells. For example, in the first row of the figure the assessor has circled the cells in the columns labeled "myself," "my mother," and "my best friend." The client is asked to consider these three people and to place an X in the cells of the two who are most similar to each other but different from the third. As shown in the first row, this (male) client considers himself and his mother to be the most similar pair. He is then asked, "In what way are you and your mother alike but different from your best friend?" In this case the client has indicated that he and his mother are both witty. This description is his con-

struct. Next he is asked, "In what way is your friend different from you and your mother?" He has responded that his friend is humorless. This description is his contrast. For this client, then, the dimension witty-humorless is one of the personal constructs he uses to interpret his interpersonal world.

Note that a construct-contrast pair need not constitute logical opposites. For example, this client might have labeled himself and his mother as witty but then labeled his best friend as serious or introverted or prefers-to-listen-to-humor-rather-than-initiate-it. If that is how he construes the two sides of the dimension, then that is what Kelly wanted to know. The Rep Test is designed to assess the individual's constructs, not the psychologist's.

This procedure is repeated with several other triads in the set. By looking at the entire set, the investigator or therapist can explore a number of themes that seem to characterize the individual's interpretation of the world. For example, some clients will reveal through this procedure that they see the entire world in authoritarian terms; dimensions like strong-weak, powerful-powerless, and so forth might appear repeatedly. Or an individual might reveal that she always pairs herself with males on the construct end of dimensions while placing other women on the contrast end.

The Rep Test is a very general procedure and is not restricted to interpretations of other people. For example, an individual may be asked to consider triads of situations or events. (Which two are alike but different from the third? Taking an examination, going out on a blind date, encountering a spider.) The technique has proved valuable both for research on people's constructs and for counseling.

SELF-SCHEMAS

A **schema** is a cognitive structure that helps us perceive, organize, process, and utilize information (Markus, 1999). Through the use of schemas, each individual develops a system for identifying what is important in his or her environment while ignoring everything else. Schemas also provide a structure within which to organize and process information. For example, most people have developed a mother schema. When asked to describe their mother, it is easy for them because the information is organized into a well-defined cognitive structure. It is easier to describe one's mother than to describe a woman one has heard about but has never met.

Schemas are relatively stable over time and therefore result in stable ways of perceiving and utilizing information. They differ from one individual to another, causing people to process information differently and to behave in different ways. They thus can be used to explain differences in personality.

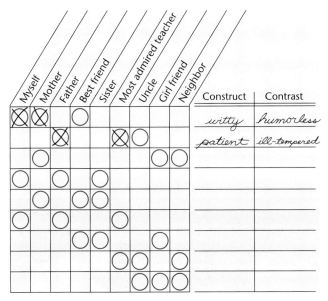

▌ Figure 13-5
The Role Construct Repertory Test
In each row, the individual compares three of the people listed at the top of the grid, placing an X under the two who are most alike. He or she then describes how they are alike by writing in the construct. Finally, the individual describes how the third person is different from the other two by writing in the contrast. This person indicates that he sees himself and his mother as being both witty and different from his best friend, who is seen as humorless. The procedure is repeated for each row in the matrix.

Perhaps the most important schema is the **self-schema**, which consists of "cognitive generalizations about the self, derived from past experience, that organize and guide the processing of self-related information" (Markus, 1977, p. 64). From an early age, we all develop a cognitive representation of who we are. The resulting self-schema is made up of the aspects of our behavior that are most important to us, and it plays a central role in the way we process information and interact with the world around us. For example, two people may both enjoy jogging and literature, but for one person exercise may be an important part of the self-schema, yet the other person's self-schema may place greater emphasis on being well-read. The first person is likely to spend more time jogging than reading, and the reverse is likely to be true of the second person.

The core of the self-schema is basic information, such as the person's name, physical appearance, and relationships with significant people. But more important from the standpoint of individual differences are particularistic features of the self-schema (Markus & Sentis, 1982; Markus & Smith, 1981). For the person whose self-schema includes an emphasis on exercise, for example, exercise is part of "who he or she is" and a part of the daily or weekly routine. For the person who enjoys jogging but does not view it as central, an occasional jog around the park will be sufficient. So, differences in self-schemas produce differences in behavior.

Self-schemas not only guide the perception and processing of information but also provide a framework for organizing and storing it. As with the mother schema mentioned earlier, we would expect people to retrieve information from memory more easily when they have a strong schema for it. This hypothesis was tested in an experiment in which college students were presented with a series of 40 questions on a video screen (Rogers, Kuiper,

Your recreational activities reflect your self-schemas.

& Kirker, 1977). The participants were asked to respond to each question by pressing a yes or no button as quickly as possible. Thirty of the questions could be answered easily without being processed through the self-schema. They asked whether a word was printed in big letters, rhymed with another word, or had the same meaning as another word. The other 10 questions required participants to decide whether a word described them, and the researchers proposed that in these cases the information had to be processed through the self-schema.

The participants were later asked to recall as many of the 40 words as they could. The results showed that when participants answered questions about themselves they were more likely to remember the information later. The researchers concluded that the participants processed this information through their self-schemas. Because information in the self-schema is easy to access, words referring to the self were easier to remember than words processed in other ways. In subsequent studies, when participants were asked whether a word described the experimenter (Kuiper & Rogers, 1979) or a celebrity (Lord, 1980), they did not recall those words as easily as words describing themselves. In sum, it appears that the superior organization and accessibility of information about ourselves makes information that is processed through the self-schema more accessible than information that is processed in other ways (Karylowski, 1990; Klein & Loftus, 1988; Klein, Loftus, & Burton, 1989).

Self-schemas differ considerably across cultures to the extent that some theorists argue that personality is a product of culture (Cross & Markus, 1999). For example, in North America we assume that the self is autonomous and separate from others and from situations and that we have individual choice over our actions and beliefs. In the North American conception of the self, a person's wishes, desires, interests, and abilities make up the self. We have the power and the responsibility to create the self we want to have, rather than allow external influences to shape our self-concepts. In contrast, in some Asian cultures, the self is not an entity separate from others but is thoroughly intertwined with one's obligations and relationships to others. The core issue in the development of the self is not to discover and express one's own wishes, desires, interests, and abilities, but to determine how one is meant to fit in with the social group and to shape oneself to best serve the social group.

AN EVALUATION OF THE COGNITIVE APPROACH

The cognitive approach has some strengths as well as some weaknesses. One positive aspect of the approach is that it is based on empirical research. As illustrated by the preceding descriptions of experiments, many cognitive structures have been subjected to extensive study in controlled laboratory experiments. Another strength of cognitive theory is that it goes beyond the trait approach in explaining personality characteristics. Rather than simply identifying traits, cognitive theorists use cognitive structures to explain individual differences in behavior.

On the other hand, a frequent criticism of the cognitive approach is that it employs vague concepts. It is difficult to state specifically what a personal construct is or to be sure when a schema is being used, and it is not entirely clear how a personal construct differs from a schema or how any of these cognitive structures relate to memory and other aspects of information processing. Moreover, behaviorists might ask whether it is really necessary to use these concepts. Perhaps personality can be explained just as well without referring to cognitions.

◆ Interim Summary

- The cognitive approach to personality is based on the idea that differences in personality stem from differences in the way individuals mentally represent information.

- Albert Bandura developed social cognitive theory, which holds that internal cognitive processes combine with environmental pressures to influence behavior, and that cognitive processes and environment have reciprocal effects on each other.

- Walter Mischel has identified a number of cognitive person variables that affect people's reactions to the environment and behaviors in the environment.

- George Kelly's personal construct theory focuses on the concepts that individuals use to interpret themselves and their social world.

- Much research has focused on the self-schema, which consists of the aspects of a person's behavior that are most important to that person. Experiments have shown that people perceive information more readily and recall it better when it is relevant to their self-schemas.

◆ Critical Thinking Questions

1. Some theorists argue that our most important schemas for ourselves and others are often nonconscious—we don't even realize we hold them and might deny we hold them if asked explicitly. Can you think of some methods by which you might be able to tap into a person's nonconscious schemas?

2. What do you think are some of the most important developmental processes or events that contribute to the type of self-schema an individual develops?

THE HUMANISTIC APPROACH

During the first half of the 20th century, the psychoanalytic and behaviorist approaches were dominant in psychology. In 1962, however, a group of psychologists founded the Association of Humanistic Psychology. They saw humanistic psychology as a "third force," an alternative to the other two approaches. To define its mission, the association adopted four principles:

1. The experiencing person is of primary interest. Humans are not simply objects of study. They must be described and understood in terms of their own subjective views of the world, their perceptions of self, and their feelings of self-worth. The central question each person must face is "Who am I?" In order to learn how the individual attempts to answer this question, the psychologist must become a partner with that person.
2. Human choice, creativity, and self-actualization are the preferred topics of investigation. People are not motivated only by basic drives like sex or aggression or physiological needs like hunger and thirst. They feel a need to develop their potentials and capabilities. Growth and self-actualization should be the criteria of psychological health, not merely ego control or adjustment to the environment.
3. Meaningfulness must precede objectivity in the selection of research problems. Humanistic psychologists argue that we should study important human and social problems, even if that sometimes means adopting less rigorous methods. And while psychologists should strive to be objective in collecting and interpreting observations, their choice of research topics can and should be guided by values. In this sense, research is not value-free.
4. Ultimate value is placed on the dignity of the person. People are basically good. The objective of psychology is to understand, not to predict or control people.

Psychologists who share these values come from diverse theoretical backgrounds. For example, the trait theorist Gordon Allport was also a humanistic psychologist, and we have already pointed out that several psychoanalysts, such as Carl Jung, Alfred Adler, and Erik Erikson, held humanistic views of motivation that diverged from Freud's views. But it is Carl Rogers and Abraham Maslow whose theoretical views lie at the center of the humanistic movement.

CARL ROGERS

Like Freud, Carl Rogers (1902–1987) based his theory on work with patients or clients in a clinic (Rogers, 1951, 1959, 1963, 1970). Rogers was impressed with

Carl Rogers believed that individuals have an innate tendency to move toward growth, maturity, and positive change. He referred to this as the *actualizing tendency*.

what he saw as the individual's innate tendency to move toward growth, maturity, and positive change. He came to believe that the basic force motivating the human organism is the **actualizing tendency**—a tendency toward fulfillment or actualization of all the capacities of the organization. A growing organism seeks to fulfill its potential within the limits of its heredity. A person may not always clearly perceive which actions lead to growth and which do not. But once the course is clear, the individual chooses to grow. Rogers did not deny that there are other needs, some of them biological, but he saw them as subservient to the organism's motivation to enhance itself.

Rogers's belief in the primacy of actualization forms the basis of his nondirective or client-centered therapy. This method of psychotherapy assumes that every individual has the motivation and ability to change and that the individual is best qualified to decide the direction such change should take. The therapist's role is to act as a sounding board while the client explores and analyzes his or her problems. This approach differs from psychoanalytic therapy, during which the therapist analyzes the patient's history to determine the problem and devise a course of remedial action. (See Chapter 16 for a discussion of various approaches to psychotherapy.)

THE SELF The central concept in Rogers's theory of personality is the **self**, or self-concept (Rogers uses the terms interchangeably). The self (or real self) consists of all the ideas, perceptions, and values that characterize "I" or "me"; it includes the awareness of "what I am" and "what I can do." This perceived self, in turn, influences both the person's perception of the world and his or her behavior. For example, a woman who perceives herself as strong and competent perceives and acts upon the world quite differently than a woman who considers herself weak and ineffectual. The self-concept does not necessarily reflect reality: A person may be highly successful and respected but still view himself or herself as a failure.

According to Rogers, the individual evaluates every experience in relation to his or her self-concept. People want to behave in ways that are consistent with their self-image, and experiences and feelings that are not consistent are threatening and may be denied entry into consciousness. This is essentially Freud's concept of repression, although Rogers felt that such repression is neither necessary nor permanent. (Freud would say that repression is inevitable and that some aspects of the individual's experiences always remain unconscious.)

The more areas of experience a person denies because they are inconsistent with his or her self-concept, the wider the gap between the self and reality and the greater the potential for maladjustment. Individuals whose self-concepts do not match their feelings and experiences must defend themselves against the truth because the truth will result in anxiety. If the gap becomes too wide, the person's defenses may break down, resulting in severe anxiety or other forms of emotional disturbance. A well-adjusted person, in contrast, has a self-concept that is consistent with his or her thoughts, experiences, and behaviors; the self is not rigid but flexible, and it can change as it assimilates new experiences and ideas.

Rogers also proposed that each of us has an ideal self, our conception of the kind of person we would like to be. The closer the ideal self is to the real self, the more fulfilled and happy the individual becomes. A large discrepancy between the ideal self and the real self results in an unhappy, dissatisfied person.

Thus, two kinds of inconsistency can develop: between the self and the experiences of reality and between the real self and the ideal self. Rogers proposed some hypotheses about how these inconsistencies may develop. In particular, Rogers believed that people are likely to function more effectively if they are brought up with **unconditional positive regard**—being given the sense that they are valued by parents and others even when their feelings, attitudes, and behaviors are less than ideal. If parents offer only conditional positive regard—valuing the child only when he or she behaves, thinks, or feels correctly—the child's self-concept is likely to be distorted. For example, feelings of competition and hostility toward a younger sibling are natural, but parents disapprove of hitting a baby brother or sister and usually punish such actions. Children must somehow integrate this experience into their self-concept. They may decide that they are bad and feel ashamed. They may decide that their parents do not like them and feel rejected. Or they may deny their feelings and decide they do not want to hit the baby. Each of these attitudes distorts the truth. The third alternative is the easiest for children to accept, but in so doing they deny their real feelings, which then become unconscious. The more people are forced to deny their own feelings and accept the values of others, the more uncomfortable they will feel about themselves. Rogers suggested that the best approach is for the parents to recognize the child's feelings as valid while explaining the reasons that hitting is not acceptable.

MEASURING REAL-IDEAL SELF-CONGRUENCE Earlier, we described a method of assessment called the *Q-sort*, in which a rater or sorter is given a set of cards, each containing a personality statement (for example, "Is cheerful"), and asked to describe an individual's personality by sorting the cards into piles. The rater places statements that are least descriptive of the individual in a pile on the left and those that are most descriptive in a pile on the right. The other statements are distributed in the intermediate piles, thereby assigning each Q item a score corresponding to the pile in which it is placed. Researchers can compare two Q-sorts by computing a correlation between their item scores, thereby assessing the degree to which the two sorts are similar.

Rogers pioneered the use of the Q-sort as a way of examining the self-concept. His Q set contains statements like "I am satisfied with myself," "I have a warm emotional relationship with others," and "I don't trust my emotions." In Rogers's procedure, individuals first sort themselves as they actually are—their real self—and then sort themselves as they would like to be—their ideal self. The correlation between the two sorts reveals the degree of incongruence between the real and ideal selves. A low or negative correlation cor-

responds to a large discrepancy, implying feelings of low self-esteem and lack of worth.

By repeating this procedure several times during the course of therapy, Rogers could assess the effectiveness of therapy. In one study, correlations between self and ideal Q-sorts of individuals seeking therapy averaged $-.01$ before therapy but increased to $+.34$ after therapy. Correlations for a matched control group that did not receive therapy did not change (Butler & Haigh, 1954). In other words, the therapy had significantly reduced these individuals' perception of the discrepancy between their real selves and their ideal selves. Note that this could occur in two ways: An individual could change his or her concept of the real self so that it was closer to the ideal self or change his or her concept of the ideal self so that it was more realistic. Therapy can produce both kinds of changes.

More recently, psychologist Tory Higgins (1987) has shown that self-discrepancies such as those described by Rogers are associated with serious depression and anxiety.

ABRAHAM MASLOW

The psychology of Abraham Maslow (1908–1970) overlaps with that of Carl Rogers in many ways. Maslow was first attracted to behaviorism and carried out studies of primate sexuality and dominance. He was already moving away from behaviorism when his first child was born, after which he remarked that anyone who observes a baby cannot be a behaviorist. He was influenced by psychoanalysis but eventually became critical of its theory of motivation and developed his own theory. Specifically, he proposed that there is a **hierarchy of needs,** ascending from the basic biological needs to the more complex psychological motivations that become important only after the basic needs have been satisfied (see Figure 13-6). The needs at one level must be at least partially satisfied before those at the

▌ Figure 13-6
Maslow's Hierarchy of Needs
Needs that are low in the hierarchy must be at least partially satisfied before needs that are higher in the hierarchy become important sources of motivation. (After Abraham H. Maslow, "Hierarchy of Needs," from *Motivation and Personality*. Copyright © 1954 by Harper and Row Publishers, Inc. Reprinted by permission of Pearson Education, Inc., Upper Saddle River, NJ.)

Self-actualization needs: to find self-fulfillment and realize one's potential

Aesthetic needs: symmetry, order, and beauty

Cognitive needs: to know, understand, and explore

Esteem needs: to achieve, be competent, and gain approval and recognition

Belongingness and love needs: to affiliate with others, be accepted, and belong

Safety needs: to feel secure and safe, out of danger

Physiological needs: hunger, thirst, and so forth

next level become important motivators of action. When food and safety are difficult to obtain, efforts to satisfy those needs will dominate a person's actions, and higher motives will have little significance. Only when basic needs can be satisfied easily will the individual have the time and energy to devote to aesthetic and intellectual interests. Artistic and scientific endeavors do not flourish in societies in which people must struggle for food, shelter, and safety. The highest motive—self-actualization—can be fulfilled only after all other needs have been satisfied.

Maslow decided to study self-actualizers—men and women who had made extraordinary use of their potential. He began by studying the lives of eminent historical figures such as Spinoza, Thomas Jefferson, Abraham Lincoln, Jane Addams, Albert Einstein, and Eleanor Roosevelt. In this way he was able to create a composite picture of a self-actualizer. The distinguishing characteristics of such individuals are listed in Table 13-2, along with some of the behaviors that Maslow believed could lead to self-actualization.

Maslow then extended his study to a population of college students. Selecting students who fit his definition of self-actualizers, he found this group to be in the healthiest 1% of the population. These students showed no signs of maladjustment and were making effective use of their talents and capabilities (Maslow, 1970).

Many people experience what Maslow called **peak experiences**: *transient moments of self-actualization.* A peak experience is characterized by happiness and fulfillment—a temporary, nonstriving, non-self-centered state of goal attainment. Peak experiences may occur in different intensities and in various contexts, such as creative activities, appreciation of nature, intimate relationships, aesthetic perceptions, or athletic participation. After asking a large number of college students to describe any experience that came close to being a peak experience, Maslow attempted to summarize their responses. They spoke of wholeness, perfection, aliveness, uniqueness, effortlessness, self-sufficiency, and the values of beauty, goodness, and truth.

A HUMANISTIC PORTRAIT OF HUMAN NATURE

As a matter of principle, humanistic psychologists have been quite explicit about the principles underlying their approach to human personality. The four principles set forth by the Association of Humanistic Psychology, which we summarized earlier, draw sharp contrasts between the humanistic portrait of human personality and the portraits drawn by the psychoanalytic and behaviorist approaches.

Most humanistic psychologists do not dispute the claim that biological and environmental variables can influence behavior, but they emphasize the individual's own

● **Table 13-2**
Self-Actualization

Listed here are the personal qualities that Maslow found to be characteristic of self-actualizers and the behaviors he considered important to the development of self-actualization. *(A. H. Maslow (1967), "Self-actualization and beyond." In* Challenges of Humanistic Psychology, *J. F. T. Bugenthal (ed.). Copyright © 1967 by Abraham H. Maslow. Used with permission of McGraw-Hill Publishers.)*

Characteristics of Self-Actualizers

Perceive reality efficiently and can tolerate uncertainty

Accept themselves and others for what they are

Spontaneous in thought and behavior

Problem-centered rather than self-centered

Have a good sense of humor

Highly creative

Resistant to enculturation, although not purposely unconventional

Concerned for the welfare of humanity

Capable of deep appreciation of the basic experiences of life

Establish deep, satisfying interpersonal relationships with a few, rather than many, people

Able to look at life from an objective viewpoint

Behaviors Leading to Self-Actualization

Experience life as a child does, with full absorption and concentration

Try something new rather than sticking to secure and safe ways

Listen to your own feelings in evaluating experiences rather than to the voice of tradition or authority or the majority

Be honest; avoid pretenses or "game playing"

Be prepared to be unpopular if your views do not coincide with those of most people

Assume responsibility

Work hard at whatever you decide to do

Try to identify your defenses and have the courage to give them up

role in defining and creating his or her destiny, and they downplay the determinism that is characteristic of the other approaches. In their view, individuals are basically good, striving for growth and self-actualization. They are also modifiable and active. Humanistic psychologists set a particularly high criterion for psychological health. Mere ego control or adaptation to the environment is not enough. Only an individual who is growing toward self-actualization can be said to be psychologically healthy. In other words, psychological health is a process, not an end state.

Such assumptions have political implications. From the perspective of humanistic psychology, anything that retards the fulfillment of individual potential—that prevents any human being from becoming all he or she can be—should be challenged. For example, if women in the 1950s were happy and well adjusted to traditional sex roles, the criterion of psychological health defined by behaviorism was satisfied. But from the humanistic perspective, consigning all women to the same role is undesirable—no matter how appropriate that role might be for some women—because it prevents many from reaching their maximum potential. It is no accident that the rhetoric of liberation movements—such as women's liberation and gay liberation—echoes the language of humanistic psychology.

Albert Einstein and Eleanor Roosevelt were among the individuals Maslow identified as self-actualizers.

AN EVALUATION OF THE HUMANISTIC APPROACH

By focusing on the individual's unique perception and interpretation of events, the humanistic approach brings individual experience back into the study of personality. More than other theories we have discussed, the theories of Rogers and Maslow concentrate on the whole, healthy person and take a positive, optimistic view of human personality. Humanistic psychologists emphasize that they study important problems, even if they do not always have rigorous methods for investigating them. They have a point—investigating trivial problems just because one has a convenient method for doing so does little to advance the science of psychology. Moreover, humanistic psychologists have succeeded in devising new methods for assessing self-concepts and conducting studies that treat the individual as an equal partner in the research enterprise. Nevertheless, critics question the quality of the evidence in support of the humanists' claims. For example, to what extent are the characteristics of self-actualizers a consequence of a psychological process called *self-actualization* and to what extent are they merely reflections of the particular value systems held by Rogers and Maslow? Where, they ask, is the evidence for Maslow's hierarchy of needs?

Humanistic psychologists are also criticized for building their theories solely on observations of relatively healthy people. Their theories are best suited to well-functioning people whose basic needs have been met, freeing them to concern themselves with higher needs. The applicability of these theories to malfunctioning or disadvantaged individuals is less apparent.

Finally, some have criticized the values espoused by the humanistic theorists. Many observers believe that Americans are already obsessed with the individual and show little concern for the welfare of the larger society. A psychology that raises individual self-fulfillment and actualization to the top of the value hierarchy may provide a "sanction for selfishness" (Wallach & Wallach, 1983). Although Maslow lists concern for the welfare of humanity among the characteristics of self-actualizers (see Table 13-2) and some of the self-actualizers identified by Maslow—such as Eleanor Roosevelt and Albert Einstein—clearly possessed this characteristic, it is not included in the hierarchy of needs.

◆ Interim Summary

- The humanistic approach is concerned with the individual's subjective experience. Humanistic psychology was founded as an alternative to psychoanalytic and behaviorist approaches.

- Carl Rogers argued that the basic force motivating the human organism is the actualizing tendency—a tendency toward fulfillment or actualization of all the capacities of the self. When the needs of the self are denied, severe anxiety can result. Children come to develop an actualized self through the experience of unconditional positive regard from their caregivers.

- Abraham Maslow proposed that there is a hierarchy of needs, ascending from the basic biological needs to the more complex psychological motivations that become important only after the basic needs have been satisfied. The needs at one level must be at least partially satisfied before those at the next level become important motivators of action.

1. Several studies suggest that people in Asian cultures are not as concerned with individualism as Americans are and instead are more concerned with the collective welfare of their family and community. To what extent do you think this refutes humanistic perspectives on personality?

2. Do you think it's always a good idea to give a child unconditional positive regard? Why or why not?

THE EVOLUTIONARY APPROACH

One of the newest and most controversial theories in personality is really an application of a very old theory. Evolutionary theory, as proposed by Darwin (1859), has played an important role in biology for well over a century. Darwin ventured some ideas about the evolutionary roots of human behavior, but the modern field of evolutionary psychology began with the work of Wilson (1975) on "sociobiology." The basic premise of sociobiology and, later, **evolutionary psychology** is that behaviors that increased the organism's chances of surviving and leaving descendants would be selected for over evolutionary history and thus would become aspects of humans' personalities.

Not surprisingly, a good deal of the research on the application of evolutionary psychology to personality has focused on mate selection. Mating involves competition—among heterosexuals, males compete with males and females compete with females. What's being competed for differs between the sexes, however, because males and females have different roles in reproduction (Trivers, 1972). Because females carry their offspring for 9 months and then nurse and care for them after birth, they have a greater investment in each offspring and can produce fewer offspring in their lifetimes than men can. This puts a premium for the female on the quality of the genetic contribution of the males with whom she reproduces, as well as on signs of his ability and willingness to help care for his offspring. In contrast, the optimal reproductive strategy for males is to reproduce as often as possible, and they will primarily be looking for females who are available and fertile.

David Buss, Douglas Kenrick, and other evolutionary psychologists have investigated personality differences between males and females that they hypothesize are the result of these differences in reproductive strategies (Buss, 1999; Kenrick, 2001; Schmitt & Buss, 1996). They reasoned that women who are interested in mating should emphasize their youth and beauty, because these are signs of their fertility, but should be choosier than men about

what partners they mate with. In contrast, men who are interested in mating should emphasize their ability to support their offspring and should be less choosy than women about their mating partners. A variety of findings have supported these hypotheses. When asked what they do to make themselves attractive to the opposite sex, women report enhancing their beauty through makeup, jewelry, clothing, and hairstyles. Women also report playing hard to get. Men report bragging about their accomplishments and earning potential, displaying expensive possessions, and flexing their muscles (Buss, 1988). Other studies have found that men are more interested in casual sex than women are (Buss & Schmitt, 1993) and are less selective in their criteria for one-night stands (Kenrick, Broth, Trost, & Sadalla, 1993).

One proxy for fertility is youth, and one proxy for economic resources is older age. Evolutionary theory suggests that men will be interested in mating with younger women, whereas women will be interested in mating with older men. These sex differences in mating preferences are have been found across 37 cultures (Buss, 1989). Kenrick and Keefe (1992) even found evidence for these mating preferences in singles ads placed in newspapers. In the ads, the older a man was, the more he expressed a preference for a younger woman. Women tended to express a preference for older men, regardless of the women's age.

Some theorists have extended evolutionary predictions far beyond mating preferences, arguing that men

Evolutionary theory provides an explanation for why older men often seek women who are much younger than they are.

are more individualistic, domineering, and oriented toward problem solving than women because these personality characteristics increased males' ability to reproduce often over history and thus were selected for (Gray, 1992; Tannen, 1990). In contrast, women are more inclusive, sharing, and communal because these personality characteristics increased the chances of survival of their offspring and thus were selected for.

In some of their more controversial work, evolutionary theorists have argued that because of sex differences in mating strategies there should be sex differences in both sexual infidelity and the sources of jealousy. Whereas men's desire to mate frequently makes them more prone to sexual infidelity than women, their concern that they are not investing their resources in offspring who are not their own makes them more concerned about sexual infidelity of their female partners. This suggests that men will be more likely than women to cheat on their female partners and more jealous than women if their spouse or partner cheats on them. Several studies have found support for these hypotheses (Buss, Larsen, Westen, & Semmelroth, 1992).

When competition among males for available females becomes fierce, it can lead to violence, particularly among males who have fewer resources to compete with, such as unemployed males. Wilson and Daly (1985; Daly & Wilson, 1990) found that homicides between nonrelatives are most likely to be among young males, whom they argued were fighting over "face" and status. They further found that homicides within families are most often husbands killing wives and argued that these killings represent the male's attempt at controlling the fidelity of the female partner.

AN EVOLUTIONARY PORTRAIT OF HUMAN NATURE

The evolutionary portrait of human nature would appear to be a rather grim one. We are this way because it has been adaptive for the species to develop in this manner, and everything about our personalities and social behavior is coded in our genes. This would seem to leave little room for positive change.

Evolutionary theorists are the first to emphasize, however, that evolution is all about change—when the environment changes, only organisms that can adapt to that change will survive and reproduce. This change just happens more slowly than we might like it to.

AN EVALUATION OF THE EVOLUTIONARY APPROACH

You should not be surprised that the evolutionary approach has taken a great deal of heat. There are important social and political implications of the arguments and findings of these theorists. Some critics argue that evolutionary psychology simply provides a thinly veiled justification for the unfair social conditions and prejudices in today's world. If women are subordinate to men in economic and political power, it's because this was evolutionarily adaptive for the species. If men beat their wives and have extramarital affairs, they can't help it; it's in their genes. If some ethnic groups have more power and wealth in society, it's because their behaviors have been selected for over evolutionary history, and their genes are superior.

Evolutionary theorists have also taken heat from the scientific community. The early arguments of sociobiologists were highly speculative and not based on hard data. Some critics argued that their hypotheses were unfalsifiable or untestable. In the last decade, there has been an upsurge of empirical research attempting to rigorously test evolutionary theories of human behavior. Some theorists have steered away from controversial topics such as sex differences in personality or abilities to investigate the role of evolution in shaping the cognitive structures of the brain (Cosmides, 1989; Cosmides & Tooby, 1989).

Still, the question remains of whether an evolutionary explanation for a given finding—whether a human sex difference or some behavior or structure that all humans share—is necessary. It is easy to develop alternative explanations for most of the findings that evolutionary theorists tend to attribute to reproductive strategies (Eagly & Wood, 1999). For example, sex differences in personality characteristics could be due to sex differences in body size and strength (for instance, men are more dominant than women because their size allows them to be, whereas women are friendlier than men because they are trying not to get beaten up by men). The causes of behavior focused on by most alternative explanations are more proximal than evolutionary causes—the explanations don't rely on claims about what has been true for millions of years and make claims only about what has been true in the relatively recent past. For many findings touted by evolutionary theorists as consistent with evolutionary history, it is difficult to conceive of experiments that could help us decide between an evolutionary explanation and an alternative explanation that focuses on more proximal causes.

Evolutionary theory is attractive in its power to explain a wide range of behaviors, however. Not since the introduction of behaviorism has psychology had a new explanatory framework that might account for most aspects of human behavior. Many evolutionary theorists are vigorously pursuing more sophisticated and persuasive empirical tests of their hypotheses. Evolutionary psychology will clearly have an important influence on personality theories in years to come.

◆ Interim Summary

- Evolutionary psychology attempts to explain human behavior and personality in terms of the adaptiveness of certain characteristics for survival and reproductive success over human history.

- Evolutionary theory is consistent with some observed sex differences in mate preferences.

- It is a controversial theory, however, both for its social implications and for the difficulty of refuting arguments derived from this theory.

◆ Critical Thinking Questions

1. To what extent do you think the political implications of a psychological theory should be of concern to its proponents?

2. Do you think evolutionary theory can predict anything about how human behavior will change in the next few centuries?

THE GENETICS OF PERSONALITY

We end with another controversial and relatively recent approach to understanding the origins of personality—the argument that personality traits are largely determined by the genes an individual was born with. Some of the best evidence that genes play a role in personality comes from the Minnesota Study of Twins Reared Apart, which we described in Chapter 12 and highlighted at the beginning of this chapter. Recall from Chapter 12 that the participants in this study were assessed on a number of ability and personality measures. In addition, they participated in lengthy interviews during which they were asked questions about such topics as childhood experiences, fears, hobbies, musical tastes, social attitudes, and sexual interests. A number of startling similarities were found. The twins with the most dramatically different backgrounds are Oskar Stohr and Jack Yufe, described at the beginning of the chapter. Another pair of twins with fairly different backgrounds are both British homemakers. They were separated during World War II and raised by families that differed in socioeconomic status. Both twins, who had never met before, arrived for their interviews wearing seven rings on their fingers.

These studies reveal that twins reared apart are just as similar to each other across a wide range of personality characteristics as twins reared together, permitting us to conclude with greater confidence that identical twins are more similar to each other on personality characteristics than fraternal twins because they are more similar genetically (Bouchard et al., 1990; Lykken, 1982; Tellegen et al., 1988).

For the most part, the correlations found in the Minnesota studies are in accord with results from many other twin studies. In general, the highest levels of heritability are found in measures of abilities and intelligence (60%–70%), the next highest levels are typically found in measures of personality (about 50%); and the lowest levels are found for religious and political beliefs and vocational interests (30%–40%).

Similar studies have examined the heritability of personality traits. For example, one study found that traits such as shyness and the tendency to become easily upset have heritabilities of between 30% and 50% (Bouchard et al., 1990; Newman, Tellegen, & Bouchard, 1998).

INTERACTIONS BETWEEN PERSONALITY AND ENVIRONMENT

GENOTYPE-ENVIRONMENT CORRELATION In shaping an individual's personality, genetic and environmental influences are intertwined from the moment of birth (McGuffin, Riley, & Plomin, 2001). First, it may take certain environments to trigger the effects of specific genes (Gottlieb, 2000). For example, a child born with a genetic tendency toward alcoholism may never become alcoholic if never exposed to alcohol. Second, parents give their biological offspring both their genes and a home environment, and both are functions of the parents' own genes. As a result, there is a built-in correlation between the child's inherited characteristics (genotype) and the environment in which he or she is raised. For example, because general intelligence is partially heritable, parents with high intelligence are likely to have children with high intelligence. But parents with high intelligence are also likely to provide an intellectually stimulating environment for their children—both through their interactions with them and through books, music lessons, trips to museums, and other intellectual experiences. Because the child's genotype and environment are positively correlated in this way, he or she will get a double dose of intellectual advantage. Similarly, children born to parents with low intelligence are likely to encounter a home environment that exacerbates whatever intellectual disadvantage they may have inherited directly.

Third, some parents may deliberately construct an environment that is negatively correlated with the child's genotype. For example, introverted parents may encourage participation in social activities to counteract the child's likely introversion: "We make an effort to have people over because we don't want Chris to grow up to be as shy as we are." Parents of a very active child may try to provide interesting quiet activities. But whether the correlation is positive or negative, the point is that

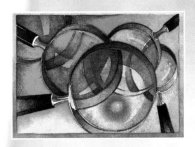

CUTTING-EDGE RESEARCH
Can You Change Your Personality With a Pill?

One way that genetics may influence personality is by influencing the neurochemistry of the brain and body. The functioning of the nervous system is affected by the amounts of various neurotransmitters available at any given time, which can vary quite widely. People also seem to differ in their average levels of those transmitters, and these differences seem to be related to particular personality traits.

Dopamine plays a role in the control of body movements and is involved in brain systems that cause the person to approach attractive objects and people. It therefore is thought to affect sociability and general activity level. Some researchers suggest that dopamine is related to extraversion and impulsivity (Depue & Collins, 1999).

Another important neurotransmitter is serotonin, which is also involved in impulsivity, and in moods such as anxiety and depression. The popular antidepressant drug Prozac is a selective serotonin reuptake inhibitor, and its effect is to raise serotonin levels. According to Peter Kramer, author of *Listening to Prozac,* the drug can actually give people new personalities. It can prevent a person from worrying needlessly and overreacting to minor stresses, thereby giving them a more cheerful outlook on life. People who have taken Prozac often report that they feel like "better people" who get more work done and are more attractive to members of the opposite sex.

Is it true that we can change our personalities by taking a pill such as Prozac? A group of scientists administered a Prozac-like drug called Paxil (paroxetine) for 4 weeks to 26 healthy volunteers who were free of depression. They chose Paxil because it is a relatively potent and specific inhibitor of serotonin reuptake compared with some of the other drugs in this category. They also administered a placebo to another group of healthy volunteers for 4 weeks. Neither the volunteers nor the researchers knew which type of pill an individual volunteer was taking. Personality and social behaviors were assessed in the volunteers 1 week and 4 weeks into the study by having them complete questionnaires and work together with other people on a puzzle task while being observed.

The volunteers who took Paxil became less irritable and hostile toward others and were more likely to engage in positive social behavior in the puzzle task than the volunteers who took the placebo. In addition, the higher the level of Paxil evident in the blood of the volunteers who took the drug, the more their irritability and hostility declined and the more their positive social behavior increased over the 4 weeks (Knutson et al., 1998).

These results seem to suggest that Paxil truly did change the personalities of the health volunteers. It seemed to do so, however, largely by changing their moods. The volunteers who took Paxil showed a significant reduction in negative mood, which fully accounted for the changes in their personalities and social behaviors. This suggests that Paxil may not have had a direct effect on personality but an indirect effect by relieving any negative mood the volunteers may have been experiencing.

Such an interpretation is fully in line with theorists who argue that a fundamental aspect of personality is mood or temperament, which influences the person's willingness to approach new challenges or to flee from them (Cloninger, Svrakic, & Przybeck, 1993; Gray, 1994). According to these theories, all personality traits derive from the individual's basic temperament, how the environment responds to that temperament (for example, did your parents punish you for being anxious or support you in overcoming anxiety?), and how your temperament leads you to make important choices in your life.

Research on the biological causes of personality is still developing. In the meantime, there are social implications to the findings summarized here: Do we want, as a society, to have people changing their personalities with pills?

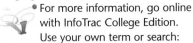 For more information, go online with InfoTrac College Edition. Use your own term or search:

- Prozac and personality
- Dopamine and personality

---

the child's genotype and environment are not simply independent sources of influence that add together to shape the child's personality. Finally, in addition to being correlated with the environment, a child's genotype shapes the environment in certain ways (Bouchard et al., 1990; Plomin, DeFries, & Loehlin, 1977; Scarr, 1996). In particular, the environment becomes a function of the child's personality through three forms of interaction: reactive, evocative, and proactive.

REACTIVE INTERACTION Different individuals who are exposed to the same environment interpret it, experience it, and react to it differently—a process known as reactive interaction. An anxious, sensitive child will experience and react to harsh parents differently than will a calm, resilient child, and the sharp tone of voice that provokes the sensitive child to tears might pass unnoticed by his sister. An extraverted child will attend to people and events around her, but her introverted brother will ignore them. A brighter child will get more out of being read to than a less bright child. In other words, each child's personality extracts a subjective psychological environment from the objective surroundings, and it is that subjective environment that shapes personality development. Even if parents provided exactly the same environment for all their children—which they

Outgoing children evoke different behavior from adults than shy children.

usually do not—it will not be psychologically equivalent for all of them. Reactive interaction occurs throughout life. One person will interpret a hurtful act as the product of deliberate hostility and react to it quite differently than a person who interprets the same act as the result of unintended insensitivity.

EVOCATIVE INTERACTION Every individual's personality evokes distinctive responses from others, which has been referred to as **evocative interaction.** An infant who squirms and fusses when picked up will evoke less nurturance from a parent than one who likes to be cuddled. Docile children will evoke a less controlling style of child rearing from parents than will aggressive children. For this reason, we cannot simply assume that an observed correlation between the child-rearing practices of a child's parents and his or her personality reflects a simple cause-and-effect sequence. Instead, the child's personality can shape the parents' child-rearing style, which, in turn, further shapes the child's personality. Evocative interaction also occurs throughout life: Gracious people evoke gracious environments; hostile people evoke hostile environments.

PROACTIVE INTERACTION As children grow older, they can move beyond the environments provided by their parents and begin to select and construct environments of their own. These environments, in turn, further shape their personalities. This process is referred to as **proactive interaction.** A sociable child will choose to go to the movies with friends rather than stay home alone and watch television because her sociable personality prompts her to select an environment that reinforces her sociability. And what she cannot select she will construct: If nobody invites her to the movies, she will organize the event

herself. As the term implies, proactive interaction is a process through which individuals become active agents in the development of their own personalities.

The relative importance of these three kinds of personality-environment interactions shifts over the course of development (Scarr, 1996; Scarr & McCartney, 1983). The built-in correlation between a child's genotype and his or her environment is strongest when the child is young and confined almost exclusively to the home environment. As the child grows older and begins to select and construct his or her own environment, this initial correlation decreases and the influence of proactive interaction increases. As we have noted, reactive and evocative interactions remain important throughout life.

SOME UNSOLVED PUZZLES Studies of twins have produced a number of puzzling patterns that still are not completely understood. For example, the estimate of heritability for IQ is higher when it is based on identical twin pairs reared apart than it is when based on a comparison of identical and fraternal twins pairs reared together. Moreover, the striking similarities of identical twins do not seem to diminish across time or separate rearing environments. In contrast, the similarities of fraternal twins (and nontwin siblings) diminish from childhood through adolescence, even when they are reared together. Instead, the longer they live together in the same home, the less similar they become (Scarr, 1996; Scarr & McCartney, 1983).

Some of these patterns would emerge if the genes themselves interact so that inheriting all one's genes in common (as identical twins do) is more than twice as effective as inheriting only half one's genes in common (as fraternal twins and nontwin siblings do). This could come about if a trait depends on a particular combination of genes. Consider, for example, the trait of having blue eyes (which we will oversimplify a bit to make the point). Suppose that two parents each have a blue-eye gene and a brown-eye gene. For one of their children to get blue eyes, the child must inherit a blue gene from the father and a blue gene from the mother; the three other combinations (brown-brown, brown-blue, blue-brown) will give the child brown eyes. In other words, any child of theirs has a one-in-four chance of getting blue eyes. But because identical twins inherit identical genes from their parents, they will also inherit the same combination of genes. If one gets blue eyes, so will the other. In contrast, if a fraternal twin inherits a blue gene from both parents, the chances that the other twin will also do so is still only one out of four and not one out of two. So, in this example, inheriting all one's genes in common is more than twice as effective as inheriting only half one's genes in common. There is evidence for this kind of gene-gene interaction for some personality traits, especially extraversion (Lykken, McGue, Tellegen,

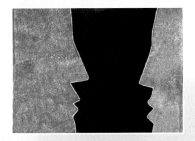

Is Freud's Influence on Psychology Still Alive?

FREUD'S INFLUENCE ON PSYCHOLOGY IS ALIVE AND VIBRANT

Joel Weinberger, Adelphi University

Is Freud still alive? Of course Freud is dead. He died on September 23, 1939. No one asks whether Isaac Newton or William James is dead. For some odd reason this is reserved for Freud. If the question is whether psychoanalysis, the branch of psychology he founded, is dead, the answer is clearly no. Psychoanalysis survived Freud and thrives today. The American Psychological Association's division of psychoanalysis is the second largest division in the association. There now exist several schools of psychoanalysis, some of which Freud would probably not recognize. That is just what you would expect from a discipline whose founder is now 60 years dead.

Are Freud's ideas dead? They certainly are not. They have entered our common vernacular. They have entered and forever changed our culture. Think of the terms of *id, ego, superego, Freudian slip,* and so on. There are psychoanalytic writers, historians, psychiatrists, and of course, psychologists. The real question, I suppose, is whether Freud's ideas are still *valid.* The answer is that some are and some are not. A surprising number remain relevant, even central, to modern psychology. So I suppose the charge is to state which of his ideas remain valid. And that is what I will address.

Let's look at some of Freud's central ideas and see how they stack up with today's psychology. Freud said that all human motives could be traced back to biological sources, specifically to sex and aggression. There is a branch of psychol-

ogy now termed evolutionary psychology (Buss, 1994); there is also sociobiology (Wilson, 1975) and ethology (Hinde, 1982). All champion the importance of biological factors in our behavior. And all have data to back up their claims. This aspect of Freud's thinking is certainly not dead. As for the importance of sex and aggression? Just look at the best selling books, hit movies, and TV shows around you. What characterizes virtually all of them? Sex and violence. Hollywood and book publishers seem all to be Freudians, and so are the people who sample their wares.

Another idea of Freud's that was very controversial in his time was his notion that children have sexual feelings. Now that is simply commonplace knowledge.

Psychoanalysts have long held that one of the major factors accounting for the effectiveness of psychotherapy is the therapeutic relationship. For many years this was not accepted, particularly by the behaviorist school (Emmelkamp, 1994). We now know that this is a critical factor in therapeutic success (Weinberger, 1996). The related idea that we carry representations of early relationships around in our heads, an idea expanded upon by object relations theory (a school of psychoanalysis) and attachment theory (the creation of a psychoanalyst, John Bowlby), is also now commonly accepted in psychology.

The most central idea usually attributed to Freud is the importance of unconscious processes. According to Freud,

we are most often unaware of why we do what we do. For a long while, mainstream academic psychology rejected this notion. Now it seems to have finally caught up to Freud. Modern thinkers now believe that unconscious processes are central and account for most of our behavior. Discussion of unconscious processes permeate research in memory (Graf & Masson, 1993), social psychology (Bargh, 1997), cognitive psychology (Baars, 1988), and so on. In fact, it is now a mainstream belief in psychology. More specific notions of Freud's such as his ideas about defense have also received empirical support (Shedler, Mayman, & Manis, 1993; D. Weinberger, 1990). So have some of his ideas about unconscious fantasies (Siegel & Weinberger, 1997). There is even some work afoot to examine Freud's conceptions of transference (Andersen & Glassman, 1996; Crits-Christoph, Cooper, & Luborsky, 1990).

Of course, many of the particulars of Freud's thinking have been overtaken by events and have turned out to be incorrect. What thinker who died over 60 yeas ago has had all of his or her ideas survive intact, without change? In broad outline however, Freud's ideas are not only alive, they are vibrant. We should probably be testing more of them. Any notion that Freud should be ignored because some of his assertions have been shown to be false is just plain silly. It is throwing out the baby with the bath water. And, he is so much fun to read!

Is Freud's Influence on Psychology Still Alive?

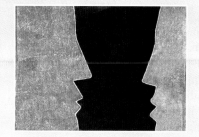

FREUD IS A DEAD WEIGHT ON PSYCHOLOGY
John F. Kihlstrom, University of California, Berkeley

If the 20th century was "The American Century," it was also the century of Sigmund Freud (Roth, 1998), because Freud changed our image of ourselves. Copernicus showed that the Earth did not lie at the center of the universe, and Darwin showed that humans were descended from "lower" animals, but Freud claimed to show that human experience, thought, and action was determined not by our conscious rationality, but by irrational forces outside our awareness and control—forces which could only be understood and controlled by an extensive therapeutic process called *psychoanalysis*.

Freud also changed the vocabulary with which we understand ourselves and others. Before you ever opened this textbook, you already knew something about the id and the superego, penis envy and phallic symbols, castration anxiety and the Oedipus complex. In popular culture, psychotherapy is virtually identified with psychoanalysis. Freudian theory, with its focus on the interpretation of ambiguous events, lies at the foundation of "postmodern" approaches to literary criticism such as deconstruction. More than anyone else, Freud's influence on modern culture has been profound and long-lasting.

Freud's cultural influence is based, at least implicitly, on the premise that his theory is scientifically valid. But from a scientific point of view, classical Freudian psychoanalysis is dead as both a theory of the mind and a mode of therapy (Crews, 1998; Macmillan, 1996). No empirical evidence supports any specific proposition of psychoanalytic theory, such as the idea that development proceeds through oral, anal, phallic, and genital stages, or that little boys lust after their mothers and hate and fear their fathers. No empirical evidence indicates

that psychoanalysis is more effective, or more efficient, than other forms of psychotherapy, such as systematic desensitization or assertiveness training. No empirical evidence indicates that the mechanisms by which psychoanalysis achieves its effects, such as they are, are those specifically predicated on the theory, such as transference and catharsis.

Of course, Freud lived at a particular period of time, and it might be argued that his theories were valid when applied to European culture at that time, even if they are no longer apropos today. However, recent historical analyses show that Freud's construal of his case material was systematically distorted by his theories of unconscious conflict and infantile sexuality, and that he misinterpreted and misrepresented the scientific evidence available to him. Freud's theories were not just a product of his time: They were misleading and incorrect even as he published them.

Drew Westen (1988), a psychologist at Harvard Medical School, agrees that Freud's theories are archaic and obsolete, but argues that Freud's legacy lives on in a number of theoretical propositions that are widely accepted by scientists: the existence of unconscious mental processes; the importance of conflict and ambivalence in behavior; the childhood origins of adult personality; mental representations as a mediator of social behavior; and stages of psychological development. However, some of these propositions are debatable. For example, there is no evidence that childrearing practices have any lasting impact on personality. More important, Westen's argument skirts the question of whether *Freud's* view of these matters was correct. It is one thing to say that unconscious motives play a role in behavior. It is something quite different to say that our

every thought and deed is driven by repressed sexual and aggressive urges; that children harbor erotic feelings toward the parent of the opposite sex; and that young boys are hostile toward their fathers, who they regard as rivals for their mothers' affections. This is what *Freud* believed, and so far as we can tell *Freud* was wrong in every respect. For example, the unconscious mind revealed in laboratory studies of automaticity and implicit memory bears no resemblance to the unconscious mind of psychoanalytic theory (Kihlstrom, 1998).

Westen also argues that psychoanalytic theory itself has evolved since Freud's time, and that it is therefore unfair to bind psychoanalysis so tightly to the Freudian vision of repressed, infantile, sexual and aggressive urges. This is true, and it is a historical fact that so-called "ego psychology" helped preserve much of what was interesting in psychology during its "Dark Ages" of radical behaviorism (Kihlstrom, 1994). But again, this avoids the issue of whether *Freud's* theories are correct. Furthermore, it remains an open question whether these "neo-Freudian" theories are any more valid than are the classically Freudian views that preceded them. For example, it is not at all clear that Erik Erikson's stage theory of psychological development is any more valid than Freud's is.

While Freud had an enormous impact on 20th century culture, he has been a dead weight on 20th century psychology. The broad themes that Westen writes about were present in psychology before Freud, or arose more recently independent of his influence. At best, Freud is a figure of only historical interest for psychologists. He is better studied as a writer than as a scientist. Psychologists can get along without him.

& Bouchard, 1992; Pedersen, Plomin, McClearn, & Friberg, 1988). But personality-environment interactions could also be partially responsible for these patterns.

Consider identical twins. Because they have identical genotypes, they also react to situations in similar ways (reactive interaction), they evoke similar responses from others (evocative interaction), and their similar, genetically guided talents, interests, and motivations lead them to seek out and construct similar environments (proactive interaction). The important point is that these processes all operate whether the twins are reared together or apart. For example, two identical twins who were separated at birth will still be treated in similar ways by other people because they evoke similar responses from others.

Proactive interaction operates in the same way. Each twin's personality prompts him or her to select friends and environments that happen to be similar to the friends and environments chosen by the other twin. But friends and environments that are similar will treat each twin in similar ways. And so it goes. Because the twins begin with identical genotypic personalities, all the processes of personality-environment interaction act together to promote and sustain their similarity across time—even if they have not met since birth.

In contrast, the environments of fraternal twins and nontwin siblings increasingly diverge as they grow older—even within the same home. They are most alike in early childhood, when parents provide the same environment for both (although even here siblings will react somewhat differently and evoke different responses from the parents). But as soon as they begin to select and construct environments outside the home, their moderately different talents, interests, and motivations will take them down increasingly divergent paths, thereby producing increasingly divergent personalities.

SHARED VERSUS NONSHARED ENVIRONMENTS Twin studies allow researchers to estimate not only how much of the variation among individuals is due to genetic variation but also how much of the environmentally related variation is due to aspects of the environment that family members share (for example, socioeconomic status) as compared with aspects of the environment that family members do not share (for example, friends outside the family). Surprisingly, some studies suggest differences due to shared aspects of the environment seem to account for almost none of the environmental variation: After their genetic similarities are subtracted out, two children from the same family seem to be no more alike than two children chosen randomly from the population (Rowe, 1997; Scarr, 1992). This implies that the kinds of variables that psychologists typically study (such as child-rearing practices, socioeconomic status, and parents' education) are contributing virtually nothing to individual differences in personality. How can this be so?

One possible explanation might be that the reactive, evocative, and proactive processes act to diminish the differences between environments as long as those environments permit some flexibility of response. A bright child from a neglecting or impoverished home is more likely than a less bright sibling to absorb information from a television program (reactive interaction), to attract the attention of a sympathetic teacher (evocative interaction), and to go to the library (proactive interaction). This child's genotype acts to counteract the potentially debilitating effects of the home environment, and therefore he or she develops differently than a less bright sibling. Only if the environment is severely restrictive will these personality-driven processes be thwarted (Scarr, 1996; Scarr & McCartney, 1983). This explanation is supported by the finding that the most dissimilar pairs of identical twins reared apart are those in which one twin was reared in a severely restricted environment.

Although this explanation seems plausible, there is no direct evidence that it is correct. In recent years, several psychologists have pointed to methodological problems in research on the heritability of individual differences that may also account for the apparent lack of effects of the environment (Turkheimer, 1998). For example, almost all the data for these studies come from self-report questionnaires, but the validity of these questionnaires, particu-

Because identical twins have identical genotypes, the process of personality-environment interaction act together to promote and sustain their similarity over time—even if they grow up in different environments.

larly as assessments of the environment of different children in the family, is questionable. In addition, the families who participate in these studies tend to be quite similar to each other in demographics—not representing the extremes of either good or bad environments. This would reduce the apparent contribution of the environment to children's abilities and personalities.

In any case, it appears that research will have to shift from the usual comparisons of children from different families to comparisons of children within the same families—with particular attention to the personality-environment interactions within those families. Similarly, more attention must be given to influences outside the family. One writer has suggested that the peer group is a far more important source of personality differences among children than the family (Harris, 1995).

◆ Interim Summary

- Evidence from twin studies suggests that genetic factors substantially influence personality traits.

- In shaping personality, genetic and environmental influences do not act independently but are intertwined from the moment of birth. Because a child's personality and his or her home environment are both a function of the parents' genes, there is a built-in correlation between the child's genotype (inherited personality characteristics) and that environment.

- Three dynamic processes of personality-environment interaction are (1) reactive interaction—different individuals exposed to the same environment experience it, interpret it, and react to it differently; (2) evocative interaction—an individual's personality evokes distinctive responses from others; and (3) proactive interaction—individuals select or create environments of their own. As a child grows older, the influence of proactive interaction becomes increasingly important.

- Studies of twins have produced a number of puzzling patterns: Heritabilities estimated from identical twins reared apart are higher than estimates based on comparisons between identical and fraternal twins; identical twins reared apart are as similar to each other as identical twins reared together, but fraternal twins and nontwin siblings become less similar over time, even when they are reared together.

- These patterns are probably due in part to interactions among genes, so that having all one's genes in common is more than twice as effective as having only half of one's genes in common. Such patterns might also be due in part to the three processes of personality-environment interaction (reactive, evocative, and proactive).

- After their genetic similarities are subtracted out, children from the same family seem to be no more alike than children chosen randomly from the population. This implies that the kinds of variables that psychologists typically study (such as child-rearing practices and the family's socioeconomic status) contribute virtually nothing to individual differences in personality.

◆ Critical Thinking Questions

1. What are some ways that reactive, evocative, and proactive interaction might have influenced the development of your personality and abilities?

2. If you have siblings, what do you think are the best explanations for the similarities and differences you see between yourself and your siblings?

CHAPTER SUMMARY

1. Although different investigators arrive at different numbers of factors, most now believe that five factors provide the best compromise. These have been labeled the "Big Five" and form the acronym OCEAN: Openness to experience, Conscientiousness, Extraversion, Agreeableness, and Neuroticism.

Although items on most inventories are composed or selected on the basis of a theory, they can also be selected on the basis of their correlation with an external criterion—the criterion-keyed method of test construction. The best-known example is the Minnesota Multi-phasic Personality Inventory (MMPI), which is designed to identify individuals with psychological disorders.

2. The Q-sort is a method of assessing personality in which raters sort cards with personality adjectives into nine piles, placing the cards that are least descriptive of the individual in pile 1 on the left and those that are most descriptive in pile 9 on the right.

3. Freud's psychoanalytic theory holds that many behaviors are caused by unconscious motivations. Personality is determined primarily by the biological drives of sex and aggression and by experiences that occur during

the first 5 years of life. Freud's theory of personality structure views personality as composed of the id, the ego, and the superego. The id operates on the pleasure principle, seeking immediate gratification of biological impulses. The ego obeys the reality principle, postponing gratification until it can be achieved in socially acceptable ways. The superego (conscience) imposes moral standards on the individual. In a well-integrated personality, the ego remains in firm but flexible control over the id and superego, and the reality principle governs.

4. Freud's theory of personality development proposes that individuals pass through psychosexual stages and must resolve the Oedipal conflict, in which the young child sees the same-sex parent as a rival for the affection of the opposite-sex parent. Over the years, Freud's theory of anxiety and defense mechanisms has fared better than his structural and developmental theories have.

5. Psychoanalytic theory has been modified by later psychologists, notably Carl Jung and Harry Stack Sullivan. Jung proposed that in addition to the personal unconscious described by Freud, there is a collective unconscious, a part of the mind that is common to all humans. Sullivan suggested that people's responses to interpersonal experiences cause them to develop personifications—mental images of themselves and others.

6. Psychologists who take the psychoanalytic approach sometimes use projective tests, such as the Rorschach Test and the Thematic Apperception Test (TAT). Because the test stimuli are ambiguous, it is assumed that the individual projects his or her personality onto the stimulus, thereby revealing unconscious wishes and motives.

7. Behavioral approaches assume that personality differences result from variations in learning experiences. Through operant conditioning, people learn to associate specific behaviors with punishment or reward. They can also learn these associations through observational learning. Through classical conditioning, people learn to associate specific situations with certain outcomes, such as anxiety.

8. The cognitive approach to personality is based on the idea that differences in personality stem from differences in the way individuals mentally represent information. Albert Bandura developed social cognitive theory, which holds that internal cognitive processes combine with environmental pressures to influence behavior and that cognitive processes and environment have reciprocal effects on each other. Walter Mischel has identified a number of cognitive person variables that affect people's reactions to the environment and behaviors in the environment. George Kelly's personal construct theory focuses on the concepts that individuals use to interpret themselves and their social world. Much research has focused on the self-schema, the aspects of a person's behavior that are most important to that person. Experiments have shown that

people perceive information more readily and recall it better when it is relevant to their self-schemas.

9. The humanistic approach is concerned with the individual's subjective experience. Humanistic psychology was founded as an alternative to psychoanalytic and behaviorist approaches. Carl Rogers argued that the basic force motivating the human organism is the actualizing tendency—a tendency toward fulfillment or actualization of all the capacities of the self. When the needs of the self are denied, severe anxiety can result. Children come to develop an actualized self through the experience of unconditional positive regard from their caregivers. Abraham Maslow proposed that there is a hierarchy of needs, ascending from the basic biological needs to the more complex psychological motivations that become important only after the basic needs have been satisfied. The needs at one level must be at least partially satisfied before those at the next level become important motivators of action.

10. Evolutionary psychology attempts to explain human behavior and personality in terms of the adaptiveness of certain characteristics for survival and reproductive success over human history. Evolutionary theory is consistent with some observed sex differences in mate preferences. It is a controversial theory, however, both for its social implications and for the difficulty of refuting arguments derived from this theory.

11. Evidence from twin studies suggests that genetic factors substantially influence personality traits. In shaping personality, genetic and environmental influences do not act independently but are intertwined from the moment of birth. Because a child's personality and his or her home environment are both a function of the parents' genes, there is a built-in correlation between the child's genotype (inherited personality characteristics) and that environment.

12. Three dynamic processes of personality-environment interaction are (1) reactive interaction—different individuals exposed to the same environment experience it, interpret it, and react to it differently; (2) evocative interaction—an individual's personality evokes distinctive responses from others; and (3) proactive interaction—individuals select or create environments of their own. As a child grows older, the influence of proactive interaction becomes increasingly important.

13. Studies of twins have produced a number of puzzling patterns: Heritabilities estimated from identical twins reared apart are higher than estimates based on comparisons between identical and fraternal twins. Identical twins reared apart are as similar to each other as identical twins reared together, but fraternal twins and nontwin siblings become less similar over time, even when they are reared together. These patterns are probably due in part to interactions among genes, so that having all one's genes in common is more than twice as effective as having only half of one's genes in

common. Such patterns might also be due in part to the three processes of personality-environment interaction (reactive, evocative, and proactive).

14. After their genetic similarities are subtracted out, children from the same family seem to be no more alike than children chosen randomly from the population. This implies that the kinds of variables that psychologists typically study (such as child-rearing practices and the family's socioeconomic status) contribute virtually nothing to individual differences in personality.

CORE CONCEPTS

personality
introversion-extraversion
neuroticism
the "Big Five"
personality inventories
Minnesota Multiphasic Personality
   Inventory
Q-sort
psychoanalytic theory
free association
conscious
preconscious
unconscious
psychological determinism
id
ego
superego
libido
defense mechanisms

repression
rationalization
reaction formation
projection
intellectualization
denial
displacement
psychosexual stages
oral stage
anal stage
phallic stage
Oedipal conflict
latency period
genital stage
collective unconscious
object relations theory
projective test
Rorschach Test
Thematic Apperception Test

behaviorist approach
operant conditioning
observational learning
classical conditioning
cognitive approach
social-learning theory
social cognitive theory
personal constructs
schema
self-schema
actualizing tendency
self
unconditional positive regard
hierarchy of needs
peak experiences
evolutionary psychology
reactive interaction
evocative interaction
proactive interaction

WEB RESOURCES

http://psychology.wadsworth.com/
atkinson14e

Take a quiz, try the activities and exercises, and explore web links.

London: http://www.freud.org.uk/
Vienna: http://freud.t0.or.at/freud/index-e.htm

Check out the chronology of Freud's life on the Vienna site or photos from the London museum, including Freud's famous couch.

http://pmc.psych.nwu.edu/

Why do people differ? This detailed site provides further insight into personality research, as well as a variety of further links to academic and nonacademic web pages.

InfoTrac Online Library

http://www.infotrac-college.com/
wadsworth

Use InfoTrac College Edition to find popular and scientific articles by using the search terms below or your own relevant terms.

- Sigmund Freud
- Abraham Maslow
- Personality tests
- Personality traits

CD-ROM LINKS

Psych Odyssey

Check out CD Chapter 15, Personality
  A. The Nature of Personality
B. Psychodynamic Approaches

Psyk.trek 2.0

Check out CD Unit 10, Personality Theory
  10a Freudian Theory
10b Behaviorist Theory
10c Humanistic Theory
10d Biological Theory

STRESS, HEALTH, AND COPING

14

Janet was feeling near the end of her rope. All day long she had endured one hassle after another. At breakfast, she spilled orange juice on the only clean blouse she had. When she got to work, there were 32 e-mail messages and 15 phone messages waiting for her. In the afternoon, her boss told her to prepare a financial report for the board meeting that was to occur at 9 A.M. the next morning, but her computer crashed and she could not access the financial records for her division. Tired and overwhelmed, when she got home, she called her mother for support, only to discover that her father had been hospitalized with chest pains. After hanging up, Janet felt disoriented, her heart was racing, and she began to get a migraine.

The kind of stress Janet was experiencing is familiar to many of us—silly mistakes that cause stress, the stress of a demanding boss, the stress in our per-

sonal relationships. Exposure to stress can lead to painful emotions like anxiety or depression. It can also lead to physical illnesses, both minor and severe.

Yet, people's reactions to stressful events differ widely: Some people faced with a stressful event develop serious psychological or physical problems, whereas other people faced with the same stressful event develop no problems and may even find the event challenging and interesting. In this chapter we discuss the concept of stress and the effects of stress on the mind and body. We also look at the differences between people's ways of thinking about and coping with stressful events, and how these differences contribute to adjustment.

Stress has become a popular topic. The media often attribute unusual behavior or illness to burnout due to stress or a nervous breakdown resulting from stress. For example, when a celebrity attempts suicide, it is often said that he or she was burnt out from the pressures of public life. On college campuses, "I'm so stressed out!" is a common claim. But what is stress? In general terms, **stress** refers to experiencing events

that are perceived as endangering one's physical or psychological well-being. These events are usually referred to as **stressors**, and people's reactions to them are termed **stress responses**.

There are some types of events that most people experience as stressful. We will describe the characteristics of such events and then describe the body's natural reaction to stress. This reaction is adaptive when it is possible to flee from or attack a stressor, but it can become maladaptive when a stressor is chronic or uncontrollable. Stress can have both direct and indirect effects on health.

The study of how stress and other social, psychological, and biological factors come together to contribute to illness is known as **behavioral medicine** or health psychology (Taylor, 1999). We will review research on how psychosocial factors interact with biological vulnerabilities to affect cardiovascular health and the functioning of the immune system. Finally, we will describe ways of managing stress to improve health.

CHARACTERISTICS OF STRESSFUL EVENTS

Countless events create stress. Some are major changes affecting large numbers of people—events such as war, nuclear accidents, and earthquakes. Others are major changes in the life of an individual—for instance, moving to a new area, changing jobs, getting married, losing a friend, suffering a serious illness. Everyday hassles can also be experienced as stressors—losing your wallet, getting stuck in traffic, arguing with your professor. Some stressors are acute: They only last a short time, such as when you are caught in an unusual traffic jam on the way to an important job interview. Other stressors are chronic: They go on for an extended period, even indefinitely, as when you are in an unsatisfying marriage. Finally, the source of stress can be within the individual, in the form of conflicting motives or desires.

Events that are perceived as stressful usually fall into one or more of the following categories: traumatic events outside the usual range of human experience, uncontrollable or unpredictable events, events that represent major changes in life circumstances, or internal conflicts. In this section we look briefly at each of these categories.

TRAUMATIC EVENTS

The most obvious sources of stress are **traumatic events**—situations of extreme danger that are outside the range of usual human experience. These include natural disasters, such as earthquakes and floods; disasters caused by human activity, such as wars and nuclear accidents; catastrophic accidents, such as car or plane crashes; and physical assaults, such as rape or attempted murder.

Many people experience a specific series of psychological reactions after a traumatic event (Horowitz, 1986). At first, survivors are stunned and dazed and appear to be unaware of their injuries or of the danger. They may wander around in a disoriented state, perhaps putting themselves at risk for further injury. For example, an earthquake survivor may wander through buildings that are on the verge of collapse. In the next stage, survivors are still passive and unable to initiate even simple tasks, but they may follow orders readily. For example, days after the assault, a rape survivor may not even think to prepare food to eat, but if a friend calls and insists that they go out for food, she will comply. In the third stage, survivors become anxious and apprehensive, have difficulty in concentrating, and may repeat the story of the catastrophe over and over again. The sur-

The causes of stress vary from one person to the next. What is overwhelming to one person may be exciting and challenging to another.

Victims of disasters such as hurricanes and tornados are often stunned and disoriented shortly after the disaster. Later they become more responsive but may still have trouble initiating even simple activities. They may remain anxious and distracted long after the disaster.

vivor of a car crash may become extremely nervous near a car, may be unable to go back to work because of inability to concentrate, and may repeatedly tell friends about the details of the crash.

One type of traumatic event that is tragically common in our society is sexual abuse. The impact of rape and other types of sexual violence on the victim's emotional and physical health appears to be great (Koss & Boeschen, 1998). Several studies have found that in the first 6 months after a rape or other assault, women and men show high levels of depression, anxiety, dismay, and many other indicators of emotional distress (Duncan, Saunders, Kilpatrick, Hanson, & Resnick, 1996; Kessler, Davis, & Kendler, 1997). For some people, this emotional distress declines over time. For others, however, emotional distress is long lasting.

In one study, Burnam and colleagues (1988) found that assault victims were twice as likely as others to have a diagnosable depressive disorder, anxiety disorder, or substance abuse disorder at some time after the assault. They were most likely to develop these disorders if they had been assaulted as a child. In fact, people who had been assaulted as children remained at higher risk for developing a psychological disorder throughout their lives.

Fortunately, most of us never experience traumatic events. More common events can lead to stress responses, however. Four characteristics of common events lead to their being perceived as stressful: controllability, predictability, major changes in life circumstances, and internal conflicts. Of course, the degree to which an event is stressful differs for each individual. That is, people differ in the extent to which they perceive an event as controllable, predictable, and a challenge to their capabilities and self-concept, and it is largely these appraisals that influence the perceived stressfulness of the event (Lazarus & Folkman, 1984).

CONTROLLABILITY

The **controllability** of an event—the degree to which we can stop it or bring it about—influences our perceptions of stressfulness. The more uncontrollable an event seems, the more likely it is to be perceived as stressful (see Chapter 7). Major uncontrollable events include the death of a loved one, being laid off from work, and serious illness. Minor uncontrollable events include such things as having a friend refuse to accept your apology for some misdeed and being bumped off a flight because the airline oversold tickets. One obvious reason uncontrollable events are stressful is that if we cannot control them, we cannot stop them from happening.

As noted earlier, however, our perceptions of the controllability of events appear to be as important to our assessment of their stressfulness as the actual controllability of those events. Consider a study in which participants were shown color photographs of victims of violent deaths. The experimental group could terminate the viewing by pressing a button. The control participants saw the same photographs for the same length of time as the experimental group, but they could not terminate the exposure. (The length of time the control group saw the photographs was determined by the length of time the experimental group saw them.) The level of arousal or anxiety in both groups was determined by measuring galvanic skin response (GSR), a drop in the electrical resistance of the skin that is widely used as an index of autonomic arousal. The experimental group showed much less anxiety in response to the photographs than the control group, even though the two groups were exposed to the photographs for the same amount of time (Geer & Maisel, 1973).

The belief that we can control events appears to reduce the impact of the events, even if we never exercise that control. This was demonstrated in a study in which two groups of participants were exposed to a loud, extremely unpleasant noise. Participants in one group were told that they could terminate the noise by pressing a button, but they were urged not to do so unless it was absolutely necessary. Participants in the other group had no control over the noise. None of the participants who had a control button actually pressed it, so the noise exposure was the same for both groups. Nevertheless, performance on subsequent problem-solving tasks was significantly worse for the group that had no control, indicating that they were more disturbed by the noise than the group that had the potential for control (Glass & Singer, 1972).

PREDICTABILITY

The **predictability** of an event—the degree to which we know if and when it will occur—also affects its stressfulness. Being able to predict the occurrence of a stressful event—even if the individual cannot control it—usually reduces the severity of the stress. As discussed in Chapter 7, laboratory experiments show that both humans and animals prefer predictable aversive events over unpredictable ones. In one study, rats were given a choice between a signaled shock and an unsignaled shock. If the rat pressed a bar at the beginning of a series of shock trials, each shock was preceded by a warning tone. If the rat failed to press the bar, no warning tones sounded during that series of trials. All of the rats quickly learned to press the bar, showing a marked preference for predictable shock (Abbott, Schoen, & Badia, 1984). Humans generally choose predictable over unpredictable shocks, too. They also show less emotional arousal and report less distress while waiting for predictable shocks to occur, and they perceive predictable shocks as less aversive than unpredictable ones of the same intensity (Katz & Wykes, 1985).

How do we explain these results? One possibility is that a warning signal before an aversive event allows the person or animal to initiate some sort of preparatory process that acts to reduce the effects of a noxious stimulus. An animal receiving the signal that a shock is about to happen may shift its feet in such a way as to reduce the experience of the shock. A man who knows he is about to receive a shot in the doctor's office can try to distract himself to reduce the pain. A woman who hears warnings of an impending hurricane can board up her windows in an attempt to prevent damage to her house.

Another possibility is that with unpredictable shock, there is no safe period, but with predictable shock, the organism (human or animal) can relax to some extent until the signal warns that shock is about to occur (Seligman & Binik, 1977). A real-life example of this phenomenon occurs when a boss who tends to criticize an employee in front of others is out of town on a business trip. The boss's absence is a signal to the employee that it is safe to relax. In contrast, an employee whose boss criticizes him unpredictably throughout the day and never goes out of town may chronically feel stressed.

Some jobs, such as fire fighting and emergency-room medicine, are filled with unpredictability and are considered very stressful. Serious illnesses often are very unpredictable. One of the major problems faced by cancer patients who receive treatment is that they cannot be sure whether they have been cured until many years have passed. Every day they must confront the uncertainty of a potentially disastrous future. Even an event as overwhelmingly negative as torture can be affected by the extent to which victims feel that the episodes of torture are predictable. Victims who are able to predict the timing and type of torture they experience while being detained recover better once they are released than victims who perceive the torture as completely unpredictable (Basoglu & Mineka, 1992).

MAJOR CHANGES IN LIFE CIRCUMSTANCES

Two pioneering stress researchers, Holmes and Rahe (1967), argued that any life change that requires numerous readjustments can be perceived as stressful. In an attempt to measure the impact of life changes, they developed the Life Events Scale shown in Table 14-1. The scale ranks life events from most stressful (death of a spouse) to least stressful (minor violations of the law). To arrive at this scale, the investigators examined thousands of interviews and medical histories to identify the kinds of events that people found stressful. Because marriage appeared to be a critical event for most people, it was placed in the middle of the scale and assigned an arbitrary value of 50. The investigators then asked approximately 400 men and women of varying ages, backgrounds, and marital status to compare marriage with a number of other life events. They were asked such questions as "Does the event call for more or less readjustment than marriage?" They were then asked to assign a point value to each event on the basis of their evaluation of its severity and the time required for adjustment. These ratings were used to construct the scale in Table 14-1.

The Holmes and Rahe scale shown in Table 14-1 had a major influence on stress research, but it has also had many critics. Although positive events often require adjustment and hence are sometimes stressful, most research indicates that negative events have a much greater impact on psychological and physical health than positive events. In addition, the Holmes and Rahe scale assumes that all people respond to a given event in the same way, but there are large differences in how people are affected by events. Some of these differences are linked to age and cultural background (Masuda & Holmes, 1978). Also, some people do not find major changes or pressure situations stressful. Rather, they experience them as challenging and are invigorated by them. Later we will discuss characteristics of individuals

Life Event	Value
Death of spouse	100
Divorce	73
Marital separation	65
Jail term	63
Death of close family member	63
Personal injury or illness	53
Marriage	50
Fired from job	47
Marital reconciliation	45
Retirement	45
Change in health of family member	44
Pregnancy	40
Sex difficulties	39
Gain of a new family member	39
Business readjustment	39
Change in financial state	38
Death of a close friend	37
Change to a different line of work	36
Foreclosure of mortgage	30
Change in responsibilities at work	29
Son or daughter leaving home	29
Trouble with in-laws	29
Outstanding personal achievement	28
Wife begins or stops work	26
Begin or end school	26
Change in living conditions	25
Revision of personal habits	24
Trouble with boss	23
Change in residence	20
Change in school	20
Change in recreation	19
Change in church activities	19
Change in social activities	18
Change in sleeping habits	16
Change in eating habits	15
Vacation	13
Christmas	12
Minor legal violations	11

© Larry L. Miller/Photo Researchers

Although marriage is a happy event, it can also be stressful.

that affect whether they view situations as stressors or as challenges.

INTERNAL CONFLICTS

So far we have discussed only external events in which something or someone in the environment challenges our well-being. Stress can also be brought about by **internal conflicts**—unresolved issues that may be either conscious or unconscious. Conflict occurs when a person must choose between incompatible, or mutually exclusive, goals or courses of action. Many of the things people desire prove to be incompatible. You want to play on your college volleyball team but cannot put in the time required and still earn the grades necessary to apply to graduate school. You want to join your friends for a pizza party but are afraid you will fail tomorrow's exam if you don't stay home and study. You don't want to go to your uncle's for dinner, but you also don't want to listen to your parents' complaints if you turn down the invitation. In each case, the two goals are incompatible because the action needed to achieve one automatically prevents you from achieving the other.

Even if two goals are equally attractive—for example, you receive two good job offers—you may agonize over the decision and experience regrets after making a choice. This stress would not have occurred if you had been offered only one job.

Conflict may also arise when two inner needs or motives are in opposition. In our society, the conflicts that are most pervasive and difficult to resolve generally occur between the following motives:

Independence versus dependence. Particularly when we are faced with a difficult situation, we may want someone to take care of us and solve our problems. But we are taught that we must stand on our own.

At other times we may wish for independence, but circumstances or other people force us to remain dependent.

Intimacy versus isolation. The desire to be close to another person and to share our innermost thoughts and emotions may conflict with the fear of being hurt or rejected if we expose too much of ourselves.

Cooperation versus competition. Our society emphasizes competition and success. Competition begins in early childhood among siblings, continues through school, and culminates in business and professional rivalry. At the same time, we are urged to cooperate and to help others.

Expression of impulses versus moral standards. Impulses must be regulated to some degree in all societies. We noted in Chapter 3 that much of childhood learning involves internalizing cultural restrictions on impulses. Sex and aggression are two areas in which our impulses frequently come into conflict with moral standards, and violation of these standards can generate feelings of guilt.

These four areas present the greatest potential for serious conflict. Trying to find a workable compromise between opposing motives can create considerable stress.

◆ Interim Summary

- Stress refers to experiencing events that are perceived as endangering one's physical or psychological well-being. These events are usually referred to as stressors, and people's reactions to them are termed stress responses.

- Traumatic events are events outside the normal range of people's experience that are highly distressing. Traumas such as rape can lead to a wide range of emotional and physical problems.

- The controllability of a situation also affects how stressful it is. Our perceptions of controllability are as important as the actual controllability of the situation.

- Unpredictable events are often perceived as stressful.

- Some researchers argue that any major change can be stressful.

- Internal conflicts—unresolved issues that may be conscious or unconscious—can cause stress.

◆ Critical Thinking Questions

1. Consider the situations in your own life you find stressful. What are the characteristics of these situations that make them so stressful?

2. To what extent do you think the need for control is influenced by culture?

PSYCHOLOGICAL REACTIONS TO STRESS

Stressful situations produce emotional reactions ranging from exhilaration (when the event is demanding but manageable) to anxiety, anger, discouragement, and depression (see the Concept Review Table). If the stressful situation continues, our emotions may switch back and forth among any of these, depending on the success of our coping efforts. Let us take a closer look at some of the more common emotional reactions to stress.

ANXIETY

The most common response to a stressor is anxiety. People who live through events that are beyond the normal range of human suffering (natural disasters, rape, kidnapping) sometimes develop a severe set of anxiety-related symptoms known as **post-traumatic stress disorder** (PTSD).

There are four sets of symptoms of PTSD. The first set represents a deep detachment from everyday life. People report feeling completely numb to the world, as if they have no emotional reactions to anything. They feel estranged from others, as if they can no longer relate to even close family and friends. They also lose their interest in their former activities and may just sit around for hours at a time, apparently staring into nothingness. The second set of symptoms is a repeated reliving of the

CONCEPT REVIEW TABLE
Reactions to Stress

Psychological Reactions

Anxiety

Anger and aggression

Apathy and depression

Cognitive impairment

Physiological Reactions

Increased metabolic rate

Increased heart rate

Dilation of pupils

Higher blood pressure

Increased breathing rate

Tensing of muscles

Secretion of endorphins and ACTH

Release of extra sugar from the liver

trauma. People may dream every night of the trauma and become afraid to go to sleep. Even while awake, they may mentally relive the trauma so vividly that they begin to behave as if they were there. A former combat soldier, when he hears a jet flying low nearby, might hit the ditch, cover his head, and feel as though he is back in combat. A rape survivor might replay scenes from her trauma over and over and see the face of her attacker in other men. The third set of symptoms includes sleep disturbances, difficulty in concentrating, and overalertness. Trauma survivors may act as though they are always vigilant for signs of the trauma recurring. They may find it impossible to concentrate on anything, including their work, conversations, or driving a car. Even if they are not having recurrent nightmares, they may have restless nights and wake up exhausted. Another symptom of PTSD that is not part of these three core sets of symptoms is survivor guilt—some people feel terribly guilty about surviving a trauma when others did not, even if they could not have saved other people.

Post-traumatic stress disorder may develop immediately after the trauma, or it may be brought on by a minor stress experienced weeks, months, or even years later. It may last a long time. A study of victims of the 1972 flood that wiped out the community of Buffalo Creek, West Virginia, found that shortly after the flood, 63% of the survivors were suffering from PTSD symptoms. Fourteen years later, 25% still experienced PTSD symptoms (Green, Lindy, Grace, & Leonard, 1992). Similarly, a study of Florida children who survived Hurricane Andrew in 1992 found that nearly 20% were still suffering from PTSD a year after the disaster (LaGreca, Sliverman, Vernberg, & Prinstein, 1996). Another study of children in South Carolina who survived Hurricane Hugo in 1993 found that, 3 years after the hurricane, a third still experienced a sense of detachment and avoided thoughts or feelings associated with the hurricane. A quarter of the children were irritable and angry, and 20% experienced chronic physiological arousal (Garrison et al., 1995).

Traumas caused by humans, such as sexual or physical assault, terrorist attacks, and war, may be even more likely to cause PTSD than natural disasters, for at least two reasons. First, such traumas challenge our basic beliefs about the goodness of life and other people, and when these beliefs are shattered, PTSD is more likely to occur (Janoff-Bulman, 1992). Second, human-caused disasters often strike individuals rather than whole communities, and suffering through a trauma alone seems to increase a person's risk of experiencing PTSD.

Studies of rape survivors have found that about 95% experience post-traumatic stress symptoms severe enough to qualify for a diagnosis of the disorder in the first 2 weeks following the rape (see Figure 14-1). About 50% still qualify for the diagnosis 3 months after the rape. As

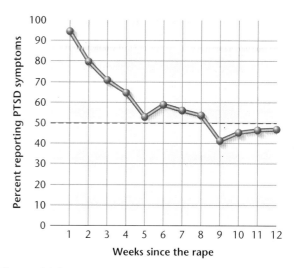

Figure 14-1
Post-Traumatic Symptoms in Rape
Almost all women who have been raped show symptoms of post-traumatic stress disorder severe enough to be diagnosed with PTSD in the first or second week following the rape. Over the 3 months following the rape, the percentage of women continuing to show PTSD declines. However, almost 50% of women continue to be diagnosed with PTSD 3 months after a rape. (After Foa & Riggs, 1995)

many as 25% still suffer from PTSD 4 to 5 years after the rape (Foa & Riggs, 1995; Resnick, Kilpatrick, Dansky, & Sanders, 1993).

Post-traumatic stress disorder became widely accepted as a diagnostic category because of difficulties experienced by Vietnam War veterans. Although stress reactions to the horrors of battle had been noted in earlier wars (in World War I it was called "shell shock" and in World War II "combat fatigue"), veterans of the Vietnam War seemed especially prone to develop the long-term symptoms we have described. The National Vietnam Veterans Readjustment Study found that nearly half a million Vietnam veterans still suffered from PTSD 15 years after their military service. Rates of PTSD were highest among Hispanic veterans, next highest among African American veterans, and lowest among European Americans (see Figure 14-2; Schlenger et al., 1992). A separate study of Native American Vietnam veterans found that as many as 70% still suffered symptoms of PTSD decades after the war ended (Manson et al., 1996). Veterans from ethnic minority groups may suffer more PTSD because they have the double jeopardy of war exposure and the stress of discrimination once they return to the United States.

Substance abuse, violence, and interpersonal problems are common correlates of post-traumatic stress disorder. In a study of 713 men who served in Vietnam, 16% reported having problems resulting from drinking

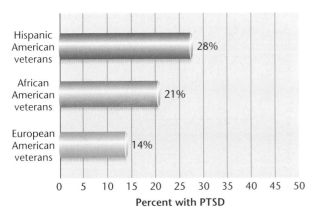

Figure 14-2
Rates of PTSD in Vietnam Veterans
A large study of Vietnam veterans showed higher rates of PTSD among veterans of color than among white veterans. (Adapted from W. E. Schlenger, R. A. Kolka, J. A. Fairbank, & R. L. Hough (1992), "The Prevalence of Post-Traumatic Stress Disorder in the Vietnam Generation: A Multi-Method, Multi-Source Assessment of Psychiatric Disorders," from *Journal of Traumatic Stress*, 5, 333–363.)

heavily, such as trouble at school or work, problems with friends, and passing out. Sixteen percent had been arrested at least once; and 44% said that they had war memories that they were still trying to forget (Yager, Laufer, & Gallops, 1984). The soldiers who fought in Vietnam were young (the average age was 19), and the conditions of warfare were unusual: absence of clear front lines, unpredictable attacks in dense jungle, difficulty distinguishing between Vietnamese allies and enemies, and lack of support for the war among the American public. To this day, some Vietnam veterans still reexperience in memories or in dreams those traumatic events. As one veteran wrote, "The war is over in history. But it never ended for me" (Marbly, 1987, p. 193).

More recent and ongoing wars and conflicts have resulted in PTSD, however, both for soldiers and for civil-

Post-traumatic stress disorder affects about one-sixth of Vietnam War veterans.

ians caught in these conflicts. For example, a study of veterans of the 1991 Persian Gulf War found that 13% were suffering from PTSD in the year after the war (Sutker, Davis, Uddo, & Ditta, 1995).

The wars in the former Yugoslavia begun in the 1990s were marked by "ethnic cleansing"—the torture and slaughter of thousands and displacement of millions of former Yugoslavians. This campaign was one of the most brutal in history, with many atrocities, concentration camps, organized mass rapes, and neighbors murdering neighbors. This woman's story is far too common:

Case Study: A woman in her 40s worked the family farm in a rural village until the day the siege began, when mortar shells turned most of their house to rubble. A few months before, she and her husband had sent their son away to be with relatives in Slovenia. The morning after the shelling, the Chetniks—Serbian nationalist forces— came and ordered everyone to leave their houses at once. Many neighbors and friends were shot dead before the woman's eyes. She and her husband were forced to sign over the title to their house, car, and bank deposits—and watched as the looting began. Looters included neighbors who were their friends. Over the next few days they traveled back from the Muslim ghetto to their land to feed the animals. One day, as she and her husband stood in the garden, the Chetniks captured them. Her husband was taken away with other men. For the next 6 months she did not know if he was dead or alive. She spent days on transport trains with no food or water, where many suffocated to death beside her. On forced marches she had to step over the dead bodies of friends and relatives. Once her group was forced across a bridge that was lined with Chetnik machine gunners randomly shooting to kill and ordering them to throw all valuables over the edge into nets. She spent weeks in severely deprived conditions in a big tent with many women and children, where constant sobbing could be heard. When she herself could not stop crying she thought that something had broken in her head and that she had gone "crazy." Now she says, "I will never be happy again." When alone, everything comes back to her. But when she is with others or busy doing chores, she can forget. "My soul hurts inside, but I'm able to pull it together." She is able to sleep without nightmares only by using a nightly ritual: "I lie down and go through every step of the house in Bosnia—the stable, everything they took, the rugs, the horses, the doors. I see it all again." (Weine et al., 1995, p. 540)

A study of Bosnian refugees conducted just after they resettled in the United States found that 65% suffered from PTSD, with older refugees more vulnerable to PTSD than younger refugees (Weine et al., 1995; see also Cardozo, Vergara, Agani, & Cotway, 2000). A follow-up study of these refugees 1 year later found that 44% were still suffering from PTSD (Weine et al., 1998).

Many refugees from Bosnia and other war-torn countries report having been tortured before they es-

Many refugees suffer from PTSD, with older refugees more vulnerable to PTSD than younger refugees.

caped their homeland, and the experience of torture significantly increases the chances that an individual will develop PTSD (Basoglu & Mineka, 1998; Shrestha et al., 1998). Torture survivors who were political activists appear less prone to develop PTSD than those who were not political activists (Basoglu et al., 1997). Political activists appeared more psychologically prepared for torture than others because they expected at some time to be tortured, often had previous experience with torture, and had a belief system whereby torture was viewed merely as an instrument of repression.

ANGER AND AGGRESSION

Another common reaction to a stressful situation is anger, which may lead to aggression. Laboratory studies have shown that some animals behave aggressively in response to a variety of stressors, including overcrowding, electric shock, and failure to receive an expected food reward. If a pair of animals is shocked in a cage from which they cannot escape, they begin fighting when the shock starts and stop fighting when it ends.

Children often become angry and exhibit aggressive behavior when they experience frustration. As noted in Chapter 11, the frustration-aggression hypothesis assumes that whenever a person's efforts to reach a goal are blocked, an aggressive drive is induced that motivates behavior designed to injure the object—or person—causing the frustration. Although research has shown that aggression is not an inevitable response to frustration, it certainly is a frequent one. When one child takes a toy from another, the second child is likely to attack the first in an attempt to regain the toy. In the late 1980s, some adults frustrated by interminable traffic jams on hot Los Angeles freeways began shooting at one another. Fortunately, adults usually express their aggression verbally rather than physically; they are more likely to exchange insults than blows.

Direct aggression toward the source of frustration is not always possible or wise. Sometimes the source is vague and intangible. The person does not know what to attack but feels angry and seeks an object on which to vent these feelings. Sometimes the individual responsible for the frustration is so powerful that an attack would be dangerous. When circumstances block direct attack on the cause of frustration, aggression may be displaced: The aggressive action may be directed toward an innocent person or object rather than toward the actual cause of the frustration. A man who is reprimanded at work may take out unexpressed resentment on his family. A student who is angry at her professor for an unfair grade may blow up at her roommate. A child frustrated by experiences at school may resort to vandalism of school property.

APATHY AND DEPRESSION

Although aggression is a frequent response to frustration, the opposite response, withdrawal and apathy, is also common. If the stressful conditions continue and the individual is unable to cope with them, apathy may deepen into depression.

The theory of learned helplessness (Seligman, 1975) explains how experience with uncontrollable negative events can lead to apathy and depression (see also Chapter 7). A series of experiments showed that dogs placed in a shuttle box (an apparatus with two compartments separated by a barrier) quickly learn to jump to the opposite compartment to escape a mild electric shock delivered to their feet through a grid on the floor. If a light is turned on a few seconds before the grid is electrified, the dogs can learn to avoid the shock by jumping to the safe compartment when signaled by the light. However, if the dog has previously been confined in another enclosure where shocks were unavoidable and inescapable—so that nothing the animal did terminated the shock—it is very difficult for the dog to learn the avoidance response in a new situation. The animal simply sits and endures the shock in the shuttle box, even though an easy jump to the opposite compartment would eliminate discomfort. Some dogs never learn, even if the experimenter demonstrates the proper procedure by carrying them over the barrier. The experimenters concluded that the animals had learned through prior experience that they were helpless to avoid the shock and therefore gave up trying to do so, even in a new situation. The animals were unable to overcome this learned helplessness (Overmeier & Seligman, 1967).

Some humans also appear to develop **learned helplessness, characterized by apathy, withdrawal, and inaction, in response to uncontrollable events.** Not all do, however. The original learned helplessness theory has had to be modified to take into account the fact that although some people become helpless after uncontrollable events, others are invigorated by the challenge posed by such events (Wortman & Brehm, 1975). This modified theory will be discussed later in the chapter.

The original learned helplessness theory is useful, however, in helping us understand why some people seem to give up when they are exposed to difficult events. For example, the theory has been used to explain why prisoners in Nazi concentration camps did not rebel against their captors more often: They had come to believe that they were helpless to do anything about their situation and therefore did not try to escape. Similarly, women whose husbands beat them frequently may not try to escape. They often say that they feel helpless to do anything about their situation because they fear what their husbands would do if they tried to leave or because they do not have the economic resources to support themselves and their children.

COGNITIVE IMPAIRMENT

In addition to emotional reactions, people often show substantial cognitive impairment when faced with serious stressors. They find it hard to concentrate and to organize their thoughts logically. They may be easily distracted. As a result, their performance on tasks, particularly complex tasks, tends to deteriorate.

This cognitive impairment may come from two sources. High levels of emotional arousal can interfere with the processing of information, so the more anxious, angry, or depressed we are after experiencing a stressor, the more likely we are to exhibit cognitive impairment. Cognitive impairment may also result from the distracting thoughts that go through our heads when we are faced with a stressor. We contemplate possible sources of action, worry about the consequences of our actions, and berate ourselves for not being able to handle the situation better. For instance, while trying to complete a test, students who suffer from test anxiety tend to worry about possible failure and about their inadequacies. They can become so distracted by these negative thoughts that they fail to follow instructions and neglect or misinterpret information. As their anxiety mounts, they have difficulty retrieving facts that they have learned well.

Cognitive impairment often leads people to adhere rigidly to behavior patterns because they cannot consider alternative patterns. People have been trapped in flaming buildings because they persisted in pushing against exit doors that opened inward; in their panic, they failed to consider other possible means of escape. Some people resort to old, childlike behavior patterns that are not appropriate to the situation. A cautious person may become even more cautious and withdraw entirely, whereas an aggressive person may lose control and strike out heedlessly in all directions.

◆ Interim Summary

- Anxiety is a common response to stress. Some people develop a severe anxiety disorder called *post-traumatic stress disorder*.
- Some people become angry in response to stress and may become aggressive.
- Withdrawal, apathy, and depression may result from stress. Some people develop learned helplessness, which is characterized by passivity and inaction and an inability to see opportunities to control their environment.
- Some people develop cognitive impairment when stressed and become unable to think clearly.

◆ Critical Thinking Questions

1. What kinds of things can family members or friends do to help the survivor of a trauma cope as well as possible with the psychological aftermath of the trauma?

2. Do you think some people are especially prone to develop PTSD following a trauma? If so, why might they be more vulnerable?

The Neural Basis of Behavior

PHYSIOLOGICAL REACTIONS TO STRESS

The body reacts to stressors by initiating a complex sequence of responses. If the perceived threat is resolved quickly, these emergency responses subside, but if the stressful situation continues, a different set of internal responses occurs as we attempt to adapt. In this section we examine these physiological reactions in detail.

THE FIGHT-OR-FLIGHT RESPONSE

Whether you fall into an icy river, encounter a knife-wielding assailant, or are terrified by your first parachute jump, your body responds in similar ways. Regardless of the stressor, your body automatically prepares to handle the emergency. Recall from Chapter 11 that this is called the **fight-or-flight response**—the body's mobilization to attack or flee from a threatening

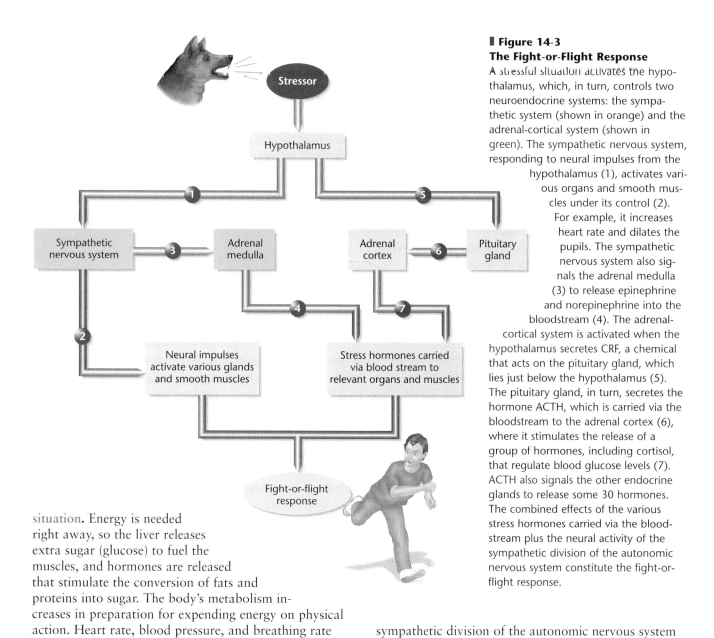

Figure 14-3
The Fight-or-Flight Response
A stressful situation activates the hypothalamus, which, in turn, controls two neuroendocrine systems: the sympathetic system (shown in orange) and the adrenal-cortical system (shown in green). The sympathetic nervous system, responding to neural impulses from the hypothalamus (1), activates various organs and smooth muscles under its control (2). For example, it increases heart rate and dilates the pupils. The sympathetic nervous system also signals the adrenal medulla (3) to release epinephrine and norepinephrine into the bloodstream (4). The adrenal-cortical system is activated when the hypothalamus secretes CRF, a chemical that acts on the pituitary gland, which lies just below the hypothalamus (5). The pituitary gland, in turn, secretes the hormone ACTH, which is carried via the bloodstream to the adrenal cortex (6), where it stimulates the release of a group of hormones, including cortisol, that regulate blood glucose levels (7). ACTH also signals the other endocrine glands to release some 30 hormones. The combined effects of the various stress hormones carried via the bloodstream plus the neural activity of the sympathetic division of the autonomic nervous system constitute the fight-or-flight response.

situation. Energy is needed right away, so the liver releases extra sugar (glucose) to fuel the muscles, and hormones are released that stimulate the conversion of fats and proteins into sugar. The body's metabolism increases in preparation for expending energy on physical action. Heart rate, blood pressure, and breathing rate increase, and the muscles tense. At the same time, certain unessential activities, such as digestion, are curtailed. Saliva and mucus dry up, thereby increasing the size of the air passages to the lungs, and an early sign of stress is a dry mouth. The body's natural painkillers, endorphins, are secreted, and the surface blood vessels constrict to reduce bleeding in case of injury. The spleen releases more red blood cells to help carry oxygen, and the bone marrow produces more white corpuscles to fight infection.

Most of these physiological changes result from activation of two neuroendocrine systems controlled by the hypothalamus: the sympathetic system and the adrenal cortical system. The hypothalamus has been called the brain's stress center because of its dual function in emergencies. Its first function is to activate the

sympathetic division of the autonomic nervous system (see Chapter 2). The hypothalamus transmits nerve impulses to nuclei in the brain stem that control the functioning of the autonomic nervous system. The sympathetic division of the autonomic system acts directly on muscles and organs to produce increased heart rate, elevated blood pressure, and dilated pupils. The sympathetic system also stimulates the inner core of the adrenal glands (the adrenal medulla) to release the hormones epinephrine (adrenaline) and norepinephrine into the bloodstream. Epinephrine has the same effect on the muscles and organs as the sympathetic nervous system (for example, it increases heart rate and blood pressure) and thus serves to perpetuate a state of arousal. Norepinephrine, through its action on the pituitary gland, is indirectly responsible for the release of extra sugar from the liver (see Figure 14-3).

The hypothalamus carries out its second function, activation of the adrenal-cortical system, by signaling the pituitary gland to secrete adrenocorticotropic hormone (ACTH), the body's "major stress hormone" (see Chapter 2). ACTH stimulates the outer layer of the adrenal glands (the adrenal cortex), resulting in the release of a group of hormones (the major one is cortisol) that regulate the blood levels of glucose and certain minerals. The amount of cortisol in blood or urine samples is often used as a measure of stress. ACTH also signals other endocrine glands to release about 30 hormones, each of which plays a role in the body's adjustment to emergency situations.

In groundbreaking work that remains influential today, researcher Hans Selye (1978) described the physiological changes we have just discussed as part of a **general adaptation syndrome,** a set of responses that is displayed by all organisms in response to stress. The general adaptation syndrome has three phases (see Figure 14-4). In the first phase, alarm, the body mobilizes to confront a threat by triggering sympathetic nervous system activity. In the second phase, resistance, the organism attempts to cope with the threat by fleeing it or fighting it. The third phase, exhaustion, occurs if the organism is unable to flee from or fight the threat and depletes its physiological resources in attempting to do so.

Selye argued that a wide variety of physical and psychological stressors can trigger this response pattern. He also argued that repeated or prolonged exhaustion of physiological resources, due to exposure to prolonged stressors that one cannot flee from or fight,

is responsible for a wide array of physiological diseases, which he called *diseases of adaptation.* He conducted laboratory studies in which he exposed animals to several types of prolonged stressors, such as extreme cold and fatigue, and found that regardless of the nature of the stressor, certain bodily changes inevitably occurred: enlarged adrenal glands, shrunken lymph nodes, and stomach ulcers. These changes decrease the organism's ability to resist other stressors, including infectious and disease-producing agents. As we will see later, chronic arousal can make both animals and people more susceptible to illness.

THE PHYSIOLOGY OF PTSD

In our discussion of PTSD, we emphasized the psychological consequences of trauma. Recent work on PTSD has also focused on apparent physiological changes that trauma survivors experience.

As we noted earlier, people with PTSD are more physiologically reactive to situations that remind them of their trauma (Southwick, Yehuda, & Wang, 1998). This activity includes changes in several neurotransmitters and hormones involved in the fight-or-flight response. In addition, studies using positron emission tomography (PET) have found some differences between PTSD sufferers and controls in activity levels in parts of the brain involved in the regulation of emotion and the fight-or-flight response (Charney et al., 1994). While imagining combat scenes, combat veterans with PTSD show increased blood flow in the anterior cingulate gyrus and the amygdala—areas of the brain that may play a role in emotion and memory. In contrast, combat veterans without PTSD did not show increases in blood flow in these regions while imagining combat scenes (see Figure 14-5; Shin et al., 1997). Some studies also show damage to the hippocampus among PTSD patients (Figure 14-6; Bremner, 1998). The hippocampus is involved in memory. Damage to it may result in some of the memory problems that PTSD sufferers report.

It is not clear whether these neurobiological abnormalities in PTSD sufferers is a cause or a consequence of their disorder. Deterioration of the hippocampus could be the result of extremely high levels of cortisol at the time of the trauma (Bremner, 1998). Interestingly, however, resting levels of cortisol among PTSD sufferers (when they are not being exposed to reminders of their trauma) tend to be lower than among people without PTSD (Yehuda, 2000). Because cortisol may act to shut down sympathetic nervous system activity after stress, the lower levels of cortisol among PTSD sufferers may result in prolonged activity of the sympathetic nervous system following stress. As a result, they may more easily develop a conditioned fear

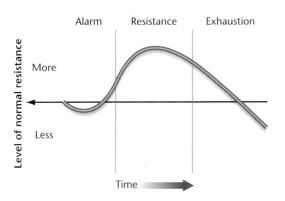

▌ Figure 14-4
The General Adaptation Syndrome
According to Hans Selye, the body reacts to a stressor in three phases. In the first phase, *alarm,* the body mobilizes to confront the threat, which temporarily expends resources and lowers resistance. In the *resistance* phase, the body actively confronts the threat, and resistance is high. If the threat continues, the body moves into the *exhaustion* phase.

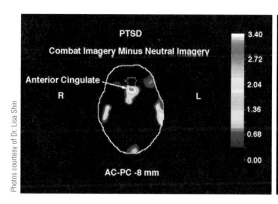 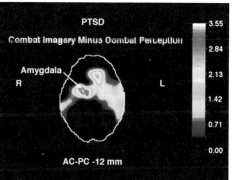

▮ Figure 14-5
PTSD and Blood Flow in the Brain
Studies using positron emission tomography show greater blood flow in the anterior cingulate and amygdala in combat veterans with PTSD than those without PTSD. (Shin, Kosslyn, Alpert, Rauch, Macklin, & Pitman (1997). "Visual Imagery and Perception in Posttraumatic Stress Disorder: A Positron Emission Tomographic Investigation." © *Archives of General Psychiatry 54*, 233–241.)

of stimuli associated with the trauma and subsequently develop PTSD. One longitudinal study assessed cortisol levels in people who had been injured in a traffic accident 1 to 2 hours previously (Yehuda, McFarlane, & Salev, 1998). Six months later, these people were evaluated for the presence of PTSD. Those who did develop the disorder had shown cortisol levels immediately after the trauma that were significantly lower than those who did not develop the disorder. Similar results were found in a study of rape survivors (Resnick et al., 1995). These data suggest that people who develop PTSD have lower baseline levels of cortisol before they experience their trauma and possibly that abnormally low cortisol levels contribute to the development of PTSD. ▮

How Stress Affects Health

Attempts to adapt to the continued presence of a stressor may deplete the body's resources and make it vulnerable to illness. The wear and tear on the body that results from chronic overactivity of the physiological response to stress is referred to as allostatic load. Chronic stress can lead to physical disorders such as ulcers, high blood pressure, and heart disease. It may also impair the immune system, decreasing the body's ability to fight invading bacteria and viruses. Indeed, doctors estimate that emotional stress plays an important role in more than half of all medical problems.

Psychophysiological disorders are physical disorders in which emotions are believed to play a central role. A common misconception is that people with psychophysiological disorders are not really sick and do not need medical attention. On the contrary, the symptoms of psychophysiological illness reflect physiological disturbances associated with tissue damage and pain. A peptic ulcer caused by stress is indistinguishable from an ulcer caused by a factor unrelated to stress, such as long-term heavy usage of aspirin.

Traditionally, research in psychophysiology focused on such illnesses as asthma, hypertension (high blood pressure), ulcers, colitis, and rheumatoid arthritis. Researchers looked for relationships between specific illnesses and characteristic attitudes toward, or ways of

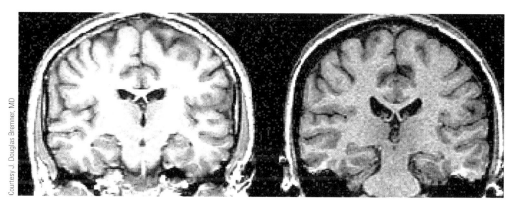

▮ Figure 14-6
PTSD and the Hippocampus
Studies using magnetic resonance imaging show deterioration in the hippocampus of people with PTSD (right scan) compared with people without PTSD (left scan). (From Bremner, 1998)

coping with, stressful life events. For example, individuals with hypertension were said to feel that life is threatening and that they must therefore be on guard at all times. Those suffering from colitis were believed to be angry but unable to express their anger. However, most studies that reported characteristic attitudes to be related to specific illnesses have not been replicated (Overmier & Murison, 1998). Thus, the hypothesis that people who react to stress in similar ways will be vulnerable to the same illnesses has generally not been confirmed. An important exception is research on coronary heart disease and Type A behavior patterns, as we will see shortly.

CORONARY HEART DISEASE The overarousal caused by chronic stressors may contribute to coronary heart disease. **Coronary heart disease** (CHD) occurs when the blood vessels that supply the heart muscles are narrowed or closed by the gradual buildup of a hard, fatty substance called plaque, blocking the flow of oxygen and nutrients to the heart. This can lead to pain, called *angina pectoris*, that radiates across the chest and arm. When the flow of oxygen to the heart is completely blocked, it can cause a myocardial infarction or heart attack.

Coronary heart disease is a leading cause of death and chronic illness. Nearly half of the deaths in the United States every year are caused by coronary heart disease, in many cases before the individual reaches age 65. There seems to be a genetic contribution to coronary heart disease: People with family histories of CHD are at increased risk for the disease. CHD is also linked to high blood pressure, high serum cholesterol, diabetes, smoking, and obesity.

People in high-stress jobs are at increased risk for CHD, particularly if their jobs are highly demanding but provide them little control (Schneiderman, Antoni, Saab, & Ironson, 2001). An example of such a job is an assembly line in which rapid, high-quality production is expected and the work is machine-paced rather than self-paced.

In one study, 900 middle-aged men and women were followed over a 10-year period and examined for the development of heart disease. Two independent methods—occupational titles and the participants' reports of their feelings about their jobs—were used to classify workers along the dimensions of job demand and job control. The results showed that both men and women in occupations classified as "high strain" (high demand combined with low control) had a risk of coronary heart disease 1.5 times greater than the risk faced by those in other occupations (Karasek, Baker, Marxer, Ahlbom, & Theorell, 1981; Karasek, Theorell, Schwartz, Pieper, & Alfredsson, 1982; Pickering et al., 1996).

A demanding family life in addition to a stressful job can adversely affect a woman's cardiovascular health.

Employed women in general are not at higher risk for CHD than homemakers. However, employed mothers are more likely to develop heart disease. The likelihood of disease increases with the number of children for working women but not for homemakers (Haynes & Feinleib, 1980). Yet women who have flexibility in and control over their work, and a good income so that they can afford to hire help with housecleaning and child-care tasks, seem not to suffer as much either physically or psychologically from their role overload (Lennon & Rosenfield, 1992; Taylor, 1999).

One group that lives in chronically stressful settings and has particularly high rates of high blood pressure is low-income African-Americans. They often do not have adequate financial resources for daily living, may be poorly educated and therefore have trouble finding good jobs, or live in violent neighborhoods. All these conditions have been linked to higher blood pressure (Williams, 1995).

Experimental studies with animals have shown that disruption of the social environment can induce pathology that resembles coronary artery disease (Manuck, Kaplan, & Matthews, 1986; Sapolsky, 1990). Some of these experiments have been conducted with a type of macaque monkey whose social organization involves the establishment of stable hierarchies of social dominance: Dominant and submissive animals can be identified within a given group on the basis of the animals' social behavior. The introduction of unfamiliar monkeys into an established social group is a stressor that leads to increased aggressive behavior as group members attempt to reestablish a social dominance hierarchy (Manuck, Kaplan, & Matthews, 1986).

In these studies, some monkey groups remained stable with fixed memberships, and other groups were stressed by the repeated introduction of new members. After about 2 years under these conditions, the high-ranking or dominant males in the unstable social condition showed more extensive atherosclerosis than the subordinate males (Sapolsky, 1990).

THE IMMUNE SYSTEM A relatively new area of research in behavioral medicine is **psychoneuroimmunology, the study of how the body's immune system is affected by stress and other psychological variables** (Ader, 2001). By means of specialized cells called *lymphocytes*, the immune system protects the body from disease-causing microorganisms. It affects the individual's susceptibility to infectious diseases, allergies, cancers, and autoimmune disorders (that is, diseases such as rheumatoid arthritis, in which the immune cells attack the normal tissue of the body). There is no single index of the quality of an individual's immune functioning, or immunocompetence. The immune system is a complex one with many interacting components, and different investigators have chosen to focus on different components of the system.

Evidence from a number of areas suggests that stress affects the immune system's ability to defend the body (Schneiderman et al., 2001). One study indicates that the common belief that we are more likely to catch a cold when we are under stress is probably correct (Cohen, Tyrel, & Smith, 1991). Researchers exposed 400 healthy volunteers to a nasal wash containing one of five cold viruses or an innocuous salt solution. The participants answered questions about the number of stressful events they had experienced in the past year, the degree to which they felt able to cope with the demands of daily life, and the frequency with which they experienced negative emotions such as anger and depression. Based on these data, each participant was assigned a stress index ranging from 3 (lowest stress) to 12 (highest stress). The volunteers were examined daily for cold symptoms and for the presence of cold viruses or virus-specific antibodies in their upper respiratory secretions.

The majority of the virus-exposed volunteers showed signs of infection, but only about a third actually developed colds. The rates of viral infection and of actual cold symptoms increased in accordance with the reported stress levels. Compared with the lowest-stress group, volunteers who reported the highest stress were significantly more likely to become infected with the cold virus and almost twice as likely to develop a cold (see Figure 14-7). These results held even after controlling statistically for a number of variables that might influence immune functioning, such as age, allergies, cigarette and alcohol use, exercise, and diet. However, the two indicators of immunocompetence that were measured in this study did not show any specific change as a result of stress, so exactly how stress lowered the body's resistance to the cold virus remains to be determined.

This study is unusual in that the participants were exposed to a virus, lived in special quarters near the laboratory for a number of days both before and after exposure, and were carefully monitored. Such controlled conditions for studying the effects of stress on health are seldom feasible. Most studies look at individuals undergoing a particularly stressful event—such as academic pressure, bereavement, or marital disruption—and evaluate their immunocompetence (Cohen, 1996). For example, a study of people who survived Hurricane Andrew in 1992 found that those who experienced more damage to their homes or whose lives were more threatened by the storm showed poorer immune system functioning than people whose homes and lives had been safer (Ironson et al., 1997). Similarly, following the 1994 Northridge earthquake in the Los Angeles area, people whose lives had been more severely disrupted showed more decline in immune system functioning than those who had not experienced as much stress as a result of the earthquake (Solomon, Segerstrom, Grohr, Kemeny, & Fahey, 1997). People who worried more about the impact of the earthquake on their lives were especially likely to show detriments in natural killer cells, a type of T-cell that seeks out and destroys cells that have been infected with a virus (Segerstrom, Solomon, Kemeny, & Fahey, 1998). It doesn't take a natural disaster to affect people's immune systems. A study of dental students found that dental wounds healed 40% more slowly if the wounds were obtained a few days before a stressful exam than if the wounds were obtained during summer vacation (Marucha et al., 1998). The slow healing of wounds during exam period was associated with poorer immune system functioning.

One factor that appears to be important is the extent to which an individual can control stress. Recall that controllability is one of the variables that determines the severity of stress. A series of animal studies demonstrated that uncontrollable shock has a much greater effect on the immune system than controllable shock (Laudenslager, Ryan, Drugan, Hyson, & Maier, 1983; Visintainer, Volpicelli, & Seligman, 1982). In these experiments, rats were subjected to electric shock. One group could press a lever to turn off the shock. The other animals received an identical sequence of shocks, but their levers were ineffective (see Figure 14-8). In one study using this procedure, the investigators looked at how readily the rats' T-cells multiplied when challenged by an invader. (T-cells are lymphocytes that secrete

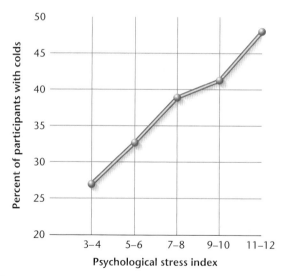

▌ Figure 14-7
Stress and Colds
This graph shows the percentage of virus-exposed people who developed colds as a function of the degree of stress reported. (After S. Cohen, D. A. J. Tyrrell, and A. P. Smith (1991) "Psychological Stress and Susceptibility to the Common Cold," *The New England Journal of Medicine*, 325:606–612. Used with permission from S. Cohen.)

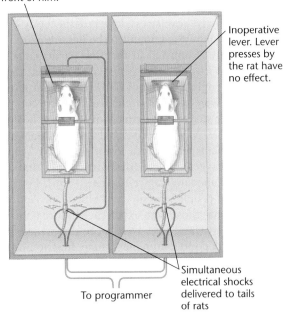

Operative lever. The rat can terminate a shock by pressing the lever in front of him.

Inoperative lever. Lever presses by the rat have no effect.

To programmer

Simultaneous electrical shocks delivered to tails of rats

▌**Figure 14-8**
Yoked Controls in a Stress Experiment
A series of electrical shocks are preprogrammed to be delivered simultaneously to the tails of the two male rats. The rat on the left can terminate a shock when it occurs by pressing the lever. The rat on the right has no control in the situation (lever is inoperative), but he is yoked to the first rat. That is, when the first rat receives a shock, the yoked rat simultaneously receives the same shock, and the shock remains on until the first rat presses his lever. The lever presses of the yoked rat have no effect on the shock sequence for either animal.

chemicals that kill harmful cells, such as cancer cells.) They found that the T-cells from rats that could control the shock multiplied as readily as those from rats that were not stressed at all. T-cells from rats exposed to uncontrollable shock, on the other hand, multiplied only weakly. Thus, shock (stress) interfered with the immune response only in rats that could not control it (Laudenslager et al., 1983).

In another study, the investigators implanted tumor cells into rats, gave them shocks, and recorded whether the rats' natural defenses rejected the cells or whether they developed into tumors. Only 27% of the rats that were given uncontrollable shocks rejected the tumors, but 63% of the rats that could turn the shocks off rejected the tumors—even though the rats received identical amounts of shock (Visintainer et al., 1982).

Perceptions of control also appear to mediate the influence of stress on the immune system in humans. In a study of the effects of marital separation or divorce on immune functioning, the partner who had initiated the separation (the one more in control of the situation) was less distressed, reported better health, and showed better immune system functioning than the other partner (Kiecolt-Glaser et al., 1988). Similarly, studies of women with breast cancer have found that those with a pessimistic perspective—that is, who felt that they had little control over events—were the most likely to develop new tumors over a 5-year period, even after the physical severity of their diseases was taken into account (Levy & Heiden, 1991; Watson et al., 1999).

Some of the best evidence that stress can affect the immune system comes from studies showing that at least some types of supportive psychological interventions can slow the progress of cancer (Baum & Posluszny, 1999). For example, several years ago researcher David Spiegel and colleagues began a study in which they randomly assigned women with metastatic breast cancer either to a series of weekly support groups or to no support groups (all of the women were receiving standard medical care for their cancers). The focus of the groups was on facing death and learning to live one's remaining days to the fullest. The researchers had no intention of affecting the course of the cancers and did not believe that it was possible to do so. They wanted only to improve the quality of life for the women in their study.

The researchers were quite surprised when, 48 months after the study began, all of the women who had not been in the support groups had died of their cancers whereas a third of the women in the support groups were still alive (Spiegel, Bloom, Kraemer, & Gottheil, 1989). The average survival time (from the time the study began) for the women in the support groups was about 40 months and about 19 months for the women who were not in the support groups. There were no differences between the groups, other than their participation in the weekly support meetings, that could explain the differences in average survival time. The two groups did not differ in the initial seriousness of their cancers, the type of therapy received, or other variables that might have affected their survival time. The researchers were forced to conclude that their intervention actually increased the number of months that the women in the support group lived (for similar results, see Helgeson et al., 1998; Richardson, Shelton, Krailo, & Levine, 1990).

How did the intervention affect the progress of these women's cancers? It is not clear, but the women in the support groups gained a great deal of psychological strength from the groups, which were intensely emotional and supportive. Members discussed their fear of dying, visited other members in the hospital, grieved when other members died, attended their funerals, and mourned the loss of abilities and friendships. In addition to sharing grief, the women in these groups derived tremendous strength from one another. They came to feel like experts in living, a wisdom that grew from their confrontation with death. They chose new life projects ranging from imparting values to their children to writing books of poetry (Spiegel, 1991). In addition, group members showed lower levels of emotional distress and learned how to control their physical pain better than women who did not participate in the support groups. Similarly, psychological interventions can substantially influence the time people need to recover from major surgery (see Kiecolt-Glaser, McGuire, Robles, & Glaser, 2002). When people are given information about what to expect before surgery and techniques for reducing pain after surgery, they show faster improvement after surgery, require less pain medication, stay in the hospital a shorter period, and have fewer postoperative complications.

The immune system is incredibly complicated, employing several different weapons that interact to defend the body. Much remains to be discovered about the immune system and even more about its relationship to the nervous system. Scientists once believed that the immune system operated quite independently, isolated from other physiological systems. But current studies are making it increasingly evident that the immune system and the nervous system have numerous anatomical and physiological connections. For example, researchers are discovering that lymphocytes have receptors for a number of neurotransmitters and that these immune system cells are equipped to receive messages from the nervous system that may alter the way they behave. The discovery of a link between neurotransmitters and the immune system is important because negative emotional states such as anxiety or depression can affect neurotransmitter levels.

In sum, as research on psychoneuroimmunology yields additional information about the links between the nervous and immune systems, we will gain a clearer understanding of how mental attitudes affect health.

HEALTH-RELATED BEHAVIORS Certain health-related behaviors can greatly increase our susceptibility to illness. Smoking is one of the leading causes of cardiovascular disease and emphysema. A high-fat diet contributes to many forms of cancer as well as to cardiovascular disease. People who do not regularly engage in a moderate amount of exercise are at increased risk for heart disease and earlier death (Baum & Posluszny, 1999). Excessive alcohol consumption can lead to liver disease and cardiovascular disease and may contribute to some cancers. And failure to use condoms during sex significantly increases the risk of contracting HIV. Scientists estimate that most of the diseases people die from in industrialized countries are heavily influenced by health-related behaviors (Taylor, 1999).

When we're stressed, we often engage in unhealthy behaviors.

When we are stressed, we may be less likely to engage in healthy behaviors. Students taking exams stay up all night, often for several nights in a row. They may skip meals and snack on junk food. Many men whose wives have died do not know how to cook for themselves and therefore may eat poorly or hardly at all. In their grief, some bereaved men increase their rates of alcohol consumption and smoking. People under stress cease normal exercise routines and become sedentary. Thus, stress may indirectly affect health by reducing rates of positive health-related behaviors and increasing rates of negative behaviors.

Engaging in unhealthy behaviors may also increase a person's subjective sense of stress. Drinking too much alcohol on a regular basis can interfere with cognitive functioning; a person who consumes excessive amounts of alcohol cannot think as clearly or quickly as one who does not drink excessively. Excessive drinking can also induce lethargy, fatigue, and a mild or moderate sense of depression that makes it difficult to overcome stressful situations or just keep up with the demands of everyday life.

Similarly, people who do not get enough sleep show impairments in memory, learning, logical reasoning, arithmetic skills, complex verbal processing, and decision making. Sleeping for only 5 hours per night for just two nights significantly reduces performance on math problems and creative thinking tasks. So, staying up late to prepare for an exam can actually decrease performance on the test (Dinges & Broughton, 1989).

Among people who already have a serious illness such as cancer or cardiovascular disease, stress can reduce their motivation or ability to engage in behaviors that are critical to their recovery or survival (Schneiderman et al., 2001). For example, they may skip appointments with their physician or fail to take necessary medications. They may not follow diets that are essential for their health; for example, a diabetic may not control sugar intake. Studies of persons infected with HIV disease suggest that those under more stress are more likely to engage in unprotected sexual activity or intravenous drug use (Fishbein et al., 1998).

In contrast, people who engage in a healthy lifestyle—eating a low-fat diet, drinking alcohol in moderation, getting enough sleep, and exercising regularly—often report that stressful events seem more manageable and that they feel more in control of their lives. Thus, engaging in healthy behaviors can help reduce the stressfulness of life as well as reducing the risk or progression of a number of serious diseases.

◆ Interim Summary

- The body reacts to stress with the fight-or-flight response. The sympathetic nervous system causes increased heart rate, elevated blood pressure, dilated pupils, and the release of extra sugar from the liver. The adrenal-cortical system causes the release of adrenocorticotropic hormone (ACTH), which stimulates the release of cortisol in the blood.

- These reactions are part of a general adaptation syndrome, a set of responses displayed by all organisms in response to stress. The syndrome consists of three phases: alarm, resistance, and exhaustion.

- Psychophysiological disorders are physical disorders in which emotions are believed to play a central role. For example, stress can contribute to coronary heart disease.

- Psychoneuroimmunology is the study of how psychological factors can affect the immune system. Stress may impair the functioning of the immune system, increasing the risk of immune-related disorders.

- Stress may affect health directly by creating chronic overarousal of the sympathetic division of the autonomic nervous system or the adrenal-cortical system or by impairing the immune system. People under stress also may not engage in positive health-related behaviors, and this may lead to illness.

◆ Critical Thinking Questions

1. How can we help people with a serious disease like cancer change in ways that might slow the progress of the disease without making them feel that they are being blamed for having the disease?

2. What are some of your unhealthiest behaviors? What prevents you from changing them?

PSYCHOLOGICAL FACTORS AND STRESS RESPONSES

As noted earlier, events that are uncontrollable or unpredictable, or that challenge our views of ourselves, tend to be experienced as stressful. Some people appear more likely than others to appraise events in these ways. There are three basic theories about why some people are prone to appraise events as stressful: the psychoanalytic, behavioral, and cognitive theories.

PSYCHOANALYTIC THEORY

Psychoanalysts distinguish between **objective anxiety,** which is a reasonable response to a harmful situation, and **neurotic anxiety,** which is anxiety out of proportion to the actual danger. Freud believed that neurotic anxiety stems from unconscious conflicts between unacceptable impulses and the constraints imposed by reality (see Chapter 13). Many impulses pose a threat to the individual because they are contradictory to personal or social values. A woman may not consciously acknowledge that she has strong hostile feelings toward her mother because these feelings conflict with her belief that a child should love her parents. If she acknowledged her true feelings, she would destroy her self-concept as a loving daughter and risk the loss of her mother's love and support. When she begins to feel angry toward her mother, the resulting anxiety serves as a signal of potential danger. Thus, this woman may experience even a minor conflict with her mother, such as a disagreement about where the family should go for vacation or what to have for dinner, as a major stressor. A woman who is not so conflicted in her feelings about her mother would experience such a conflict as a less severe stressor.

According to psychoanalytic theory, we all have unconscious conflicts. For some people, however, these conflicts are more numerous and severe, and as a result these people experience more events as stressful.

BEHAVIORAL THEORY

Although Freud saw unconscious conflicts as the internal source of stress responses, behaviorists have focused on ways in which individuals learn to associate stress responses with certain situations. People may also react to specific situations with fear and anxiety because those situations caused them harm or were stressful in the past. Some phobias develop through such classical conditioning (see Chapter 7). For example, a person whose car nearly slid off the road on the side of a steep mountain may now experience anxiety every time she is in a high place. Or a student who failed a final exam in a particular classroom may feel anxious the next year when he reenters that room to take another class.

Sometimes fears are difficult to extinguish. If your first reaction is to avoid or escape the anxiety-producing situation, you may not be able to determine when the situation is no longer dangerous. A little girl who has been punished for assertive behavior in the past may never learn that it is acceptable for her to express her wishes in new situations because she never tries. People can continue to have fears about particular situations because they chronically avoid the situation and therefore never challenge their fears.

COGNITIVE THEORY

A modification of the learned helplessness theory proposed by Abramson, Seligman, & Teasdale (1978) focuses on the attributions or causal explanations people give for important events. These researchers argued that when people attribute negative events to causes that are internal to them ("it's my fault"), are stable in time ("it's going to last forever"), and are global, affecting many areas of their lives, they are likely to show a helpless, depressed response to negative events. For example, if a man whose wife left him attributed the breakup of his marriage to his "bad" personality (an internal, stable, and global attribution), he would tend to lose self-esteem and expect future relationships to fail as well. In turn, he would show lowered motivation, passivity, and sadness. In contrast, if he made a less pessimistic attribution, such as attributing the failure of his marriage to incompatibility between himself and his wife, he would tend to maintain his self-esteem and motivation for the future.

Abramson and colleagues propose that people have consistent **attributional styles,** or styles of making attributions for the events in their lives, and that these styles influence the degree to which people view events as stressful and have helpless, depressed reactions to difficult events. A number of studies support this theory (Peterson & Bossio, 2001). In one study, researchers assessed the attributional styles of students a few weeks before a midterm exam. Just before the exam, they also asked the students

what grade they would consider a failure and what grade they would be happy with. After the students received their grades, they measured the students' levels of sadness and depression. Among students who received a grade below their standards, those who had a pessimistic attributional style were significantly more depressed than those who had a more optimistic attributional style (Metalsky, Halberstadt, & Abramson, 1987).

Pessimism is also linked to physical illness (Taylor, Kemeny, Reed, Bower, & Gruenewald, 2000). Students who are more pessimistic report more illness and make more visits to the health center than students with a more optimistic attributional style. In a 35-year study of men in the Harvard classes of 1939–1940, researchers found that men who had a pessimistic attributional style at age 25 were more likely to develop physical illness over the subsequent years than men with a more optimistic attributional style (Peterson, Seligman, & Vaillant, 1988). Other studies have found that pessimists recover more slowly from coronary bypass surgery and have more severe angina than optimists (Scheier et al., 1989).

How does pessimism affect health? People who are pessimistic tend to appraise events as more stressful. In turn, this greater sense of stress may contribute to poor health by causing the chronic arousal of the body's fight-or-flight response, resulting in the type of physiological damage discussed earlier. Several studies have found evidence for this. In one, the blood pressure of pessimists and optimists was monitored daily for 3 days. The pessimists had chronically higher blood pressure levels than the optimists across the 3 days (Raikkonen et al., 1999).

The chronic physiological arousal associated with pessimism has also been linked to lowered immune system functioning. For example, a study of older adults found that those who were pessimistic had poorer im-

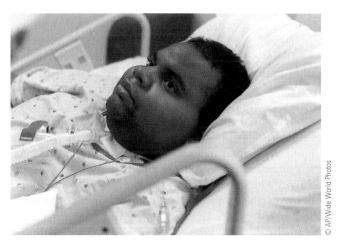

People who are pessimistic do not recover from illnesses or surgery as quickly as people who are optimistic.

mune system functioning than those who were optimistic (Kamen-Siegel, Rodin, & Seligman, 1991). A study of gay men who were HIV-positive found that those who blamed themselves for negative events showed more decline in immune functioning over 18 months than those who engaged in less self-blaming attributions (Segerstrom, Taylor, Kemeny, Reed, & Visscher, 1996). Another study of gay men found that among both HIV-positive and HIV-negative men, those who were more pessimistic and fatalistic were less likely to engage in healthy behaviors, such as maintaining a proper diet, getting enough sleep, and exercising (Taylor et al., 1992). This is particularly important for the HIV-positive men, because engaging in these behaviors can reduce the risk of developing AIDS. Thus, a pessimistic outlook may affect health directly, by reducing immune system functioning, or indirectly, by reducing a person's tendency to engage in health-promoting behavior.

HARDINESS Another line of research has focused on people who are most resistant to stress—who do not become physically or emotionally impaired even in the face of major stressful events (Kobasa, 1979; Kobasa, Maddi, & Kahn, 1982). This characteristic is referred to as **hardiness.** In one study, more than 600 men who were executives or managers in the same company were given checklists and asked to describe all of the stressful events and illnesses they had experienced over the previous 3 years. Two groups were selected for comparison. The first group scored above average on both stressful events and illness; the second group scored equally high on stress but below average on illness. Members of both groups then filled out detailed personality questionnaires. Analysis of the results indicated that the high-stress, low-illness men differed from the men who became ill under stress on three major dimensions: They were more actively involved in their work and social lives, they were more oriented toward challenge and change, and they felt more in control of events in their lives (Kobasa, 1979).

These personality differences could be the result rather than the cause of illness. For example, it is hard for people to be involved in work or in social activity when they are ill. The investigators therefore conducted a longitudinal study that considered the personality characteristics of business executives before they became ill and then monitored their life stress and the extent of their illnesses for 2 years. The results showed that the executives whose attitudes toward life could be rated high on involvement, feelings of control, and positive responses to change remained healthier over time than men who scored low on these dimensions (Kobasa, Maddi, & Kahn, 1982). The most important factors appear to be a sense of control and commitment to goals

(Cohen & Edwards, 1989). Other studies of women (Wiebe & McCallum, 1986) and persons symptomatic with HIV disease (Farber, Schwartz, Schaper, Moonen, & McDaniel, 2000) have also found that hardiness predicts better psychological and physical health.

The personalities of stress-resistant or hardy individuals are characterized by commitment, control, and challenge. These characteristics are interrelated with the factors that influence the perceived severity of stressors. For example, the sense of being in control of life events reflects feelings of competence and also influences the appraisal of stressful events. Challenge also involves cognitive evaluation, the belief that change is normal in life and should be viewed as an opportunity for growth rather than as a threat to security.

FINDING MEANING In a related line of work, researchers have been examining a somewhat surprising but heart-warming phenomenon: Many people confronted with a major trauma say that they feel their lives have changed in extremely positive ways as a result of their experiences. Studies of bereaved people, cancer patients, myocardial infarction patients, bone marrow transplant patients, stroke victims and their caregivers, and men testing positive for HIV find that, as a consequence of their experience, they feel their lives have more meaning and they have grown in important ways (Tennen & Affleck, 1999). Take, for example, this quote from a woman who recently lost someone she loved very dearly.

> I tend to look at it generally as if all the things that happen in my life are a gift, for whatever reason, or however they happen. It doesn't necessarily have to be only pleasant gifts, but everything that happens . . . there's a meaning. I've had a lot of suffering in my life . . . and through that I've learned a great deal. While I wouldn't want to go back and relive that, I'm grateful for it because it makes me who I am. There's a lot of joys and sorrows, but they all enrich life. (Alicia, quoted in Nolen-Hoeksema & Larson, 1999, p. 143)

People often say that they feel they grew in character as a result of their experience, discovering new strengths they didn't know they had. They also say they gained a healthier perspective on what is important in their lives and made major changes in their lives based on this new perspective. Many people report that their relationships with friends and family members are deeper and more meaningful now.

In turn, finding meaning or positive growth in a trauma seems to help people adjust, both physically and psychologically. Several studies have found that people who finding meaning or growth in traumatic events show less depression and anxiety after the event than others. For example, in a study of recently bereaved peo-

Finding meaning in a loss can help people cope with it.

ple, Davis and colleagues (1998) showed that those who found some meaning in their loss or felt they grew positively showed less depression and fewer symptoms of post-traumatic stress disorder than those who did not over the 18 months following their loss. It did not matter to psychological health what type of meaning or growth people found, as long as they found some sort of meaning or growth in their experience.

Some studies also suggest that finding meaning is related to the course of physiological disease. For example, Affleck and colleagues found that men who had had a heart attack and who felt they had grown personally as a result of the heart attack, such as changing their philosophy of life or values, were less likely to have a subsequent heart attack and had less cardiac disease over the next 8 years (Affleck, Tennen, Croog, & Levine, 1987). In a study of men who were HIV positive, Bower and colleagues found that those who had found some meaning in the loss of a friend or partner to AIDS maintained healthier immune systems (indexed by CD4 T helper cells) and were less likely to die from AIDS over a 2- to 3 follow-up period (Bower, Kemeny, Taylor, & Fahey, 1998).

Why are some people able to find meaning or growth in trauma and others do not? Optimism seems to play a role. Optimists are more likely to report positive changes, benefits, or growth following stressful events (see Taylor et al., 2000). Similarly, hardy people appear to perceive more benefits from their stressful experiences. For example, a study of U.S. soldiers participating in a peacekeeping mission to Bosnia showed that those who scored high on measures of hardiness during their deployment were more likely to believe they had obtained benefits, such as personal growth, from their work in Bosnia than those who were not hardy (Britt, Adler, & Bartone, 2001).

THE TYPE A PATTERN

A behavior pattern or personality style that has received a great deal of attention is the **type A pattern.** Over the years, physicians had noticed that heart attack victims tend to be hostile, aggressive, impatient individuals who were overinvolved in their work. In the 1950s, two cardiologists defined a set of behaviors that seemed to characterize patients with coronary heart disease, which were labeled the type A pattern (Friedman & Rosenman, 1974). People who exhibit this behavior pattern are extremely competitive and achievement oriented; they have a sense of time urgency, find it difficult to relax, and become impatient and angry when confronted with delays or with people whom they view as incompetent. Although outwardly self-confident, they are prey to constant feelings of self-doubt, and they push themselves to accomplish more and more in less and less time. Some common type A behaviors are listed in Table 14-2.

Type B people do not exhibit the characteristics listed for type A. They are able to relax without feeling guilty and work without becoming agitated. They lack a sense of time urgency, with its accompanying impatience, and are not easily roused to anger.

To examine the relationship between type A behavior and coronary heart disease, more than 3,000 healthy, middle-aged men were evaluated by means of a structured interview that was designed to be irritating. The interviewer kept the participant waiting without explanation and then asked a series of questions about being competitive, hostile, and pressed for time, such as "Do you ever feel rushed or under pressure?" "Do you eat quickly?" "Would you describe yourself as ambitious and hard driving or relaxed and easy-going?" and "Do you resent it if someone is late?" The interviewer interrupted, asked questions in a challenging manner, and made irrelevant remarks. The interview was scored more on the way the person behaved in answering the questions than on the answers themselves. For example, type A men spoke loudly in an explosive manner, talked over

● Table 14-2
Type A Behaviors

Some behaviors that characterize people prone to coronary heart disease. *(From Type A Behavior and Your Heart by Meyer Friedman and R. N. Rosenman, copyright © 1974 by Meyer Friedman. Used by permission of Alfred A. Knopf, a division of Random House, Inc.)*

Thinking of or doing two things at once

Scheduling more and more activities into less and less time

Failing to notice or be interested in the environment or things of beauty

Hurrying the speech of others

Becoming unduly irritated when forced to wait in line or when driving behind a car you think is moving too slowly

Believing that if you want something done well, you have to do it yourself

Gesticulating when you talk

Frequent knee jiggling or rapid tapping of your fingers

Explosive speech patterns or frequent use of obscenities

Making a fetish of always being on time

Having difficulty sitting and doing nothing

Playing nearly every game to win, even when playing with children

Measuring your own and others' success in terms of numbers (number of patients seen, articles written, and so on)

Lip clicking, head nodding, fist clenching, table pounding, or sucking in of air when speaking

Becoming impatient while watching others do things you think you can do better or faster

Rapid blinking or tic-like eyebrow lifting

---

the interviewer so as not to be interrupted, appeared tense and tight-lipped, and described hostile incidents with great emotional intensity. Type B men sat in a relaxed manner, spoke slowly and softly, were easily interrupted, and smiled often.

After the participants had been classified as type A or type B, they were studied for 8½ years. During that period, type A men had twice as many heart attacks or other forms of coronary heart disease as type B men. These results held up even after diet, age, smoking, and other variables were taken into account (Rosenman et al., 1976). Other studies confirmed this twofold risk and linked type A behavior to heart disease in both men and women (Kornitzer et al., 1982; Haynes, Feinleib, & Kannel, 1980). In addition, type A behavior correlates with severity of coronary artery blockage, as determined at autopsy or in x-ray studies of the inside of coronary blood vessels (Friedman et al., 1968; Williams et al., 1988).

In 1981, the American Heart Association concluded that type A behavior should be classified as a risk factor for coronary heart disease. However, two subsequent studies failed to find a link between type A behavior and heart disease (Case, Heller, Case, & Moss, 1985; Shekelle, Neaton, Jacobs, Hulley, & Blackburn, 1983). Although some researchers attribute this failure to the way type A individuals were assessed in these studies, others believe that the original definition of type A behavior is too diffuse. They argue that time urgency and competitiveness are not the most important components. Instead, the crucial variable may be hostility.

Several studies have found that a person's level of hostility is a better predictor of heart disease than his or her overall level of type A behavior. Accordingly, several studies have used personality tests rather than interviews to measure hostility. For example, a 25-year study of 118 male lawyers found that those who scored high in hostility on a personality inventory taken in law school were five times more likely to die before age 50 than other classmates (Barefoot et al., 1989). In a similar follow-up study of physicians, hostility scores obtained in medical school predicted the incidence of coronary heart disease, as well as mortality from all causes (Barefoot, Williams, & Dahlstrom, 1983). In both studies, this relationship was independent of the effects of smoking, age, and high blood pressure. There is some evidence that when anger is repressed or held in, it may be even more destructive to the heart than anger that is expressed (Spielberger et al., 1985; Wright, 1988).

How does type A behavior or hostility lead to coronary heart disease? A possible biological mechanism is the way the sympathetic nervous system responds to stress. When exposed to stressful experimental situations (for example, when faced with the threat of failure, harassment, or competitive task demands), most participants report feeling angry, irritated, and tense. However, participants who score high on hostility as a trait show much larger increases in blood pressure, heart rate, and secretion of stress-related hormones than participants with low hostility scores (Raeikkoenen, Matthews, Flory, & Owens, 1999; Suarez, Kuhn, Schanberg, Williams, & Zimmerman, 1998). The same results are found when type A participants are compared with type B participants. The sympathetic nervous systems of hostile and/or type A individuals appear to be hyperresponsive to stressful situations. All of these physiological changes can damage the heart and blood vessels.

Not surprisingly, hostile people also report higher degrees of interpersonal conflict and less social support than other people (Benotsch et al, 1997). Reductions in social support have direct negative effects on a number of objective and subjective indices of health (see Uchino, Uno, & Holt-Lunstad, 1999). Thus, hostility may have both di-

Type A people lose their temper easily

rect effects on cardiovascular health by increasing chronic arousal and indirect effects by lowering social support.

The good news about the type A behavior pattern is that it can be modified through well-established therapy programs, and people who are able to reduce their type A behavior show lowered risk of coronary heart disease. We will discuss this therapy later in the chapter.

◆ Interim Summary

- Psychoanalytic theory suggests that events are stressful when they arouse our unconscious conflicts.

- Behaviorists argue that people react to specific situations with fear and anxiety because those situations caused them harm or were stressful in the past.

- Cognitive theorists argue that people's attributions or causal explanations influence their stress responses. People who tend to attribute bad events to internal, stable, and global causes are more likely to develop learned helplessness after experiencing such events and to become ill.

- Hardy people tend to see stressful events as challenges and have a strong sense of personal control; these characteristics may protect against the development of illness in the face of stress.

- People who are able to find meaning in a traumatic event are less likely to develop emotional problems.

- People with the type A behavior pattern tend to be hostile, aggressive, impatient individuals who are overinvolved in their work. Studies of men and women show that people who exhibit this pattern are at increased risk for coronary heart disease.

◆ Critical Thinking Questions

1. What might be the benefits of the type A behavior pattern for people with this pattern?

2. What might make some cultures more prone to stress-related health problems than others?

COPING SKILLS

The emotions and physiological arousal created by stressful situations are highly uncomfortable, and this discomfort motivates the individual to do something to alleviate it. The term **coping** is used to refer to the process by which a person attempts to manage stressful demands, and it takes two major forms. A person can focus on the specific problem or situation that has arisen, trying to find some way of changing it or avoiding it in the future. This is called **problem-focused coping**. A person can also focus on alleviating the emotions associated with the stressful situation, even if the situation itself cannot be changed. This is called **emotion-focused coping** (Lazarus & Folkman, 1984). When dealing with a stressful situation, most people use both problem-focused and emotion-focused coping.

PROBLEM-FOCUSED COPING

There are many strategies for solving problems. First, you must define the problem. Then you can generate alternative solutions and weigh the costs and benefits of the alternatives. Eventually, you must choose between alternative solutions and then act upon your choice. Problem-focused strategies can also be directed inward: You can change something about yourself instead of changing the environment. You can change your goals, find alternative sources of gratification, or learn new skills in inward-directed strategies. How skillfully people employ these strategies depends on their range of experiences and capacity for self-control.

Suppose you receive a warning that you are about to fail a course required for graduation. You might confer with the professor, devise a work schedule to fulfill the requirements and then follow it, or you might decide that you cannot fulfill the requirements in the time remaining and sign up to retake the course in summer school. Both of these actions are problem-focused methods of coping.

People who tend to use problem-focused coping in stressful situations show lower levels of depression both during and after the stressful situation (Billings & Moos, 1984). Of course, people who are less depressed may find it easier to use problem-focused coping. But longitudinal studies show that problem-focused coping leads to shorter periods of depression, even taking into account people's initial levels of depression. In addition, therapies that teach depressed people to use problem-focused coping can be effective in helping them overcome their depression and react more adaptively to stressors (Nezu, Nezu, & Perri, 1989).

EMOTION-FOCUSED COPING

People engage in emotion-focused coping to prevent their negative emotions from overwhelming them and making them unable to take action to solve their problems. They also use emotion-focused coping when a problem is uncontrollable.

We try to cope with our negative emotions in many ways. Some researchers have divided these into behavioral strategies and cognitive strategies (Moos, 1988). Behavioral strategies include engaging in physical exercise, using alcohol or other drugs, venting anger, and seeking emotional support from friends. Cognitive strategies include temporarily setting the problem aside ("I decided it wasn't worth worrying about") and reducing the threat by changing the meaning of the situation ("I decided that her friendship wasn't that important to me"). Cognitive strategies often involve reappraising the situation. Obviously, we would expect some behavioral and cognitive strategies to be adaptive and others (such as drinking heavily) to merely cause more stress.

One strategy that appears to help people adjust emotionally and physically to a stressor is seeking emotional support from others. In a study of women who had just undergone surgery for breast cancer, Levy and colleagues (1990) found that those who actively sought social support had higher natural killer cell activity, indicating that

Talking with supportive friends about your problems can be an adaptive coping strategy.

their immune system was attacking the cancer more aggressively. Pennebaker (1990) has found that people who reveal personal traumas, such as being raped or having a spouse commit suicide, to supportive others tend to show more positive physical health both shortly after the trauma and in the long run.

The quality of the social support a person receives after experiencing a trauma strongly influences the impact of that support on the individual's health, however (Rook, 1984). Some friends or relatives can be burdens instead of blessings in times of stress. People whose social networks are characterized by a high level of conflict tend to show poorer physical and emotional health after a major stressor such as bereavement (Windholz, Marmar, & Horowitz, 1985). Conflicted social relationships may affect physical health through the immune system. Kiecolt-Glaser, Glaser, Cacioppo, and Malarkey (1998) found that newlywed couples who became hostile and negative toward each other while discussing a marital problem showed greater decreases in four indicators of immune system functioning than couples who remained calm and nonhostile in discussing marital problems. Couples who became hostile during these discussions also showed elevated blood pressure for a longer period than those who did not become hostile.

Some people engage in a more maladaptive way of coping with negative emotions: They simply deny that they have any negative emotions and push those emotions out of conscious awareness, a strategy that is referred to as repressive coping. People who engage in repressive coping tend to show more autonomic nervous system activity (such as a higher heart rate) in response to stressors than people who do not engage in repressive coping (Brown et al., 1996; Weinberg, Schwartz, & Davidson, 1979). Pushing emotions out of awareness may require real physical work, which results in chronic overarousal and, in turn, in physical illness.

Repressing important aspects of one's identity may also be harmful to one's health. An intriguing study showed that gay men who conceal their homosexual identity may suffer health consequences (Cole et al., 1996). Men who concealed their homosexuality were about three times more likely to develop cancer and certain infectious disease (pneumonia, bronchitis, sinusitis, tuberculosis) over a 5-year period than men who were open about their homosexuality (see Figure 14-9). All of these men were HIV-negative. But another study by the same researchers focused on HIV-positive gay men and found that the disease progressed faster in those who concealed their homosexuality than in those who did not (Cole et al., 1995). The differences in health between the men who were "out" and those who were "closeted" did not reflect differences in health-related behaviors (smoking, exercise). It may be that chronic inhibition of one's

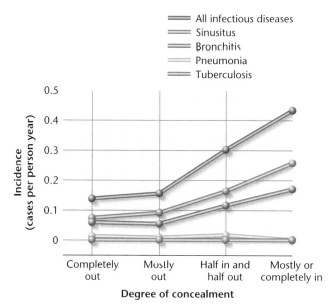

Figure 14-9
Infectious Diseases as a Function of Concealing One's Sexual Orientation
Homosexual men who concealed their homosexuality from others were more prone to several infectious diseases. (From S. W. Cole, M. E. Kemeny, S. E. Taylor, and B. R. Visscher (1996), "Elevated Physical Health Risk Among Gay Men Who Conceal Their Homosexual Identity," *Health Psychology*, 15, pp. 243–251. Copyright © 1996 by the American Psychological Association. Reprinted with permission.)

identity, like chronic inhibition of emotions, can have direct effects on health.

In contrast, talking about negative emotions and important issues in one's life appears to have positive effects on health. In a large series of studies, Pennebaker (1990) has found that encouraging people to reveal personal traumas in diaries or essays improves their health. In one study, 50 healthy undergraduates were randomly assigned to write either about the most traumatic and upsetting events in their lives or about trivial topics for 20 minutes on 4 consecutive days. Blood samples were taken from the students on the day before they began writing, on the last day of writing, and 6 weeks after writing, and it was tested for several markers of immune system functioning. The number of times the students visited the college health center over the 6 weeks after the writing task was also recorded and compared with the number of health center visits the students had made before the study. As Figure 14-10 shows, students who revealed their personal traumas in essays showed more positive immune system functioning and visited the health center less frequently than students in the control group (Pennebaker, Kiecolt-Glaser, & Glaser, 1988). In contrast, the group who wrote about trivial events experienced a slight increase in health center visits and a decrease in lymphocyte response, for unknown reasons. Pennebaker (1997) believes that writ-

ing is helpful because it assists people in finding meaning in the events that happen to them and helps them understand them. Finding meaning and understanding then reduces the negative emotions people feel about events and may therefore reduce the physiological wear and tear associated with chronic negative emotions (see also Bower et al., 1998).

Positive social support may help people adjust better emotionally to stress by leading them to avoid ruminat-

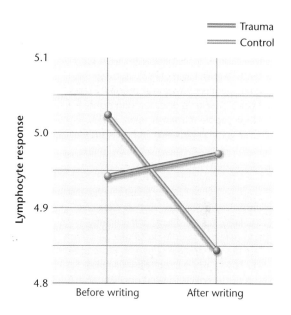

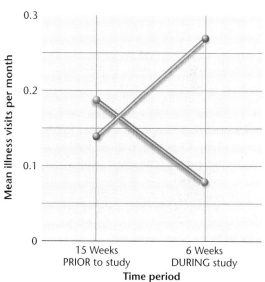

Figure 14-10
Students' Health After Writing About Traumas or Trivialities
Students who revealed personal traumas in a series of essays had stronger immune system functioning and fewer health care visits than students who wrote about trivial events in their essays. (After Pennebaker, Kiecolt-Glaser, & Glaser, 1988)

CUTTING-EDGE RESEARCH
Is Religion Good for Your Health?

Psychologists have had an ambivalent relationship with religion. In recent years, however, an increasing number of studies have suggested that religious people are happier and healthier, on average, than nonreligious people (for reviews, see Ellison & Levin, 1998). Actively religious people show lower mortality rates from a variety of diseases than nonreligious people (Oman & Reed, 1998). They are also generally in better physical health (Koenig et al., 1997). Religious beliefs may have an impact on health because they influence health behaviors. Many religions have prohibitions against unhealthy behaviors, such as excessive drinking, taking drugs, and smoking, and religious people do smoke and drink less than nonreligious people (Koenig et al., 1997). In addition, positive social support is linked to better health, and religious groups offer social support to their members.

There is a much longer tradition of researching the links between religion and mental health. In the past, many psychologists have viewed religion as bad for mental health. They argued that religious beliefs do not help people cope with adversity. Instead, they lead people to accept adversity as "God's will" rather than doing what they can to overcome that adversity. And, they said, if religious people look psychologically healthier in some studies, it is only because they are more prone to deny their psychological problems, or because these studies were biased in favor of finding a positive relationship between religion and psychological health.

It is true that many of the studies on religion and health done over the years were conducted by people who had a stake in the outcome of the study—religious people who wanted to find a positive relationship or nonreligious people who wanted to find a negative relationship. There is an increasing body of well-done psychological science, however, that is consistently finding that people who have a strong religious faith and are active in a religious community

recover better psychologically after traumas than nonreligious people (Ellison & Levin, 1998). For example, a study of parents who had lost an infant to sudden infant death syndrome found that those parents who were active in their churches were better able to cope with the loss of their child (McIntosh, Silver, & Wortman, 1993).

For now, just how religiosity affects mental and physical health is largely unknown (Ellison & Levin, 1998). In addition, most of the research to date has been on people who ascribe to Christian or Jewish beliefs, and little work has been done with people of other faiths. But old assumptions that religion is a danger to health and that religiosity is an unhelpful defense mechanism are being replaced by more open-minded views on the benefits religion offers to people.

 For more information, go online with InfoTrac College Edition. Use your own term or search:

- Religion health
- Religion and psychology

---

ing about the stressor (Nolen-Hoeksema, 1991). Rumination involves isolating ourselves to think about how bad we feel, worrying about the consequences of the stressful event or our emotional state, or repeatedly talking about how bad things are without taking any action to change them. One longitudinal study of recently bereaved people found that those who ruminated in response to their grief were depressed for longer periods (Nolen-Hoeksema & Larson, 1999). In addition, those who were more socially isolated or had a lot of conflict in their social networks were most likely to ruminate.

Another longitudinal study was conducted quite by accident. A group of researchers at Stanford University happened to have obtained measures of emotion-focused coping tendencies and levels of depression and anxiety in a large group of students 2 weeks before the major earthquake that hit the San Francisco Bay area in 1989. They remeasured the students' levels of depression and anxiety 10 days and 7 weeks following the earthquake. They also estimated how much environmental stress the students experienced as a result of the earthquake (that

is, injury to themselves, to their friends or family, and to their homes). The results showed that students who exhibited a ruminative style of coping with emotions before the earthquake were more likely to be depressed and anxious 10 days after the earthquake and 7 weeks later. This was true even after the students' levels of depression and anxiety before the earthquake were taken into account (Nolen-Hoeksema & Morrow, 1991). Students who engaged in dangerous activities, such as drinking alcohol, to avoid their negative moods also tended to remain depressed and anxious. In contrast, students who used pleasant activities to improve their mood and regain a sense of control experienced short and mild periods of depression and anxiety.

You might ask whether people who engage in ruminative coping are more likely to solve their problems. The available evidence suggests that the answer is no. People who engage in ruminative coping are less likely to engage in active problem solving in response to stressors. In contrast, people who use pleasant activities to take a breather from their negative moods are more likely to turn to active problem solving to deal with stressors (Nolen-Hoeksema & Larson, 1999; Nolen-Hoeksema & Morrow, 1991). In addition, people who use ruminative coping may actually do a poorer job of problem solving when they do try. Two laboratory studies have shown that depressed people who spend 10 minutes ruminating and then do a problem-solving task show poorer performance at problem solving than depressed people who are distracted for 10 minutes before attempting the problem-solving task (Lyubomirsky & Nolen-Hoeksema, 1995; Nolen-Hoeksema & Morrow, 1991). Rumination thus may get in the way of good problem solving.

◆ Interim Summary

- Coping strategies are divided into problem-focused strategies and emotion-focused strategies.

- People who take active steps to solve problems are less likely to experience depression and illness following negative life events.

- People who use rumination or avoidance strategies to cope with negative emotions show longer and more severe distress after negative events than people who seek social support or reappraise an event to cope with their emotions.

◆ Critical Thinking Questions

1. In what way might the environment in which a child is raised affect the development of his or her coping strategies?

2. How might you differentiate between people who repress or deny that they are distressed and people who really do not experience much distress in the face of difficult events?

MANAGING STRESS

In addition to seeking positive social support in times of stress, people can learn other techniques to reduce the negative effects of stress on the body and the mind. In this section, we discuss some behavioral and cognitive techniques that have been shown to help people reduce the effects of stress. We then discuss in detail how these techniques are applied to reduce type A behavior and coronary heart disease.

BEHAVIORAL TECHNIQUES

Among the behavioral techniques that help people control their physiological responses to stressful situations are biofeedback, relaxation training, meditation, and aerobic exercise.

BIOFEEDBACK In **biofeedback** training, individuals receive information (feedback) about an aspect of their physiological state and then attempt to alter that state. For example, in a procedure for learning to control tension headaches, electrodes are attached to the participant's forehead so that any movement in the forehead muscle can be electronically detected, amplified, and fed back to the person as an auditory signal. The signal, or tone, increases in pitch when the muscle contracts and decreases when it relaxes. By learning to control the pitch of the tone, the individual learns to keep the muscle relaxed. (Relaxation of the forehead muscle usually ensures relaxation of scalp and neck muscles as well.) After 4 to 8 weeks of biofeedback training, the participant learns to recognize the onset of tension and to reduce it without feedback from the machine (Thorpe & Olson, 1997).

RELAXATION TRAINING **Relaxation training** involves teaching people techniques to deeply relax their muscles and slow down and focus their thoughts. Physiological processes that are controlled by the autonomic nervous

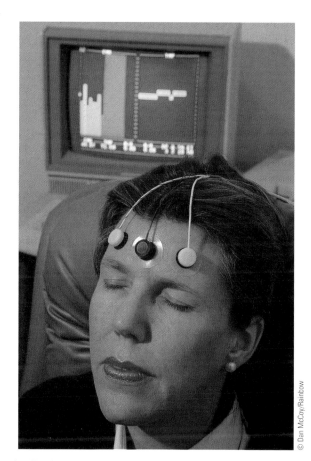

Biofeedback has proven useful in reducing some chronic health problems.

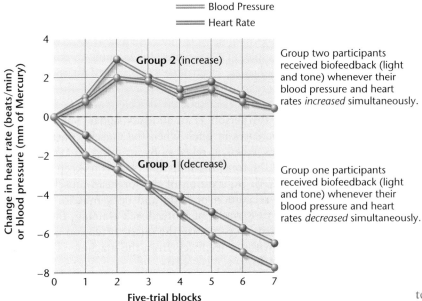

■ **Figure 14-11**
Operant Conditioning of Blood Pressure and Heart Rate
Parrticipants in both groups achieved significant simultaneous control of blood pressure and heart rate during a single conditioning session. The group reinforced for lowering both functions (group 1) achieved increasingly greater control over trials; the group reinforced for raising both functions (group 2) was less consistent. (G. E. Schwartz (1975) "Biofeedback, Self-Regulation, and the Patterning of Physiological Processes," in *American Scientist,* 63:316. Reprinted by permission of The Scientific Research Society.)

system, such as heart rate and blood pressure, have traditionally been assumed to be automatic and not under voluntary control. However, laboratory studies have demonstrated that people can learn to modify heart rate and blood pressure (see Figure 14-11). The results of these studies have led to relaxation procedures for treating patients with high blood pressure (hypertension). One procedure is to show patients a graph of their blood pressure while it is being monitored and to teach them techniques for relaxing different muscle groups. Patients are instructed to tense their muscles (for example, to clench a fist or tighten the abdomen), release the tension, and notice the difference in sensation. By starting with the feet and ankle muscles and progressing through the body to the muscles that control the neck and face, patients learn to modify muscular tension. This combination of biofeedback with relaxation training has proved effective in lowering blood pressure for some individuals (Mukhopadhyay & Turner, 1997).

Reviews of numerous studies using biofeedback and relaxation training to control headaches and hypertension conclude that the most important variable is learning how to relax (Thorpe & Olson, 1997). Some people may learn to relax faster when they receive biofeedback. Others may learn to relax equally well when they receive training in muscle relaxation without any specific biofeedback. The usefulness of relaxation training seems to depend on the individual. Some people who are not conscientious about taking drugs to relieve high blood pressure are more responsive to relaxation training, whereas others who have learned to control their blood pressure through relaxation may eventually drop the procedure because they find it too time-consuming.

MEDITATION Meditation is an effective technique for inducing relaxation and reducing physiological arousal. Almost all studies of the phenomenon report a significant lowering of the respiratory rate, a decrease in oxygen consumption, and less elimination of carbon dioxide. The heart rate is lowered, blood flow stabilizes, and the concentration of lactate in the blood is decreased (Dillbeck & Orme-Johnson, 1987). Also, there are changes in EEG brain wave activity that suggest that cortical arousal is decreased during meditation, reflecting a reduced level of mental activity (Fenwick, 1987). Meditation has also proved effective in helping people with chronic feelings of anxiety, in improving self-esteem, and in reducing relapse in people prone to serious depression (Snaith, 1998). In a study of cancer patients, those who were taught to meditate showed significant reductions in symptoms of depression, anger, and anxiety and fewer cardiopulmonary and gastrointestinal symptoms than those who were not taught to meditate (Speca, Carlson, Goodey, & Angen, 2000).

However, a leading researcher in this field contends that the same effects can be achieved through simple rest. After a thorough study of the research evidence, he concludes that there are no consistent differences between meditating and resting participants in heart rate, respiration rate, oxygen consumption, blood flow, and other physiological measures (Holmes, 1984, 1985a, 1985b). So, simply resting may produce stress-reduction effects similar to those produced by meditation.

EXERCISE Another factor that is important in controlling stress is physical fitness. Individuals who regularly engage in aerobic exercise (any sustained activity that increases heart rate and oxygen consumption, such as jogging, swimming, or cycling) show significantly lower heart rates and blood pressure in response to stressful situations than others (Taylor, 1999). In turn, Brown (1991) found that physically fit people were much less likely to become physically ill following stressful events than people who were not fit. Because of these findings, many stress management programs also emphasize physical fitness.

COGNITIVE TECHNIQUES

People who are able to control their physiological or emotional responses through biofeedback and relaxation training in the laboratory will have more difficulty doing so in actual stressful situations, particularly if they continue to interact in ways that make them tense. Consequently, an additional approach to stress management focuses on changing the individual's cognitive responses to stressful situations. **Cognitive behavior therapy** attempts to help people identify the kinds of stressful situations that produce their physiological or emotional symptoms and alter the way they cope with these situations. For example, a man who suffers from tension headaches would be asked to keep a record of their occurrence and rate the severity of each headache and the circumstances in which it occurred. Next he would be taught how to monitor his responses to these stressful events and asked to record his feelings, thoughts, and behavior prior to, during, and following the event. After a period of self-monitoring, certain relationships often become evident among situational variables (for example, criticism by a supervisor or coworker), thoughts ("I can't do anything right"), and emotional, behavioral, and physiological responses (depression, withdrawal, and headache).

The next step is trying to identify the expectations or beliefs that might explain the headache reactions (for example, "I expect to do everything perfectly, so the slightest criticism upsets me" or "I judge myself harshly, become depressed, and end up with a headache"). The final and most difficult step is trying to change something about the stressful situation, the individual's way of thinking about it, or the individual's behavior. The options might include finding a less stressful job, recognizing that the need to perform perfectly leads to unnecessary anguish over errors, and learning to behave more assertively in interactions instead of withdrawing.

Biofeedback, relaxation training, exercise, and cognitive therapy have all proved useful in helping people control their physiological and emotional responses to stress. Some research suggests that the improvement is more likely to be maintained over time with a combination of cognitive and behavior therapy (Holroyd, Appel, & Andrasik, 1983). Because the complex demands of everyday life often require flexible coping skills, being able to relax may not be an effective method of coping with some of life's stresses. Programs for stress management frequently employ a combination of biofeedback, relaxation training, exercise, and cognitive modification techniques.

MODIFYING TYPE A BEHAVIOR

A combination of cognitive and behavioral techniques has been shown to reduce type A behavior (Friedman et al., 1994). The participants were more than 1,000 individuals who had experienced at least one heart attack. Participants in the treatment group were helped to reduce their sense of time urgency by practicing standing in line (a situation that type A individuals find extremely irritating) and using the opportunity to reflect on things that they do not normally have time to think about, to watch people, or to strike up a conversation with a stranger. Treatment also included helping participants learn to express themselves without exploding at people and to alter certain specific behaviors (such as interrupting others or talking or eating hurriedly). Therapists helped the participants reevaluate certain beliefs (such as the notion that success depends on the quantity of work produced) that might lead to urgent and hostile behavior. Finally, participants found ways to make their home and work environments less stressful (such as reducing the number of unnecessary social engagements).

The critical dependent variable in this study was the occurrence of another heart attack. By the end of the study 4½ years later, the experimental group had a heart attack recurrence rate almost half that of control participants who were not taught how to alter their lifestyles. Clearly, learning to modify type A behavior was beneficial to these participants' health (Friedman et al., 1994).

Like other research described in this chapter, this study was based on the premise that the mind and the body influence each other. Simple models of how stress affects health are being replaced by complex models that explain how biological, psychological, and social factors intertwine to create disease or health. As we have seen, the body has characteristic physiological reactions to stress. For people with preexisting biological vulnerabilities, such as a genetic predisposition to heart disease, these physiological reactions to stress can cause deterioration in health. Yet an individual's perception of stress is determined by characteristics of events in the environment and by his or her personal history, appraisals of the event, and coping styles. Thus, the extent to which the individual experiences psychological distress or ill health following potentially stressful situations is determined by the biological and psychological vulnerabilities and strengths he or she brings to these situations.

Is Unrealistic Optimism Good for Your Health?

UNREALISTIC OPTIMISM CAN BE BAD FOR YOUR HEALTH
Neil D. Weinstein, Rutgers University

Are you more likely or less likely to develop a drinking problem than the other people in your psychology class? How about your chances of getting a sexually transmitted disease (STD) or your chances of having a heart attack some day? When asked questions like these, few people admit to having above-average risk. Typically, 50% to 70% of a group claim that their risk is below average, another 30% to 50% say that their risk is average, but less than 10% acknowledge that their risk is above average.

Obviously, this cannot be correct. Your own risk of heart disease might actually be below average, but the number of people who make such a claim is simply too great for them all to be right. The "average" person has, by definition, an "average" risk. So when the people who claim below-average risk greatly outnumber those who say their risk is higher than average, something must be wrong with their risk judgments.

The data show that most of the individuals whose actions, family history, or environment put them at high risk either don't realize it or won't admit it. In general, we summarize these findings by saying that people are unrealistically optimistic about future risks. This unrealistic optimism is especially strong with risks that are somewhat under our own control, such as alcoholism, lung cancer, and STDs. Apparently, we are quite confident that we will do a better job of avoiding these problems than will our peers.

What unrealistic optimism demonstrates is that we are not impartial and open-minded when it comes to health risk information. Most of us want to be informed and make good decisions, but we also want to feel that our lifestyles are already healthful, that changes are not needed, and that we don't have to worry. Unfortunately, this search for a rosy interpretation can get us into trouble. If everything is fine as is, then we don't need to take precautions. We can continue to get drunk with our friends, eat as much pizza, fries, and hamburgers as we want, and use condoms only with sexual partners we know are promiscuous (curiously, we rarely think that any of them are). Most of the time, such risky behavior does not get us into trouble, but the odds of getting into trouble are certainly increased. The millions of college students who get STDs every year or who get into automobile accidents after too many beers are clear examples of people doing things that they know are supposed to be risky. But they have concluded that, for them, it will be okay. This is not ignorance; it is unrealistic optimism.

An especially upsetting example is college students who smoke cigarettes. They have all kinds of illusions to make them feel comfortable. They will smoke for only a couple of years and then they will quit. (Others may get hooked, but not them.) Their cigarettes are low in tar, or they don't inhale. They exercise a lot, which will counteract the effects of smoking. Smokers don't deny that cigarettes are bad for people. They just think the effects won't be bad for them. Typically, they say that their risk of heart disease, lung cancer, and emphysema is lower than that of other smokers and only "a little" above the risk of the average person.

Optimism does have its advantages. When people already have a severe illness and are coping with it—illnesses such as cancer or AIDS—maintaining optimism is important. It helps people put up with sometimes unpleasant treatments, and a positive mood may itself help by improving the body's ability to resist disease. Even being overly optimistic about the future is unlikely to lead someone who has a life-threatening disease to pretend that he or she is not sick or to stop treatment. However, the perils of unrealistic optimism are greater when the issue is preventing harm from occurring. If you think you can handle a car after a night of drinking, if none of your dates could carry an STD, or if, unlike your classmates, you can stop smoking any time you want, your unrealistic optimism is likely to lead to health consequences you will regret.

Neil Weinstein

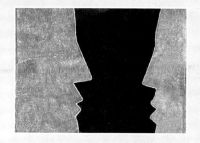

Is Unrealistic Optimism Good for Your Health?

UNREALISTIC OPTIMISM CAN BE GOOD FOR YOUR HEALTH
Shelley E. Taylor, University of California, Los Angeles

Is unrealistic optimism bad for your health? It seems like it should be. After all, if people believe they are relatively invulnerable to disorders ranging from tooth decay to heart disease, logically, shouldn't that interfere with practicing good health behaviors? Ample evidence suggests that most people are indeed unrealistically optimistic about their health. But, if anything, unrealistic optimism seems to be good for your health.

Consider the practice of health habits, such as wearing a seat belt, getting exercise, and avoiding harmful substances such as tobacco and alcohol. Rather than undermining such habits, as some have assumed, unrealistic optimism may actually lead people to practice better health habits.

Shelley E. Taylor

Aspinwall and Brunhart (1996) found that people with optimistic expectations about their health actually pay *more* attention to personally relevant risk-related information than pessimistic people, apparently so that they can take preventive action to offset those risks. People who are optimistic about their health may be so precisely because they practice better health habits than more pessimistic people (Armor & Taylor, 1998).

Perhaps the most persuasive evidence for beneficial health effects of unrealistic optimism has come from studies of gay men with the HIV virus. In one study, men who were unrealistically optimistic

about their ability to avoid AIDS (such as believing that their bodies might shake off the virus) practiced more health-promoting behaviors than those who were less optimistic (Taylor, Kemeny, Aspinwall, Schneider, Rodriguez, & Herbert, 1992). Reed, Kemeny, Taylor, Wang, and Visscher (1994) found that, among men diagnosed with AIDS, maintaining an unrealistically optimistic outlook, as opposed to a realistic one, was associated with an increased length of life of nine months. In a parallel finding, Richard Schulz found that pessimistic cancer patients died earlier than those who were more optimistic (Schulz, Bookwala, Knapp, Scheier, & Williamson, 1996).

Optimists also seem to recover faster from illnesses. Leedham, Meyerowitz, Muirhead, and Frist (1995) found that optimistic expectations among heart transplant patients were associated with better mood, quality of life, and adjustment to illness. Similar findings are reported by Scheier and his associates (Scheier et al., 1989) in their study of people adjusting to coronary artery bypass surgery. What accounts for findings like these?

Optimism is associated with good coping strategies, as well as with good health habits. Optimists are active copers who try to solve problems rather than avoid them (e.g., Scheier & Carver, 1992). Optimistic people are also more interpersonally successful, and so they may do a better job of attracting social support. Social support is known to reduce the likelihood of illness and promote recovery, and so, optimistic people may recruit this special resource for dealing with stress and with illness.

Scientists are now realizing that optimism may create or be associated with a

bodily state conducive to health or to rapid recovery from illness. Suzanne Segerstrom and her associates (Segerstrom, Taylor, Kemeny, & Fahey, 1998) studied a group of law students under intense academic stress during the first semester of law school. They found that the optimistic law students showed an immunological profile suggestive of greater resistance to illness and infection. Other studies are showing similar findings (Bower, Kemeny, Taylor, & Fahey, 1998).

Why do some people think that optimism is bad for your health? Some researchers have indicted unrealistic optimism as a culprit that promotes health risk without the evidence. For example, although smokers seemingly underestimate their risk for lung cancer, there is no evidence that their unrealistic optimism led them to smoke or justifies their continued smoking. Indeed, smokers are well aware that they are more vulnerable to lung disorders than are nonsmokers.

Does this mean that unrealistic optimism is always beneficial for your health or is beneficial to all people? Seymour Epstein and his associates (Epstein & Meier, 1989) have suggested that most optimists are "constructive optimists" who take active efforts to protect their health and safety. But a few optimists are "naïve optimists" who believe that everything will turn out all right without any active efforts on their part. If optimists are ever at risk for poorer health habits, it may be this small group of avoidant copers.

Before you write off unrealistic optimism as a state that blinds people to the realistic risks we all face, look at its benefits. It keeps people happier, healthier, and more likely to recover from illness.

◆ Interim Summary

- Biofeedback and relaxation training attempt to teach people how to control their physiological responses by learning to recognize tension and reduce it through deep muscle relaxation and concentration.

- Exercise can help people cope with stress over the long term.

- Cognitive behavior therapy attempts to help people recognize and modify their cognitive and behavioral responses to stress.

- Type A behavior can be changed through behavioral and cognitive techniques, resulting in reduced risk of coronary heart disease.

◆ Critical Thinking Questions

1. Some people claim to be "addicted to stress." If this is possible, what might it mean to be addicted to stress?

2. What do you expect would be the greatest challenges to helping a type A person change his or her behavior?

CHAPTER SUMMARY

1. Stress refers to experiencing events that are perceived as endangering one's physical or psychological well-being. These events are usually referred to as stressors, and people's reactions to them are termed stress responses. Traumatic events are usually perceived as stressful, as are uncontrollable and unpredictable events. Some researchers believe that any major change, as well as internal conflicts, can be stressful.

2. Some people become angry in response to stress and may become aggressive. Withdrawal, apathy, and depression may result from stress. Some people develop learned helplessness, which is characterized by passivity and inaction and the inability to see opportunities to control one's environment. Some people develop cognitive impairment when stressed and cannot think clearly.

3. The body reacts to stress with the fight-or-flight response. The sympathetic nervous system causes increased heart rate, elevated blood pressure, dilated pupils, and release of extra sugar from the liver. The adrenal-cortical system causes the release of adrenocorticotropic hormone (ACTH), which stimulates the release of cortisol in the blood.

4. These reactions are part of a general adaptation syndrome, a set of responses displayed by all organisms in response to stress. The syndrome consists of three phases: alarm, resistance, and exhaustion.

5. Stress may affect health directly by creating chronic overarousal of the sympathetic division of the autonomic nervous system or the adrenal-cortical system or by impairing the immune system. People under stress also may not engage in positive health-related behaviors, and this may lead to illness. Psychophysiological disorders are physical disorders in which emotions are believed to play a central role. For example, stress can contribute to coronary heart disease. Psychoneuroimmunology is the study of how psychological factors can affect the immune system. Stress may impair the functioning of the immune system, increasing the risk of immune-related disorders.

6. Psychoanalytic theory suggests that events are stressful when they arouse our unconscious conflicts. Behaviorists argue that people react to specific situations with fear and anxiety because those situations caused them harm or were stressful in the past. Cognitive theorists argue that people's attributions or causal explanations influence their stress responses. People who tend to attribute bad events to internal, stable, and global causes are more likely to develop learned helplessness and become ill after experiencing such events.

7. Hardy people tend to see stressful events as challenges and have a strong sense of personal control, characteristics that may protect against the development of illness in the face of stress. People who are able to find meaning in a traumatic event are less likely to develop emotional problems.

8. People with the type A behavior pattern tend to be hostile, aggressive, impatient individuals who are overinvolved in their work. Studies of men and women show that people who exhibit this pattern are at increased risk for coronary heart disease.

9. Coping strategies are divided into problem-focused strategies and emotion-focused strategies. People who take active steps to solve problems are less likely to experience depression and illness following negative life

events. People who use rumination or avoidance strategies to cope with negative emotions show longer and more severe distress after negative events than people who seek social support or reappraise an event to cope with their emotions.

10. Biofeedback and relaxation training attempt to teach people how to control their physiological responses by learning to recognize tension and reduce it through deep muscle relaxation and concentration.

11. Exercise can help people cope with stress over the long term.

12. Cognitive behavior therapy attempts to help people recognize and modify their cognitive and behavioral responses to stress.

13. Type A behavior can be changed through behavioral and cognitive techniques, resulting in reduced risk of coronary heart disease.

CORE CONCEPTS

stress
stressor
stress response
behavioral medicine
traumatic event
controllability
predictability
internal conflicts
anxiety
post-traumatic stress disorder

learned helplessness
fight-or-flight response
general adaptation syndrome
psychophysiological disorders
coronary heart disease
psychoneuroimmunology
objective anxiety
neurotic anxiety
attributional style
hardiness

type A pattern
coping
problem-focused coping
emotion-focused coping
biofeedback
relaxation training
meditation
cognitive behavior therapy

 WEB RESOURCES

http://psychology.wadsworth.com/ atkinson14e

Take a quiz, try the activities and exercises, and explore web links.

http://wellness.uwsp.edu/Health_Service/Services/ stress.htm

How stressed are you? Answer the questions on this site and find out.

http://www.coolware.com/health/medical_ reporter/stress.html

Learn more about stress, health, and how to cope with the stress in your life.

http://sdoublet.freeyellow.com/problem.htm

This site provides an extensive discussion of the history of stress research.

 InfoTrac Online Library

http://www.infotrac-college.com/ wadsworth

Use InfoTrac College Edition to find popular and scientific articles by using the search terms below or your own relevant terms.

- Type A behavior
- Biofeedback
- Health psychology
- Meditation
- Posttraumatic stress disorder

CD-ROM LINKS

 Psych Odyssey

Check out CD Chapter 18, Health Psychology
A. Stress and Coping

 Psyk.trek 2.0

Check out CD Unit 11, Abnormal Behavior and Therapy
10f Types of Stress
10g Responding to Stress

PSYCHOLOGICAL DISORDERS

Mike was a 32-year-old father who had many concerns. When driving, he felt compelled to stop the car often to check whether he had run over people, although there was no reason to think he had. Before flushing the toilet, Mike inspected the toilet to be sure that a live insect had not fallen into it—he did not want to be responsible for killing any live creature. In addition, he repeatedly checked the doors, stoves, lights, and windows of his house, making sure that all were shut or turned off so that no harm, such as fire or burglary, would befall his family as the result of his "irresponsible" behavior. In particular, he worried about the safety of his 15-month-old daughter, repeatedly checking the gate to the basement to be sure

that it was locked. He did not carry his daughter while walking on concrete floors, in order to avoid killing her by accidentally dropping her. Mike performed these and many other checks for an average of 4 hours a day. (Adapted from Foa & Steketee, 1989, p. 189)

Most of us have concerns, but Mike's concerns seem extreme. Some people might say they are so extreme as to be abnormal, even crazy. In this chapter, we explore the concept of abnormality. We will see that sometimes the line between normal and abnormal is clear, but most of the time it is fuzzy. We will investigate in detail several specific types of abnormality and theories of

why some people develop psychological disorders and others do not.

A word of warning may be appropriate before we proceed. It is common for students studying abnormal psychology for the first time to diagnose mental disorders in themselves, just as medical students diagnose themselves as suffering from every new disease they read about. Most of us have had some of the symptoms we will be describing, and that is not cause for alarm. However, if you have been bothered by distressing feelings for a long time, it never hurts to talk to someone about them—perhaps someone in your school's counseling service or student health service.

DEFINING ABNORMALITY

What do we mean by "abnormal" behavior? By what criteria do we distinguish it from "normal" behavior? In this age of rapid technological advances, you might think that there would be some objective test—a blood test or brain scan—that could determine whether an individual has a mental disorder. There is no such test currently, however. Instead, we must rely on signs and symptoms, and on subjective criteria for deciding when those symptoms constitute abnormality. A number of different types of criteria for defining abnormality have been proposed.

DEVIATION FROM CULTURAL NORMS

Every culture has certain standards, or norms, for acceptable behavior, and behavior that deviates markedly from those norms is considered abnormal. Proponents of a **cultural relativist perspective** argue that we should respect each culture's definitions of abnormality for the members of that culture. By doing so, we do not impose one culture's standards for behavior on another. Opponents of this position point to a number of dangers, however (Szasz, 1971). Throughout history, societies have labeled individuals as abnormal to justify controlling or silencing them, as Hitler branded the Jews abnormal to justify the Holocaust. Another problem is that the concept of abnormality changes over time within the same society. Forty years ago, most Americans would have considered men wearing earrings abnormal. Today, such behaviors tend to be viewed as differences in lifestyle rather than as signs of abnormality. Thus, ideas of normality and abnormality differ from one society to another and over time within the same society.

DEVIATION FROM STATISTICAL NORMS

The word **abnormal** means away from the norm. Many characteristics, such as height, weight, and intelligence, cover a range of values when measured over an entire population. Most people, for example, fall within the middle range of height, and a few are abnormally tall or abnormally short. One definition of abnormality therefore is based on deviation from statistical norms: Abnormal behavior is statistically infrequent or deviant from the norm. But according to this definition, a person who is extremely intelligent or extremely happy would be classified as abnormal. Thus, in defining abnormal behavior, we must consider more than statistical frequency.

MALADAPTIVENESS OF BEHAVIOR

Rather than defining abnormal behavior in terms of deviance from either statistical or societal norms, many social scientists believe that the most important criterion is how the behavior affects the well-being of the individual or the social group. According to this criterion, behavior is abnormal if it is **maladaptive**—that is, if it has adverse effects on the individual or on society. Some kinds of deviant behavior interfere with the welfare of the individual (a man who is so fearful of crowds that he cannot ride the bus to work, alcoholics who drink so heavily that they cannot hold a job, a woman who attempts suicide). Other forms of deviant behavior are harmful to society (an adolescent who has violent aggressive outbursts, a paranoid individual who plots to assassinate national leaders). If we use the criterion of maladaptiveness, all of these behaviors would be considered abnormal.

PERSONAL DISTRESS

A fourth criterion considers abnormality in terms of the individual's subjective feelings of **distress**—their feelings of anxiety, depression, or agitation, or experiences such as insomnia, loss of appetite, or numerous aches and pains. Most people who are diagnosed with a mental disorder feel acutely miserable. Sometimes personal distress may be the only symptom of abnormality, and the individual's behavior may appear normal to the casual observer.

Fashions change over time—just as definitions of abnormality do.

© Bettmann Corbis

© Wartenberg/Picture Press/Corbis

None of these definitions provides a completely satisfactory description of abnormal behavior. In most instances, all four criteria—social deviation, statistical frequency, maladaptive behavior, and personal distress—are considered in diagnosing abnormality.

What Is Normality?

Normality is even more difficult to define than abnormality, but most psychologists would agree that the characteristics in the following list indicate emotional well-being. (Note that these characteristics do not make sharp distinctions between the mentally healthy and the mentally ill. Rather, they represent traits that a normal person possesses to a greater degree than an individual who is diagnosed as abnormal.)

1. *Appropriate perception of reality.* Normal individuals are fairly realistic in appraising their reactions and capabilities and in interpreting what is going on in the world around them. They do not consistently misperceive what others say and do, and they do not consistently overrate their abilities and tackle more than they can accomplish, nor do they underestimate their abilities and shy away from difficult tasks.
2. *Ability to exercise voluntary control over behavior.* Normal individuals feel fairly confident about their ability to control their behavior. Occasionally they may act impulsively, but they are able to restrain their sexual and aggressive urges when necessary. They may fail to conform to social norms, but in such instances their decisions are voluntary rather than the result of uncontrollable impulses.
3. *Self-esteem and acceptance.* Well-adjusted people have some appreciation of their own worth and feel accepted by those around them. They are comfortable with other people and are able to react spontaneously in social situations. At the same time, they do not feel obligated to completely subjugate their opinions to those of the group. Feelings of worthlessness, alienation, and lack of acceptance are prevalent among individuals who are diagnosed as abnormal.
4. *Ability to form affectionate relationships.* Normal individuals are able to form close and satisfying relationships with other people. They are sensitive to the feelings of others and do not make excessive demands on others to gratify their own needs. Often, mentally disturbed people are so concerned with protecting their own security that they become extremely self-centered. Preoccupied with their own feelings and strivings, they seek affection but are unable to reciprocate. Sometimes they fear intimacy because their past relationships have been destructive.
5. *Productivity.* Well-adjusted people are able to channel their abilities into productive activity. They are

Well-adjusted people are able to channel their abilities into productive activity.

enthusiastic about life and do not need to drive themselves to meet the demands of the day. Chronic lack of energy and excessive susceptibility to fatigue are often symptoms of psychological tension resulting from unsolved problems.

Classifying Abnormal Behaviors

A broad range of behaviors have been classified as abnormal. Some abnormal behaviors are acute and transitory, resulting from particularly stressful events, whereas others are chronic and lifelong. Each person's behavior and emotional problems are unique, and no two individuals behave in exactly the same manner or share the same life experiences. However, enough similarities exist for mental health professionals to classify cases into categories.

A good classification system has many advantages. If the various types of abnormal behavior have different causes, we can hope to uncover them by grouping individuals according to similarities in behavior and then looking for other ways in which they may be similar. A diagnostic label also enables those who work with disturbed individuals to communicate information more quickly and concisely. The diagnosis of schizophrenia indicates quite a bit about a person's behavior. Knowing that an individual's symptoms are similar to those of other patients is also helpful in deciding how to treat the patient. Disadvantages arise, however, if we allow a diagnostic label to carry too much weight. Labeling induces us to overlook the unique features of each case and expect the person to conform to the classification. We may also forget that a label for maladaptive behavior is not an explanation of that behavior

CONCEPT REVIEW TABLE
Categories of Mental Disorders

Listed here are the main diagnostic categories of DSM-IV. Each category includes numerous subclassifications. *(From Diagnostic and Statistical Manual of Mental Disorders, Fourth Edition, Washington, DC: American Psychiatric Association, 1994.)*

1. **Disorders usually first evident in infancy, childhood, or adolescence**	Includes mental retardation, autism, attention deficit disorder with hyperactivity, separation anxiety, speech disorders, and other deviations from normal development.
2. **Delirium, dementia, amnestic, and other cognitive diorders**	Disorders in which the functioning of the brain is known to be impaired, either permanently or transiently; may be the result of aging, degenerative diseases of the nervous system (for example, syphilis or Alzheimer's disease), or the ingestion of toxic substances (for example, lead poisoning or drugs).
3. **Psychoactive substance use disorders**	Includes excessive use of alcohol, barbiturates, amphetamines, cocaine, and other drugs that alter behavior. Marijuana and tobacco are also included in this category, which is controversial.
4. **Schizophrenia**	A group of disorders characterized by loss of contact with reality, marked disturbances of thought and perception, and bizarre behavior. At some phase, delusions or hallucinations almost always occur.
5. **Mood disorders**	Disturbances of normal mood; the person may be extremely depressed, abnormally elated, or may alternate between periods of elation and depression.
6. **Anxiety disorders**	Includes disorders in which anxiety is the main symptom (generalized anxiety or panic disorders) or anxiety is experienced unless the individual avoids feared situations (phobic disorders) or tries to resist performing certain rituals or thinking persistent thoughts (obsessive-compulsive disorders). Also includes post-traumatic stress disorder.
7. **Somatoform disorders**	The symptoms are physical, but no organic basis can be found and psychological factors appear to play the major role. Included are conversion disorders (for example, a woman who resents having to care for her invalid mother suddenly develops a paralyzed arm) and hypochondriasis (excessive preoccupation with health and fear of disease when there is no basis for concern.) Does *not* include psychosomatic disorders that have an organic basis. (See Chapter 14)
8. **Dissociative disorders**	Temporary alterations in the functions of consciousness, memory, or identity due to emotional problems. Included are amnesia (the individual cannot recall anything about his or her history following a traumatic experience) and dissociative identity disorder (better known as multiple personality disorder, involving two or more independent personality systems existing within the same individual).
9. **Sexual Disorders**	Includes problems of sexual identity (for example, transsexualism), sexual performance (for example, impotence, premature ejaculation, and frigidity), and sexual aim (for example, sexual interest in children, sadism, and masochism).
10. **Eating disorders**	Self-induced starvation (anorexia) or patterns of binge eating followed by self-induced purging (bulimia).
11. **Sleep disorders**	Includes chronic insomnia, excessive sleepiness, sleep apnea, sleepwalking, and narcolepsy.
12. **Factitious disorders**	Physical or psychological symptoms that are intentionally produced or feigned. Differs from malingering in that there is no obvious goal, such as disability payments or the avoidance of military service. The best-studied form of this disorder is called Münchausen syndrome: The individual's plausible presentation of factitious physical symptoms results in frequent hospitalizations.
13. **Impulse control disorder**	Includes kleptomania (compulsive stealing of objects not needed for personal use or their monetary value), pathological gambling, and pyromania (setting fires for the pleasure or relief of tension derived thereby).
14. **Personality disorders**	Long-standing patterns of maladaptive behavior that constitute immature and inappropriate ways of coping with stress or solving problems. Antisocial personality disorder and narcissistic personality disorder are two examples.
15. **Other conditions that may be the focus of clinical attention**	This category includes many of the problems for which people seek help, such as marital problems, parent-child difficulties, and academic or occupational problems.

The classification does not tell us how the behavior originated or what causes it to continue.

The classification of mental disorders used by most mental health professionals in the United States is the *Diagnostic and Statistical Manual of Mental Disorders,* **4th edition** (DSM-IV for short), which corresponds generally to the international system formulated by the World Health Organization. The major categories of mental disorders classified by DSM-IV are listed in the Concept Review Table. DSM-IV provides an extensive list of subcategories under each of these headings, as well as a description of the symptoms that must be present for the diagnosis to be applicable.

You have probably heard the terms *neurosis* and *psychosis* and may be wondering where they fit into the categories of mental disorders listed in the Concept Review Table. Traditionally, these terms denoted major diagnostic categories. **Neuroses** (the plural of *neurosis*) included a group of disorders characterized by anxiety, unhappiness, and maladaptive behavior that were seldom serious enough to require hospitalization. The individual could usually function in society, though not at full capacity. **Psychoses** (the plural of *psychosis*) included more serious mental disorders. The individual's behavior and thought processes were so disturbed that he or she was out of touch with reality, could not cope with the demands of daily life, and usually had to be hospitalized.

Neither neuroses nor psychoses appear as major categories in DSM-IV. There are several reasons for this departure from earlier classification systems, but the main one concerns precision of diagnosis. Both categories were fairly broad and included a number of mental disorders with quite dissimilar symptoms. Consequently, mental health professionals did not always agree on the diagnosis for a particular case. DSM-IV attempts to achieve greater consensus by grouping disorders according to very specific behavioral symptoms without implying anything about their origins or treatment. The intention is to describe observations of individuals who have psychological problems in a way that ensures accurate communication among mental health professionals. Consequently, DSM-IV includes many more categories than previous editions of the manual.

Although psychosis is no longer a major category, DSM-IV recognizes that people who are diagnosed as having schizophrenia, delusional disorders, and some mood disorders exhibit psychotic behavior at some point during their illness. Their thinking and perception of reality are severely disturbed, and they may have hallucinations (false sensory experiences, such as hearing voices or seeing strange visions) and/or delusions (false beliefs, such as the conviction that all thoughts are controlled by a powerful being from another planet). These issues will become clearer as we look more closely at some of the mental disorders listed in the Concept Review Table. We will examine anxiety disorders, mood disorders, schizophrenia, and two types of personality disorder. Alcoholism and drug dependence (both classified as psychoactive substance use disorders) are covered in Chapter 6.

Table 15-1 indicates the likelihood of the major mental disorders during one's lifetime. The study on which this table is based found that mental disorders are more common among people under age 45. Although the overall rates of disorders are not different in men and women, there are sex differences in the incidence of specific disorders. For example, men are twice as likely as women to abuse alcohol or other drugs. Antisocial personality disorders affect three times as many men as women, but more women suffer from mood and anxiety disorders.

Many cultures recognize mental disorders that do not correspond to any disorders listed in the DSM-IV (see Table 15-2). Some of these disorders may have the same underlying causes as certain disorders recognized by the DSM-IV but are manifested by different symptoms in other cultures. Other disorders may be truly unique to the cultures in which they are found. The presence of such culture-bound syndromes suggests that the disorders listed in DSM-IV represent only the disorders that occur in mainstream American culture rather than a universal list of disorders to which all humans are susceptible. This supports the views of those who argue that we cannot define abnormality without reference to the norms of a particular culture.

● Table 15-1
Lifetime Prevalence Rates of Selected Disorders

Listed here are the percentage of individuals in the U.S. population who have experienced one of these mental disorders during their lifetime. These percentages are based on interviews with a sample of 8,098 individuals, age 18 to 54, all around U.S. cities. (*From R. C. Kessler, K. A. McGonagle, S. Zhao, and C. B. Nelson (1994), "Lifetime and 12-month prevalence of DSM-III-R psychiatric disorders in the United States: Results from the National Comorbidity Study,"* Archives of General Psychiatry, *51(1):8–19. Copyright © 1994 by the American Medical Association.*)

Disorder	Rate
Anxiety disorders	24.9
Mood disorders	19.3
Schizophrenia and related disorders	0.7
Antisocial personality	3.5
Substance use disorder	26.6

● **Table 15-2**
Culture-Bound Syndromes

Some cultures have syndromes or mental disorders that are found only in that culture and that do not correspond to any DSM-IV categories. (*Based on APA, 2000*)

Syndrome	Cultures Where Found	Symptoms
amok	Malaysia, Laos, Philippines, Papua New Guinea, Puerto Rico, Navajos	Brooding, followed by violent behavior, persecutory ideas, amnesia, exhaustion. More often seen in men than in women.
ataque de nervios	Latin America	Uncontrollable shouting, crying, trembling, heat in the chest rising to the head, verbal or physical aggression, seizures, fainting.
ghost sickness	American Indians	Nightmares, weakness, feelings of danger, loss of appetite, fainting, dizziness, hallucinations, loss of consciousness, sense of suffocation.
koro	Malaysia, China, Thailand	Sudden and intense anxiety that the penis (in males) or the vulva and nipples (in females) will recede into body and cause death.
latah	East Asia	Hypersensitivity to sudden fright, trance-like behavior. Most often seen in middle-aged women.
susto	Mexico, Central America	Appetite disturbances, sleep disturbances, sadness, loss of motivation, feelings of low self-worth following a frightening event. Sufferers believe that their soul has left their body.
taijin kyofusho	Japan	Intense fear that one's body displeases, embarrasses, or is offensive to others.

PERSPECTIVES ON MENTAL DISORDERS

Attempts to understand the causes of mental disorders generally fall under one of the three broad perspectives we have discussed throughout this book. The **biological perspective,** also called the *medical* or *disease model,* suggests that mental disorders are brain disorders. Researchers using this approach look for genetic irregularities that may predispose a person to develop a particular mental disorder by affecting the functioning of the brain. They also look for abnormalities in specific parts of the brain and dysfunction in neurochemical systems in the brain and other parts of the body. Proponents of this perspective generally favor the use of drugs to treat disorders.

There are a number of specific **psychological perspectives** that see mental disorders as problems in the functioning of the mind. The **psychoanalytic perspective** emphasizes unconscious conflicts, usually originating in early childhood, and the use of defense mechanisms to handle the anxiety generated by the repressed impulses and emotions. Bringing the unconscious conflicts and emotions into awareness presumably eliminates the need for the defense mechanisms and alleviates the disorder.

The **behavioral perspective** investigates how fears become conditioned to specific situations and the role of reinforcement in the origin and maintenance of inappropriate behaviors. This approach looks at mental disorders from the standpoint of learning theory and assumes that maladaptive behaviors are learned.

The **cognitive perspective** suggests that some mental disorders stem from disordered cognitive processes and can be alleviated by changing these faulty cognitions. Rather than stressing hidden motivations, emotions, and conflicts, however, it emphasizes conscious mental processes. The way we think about ourselves, the way we appraise stressful situations, and our strategies for coping with them are all interrelated.

Cultural or **sociological perspectives** take the view that mental disorders are not situated in the brain or mind of the individual but in the social context in which the individual lives. Proponents of this perspective look to stresses in the physical and social environment, such as discrimination and poverty, that can interfere with people's functioning. They also pay attention to how culture shapes the types of mental disorders people are most susceptible to and how they manifest their distress.

The ideas embodied in these brief summaries will become clearer as we discuss them in relation to specific mental disorders. Each of these approaches has something important to say about mental disorders, but none has the complete answer. One way of integrating these factors is the **vulnerability-stress model,** which considers the interaction between a predisposition, which makes a person vulnerable for developing a particular disorder, and stressful environmental conditions encountered by that person. At the biological level, vulnerability might stem from genetic factors. This is evident in disorders in which having a close relative with the disorder increases a person's risk of developing it. At the psychological level, a chronic feeling of hopelessness and inadequacy might make an individual vulnerable to depression. Having a predisposition for a particular disorder does not guarantee that the person will develop the disorder. Whether the predisposition leads to an actual disorder often depends on the kinds of stressors, including poverty, malnutrition, frustration, conflicts, and traumatic life events, the individual encounters.

The key point of the vulnerability-stress model is that both vulnerability and stress are necessary. It helps explain why some people develop serious psychological problems when confronted with a minimum of stress while others remain healthy regardless of how difficult their lives may become.

◆ Interim Summary

- The diagnosis of abnormal behavior is based on social norms, statistical frequency, adaptiveness of behavior, and personal distress.

- Characteristics of good mental health include efficient perception of reality, control of behavior, self-esteem, ability to form affectionate relationships, and productivity.

- DSM-IV classifies mental disorders according to specific behavioral symptoms. Such a classification system helps communicate information and provides a basis for research. However, each case is unique, and diagnostic labels should not be used to pigeonhole individuals.

- Theories about the causes of mental disorders and proposals for treating them can be grouped according to those that focus on the brain and other biological factors; those that focus on the mind, including psychoanalytic, behavioral, and cognitive perspectives; and those that focus on sociocultural and environmental factors.

- The vulnerability-stress model emphasizes the interaction between a predisposition (biological and/or psychological) that makes a person vulnerable to a particular disorder and stressful environmental conditions encountered by the individual.

◆ Critical Thinking Questions

1. Studying any mental disorder from one theoretical perspective holds the danger that the investigator will be biased to look for particular causes of the disorder and to ignore other causes. But is it possible to study a mental disorder from a totally atheoretical perspective—that is, to approach the disorder with no presumptions about its likely causes? Why or why not?

2. People who are diagnosed with a mental disorder often say it is a relief to have a label for their distress. Why might this be true?

ANXIETY DISORDERS

Most of us feel anxious and tense in the face of threatening or stressful situations. Such feelings are normal reactions to stress. Anxiety is considered abnormal only when it occurs in situations that most people can handle with little difficulty. **Anxiety disorders** include a group of disorders in which anxiety either is the main symptom (generalized anxiety and panic disorders) or is experienced when the individual attempts to control certain maladaptive behaviors (phobic and obsessive-compulsive disorders). (Post-traumatic stress disorder, which involves anxiety following a traumatic event, was discussed in Chapter 14.) The following passage describes a person suffering from an anxiety disorder:

> Hazel was walking down a street near her home one day when she suddenly felt flooded with intense and frightening physical symptoms. Her whole body tightened up, she began sweating and her heart was racing, and she felt dizzy and disoriented. She thought, "I must be having a heart attack! I can't stand this! Something terrible is happening! I'm going to die." Hazel just stood frozen in the middle of the street until an onlooker stopped to help her.

There are four types of symptoms of anxiety, and Hazel was experiencing symptoms of each type. First, she had physiological or somatic symptoms: Her heart was racing, she was perspiring, and her muscles tensed. You may recognize these symptoms as part of the fight-or-flight response discussed in Chapter 14. This is the body's natural reaction to a challenging situation—the physiological changes of the fight-or-flight response prepare the body to fight a threat or to flee from it.

Second, Hazel had cognitive symptoms of anxiety: She was sure she was having a heart attack and dying. Third, Hazel had a behavioral symptom of anxiety: She froze, unable to move until help arrived. Fourth, she had the sense of dread and terror that make up the emotional symptoms of anxiety.

All of these symptoms can be highly adaptive when we are facing a real threat, such as a saber-toothed tiger in prehistoric times or a burglar today. They become maladaptive when there is no real threat to fight against or flee from. Hazel's symptoms were not triggered by a dangerous situation but came "out of the blue." Even when these symptoms do arise in response to some perceived threat, they can be maladaptive when they are out of proportion to the threat or persist after the threat has passed. Many people with anxiety disorders seem to view situations as highly threatening that most of us would consider benign, and they worry about those situations even when they are highly unlikely to occur. For example, people with social phobias are terrified of the possibility that they might embarrass themselves in public, and they therefore go to great lengths to avoid social situations.

● Table 15-3
Generalized Anxiety

The statements listed in this table are self-descriptions by individuals who have chronically high levels of anxiety. (*From Abnormal Psychology"* The Problem of Maladaptive Behavior, *7/e, by I. G. Sarason & B. R. Sarason. Copyright © 1993 by I. G. Sarason and B. R. Sarason. Adapted by permission of Prentice-Hall, Upper Saddle River, NJ.)*

I am often bothered by the thumping of my heart.

Little annoyances get on my nerves and irritate me.

I often become suddenly scared for no good reason.

I worry continuously, and that gets me down.

I frequently get spells of complete exhaustion and fatigue.

It is always hard for me to make up my mind.

I always seem to be dreading something.

I feel nervous and high-strung all the time.

I often feel I cannot overcome my difficulties.

I feel constantly under strain.

In one form of anxiety disorder, **generalized anxiety disorder,** the person experiences a constant sense of tension and dread. Inability to relax, disturbed sleep, fatigue, headaches, dizziness, and rapid heart rate are the most common physical complaints. In addition, the individual continually worries about potential problems and has difficulty concentrating or making decisions. When the individual finally makes a decision, it becomes a source of further worry ("Did I foresee all the possible consequences?"). Some self-descriptions provided by people with chronically high levels of anxiety appear in Table 15-3. Other anxiety disorders, such as panic disorder, phobias, and obsessive-compulsive disorder, are characterized by more focused anxiety and are discussed in more detail in the rest of this section.

PANIC DISORDERS

Hazel's symptoms suggest that she experienced a **panic attack**—an episode of acute and overwhelming apprehension or terror. During panic attacks, the individual feels certain that something dreadful is about to happen. This feeling is usually accompanied by such symptoms as heart palpitations, shortness of breath, perspiration, muscle tremors, faintness, and nausea. The symptoms result from excitation of the sympathetic division of the autonomic nervous system (see Chapter 2) and are the same reactions that an individual experiences when extremely frightened. During severe panic attacks, the person fears that he or she will die.

As many as 40% of young adults have occasional panic attacks, especially during times of stress (King, Gullone, Tonge, & Ollendick, 1993). For most of these people, the panic attacks are annoying but isolated events that do not change how they live their lives. When panic attacks become a common occurrence and the individual begins to worry about having attacks, he or she may receive a diagnosis of **panic disorder.** Panic disorder is relatively rare: Only about 1.5% to 3.5% of the population will ever develop a panic disorder (American Psychiatric Association, 2000). Usually panic disorder appears sometime between late adolescence and the mid-30s. Without treatment, panic disorder tends to become chronic (Weiss & Last, 2001).

Panic-like symptoms may take a different form across cultures. People from Latino cultures, particularly in the Caribbean, sometimes experience a sudden rush of anxiety symptoms known as *ataque de nervios.* The symptoms of *ataque* include trembling, feelings of out of control, sudden crying, screaming uncontrollably, verbal and physical aggression, and sometimes seizure-like or fainting episodes and suicidal gestures (Lopez & Guarnaccia, 2000). When *ataque de nervios* comes out of the blue, it is often attributed to the stresses of daily living or to spiritual causes. A study of Puerto Ricans after the 1985 floods found that 16% of the victims reported experiencing an *ataque* (Guarnaccia Canino, Rubio-Stipec, & Bravo, 1993).

People with panic disorder may believe that they have a life-threatening illness, such as heart disease or susceptibility to stroke, even after such illnesses have been ruled out by medical examinations. They may go from one physician to another, searching for the one who can diagnose their ailments. They may also believe that they are "going crazy" or "losing control." If their symptoms go untreated, they may become depressed and demoralized.

About a third to half of people with panic disorder also develop agoraphobia (American Psychiatric Association, 2000). People with **agoraphobia** fear any place where they might be trapped or unable to receive help in an emergency. The emergency they most often fear is having a panic attack. The term *agoraphobia* comes from the ancient Greek words meaning "fear of the marketplace." People with agoraphobia fear being in a busy, crowded place such as a mall. They may also fear being in tightly enclosed spaces from which it can be difficult to escape, such as a bus, elevator, or subway, or being alone in wide-open spaces such as a meadow or a deserted beach. All of these places are frightening for people with agoraphobia because if a panic attack or some other emergency occurred, it would be very difficult for them to escape or get help. They may also fear that they will embarrass themselves when others see that they are having a panic attack, even though other people usually cannot tell when a person is having a panic attack.

People with agoraphobia avoid all the places they fear. They significantly curtail their activities, remaining in a few "safe" places, such as the area within a few blocks of home. Sometimes they can venture into "unsafe" places if a trusted family member or friend accompanies them. If they attempt to enter "unsafe" places on their own, however, they may experience a great deal of general anxiety beforehand and have a full panic attack when in the unsafe place. Hazel, whom we met earlier in the chapter, provides an example:

> Hazel continued to have panic attacks every few days, sometimes on the same street where she had the first panic attack, but increasingly in places where she'd never had a panic attack before. It seemed she was especially likely to have a panic attack if there were lots of people standing around her, and she became confused about how she would get out of the crowd if she began to panic. The only place Hazel had not had any panic attacks was in her apartment. She began to spend more and more time in her apartment and refused to go anyplace she had previously had a panic attack. After a few months, she had called in sick to work so often that she was fired. Yet, Hazel could not bring herself to leave her apartment at all. She had her groceries delivered to her so she wouldn't have to go out to get them. She would see friends only if they would come to her apartment. Hazel's savings were becoming depleted, however, because she had lost her job. Hazel began looking for a job that she could do from her apartment.

Although people can develop agoraphobia without panic attacks, the vast majority of people with agoraphobia do have panic attacks or panic-like symptoms in social situations (Craske & Barlow, 2001). Agoraphobia usually develops within a year of the onset of recurrent panic attacks. Obviously, the symptoms of agoraphobia can severely interfere with the ability to function in daily life. People with agoraphobia often turn to alcohol and other drugs to cope with their symptoms. Fortunately, we have learned a great deal about the causes of panic and agoraphobia in recent years.

UNDERSTANDING PANIC DISORDER AND AGORAPHOBIA

Many people who develop panic disorder probably have a genetic or other biological vulnerability to the disorder. Panic disorder runs in families (Foley et al., 2001; van den Heuvel, van de Wetering, Veltman, & Pauls, 2000). This does not mean, of course, that panic disorders are entirely hereditary, in that family members live in the same environment. However, the results of twin studies provide firmer evidence for an inherited predisposition for panic disorder. Recall that identical twins share the same heredity; thus, if a disorder is transmitted entirely genetically, when one identical twin suffers from the disorder, the other twin should be highly likely to suffer from the disorder. In contrast, fraternal twins are no more alike genetically than ordinary siblings, so that when one twin suffers from the disorder, the other twin should not be at greatly increased risk for the disorder.

Twin studies have shown than an identical twin is twice as likely to suffer panic disorder if the other twin does than Is true for fraternal twins (Kendler, Neale, Kessler, & Heath, 1992, 1993; van den Heuvel et al., 2000).

One characteristic that may be inherited in people who are prone to panic attacks is an overreactive fight-or-flight response (McNally, 2001). A full panic attack can be induced easily by having such individuals engage in activities that stimulate the initial physiological changes of the fight-or-flight response. For example, when people with panic disorder purposely hyperventilate, breathe into a paper bag, or inhale a small amount of carbon dioxide, they experience an increase in subjective anxiety, and many will experience a full panic attack (see Figure 15-1; Bourin, Baker, & Bradwejn, 1998; Craske & Barlow, 2001). In contrast, people without a history of panic attacks may experience some physical discomfort while performing these activities, but they rarely experience a full panic attack.

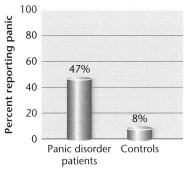

a) After hyperventilating

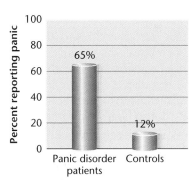

b) After inhaling carbon dioxide

❚ **Figure 15-1**
Panic Attacks of Patients and Controls
People with panic disorder are much more likely than people without panic disorder to have a panic attack when made to hyperventilate or inhale small amounts of carbon dioxide in laboratory experiments. (Adapted from R. M. Rapee, T. A. Brown, M. M. Anthony, & D. H. Barlow (1992), "Response to hyperventilation and inhalation of 5.5% carbon-dioxide-enriched air across the DSM-III-R anxiety disorders," *Journal of Abnormal Psychology*, 101, 538–552. Copyright © 1992 by the American Psychological Association. Adapted with permission.)

This overreactive fight-or-flight response may be the result of deficiencies in areas of the brain that regulate this response, especially the limbic system (Deakin & Graeff, 1991; Gray, 1982; Reiman, Lane, Ahern, Schwartz, & Davidson, 2000). Some studies show that people with panic disorder have low levels of the neurotransmitter serotonin in the limbic system and other brain circuits involved in the fight-or-flight response (Bell & Nutt, 1998). Serotonin deficiencies cause chronic hyperactivation of these areas of the brain, putting the individual on the verge of a panic attack most of the time.

An overreactive fight-or-flight response may not be enough to create a full panic disorder, however. Cognitive-behavioral theories of panic and agoraphobia suggest that people who are prone to panic attacks tend to pay very close attention to their bodily sensations, misinterpret bodily sensations in a negative way, and engage in catastrophic thinking (Bouton, Mineka, & Barlow, 2001; Clark, 1988; Craske & Barlow, 2001). In the case described earlier, when Hazel felt her muscles tightening, she began thinking, "I'm having a heart attack! I'm going to die!" Not surprisingly, these thoughts increased her emotional symptoms of anxiety, which in turn made her physiological symptoms worse—her heart rate increased even more, and her muscles felt even tighter. Interpreting these physiological changes catastrophically led to a full panic attack. Between attacks, Hazel is hypervigilant, paying close attention to any bodily sensation. Her constant vigilance causes her autonomic nervous system to be chronically aroused, making it more likely that she will have another panic attack.

How does agoraphobia develop out of panic disorder? According to the cognitive-behavioral theory, people with panic disorder remember vividly the places where they have had attacks. They greatly fear those places, and that fear generalizes to all similar places. By avoiding those places, they reduce their anxiety, and their avoidance behavior thus is highly reinforced. They may also find that they experience little anxiety in particular places, such as their own homes, and this reduction of anxiety is also highly reinforcing, leading them to confine themselves to these "safe" places. Thus, through classical and operant conditioning, their behaviors are shaped into what we call agoraphobia.

What evidence is there for this theory? Several laboratory studies support the contentions that cognitive factors play a strong role in panic attacks and that agoraphobic behaviors may be conditioned through learning experiences (McNally, 2001). In one study, researchers asked two groups of patients with panic disorder to wear masks through which they would inhale slight amounts of carbon dioxide. Both groups were told that, although inhaling a slight amount of carbon dioxide was not dangerous to their health, it could induce a panic attack.

One group was told that they could not control the amount of carbon dioxide that came through their masks. The other group was told that they could control how much carbon dioxide they inhaled by turning a knob. Actually, neither group had any control over the amount of carbon dioxide they inhaled, and both groups inhaled the same small amount. Eighty percent of the patients who believed that they had no control experienced a panic attack, but only 20% of those who believed that they could control the carbon dioxide had an attack. These results clearly suggest that beliefs about control over panic symptoms play a strong role in panic attacks (Sanderson, Rapee, & Barlow, 1989).

In a study focusing on agoraphobic behaviors, researchers examined whether people with panic disorder could avoid having a panic attack, even after inhaling carbon dioxide, by having a "safe person" nearby. Panic patients who were exposed to carbon dioxide with their safe person present were much less likely to experience the emotional, cognitive, and physiological symptoms of panic than panic patients who were exposed to carbon dioxide without their safe person present (see Figure 15-2; Carter, Hollon, Caron, & Shelton, 1995). These results show that the symptoms of panic become associated with certain situations and that operant behaviors such as sticking close to a "safe person" can be reinforced by the reduction of panic symptoms.

The biological and cognitive-behavioral theories of panic disorder and agoraphobia thus can be integrated

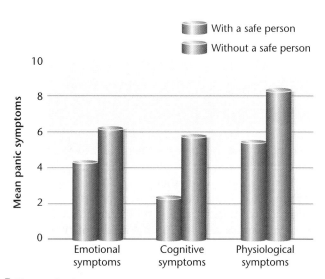

▌Figure 15-2
Panic Symptoms in Panic Patients With and Without a Safe Person Available
Panic patients were much more likely to show symptoms of panic when a safe person was not with them. (After Carter, Hollon, Caron, & Shelton, 1995)

Biological predisposition to overreactive
fight-or-flight response

Cognitive predisposition to catastrophizing cognitions

Excessive fight-or-flight response easily triggered

Frequent panic attacks

Person avoids places associated with panic

Avoidance reinforced by reduction of anxiety

Agoraphobia develops

▌**Figure 15-3**
A Vulnerability-Stress Model of Panic and Agoraphobia
A combination of biological vulnerability to an overreactive
fight-or-flight response plus cognitive vulnerability to catastrophizing cognitions may begin a chain of processes leading to
panic and agoraphobia.

into a vulnerability-stress model (Craske & Barlow,
2001; see Figure 15-3). People who develop panic disorder may have a genetic or biochemical vulnerability to
an overreactive fight-or-flight response, so that even
with only a slight triggering stimulus, their bodies experience all the physiological symptoms of the response.
For a full panic disorder to develop, however, it may be
necessary for these individuals to also be prone to catastrophizing these symptoms and worrying excessively
about having panic attacks. These cognitions further
heighten their physiological reactivity, making it even
more likely that they will experience a full fight-or-flight
response. Agoraphobia develops when they begin to
avoid places that they associate with their panic symptoms and confine themselves to places where they experience less anxiety. This vulnerability-stress model has
led to exciting breakthroughs in the treatment of panic
disorder and agoraphobia, which we will discuss in
Chapter 16.

PHOBIAS

A **phobia** is an intense fear of a stimulus or situation that
most people do not consider particularly dangerous. The
individual usually realizes that this fear is irrational but
still feels anxiety (ranging from strong uneasiness to
panic) that can be alleviated only by avoiding the feared
object or situation.

Many of us have one or two irrational fears—of
snakes, insects, and heights, for example. However, a
fear is usually not diagnosed as a phobic disorder unless
it interferes considerably with the person's daily life. Examples might include a woman whose fear of enclosed
places prevents her from entering elevators or a man
whose fear of crowds prevents him from attending the
theater or walking along congested sidewalks.

DSM-IV divides phobic disorders into three broad
categories: simple phobias, social phobias, and agoraphobia. A **simple phobia** is a fear of a specific object, animal, or situation. Irrational fears of snakes, germs, enclosed places, and darkness are examples. Some people
may develop a simple phobia but be normal in other respects. In more serious cases, the individual has a number of phobias that interfere with many aspects of life

© John Cancalosi/Peter Arnold

One of the most common phobias is a snake phobia.

and may be intertwined with obsessive or compulsive behavior. People with **social phobias** feel extremely insecure in social situations and have an exaggerated fear of embarrassing themselves. Often they are afraid that they will betray their anxiety by such signs as hand tremors, blushing, or a quavering voice. These fears are usually unrealistic: Individuals who fear that they might shake do not do so; those who fear that they will stutter or quaver actually speak quite normally. Fear of public speaking or of eating in public are the most common complaints of socially phobic individuals.

People with social phobias will go to great lengths to avoid situations in which others might evaluate them. They may take jobs that are solitary and isolating to avoid other people. If they find themselves in a feared social situation, they may begin trembling and perspiring, feel confused and dizzy, have heart palpitations, and eventually have a full panic attack. They are sure that others see their nervousness and are judging them as inarticulate, weak, stupid, or "crazy."

Social phobia is quite common, with about 8% of the U.S. adult population qualifying for the diagnosis in a 12-month period and 1 in 8 people experiencing the disorder at some time in their lives (Kessler et al., 1998; Schneider et al., 1992). Social phobia typically begins in adolescence (Blazer, George, & Hughes, 1991) and tends to be a chronic problem if it is not treated (Kessler et al., 1998).

UNDERSTANDING PHOBIAS

Historically, phobias have been the subject of a major clash between psychodynamic theories and behavioral theories. Freud's theory of the development of phobias was one of his most famous and controversial. Freud argued that phobias result when people displace anxiety over unconscious motives or desires onto objects that symbolize those motives or desires. His classic example was the case of Little Hans, a 5-year-old who developed an intense fear of horses. Freud interpreted the boy's phobia in terms of Oedipal fears (see Chapter 13) through the following analysis: Hans was in love with his mother, jealously hated his father, and wanted to replace him (the Oedipal conflict); he feared that his father would retaliate by castrating him; the anxiety produced by this conflict was enormous because the wishes were unacceptable to the child's conscious mind; the anxiety was displaced onto an innocent object (a large horse that Hans had seen fall down and thrash about violently in the street).

Freud's evidence for his explanation of Hans's horse phobia consisted of Hans's answers to a series of rather leading questions about what he was "really" afraid of, along with the fact that Hans appeared to lose his horse phobia after his conversations with Freud. Freud suggested that Hans had gained insight into the true source of his phobia and that this insight had cured the phobia. Critics pointed out, however, that Hans never provided any spontaneous or direct evidence that his real concern was his father rather than the horse. They also noted that Hans's phobia diminished gradually over time rather than abruptly in response to some sudden insight.

Some of the severest critics of Freud's analysis of phobias were behaviorists (Watson & Raynor, 1920). They argued that phobias do not develop from unconscious anxieties but rather from classical and operant conditioning. Many phobias emerge after a traumatic experience—a child nearly drowns and develops a phobia of water, another child is bitten by a dog and develops a phobia of dogs, an adolescent who stumbles through a speech in class is laughed at by peers and develops a phobia of public speaking. In these cases, a previously neutral stimulus (water or dogs or public speaking) is paired with a traumatic event (drowning or biting or embarrassment) that elicits anxiety. Through classical conditioning, the previously neutral stimulus now is able to elicit the anxiety reaction. In addition, many people with such fears avoid the phobic object because avoidance helps reduce their anxiety, and the phobic behavior is maintained through operant conditioning.

Although some phobias appear to result from actual frightening experiences, others may be learned vicariously through observation (Bandura, 1969; Mineka, Davidson, Cook, & Keir, 1984). Fearful parents tend to produce children who share their fears. A child who observes parents react with fear to a variety of situations may develop the same reactions to those situations. Indeed, studies find that phobias clearly run in families (Kessler et al., 1998; Fyer, Mannuzza, Chapman, & Liebowitz, 1993). It is unclear whether this is due largely to children learning phobias from their parents or also partially due to genetic transmission of phobias. The first-degree relatives of people with phobias are three to four times more likely than others to also have a phobia, and twin studies suggest that this is due, at least in part, to genetics (Hettema et al., 2001). What is likely to be inherited is a fearful temperament rather than the phobia per se (Hudson & Rapee, 2000).

Behavioral theories have led to highly successful treatments for phobias, lending further support to these theories. In contrast, treatments based on psychodynamic theories of phobias tend to be unsuccessful, and current drug treatments tend to relieve phobic symptoms only in the short term.

OBSESSIVE-COMPULSIVE DISORDER

A man gets out of bed several times each night and checks all the doors to make sure they are locked. Upon returning to bed, he is tormented by the thought that he may have missed one. Another man takes three or four showers in succession, scrubbing his body thoroughly with a special disinfectant each time, fearful that he may be contaminated by germs. A woman has recurrent thoughts about stabbing her infant and feels panic-stricken whenever she has to handle scissors or knives. A teenage girl is always late to school because she feels compelled to repeat many of her actions (replacing her brush on the dresser, arranging the school supplies in her book bag, crossing the threshold to her bedroom) a set number of times, usually some multiple of the number 4.

All of these people have symptoms of **obsessive-compulsive disorder:** Their lives are dominated by repetitive acts or thoughts. Obsessions **are** persistent intrusions of unwelcome thoughts, images, or impulses that elicit anxiety. Compulsions **are** irresistible urges to carry out certain acts or rituals that reduce anxiety. Obsessive thoughts are often linked with compulsive acts (for example, thoughts of lurking germs, which lead to the compulsion to wash eating utensils many times before using them). Regardless of whether the repetitive element is a thought (obsession) or an act (compulsion), the central feature of the disorder is the subjective experience of loss of control. The victims struggle mightily to rid themselves of the troublesome thoughts or resist performing the repetitive acts but are unable to do so.

At times, all of us have persistently recurring thoughts ("Did I leave the gas on?") and urges to perform ritualistic behavior (arranging items on a desk in a precise order before starting an assignment). But for people with obsessive-compulsive disorders, such thoughts and acts occupy so much time that they seriously interfere with daily life. These individuals recognize their thoughts as irrational and repugnant but are unable to ignore or suppress them. They realize the senselessness of their compulsive behavior but become anxious when they try to resist their compulsions, and feel a release of tension once the acts are carried out.

Obsessive thoughts cover a variety of topics, but most often they are concerned with causing harm to oneself or others, fear of contamination, and doubt that a completed task has been accomplished satisfactorily (Hewlett, 2000; Rachman & Hodgson, 1980). Interestingly, the content of obsessions changes with the times. In earlier days, obsessive thoughts about religion and sex were common—for example, blasphemous thoughts or impulses to shout obscenities in church or expose one's genitals in public. These types of obsessions are less frequent today. And whereas obsessions about contamination used to focus on syphilis, AIDS has now become the object of many contamination fears (Rapaport, 1989).

Some people with an obsessive-compulsive disorder have intrusive thoughts without engaging in repetitious actions. However, the majority of patients with obsessive thoughts also exhibit compulsive behavior (Akhtar, Wig,

Varma, Pershard, & Verma, 1975). Compulsions take a variety of forms, of which the two most common are washing and checking (Foa & Steketee, 1989). "Washers" feel contaminated when exposed to certain objects or thoughts and spend hours performing washing and cleaning rituals. "Checkers" check doors, lights, ovens, or the accuracy of a completed task 10, 20, or 100 times or repeat ritualistic acts over and over again. They believe that their actions will prevent future "disasters" or punishments. Sometimes these rituals are related to the anxiety-evoking obsessions in a direct way (for example, repeatedly checking to see if the stove has been turned off to avoid a possible fire); other rituals are not rationally related to the obsessions (for example, dressing and undressing in order to prevent one's spouse from having an accident). The common theme behind all of these repetitive behaviors is doubt. Obsessive-compulsive individuals cannot trust their senses or their judgment; they can't trust their eyes, even though they see no dirt, or really believe that the door is locked.

Obsessive-compulsive disorders are related to phobic disorders in that both involve severe anxiety and both may appear in the same patient. However, there are important differences. Phobic patients seldom ruminate about their fears, nor do they show ritualistic compulsive behavior. And the two disorders are evoked by different stimuli. Dirt, germs, and harm to others—common obsessive-compulsive preoccupations—seldom cause major problems for phobic individuals.

Obsessive-compulsive disorder often begins at a young age (Foa & Franklin, 2001). It tends to be chronic if left untreated. Obsessional thoughts are very distressing, and engaging in compulsive behaviors can take a great deal of time and be highly maladaptive (for example, washing one's hands so often that they bleed). People with this disorder thus are quite psychologically impaired. Between 1% and 3% of people develop obsessive-compulsive disorder at some time in their lives (Hewlett, 2000). The prevalence of OCD does not seem to differ greatly across countries that have been studied, including the United States, Canada, Mexico, England, Norway, Hong Kong, India, Egypt, Japan, and Korea (Escobar, 1993; Insel, 1984; Kim, 1993).

UNDERSTANDING OBSESSIVE-COMPULSIVE DISORDER

Considerable research evidence suggests that obsessive-compulsive disorder may have biological causes. Some family research suggests that disordered genes may play a role in determining who is vulnerable to OCD (Hettema et al., 2001; Nestadt et al., 2000). Most of the biological research on OCD, however, has focused on a critical circuit in the brain. People with this disorder may have defi-

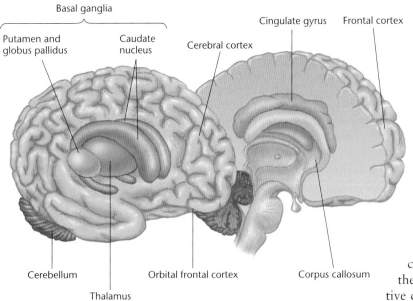

Basal ganglia

Putamen and globus pallidus

Caudate nucleus

Cerebral cortex

Cingulate gyrus

Frontal cortex

Cerebellum

Orbital frontal cortex

Corpus callosum

Thalamus

▊ Figure 15-4
The Human Brain and OCD
This three-dimensional view of the human brain shows the locations of the orbital frontal cortex and the basal ganglia—areas implicated in obsessive-compulsive disorder. Among the basal ganglia's structures are the caudate nuclei, which filter powerful impulses that arise in the orbital frontal cortex so that only the most powerful ones reach the thalamus.

ciencies in the neurotransmitter serotonin in the areas of the brain that regulate primitive impulses about sex, violence, and cleanliness—impulses that are often the focus of obsessions (Baxter, Schwartz, Bergman, & Szuba,

1992; Rapaport, 1990; Swedo, Pietrini, & Leonard, 1992). An elaborate circuit in the brain seems to be involved, beginning with the frontal cortex (see Figure 15-4). Impulses arise here and are carried to a part of the basal ganglia called the *caudate nucleus*. The strongest impulses then travel to the thalamus, where they may be acted upon. As a result, primitive impulses may break through into consciousness and motivate the execution of stereotyped behaviors much more often in people with obsessive-compulsive disorder than in normal individuals.

PET scans of people with obsessive-compulsive disorder show more activity in the areas of the brain involved in this primitive circuit than do PET scans of people without the disorder (Baxter, Schwartz, Guze, & Bergman, 1990) (see Figure 15-5; Saxena et al., 1998). In addition, people with the disorder often get some relief from their symptoms when they take drugs that regulate serotonin levels (Rapaport, 1991). Finally, patients who respond well to these drugs tend to show greater reductions in the rate of activity in these brain areas than patients who do not respond well to these drugs (Baxter et al., 1992; Swedo et al., 1992). Interestingly, OCD patients who respond to behavior therapies also tend to show decreases in activity in the caudate nucleus and thalamus (see Figure 15-6; Schwartz, Snidman, & Kagan, 1996).

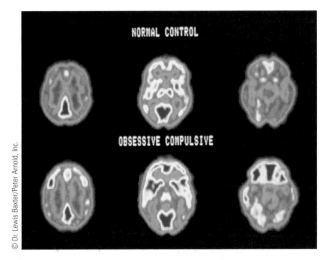

▊ Figure 15-5
A Normal Brain Versus an Obsessive-Compulsive Brain
This PET scan shows the metabolic differences between areas of the brain of a person with obsessive-compulsive disorder and the same areas in the brain of a normal person.

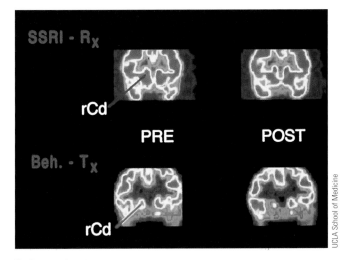

▊ Figure 15-6
OCD Pretreatment Versus Posttreatment
PET studies show decreases in metabolic activity in the caudate nucleus in OCD patients after they have received behavior therapy. (From Schwartz, Stoessel, Baxter, Martin, & Phelps, 1996)

As with panic disorder, however, people may go on to develop a full obsessive-compulsive disorder only if they also have certain cognitive and behavioral vulnerabilities in addition to a biological vulnerability. Cognitive and behavioral theorists suggest that people with obsessive-compulsive disorder have more trouble "turning off" intrusive thoughts because they have a tendency toward rigid, moralistic thinking (Rachman, 1993; Salkovskis, 1989). They are more likely to judge their negative, intrusive thoughts as unacceptable, and they become more anxious and guilty about these thoughts. This anxiety then makes it even harder to dismiss the thought (Clark & de Silva, 1985). People with obsessive-compulsive disorder may also believe that they should be able to control all thoughts and have trouble accepting the fact that everyone has negative thoughts occasionally (Clark & Purdon, 1993; Freeston, Ladouceur, Thibodeau, & Gagnon, 1992). They tend to believe that having these thoughts means they are going crazy, or they equate having the thought with actually engaging in the behavior ("If I'm thinking about hurting my child, I'm as guilty as if I actually did hurt my child"). Of course, this just makes them even more anxious when they have thoughts, because it's harder to dismiss them.

Compulsions may develop when the obsessional person discovers that some behavior temporarily quells the obsession and the anxiety it arouses. This reduction in anxiety reinforces the behavior, and a compulsion is born: Every time the person has the obsession, he or she will feel compelled to engage in the behavior to reduce anxiety.

Again, some of the best evidence in favor of cognitive and behavioral perspectives on obsessive-compulsive disorder can be seen in the fact that therapies based on these perspectives are helpful to people with the disorder, as we will discuss in Chapter 16. In contrast, psychodynamic theories of obsessive-compulsive disorder have not led to successful treatments. According to those theories, obsessions are unacceptable impulses (hostility, destructiveness, inappropriate sexual urges) that have been repressed and reappear in a disguised form. The individual feels that they are not a part of himself or herself, and may engage in compulsive acts to undo or atone for them. A mother who is obsessed with thoughts of murdering her child may feel compelled to check many times during the night to assure herself that the child is well. Compulsive rituals also serve to keep threatening impulses out of the individual's conscious awareness: A person who is continually busy has little opportunity to think improper thoughts or commit improper actions. According to psychodynamic theory, bringing the unconscious conflict to light and gaining insight into it should cure an obsessive-compulsive disorder. What little research has been done to test this theory, however, suggests that insight-oriented therapy does not cure obsessive-compulsive disorder in most cases.

In sum, biological and psychological factors probably combine in creating many of the anxiety disorders. Many people who develop these disorders probably have a genetic, neurological, or biochemical vulnerability to anxiety. But it may be necessary for them also to have a tendency toward catastrophizing and engaging in maladaptive avoidant behaviors that reduce anxiety for a full anxiety disorder to develop.

◆ Interim Summary

- Anxiety disorders include generalized anxiety (constant worry and tension), panic disorders (sudden attacks of overwhelming apprehension), phobias (irrational fears of specific objects or situations), and obsessive-compulsive disorders (persistent unwanted thoughts, or obsessions, combined with urges, or compulsions, to perform certain acts).

- Biological theories of anxiety disorders attribute them to genetic predispositions or to biochemical or neurological abnormalities. Most anxiety disorders run in families, and twin studies strongly suggest that panic disorder and obsessive-compulsive disorder have an inherited component.

- People who suffer panic attacks have an overreactive fight-or-flight response, perhaps because of serotonin deficiencies in the limbic system.

- People with obsessive-compulsive disorder may have serotonin deficiencies in areas of the brain that regulate primitive impulses.

- Cognitive and behavioral theorists suggest that people with anxiety disorders are prone to catastrophizing cognitions and to rigid, moralistic thinking. Maladaptive behaviors such as avoidant behaviors and compulsions arise through operant conditioning when the individual discovers that the behaviors reduce anxiety. Phobias may emerge through classical conditioning.

- Psychodynamic theories attribute anxiety disorders to unconscious conflicts that are disguised as phobias, obsessions, or compulsions.

◆ Critical Thinking Questions

1. Women are more likely than men to suffer from the anxiety disorders (except for obsessive-compulsive disorder). Can you generate some hypotheses for this gender difference?

2. Humans are much more likely to develop phobias of snakes and spiders than of guns or other modern weapons that are a greater danger to them. Can you generate an evolutionary explanation for this?

MOOD DISORDERS

Individuals with **mood disorders** may be severely depressed or manic (wildly elated), or may experience periods of depression as well as periods of mania. Mood disorders are divided into **depressive disorders,** in which the individual has one or more periods of depression without a history of manic episodes, and **bipolar disorders,** in which the individual alternates between periods of depression and periods of mania, usually with a return to normal mood between the two extremes. Manic episodes without some history of depression are uncommon.

DEPRESSION

> From the time I woke up on the morning until the time I went to bed at night, I was unbearably miserable and seemingly incapable of any kind of joy or enthusiasm. Everything—every thought, word, movement—was an effort. Everything that once was sparkling now was flat. I seemed to myself to be dull, boring, inadequate, thick brained, unlit, unresponsive, chill skinned, bloodless and sparrow drab. I doubted, completely, my ability to do anything well. It seemed as though my mind had slowed down and burned out to the point of being virtually useless. The wretched, convoluted, and pathetically confused mass of gray worked only well enough to torment me with a dreary litany of my inadequacies and shortcomings in character and to taunt me with the total, the desperate hopelessness of it all. (Jamison, 1995, p. 110)

Most of us have periods when we feel sad, lethargic, and uninterested in any activities—even pleasurable ones. Mild depressive symptoms are a normal response to many of life's stresses, especially important losses. Depression becomes a disorder when the symptoms become so severe that they interfere with normal functioning, and when they continue for weeks at a time. Depressive disorders are relatively common, with about 17% of people having an episode of severe depression such as Jamison describes at some time in their lives (Kessler et al., 1994). Women are twice as likely as men to develop depression (Nolen-Hoeksema, 2002).

Although depression is characterized as a mood disorder, it is truly a disorder of the whole person, affecting bodily functions, behaviors, and thoughts as well as emotions (see Figure 15-7). A person need not have all the symptoms of depression to be diagnosed with a disorder, but the more symptoms he or she has and the more intense they are, the more certain we can be that the individual is suffering from depression.

The emotional symptoms of depression are not the everyday blues that we all experience from time to time, but an unrelenting pain and despair. People also report that they have lost the ability to experience joy, even in response to the most joyous occasions, a symptom re-

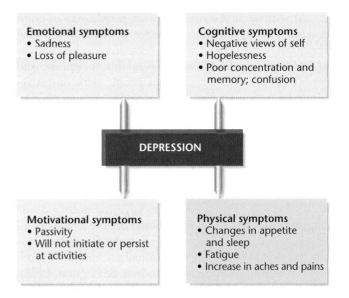

▌Figure 15-7
The Symptoms of Depression
Depression includes emotional, cognitive, motivational, and physical symptoms.

ferred to as **anhedonia.** They say that they don't find interacting with family or friends, their work, or their hobbies enjoyable anymore.

The cognitive symptoms consist primarily of negative thoughts, with themes of worthlessness, guilt, hopelessness, and even suicide. Motivation is at a low ebb: The depressed person tends to be passive and has difficulty initiating activities. The following conversation between a patient and his therapist illustrates this passivity. The man, who had been hospitalized after a suicide attempt, spent his days sitting motionless in the lounge. His therapist decided to try to engage him in some activities:

> Therapist: I understand that you spend most of your day in the lounge. Is that true?
>
> Patient: Yes, being quiet gives me the peace of mind I need.
>
> Therapist: When you sit here, how's your mood?
>
> Patient: I feel awful all the time. I just wish I could fall in a hole somewhere and die.
>
> Therapist: Do you feel better after sitting for 2 or 3 hours?
>
> Patient: No, the same.
>
> Therapist: So you're sitting in the hope that you'll find peace of mind, but it doesn't sound like your depression improves.
>
> Patient: I get so bored.
>
> Therapist: Would you consider being more active? There are a number of reasons why I think increasing your activity level might help.

Some people suffer depression for years.

Patient: There's nothing to do around here.

Therapist: Would you consider trying some activities if I could come up with a list?

Patient: If you think it will help, but I think you're wasting your time. I don't have any interests. (Beck, Rush, Shaw, & Emery, 1979, p. 200)

The physical symptoms of depression include changes in appetite, sleep disturbances, fatigue, and loss of energy. Because a depressed person's thoughts are focused inward rather than toward external events, he or she may magnify minor aches and pains and worry about health.

As we see from this description of its symptoms, depression can be a debilitating disorder. Unfortunately, severe depression can also be long-lasting. One study of people with severe depression found that over a 9-year period they were symptom-free only 27% of the time (Judd et al., 1998). Even if they recover from one bout of depression, people remain at high risk for relapses into new episodes. There is some good news, however. Episodes of depression can be greatly shortened—and new episodes prevented—with either drug therapy or psychotherapy, as we discuss in Chapter 16.

BIPOLAR DISORDER

The majority of depressions occur without episodes of mania. But some people with a mood disorder will experience both depression and mania and hence can be diagnosed with bipolar disorder, also known as manic-depression. The individual alternates between depression and extreme elation. In some cases the cycle between depressive episodes and manic episodes is swift, with only a brief return to normality in between.

People experiencing **manic episodes** behave in a way that appears on the surface to be the opposite of depression. During mild manic episodes, they are energetic, enthusiastic, and full of self-confidence. They talk continually, rush from one activity to another with little need for sleep, and make grandiose plans, paying little attention to their practicality, as Jamison (1995, pp. 36–37) describes:

I was a senior in high school when I had my first attack. At first, everything seemed so easy. I raced about like a crazed weasel, bubbling with plans and enthusiasms, immersed in sports, and staying up all night, night after night, out with friends, reading everything that wasn't nailed down, filling manuscript books with poems and fragments of plays, and making expansive, completely unrealistic plans for my future. The world was filled with pleasure and promise; I felt great. Not just great, I felt *really* great. I felt I could do anything, that no task was too difficult. My mind seemed clear, fabulously focused, and able to make intuitive mathematical leaps that had up to that point entirely eluded me. Indeed, they elude me still. At the time, however, not only did everything make perfect sense, but it all began to fit into a marvelous kind of cosmic relatedness. My sense of enchantment with the laws of the natural world caused me to fizz over, and I found myself buttonholing my friends to tell them how beautiful it all was. They were less than transfixed by my insights into the webbings and beauties of the universe although considerably impressed at how exhausting it was to be around my enthusiastic ramblings: You're talking too fast, Kay. Slow down, Kay. You're wearing me out, Kay. Slow down, Kay. And those times when they didn't actually come out and say it, I still could see it in their eyes: For God's sake, Kay, slow down.

This kind of energy, self-confidence, and enthusiasm may actually seem quite attractive to you, and indeed, many people in the midst of a manic episode do not want to get rid of their symptoms. At some point, however, manic symptoms often cross a line from joyful exuberance into hostile agitation. People may become angered by attempts to interfere with their activities and become abusive. Impulses (including sexual ones) are immediately expressed in actions or words. People may become confused and disoriented and may experience delusions of great wealth, accomplishment, or power. Eventually, most manic episodes revert into episodes of depression, sometimes extremely severe.

Bipolar disorders are relatively uncommon. Whereas about 21% of adult females and 13% of adult males in the United States have experienced depression, less than 2% of the adult population has had a bipolar disorder. Bipolar disorder, which appears to be equally common in men and women (Kessler et al., 1994), differs from other mood disorders in that it tends to occur at an earlier age, is more likely to run in families, responds to different medications, and almost always recurs if not treated.

UNDERSTANDING MOOD DISORDERS

As with the anxiety disorders, a combined biological and psychological model may best explain the mood disorders. Most people who develop depression—and particularly bipolar disorder—may have a biological vulnerability to these disorders. But the experience of certain types of life events, along with a tendency to think in negative ways, also clearly increases the likelihood of developing these disorders.

 The Neural Basis of Behavior

THE BIOLOGICAL PERSPECTIVE A tendency to develop mood disorders, particularly bipolar disorders, appears to be inherited (Wallace, Schneider, & McGuffin, 2002). Family history studies of people with bipolar disorder find that their first-degree relatives (parents, children, and siblings) have at least two to three times higher rates of both bipolar disorder and depressive disorders than relatives of people without bipolar disorder (Wallace et al., 2002; MacKinnon, Jamison, & De Paulo, 1997). Twin studies of bipolar disorder have also consistently suggested that the disorder has a genetic component. Indeed, the concordance rates between identical twins (the likelihood that both twins will have the disorder if one twin has the disorder) range from 50% to 100% across recent studies (Stoll, Renshaw, Yurgelun-Todd, & Cohen, 2000).

There is increasing evidence that depression, particularly recurrent depression, also is heritable. Family history studies find that first-degree relatives of people with depression have two to four times higher rates of depression than others (Sullivan, Neale, & Kendler, 2000). Interestingly, relatives of depressed people do not have any greater risk of developing bipolar disorder than relatives of people with no mood disorder. This suggests that bipolar disorder has a different genetic basis from that of depression. Twin studies also suggest that depression is heritable but to a lesser degree than bipolar disorder (Sullivan et al., 2000).

The specific role that genetic factors play in mood disorders is unclear. However, it seems likely that a biochemical abnormality is involved. The neurotransmitters norepinephrine and serotonin are believed to play an important role in mood disorders. Recall from Chapter 2 that neurotransmitters and their receptors interact like locks and keys (see Figure 15-8). Each neurotransmitter will fit into a particular type of receptor on the neuronal membrane. If there are the wrong number of receptors for a given type of neurotransmit-

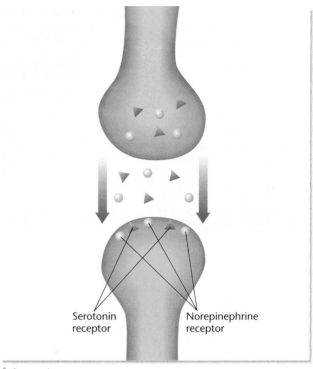

▲ Serotonin

○ Norepinephrine

❚ Figure 15-8
Neurotransmission in Depression
The neuronal receptors for norepinephrine and serotonin may not work efficiently in depressed people, so that norepinephrine and serotonin released from one neuron cannot bind to receptor sites on other neurons.

ter or the receptors for that neurotransmitter are too sensitive or not sensitive enough, the neurons do not efficiently use the available amounts of neurotransmitter. Several studies suggest that people with depression or bipolar disorder may have abnormalities in the number and sensitivity of receptor sites for serotonin and norepinephrine, particularly in areas of the brain that are involved in the regulation of emotion, such as the hypothalamus (Thase et al., 2002). In major depressive disorder, receptors for these neurotransmitters appear to be insensitive or too few in number. The picture is less clear for bipolar disorder, but it is likely that receptors for these neurotransmitters undergo poorly timed changes in sensitivity that are correlated with mood changes (Kujawa & Nemeroff, 2000).

The structure and functioning of the brain also appears to be altered in people with mood disorders. Neuroimaging studies using computed tomography (CT) scans and magnetic resonance imaging (MRI) have found deterioration in the prefrontal cortex of people with severe unipolar depression or bipolar dis-

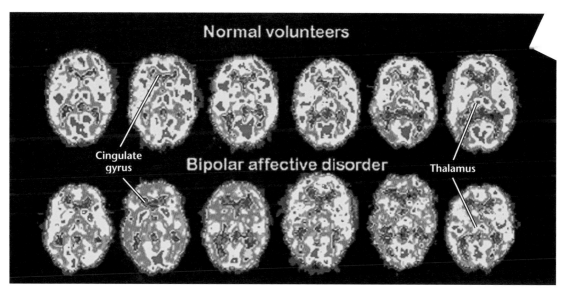

▌ Figure 15-9
PET Scans of Bipolar Disorder
PET scans in six control subjects and six patients with bipolar disorder. Note decreases in relative metabolic rate in the cingulate gyrus and thalamus in bipolar subjects. (Courtesy of Monte S. Buschbaum, M.D., Mt. Sinai School of Medicine, New York)

order (Drevets, 2000; Liotti & Mayberg, 2001). This is associated with abnormalities in metabolism in this area of the brain, according to positron emission tomography (PET) studies (see Figure 15-9; Buchsbaum

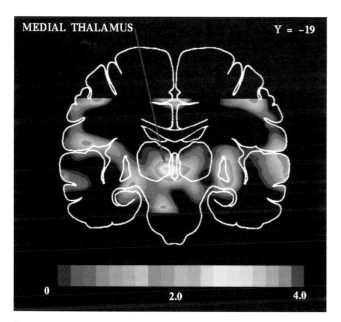

▌ Figure 15-10
Brain Functioning in Depression
This brain image shows increased metabolism in the medial thalamus of people with depression compared with those without depression. (Source: Drevets, W.C. (2000). Neuroimaging studies of mood disorders. *Biological Psychiatry, 48,* 813–829)

et al., 1997). The prefrontal cortex is involved in many aspects of cognitive functioning and in the regulation of emotion. The prefrontal cortex also has extensive connections with many other areas of the brain, including the thalamus, hypothalamus, amygdala, and hippocampus, which are involved in the regulation of responses to stress and in sleep, appetite, sexual drive, motivation, and memory. These areas of the brain show abnormalities in metabolism in people with the mood disorders as well (see Figure 15-10; Drevets et al., 1992, 1995). These structural and functional brain abnormalities could be precursors and causes of mood disorders, or they could be the result of biochemical processes in the mood disorders that have a toxic effect on the brain. We do not yet know the precise meaning of these abnormalities, but the rapid advances in neuroimaging technologies are sure to bring exciting new clues in the future. ▧

THE COGNITIVE PERSPECTIVE Cognitive theories focus primarily on depression. According to these theories, people become depressed because they tend to interpret events in their lives in pessimistic, hopeless ways (Abramson, Metalsky, & Alloy, 1989; Beck et al., 1979; Peterson & Seligman, 1984). One of the most influential cognitive theorists, Aaron Beck, grouped the negative thoughts of depressed individuals into three categories, which he called the *cognitive triad*: negative thoughts about the self, about present experiences, and about the future. Negative thoughts about the self include the de-

CUTTING-EDGE RESEARCH
The Biology of Suicide

The most disastrous consequence of depression is suicide. Not everyone who attempts or commits suicide is depressed, however, and suicidal thoughts and actions are alarmingly common. Nearly half of all teenagers in the United States say they know someone who has tried to commit suicide (see figure). One in five teenagers admits to attempting or seriously contemplating suicide (National Institute of Mental Health, 2000). Suicide is the ninth leading cause of the death in the United States and third leading cause among people 15 to 24 years of age (NIMH, 2000). More people die from suicide than from homicide.

Women attempt to commit suicide about three times more often than men do, but men succeed more often than women in killing themselves. The greater number of suicide attempts by women is probably related to the greater incidence of depression among women. The fact that men are more successful in their attempts is related to the choice of method. Until recently, women have tended to use less lethal means, such as cutting their wrists or overdosing on sleeping pills; men are more likely to use firearms or carbon

monoxide fumes or to hang themselves (Crosby, Cheltenham, & Sacks, 1999). However, with the marked increase in the number of women owning guns, suicide by firearms has now become women's method of first choice. Consequently, the fatality rate for women is changing. (Attempted suicides are successful 80% of the time when firearms are involved, but only 10% of drug or poison ingestions are fatal—a powerful argument for not keeping firearms in the home.)

Within the United States, there are substantial differences between ethnic-racial groups in rates of suicide (McIntosh, 1991; NIMH, 2000). Whites have higher suicide rates than all other groups except for Native Americans, whose suicide rate is more than twice the national average. There are also cross-national differences in suicide

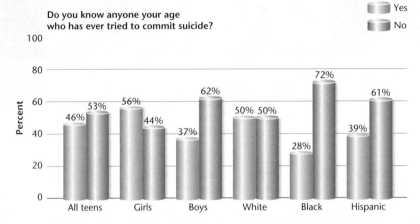

Do you know anyone your age who has ever tried to commit suicide?

Yes / No

	All teens	Girls	Boys	White	Black	Hispanic
Yes	46%	56%	37%	50%	28%	39%
No	53%	44%	62%	50%	72%	61%

Note: Hispanic may be of any race. There were too few Asian respondents to give separate percentages.

Based on surveys of 13- to 17-year-olds nationwide. The latest poll was conducted Oct. 11 to 14, 1999, with 1,038 teenagers. Those with no answer are not shown.

Teenager's Experience With Suicide
Percentages of teenagers in a national poll who answered "yes" or "no" to the question, "Do you know anyone your age who has ever tried to commit suicide?" (Source: *New York Times*, October 20, 1999, page 1)

pressed person's belief that he or she is worthless and inadequate. The depressed person's negative view of the future is one of hopelessness. Depressed people believe that their inadequacies and defects will prevent them from ever improving their situation.

Beck proposes that the depressed person's negative beliefs about self ("I am worthless," "I can't do anything right") are formed during childhood or adolescence through such experiences as loss of a parent, social rejection by peers, criticism by parents or teachers, or a series of tragedies. These negative beliefs are activated whenever a new situation resembles in some way—perhaps only remotely—the conditions in which the beliefs were learned, and depression may result. Moreover, according to Beck, depressed individuals make some systematic errors in thinking that lead them to misperceive reality in a way that contributes to their negative beliefs

about themselves. These cognitive distortions are listed in Table 15-4.

Another cognitive approach to depression, which focuses on the kinds of attributions, or causal explanations, that people make when bad things happen, was discussed in Chapter 14. This theory proposes that people who tend to attribute negative events to causes that are internal ("it's my fault"), are stable over time ("it's going to last forever"), and affect many areas of their lives are more prone to depression than individuals who have a less pessimistic attributional style (Abramson, Metalsky, & Alloy, 1989; Peterson & Seligman, 1984).

Critics of cognitive theories of depression have argued that these negative cognitions are symptoms or consequences of depression rather than causes. Although it is clear that depressed people have negative cognitions, there is less evidence that negative cognitive styles pre-

rates, with higher rates in Hungary, Germany, Austria, Denmark, and Japan and lower rates in Egypt, Mexico, Greece, and Spain (WHO, 1992). The United States, Canada, and England have suicide rates that fall between these two extremes.

Among the reasons most frequently cited by those who have attempted suicide are depression, loneliness, ill health, marital problems, and financial or job difficulties (Jamison, 1999; NIMH, 1999).

Another psychological problem contributing to suicide, in addition to depression, is drug abuse. For example, a prospective study of suicide attempts found that 33% of attempters were identified as heavy drinkers, compared to less than 3% of nonattempters. When alcoholism co-occurs with depression, the risk of suicide is especially high (Waller, Lyons, & Constantini-Ferrando, 1999). Alcohol lowers people's inhibitions to engage in impulsive acts, even self-destructive acts like suicide attempts.

There have been many theories of suicide risk. Much of the most recent research focuses on biological causes. There is some evidence that suicide runs in families (Tsuang, 1983), although this may not represent a specific genetic risk for suicide but rather a genetic risk for depression and other psychological problems. One twin study found a concordance rate for serious suicide attempts of 23% among identical twins and 0% among nonidentical twins (Statham et al., 1998), providing stronger evidence of a genetic risk.

Several studies have linked suicide to low serotonin levels (Mann, Brent & Arango, 2001). For example, postmortem studies of the brains of people who committed suicide find low levels of serotonin (Gross-Isseroff, Biegon, Voet, & Weizman, 1998). Suicide attempters with low serotonin levels are 10 times more likely to make another suicide attempt than those with higher serotonin levels (Roy, 1992). Low serotonin levels are linked with suicide even among people who are not depressed, suggesting that the connection between serotonin and suicidality is not due entirely to a common connection to depression. Serotonin may generally be linked to impulsive and aggressive behavior (Linnoila & Virkkunen, 1992). Low serotonin levels are most strongly associated with impulsive and violent suicides.

Controversial research suggests that there might be a link between low cholesterol levels and suicide (Brunner, Parhofer, Schwandt, & Bronisch, 2002). Studies of medical and death statistics show that people with low cholesterol levels, because they were on low-cholesterol diets, taking cholesterol-lowering medications, exercising more, or just naturally had low levels, have higher rates of suicide than people with higher cholesterol levels (Ellison & Morrison, 2001; Jamison, 1999; Kaplan & Kaufmann, 1993). Initially, researchers thought the link between low cholesterol and suicide might be false and due to both factors being tied to depression. Depressed people eat less and thus may have lower cholesterol levels, and they are more likely to commit suicide. When studies controlled for the link between depression and suicide, however, the link between low cholesterol and suicide remained (Fawcett, Busch, Jacobs, Kravitz, & Fogg, 1997).

How could low cholesterol contribute to suicidality? Speculations focus on a possible link between cholesterol and serotonin. Studies of monkeys show that feeding them a low-fat diet leads to increases in physical violence (Kaplan, Muldoon, Manuck, & Mann, 1997). Researchers speculate that lowering cholesterol lowers serotonin, which in turn increases impulsive, violent behavior, perhaps including suicide. Although there is a great deal more research to be done on this and other theories of suicidality, understanding the sources of self-destructive behavior is clearly an important goal for the future.

 For more information, go online with InfoTrac College Edition. Use your own term or search:

- Psychology and suicide
- Diet and suicide

● **Table 15-4**
Cognitive Distortions in Depression

According to Beck's theory, these are the principal errors in thinking that characterize depressed individuals.

Overgeneralization	Drawing a sweeping conclusion on the basis of a single event. For example, a student concludes from his poor performance in one class on a particular day that he is inept and stupid.
Selective Abstraction	Focusing on an insignificant detail while ignoring the more important features of a situation. For example, from a conversation in which her boss praises her overall job performance, a secretary remembers the only comment that could be construed as mildly critical.
Magnification and Minimization	Magnifying small bad events and minimizing major good events in evaluating performance. For example, a woman gets a small dent in her car fender and views it as a catastrophe (magnification), while the fact that she gave an excellent presentation in class does nothing to raise her self-esteem (minimization).
Personalization	Incorrectly assuming responsibility for bad events in the world. For example, when rain dampens spirits at an outdoor buffet, the host blames himself rather than the weather.
Arbitrary Inference	Drawing a conclusion when there is little evidence to support it. For example, a man concludes from his wife's sad expression that she is disappointed in him; if he had checked out the situation, he would have discovered that she was distressed by a friend's illness.

cede and cause depressive episodes (Haaga, Dyck, & Ernst, 1991). Also, there is some evidence that depressed people may actually perceive reality more accurately than normal people: When asked to make judgments about how much control they have over situations that are actually uncontrollable, depressed people are quite accurate. In contrast, nondepressed people greatly overestimate the amount of control they have, especially over positive events (Alloy & Abramson, 1979).

A recent study that followed students through their college careers provides strong evidence that negative cognitive styles do precede and predict depression. Researchers measured the students' tendencies toward negative thinking patterns early in their first year of college and followed them for the next few years. Students who evidenced a negative cognitive triad or a pessimistic attributional style were much more likely to experience episodes of depression during their college years than those who did not, even if they had never been depressed before going to college (Abramson et al., 1999; Alloy, Abramson, Safford, & Gibb (in press); Alloy et al., 1999).

THE PSYCHOANALYTIC PERSPECTIVE Psychoanalytic theories interpret depression as a reaction to loss (Figure 15-11). Whatever the nature of the loss (rejection by a loved one, being fired from a job), the depressed person reacts to it intensely because the current situation brings back all the fears of an earlier loss that occurred in childhood—the loss of parental affection. The indi-

vidual's needs for affection and care were not satisfied in childhood. A loss in later life causes him or her to regress to the helpless, dependent state of childhood, when the original loss occurred. Part of the depressed person's behavior, therefore, represents a cry for love—a display of helplessness and an appeal for affection and security (Bibring, 1953; Blatt, 1974).

Reaction to loss is complicated by angry feelings toward the deserting person. An underlying assumption of psychoanalytic theories is that people who are prone to depression have learned to repress their hostile feelings because they are afraid of alienating those on whom they depend for support. When things go wrong, they turn their anger inward and blame themselves. For example, a woman may feel extremely hostile toward an employer who fired her, but because her anger arouses anxiety, she internalizes her feelings: She is not angry; rather, others are angry at her. She assumes that the employer had a reason for rejecting her: She is incompetent and worthless.

Psychoanalytic theories suggest that the depressed person's low self-esteem and feelings of worthlessness stem from a childlike need for parental approval. A small child's self-esteem depends on the approval and affection of the parents. But as a person matures, feelings of worth should also be derived from the individual's sense of his or her own accomplishments and effectiveness. The self-esteem of a person prone to depression depends primarily on external sources: the approval and support of others. When these supports fail, the individual may be thrown into a state of depression.

Psychoanalytic theories of depression thus focus on loss, overdependence on external approval, and internalization of anger. They seem to provide a reasonable explanation for some of the behaviors exhibited by depressed individuals, but they are difficult to prove or to refute.

◆ Interim Summary

- The mood disorders are divided into depressive disorders, in which individuals experience only depressed mood, and bipolar disorder (or manic-depression), in which individuals experience both depression and mania.

- Biological theories attribute mood disorders to genetic factors and to problems in regulation of the neurotransmitters serotonin and norepinephrine.

- Cognitive theories attribute depression to pessimistic views of the self, the world, and the future and to maladaptive attributional styles.

- Psychodynamic theories view depression as a reactivation of loss of parental affection in a person who is dependent on external approval and tends to turn anger inward.

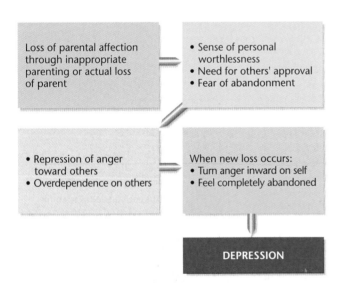

❙ Figure 15-11
Psychodynamic Theories of Depression
Psychodynamic theories suggest that depressed people did not receive enough parental affection in childhood and that subsequent losses in adulthood trigger feelings of dejection and worthlessness.

1. There is evidence that depression is much more common among people born in recent generations (since the 1950s) than in people born in earlier generations (around the turn of the 20th century). Can you generate some hypotheses for this historical trend?

2. Many famous artists and writers have suffered from depression or bipolar disorder, including composer Robert Schumann, writers Sylvia Plath and William Styron, and comedian Drew Carey. Could there be a link between mood disorders and creativity, and if so, what might be the nature of that link?

SCHIZOPHRENIA

What then does schizophrenia mean to me? It means fatigue and confusion, it means trying to separate every experience into the real and the unreal and not sometimes being aware of where the edges overlap. It means trying to think straight when there is a maze of experiences getting in the way, and when the thoughts are continually being sucked out of your head so that you become embarrassed to speak at meetings. It means feeling sometimes that you are inside your head and visualizing yourself walking over your brain, or watching another girl wearing your clothes and carrying out actions as you think them. It means knowing that you are continually "watched," that you can never succeed in life because the laws are all against you and knowing that your ultimate destruction is never far away. (quoted in Rollin, 1980, p. 162)

Some of the feelings and experiences this woman is describing may sound familiar—difficulty in thinking straight, feeling as though you are watching yourself act, not being sure how to interpret events that happen. People with **schizophrenia**, however, have such difficulty in sorting out the real from the unreal, in keeping track of their thoughts, in responding to the everyday events of life, that they often become immobilized. Schizophrenia occurs in all cultures, even those that are remote from the stresses of industrialized civilization, and appears to have plagued humanity for at least 200 years. The disorder affects about 1% of the population and occurs equally in men and women. Schizophrenia exacts heavy costs both on the individual and on his or her family and community. People with schizophrenia must seek psychiatric and medical help frequently, and the direct medical costs amount to more than $20 billion per year in the United States alone (Torrey, 1995). The disorder usually begins in late adolescence or early adulthood, just when an individual is beginning a career and starting a family.

Unfortunately, schizophrenia is one of the most stigmatized disorders, so individuals with this disorder and their families often carry tremendous shame.

CHARACTERISTICS OF SCHIZOPHRENIA

Sometimes schizophrenia develops slowly as a gradual process of increasing seclusiveness and inappropriate behavior. Sometimes the onset is sudden, marked by intense confusion and emotional turmoil. Such acute cases are usually precipitated by a period of stress in individuals whose lives have tended toward isolation, preoccupation with self, and feelings of insecurity. Whether schizophrenia develops slowly or suddenly, the symptoms are many and varied. The primary characteristics of schizophrenia can be summarized under the following headings, although not every person diagnosed as having the disorder will exhibit all of these symptoms.

DISTURBANCES OF THOUGHT AND ATTENTION In schizophrenia, both the process of thinking and the content of thought may be disordered. The following excerpt from the writings of a person with schizophrenia illustrates how difficult it is to understand schizophrenic thinking.

> If things turn by rotation of agriculture or levels in regards and timed to everything; I am referring to a previous document when I made some remarks that were facts also tested and there is another that concerns my daughter she has a lobed bottom right ear, her name being Mary Lou. Much of abstraction has been left unsaid and undone in these products milk syrup, and others, due to economics, differentials, subsidies, bankruptcy, tools, buildings, bonds, national stocks, foundation craps, weather, trades, government in levels of breakages and fuses in electronics too all formerly states not necessarily factuated. (Maher, 1966, p. 395)

By themselves, the words and phrases make sense, but they are meaningless in relation to each other. The juxtaposition of unrelated words and phrases and the idiosyncratic word associations (sometimes called **word salad**) are characteristic of schizophrenic writing and speech. They reflect a **loosening of associations** in which the individual's ideas shift from one topic to another in ways that appear unrelated. Moreover, the train of thought often seems to be influenced by the sound of words rather than by their meaning. The following account by a woman with schizophrenia of her thoughts in response to her doctor's questions illustrates this tendency to form associations by rhyming words, referred to as clang associations:

> Doctor: How about the medication? Are you still taking the Haldol? [an antipsychotic drug]
>
> Patient Thinks: Foul Wall. (She nods but does not reply.)

Doctor: What about the vitamins?

Patient Thinks: Seven sins. Has-beens. (She nods.)

Doctor: I don't think you're taking all your meds.

Patient Thinks: Pencil leads. (North, 1987, p. 261)

The confused thought processes that are the hallmark of schizophrenia seem to stem from a general difficulty in focusing attention and filtering out irrelevant stimuli. Most of us are able to focus our attention selectively. From a mass of incoming sensory information, we are able to select the stimuli that are relevant to the task at hand and ignore the rest. A person who suffers from schizophrenia is receptive to many stimuli at the same time and has trouble making sense of the profusion of inputs, as the following statement by a schizophrenic patient illustrates:

> I can't concentrate. It's diversions of attention that trouble me. I am picking up different conversations. It's like being a transmitter. The sounds are coming through to me, but I feel my mind cannot cope with everything. It's difficult to concentrate on any one sound. (McGhie & Chapman, 1961, p. 104)

A sense of being unable to control one's attention and focus one's thoughts is central to the experience of schizophrenia.

In addition to disorganized thought processes, people with schizophrenia experience disturbances in the content of thought. Most individuals suffering from schizophrenia show a lack of insight. When asked what is wrong or why they are hospitalized, they seem to have no appreciation of their condition and little realization that their behavior is unusual. They are also subject to **delusions,** beliefs that most people would view as misinterpretations of reality. The most common delusions are beliefs that external forces are trying to control one's thoughts and actions. These delusions of influence include the belief that one's thoughts are being broadcast to the world so that others can hear them, that strange thoughts (not one's own) are being inserted into one's mind, or that feelings and actions are being imposed on one by some external force. Also frequent are beliefs that certain people or certain groups are threatening or plotting against one (delusions of persecution). Less common are beliefs that one is powerful and important (delusions of grandeur).

The term **paranoid** is used to refer to an individual who has delusions of persecution. Such a person may become suspicious of friends and relatives, fear being poisoned, or complain of being watched, followed, and talked about. So-called motiveless crimes, in which an

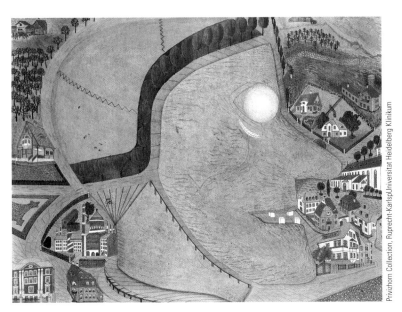

The German psychiatrist Hans Privizhorn has assembled an extensive collection of artwork by mental patients. This painting, by August Neter, illustrates the hallucinations and paranoid fantasies experienced by many schizophrenic patients.

Privizhorn Collection, Ruprecht-KarlspUniversitat Heidelberg Klinikum

individual attacks or kills someone for no apparent cause, are sometimes committed by people who are later diagnosed as having paranoid schizophrenia. These incidents are quite rare, however. Most people with schizophrenia are not a danger to others, although their confusion may make them a danger to themselves.

The specific content of delusions in schizophrenia may vary across cultures (Tateyama, Asai, Hashimoto, Bartels, & Kasper, 1998). For example, delusions of persecution often focus on persons of authority in the culture. Thus, Americans with persecutory delusions may fear that the Central Intelligence Agency is out to get them, whereas Afro Caribbeans may believe that people are trying to kill them with curses (Westermeyer, 1993). Among the Japanese, people with schizophrenia might have delusions of being slandered, whereas Western Europeans with schizophrenia are more likely to have religious delusions of having committed a sin. These differences in the content of delusions probably reflect differences in a culture's belief systems as well as structures of authority.

DISTURBANCES OF PERCEPTION People experiencing acute schizophrenic episodes often report that the world appears different (noises seem louder, colors more intense). Their own bodies may no longer appear the same (their hands may seem too large or too small, their legs overly extended, their eyes dislocated in the face). Some people fail to recognize themselves in a mirror, or see their reflection as a triple image. The most dramatic disturbances of perception are **hallucinations,** sensory experiences in the absence of relevant or adequate external stimulation. Auditory hallucinations (usually voices telling one what to do or commenting on one's actions) are the most common. Visual hallucinations (such as seeing strange creatures or heavenly beings) are somewhat less frequent. Other sensory hallucinations (a bad odor emanating from one's body, the taste of poison in food, the feeling of being pricked by needles) occur infrequently.

Hallucinations are often frightening, even terrifying, as the following example illustrates:

> At one point, I would look at my co-workers and their faces would become distorted. Their teeth looked like fangs ready to devour me. Most of the time I couldn't trust myself to look at anyone for fear of being swallowed. I had no respite from the illness. Even when I tried to sleep, the demons would keep me awake, and at times I would roam the house searching for them. I was being consumed on all sides whether I was awake or asleep. I felt I was being consumed by demons. (Long, 1996)

In one sense, hallucinations are not far removed from ordinary experiences. We all know what visual hallucinations are like because we have them in dreams. But for most people dreams occur only during sleep. It is possible that some sort of neurotransmitter-mediated process inhibits dreams during the waking state and that this process has failed in schizophrenics who hallucinate (Assad & Shapiro, 1986).

Auditory hallucinations may have their origin in ordinary thought. We often carry on internal dialogues—for example, commenting on our actions or having an imaginary conversation with another person. We may even occasionally talk to ourselves aloud. The voices that people with schizophrenia hear, calling them names or telling them what to do, are similar to internal dialogues. But a person experiencing an auditory hallucination does not believe that the voices originate within the self or that they can be controlled. The inability to distinguish between external and internal, real and imagined, is central to the schizophrenic experience.

DISTURBANCES OF EMOTIONAL EXPRESSION People suffering from schizophrenia usually fail to exhibit normal emotional responses. They often are withdrawn and unresponsive in situations that should make them sad or happy. For example, a man may show no emotional response when informed that his daughter has cancer. However, this blunting of emotional expression can conceal inner turmoil, and the person may erupt with angry outbursts.

Sometimes individuals with schizophrenia express emotions that are inappropriately linked to the situation or to the thought being expressed, such as smiling while speaking of tragic events. Because our emotions are influenced by cognitive processes, it is not surprising that disorganized thoughts and perceptions are accompanied by changes in emotional responses. This point is illustrated in the following comments:

> Hall the time I am talking about one thing and thinking about half a dozen other things at the same time. It must look queer to people when I laugh about something that has got nothing to do with what I am talking about, but they don't know what's going on inside and how much of it is running around in my head. You see I might be talking about something quite serious to you and other things come into my head at the same time that are funny and this makes me laugh. If I could only concentrate on one thing at the one time I wouldn't look half so silly. (McGhie & Chapman, 1961, p. 104)

MOTOR SYMPTOMS AND WITHDRAWAL FROM REALITY

People with schizophrenia often exhibit bizarre motor activity. They may grimace, adopt strange facial expressions, or gesture repeatedly using peculiar sequences of finger, hand, and arm movements. Some may become very agitated and move about in continual activity, as in a manic state. Some, at the other extreme, may become totally unresponsive and immobile, adopting an unusual posture and maintaining it for long periods of time. For example, a person may stand like a statue with one foot extended and one arm raised toward the ceiling, maintaining this state of catatonic immobility for hours. Such an individual, who appears to have completely withdrawn from reality, may be responding to inner thoughts and fantasies.

DECREASED ABILITY TO FUNCTION Besides the specific symptoms we have described, people with schizophrenia are impaired in their ability to carry out the daily routines of living. If the disorder occurs in adolescence, the individual shows a decreasing ability to cope with school and has limited social skills and few friends. Adults suffering from schizophrenia are often unsuccessful in obtaining or holding a job. Personal hygiene and grooming deteriorate, and the individual avoids the company of other people. The signs of schizophrenia are many and varied. Trying to make sense of the variety of symptoms is complicated by the fact that some may result directly from the disorder, whereas others may be a reaction to life in a mental hospital or to the effects of medication.

CULTURE AND THE PROGRESSION OF SCHIZOPHRENIA

Generally, schizophrenia is more chronic and debilitating than other psychological disorders. Between 50% and 80% of people who are hospitalized with one episode of schizophrenia are eventually rehospitalized for another episode at some time in their lives (Eaton et al., 1992). Not everyone with schizophrenia shows progressive deterioration in functioning, however. Between 20% and 30% of people treated for schizophrenia recover substantially from the illness within 10 to 20 years of its onset (Eaton et al., 1998; Jablensky, 2000).

Culture seems to play a strong role in the course of schizophrenia. People who have schizophrenia in developing countries, such as India, Nigeria, and Colombia, are less likely to remain incapacitated by the disorder for the long term than people who have schizophrenia in developed countries such as the United States, Great Britain, or Denmark (see Figure 15-12; Jablensky, 1989). Why might this be? It may be due partially to variations in the genes for schizophrenia across cultural groups (Jablensky, 2000). Differences in how cultures treat their schizophrenic members probably play a strong role also. In developing countries, people with schizophrenia are more likely cared for at home by a broad network of family members who share responsibility for the individual (Karno & Jenkins, 1993). In contrast, in developed countries, it is less likely that the person with schizophrenia lives with family or that his or her immediate family has other family members nearby who share in the care. Caring for a family member with schizophrenia can be a huge burden. When this burden is shouldered by only a few people, there can be tremendous conflict in the family, which may exacerbate the symptoms of the person with schizophrenia.

The odds of all four of a set of identical quadruplets being diagnosed as schizophrenic are 1 in 2 billion—yet these quadruplets, the Genain sisters, all suffer from schizophrenia and have been hospitalized at various times since high school.

UNDERSTANDING SCHIZOPHRENIA

Schizophrenia probably has strong biological roots, but environmental stress may push people who are vulnerable to schizophrenia into more severe forms of the disorder or new episodes of psychosis.

The Neural Basis of Behavior

THE BIOLOGICAL PERSPECTIVE

Family studies show that there is a hereditary predisposition for schizophrenia. Relatives of people with schizophrenia are more likely to develop the disorder than people from families that are free of schizophrenia (Cardno, O'Donovan, & Owen, 2000; Lichtermann, Karbe, & Maier, 2000). Figure 15-13 shows the lifetime risk of developing schizophrenia as a function of how closely an individual is genetically related to a person diagnosed as schizophrenic. Note that an identical twin of a schizophrenic is 3 times more likely than a fraternal twin to develop schizophrenia and 46 times more likely than an unrelated person to develop the disorder. However, fewer than half of identical twins of people with schizophrenia develop schizophrenia themselves, even though they share the same genes. This fact demonstrates the importance of nongenetic variables.

How do the genetic abnormalities that predispose an individual to schizophrenia affect the brain? Current research focuses on two areas: brain structure and biochemistry. Two types of structural deficits have been found in the brains of people with schizophrenia. First, the prefrontal cortex is smaller and shows less activity

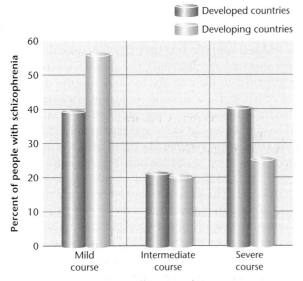

▌ Figure 15-12
Cultural Differences in the Course of Schizophrenia
People with schizophrenia in developing countries are more likely to have a mild course of the disorder than are people in developed countries, whereas people in developed countries are more likely to have a severe course of the disorder than are people in developing countries. (A. Jablensky (1989). "Epidemiology and cross-cultural aspects of schizophrenia," in *Psychiatric Annals*, 19, 516–524. Reprinted by permission of SLACK, Inc.)

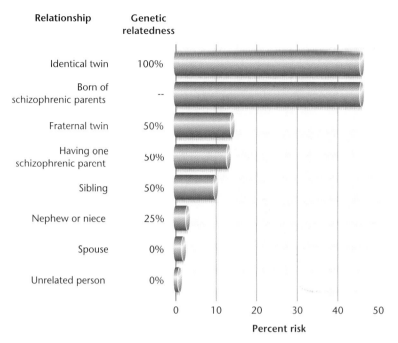

Relationship	Genetic relatedness	
Identical twin	100%	
Born of schizophrenic parents	--	
Fraternal twin	50%	
Having one schizophrenic parent	50%	
Sibling	50%	
Nephew or niece	25%	
Spouse	0%	
Unrelated person	0%	

Percent risk

▌ Figure 15-13
Genetic Relationships and Schizophrenia
The lifetime risk of developing schizophrenia is largely a function of how closely an individual is genetically related to a schizophrenic person and not a function of how much their environment is shared. In the case of an individual with two schizophrenic parents, genetic relatedness cannot be expressed in terms of percentages, but the regression of the individual's "genetic value" on that of the parents is 100%, the same as it is for identical twins.

(*Schizophrenia: The Epigenetic Puzzle,* by I. I. Gottesman & J. Shields. Copyright © 1992 Cambridge University Press. Reprinted by permission of the publisher.)

in some people with schizophrenia than in people without the disorder (Andreasen, 2001; Buchsbaum, Haier, Potkin, & Nuechterlein, 1992; Vance et al., 2000; see Figure 15-14). The prefrontal cortex is the largest re-

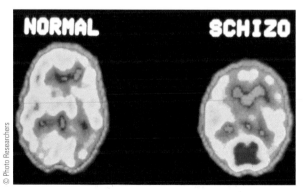

▌ Figure 15-14
A Normal Brain Versus a Schizophrenic Brain
This PET scan shows the metabolic differences between the prefrontal cortex of a schizophrenic individual and the same areas in the brain of a normal individual.

gion of the brain in human beings, nearly 30% of the total cortex, and it has connections to all the other cortical regions, as well as to the limbic system, which is involved in emotion and cognition, and the basal ganglia, which is involved in motor movement. The prefrontal cortex plays important roles in language, emotional expression, planning and producing new ideas, and mediating social interactions. Thus, it seems logical that people whose prefrontal cortex is unusually small or inactive would show a wide range of deficits in cognition, emotion, and social interaction, as people with schizophrenia do.

Second, people with schizophrenia have enlarged ventricles and fluid-filled spaces in the brain (see Figure 15-15; Eyler Zorrilla et al., 1997; Galderisi et al., 2000). The presence of enlarged ventricles suggests atrophy or deterioration in other brain tissue. The specific areas of the brain that have deteriorated, resulting in ventricular enlargement, could lead to different manifestations of schizophrenia (Breier, Schreiber, Dyer, & Pickar, 1992).

Although neurochemical theories of mood disorders center on norepinephrine and serotonin, the culprit in schizophrenia is believed to be dopamine. Early dopamine theories of schizophrenia held that the disorder was the result of the presence of too much dopamine in key areas of the brain. This view is now considered too simple. The most recent theories suggest that there is a complicated imbalance in levels of dopamine in different areas of the brain (Conklin & Iacono, 2002). First, there may be excess dopamine activity in the mesolimbic system, a subcortical part of the brain involved in cognition and emotion, which leads to the "positive" symptoms of schizophrenia—hallucinations, delusions, disordered thought. On the other hand, there may be unusually low dopamine activity in the prefrontal area of the brain, which is involved in attention, motivation, and organization of behavior (see Figure 15-16; Taber, Lewis, & Hurley, 2001). Low dopamine activity in the prefrontal area may lead to the "negative" symptoms of schizophrenia—lack of motivation, inability to care for oneself, inappropriate emotional expression.

As we mentioned, these abnormalities in brain structure and neurochemical functioning could be due to genetics, but they also could be the result of insults to the brain of a fetus or young child. Studies have found that people who have schizophrenia are more likely to have a history of birth complications, perinatal brain damage, infections in the central nervous system (such as meningitis) in infancy, and maternal pregnancy complications or influenza in pregnancy (Jablensky,

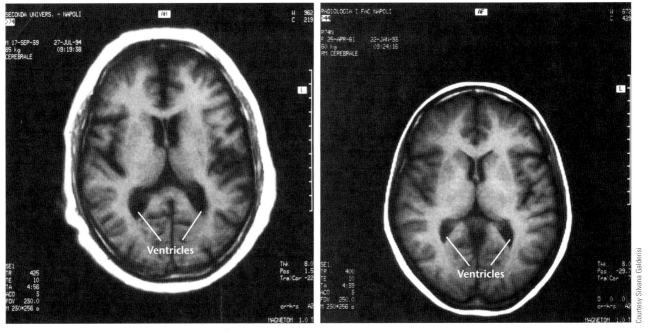

▌ Figure 15-15
Brain Functioning in Schizophrenia
The MRI on the left shows evidence of ventricular enlargement in the brain of a schizophrenic person compared with that of a nonschizophrenic person in the image on the
right. (Courtesy of Silvana Galderisi, from Galderisi, Vita, Rossi, Stratta, Leonardi and Invernizzi, (2000) "Qualitative MRI findings in patients with schizophrenia," *Psychiatry Research: Neuroimaging Section* 98:117–126,
reprinted by permission.)

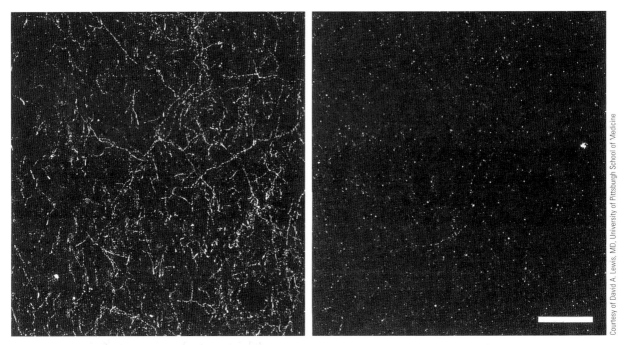

▌ Figure 15-16
Dopamine Axons in Prefrontal Cortex and Schizophrenia
The photomicrograph on the left is from a nonschizophrenic person and shows a much
denser network of dopamine axons in the prefrontal cortex than the photomicrograph on
the right, which is from a person with schizophrenia (bar = 200 microns).

2000). Each of these might cause permanent damage to the central nervous system of the fetus or young child, perhaps contributing to risk for schizophrenia.

THE SOCIAL AND PSYCHOLOGICAL PERSPECTIVE

Although it is clear that stressful events cannot cause a person to develop the full syndrome of schizophrenia, psychosocial factors may play an important role in determining the eventual severity of the disorder in people with a biological predisposition, as well as in triggering new episodes of psychosis. The type of stress that has received the most attention in recent studies is family-related stress. Members of families that are high in expressed emotion are overinvolved with one another, overprotective of the disturbed family member, and, at the same time, critical, hostile, and resentful toward the disturbed member (Brown, Birley, & Wing, 1972; Vaughn & Leff, 1976). People with schizophrenia whose families are high in expressed emotion are three to four times more likely to suffer a new psychotic episode than those whose families are low in expressed emotion (Brown, Birley, & Wing, 1972; Leff & Vaughn, 1981; Mintz, Lieberman, Miklowitz, & Mintz, 1987). Being in a family with high levels of expressed emotion may create stresses that trigger new episodes of psychosis by overwhelming the schizophrenic person's ability to cope.

The link between expressed emotion and relapse in schizophrenia may help to explain the cross-cultural differences in the prognosis of this disorder. One study found that families of people with schizophrenia in Mexico and India scored lower on measures of expressed emotions than did families of people with schizophrenia in Europe and the United States (see Figure 15-17; Karno et al., 1987; Karno & Jenkins, 1993).

Critics of the research on expressed emotion argue that the hostility and intrusiveness observed in some families of people with schizophrenia might be the result of the symptoms exhibited by the disturbed member, rather than a factor contributing to the disorder (Parker, Johnston, & Hayward, 1988). Although families are often forgiving of positive symptoms like hallucinations, viewing them as uncontrollable, they can be unforgiving of the negative symptoms like lack of motivation (Brewin, MacCarthy, Duda, & Vaughn, 1991; Hooley, Richters, Weintraub, & Neale, 1987; Lopez & Guarnaccia, 2000). People with these symptoms may elicit more negative expressed emotion and may be especially prone to relapse.

Another alternative explanation for the link between expressed emotion and relapse comes from evidence that family members who are especially high in expressed emotion are themselves more likely to exhibit some form of psychopathology (Goldstein, Talovic, Nuechterlein, & Fogelson, 1992). In such families, people with schizophrenia may have high rates of relapse

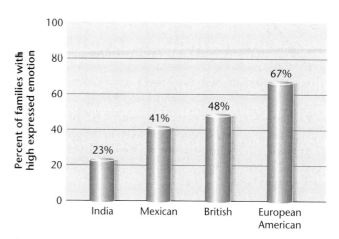

Figure 15-17
Cultural Differences in the Prevalence of Expressed Emotion in Families of Schizophrenics
Families of schizophrenics from developing countries tend to show lower levels of expressed emotion than do families of schizophrenics from developed countries. This may be one reason that schizophrenics from developing countries have fewer relapses than do schizophrenics from developed countries. (M. Karno & J. H. Jenkins (1993). "Cross-Cultural Issues in the Course and Treatment of Schizophrenia." *Psychiatric Clinics of North America, 16*, 339–350. Reprinted by permission of W. B. Saunders Co.)

because they have a greater genetic predisposition toward psychopathology, as evidenced by the presence of psychopathology in their families, rather than because their families are high in expressed emotion. Perhaps the best evidence that expressed emotion actually influences relapse is that treatments that reduce expressed emotion tend to reduce the relapse rate in schizophrenic family members.

◆ Interim Summary

- Schizophrenia is characterized by disturbances in thought, including disorganized thought processes, delusions, and lack of insight.

- Other symptoms include perceptual disturbances (such as hallucinations), inappropriate emotional expression, bizarre motor activity, withdrawal, and impaired functioning.

- Schizophrenia clearly is transmitted genetically.

- People with schizophrenia also have problems in dopamine regulation.

- Two types of brain abnormalities are consistently seen in schizophrenia: The prefrontal cortex is smaller and less active, and the ventricles are enlarged.

- Difficult environments probably cannot cause schizophrenia, but they may worsen the disorder and contribute to relapses.

1. What might be the mechanisms by which living in a family with high expressed emotion contributes to relapse in people with schizophrenia?

2. There is evidence that people with schizophrenia are more likely to have been born in the winter or spring of the year than in the summer or fall. Can you generate some hypotheses about why this might be so?

PERSONALITY DISORDERS

Personality disorders are long-standing patterns of maladaptive behavior. In Chapter 13, we described personality traits as enduring ways of perceiving or relating to the environment and thinking about oneself. When personality traits become so inflexible and maladaptive that they significantly impair the individual's ability to function, they are referred to as personality disorders. People with personality disorders experience themselves and the world in ways that are highly distressing to them and/or impair their ability to function in daily life. These experiences begin in childhood or adolescence and persist over time and across situations, affecting most areas of the person's life. The particular emotions, thoughts, and behaviors that an individual experiences vary according to the specific disorder.

Personality disorders are immature and inappropriate ways of coping with stress or solving problems. They are usually evident by early adolescence and may continue throughout the life span. Unlike people with mood or anxiety disorders, which also involve maladaptive behavior, people who have personality disorders often do not feel upset or anxious and may not be motivated to change their behavior. They do not lose contact with reality or display marked disorganization of behavior.

DSM-IV lists several personality disorders (see the Concept Review Table). The characteristics of these disorders tend to overlap, making it difficult to agree on how to classify some individuals. Moreover, it is difficult to say when a person's behavior is simply different from other people's behaviors and when the behavior is so severe that it warrants a diagnosis. The personality disorder that has been studied the most and is the most reliably diagnosed is the antisocial personality (formerly termed psychopathic personality and sometimes referred to as sociopathy). We discuss it in this section, along with borderline personality disorder, a controversial personality disorder that has received much attention in recent years.

CONCEPT REVIEW TABLE
Types of Personality Disorders

The DSM-IV recognizes several different personality disorders.

Diagnosis	Description
Antisocial Personality Disorder	Impulsive, callous behavior based on disregard for others and lack of respect for social norms.
Borderline Personality Disorder	Chronic instability of mood, relationships, and self-concept; self-destructive impulsiveness.
Histrionic Personality Disorder	Chronic intense need for attention and approval sought by dramatic behavior, seductiveness, and dependence.
Narcissistic Personality Disorder	Frequent grandiosity and obliviousness to others' needs; exploitative behavior; arrogance.
Paranoid Personality Disorder	Chronic and pervasive mistrust of others that is unwarranted.
Schizoid Personality Disorder	Chronic lack of interest in interpersonal relationships; emotional coldness.
Schizotypal Personality Disorder	Chronically inhibited or inappropriate emotional and social behavior; aberrant cognitions; disorganized speech.
Avoidant Personality Disorder	Avoidance of social interactions and restrictiveness in interactions due to chronic worry over being criticized.
Dependent Personality Disorder	Pervasive selflessness, need to be cared for, and fear of rejection.
Obsessive-Compulsive Personality Disorder	Pervasive rigidity in activities and relationships; extreme perfectionism.

ANTISOCIAL PERSONALITY

People who have **antisocial personality disorder** have little sense of responsibility, morality, or concern for others. Their behavior is determined almost entirely by their own needs. In other words, they lack a conscience. Whereas the average person realizes at an early age that some restrictions are placed on behavior and that pleasures must sometimes be postponed in consideration of the needs of others, individuals who have antisocial personalities seldom consider any desires except their own. They behave impulsively, seek immediate gratification of their needs, and cannot tolerate frustration. Extreme versions of this disorder were depicted by Woody Harrelson in the movie *Natural Born Killers* and by Anthony Hopkins in *The Silence of the Lambs*.

Antisocial behavior results from a number of causes, including membership in a delinquent gang or a criminal subculture, the need for attention and status, loss of contact with reality, and inability to control impulses. However, most juvenile delinquents and adult criminals show some concern for others (for example, family or gang members) and adhere to some code of moral conduct (never betray a friend). In contrast, people with antisocial personalities have little feeling for anyone except themselves and seem to experience little guilt or remorse, regardless of how much suffering their behavior may cause. Other characteristics of the antisocial personality (or sociopath) include a great facility for lying, a need for thrills and excitement with little concern for possible injury, and inability to alter behavior as a consequence of punishment. Such individuals are often attractive, intelligent, charming people who are adept at manipulating others—in other words, good con artists. Their façade of competence and sincerity wins them promising jobs, but they have little staying power. Their restlessness and impulsiveness soon lead them into an escapade that reveals their true nature; they accumulate debts, desert their families, squander company money, or commit crimes. When they are caught, their declarations of repentance are so convincing that they often escape punishment and are given another chance. But antisocial personalities seldom live up to these declarations; what they say has little relation to what they feel or do. Deceitfulness is one of the defining characteristics of antisocial personality (Kraus & Reynolds, 2001).

Fortunately, the full syndrome of antisocial personality disorder is relatively rare. It is much more common in men than in women, with about 3% of men and 1% of women having this disorder at some time in their lives (Kraus & Reynolds, 2001).

UNDERSTANDING ANTISOCIAL PERSONALITY DISORDER

What factors contribute to the development of an antisocial personality? Current research focuses on biological determinants, the quality of the parent-child relationship, and ways of thinking that promote antisocial behaviors.

 The Neural Basis of Behavior

BIOLOGICAL FACTORS Genetic factors appear to play a role in the development of antisocial personality. Twin studies show that if one identical twin has antisocial personality characteristics, the other twin also has these characteristics about 50% of the time. In contrast, among fraternal twins the concordance rate for antisocial personality is only about 20% (Carey & Goldman, 1997; Rutter et al., 1990). Adoption studies find that the criminal records of adopted sons are more similar to the records of their biological fathers than to those of their adoptive fathers (Cloninger & Gottesman, 1987; Mednick, Reznick, Hocevar, & Baker, 1987).

One of the cardinal features of antisocial personality is impulsivity (Rutter, 1997). Many animal studies and some human studies suggest that impulsive and aggressive behaviors are linked to low levels of the neurotransmitter serotonin (Berman, Kavoussi, & Coccaro, 1997; Ferris & de Vries, 1997; Moffitt et al., 1998). Could low serotonin levels be a cause of antisocial personality? We do not yet know.

People with antisocial personalities also show deficits in the ability to sustain concentration, in abstract reasoning and concept formation, in formulating and implementing goals, in self-monitoring and self-awareness, and in shifting from maladaptive patterns of behavior to more adaptive ones (Henry & Moffitt, 1997). Collectively, these are known as executive functions, and their control resides largely in the temporal and frontal lobes of the brain. In turn, some studies have found differences between antisocial adults (usually prison inmates) and the general population in the structure or functioning of these areas of the brain (Blake, Pincus & Buckner, 1995). These brain anomalies could be the result of medical illnesses and exposure to toxins during infancy and childhood, which are both more common in antisocial people than in controls, or to genetic abnormalities. Whatever their causes, deficits in executive functions could contribute to poor impulse control and difficulty in anticipating the consequences of one's actions.

Many studies have argued that people with antisocial personality disorder have low levels of arousability, which may lead them to seek stimulation and sensation through impulsive and dangerous acts (Raine, 1997). For example, one study compared two groups of adolescent male delinquents selected from the detention unit of a juvenile court. One group had been diagnosed as having antisocial personality disorder; the other group was diagnosed as exhibiting adjustment reactions to negative life events. The experimenters measured galvanic skin response (GSR) under stress (see Chapter 11). Dummy electrodes were attached to each participant's leg, and he was told that in 10 minutes he would be given a very strong but not harmful shock. A large clock was visible so that the participant knew precisely when the shock was supposed to occur. No shock was actually administered. The two groups showed no difference in GSR measures during periods of rest or in response to auditory or visual stimulation. However, during the 10 minutes of shock anticipation, the group with adjustment reactions showed significantly more tension than the antisocial group. At the moment when the clock indicated the shock was due, most members of the group with adjustment reactions showed GSR responses indicating a sharp increase in anxiety. None of the antisocial participants showed this reaction (Lippert & Senter, 1966). Low arousability to anxiety-provoking stimuli may also make it more difficult for people with antisocial personality disorder to learn from punishment because punishment is less aversive for them than for most people, and they will not be anxious in anticipation of the punishment.

SOCIAL FACTORS Although children who develop antisocial personalities may have a biological predisposition for the disorder, studies suggest that they are unlikely to develop the disorder unless they are also exposed to environments that promote antisocial behavior (Dishion & Patterson, 1997; Kraus & Reynolds, 2001). The parents of children with antisocial personalities often appear to be simultaneously neglectful and hostile toward their children. The children are frequently unsupervised for long periods. The parents often are not involved in the children's everyday lives, not knowing where they are or who their friends are. But when these parents do interact with their children, the interactions are often characterized by hostility, physical violence, and ridicule (Patterson, DeBaryshe, & Ramsey, 1989). This description does not fit all parents of such children, but parental noninvolvement and hostility are good predictors of children's vulnerability to antisocial personality disorder.

The biological and family factors that contribute to antisocial personality often coincide. Children who behave in antisocial ways often suffer from neuropsychological problems that are the result of maternal drug use, poor prenatal nutrition, prenatal and postnatal exposure to toxic agents, child abuse, birth complications, and low birth weight (Moffitt, 1993). Children with these neuropsychological problems are more irritable, impulsive, awkward, overreactive, and inattentive, and they learn more slowly than their peers. This makes them difficult to care for, and they are therefore at increased risk for maltreatment and neglect. In turn, the parents of these children are more likely to be teenagers or to have psychological problems of their own that contribute to ineffective, harsh, or inconsistent parenting. Thus, for these children a biological predisposition to disruptive, antisocial behaviors may be combined with a style of parenting that contributes to these behaviors. In a study of 536 boys, Moffitt (1990) found that those who had both neuropsychological deficits and adverse home environments scored four times higher on an aggression scale than those with neither neuropsychological deficits nor adverse home environments.

PERSONALITY FACTORS Children with antisocial personalities tend to process information about social interactions in ways that promote aggressive reactions to these interactions (Crick & Dodge, 1994). They assume that other children will be aggressive toward them, and they interpret other children's actions in line with these assumptions rather than using cues from the specific situations they actually face. In addition, they tend to believe that any negative action by a peer—such as taking their favorite pencil—are intentional rather than accidental. When deciding what action to take in response to a perceived provocation by a peer, children with antisocial personalities tend to think of a narrow range of responses, usually including aggression. When pressed to consider responses other than aggression, they make ineffective or vague responses and often consider responses other than aggression to be useless or unattractive.

Children who think about their social interactions in this way are likely to engage in aggressive behaviors toward others and may therefore suffer retaliation. Other children will hit them, parents and teachers will punish them, and they will be perceived more negatively by others. These actions may feed their assumptions that the world is against them, causing them to misinterpret future actions by others. In this way, a cycle of interactions can be established that maintains and encourages aggressive, antisocial behaviors.

BORDERLINE PERSONALITY DISORDER

Borderline personality disorder is a lifelong disorder characterized by extreme variability in mood, relationships, and self-perceptions. It has been the focus of considerable attention in the popular press and in clinical and research writings in psychology in the last couple of decades. The diagnosis of borderline personality disorder was added to the DSM in 1980, but clinicians have long used the label "borderline" to refer to people who seem to teeter between severe neurotic traits (such as emotional instability) and bouts of psychosis (see Millon, 1981).

Instability is a key feature of borderline personality disorder. The mood of individuals with this disorder is unstable, with bouts of severe depression, anxiety, or anger seeming to arise frequently, often without good reason. The self-concept is unstable, with periods of extreme self-doubt and grandiose self-importance. Interpersonal relationships are extremely unstable, and the person can switch from idealizing other people to despising them without provocation. A classic movie depiction of borderline personality disorder was given by Glenn Close in *Fatal Attraction*. People with borderline personality disorder often feel desperately empty and will initially cling to a new acquaintance or therapist in the hope that he or she will fill the tremendous void they feel in themselves. At the same time, they may misinterpret other people's innocent actions as signs of abandonment or rejection. For example, if a therapist has to cancel an appointment because she is ill, a person with borderline personality disorder might interpret this as a rejection and become extremely depressed or angry. Along with instability of mood, self-concept, and interpersonal relationships comes a tendency toward impulsive self-damaging behaviors, including self-mutilation and suicidal behavior. Self-mutilation often takes the form of burning or cutting. Finally, people with borderline personality disorder are prone to transient episodes in which they feel unreal, lose track of time, and may even forget who they are. The following case describes a person with borderline personality disorder (McGlashan, 1983, pp. 87–88).

Ms. Q was a 28-year-old, white single woman when admitted voluntarily [to a psychiatric hospital]. . . . In late adolescence, Ms. Q became romantically and sexually involved with a young artist. When he informed her that she was "just another woman" in his life, she became morose and moody. She began hallucinating his face on movie screens and newspapers. Shortly after the accidental drowning of a young boy from her neighborhood, Ms. Q started feeling guilty for his death and feared imminent apprehension by the police. In an act later described as a "manipulative gesture," she took an overdose of sleeping medication and was hospitalized briefly.

Over the next five years, Ms. Q attended college sporadically. She moved often between a variety of living situations: alone in hotels or dormitories or with one or the other of her divorced parents. Changes of domicile were often precipitated by quarrels. Although seldom alone, she developed relatively superficial social relationships. The few women whom she befriended tended to be older. She would fre-

quently become attached to their parents and call them "mama and papa." Sexually she had three or four intense affairs, each lasting less than six months and each terminating painfully with one or the other partner refusing to marry. In all of her relationships, Ms. Q was described as manipulative, dependent, masochistic, hostile, and derogatory.

Mood swings between anger and despondency occurred weekly and sometimes daily. She frequently abused alcohol and barbiturates and made numerous manipulative suicidal threats. For the latter she was hospitalized briefly on two more occasions (one month or less in duration). . . .

In her mid-20s, Ms. Q joined the armed services. After an initial honeymoon period, she performed miserably. She cried "for hours over her typewriter and stayed in her room not eating." After ten months, she received a "neuropsychiatric" medical discharge. She began moving around again, trying various jobs, which she was unable to hold for more than a few days. She became more seclusive, even with fellow employees.

At age 26 Ms. Q began two years of intensive psychotherapy (up to four times per week). Her therapist recorded that Ms. Q tried "very hard to be sick" and was intent on causing "trouble with everyone she did not like" by "upsetting everyone during her bad spells."

Her hospitalization at [the psychiatric hospital] arose out of a visit home to her mother. She felt slighted in several ways. First, her mother's welcome was less than "gushing." Second, she felt insulted when her mother's boyfriend showed her a brochure describing a psychiatric residential treatment facility. Third, she discovered that a certain choice piece of family real estate was being willed to her least favorite sibling. Feeling rejected, she took an overdose of aspirin and was hospitalized at]the psychiatric hospital] shortly thereafter.

People with borderline personality disorder also tend to receive diagnoses of one of the acute disorders, including substance abuse, depression, generalized anxiety disorder, simple phobias, agoraphobia, post-traumatic stress disorder, and panic disorder (Kraus & Reynolds, 2001). Longitudinal studies of people with this disorder indicate that about 10% die by suicide, and perhaps 75% have attempted suicide (Kraus & Reynolds, 2001; Perry, 1993). The greatest risk of suicide appears to be in the first year or two after receiving a diagnosis of borderline personality disorder. This may be due to the fact that a person is often not diagnosed with this disorder until a crisis brings him or her into therapy.

The lifetime prevalence of borderline personality disorder is between 1% and 2% (Weissman, 1993). The disorder is diagnosed much more often in women than in men (Fabrega, Ulrich, Pilkonis, & Mezzich, 1991; Swartz, Blazer, George, & Winfield, 1990). People with this disorder tend to have stormy marital relationships, more job difficulties, and a higher rate of physical disability than average.

Understanding Borderline Personality Disorder

Psychoanalytic theorists have provided the most comprehensive explanation of borderline personality disorder. They suggest that individuals with borderline personalities retain a foothold in the real world but rely on primitive defenses such as denial rather than more advanced defenses against their conflicts (Kernberg, 1979). In addition, such individuals have very poorly developed views of self and others, stemming from poor early relationships with caregivers. The caregivers of people with borderline personality disorder are characterized as deriving much gratification from the child's dependence on them early in life. They do not encourage the child to develop a separate sense of self and may punish attempts at individuation and separation. As a result, people with borderline personality disorder never learn to fully differentiate between their views of self and others. This makes them extremely sensitive to others' opinions of them and to the possibility of being abandoned. When others are perceived as rejecting them, they reject themselves and may engage in self-punishment or self-mutilation.

Individuals with borderline personalities also have never been able to integrate the positive and negative qualities of either their self-concept or their concept of others, because their early caregivers were comforting and rewarding when they remained dependent and compliant toward them but hostile and rejecting when they tried to separate from them. People with borderline personalities therefore tend to see themselves and others as either "all good" or "all bad" and vacillate between these two views. This process is referred to as splitting. The changeability of borderline individuals' emotions and interpersonal relationships is caused by splitting—their emotions and their perspectives on their relationships reflect their vacillation between the "all good" and the "all bad" self or other.

Other research suggests that many people with borderline personality disorder have a history of physical and sexual abuse during childhood (Perry, 1993). This abuse could lead to the problems in self-concept that most theorists believe to be at the core of this disorder. In addition, a child whose parent alternates between being abusive and being loving could develop a fundamental mistrust of others and a tendency to see others as all good or all bad.

◆ Interim Summary

- Personality disorders are lifelong patterns of maladaptive behavior that constitute immature and inappropriate ways of coping with stress or solving problems.
- Individuals with antisocial personality disorder are impulsive, show little guilt, are concerned only with their own needs, and are frequently in trouble with the law.
- Antisocial personality disorder probably has genetic and biological roots, but neglectful and hostile parenting may also contribute to the disorder.
- People with borderline personality disorder show instability in mood, self-concept, and interpersonal relationships.
- Psychodynamic theories suggest that the caregivers of people with this disorder required their children to be highly dependent and alternated between extreme expressions of love and hostility.

◆ Critical Thinking Questions

1. Do personality disorders seem to be just the extremes of normal personality traits or distinct entities that are qualitatively different from normal personality traits?

2. What similarities do you see between antisocial personality disorder and borderline personality disorder?

DISSOCIATIVE IDENTITY DISORDER

Dissociative identity disorder, also called *multiple personality disorder,* is the existence in a single individual of two or more distinct identities or personalities that alternate in controlling behavior. Usually, each personality has its own name and age and a specific set of memories and characteristic behaviors. In most cases, there is a primary identity that carries the individual's given name and is passive, dependent, and depressed. The alternate identities typically have characteristics that contrast with the primary identity—for example, hostile, controlling, and self-destructive (American Psychiatric Association, 2000). In some cases the personalities may even differ in such characteristics as handwriting, artistic or athletic abilities, and knowledge of a foreign language. The primary identity often has no awareness of the experiences of the other identities. Periods of unexplained amnesia—loss of memory for hours or days each week—can be a clue to the presence of dissociative identity disorder.

We should make clear that dissociative identity disorder is not classified as a personality disorder, like antisocial personality disorder or borderline personality disorder. Instead, it is classified as a dissociative disorder, because at the core of this disorder is the chronic tendency to dissociate—to split off different facets of one's sense of self, memories, or consciousness.

One of the most famous cases of multiple personality is that of Chris Sizemore, whose alternative personalities—Eve White, Eve Black, and Jane—were portrayed in the movie *The Three Faces of Eve* (Thigpen & Cleckley, 1957) and later described extensively in her autobiography, *I'm Eve* (Sizemore & Pittillo, 1977). Another well-studied case is that of Jonah, a 17-year-old who was admitted to a hospital complaining of severe headaches that were often followed by memory loss. Hospital attendants noticed striking changes in his personality on different days, and the psychiatrist in charge detected three distinct secondary identities. The relatively stable personality structures that emerged are diagrammed in Figure 15-18 and can be characterized as follows:

Jonah. The primary personality. Shy, retiring, polite, and highly conventional, he is designated "the square." Sometimes frightened and confused during interviews, Jonah is unaware of the other personalities.

Sammy. He has the most intact memories. Sammy can coexist with Jonah or set Jonah aside and take over. He claims to be ready when Jonah needs legal advice or is in trouble; he is designated "the mediator." Sammy remembers emerging at age 6, when Jonah's mother stabbed his stepfather and Sammy persuaded the parents never to fight again in front of the children.

King Young. He emerged when Jonah was 6 or 7 years old to straighten out Jonah's sexual identity after his mother occasionally dressed him in girls' clothing at home and Jonah became confused about boys' and girls' names at school. King Young has looked after Jonah's sexual interests ever since; hence, he is designated "the lover." He is only dimly aware of the other personalities.

Usoffa. A cold, belligerent, and angry person, Usoffa is capable of ignoring pain. It is his sworn duty to watch over and protect Jonah; thus, he is designated "the warrior." He emerged at age 9 or 10, when a gang of boys beat up Jonah without provocation. Jonah was helpless, but Usoffa emerged and fought viciously against the attackers. He, too, is only dimly aware of the other personalities.

The four personalities tested very differently on all measures having to do with emotionally laden topics but scored essentially alike on tests relatively free of emotion or personal conflict, such as intelligence or vocabulary tests.

Dissociative identity disorder reflects a failure to integrate various aspects of identity, memory, and consciousness. The dissociation is so complete that several different personalities seem to be living in the same body.

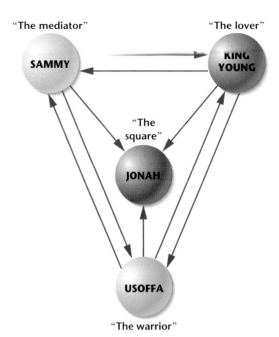

▌Figure 15-18
Jonah's Four Component Identities
The three personalities on the periphery have superficial knowledge of each other but are intimately familiar with Jonah, who in turn is totally unaware of them. (A. M. Ludwig, J. M. Brandsma, C. B. Wilbur, F. Benfeldt & D. H. Jameson (1972), "The Objective Study of a Multiple Personality," in *Archives of General Psychiatry*, 26:298–310. Copyright © 1972 by the American Medical Association.)

Observers note that the switch from one personality to another is often accompanied by subtle changes in posture and tone of voice. The new personality talks, walks, and gestures differently. There may even be changes in physiological processes such as blood pressure and brain activity (Putnam, 1991).

Individuals with dissociative identity disorder frequently report having experienced physical and sexual abuse during childhood (Ellason et al., 1996). The accuracy of such reports is controversial, because childhood memories may be subject to distortion, and individuals with this disorder tend to be very vulnerable to suggestion. Nevertheless, many theorists believe that this disorder develops as a defense against traumatic childhood experiences. The child copes with a painful problem by creating another personality to bear the brunt of the difficulty (Ross, 1997). In Jonah's case, Sammy (the mediator) emerged when Jonah had to deal with his mother's attack on his stepfather.

The child presumably learns to defend himself from the pain of abuse by dissociating the memory from consciousness. If the child is severely and repeatedly abused, this method of defense leads over time to dissociative identities in which only one or two subpersonalities are conscious of the abuse and the others have no memory of the pain. It is adaptive for the child to keep the personalities separate in order to keep awareness of the abuse from his or her other selves. That way the feeling and memories of abuse do not continually flood the child's consciousness when he or she cannot handle it—for instance, while at school or playing with friends (Braun, 1986).

Another factor in the development of dissociative identity disorder appears to be an enhanced susceptibility to self-hypnosis, a process by which one is able at will to put oneself into the kind of trance state characteristic of hypnosis. Patients with dissociative identity disorder often make excellent hypnotic subjects, and they report that the trance experience is identical to experiences they have had, dating back to childhood (Kihlstrom, Glisky, & Angiulo, 1994). One of the personalities of a patient said, "She creates personalities by blocking everything from her head, mentally relaxes, concentrates very hard, and wishes" (Bliss, 1980, p. 1392).

Once individuals discover that creating another identity relieves them of emotional pain, they are likely to create other personalities when confronted by emotional problems. Thus, when Jonah was beaten by a gang of boys at age 10, he created another personality, Usoffa Abdulla, to handle the problem. Some dissociative identity patients become so accustomed to defending against problems by means of alternate personalities that they continue the process throughout adulthood, creating new personalities in response to new problems, and they may end up with a dozen or more different personalities (Putnam, 1991).

Cases of dissociative identity disorder have always been fascinating but rare. However, recent years have seen a sharp rise in the number of cases reported in the United States. Some believe that this increase reflects increased awareness of the disorder among mental health professionals and, hence, identification of cases that previously were undiagnosed. Others believe that the disorder has been overdiagnosed in individuals who are highly suggestible (American Psychiatric Association, 2000). Dissociative identity disorder is much more frequently diagnosed in the United States than in Europe, India, or Japan (Ross, 1989). Within the United States, dissociative identity disorder is rarely diagnosed in Latinos (Martinez-Taboas, 1989). Some theorists believe that Latinos confronted by traumatic stressors are more likely to develop *ataque de nervios*, which we described earlier, rather than dissociative identity disorder.

◆ Interim Summary

- In dissociative identity disorder, two or more well-developed personalities alternate within the same individual.

- Many theorists attribute this disorder to child abuse.

- The ability to hypnotize oneself may also be key to the development of dissociative identity disorder.

- This is a rare disorder, although the frequency with which it is diagnosed has increased in recent decades, particularly in the United States.

◆ Critical Thinking Questions

1. Childhood abuse is more likely to contribute to dissociative identity disorder if it occurs chronically over a long period of time. Can you think of other traumas in the lives of modern children that might contribute to the development of dissociative identity disorder?

2. Most people experience mild dissociative experiences, such as finding themselves someplace but not knowing how they got there, or becoming so involved in a fantasy that it seems real, particularly when they are very tired, stressed, or have been drinking or taking drugs. Can you identify other common dissociative experiences and their possible sources?

INSANITY AS A LEGAL DEFENSE

Before leaving the subject of mental disorders, we should look briefly at the controversial issue of insanity. How should the law treat a mentally disturbed person who commits a criminal offense? Should individuals whose mental faculties are impaired be held responsible for their actions? These questions are of concern to behavioral and social scientists, members of the legal profession, and others who work with criminal offenders.

Over the centuries, an important part of Western law has been the concept that a civilized society should not punish a person who is mentally incapable of controlling his or her conduct. In 1724 an English court maintained that a man was not responsible for an act if "he doth not know what he is doing, no more than . . . a wild beast." Modern standards of legal responsibility, however, have been based on the M'Naghten decision of 1843. The **M'Naghten Rule** states that a defendant may be found not guilty by reason of insanity only if he was so severely disturbed at the time of his act that he did not know what he was doing, or if he did know what he was doing, did not know that it was wrong.

The M'Naghten Rule was adopted in the United States, and the distinction of knowing right from wrong remained the basis for most decisions of legal insanity for over a century. Some states added to their statutes the doctrine of "irresistible impulse," which recognizes that some mentally ill individuals may respond correctly when asked if a particular act is morally right or wrong but may be unable to control their behavior.

During the 1970s, a number of state and federal courts adopted the **American Law Institute Rule,** a broader legal definition of insanity proposed by the American Law Institute, which states: "A person is not responsible for criminal conduct if at the time of such conduct, as a result of mental disease or defect, he lacks substantial capacity either to appreciate the wrongfulness of his conduct or to conform his conduct to the requirements of the law." The word *substantial* suggests that any incapacity is not enough to avoid criminal responsibility but that total incapacity is not required either. The use of the word *appreciate* rather than *know* implies that intellectual awareness of right or wrong is not enough; individuals must have some understanding of the moral or legal consequences of their behavior before they can be held criminally responsible.

The problem of legal responsibility in the case of mentally disordered individuals became a topic of increased debate in the wake of John Hinckley Jr.'s acquittal, by reason of insanity, for the attempted assassination of President Reagan in 1981. Many Americans were outraged by the verdict and felt that the insanity defense was a legal loophole that allowed too many guilty people to go free. In response, Congress enacted the Insanity Defense Reform Act (1984), which contains a number of provisions designed to make it more difficult to absolve a defendant of legal responsibility. For example, the act changes the American Law Institute's "lacks substantial capacity . . . to appreciate" to "unable to appreciate"; it stipulates that the mental disease or defect be "severe" (the intent being to exclude nonpsychotic disorders such as antisocial personality); and it shifts the burden of proof from the prosecution to the defense (instead of the prosecution having to prove that the person was sane beyond a reasonable doubt at the time of the crime, the defense must prove he or she was not sane, and must do so with "clear and convincing evidence"). This law applies to all cases tried in federal courts and about half the state courts.

Another attempt to clarify the legal defense of insanity is the verdict "guilty but mentally ill." Initially proposed by Michigan, it has been adopted by 11 states. (In some of these states, this verdict replaces the not guilty by reason of insanity verdict; in others, it is an additional option.) Generally, the laws permit a finding of **guilty but mentally ill** when a defendant is found to have a substantial disorder of thought or mood that afflicted him at the time of the crime and significantly impaired his judgment, behavior, capacity to recognize reality, or ability to cope with the ordinary demands of life. The effect of this mental illness, however, falls short of legal insanity. The verdict of guilty but mentally ill allows jurors to convict a person whom they perceive as dangerous while attempting also to ensure that he or she receives treatment for the disorder. The individual could be given treatment in prison or be treated in a mental hospital and returned to prison when deemed fit to complete the sentence.

Public concern that the insanity defense may be a major loophole in the criminal law is largely groundless. The defense is rarely used, and actual cases of acquittal by reason of insanity are even rarer. Jurors seem reluctant to believe that people are not morally responsible for their acts, and lawyers, knowing that an insanity plea is likely to fail, tend to use it only as a last resort. Fewer than 1% of defendants charged with serious crimes are found not guilty by reason of insanity.

◆ Interim Summary

- Although the use of insanity as a legal defense is a subject of considerable controversy, in reality the defense is rarely used and even more rarely successful.

- The M'Naghten Rule states that a defendant may be found not guilty by reason of insanity only if he was so severely disturbed at the time of his act that he did not know what he was doing, or if he did know what he was doing, did not know that it was wrong.

- The American Law Institute Rule states: "A person is not responsible for criminal conduct if at the time of such conduct, as a result of mental disease or defect, he lacks substantial capacity either to appreciate the wrongfulness of his conduct or to conform his conduct to the requirements of the law."

- Courts now allow a finding of guilty but mentally ill when a defendant is found to have a substantial disorder of thought or mood that afflicted him at the time of the crime and significantly impaired his judgment, behavior, capacity to recognize reality, or ability to cope with the ordinary demands of life.

◆ Critical Thinking Questions

1. Most of the people judged guilty but mentally ill never receive adequate psychiatric treatment in prison. Do you think this invalidates this verdict as an alternative to the insanity defense? Why or why not?

2. Why do you think most people believe that many criminals "get off" on the insanity defense?

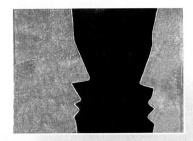

Is Attention Deficit/Hyperactivity Disorder (ADHD) Overdiagnosed?

ADHD IS OVERDIAGNOSED

Caryn L. Carlson, The University of Texas at Austin

The growing public attention to ADHD over the past decade has increased the detection of legitimate cases and led to much-needed research. We must be cautious, however, that we do not allow the diagnostic pendulum to swing too far, since finding answers about ADHD depends on the rigor and integrity of our classification system.

There is reason to believe that ADHD is currently being overdiagnosed in some areas of the United States. Prescriptions of stimulant medications, which are almost exclusively for ADHD, provide a "proxy" for diagnostic rates and afford an examination of trends over time and place. Use of methylphenidate in the United States, already high by worldwide standards (International Narcotics Control Board, 1998), skyrocketed in the early 1990s, more than doubling from 1990 through 1995 (Safer, Zito, & Fine, 1996) and has continued to increase since then. While rates are up for all age groups, the largest increase is for teenagers and adults; among school-age children in one region, the proportion of high school students using stimulant medication tripled from 1991 through 1995 (Safer, Zito, & Fine, 1996). Certainly the true prevalence of ADHD has not increased at this rate, although part of the increase no doubt reflects the detection of previously unrecognized ADHD. While some reports suggest that even now many ADHD children may not be recognized or treated (Wolraich, Hannah, Baumgaertel, & Feurer, 1998), the average rates are now quite high (Safer, Zito, & Fine, 1996).

Part of the dramatic increase probably reflects overdiagnosis, particularly when considered in light of the vast disparities across geographical locales in the United States. The rate of methylphenidate consumption per capita in 1995 was 2.4 times higher in Virginia than in neighboring West Virginia, and nearly 4 times higher than in California (Spanos, 1996). Even more troubling are the high discrepancies across counties within states. For example, although the per capita rate for males of ages 6–12 in 1991 in New York was 4.1% statewide, rates varied by a factor of 10 among counties, ranging up to 14% (Kaufman, 1995).

What factors might lead to overdiagnosis of ADHD? We know from epidemiological research that unreasonable prevalence rates (e.g., up to nearly 23% of school-age boys [Wolraich, Hannah, Baumgaertel, & Feurer, 1998]) are obtained when ADHD is identified based merely on simple ratings from one source, but become much lower when full diagnostic criteria—including age of onset by 7, presence across settings, and confirmation of impairment—are imposed. The wide variability in diagnostic rates across locations suggests that clinicians are applying diagnostic criteria inconsistently. Some clinicians diagnose without assessing all criteria, and often they rely only on parent reports. While underdiagnosis may be occurring in some places, overdiagnosis is occurring in others.

When is overdiagnosis most likely? It seems that the diagnosis of ADHD has become fashionable for those who experience some negative life event—such as school failure or job loss—and desire to attribute such problems to a disorder rather than accept personal responsibility. This tendency is apparent even in more mundane arenas, such as feeling bored or unmotivated—"What a relief: the fact that I find it difficult to pay attention in my 'history of Swedish cartographers' class isn't my fault. I have ADHD."

One safeguard against misdiagnosis is the current criteria that symptoms must appear by age 7. But how early and by what means can we detect ADHD if we agree that it is present from an early age? Since objective measures that can reliably identify ADHD are currently unavailable, we must rely on symptom reports from others. Setting the age of onset at 7 years recognizes that normal behavior patterns may be similar to symptoms of ADHD up to about age 5, when normally activity decreases and attention increases (but not in children with ADHD). Also, impairment may not occur outside the demands of a classroom environment. But if individuals do not have symptoms early but develop them later for a variety of reasons, including life situations or stress, then diagnosis does not seem warranted. Should such problems be recognized? By all means. Should they be treated? Of course, by teaching people organizational and behavior management strategies, and possibly even with medication. But significant problems in living are not the

Caryn Carlson

equivalent of disorders, and to call them that will deter us in the search for etiologies of ADHD.

Is Attention Deficit/Hyperactivity Disorder (ADHD) Overdiagnosed?

ADHD IS NEITHER OVERDIAGNOSED NOR OVERTREATED
William Pelham, SUNY Buffalo

Because ADHD is the most widely diagnosed mental health disorder of childhood and because its frequency of treatment with medication has been increasing exponentially through the 1990s, it has become fashionable in many quarters—particularly among educators—to argue that it is overdiagnosed and consequently overtreated. Histrionic diatribes aside, there is no solid empirical evidence that ADHD is overdiagnosed or overtreated.

First, consider the accusation that ADHD is only a relatively recent phenomenon. To the contrary, the diagnosis was often widely used in the past but played second fiddle to other diagnoses. For example, one of the more important early studies in treatment of conduct disordered children (Patterson, 1974) noted, almost as an aside that more than two-thirds of the boys had hyperkinesis, an early label for ADHD. Thus while ADHD may well be *diagnosed* more often than in the past 30 years, it is simply being diagnosed more appropriately and given the prominence it deserves.

It is important to note that the major reason for the increasing rate of ADHD identification in the 1990s is a result of the 1991 change in the status of ADHD in the Individuals with Disabilities Education Act (IDEA), the federal law that governs special education throughout the United States. This change included ADHD as a handicapping condition. Further, the U. S. Office of Education sent a memorandum to all state officers of education directing them to consider ADHD as a condition eligible for special education. As a result of this directive, school districts throughout the country for the

first time were required to establish screening and diagnostic procedures for ADHD. The increase in diagnosis for ADHD is thus not a conspiracy or a fatal flaw in education or an indictment of current parenting practices, but is instead a natural by-product of a change in federal regulations governing education in the United States.

What about the criticism that ADHD is a disorder with diagnostic rates that vary widely both within North America and across the world? The explanation is that local school districts and states vary dramatically in the degree to which they have implemented the mandated changes in the IDEA. Furthermore, ADHD when similar diagnostic criteria are applied, comparable rates to those in North America exist in a diverse collection of countries that include Italy, Spain, South Africa, Israel, Argentina, and Vietnam.

The most important factor in deciding whether a mental health disorder is overdiagnosed is whether the diagnosed individuals have impairments in daily life functioning sufficient to justify the label. ADHD is a particularly compelling example of this issue because the children suffer from dramatic impairment in relationships with peers, parents, teachers, and siblings, as well as in classroom behavior and academic performance. To take a single example, in one classic study of consecutive referrals to a clinic, 96% of ADHD children were rejected by their peers on sociometric nominations at a rate higher than their class averages (Pelham & Bender, 1982). In the field of child psychopathology, the number of negative nominations received on a classroom peer nomination inventory in

elementary school is widely thought to be the best indicator of severe impairment in childhood and poor outcome in adulthood, so this elevated rate of negative nominations highlights the impairment that ADHD children suffer in the peer domain.

A corollary of the argument that many children are inappropriately diagnosed with ADHD is the complaint that these children are being inappropriately treated—usually with medication. In fact, the literature shows that only a small minority of diagnosed ADHD children (or all children with mental health disorders for that matter) receive treatment—medication or otherwise. We should be happy that treatment rates for the disorder are increasing. The dramatic rise in the treatment of ADHD—pharmacological or otherwise—clearly results from the increase in the rates of diagnosis, which are secondary to the change in the IDEA noted above. Notably, one of the studies that supports these arguments regarding impairment and treatment was conducted with children identified using only teacher ratings, which have been the main target for complaints of overdiagnosis (Wolraich et al, 1998).

In summary, ADHD is the most common mental health disorder of childhood, and it is one of the most impairing and refractory, and one with poor long-term prognosis. Current diagnostic rates are in line with scientific views of the nature of the disorder. If anything, we need to accurately identify *more* children with ADHD and provide the evidence-based treatments—both behavioral and pharmacological—that they need.

CHAPTER SUMMARY

1. The diagnosis of abnormal behavior is based on social norms, statistical frequency, adaptiveness of behavior, and personal distress. Characteristics of good mental health include efficient perception of reality, control of behavior, self-esteem, ability to form affectionate relationships, and productivity.

2. DSM-IV classifies mental disorders according to specific behavioral symptoms. Such a classification system helps communicate information and provides a basis for research. However, each case is unique, and diagnostic labels should not be used to pigeonhole individuals.

3. Theories about the causes of mental disorders and proposals for treating them can be grouped according to those that focus on the brain and other biological factors, those that focus on the mind, including psychoanalytic, behavioral, and cognitive perspectives, and those that focus on sociocultural and environmental factors. The vulnerability-stress model emphasizes the interaction between a predisposition (biological and/or psychological) that makes a person vulnerable to a particular disorder, and stressful environmental conditions encountered by the individual.

4. Anxiety disorders include generalized anxiety (constant worry and tension), panic disorders (sudden attacks of overwhelming apprehension), phobias (irrational fears of specific objects or situations), and obsessive-compulsive disorders (persistent unwanted thoughts, or obsessions, combined with urges, or compulsions, to perform certain acts).

5. Biological theories of anxiety disorders attribute them to genetic predispositions or to biochemical or neurological abnormalities. Most anxiety disorders run in families, and twin studies strongly suggest that panic disorder and obsessive-compulsive disorder have an inherited component. People who suffer panic attacks have an overreactive fight-or-flight response, perhaps because of serotonin deficiencies in the limbic system. People with obsessive-compulsive disorder may have serotonin deficiencies in areas of the brain that regulate primitive impulses.

6. Cognitive and behavioral theorists suggest that people with anxiety disorders are prone to catastrophizing cognitions and to rigid, moralistic thinking. Maladaptive behaviors such as avoidant behaviors and compulsions arise through operant conditioning when the individual discovers that the behaviors reduce anxiety. Phobias may emerge through classical conditioning. Psychodynamic theories attribute anxiety disorders to unconscious conflicts that are disguised as phobias, obsessions, or compulsions.

7. Mood disorders are divided into depressive disorders (in which the individual has one or more periods of depression) and bipolar disorders (in which the individual alternates between periods of depression and periods of elation, or mania). Sadness, loss of gratification in life, negative thoughts, and lack of motivation are the main symptoms of depression.

8. Biological theories attribute mood disorders to genetic factors and to problems in regulation of the neurotransmitters serotonin and norepinephrine. Cognitive theories attribute depression to pessimistic views of the self, the world, and the future and to maladaptive attributional styles. Psychodynamic theories view depression as a reactivation of loss of parental affection in a person who is dependent on external approval and tends to turn anger inward.

9. Schizophrenia is characterized by disturbances in thought, including disorganized thought processes, delusions, and lack of insight. Other symptoms include perceptual disturbances (such as hallucinations), inappropriate emotional expression, bizarre motor activity, withdrawal, and impaired functioning.

10. Schizophrenia clearly is transmitted genetically. People with schizophrenia also have problems in dopamine regulation, as well as two types of brain abnormalities: The prefrontal cortex is smaller and less active, and the ventricles are enlarged. Difficult environments probably cannot cause schizophrenia, but they may worsen the disorder and contribute to relapses.

11. Personality disorders are lifelong patterns of maladaptive behavior that are immature and inappropriate ways of coping with stress or solving problems. Individuals with antisocial personalities are impulsive, show little guilt, are concerned only with their own needs, and are frequently in trouble with the law. Antisocial personality disorder probably has genetic and biological roots, but neglectful and hostile parenting may also contribute to the disorder.

12. People with borderline personality disorder show instability in mood, self-concept, and interpersonal relationships. Psychodynamic theories suggest that the caregivers of people with this disorder required their children to be highly dependent and alternated between extreme expressions of love and hostility.

13. In dissociative identity disorder, two or more well-developed personalities alternate within the same individual. Many theorists attribute this disorder to child abuse.

14. Although the use of insanity as a legal defense is a subject of considerable controversy, in reality the defense is rarely used and even more rarely successful.

CORE CONCEPTS

cultural relativist perspective
abnormal
maladaptive
distress
normality
*Diagnostic and Statistical Manual
    of Mental Disorders,* **4th edition**
    (DSM-IV)
neuroses
psychoses
biological perspective
psychological perspective
psychoanalytic perspective
behavioral perspective
cognitive perspective
cultural or sociological perspective

vulnerability-stress model
anxiety disorders
generalized anxiety disorder
panic attack
panic disorder
ataque de nervios
agoraphobia
phobia
simple phobia
social phobia
obsessive-compulsive disorder
obsession
compulsion
mood disorders
depressive disorders
bipolar disorders

anhedonia
manic episode
schizophrenia
word salad
loosening of associations
delusion
paranoid
hallucination
personality disorder
antisocial personality disorder
borderline personality disorder
dissociative identity disorder
M'Naghten Rule
American Law Institute Rule
guilty but mentally ill

 # WEB RESOURCES

http://psychology.wadsworth.com/
atkinson14e

Take a quiz, try the activities and exercises, and explore
web links.

http://bama.ua.edu/~jhooper/tableofc.html

This forensic psychiatry resource page by James Hooper
offers a discussion of insanity and the law, as well as a
listing of landmark cases that involve the insanity defense.

http://www.chovil.com/

This personal site by schizophrenic patient Ian Chovil includes a marvelous life story that helps give a "face" to
schizophrenia. Chovil also explains the biology of schizophrenia and therapy for people with the disease.

http://www2.health-center.com/mentalhealth/
therapy/

This site outlines a variety of different psychological disorders, discusses the major kinds of therapy, and provides
links to related articles.

 InfoTrac Online Library
http://www.infotrac-college.com/
wadsworth

Use InfoTrac College Edition to find popular and scientific articles by using the search terms below or your
own relevant terms.

- Antisocial personality disorder
- Bipolar disorder
- Dissociative identity disorder
- Schizophrenia

CD-ROM LINKS

 Psych Odyssey

Check out CD Chapter 16, Abnormal
Psychology

A. Classifying and Diagnosing Abnormal Behavior
B. Mood Disorders
C. Schizophrenic Disorders

 Psyk.trek 2.0

Check out CD Unit 11, Abnormal Behavior
and Therapy

11a Anxiety Disorders
11b Mood Disorders
11c Schizophrenic Disorders

TREATMENT OF PSYCHOLOGICAL DISORDERS

16

Steve M. has paranoid schizophrenia. He frequently hears voices berating him and accusing him of having done something wrong. He was convinced that a transmitter had been implanted in his head, through which he was receiving these messages. When he takes his medications, the voices are quieted and the paranoid beliefs begin to recede.

Over the last 5 years, Steve has been hospitalized three times. Each time he had stopped his medication, twice believing himself well and once, just tired of the whole thing. In between hospitalizations, he has spent some time in a day treatment program and some time taking classes at college. He still struggles with determining what is real and what is not, but he has learned through ther-

apy that he can check this out with the people he trusts, principally his stepmother, brother, and father. Steve has developed a long-term relationship with a psychologist from the clinic whom he sees once a week (in addition to his medication checks with the psychiatrist). Together they confront the very real challenges that his illness and the stigma attached to it poses. His parents, through the parent-support group they have joined, are learning to do the same. (Adapted from Bernheim, 1997, pp. 126–130).

Steve and his family are making use of a variety of types of treatment to control his paranoid schizophrenia. The medications he is taking are one form

of biological treatment for psychological disorders. He is also seeing a psychotherapist to learn new ways of coping with his disorder. His parents are making use of community-based resources to understand Steve's problems.

In this chapter we look at methods for treating abnormal behavior. The most frequently used methods are listed in the Concept Review Table. Each of these treatments is linked to a particular theory of the causes of mental disorders. As we discuss in the next section, our theories of mental disorders, and therefore our treatment of these disorders, has changed a great deal over history.

CONCEPT REVIEW TABLE
Methods of Therapy

Type of Therapy	Example	Description
Psychodynamic Therapies	Traditional psychoanalysis	Through free association, dream analysis, and transference, attempts to discover the unconscious basis of the client's current problems so as to deal with them in a more rational way.
	Contemporary psychodynamic therapies (e.g., interpersonal therapy)	More structured and short-term than traditional psychoanalysis; emphasize the way the client is currently interacting with others.
Behavior Therapies	Systematic desensitization	The client is trained to relax and then presented with a hierarchy of anxiety-producing situations and asked to relax while imagining each one.
	In vivo exposure	Similar to systematic desensitization except that the client actually experiences each situation.
	Flooding	A form of in vivo exposure in which a phobic individual is exposed to the most feared object or situation for an extended period without an opportunity to escape.
	Selective reinforcement	Reinforcement of specific behaviors, often through the use of tokens that can be exchanged for rewards.
	Modeling	A process in which the client learns behaviors by observing and imitating others; often combined with behavioral rehearsal (e.g., in assertiveness training).
Cognitive-Behavior Therapies		Treatment methods that use behavior modification techniques but also incorporate procedures designed to change maladaptive beliefs.
Humanistic Therapies (e.g., client-centered therapy)		In an atmosphere of empathy, warmth, and genuineness, the therapist attempts to facilitate the process through which the client works out solutions to his or her own problems.
Biological Therapies	Psychotherapeutic drugs	Use of drugs to modify mood and behavior.
	Electroconvulsive therapy (ECT)	A mild electric current is applied to the brain to produce a seizure.

HISTORICAL BACKGROUND

Among the earliest beliefs about mental disorders, dating back to the Stone Age, was that a person who behaved in unusual ways was possessed by evil spirits. These demons were removed or exorcised through such techniques as prayer, incantation, and magic. If these techniques were unsuccessful, more extreme measures were taken to ensure that the body would be an unpleasant dwelling place for the evil spirit. Flogging, starving, burning, and causing the person to bleed profusely were frequent forms of "treatment."

Some of the earliest written texts on mental disorders are from the Chinese, who viewed the human body as containing both a positive and negative force. If the two forces were not in balance, illness, including insanity, could result. The ancient Chinese also believed that emotions could be caused when "vital air" flows on specific internal organs. For example, sorrow was caused when air flowed on the lungs, anger was caused when air flowed on the liver, and worry was caused when air flowed on the spleen.

In the Western world, the Greek physician Hippocrates (circa 460–377 B.C.) is credited with bringing a medical perspective to the study of mental disorders. He believed that unusual behaviors were the result of a disturbance in the balance of bodily fluids. Hippocrates, and the Greek and Roman physicians who followed him, argued for more humane treatment of the mentally ill. They stressed the importance of pleasant surroundings, exercise, proper diet, massage, and soothing baths, as well as some less desirable treatments, such as purging and mechanical restraints. Although there were no institutions for the mentally ill, many individuals were

Philippe Pinel in the courtyard of the hospital of Salpetriere.

cared for with great kindness in temples dedicated to the gods of healing.

This progressive view of mental illness did not continue, however. Primitive superstitions and belief in demon possession were revived during the Middle Ages. The mentally ill were considered to be in league with Satan and to possess supernatural powers with which they could cause floods, pestilence, and injuries to others. Seriously disturbed individuals were treated cruelly: It was believed that beating, starving, and torturing the mentally ill served to punish the devil. This type of cruelty culminated in the witchcraft trials of the 15th, 16th, and 17th centuries, in which thousands of people, many of whom may have been mentally ill, were sentenced to death.

EARLY ASYLUMS

In the late Middle Ages, cities created asylums to cope with the mentally ill. These asylums were simply prisons; the inmates were chained in dark, filthy cells and treated more as animals than as human beings. It was not until 1792, when Philippe Pinel was placed in charge of an asylum in Paris, that some improvements were made. As an experiment, Pinel removed the chains that restrained the inmates. Much to the amazement of skeptics who thought Pinel was mad to unchain such "animals," the experiment was a success. When released from their restraints, placed in clean, sunny rooms, and treated kindly, many people who for years had been considered hopelessly insane improved enough to leave the asylum.

By the beginning of the 20th century, the fields of medicine and psychology were making great advances. In 1905, a mental disorder known as general paresis was shown to have a physical cause: a syphilis infection acquired many years before the symptoms of the disorder appeared. The syphilis spirochete remains in the body after the initial genital infection disappears, and it gradually destroys the nervous system. The results include the syndrome known as **general paresis—a gradual decline in mental and physical functioning, marked changes in personality, and delusions and hallucinations.** If the disorder is not treated, death occurs within a few years. At one time, general paresis accounted for more than 10% of all admissions to mental hospitals, but today few cases are reported, owing to the effectiveness of penicillin in treating syphilis (Dale, 1975).

The discovery that general paresis was the result of a disease encouraged those who believed that mental illness has biological causes. Nevertheless, in the early 1900s the public still did not understand mental illness and viewed mental hospitals and their inmates with fear and horror. Clifford Beers undertook the task of educating the public about mental health. As a young man, Beers had developed a bipolar disorder and been confined for 3 years in several private and state hospitals. At the time, lack of funds made the average state mental hospital—with its overcrowded wards, poor food, and badly trained attendants—a highly unpleasant place to live. After his recovery, Beers described his experiences in a book titled *A Mind That Found Itself* (1908), which attracted considerable public attention. Beers worked ceaselessly to educate the public about mental illness and helped organize the National Committee for Mental Hygiene. The mental hygiene movement played an invaluable role in stimulating the organization of child-guidance clinics and community mental health centers to aid in the prevention and treatment of mental disorders.

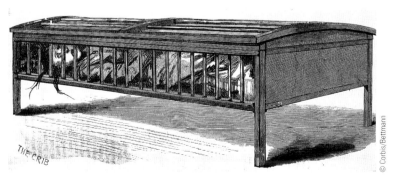

The crib, a restraining device used in a New York mental institution in 1882.

Modern Treatment Facilities

Mental hospitals have been upgraded markedly since Beers's day, but there is still much room for improvement. The best mental hospitals are comfortable and well-kept places that provide therapeutic activities: individual and group psychotherapy, recreation, occupational therapy (designed to teach skills as well as provide relaxation), and educational courses to help patients prepare for jobs upon release from the hospital. The worst are primarily custodial institutions where patients lead a boring existence in run-down, overcrowded wards and receive little treatment beyond medication. Most mental hospitals fall somewhere between these extremes.

Beginning in the early 1960s, emphasis shifted from treating mentally disturbed individuals in hospitals to treating them in their own communities. This movement toward deinstitutionalization was motivated partly by the recognition that hospitalization has some inherent disadvantages, regardless of how good the facilities may be. Hospitals remove people from the social support of family and friends and the familiar patterns of daily life, and they encourage dependence. They are also very expensive.

During the 1950s, psychotherapeutic drugs (discussed later in the chapter) were discovered that could relieve depression and anxiety and reduce psychotic behavior. When these drugs became widely available in the 1960s, many hospitalized patients could be discharged and returned home to be treated as outpatients. The Community Mental Health Centers Act of 1963 made federal funds available for the establishment of community treatment centers designed to provide outpatient treatment and other services, including short-term and partial hospitalization. In partial hospitalization, individuals may receive treatment at the center during the day and return home in the evening, or they can work during the day and spend nights at the center. The movement toward discharge of institutionalized mental patients to community-based services became known as **deinstitutionalization.**

As Figure 16-1 shows, the number of patients treated in state and county mental hospitals has decreased dramatically. For some patients, deinstitutionalization has been successful. The services of mental health centers and private clinicians, along with help from their families and the use of psychotherapeutic drugs, have enabled them to resume satisfactory lives. For others, however, deinstitutionalization has had unfortunate consequences, largely because the facilities in most communities are far from adequate.

Many individuals who improve with hospitalization and could manage on their own with assistance do not receive adequate follow-up care in terms of outpatient therapy, monitoring of medication, or help in finding friends, housing, and jobs. As a consequence, they lead a "revolving-door" existence, going in and out of institutions between unsuccessful attempts to cope on their own. About half of all patients discharged from state hospitals are readmitted within a year.

Some discharged patients are too incapacitated to even attempt to support themselves or function without custodial care. They often live in dirty, overcrowded housing or on the streets. The disheveled man standing on the corner talking to himself and shouting gibberish may be one victim of deinstitutionalization. The woman with all her possessions in a shopping bag who spends one night in the doorway of an office building and the next in a subway station may be another. At least a third of street people suffer from some sort of mental disorder (Rossi, 1990).

The increasing visibility of homeless mentally ill individuals, particularly in large cities, has aroused public concern and prompted a move toward reinstitutionalization. However, this raises an important ethical issue. If such people are not readjusting to society, should they be involuntarily committed to a mental hospital? One of the most cherished civil rights in a democratic society is the right to liberty.

Some experts believe that legal action is warranted only if a person is potentially dangerous to others. The rare, but highly publicized, occasions when a mentally ill person experiencing a psychotic episode attacks an innocent bystander have generated fears for public safety. But dangerousness is difficult to predict (Monahan, 2001). Recent studies suggest that people who have both serious mental disorders and a substance abuse problem (such as alcoholism) do appear to commit violent crimes more often than mentally healthy people (Steadman et

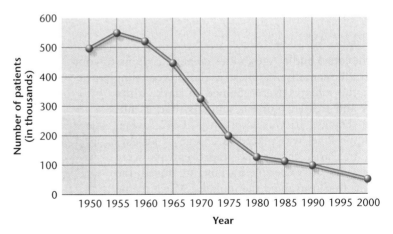

▌ Figure 16-1
Patients in Mental Hospitals
The number of patients cared for in U.S. state and county mental hospitals has decreased dramatically since 1955. (After Lamb, 2001)

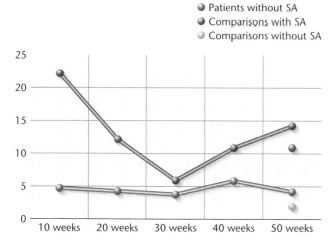

▌Figure 16-2
Likelihood of Violence

The percent of patients with or without a substance abuse problem, and community comparisons with or without a substance abuse problem, who committed a violent act in the previous 10 weeks. Note that the community comparison group was assessed only at one time—at the end of the day. SA refers to substance abuse. (H. J. Steadman, E. P. Mulvey, J. Monahan, P. C. Robbins, P. S. Applebaum, T. Grisso, L. Roth, & E. Silver (1998). Violence by people discharged from acute psychiatric inpatient facilities and by others in the same neighborhoods. *Archives of General Psychiatry, 55*, 393–401. © 1998 American Medical Association.)

al., 1998). Figure 16-2 provides data from a large study in which patients with mental disorders were compared with mentally healthy people in the community. Those with mental disorders and a substance abuse problem were more likely to commit a serious violent act than the community comparison group or than the patients with mental disorders but no substance abuse problem. In addition, patients with mental disorders but no substance abuse problem were slightly more likely to commit violent acts than mentally healthy people with no substance abuse problem. Note, however, that the presence of a substance abuse problem was as strong a predictor of violence as the presence of a mental disorder in this study. In general, experts' opinions regarding whether a given individual with a mental disorder will commit violent crimes are often incorrect, particularly for the long term (Gardner, Lidz, Mulvey, & Shaw, 1996).

Moreover, our legal system is designed to protect people from preventive detention. A person is assumed to be innocent until proven guilty by the courts, and prisoners are released from penitentiaries even though statistics show that most will commit additional crimes. Should mentally ill individuals not have the same rights? And what about people who appear more dangerous to themselves than to others? Should they be committed? These complex issues have yet to be resolved.

Aside from the legal issues, the problem of providing care for the mentally ill remains. Many people with mental disorders might voluntarily seek treatment but cannot because they do not have the means to pay for good treatment. About 40% of people with a serious mental disorder receive little or no regular care (Torrey, 1997).

PROFESSIONALS WHO PROVIDE PSYCHOTHERAPY

Whether a person receives therapy in a hospital, a community mental health center, or a private office, several different types of professionals may be involved.

A psychiatrist has an M.D. degree and has completed a three-year residency (after medical school) in a mental health facility, during which he or she received supervision in the diagnosis of abnormal behavior, drug therapy, and psychotherapy. As a physician, the psychiatrist can prescribe medication and, in most states, hospitalization.

The term *psychoanalyst* is reserved for individuals who have received specialized training at a psychoanalytic institute learning the methods and theories derived from Freud. The program usually takes several years, during which the trainees must undergo their own psychoanalyses as well as treat several clients psychoanalytically while under supervision.

Psychologists who work as therapists have obtained graduate training in clinical, counseling, or school psychology. Usually, they hold a Ph.D. (Doctor of Philosophy) or Psy.D. (Doctor of Psychology) degree. The Ph.D. emphasizes training in research as well as diagnosis and therapy. The Psy.D. is a more applied degree, focusing mainly on diagnosis and therapy. Both degrees require 4 to 5 years of postgraduate study, plus a year or more of internship. In addition, most states require psychologists to pass a licensing or certification examination.

Clinical psychologists work with people suffering from a broad range of mental disorders. Counseling psychologists focus more on problems of adjustment and often concentrate on specific areas such as student, marriage, or family counseling. School psychologists are concerned with young people who have academic difficulties.

Psychiatric social workers have completed a 2-year master's degree program (M.S.W.), which includes training in interviewing, therapy, and in extending treatment procedures to the home and community. Some psychiatric social workers also go on to complete a doctorate in social work. A psychiatric social worker often is called on to collect information about a patient's home situation and to assist the patient in getting help from community resources (such as hospitals, clinics, and social agencies).

Sometimes these professionals work as a team. The psychiatrist prescribes psychotherapeutic medications and monitors their effectiveness; the psychologist sees the same client in individual or group psychotherapy; the social worker monitors the home environment and acts as a liaison with community agencies for the client. In mental hospitals, a fourth professional is available: the psychiatric nurse. Psychiatric nursing is a field within the nursing profession that requires special training in the understanding and treatment of mental disorders. In our discussion of psychotherapeutic techniques, we will not specify the profession of the psychotherapists. Instead, we will assume that they are trained and competent members of any one of these professions.

◆ Interim Summary

- Treatment of the mentally ill has progressed from the ancient notion that abnormal behavior resulted from possession by evil spirits that needed to be punished, to custodial care in asylums, to modern mental hospitals and community mental health centers.

- The policy of deinstitutionalization was intended to move hospitalized mental patients into the community, where they would receive outpatient services.

- The deinstitutionalization movement was never adequately funded and, despite its good intentions, has added to the number of homeless mentally ill individuals, causing concern about civil rights and adequate care.

- Several different mental health professionals provide service to people with mental disorders, including psychiatrists, psychologists, psychiatric social workers, and psychiatric nurses.

◆ Critical Thinking Questions

1. What do you think society's obligations are to people with serious mental disorders? What laws should be enacted to protect the rights of these people?

2. Does society have any right or obligation to see to it that children with serious mental disorders receive treatment, even if their parents do not agree to the treatment?

TECHNIQUES OF PSYCHOTHERAPY

Psychotherapy refers to the variety of psychological interventions that share the goal of alleviating human problems and facilitating effective functioning in society. Some psychotherapists (such as psychoanalysts) believe that modification of behavior is dependent on the indi-

vidual's understanding of his or her unconscious motives and conflicts. Others (such as behavior therapists and cognitive-behavior therapists) focus on changing habitual patterns of thinking and behavior rather than on unconscious conflicts. Despite differences in techniques, most methods of psychotherapy have certain basic features in common. They involve a helping relationship between two people: the client (patient) and the therapist. The client is encouraged to discuss intimate concerns, emotions, and experiences freely without fear of being judged by the therapist or having confidences betrayed. The therapist, in turn, offers empathy and understanding, engenders trust, and tries to help the client develop more effective ways of handling problems.

PSYCHODYNAMIC THERAPIES

A key assumption of **psychodynamic therapies** is that a person's current problems cannot be resolved successfully without a thorough understanding of their unconscious basis in early relationships with parents and siblings. The goal of these therapies is to bring conflicts (repressed emotions and motives) into awareness so that they can be dealt with in a more rational and realistic way. The psychodynamic therapies include traditional Freudian psychoanalysis and more recent therapies based on it (see Vakoch & Strupp, 2000).

One of the main techniques that psychodynamic therapists use to recover unconscious conflicts is **free association,** in which the client is encouraged to give free rein to thoughts and feelings and to say whatever comes to mind without editing or censoring it. This is not easy to do, however. In conversation, we usually try to keep a connecting thread running through our remarks and exclude irrelevant ideas. With practice, free association becomes easier. But even individuals who conscientiously try to give free rein to their thoughts will occasionally find themselves blocked, unable to recall the details of an event or finish a thought. Freud believed that blocking, or resistance, results from the individual's unconscious control over sensitive areas and that these are precisely the areas that need to be explored.

Another technique often used in traditional psychoanalytic therapy is **dream analysis,** which consists of talking about the content of one's dreams and then free associating to that content. Freud believed that dreams are "the royal road to the unconscious"; they represent an unconscious wish or fear in disguised form. He distinguished between dreams' manifest content (the obvious, conscious content) and their latent content (the hidden, unconscious content). By talking about the manifest content of a dream and then free associating to that content, the analyst and client attempt to discover the dream's unconscious meaning.

"HAVE A COUPLE OF DREAMS, AND CALL ME IN THE MORNING."

As the therapist and client interact during therapy, the client will often react to the therapist in ways that seem exaggerated or inappropriate. The client may become enraged when the therapist must reschedule an appointment, or may be excessively deferential to the therapist. The term **transference** refers to the tendency for the client to make the therapist the object of thoughts and emotions: The client expresses attitudes toward the analyst that are actually felt toward other people who are, or were, important in his or her life. By pointing out how their clients are reacting to them, therapists help their clients achieve a better understanding of how they react to others. The following passage illustrates an analyst's use of transference, followed by the use of free association:

> Client: I don't understand why you're holding back on telling me if this step is the right one for me at this time in my life.
>
> Therapist: This has come up before. You want my approval before taking some action. What seems to be happening here is that one of the conflicts you have with your wife is trying to get her approval of what you have decided you want to do, and that conflict is occurring now between us.
>
> Client: I suppose so. Other people's approval has always been very important to me.
>
> Therapist: Let's stay with that for a few minutes. Would you free associate to that idea of getting approval from others. Just let the associations come spontaneously—don't force them. (Adapted from Woody & Robertson, 1988, p. 129)

Traditional psychoanalysis is a lengthy, intensive, and expensive process. Client and analyst usually meet for 50-minute sessions several times a week for at least a year and often for several years. Many people find self-exploration under traditional psychoanalysis to be of value; however, for some people it is unaffordable. In addition, people suffering from acute depression, anxiety, or psychosis typically cannot tolerate the lack of structure in traditional psychoanalysis and need more immediate relief from their symptoms.

In response to these needs, as well as to changes in psychoanalytic theory since Freud's time, newer psychodynamic therapies tend to be more structured and short-term than traditional psychoanalysis. One such therapy is called **interpersonal therapy** (Klerman, Weissman, Rounsaville, & Chevron, 1984). Sessions are scheduled less frequently, usually once a week. There is less emphasis on complete reconstruction of childhood experiences and more attention to problems arising from the way the individual is currently interacting with others. Free association is often replaced with direct discussion of critical issues, and the therapist may be more direct, raising pertinent topics when appropriate rather than waiting for the client to bring them up. Although transference is still considered an important part of the therapeutic process, the therapist may try to limit the intensity of the transference process. Research has found interpersonal therapy to be helpful in the treatment of depression, anxiety, drug addiction, and eating disorders (Markowitz & Weissman, 1995).

Still central, however, is the psychoanalytic therapist's conviction that unconscious motives and fears are at the core of most emotional problems and that insight is essential to a cure (Auld & Hyman, 1991). As we will see in the next section, behavior therapists do not agree with these views.

BEHAVIOR THERAPIES

The term **behavior therapy** includes a number of therapeutic methods based on the principles of learning and conditioning (see Chapter 7). Behavior therapists assume that maladaptive behaviors are learned ways of coping with stress and that some of the techniques developed in experimental research on learning can be used to substitute more appropriate responses for maladaptive ones (Follette & Hayes, 2000). Whereas psychoanalysis is concerned with understanding how the individual's past conflicts influence behavior, behavior therapy focuses more directly on the behavior itself.

Behavior therapists point out that although the achievement of insight is a worthwhile goal, it does not ensure behavioral change. Often we understand why we behave the way we do in a certain situation but are unable to change our behavior. If you are unusually timid about speaking in class, you may be able to trace this fear to past events (your father criticized your opinions whenever you expressed them, your mother made a point of correcting your grammar, you had little experience in public speaking during high school because you were afraid to compete with your older brother, who was captain of the debate team). Understanding the reasons behind your fear does not necessarily make it easier for you to contribute to class discussions.

In contrast to psychodynamic therapy, which attempts to change certain aspects of the personality, behavior therapies attempt to modify behaviors that are maladaptive in specific situations. In the initial session, the therapist listens carefully to the client's statement of the problem. What exactly does the client want to change? Is it a fear of flying or of speaking in public? Difficulty in controlling eating or drinking? Feelings of inadequacy and helplessness? Inability to concentrate and get work done? The first step is to define the problem clearly and break it down into a set of specific therapeutic goals. If, for example, the client complains of general feelings of inadequacy, the therapist will try to get the client to describe these feelings more specifically: to pinpoint the kinds of situations in which they occur and the kinds of behaviors associated with them. Inadequate to do what? To speak up in class or in social situations? To get assignments completed on time? To control eating? Once the behaviors that need to be changed have been specified, the therapist and client work out a treatment program, choosing the treatment method that is most appropriate for the particular problem.

SYSTEMATIC DESENSITIZATION AND IN VIVO EXPOSURE Systematic desensitization is a method of eliminating fears by substituting a response that is incompatible with anxiety—namely, relaxation. (It is difficult to be both relaxed and anxious at the same time.) The client is first trained to relax deeply. One way is to progressively relax various muscles, starting, for example, with the feet and ankles and proceeding up the body to the neck and face. The person learns what muscles feel like when they are truly relaxed and how to discriminate among various degrees of tension. Sometimes drugs and hypnosis are used to help people who cannot relax otherwise.

The next step is to make up a hierarchy of the anxiety-producing situations. The situations are ranked in order from the one that produces the least anxiety to the one that produces the most. In systematic desensitization, the client is then asked to relax and imagine each situation in the hierarchy, starting with the one that is least anxiety-producing. In vivo exposure is a method highly similar to systematic desensitization that requires the client to actually experience the anxiety-producing situations. In vivo exposure is more effective than simply imagining anxiety-producing situations, but some clients need to begin with

imagination and eventually move to actually experiencing feared situations.

An example will make these procedures clearer. Suppose that the client is a woman who suffers from a phobia of snakes. The phobia is so strong that she is afraid to walk in her own back yard, let alone go for a walk in the countryside or on a vacation in a wooded area. Her anxiety hierarchy might begin with a picture of a snake in a book. Somewhere around the middle of the hierarchy might be viewing a snake in a glass cage at the zoo. At the top of the hierarchy would be actually handling a snake. After this woman has learned to relax and has constructed the hierarchy, the therapist begins taking her through her list. In systematic desensitization, she sits with her eyes closed in a comfortable chair while the therapist describes the least anxiety-provoking situation. If she can imagine herself in the situation without any increase in muscle tension, the therapist proceeds to the next item on the list. If the woman reports any anxiety while visualizing a scene, she concentrates on relaxing, and the same scene is visualized until all anxiety has been neutralized. This process continues through a series of sessions until the situation that originally provoked the most anxiety now elicits only relaxation. At this point, the woman has been systematically desensitized to anxiety-provoking situations through the strengthening of an incompatible response—relaxation.

During in vivo exposure, the woman would actually experience each of the situations on her list, beginning with the least feared one, with the coaching of the therapist. Before she actually handled a snake herself, the therapist might model handling the snake without being fearful—the therapist would hold the snake in the client's presence, displaying confidence and no anxiety. Eventually the client would handle the snake herself, allowing it to crawl on her while using relaxation to control her anxiety. In vivo exposure therapy of this sort has proven extremely effective in the treatment of phobias (Bandura, Blanchard, & Ritter, 1969).

The specific learning process operating in in vivo exposure may be extinction. Exposing oneself to a fear-arousing stimulus and discovering that nothing bad happens extinguishes the conditioned fear response. Relaxation may be merely a useful way to encourage a person to confront the feared object or situation. Indeed, if phobic individuals can force themselves to stay in the feared situation for a long period (for example, a claustrophobic person sits in a closet for hours or someone who fears contamination goes for days without washing), the initial terror gradually subsides. The term *flooding* is used to refer to this procedure, a type of in vivo therapy in which a phobic individual is exposed to the most feared object or situation for an extended period without an opportunity to escape. This approach has proved to be

Behavioral treatments for phobias require people to actually confront the object of their phobia.

particularly effective in the treatment of agoraphobia and obsessive-compulsive disorders (Thorpe & Olson, 1997).

SELECTIVE REINFORCEMENT Systematic desensitization and in vivo exposure are based on principles of classical conditioning. **Selective reinforcement,** or strengthening of specific desired behaviors, is based on the principles of operant conditioning and has also proved to be an effective method of modifying behavior, especially with children.

The procedure can be illustrated by the case of a third-grade student who was inattentive in school, refused to complete assignments or participate in class, and spent most of her time daydreaming. In addition, her social skills were poor and she had few friends. The behavior to be reinforced was defined as "on-task" behavior, which included paying attention to schoolwork or instructions from the teacher, completing reading assignments, and taking part in class discussions. The reinforcement consisted of beans that were used as tokens to be exchanged for special privileges that the girl valued, such as standing first in line (three beans) or being allowed to stay after school to help the teacher with special projects (nine beans). Whenever the teacher observed the student performing on-task behaviors, she placed one bean in a jar.

During the first 3 months of treatment, the girl completed 12 units of work, compared with none during the previous 3 months. In the final 3 months, she completed 36 units and was performing at the same level as the rest of the class. A follow-up the next year showed that the girl was maintaining her academic performance. She also showed marked improvement in social skills and was accepted more by the other children (Walker, Hedberg, Clement, & Wright, 1981). This is a common finding: Improving behavior in one area of life often produces benefits in other areas (Kazdin, 1982).

Reinforcement of desirable responses can be accompanied by extinction of undesirable ones. For example, a boy who habitually shouts to get his mother's attention could be ignored whenever he does so and reinforced by her attention only when he comes to her and speaks in a conversational tone.

Operant conditioning procedures involving rewards for desirable responses and no rewards for undesirable ones have been used successfully in dealing with a broad range of childhood problems, including bed-wetting, aggression, tantrums, disruptive classroom behavior, poor school performance, and social withdrawal. Similar procedures have been used with autistic children, retarded adults, and severely disordered mental patients.

MODELING Another effective means of changing behavior is modeling. Modeling is the process by which person learns behaviors by observing and imitating others. Because observing others is a major way in which humans learn, watching people who are displaying adaptive behavior should teach people with maladaptive responses better coping strategies. Observing the behavior of a model (either live or videotaped) has proved effective in reducing fears and teaching new skills. For example, observing a therapist handle a snake can reduce the fears of a person with a snake phobia, making it possible for him or her to eventually handle the snake also.

Modeling is effective in overcoming fears and anxieties because it provides an opportunity to observe someone else go through the anxiety-provoking situation without getting hurt. Watching videotapes of models enjoying a visit to the dentist or going through various hospital procedures has proved successful in helping both children and adults overcome their fears of such experiences (Melamed & Siegel, 1975; Shaw & Thoresen, 1974).

BEHAVIORAL REHEARSAL In a therapy session, modeling is often combined with **behavioral rehearsal,** or role playing. The therapist helps the client rehearse or practice more adaptive behaviors. In the following excerpt, a therapist helps a young man overcome his anxieties about asking women for dates. The young man has been pretending to talk to a woman over the phone and finishes by asking for a date.

> Client: Um, I was wondering, you wouldn't want to go out on a date Saturday night, or anything, would you?
>
> Therapist: Okay, that's a start. Can you think of another way of asking her out that sounds a bit more positive and confident? For example, "There's a concert I'd like to see on Saturday night and I'd like very much to take you, if you are free."

Client: That's great!

Therapist: Okay, you try it.

Client: Um, I've got two tickets to the concert Saturday night. If you don't have anything to do, you might want to come along.

Therapist: That's better. Try it one more time, but this time try to convey to her that you'd really like her to go.

Client: I've got two tickets for Saturday's concert. It would be great if you'd go with me, if you're not busy.

Therapist: Great! Just practice it a couple of more times, and you're ready to pick up the phone.

This example illustrates the use of behavioral rehearsal in a type of behavior therapy known as assertiveness training. Like the young man in the example, many people have trouble asking for what they want or refusing to allow others to take advantage of them. By practicing assertive responses (first in role-playing with the therapist and then in real-life situations), the individual not only reduces anxiety but also develops more effective coping techniques. The therapist determines the kinds of situations in which the person is passive and then helps him or her think of and practice some assertive responses that might be effective. The following are examples of situations that might be worked through during a sequence of therapy sessions:

Someone steps in front of you in line.

A friend asks you to do something that you do not want to do.

Your boss criticizes you unjustly.

You return defective merchandise to a store.

You are annoyed by the conversation of people behind you in a movie theater.

The mechanic did an unsatisfactory job of repairing your car.

Most people do not enjoy dealing with such situations, but some are so fearful of asserting themselves that they say nothing and instead build up feelings of resentment and inadequacy. In assertiveness training, the client rehearses with the therapist effective responses that could be made in such situations and then gradually tries them out in real life. The therapist tries to teach the client to express his or her needs in a way that is straightforward and forceful but is not seen by others as hostile or threatening (see Table 16-1).

SELF-REGULATION Because the client and therapist seldom meet more than once per week, the client must learn to control or regulate his or her own behavior so

● **Table 16-1**
Some Elements of an Assertive Response

Decide what you want to say and stick with it rather than giving in to others the minute they disagree with you. For example, when a clerk says you cannot return a defective product, say, "This is defective and I want to return it" repeatedly until the clerk allows you to return it or at least calls the manager, whom you tell, "This is defective and I want to return it" until you get your money back.

Ask for small, specific changes in a situation or another person's behavior rather than requesting global changes. For example, rather than saying, "I want you to be more loving," say, "I want you to listen to me when I talk."

Use "I" phrases instead of accusatory phrases when discussing a difficult situation with another person. Four pieces to an "I" statement are:
I feel . . .
when you . . .
because . . .
what I want . . .
For example, "*I feel* angry *when you* don't show up for an appointment *because* it wastes my time. *What I want* is for you to call me and cancel our appointment when you think you won't be able to make it."

that progress can be made outside the therapy hour. Moreover, if people feel that they are responsible for their own improvement, they are more likely to maintain whatever gains they make. **Self-regulation** involves monitoring, or observing, one's own behavior and using various techniques—self-reinforcement, self-punishment, control of stimulus conditions, development of incompatible responses—to change maladaptive behavior. An individual monitors his or her behavior by keeping a careful record of the kinds of situations that elicit the maladaptive behavior and the kinds of responses that are incompatible with it. For example, a person who is concerned with alcohol abuse would note the kinds of situations in which he or she is most tempted to drink and would try to control such situations or devise a response that is incompatible with drinking (see Marlatt's Seeing Both Sides essay for an application of these techniques). A man who finds it hard not to join his coworkers in a noontime cocktail might plan to eat lunch at his desk, thereby controlling his drinking behavior by controlling his environment. If he is tempted to relax with a drink upon arriving home from work, he might substitute a game of tennis or a jog around the block as a means of relieving tension. Both of these activities would be incompatible with drinking.

Self-reinforcement is rewarding yourself immediately for achieving a specific goal. The reward could be praising yourself, watching a favorite television program, telephoning a friend, or eating a favorite food. Self-punishment is arranging for an aversive consequence for failing to

This program illustrates the use of learning principles to help control food intake. (After Stuart & Davis, 1972; O'Leary & Wilson, 1975)

Self-Monitoring

Daily Log
Keep a detailed record of everything you eat. Note the amount eaten, the type of food and its caloric value, the time of day, and the circumstances of eating. This record will establish the caloric intake that is maintaining your present weight. It will also help identify the stimuli that elicit and reinforce your eating behavior.

Weight Chart
Decide how much weight you want to lose, and set a weekly weight loss goal. Your weekly goal should be realistic (between 1 and 2 pounds). Record your weight each day on graph paper. In addition to showing how your weight varies with food intake, this visual record will reinforce your dieting efforts as you observe progress toward your goal.

Controlling Stimulus Conditions

Use these procedures to narrow the range of stimuli associated with eating:

1. Eat only at predetermined times, at a specific table, using a special place mat, napkin, dishes, and so forth. Do *not* eat at other times or in other places (for example, while standing in the kitchen).
2. Do *not* combine eating with other activities, such as reading or watching television.
3. Keep in the house only the foods that are permitted on your diet.
4. Shop for food only after having had a full meal; buy only items that are on a previously prepared list.

Modifying Actual Eating Behavior

Use these procedures to break the chain of responses that makes eating automatic.

1. Eat very slowly, paying close attention to the food.
2. Finish chewing and swallowing before putting more food on the fork.
3. Put your utensils down for periodic short breaks before continuing to eat.

Developing Incompatible Responses

When tempted to eat at times other than those specified, find a substitute activity that is incompatible with eating. For example, exercise to music, go for a walk, talk with a friend (preferably one who knows that you are dieting), or study your diet plan and weight graph, noting how much weight you have lost.

Self-Reinforcement

Arrange to reward yourself with an activity that you enjoy (watching television, reading, planning a new wardrobe, visiting a friend) when you have maintained appropriate eating behavior for a day. Plan larger rewards (for example, buying something you want) for a specified amount of weight loss. Self-punishment (other than forgoing a reward) is probably less effective because dieting is a fairly depressing business anyway. But you might decrease the frequency of binge eating by immediately reciting to yourself the aversive consequences or by looking at an unattractive picture of yourself in a bathing suit.

achieve a goal, such as depriving yourself of something you enjoy (not watching a favorite television program, for instance) or making yourself do an unpleasant task (such as cleaning your room). Depending on the kind of be- havior you want to change, various combinations of self-reinforcement, self-punishment, or control of stimuli and responses may be used. Table 16-2 outlines a program for self-regulation of eating.

Often, many of the techniques of behavior therapy are used in combination to treat people with serious mental disorders. Behavior therapy has proven effective for several of the anxiety disorders, including panic disorder, phobias, and obsessive-compulsive disorders (Fals-Stewart & Allen, 1993; Lindsay, Crino, & Andrews, 1997; Ollendick & King, 1998, 2000), for depression (Jacobson & Hollon, 1996), for problems in sexual functioning (Rosen & Leiblum, 1995), and for several childhood disorders (Thorpe & Olson, 1997).

COGNITIVE-BEHAVIOR THERAPIES

The behavior therapy procedures discussed so far have focused on modifying behavior directly. They devote little attention to the individual's thinking and reasoning processes. Initially, behavior therapists discounted the importance of cognition, preferring a strict stimulus-response approach. However, in response to evidence that cognitive factors—thoughts, expectations, and interpretations of events—are important determinants of behavior, many behavior therapists now incorporate cognitions in their approaches to therapy (Bandura, 1986).

Cognitive-behavior therapy is a general term for treatment methods that use behavior modification techniques but also incorporate procedures designed to change maladaptive beliefs (A. T. Beck, Rush, Shaw, & Emery, 1979; J. S. Beck, 1995). The therapist helps the client control disturbing emotional reactions, such as anxiety and depression, by teaching more effective ways of interpreting and thinking about experiences. For example, as we noted in discussing Beck's cognitive theory of depression (see Chapter 15), depressed individuals tend to appraise events from a negative and self-critical viewpoint. They expect to fail rather than succeed, and they tend to magnify failures and minimize successes in evaluating their performance. In treating depression, cognitive-behavior therapists help clients recognize the distortions in their thinking and make changes that are more in line with reality. The following dialogue illustrates how a therapist, through carefully directed questioning, makes a client aware of the unrealistic nature of her beliefs.

> Therapist: Why do you want to end your life?
>
> Client: Without Raymond, I am nothing. . . . I can't be happy without Raymond. . . . But I can't save our marriage.
>
> Therapist: What has your marriage been like?
>
> Client: It has been miserable from the very beginning. . . . Raymond has always been unfaithful. . . . I have hardly seen him in the past five years.
>
> Therapist: You say that you can't be happy without Raymond. . . . Have you found yourself happy when you are with Raymond?

> Client: No, we fight all the time and I feel worse.
>
> Therapist: You say you are nothing without Raymond. Before you met Raymond, did you feel you were nothing?
>
> Client: No, I felt I was somebody.
>
> Therapist: If you were somebody before you knew Raymond, why do you need him [in order] to be somebody now?
>
> Client: (puzzled) Hmmm. . . .
>
> Therapist: If you were free of the marriage, do you think that men might be interested in you—knowing that you were available?
>
> Client: I guess that maybe they would be.
>
> Therapist: Is it possible that you might find a man who would be more constant than Raymond?
>
> Client: I don't know. . . . I guess it's possible. . . .
>
> Therapist: Then what have you actually lost if you break up the marriage?
>
> Client: I don't know.
>
> Therapist: Is it possible that you'll get along better if you end the marriage?
>
> Client: There is no guarantee of that.
>
> Therapist: Do you have a real marriage?
>
> Client: I guess not.
>
> Therapist: If you don't have a real marriage, what do you actually lose if you decide to end the marriage?
>
> Client: (long pause) Nothing, I guess. (Beck, 1976, pp. 280–291)

The behavioral component of the treatment comes into play when the therapist encourages the client to formulate alternative ways of viewing her situation and then test the implications of those alternatives. For example, the woman client in the preceding dialogue might be asked to record her moods at regular intervals and then note how her depression and feelings of self-esteem fluctuate as a function of what she is doing. If she finds that she feels worse after interacting with her husband than when she is alone or is interacting with someone else, this information could serve to challenge her belief that she "can't be happy without Raymond."

A cognitive-behavioral program to help someone overcome agoraphobia might include training in more adaptive thinking, along with in vivo exposure (accompanied excursions that take the individual progressively farther from home). The therapist teaches the client to replace self-defeating internal dialogues ("I'm so nervous, I know I'll faint as soon as I leave the house") with positive self-instructions ("Be calm; I'm not alone; even if I have a panic attack, I can cope"). Table 16-3 de-

● Table 16-3
Coping With Depression

A program for the treatment of depression that combines behavioral and cognitive techniques. This is a condensed description of a 12-session course used to treat depressed individuals in small groups. *(Reprinted with permission from The Coping With Depression Course: Psychoeducational Intervention for Unipolar Depression, by P. M. Lewnsohn, D. O. Antonucio, J. L. Skinmetz, & L. Teri. Copyright © 1984 by Castalia Publishing Company. All rights reserved.)*

Instruction in Self-Change Skills

Pinpointing the target behavior and recording its baseline rate of occurrence; discovering the events or situations that precede the target behavior and the consequences (either positive or negative) that follow it; setting goals for change and choosing reinforcers.

Relaxation Training

Learning progressive muscle relaxation to handle the anxiety that often accompanies depression; monitoring tension in daily situations; and applying relaxation techniques.

Increasing Pleasant Activities

Monitoring the frequency of enjoyable activities and planning weekly schedules so that each day contains a balance between negative/neutral activities and pleasant ones.

Cognitive Strategies

Learning methods for increasing positive thoughts and decreasing negative ones; for identifying irrational thoughts and challenging them; and for using self-instructions to help handle problem situations.

Assertiveness Training

Identifying situations in which being nonassertive adds to feelings of depression; learning to handle social interactions more assertively via modeling and role playing.

Increasing Social Interaction

Identifying the factors that are contributing to low social interaction (such as getting into the habit of doing things alone, feeling uncomfortable due to few social skills); deciding on activities that need to be increased (such as calling friends to suggest getting together) or decreased (such as watching television) in order to increase the level of pleasant social interaction.

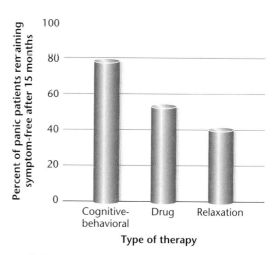

▌Figure 16-3
Percentage of Panic Patients Remaining Symptom-Free After 15 Months

People receiving cognitive-behavioral therapy for panic disorder were more likely to remain symptom-free over 15 months than people receiving only drug therapy or relaxation training. (After Clark et al., 1994)

scribes a program for the treatment of depression that includes techniques for modifying behavior and changing attitudes.

Cognitive-behavior therapists agree that it is important to alter a person's beliefs in order to bring about an enduring change in behavior. Most maintain that behavioral procedures are more powerful than strictly verbal ones in affecting cognitive processes. For example, to overcome anxiety about giving a speech in class, it is helpful to think positively: "I know the material well, and I'm sure I can present my ideas effectively" and "The topic is interesting, and the other students will enjoy what I have to say." But first presenting the speech to a roommate and again before a group of friends will probably do more to reduce anxiety. Successful performance increases our feeling of mastery. In fact, it has been suggested that all therapeutic procedures that are effective give the client a sense of mastery or self-efficacy. Observing others cope and succeed, being verbally persuaded that we can handle a difficult situation, and judging from internal cues that we are relaxed and in control contribute to feelings of self-efficacy. But the greatest sense of efficacy comes from actual performance, from the experience of mastery. In essence, nothing succeeds like success (Bandura, 1995).

Cognitive-behavioral therapies have proven highly effective in treating an array of nonpsychotic conditions, including depression, anxiety disorders, eating disorders, drug and alcohol dependence, and sexual dysfunctions (Chambless & Ollendick, 2001; Fairburn et al., 1995; Jacobson & Hollon, 1996; Margraf, Barlow, Clark, & Telch, 1993; Marlatt, Larimer, Baer, & Quigley, 1993; Rosen & Lieblum, 1995; see Figure 16-3). These therapies tend not only to help people overcome troubling thoughts, feelings, and behaviors but also to prevent relapses after therapy has ended.

HUMANISTIC THERAPIES

Humanistic therapies are based on the humanistic approach to personality discussed in Chapter 13. They emphasize the individual's natural tendency toward growth and self-actualization. Psychological disorders are assumed to arise when circumstances or other people (parents, teachers, spouses) prevent the individual from achieving his or her potential. When this occurs, people begin to deny their true desires, and their potential for growth is reduced. Humanistic therapies seek to help people get in touch with their real selves and make deliberate choices regarding their lives and behavior rather than being controlled by external events.

Like the psychoanalyst, the humanistic therapist attempts to increase the client's awareness of underlying emotions and motives. But the emphasis is on what the individual is experiencing in the here and now, rather than in the past. The humanistic therapist does not interpret the client's behavior (as a psychoanalyst might) or try to modify it (as a behavior therapist would), because this would amount to imposing the therapist's views on the patient. The goal of the humanistic therapist is to facilitate exploration of the individual's own thoughts and feelings and to assist the individual in arriving at his or her own solutions. This approach will become clearer as we look at client-centered therapy (also called *nondirective therapy*), one of the first humanistic therapies.

Client-centered therapy, developed in the 1940s by the late Carl Rogers, is based on the assumption that each individual is the best expert on himself or herself and that people are capable of working out solutions to their own problems. The task of the therapist is to facilitate this process—not to ask probing questions, make interpretations, or suggest courses of action. In fact, Rogers preferred the term *facilitator* to *therapist*, and he called the people he worked with *clients* rather than *patients* because he did not view emotional difficulties as indications of an illness to be cured.

The therapist facilitates the client's progress toward self-insight by restating what the client says about his or her needs and emotions. Rogers believed that the most important qualities for a therapist are empathy, warmth, and genuineness. Empathy refers to the ability to understand the feelings the client is trying to express and the ability to communicate this understanding to the client. The therapist must adopt the client's frame of reference and strive to see the problems as the client sees them. By warmth, Rogers meant acceptance of individuals the way they are, including the conviction that they have the capacity to deal constructively with their problems. A therapist who is genuine is open and honest and does not play a role or operate behind a professional façade. People are reluctant to reveal themselves to those whom they perceive as phony. Rogers believed that a therapist who possesses these three attributes will facilitate the client's growth and self-exploration (Rogers, 1970).

Rogers was the first therapist to make tape recordings of therapy sessions and permit them to be studied and analyzed. He and his colleagues have contributed much to psychotherapy research. Client-centered therapy has some limitations, however. Like psychoanalysis, it appears to be successful only with individuals who are fairly verbal and are motivated to discuss their problems. For people who do not voluntarily seek help or are seriously disturbed and unable to discuss their feelings, more directive methods are usually necessary. In addition, by using the client's self-reports as the only measure of psychotherapeutic effectiveness, the client-centered therapist ignores behavior outside the therapy session. Individuals who feel insecure and ineffective in their interpersonal relationships often need more structured help in modifying their behavior.

SOCIOCULTURAL APPROACHES TO THERAPY

Sociocultural approaches to treatment view the individual as part of a larger system of relationships, influenced by social forces and culture, and believe that this larger system must be addressed in therapy.

GROUP THERAPY Many emotional problems involve difficulties in relating to others, including feelings of isolation, rejection, and loneliness and an inability to form meaningful relationships. Although the therapist can help the client work out some of these problems, the final test lies in how well the person can apply the attitudes and responses learned in therapy to relationships in everyday life. **Group therapy** permits clients to work out their problems in the presence of others, observe how other people react to their behavior, and try out new ways of responding when old ones prove unsatisfactory (Forsyth & Corazzini, 2000). It is often used as a supplement to individual psychotherapy.

Psychoanalytic, humanistic, and cognitive-behaviorist therapists have modified their techniques so that they can be used with groups. Group therapy has been used in a variety of settings: in hospital wards and outpatient psychiatric clinics, with parents of disturbed children, and with teenagers in correctional institutions, to name a few. Typically, a group consists of a small number of individuals (six to eight is considered optimal) who have similar problems. The therapist usually remains in the background, allowing group members to exchange experiences, comment on one another's behavior, and discuss their own problems as well as those of the other members. However, in some groups the therapist is quite active. For example, in a group desensitization session, people who share the same phobias (such as fear of flying or anxiety about tests) may be led through a systematic desensitization hierarchy. Or in a session for training social skills, a group of shy and unassertive individuals may be coached in a series of role-playing scenes.

Group therapy has several advantages over individual therapy. It uses the therapist's resources more efficiently because one therapist can help several people at once. An individual can derive comfort and support from observing that others have similar, perhaps more severe problems. A person can learn vicariously by watching how others behave and can explore attitudes and reactions by interacting with a variety of people, not just with the therapist. Groups are particularly effective when they give participants opportunities to acquire new social skills through modeling and to practice these skills in the group.

Most groups are led by a trained therapist. However, the number and variety of self-help groups—groups that are conducted without a professional therapist—are increasing. **Self-help groups** are voluntary organizations of people who meet regularly to exchange information and support one another's efforts to overcome a common problem. Alcoholics Anonymous is the best known of these groups (see Humphreys's Seeing Both Sides essay for a discussion of AA). Other groups help people cope with specific stressful situations, such as bereavement, divorce, and single parenthood. Table 16-4 lists a variety of self-help groups.

MARITAL AND FAMILY THERAPY Problems in communicating feelings, satisfying one's needs, and responding appropriately to the needs and demands of others become intensified in the intimate context of marriage and family life. To the extent that they involve more than one client and focus on interpersonal relationships, **marital therapy**—in which a married or partnered couple undergoes therapy—and **family therapy**—in which the entire family undergoes therapy together—can be considered specialized forms of group therapy.

The high divorce rate and the number of couples seeking help for difficulties in their relationships have made marital or couples therapy a growing field. Studies show that joint therapy for both partners is more effective in solving marital problems than individual therapy for only one partner (Baucom, Epstein, & Gordon, 2000). Marital therapy can also be very helpful when one partner has a psychological disorder whose symptoms or consequences are disrupting the marriage.

There are many approaches to marital therapy, but most focus on helping the partners communicate their feelings, develop greater understanding and sensitivity to each other's needs, and work on more effective ways of

● **Table 16-4**
Examples of Self-Help Groups

Listed here are some of the self-help groups available in one large community. (After San Diego Mental Health Association, 1989)

AIDS Counseling Program
AIRS (teenage chemical dependency)
Adult Children of Alcoholics
Adults Molested as Children
Affective Disorders Group (mood disorders)
Al-Anon (families of alcoholics)
Ala-Teen (teenage alcohol abuse)
Alcoholics Anonymous
Alzheimer's Disease Family Support Group
Arthritis Support Group
Battered Women's Support Group
Bi-Polar Support Group (manic-depression)
CREATE (college students recovering from mental illness)
Emotional Health Anonymous
Epilepsy Support Group
Gay Men's Coming-Out Group
Grandmothers' Support Group (mothers of teenage mothers)
Lesbian Support Group
Loss Support (grief recovery)
Make Today Count (breast cancer support)
PMS Association (premenstrual syndrome)
Parent Aid (parents at risk for child abuse)
Parents United (sexual abuse)
Parkinson's Disease Support Group
Pre Ala-Teen (child alcohol dependency)
Project Return (recovering mental patients)
Recovery, Inc.
Phobia Foundation
Single Parent Support Group
Survivors of Suicide
Teen Mothers Support Group
Victims of Homicide (family and loved ones)
Voices (schizophrenic support group)

handling their conflicts. Some couples enter marriage with very different and often unrealistic expectations about the roles of husband and wife. The therapist can help them clarify their expectations and work out a mutually agreeable compromise. Sometimes the couple negotiates behavioral contracts, agreeing on the behavior changes each person is willing to make in order to create a more satisfying relationship, and specifying rewards and penalties for making, or not making, the desired changes.

Family therapy overlaps with marital therapy but has a somewhat different origin. It developed in response to the discovery that many people who improved in individual therapy away from their families—often in institutional settings—relapsed when they returned home. It became apparent that many of these people came from disturbed family settings that must be modified if the individual's gains were to be maintained. In the case of children with psychological problems, it is particularly important that the family be treated. The basic premise of family therapy is that the problem shown by the identified patient is a sign that something is wrong with the entire family; the family system is not operating properly. The difficulty may lie in poor communication among family members or in an alliance between some family members that excludes others. For example, a mother whose relationship with her husband is unsatisfactory may focus all her attention on her son. As a result, the husband and daughter feel neglected, and the son, upset by his mother's excessive attention and the resentment directed toward him by his father and sister, develops problems in school. Although the boy's school difficulties may be the reason for seeking treatment, it is clear that they are only a symptom of a more basic family problem.

In family therapy, the family meets regularly with one or two therapists (usually a male and a female). The therapist observes the interactions among family members and tries to help each member become aware of the way he or she relates to the others and how his or her actions may be contributing to the family's problems. Sometimes videotape recordings are played back to make the family members aware of how they interact. At other times, the therapist may visit the family at home to observe conflicts and verbal exchanges as they occur in their natural setting. It often becomes apparent that problem behaviors are being reinforced by the responses of family members. For example, a child's temper tantrums or a teenager's eating problems may be inadvertently reinforced by the attention they elicit from the parents. The therapist can teach the parents to monitor their own and their children's behavior, determine how their reactions may be reinforcing the problem behavior, and then alter the reinforcement contingencies.

An important application of family therapy is in teaching families of people with schizophrenia to communicate more positively and clearly (Goldstein, 1987). People with schizophrenia in families in which conflict and hostility are expressed in hurtful ways and in which family members are overinvolved in each other's lives tend to have more frequent relapses than those in families in which conflict and hostility are expressed more calmly and family members respect each other's independence. Training programs that enhance family members' skills in expressing negative emotion and interacting in positive ways can reduce relapse rates for people with schizophrenia.

Family therapies seek to treat the family as a whole.

COMMUNITY-BASED PROGRAMS A variety of community resources have been developed to serve the psychological needs of different groups. One such resource is the **halfway house,** where patients who have been hospitalized can live while making the transition back to independent living in the community. Residential centers are also available for people who are recovering from alcohol and drug problems, for delinquent or runaway youths, and for battered wives. Rap centers, where troubled teenagers can discuss their problems with other teenagers and with sympathetic counselors, play an important role in many communities, and youth centers provide job counseling, remedial education, and help with family and personal problems.

Crisis intervention provides immediate help for individuals and families undergoing intense stress. During periods of acute emotional turmoil, people often feel overwhelmed and incapable of dealing with the situation. They may not be able to wait for a therapy appointment, or they may not know where to turn. One form of crisis intervention is provided by 24-hour walk-in services, often in a community mental health center, where a person can receive immediate attention. A therapist helps clarify the problem, provides reassurance, suggests a plan of action, and mobilizes the support of other agencies or family members. This kind of therapy is usually short-term (five or six sessions) and provides the support the person requires to handle the crisis at hand. Such short-term intervention often makes hospitalization unnecessary.

Another form of crisis intervention is the telephone hot line. Telephone crisis centers are usually staffed by volunteers under the direction of mental health professionals. Some focus specifically on suicide prevention; others help distressed callers find the particular kind of assistance they need. The volunteers usually receive training that emphasizes listening with care, evaluating the potential for suicide, conveying empathy and understanding, providing information about community resources, offering hope and reassurance, and recording the caller's name and phone number before he or she hangs up so that a professional can follow up on the problem. Most major cities in the United States have developed some form of telephone hot line to help people who are undergoing periods of severe stress, as well as specialized hot lines to deal with child abuse, rape victims, battered wives, and runaways. The phone numbers are widely publicized in the hope of reaching those who need help.

Most of the community programs we have discussed could not function without the help of paraprofessionals. Because the need for psychological services outstrips the supply of available therapists, concerned citizens can play a valuable role. People of all ages and backgrounds have been trained to work in the field of community mental health. College students have served as companions for hospitalized patients. Older individuals who have raised families have been trained to work with adolescents in community clinics, to counsel parents of youngsters with behavior problems, and to work with schizophrenic children. Former mental patients, recovered drug addicts, and ex-convicts have been trained to help individuals faced with problems similar to the ones they have experienced.

Many residential mental health programs are run by nonprofessionals in consultation with trained therapists. An outstanding example is Achievement Place, a home-style facility in Kansas where couples act as surrogate parents for a group of youngsters who have been referred by the courts because of delinquent behavior. Behavior therapy methods are used to extinguish aggressive behavior and reward social skills. Follow-up data show that youths who graduate from Achievement Place have fewer contacts with courts and police and achieve slightly higher grades than youths who are placed on probation or in a traditional institution for delinquents (Fixsen, Phillips, Phillips, & Wolf, 1976). There are numerous other Achievement Places throughout the United States modeled after the original Kansas facility.

CULTURALLY SPECIFIC THERAPIES Many cultural groups, both within modern industrialized countries and in developing countries, have their own forms of therapy for distressed people. Native American treatments focus on the religious practices, psychological well-being, and physical health of the individual (LaFromboise, Trimble, & Mohatt, 1998). Distressed persons are encouraged to view themselves as embedded in their community and as an expression of the community. Their family and friends participate with them in ceremonies involving prayers, songs, and dances that emphasize their cultural heritage and the reintegration of the individual into the cultural network. In addition, the individual may be pre-

Some Native American groups have their own healing rituals for people with psychological distress.

scribed herbal medicines that have been used for hundreds of years.

Latinos in the southwestern United States and Mexico may consult folk healers, known as *curanderos* or *curanderas* (Koss-Chioino, 1995; Martinez, 1993). *Curanderos* use religiously based rituals to overcome the folk illnesses believed to cause psychological and physical problems. These illnesses may be the result of curses placed on the individuals. Healing rituals include prayers, the use of holy palm, and incantations. *Curanderos* may also apply healing ointments or oils and prescribe herbal medicines.

AN ECLECTIC APPROACH

There are many variations of psychotherapy besides the ones described here. Several are listed in Table 16-5. Most psychotherapists do not adhere strictly to any single method. Instead, they take an eclectic approach, selecting from the different techniques the ones that they

● **Table 16-5**
Other Approaches to Psychotherapy

Listed here are several psychotherapies that are not discussed in the text.

Name	Focus of Therapy	Principal Methods
Gestalt therapy	To become aware of the whole personality by working through unresolved conflicts and discovering aspects of the individual's being that are blocked from awareness. Emphasis is on becoming intensely aware of how one is feeling and behaving at the moment.	Therapy in a group setting, but therapist works with one individual at a time. Acting out fantasies, dreams, or the two sides to a conflict are methods used to increase awareness. Combines psychoanalytic emphasis on resolving internal conflicts with behaviorist emphasis on awareness of one's behavior and humanistic concern for self-actualization.
Reality therapy	To clarify the individual's values and evaluate current behavior and future plans in relation to these values. To force the individual to accept responsibility.	Therapist helps the individual perceive the consequences of possible courses of action and decide on a realistic solution or goal. Once a plan of action has been chosen, a contract may be signed in which the client agrees to follow through.
Rational-emotive therapy	To replace irrational ideas (It is essential to be loved and admired by everyone all the time; I should be competent in all respects; people have little control over their sorrow and unhappiness) with more realistic ones. Assumes that cognitive change will produce emotional changes.	Therapist attacks and contradicts the individual's ideas (sometime subtly, sometimes directly) in an attempt to persuade her or him to take a more rational view of the situation. Similar to Beck's cognitive therapy, but the therapist is more direct and confrontive.
Transactional analysis	To become aware of the intent behind the individual's communications; to eliminate subterfuge and deceit so that the individual can interpret his or her behavior accurately.	Therapy in a group setting. Communications between married couples or group members are analyzed in terms of the part of the personality that is speaking—"parent," "child," or "adult" (similar to Freud's superego, id, and ego)—and the intent of the message. Destructive social interactions or "games" are exposed for what they are.
Hypnotherapy	To relieve the symptoms and strengthen ego processes by helping the individual set reality aside and make constructive use of imagery.	Therapist uses various hypnotic procedures in an attempt to reduce conflict and doubt by focusing the individual's attention, to modify symptoms through direct suggestion or displacement, and to strengthen the individual's ability to cope.

feel are most appropriate, given the client's personality and specific symptoms. Although their theoretical orientation may be toward a particular method or school (for example, more psychoanalytic than behaviorist), eclectic psychotherapists feel free to discard concepts that they view as not especially helpful and to select techniques from other schools. In addition, many psychotherapists use both psychotherapeutic techniques and drug therapies in treating clients with more severe problems. (Psychotherapists who are not physicians will work with a psychiatrist who will prescribe drugs for their patients.)

In dealing with a highly anxious individual, for instance, an eclectic psychotherapist might first prescribe tranquilizers or relaxation training to help reduce the client's level of anxiety. (Most psychoanalysts would not take this approach, however, because they believe that anxiety is necessary to motivate the client to explore his or her conflicts.) To help the client understand the origins of his or her problems, the therapist might discuss certain aspects of the patient's history but might consider it unnecessary to explore childhood experiences to the extent that a psychoanalyst would. The therapist might use educational techniques, such as providing information about sex and reproduction to help relieve the anxieties of an adolescent boy who feels guilty about his sexual impulses, or explaining the functioning of the autonomic nervous system to reassure an anxious woman that some of her symptoms, such as heart palpitations and hand tremors, are not indications of a disease.

Recognizing that often no single therapeutic approach deals successfully with all aspects of a problem, more and more therapists are specializing in specific problems. For example, some clinicians specialize in sexual dysfunction. They learn all they can about the

"I UTILIZE THE BEST FROM FREUD, THE BEST FROM JUNG AND THE BEST FROM MY UNCLE MARTY, A VERY SMART FELLOW."

physiological processes that lead to orgasm; the effects of drugs such as alcohol, tranquilizers, and other medications on sexual performance; and how such factors as anxiety, sexual traumas, and poor communication between partners contribute to sexual dysfunction. Once they have learned all they can about the variables involved in normal and abnormal sexual functioning, they examine the various therapeutic systems to see what techniques can be applied to specific problems. Although sex therapists may draw upon all of the approaches we have discussed, biological and cognitive-behavioral methods are most often used in treating sexual dysfunctions.

Other therapists specialize in anxiety, depression, alcoholism, and marital problems. Some concentrate on certain age groups, seeking to learn all they can about the problems of children, adolescents, or the aged. Within their area of specialization, therapists generally use an eclectic approach.

SPECIAL ISSUES IN TREATING CHILDREN

Every therapy we have described has probably been used at one time or another to treat children and adolescents with psychological disorders. Studies of the effectiveness of psychological and biological therapies generally show that children and adolescents who receive therapy have better outcomes than those who receive no therapy (Roberts, Vernberg, & Jackson, 2000). The effectiveness of any specific type of therapy may depend largely on the type of disorder the child or adolescent has.

Designing and applying effective therapies for children and adolescents is made difficult by a number of factors. First, the therapy must be matched to the child's developmental level. Children must be able to under-

stand what the therapist is saying and participate in the therapy to benefit from it. Therapies that are over their heads do them little good. Second, children are embedded in families, and often the family as well as the child must be treated. Yet, sometimes the family refuses to be treated or to recognize how they may be contributing to the child's problems. Finally, children and adolescents seldom refer themselves for treatment but instead are most often brought to treatment by their parents or other adults. This can substantially reduce their motivation to engage in therapy.

Unfortunately, most children who could benefit from therapy do not receive it. Treatment facilities specializing in children's problems are not available in many parts of the United States. Perhaps 50% of psychologically disturbed children receive advice or medications only from their family physicians, who are not trained in the assessment and treatment of psychological disorders (Tuma, 1989). The child welfare system sees many troubled children, often the victims of abuse and neglect. Increasingly, such children are placed in long-term foster care rather than given specialized psychological treatment. Many children in the juvenile justice system suffer from psychological disorders, but few receive long-term intensive treatment (Tuma, 1989). There is considerable room for the expansion of services to psychologically disturbed children.

THE EFFECTIVENESS OF PSYCHOTHERAPY

How effective is psychotherapy? Which methods work best? One survey of the American public found that most people who have had psychotherapy think it helped them (Figure 16-4; Seligman, 1995). In describing each of the psychotherapies, we mentioned some studies of their effectiveness. In this section, we look briefly at how research on the effectiveness of therapy is done (see Haaga & Stiles, 2000).

EVALUATING PSYCHOTHERAPY It is difficult to objectively evaluate the effectiveness of psychotherapy because so many variables must be considered. For instance, some people with psychological problems get better without any professional treatment. This phenomenon is called *spontaneous remission*. People with some types of mental disorders do improve simply with the passage of time. More often, however, improvement that occurs in the absence of treatment is not spontaneous. Rather, it is the result of external events such as the help of another person or changes in the individual's life situation.

Many emotionally disturbed people who do not seek professional assistance improve with the help of a nonprofessional, such as a friend, teacher, or religious ad-

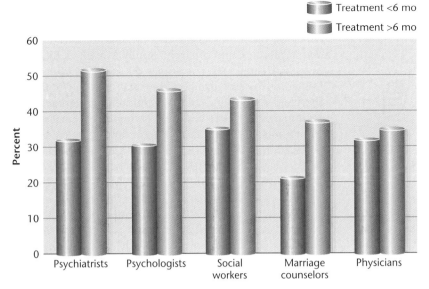

Treatment <6 mo
Treatment >6 mo

▌Figure 16-4
Percentage of People Who Reported That Treatment "Made Things a Lot Better" in a Study by *Consumer Reports* (1995)

A novel study by the magazine *Consumer Reports* simply asked people who had received some treatment for psychological symptoms whether it had been helpful or not. (M. E. P. Seligman (1995). The effectiveness of psychotherapy: The Consumer Reports study. *American Psychologist, 50,* 965–974. Copyright © 1995 by the American Psychological Association. Reprinted with permission.)

viser. We cannot consider these recoveries to be spontaneous, but because they are not due to psychotherapy, they are included in the rate of spontaneous remission, which ranges from about 30% to 60%, depending on the particular disorder being studied (Haaga & Stiles, 2000). To allow for those who would have improved without treatment, any evaluation of psychotherapy must compare a treated group with an untreated control group. Psychotherapy is judged to be effective if the client's improvement after therapy is greater than any improvement that occurs without therapy over the same period. The ethical problem of allowing someone to go without treatment is usually resolved by composing the control group of individuals on a waiting list. Members of the waiting-list control group are interviewed at the beginning of the study to gather baseline information, but they receive no treatment until after the study. Unfortunately, the longer the study (and time is needed to measure improvement, especially with insight therapies), the harder it is to keep people on a waiting list.

A second major problem in evaluating psychotherapy is measuring the outcome. How do we decide whether a person has been helped by therapy? We cannot always rely on the individual's own assessment. Some people report that they are feeling better simply to please the therapist or to convince themselves that their money was well spent. The therapist's evaluation of the treatment as successful cannot always be considered an objective criterion, either. The therapist has a vested interest in proclaiming that the client is better. And sometimes the changes that the therapist observes during the therapy session do not carry over into real-life situations. Assessment of improvement, therefore, should include at least three independent measures: the client's evaluation of progress, the therapist's evaluation, and the judgment of third parties such as family members and friends or a clinician not involved in the treatment.

Despite these problems, researchers have been able to conduct many psychotherapy evaluation studies. In 1952, the well-known British psychologist Hans Eysenck stunned the field when he reviewed studies evaluating the effectiveness of psychotherapy and concluded that psychotherapy did not work. People who had received psychotherapy apparently fared no better than people who were not treated or were placed on a waiting list. The number and quality of studies evaluating psychotherapies prior to 1952 was limited, however. Not surprisingly, Eysenck's review prompted a great deal of new research.

Several reviews of this research over the last five decades have concluded that psychotherapy does indeed have positive effects and is better than no treatment at all or various placebos (Lambert & Bergin, 1994; Luborsky, Singer, & Luborsky, 1975; Smith, Glass, & Miller, 1980; Wampold et al., 1997). In 1980, for example, a group of investigators located 475 published studies that compared at least one therapy group with an untreated control group. Using the statistical procedure known as meta-analysis (see Chapter 6), they determined the magnitude of effect for each study by comparing the average change produced in treatment (on measures such as self-esteem, anxiety, and achievement in work and school) with that experienced by the control group. They concluded that individuals receiving therapy were better off than those who had received no treatment. The average psychotherapy patient showed greater improvement than 80% of the untreated patients (Smith, Glass, & Miller, 1980). A subsequent review that analyzed a new sample of studies yielded comparable results (Shapiro & Shapiro, 1982).

COMPARING PSYCHOTHERAPIES Psychotherapy produces greater improvement than no treatment, but are the different therapeutic approaches equally effective? A number of reviews have analyzed studies in which the results of different psychotherapies (usually including behavioral, cognitive-behavioral, and sometimes client-centered therapies) were compared (Bergin & Lambert, 1979; Rachman & Wilson, 1980; Smith, Glass, & Miller, 1980). The conclusion of most of these reviews is that there is little difference in effectiveness between therapies. How can therapies that espouse such different methods produce such similar results? Numerous possible explanations have been suggested (Stiles, Shapiro, & Elliott, 1986). We will discuss two of them here.

Perhaps certain therapies are effective for certain problems or disorders but relatively ineffective for others. When specific therapies are used to treat a wide range of disorders, they may help in some cases but not in others. Thus, averaging results over cases may conceal the special strengths of a particular therapy. We need to know which treatment is effective for which problem (Chambless & Hollon, 1998). In several controlled studies, different types of psychotherapy were compared with drug therapy or with controls in which people received no therapy for a specific disorder. These studies clearly suggest that certain forms of psychotherapy can be highly effective in the treatment of depression, anxiety disorders, eating disorders, substance abuse disorders, and several childhood disorders (De Rubeis & Crits-Cristoph, 1998; Kazdin & Weisz, 1998; Roth et al., 1996). Psychotherapy can also help reduce symptoms of autism and schizophrenia and lower the risk of relapse in schizophrenia (Hogarty, 1986; Kazdin & Weisz, 1998).

Not all forms of psychotherapy have undergone rigorous empirical tests for effectiveness, however. In general, proponents of behavioral and cognitive approaches have been interested in testing the efficacy of their therapies, so many studies have focused on these types of therapies. In contrast, proponents of psychodynamic and humanistic therapies have been less concerned with empirical tests of their therapies (De Rubeis & Crits-Cristoph, 1998).

Another reason why different psychotherapies may be equally effective in helping clients is because they all share certain factors. It may be these common factors, rather than the specific therapeutic techniques employed, that promote positive change.

COMMON FACTORS IN PSYCHOTHERAPIES

One school of therapy emphasizes insight; another, modeling and reinforcement; yet another, rational cognitions. But perhaps these variables are not the crucial ones. Other factors that are common to most psychotherapies may be more important (Garfield, 1994; Orlinsky & Howard, 1987; Snyder, Ilardi, Michael, & Cheavens,

2000). They include a strong alliance between the therapist and client, reassurance and support, desensitization, reinforcement of adaptive responses, and insight.

AN INTERPERSONAL RELATIONSHIP OF WARMTH AND TRUST Regardless of the type of therapy, in a good therapeutic relationship the client and the therapist have mutual respect and regard. The client must believe that the therapist understands and is concerned with his or her problems. A therapist who understands our problems and believes we can solve them earns our trust, which increases our sense of competence and our confidence that we can succeed.

Our problems often seem insurmountable and unique to us. Discussing them with an expert who accepts our difficulties as not unusual and indicates that they can be resolved is reassuring. Having someone help us with problems that we have not been able to solve alone also provides a sense of support and a feeling of hope, and hope may be critical to recovery from psychological problems (Snyder et al., 2000). In fact, the most successful therapists, regardless of method, are those who form a helpful, supportive relationship with their clients (Luborsky, McLellan, Woody, O'Brien, & Auerbach, 1985).

DESENSITIZATION We have already talked about systematic desensitization, the specific techniques of behavior therapy aimed at helping individuals lose their fear of certain objects or situations. But many types of psychotherapy can encourage a broader kind of desensitization. When we discuss troubling events and emotions in the accepting atmosphere of a therapy session, they gradually lose their threatening quality. Problems that we brood about alone can become magnified beyond proportion, and sharing those problems with someone else often makes them seem less serious. Several other hypotheses can also explain how desensitization occurs in psychotherapy. For example, putting disturbing events into words may help us reappraise the situation in a more realistic manner. From the viewpoint of learning theory, repeatedly discussing distressing experiences in the security of a therapeutic setting may gradually extinguish the anxiety associated with them. Whatever the process, desensitization does appear to be common to many kinds of psychotherapy.

REINFORCEMENT OF ADAPTIVE RESPONSES Behavior therapists use reinforcement as a technique to increase positive attitudes and actions. But any therapist who wins the trust of a patient serves as a reinforcing agent because the therapist tends to express approval of behaviors or attitudes that are conducive to better adjustment, while ignoring or expressing disapproval of maladaptive attitudes or responses. Which responses are re-inforced depends on the therapist's orientation and therapeutic goals. The use of reinforcement may be intentional or unintentional; in some instances, the therapist may be unaware that he or she is reinforcing or failing to reinforce a particular behavior. For example, client-centered therapists believe in letting the client determine what is discussed during the therapy sessions, and they do not wish to influence the trend of the client's conversation. However, reinforcement can be subtle; a smile, a nod, or a simple "um hmm" in response to certain statements may increase the likelihood of their recurrence.

Because the goal of all psychotherapies is to bring about a change in the client's attitudes and behaviors, some type of learning must take place in therapy. The therapist needs to be aware of his or her role in influencing the client by means of reinforcement and should use this knowledge to facilitate desired changes.

UNDERSTANDING OR INSIGHT All of the psychotherapies we have been discussing provide an explanation of the client's difficulties—how they arose, why they persist, and how they can be changed (Frank & Frank, 1991). For a patient in psychoanalysis, this explanation may take the form of gradual understanding of repressed childhood fears and the ways in which these unconscious feelings have contributed to current problems. A behavior therapist might inform the client that current fears are the result of previous conditioning and can be conquered by learning responses that are incompatible with the current ones. A client in a cognitive-behavior treatment program might be told that his or her difficulties stem from the irrational belief that one must be perfect or must be loved by everyone.

How can such different explanations all produce positive results? Perhaps the precise nature of the insights and understanding provided by the therapist is relatively unimportant. It may be more important to provide the client with an explanation for the behavior or feelings that are so distressing and to present a set of activities (such as free association or relaxation training) that both the therapist and the client believe will alleviate the distress. A person who is experiencing disturbing symptoms and is unsure of their cause or how serious they might be will feel reassured by a professional who seems to know what the problem is and offers ways of relieving it. The knowledge that change is possible gives rise to hope, and hope is an important variable in facilitating change.

Our discussion of the factors shared by all forms of psychotherapy is not intended to deny the value of some specific treatment methods. Perhaps the most effective therapist is one who recognizes the importance of these common factors and utilizes them in a planned manner

for all patients but also selects the specific procedures that are most appropriate for each individual.

◆ Interim Summary

- Psychotherapy is the treatment of mental disorders by psychological means. One type of psychotherapy is psychoanalysis, which was developed by Freud. Free association, dream analysis, and transference are used to help the patient gain insight into problems. Contemporary psychodynamic therapies are briefer than traditional psychoanalysis and place more emphasis on the client's current interpersonal problems.

- Behavior therapies apply methods based on learning principles to modify the client's behavior, including systematic desensitization, in vivo exposure, reinforcement of adaptive behaviors, modeling and rehearsal of appropriate behavior, and techniques for self-regulation of behavior.

- Cognitive-behavior therapies use behavior modification techniques but also incorporate procedures for changing maladaptive beliefs. The therapist helps the client replace irrational interpretations of events with more realistic ones.

- Humanistic therapies help clients become aware of their real selves and solve their problems with a minimum of intervention by the therapist. Carl Rogers, who developed client-centered psychotherapy, believed that the therapist must have three characteristics in order to promote the client's growth and self-exploration: empathy, warmth, and genuineness.

- Sociocultural approaches view individuals as embedded in larger social systems, including families and societies. Community-based programs seek to integrate people with mental disorders back into the community while providing treatment. Several cultures have treatments specific to that culture and based on their own religious and cultural beliefs.

- The effectiveness of psychotherapy is hard to evaluate because of the difficulty of defining a successful outcome and controlling for spontaneous remission. Factors common to the various psychotherapies—a warm and trustful interpersonal relationship, reassurance and support, desensitization, insight, and reinforcement of adaptive responses—may be more important in producing positive change than the specific therapeutic methods used.

◆ Critical Thinking Questions

1. How might a psychotherapist adapt the therapeutic methods described in this section to help a person

with schizophrenia? Which methods do you think would be helpful for a person with schizophrenia? Which methods would not be helpful?

2. A major controversy these days is whether medical insurance should cover the cost of psychotherapy. Do you think it should or should not? What is your judgment based upon?

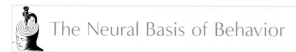 The Neural Basis of Behavior

BIOLOGICAL THERAPIES

The biological approach to abnormal behavior assumes that mental disorders, like physical illnesses, are caused by biochemical or physiological dysfunctions of the brain. Biological therapies include the use of drugs and electroconvulsive shock.

PSYCHOTHERAPEUTIC DRUGS

By far the most successful biological therapy is the use of drugs to modify mood and behavior (see the Concept Review Table for a review). The discovery in the early 1950s of drugs that relieved some of the symptoms of schizophrenia represented a major breakthrough in the treatment of severely disturbed individuals. Intensely agitated patients no longer had to be physically restrained by straitjackets, and patients who had been spending

most of their time hallucinating and exhibiting bizarre behavior became more responsive and functional. As a result, psychiatric wards became more manageable, and patients could be discharged more quickly. A few years later, the discovery of drugs that could relieve severe depression had a similar beneficial effect on hospital management and population. We saw in Figure 16-1 the reduction in the number of mental hospital residents after the introduction of antipsychotic and antidepressant drugs. At about the same time, drugs were being developed to relieve anxiety.

ANTIPSYCHOTIC DRUGS The first drugs that were found to relieve the symptoms of schizophrenia belonged to the family called **phenothiazines.** Examples are Thorazine (chlorpromazine) and Prolixin (fluphenazine). These drugs have been called *major tranquilizers,* but this term is not really appropriate because they do not act on the nervous system in the same way as barbiturates or antianxiety drugs. They may cause some drowsiness and lethargy, but they do not induce deep sleep, even in massive doses. They also seldom create the pleasant, slightly euphoric feeling associated with low doses of antianxiety drugs. In fact, the psychological effects of the antipsychotic drugs when administered to normal individuals are usually unpleasant. These drugs are seldom abused.

In Chapter 15, we discussed the theory that schizophrenia is caused by excessive activity of the neurotransmitter dopamine. Antipsychotic drugs block dopamine receptors. Because the drugs' molecules are structurally similar to dopamine molecules, they bind to the postsynaptic receptors of dopamine neurons,

CONCEPT REVIEW TABLE
Drug Treatments for Mental Disorders

These are the major types of drugs used to treat several kinds of mental disorders.

Type of Drug	Purpose	Mode of Action
Antipsychotic drugs (e.g., Thorazine, Haldol, Clozaril)	Reduce symptoms of psychosis (loss of reality testing, hallucinations, delusions)	Block dopamine receptors
Antidepressant drugs (e.g., Elavil, Prozac)	Reduce symptoms of depression	Increase functional levels of serotonin and norepinephrine
Lithium	Reduce symptoms of bipolar disorder (mania and depression)	Regulates levels of serotonin, norepinephrine, and other neurotransmitters
Antianxiety drugs (e.g., Valium, Xanax)	Reduce symptoms of anxiety	Depresses central nervous system
Stimulants (e.g., Ritalin, Dexedrine)	Increase attention and concentration	Possibly by increasing levels of dopamine

thereby blocking the access of dopamine to its receptors. (The drug itself does not activate the receptors.) A single synapse has many receptor molecules. If all of them are blocked, transmission across the synapse will fail. If only some of them are blocked, transmission will be weakened. The clinical potency of an antipsychotic drug is directly related to its ability to compete for dopamine receptors.

Antipsychotic drugs are effective in alleviating hallucinations and confusion and restoring rational thought processes. These drugs do not cure schizophrenia, and most patients must continue to use the drugs to function outside of a hospital. Many of the characteristic symptoms of schizophrenia—emotional blunting, seclusiveness, difficulties in sustaining attention—remain. Nevertheless, antipsychotic drugs shorten the length of time patients must be hospitalized, and they prevent relapse. Studies of people with schizophrenia living in the community find that the relapse rate for those taking one of the phenothiazines is typically half the relapse rate for those receiving a placebo (Hogarty et al., 1979).

Unfortunately, antipsychotic drugs do not help all people with schizophrenia. In addition, the drugs have unpleasant side effects—dryness of the mouth, blurred vision, difficulty in concentrating—that prompt many patients to discontinue their medication. One of the most serious side effects is a neurological disorder known as **tardive dyskinesia,** which involves involuntary movements of the tongue, face, mouth, or jaw. Patients with this disorder may involuntarily smack their lips, make sucking sounds, stick out their tongue, puff their cheeks, or make other bizarre movements, over and over again. Tardive dyskinesia is often irreversible and may occur in more than 20% of people who use antipsychotic drugs for long periods (Morgenstern & Glazer, 1993).

In recent years, new drugs called **atypical antipsychotics** have been found to reduce symptoms of schizophrenia without causing so many side effects (Wilson & Clausen, 1995). These drugs include clozapine and risperidone. They appear to work by binding to a different type of dopamine receptor than the other drugs, although they also influence several other neurotransmitters, including serotonin.

ANTIDEPRESSANT DRUGS Antidepressant drugs help elevate the mood of depressed individuals. These drugs energize, apparently by increasing the availability of two neurotransmitters (norepinephrine and serotonin) whose levels are deficient in some cases of depression (see Chapter 15). Antidepressant drugs act in different ways to increase neurotransmitter levels. **Monoamine oxidase (MAO) inhibitors** block the activity of an enzyme that can destroy both norepinephrine and serotonin, thereby increasing the concentration of these two

neurotransmitters in the brain. **Tricyclic antidepressants** prevent the reuptake of serotonin and norepinephrine, thereby prolonging the action of the neurotransmitter. (Recall that reuptake is the process by which neurotransmitters are drawn back into the nerve terminals that released them.) Both classes of drugs have proved effective in relieving depression.

Like the antipsychotic drugs, the antidepressants can produce some undesirable side effects. The most common of these are dry mouth, blurred vision, constipation, and urinary retention. They can also cause a severe drop in blood pressure when a person stands up, as well as changes in heart rate and rhythm. An overdose of tricyclic antidepressants can be fatal, a serious concern when a depressed patient may be suicidal. The MAO inhibitors can interact with certain foods, including cheese, chocolate, and red wine, to create severe cardiac problems.

The search for drugs that are more effective, have fewer side effects, and act more quickly has intensified in the past 20 years. As a result, new drugs appear on the market almost daily. The **serotonin reuptake inhibitors** selectively increase serotonin levels by blocking its reuptake. Examples are Prozac (fluoxetine), Paxil (paroxetine), and Zoloft (sertraline). Even more recent drugs increase the availability of both serotonin and norepinephrine (such as Remeron). In addition to relieving depression, these drugs have proved helpful in treating the anxiety disorders, including obsessive-compulsive disorder and panic disorder (Schatzberg, 2000). They tend to produce fewer side effects than the other antidepressants, although they can cause inhibited orgasm, nausea and diarrhea, dizziness, and nervousness.

People with bipolar disorder often take an antidepressant medication to control their depression but must take other drugs to control their mania. **Lithium reduces extreme mood swings and returns the individual to a more normal emotional state.** It appears to do so by stabilizing a number of neurotransmitter systems, including serotonin and dopamine, and may also stabilize levels of the neurotransmitter glutamate (Thase et al., 2002). People with bipolar disorder who take lithium must take it even when they are not suffering from acute mania. Otherwise, about 80% will lapse into new episodes of mania or depression (Maj, Pirozzi, Magliano, & Bartoli, 1998).

Unfortunately, only about 30% to 50% of people with bipolar disorder respond to lithium (Bowden, 2000; Thase et al., 2002). In addition, it has severe side effects, including abdominal pain, nausea, vomiting, diarrhea, tremors, and twitches (Jamison, 1995). Patients complain of blurred vision and problems in concentration and attention that interfere with their ability to work. Lithium can cause kidney dysfunction, birth defects, and a form of diabetes if taken by women during the first trimester of pregnancy.

Anticonvulsant medications (such as Tegretol, Valproate and Depakote) are now commonly used to treat bipolar disorder. These drugs can be highly effective in reducing the symptoms of severe and acute mania but do not seem to be as effective as lithium for long-term treatment of bipolar disorder (Post et al., 1998). The side effects of the anticonvulsants include dizziness, rash, nausea, and drowsiness. Antipsychotic medications may also be prescribed for people who suffer severe mania (Post et al., 1998).

ANTIANXIETY DRUGS Several drugs traditionally used to treat anxiety belong to the family known as **benzodiazepines.** They are commonly known as tranquilizers and are marketed under such trade names as Valium (diazepam), Librium (chlordiazepoxide), and Xanax (alprazolam). Antianxiety drugs reduce tension and cause drowsiness. Like alcohol and the barbiturates, they depress the action of the central nervous system. Family physicians often prescribe tranquilizers to help people cope during difficult periods in their lives. The drugs are also used to treat anxiety disorders, withdrawal from alcohol, and physical disorders related to stress. For example, in the treatment of a phobia, antianxiety drugs may be combined with systematic desensitization to help the individual relax when confronting the feared situation.

Although tranquilizers may be useful on a short-term basis, their overall benefits are debatable and they clearly are overprescribed and misused. Until quite recently (before some of the dangers became apparent), Valium and Librium were the two most widely prescribed drugs in this country (Julien, 1992). Long-term use of tranquilizers can lead to physical dependence (see Chapter 6). Although tranquilizers are not as addictive as barbiturates, tolerance does develop with repeated use, and the individual experiences severe withdrawal symptoms if use of the drug is discontinued. In addition, tranquilizers impair concentration, including driving performance, and can cause death if combined with alcohol.

In recent years, researchers have discovered that certain antidepressant drugs also reduce symptoms of anxiety. This is particularly true of the serotonin reuptake inhibitors discussed previously. These drugs may relieve anxiety as well as depression because they affect biochemical disturbances that are common to both conditions.

STIMULANTS Stimulant drugs are used to treat the attentional problems of children with attention deficit hyperactivity disorder (ADHD). One of the most commonly used stimulants has the trade name Ritalin.

Although it may seem odd to give a stimulant to a hyperactive child, between 60% and 90% of children with ADHD respond to these drugs with decreases in disruptive behavior and increases in attention (Gadow, 1992). Stimulant drugs may work by increasing levels of dopamine in the synapses of the brain.

The use of Ritalin is a subject of controversy because some schools and physicians have been too quick to diagnose ADHD in schoolchildren and to prescribe Ritalin for them (Hinshaw, 1994). Stimulant drugs have significant side effects, including insomnia, headaches, tics, and nausea (Gadow, 1991, 1992). Children must be accurately diagnosed with ADHD before stimulant drugs are prescribed.

In sum, drug therapy has reduced the severity of some types of mental disorders. Many individuals who would require hospitalization otherwise can function within the community with the help of these drugs. On the other hand, there are limitations to the application of drug therapy. All therapeutic drugs can produce undesirable side effects. Many people with medical problems, as well as women who are pregnant or nursing, often cannot take psychoactive drugs. In addition, many psychologists feel that these drugs alleviate symptoms without requiring the patient to face the personal problems that may be contributing to the disorder or may have been caused by the disorder (such as marital problems caused by the behaviors of a manic person).

ELECTROCONVULSIVE THERAPY

In **electroconvulsive therapy (ECT),** also known as electroshock therapy, a mild electric current is applied to the brain to produce a seizure similar to an epileptic convulsion. ECT was a popular treatment from about 1940 to 1960, before antipsychotic and antidepressant drugs became readily available. Today it is used primarily in cases of severe depression when the patient has failed to respond to drug therapy.

ECT has been the subject of much controversy. At one time it was used indiscriminately in mental hospitals to treat such disorders as alcoholism and schizophrenia, for which it produced no beneficial results. Before more refined procedures were developed, ECT was a frightening experience for the patient, who was often awake until the electric current triggered the seizure and produced momentary unconsciousness. The patient frequently suffered confusion and memory loss afterward. Occasionally, the intensity of the muscle spasms accompanying the brain seizure resulted in physical injuries.

Today, ECT is much safer. The patient is given a short-acting anesthesia and injected with a muscle

Can Common Herbs Treat Mental Disorders?

You've heard of them—St. John's wort, kava, valerian, gingko biloba—herbal medicines once used only by counterculture folks. These herbals are now a $4 billion industry, and it is estimated that one of every three Americans has used herbal medicines (Brevoort, 1998). One of the most common uses for herbals is in the treatment for psychological symptoms such as depression and anxiety. But do they work, and are they safe?

Herbal medicines have actually been part of mainstream treatment for psychological problems in Europe and Asia for centuries. St. John's wort, an aromatic perennial that is native to Europe but also grows wild in parts of Asia, North America, and South America, is used more often to treat depression in Germany than standard antidepressant medications manufactured by pharmaceutical companies (Beaubrun & Gray, 2000). Dozens of studies, most conducted in Germany, suggested that St. John's wort is effective in the treatment of mild to moderate depression, although it may not be potent enough to relieve more serious depression (Linde et al., 1996). Criticisms were raised of the methods of these studies, however, so the National Institute of Health initiated a large study in America comparing St. John's wort to placebo in treating serious depression (Shelton et al., 2001). St. John's wort did not fare well in this study—it proved no more effective than placebo on several measures of depression.

One reason people had hoped that St. John's wort would prove helpful for depression is that its side effects tend to be less severe than the side effects of antidepressant drugs. One study found that less than 3% of people taking St. John's wort experienced any side effects (Woelk, Burkard, & Grunwald, 1994). The most common side effects are gastrointestinal irritation, allergic reactions, dry mouth, sedation, headache, and increased sensitivity to light.

In the last few years, however, the safety of St. John's wort has been seriously questioned by evidence that it can interact with medications people take for medical ailments. For example, there are several reports that St. John's wort interferes with the efficacy of drugs used to treat patients who have recently received organ transplants, resulting in the rejection of the new organs. It may also interfere with drugs used to treat heart disease, seizures, and certain cancers (see http://www.nimh.nih.gov/events/stjohnwort.cfm). Thus, there are increasing concerns about the widespread use of St. John's wort, because people may be exposing themselves to potential drug-drug interactions with little reason for hope that they will gain relief from depressive symptoms.

Two products used to treat anxiety, valerian and kava, have also received some scientific scrutiny. Kava is the psychoactive member of the pepper family, widely used in Polynesia, Micronesia, and Melanesia as a ceremonial, tranquilizing beverage, and in Europe and the United States for anxiety and insomnia (Beaubrun & Gray, 2000; Fugh-Berman & Cott, 1999). Kava appears to have few side effects in moderate dosages, although some people experience gastrointestinal distress or allergic reactions. Valerian is a perennial native to Europe and Asia. Some studies suggest it can relieve insomnia, although not all studies show it is better than placebo (Beaubrun & Gray, 2000). Again, side effects from valerian are rare but can include gastrointestinal upset, allergies, headache, and restless sleep. Both kava and valerian can enhance the effects of other sedatives, leading to severe side effects, and thus should not be taken in combination with benzodiazepines, other prescription antianxiety drugs, or alcohol.

Particularly with the aging of the baby-boomer generation, claims that gingko biloba can improve memory have gotten a lot of media attention (see Chapter 8 for more information). Gingko biloba is an antioxidant that has been used for more than 2,000 years in China as a treatment for asthma. A widely publicized study in the United States showed that gingko biloba can enhance cognitive functioning in people with Alzheimer's disease and other forms of dementia (Le Bars et al., 1997). Although side effects of gingko biloba are unusual (and include gastrointestinal upset, allergic reactions, and headaches), it does have anticoagulant effects and in rare cases has been associated with serious bleeding problems, usually in people who are already taking anticoagulant drugs.

One of the greatest dangers of the tremendous increase in popularity of the herbal medicines is that many people are taking them without medical supervision. They are widely available in supermarkets and drug stores, and many people who take these substances are also taking prescription medications that may interact with the herbal remedies. The emerging evidence that St. John's wort is not as safe, nor as effective, as was thought even 5 years ago raises concerns that, as millions more people try herbal medicines, we will discover additional dangers associated with these medicines.

In addition, the herbals are not as tightly regulated in the United States as in Germany. Products can vary greatly in their potency, depending on variations in the raw plant material and in the methods of preparing the final product (Beaubrun & Gray, 2000). An analysis of 10 different brands of St. John's wort showed that the amount of hypericin, a component of St. John's wort often used for standardization purposes, varied from 20% to 140% of the amount claimed on the label, with half of the brands containing less than 80% of the labeled amount and two brands containing more than 120% of the labeled amount (Monmaney, 1998).

Although people think of herbal medicines as natural and therefore safe, they must be considered and treated like a drug.

 For more information, go online with InfoTrac College Edition. Use your own term or search:

- St. John's wort
- Kava
- Valerian
- Gingko

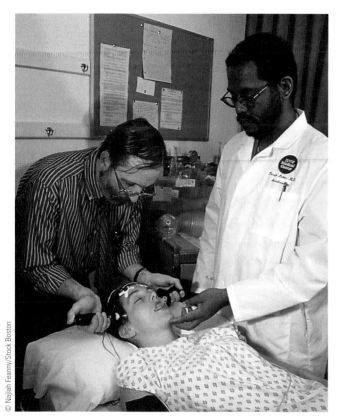

Electroconvulsive therapy is relatively effective in the treatment of depression.

relaxant. A brief, very weak electric current is applied to the brain, typically to the temple on the side of the nondominant cerebral hemisphere. The minimum current required to produce a brain seizure is administered, because the seizure itself—not the electricity—is therapeutic. The muscle relaxant prevents convulsive muscle spasms. The individual awakens within a few minutes and remembers nothing about the treatment. Four to six treatments are usually administered over a period of several weeks.

The most troublesome side effect of ECT is memory loss. Some patients report a gap in memory for events that occurred up to 6 months before ECT, as well as impaired ability to retain new information for a month or two after the treatment. However, if very low dosages of electricity are used (the amount is carefully calibrated for each patient to be just sufficient to produce a seizure) and administered only to the nondominant side of the brain, memory problems are minimal (Schwartz, 1995).

No one knows how the electrically induced seizures relieve depression. Brain seizures cause massive release of norepinephrine and serotonin, and, as noted in Chapter 15, deficiencies of these neurotransmitters may be an important factor in some cases of depression.

Currently, researchers are trying to determine the similarities and dissimilarities between ECT and antidepressant drugs in terms of the way each affects neurotransmitters. However it works, ECT is effective in bringing some people out of severe, immobilizing depression, and it does so faster than drug therapy.

COMBINING BIOLOGICAL AND PSYCHOLOGICAL THERAPIES

Although in this chapter we divided therapies into psychological and biological therapies, today there is a movement toward combined biological and psychological treatments. In depression and the anxiety disorders, often both the patient's biochemistry and his or her functioning in social and occupational settings are affected by the disorder, and it can be helpful to provide treatment at both the biological and psychosocial levels. Even in disorders like schizophrenia, whose primary cause is biological, the patient often experiences severe losses in social skills and ability to function on a job. Supplementing antipsychotic drugs with psychotherapy designed to help the person cope with the consequences of schizophrenia can be very useful.

The fact that a wide range of both psychotherapies and drugs are effective in the treatment of some disorders (especially depression) suggests that intervening at one level of a person's bio-psycho-social system can affect all levels of the system. For example, intervening at the psychological level may cause changes in the patient's biochemistry and social behaviors. When this occurs, it is because our biochemistry, our personalities and thought processes, and our social behaviors are so thoroughly intertwined that each can affect the other in both positive and negative ways.

◆ Interim Summary

- Biological therapies include electroconvulsive therapy (ECT) and the use of psychotherapeutic drugs. Of the two, drug therapy is by far the more widely used.

- Antipsychotic drugs, which alter levels of the neurotransmitter dopamine, have proved effective in the treatment of schizophrenia.

- Antidepressants help to elevate the mood of depressed patients by affecting levels of the neurotransmitters serotonin and norepinephrine. Lithium has been effective in treating bipolar disorders.

- Antianxiety drugs depress the action of the central nervous system and are used to reduce severe anxiety and help clients cope with life crises.

- Stimulant drugs are used to treat attention deficit hyperactivity disorder in children.

1. Many people currently using psychoactive drugs, particularly the serotonin reuptake inhibitors, are not suffering from a severe mood disorder but from the stresses of everyday living. Do you think this is an appropriate use of these drugs? Why or why not?

2. Do you think people with mental disorders should be forced to take drugs to control their symptoms? Would your answer depend on the type of symptoms they suffered?

EFFECTS OF CULTURE AND GENDER ON THERAPY

Culture and gender can influence the process of psychotherapy at many stages (Gray-Little & Kaplan, 2000). A person's cultural background and gender can affect the type of diagnosis they are given for their symptoms. They can affect their willingness to seek psychotherapy and to remain in psychotherapy. And they can affect the type of therapy an individual feels is appropriate.

For example, studies using standardized criteria to make psychiatric diagnoses find that the rates of severe mood disorders and schizophrenia are very similar among African Americans, whites, and Hispanics (Robins et al., 1984). (Rates of these disorders among Native Americans and Asian Americans are not available.) African Americans may be more frequently misdiagnosed as suffering from schizophrenia than whites, however (Mukherjee, Shukla, Woodle, Rosen, & Olarte, 1983). Because this diagnosis often leads to hospitalization, it may explain the overrepresentation of African Americans among hospitalized mental patients.

Men and women are hospitalized at about the same rate for mental disorders (Narrow, Regier, Rae, Manderscheid, & Locke, 1993), but the types of disorders for which they are hospitalized differ considerably. Men are more often hospitalized for substance abuse than women, but women are more often hospitalized for a mood disorder than men. There are no gender differences in the rate of hospitalization for schizophrenia.

Most people who seek treatment for a psychological disorder are not hospitalized. They are more likely to receive treatment from private-practice psychologists, psychiatrists, or general-practice physicians. In fact, one

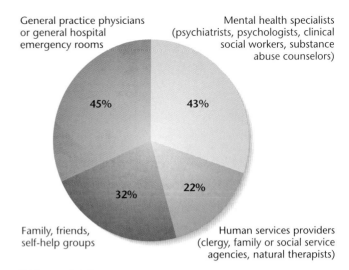

Figure 16-5
Sources of Mental Health Care for People with Mental Disorders
People receive mental health care from several sources in addition to mental health specialists. (After Narrow, Regier, Rae, Maunderscheid, & Locke, 1993)

large study found that people in the United States are twice as likely to seek help for emotional or mental problems from their general-practice physicians than from a mental health professional (Figure 16-5; Narrow et al., 1993). Women are much more likely than men to talk to their general-practice physicians about mental and emotional problems and somewhat more likely to seek help from a mental health professional for these problems.

Hispanics and Asian Americans appear to be more likely to care for a family member who is suffering from a major mental disorder in the home than non-Hispanic whites (Gaw, 1993; Gray-Little & Kaplan, 2000). These trends may be due both to emphasis on the family as the center of problem solving and to the stigma associated with seeking mental health care. In contrast, African Americans tend to seek mental health treatment more quickly after the onset of symptoms than members of other groups.

Several cross-cultural theorists have made recommendations about the type of psychotherapy that might prove most acceptable to members of specific ethnic groups (see Sue & Sue, 1999, for a review). For example, some studies suggest that people from Latino, Asian, and Native American cultures are more comfortable with structured and action-oriented therapies, such as behavior or cognitive-behavior therapies, than with unstructured therapies (Apointe, Rivers, & Wohl,

Therapists and clients from different backgrounds sometimes must struggle to understand each other.

1995; Atkinson & Hackett, 1998). Although some clinicians have suggested that women find therapies that focus on interpersonal relations and expression of feelings more appealing and helpful than other types of therapies, there is little evidence for this assertion (Garfield, 1994). For example, in the largest study of the treatment of depression, clients who were matched with a therapist of their gender did not recover more quickly or fully than clients who were matched with a therapist of the other gender (Zlotnick, Elkin & Shea, 1998).

The specific form of therapy may not matter as much as the cultural and gender sensitivity exhibited by the therapist. Members of minority groups are much more likely than whites to drop out of therapy (Atkinson & Hackett, 1998). Although there has been much effort put into recruiting persons from ethnic minority groups to become psychotherapists, the majority of therapists are still white. Minority clients may find the suggestions of white therapists strange and unhelpful.

Therapists and clients who are members of the same ethnic or racial group do not necessarily share the same value system, however. For example, a fourth-generation Japanese American who has fully adopted the competitive and individualistic values of U.S. society may clash with a recent immigrant from Japan who adheres to the self-sacrificing, community-oriented values of Japanese culture. Similarly, a woman therapist who has strong feminist values may clash with a woman client who holds traditional sex-role expectations. These value differences among people of the same ethnic-racial group or the same gender may explain why studies show that

matching the ethnicity or race or gender of therapist and client does not necessarily lead to a better outcome (Sue & Sue, 1999).

Some clients care deeply about having a therapist of the same ethnic group or gender, but others may trust only a therapist who corresponds to their stereotype of a "doctor," and still others have no preferences regarding the ethnicity or gender of their therapist. For clients who wish to be matched with a therapist of the same ethnic or gender group, this matching may be necessary if the client is to trust the therapist and have faith in the therapy. As noted earlier, the relationship between client and therapist and the client's beliefs about the likely effectiveness of therapy contribute strongly to the effectiveness of the therapy.

◆ Interim Summary

- Ethnic differences in treatment-seeking may be caused by differences in attitudes toward hospitalization and in the availability of nonprofessional sources of care. In addition, African Americans may be over-diagnosed with schizophrenia, which leads to their higher hospitalization rates.

- Men and women are equally likely to be hospitalized or to seek a mental health professional for psychological problems, but men more frequently seek care for substance abuse than women, and women more frequently seek care for a mood disorder than men. Women are also more likely than men to talk with their general-practice physician about mental health problems.

- Some clients may wish to work with a therapist of the same culture or gender, but it is unclear whether matching the therapist and the client is necessary for therapy to be effective.

- It is important for therapists to be sensitive to the influences of culture and gender on a client's attitudes toward therapy and on the acceptability of different types of solutions to their problems.

◆ Critical Thinking Questions

1. Should society fund more research on alternative therapies, such as those based on the beliefs of specific cultures? Why or why not?

2. Why might African Americans be more frequently misdiagnosed with schizophrenia than European Americans?

Is Alcoholics Anonymous (AA) an Effective Intervention for Alcohol Abuse?

AA HELPS PROBLEM DRINKERS

Keith Humphreys, Stanford University and Veterans Affairs Palo Alto Health Care System

Alcoholics Anonymous (AA) is a worldwide fellowship of approximately 2 million alcohol-dependent individuals who are committed to helping each other permanently abstain from alcohol, as well as become more honest, humble, compassionate, and spiritually serene. In over 50 nations, AA members meet in mutual help groups on a regular basis, where they use AA principles (e.g., the "Twelve Steps") and their personal "experience, strength, and hope" to promote sobriety. In the United States, AA is the most commonly sought source of help for alcohol problems (Weisner, Greenfield, & Room, 1995), far outstripping all professional interventions combined. AA also enjoys an excellent reputation among most treatment professionals. At the same time, some clinicians and researchers doubt AA's effectiveness (Ogborne, 1993), noting that the organization offers a loosely monitored and unstandardized program based primarily on the experience and spiritual outlook of its members rather than a standardized professional treatment derived from objective, scientific research. AA attempts to change many aspects of members' lives, and hence the question of whether AA "works" can be framed in many different ways. Here, I focus on one of AA's intended benefits—abstinence from alcohol—and describe how recent studies provide credible evidence that AA helps problem drinkers stop consuming alcohol.

For example, Cross and colleagues (Cross, Morgan, Martin, & Rafter, 1990) followed up a sample of 158 alcohol de-

pendent patients 10 years after treatment to determine what factors (e.g., problem severity, age, sex) predicted long-term abstinence from alcohol. Of all the variables examined, only AA involvement increased the likelihood of abstinence. These findings supporting AA's effectiveness were essentially replicated in an 8-year follow-up of a sample of 628 alcohol-abusing individuals conducted by a different research group (Humphreys, Moos, & Cohen, 1997). Although not a study of AA per se, the randomized clinical trial known as Project Match (Project Match Research Group, 1997) demonstrated that counseling facilitating AA involvement is as effective at reducing alcohol consumption as are other established psychotherapies for alcohol-dependent clients.

Because AA attendance is free of charge, the organization is probably the most cost-effective way for alcohol-dependent individuals to become abstinent. One study of 201 alcohol abusers illustrating this point compared 135 individuals who initially chose to attend AA with 66 individuals who initially chose to seek professional outpatient treatment (Humphreys & Moos, 1996). Despite the fact that individuals were not randomly assigned to each condition, at baseline, there were no significant differences between groups on demographic variables, alcohol problems, or psychopathology. By the three-year follow-up, the AA attenders had reduced their daily alcohol intake an average of 75% and had decreased their alcohol dependence symptoms (e.g., blackouts) an average of

71%. Individuals receiving professional treatment improved comparably. However, alcohol-related health care costs over the three-year study were 45% ($1,826 per person) lower in the AA group than in the treated group. Hence, AA not only promotes abstinence, but does so in a cost-effective fashion that probably takes a substantial burden off of the formal health care system.

Research on the effects of AA participation has improved substantially in recent years, but still has considerable room for growth. Confidence in AA's effectiveness would be increased if more studies employed longitudinal designs, included comparison groups, and used biological tests or collateral data sources to confirm self-reports of abstinence. Further, even well-designed studies do not show that AA works for every participant or that its benefits are always substantial. However, the same could be said for virtually every professional psychosocial treatment for alcohol dependence. Therefore, particularly in light of AA's availability and minimal financial cost, it

Keith Humphreys

clearly is one of society's more important resources for helping alcohol-dependent individuals recover.

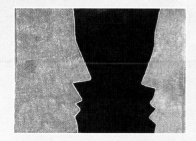

Is Alcoholics Anonymous (AA) an Effective Intervention for Alcohol Abuse?

AA IS NOT THE ONLY WAY

G. Alan Marlatt, University of Washington

Although Alcoholics Anonymous (AA) is the most well-known self-help group for many people who are recovering from alcoholism, it is not the only way to help many individuals to stop drinking, and for some problem drinkers, AA may be a barrier to successful treatment. Studies show that of every two people who attend their first meeting of AA, only one returns for a second or subsequent meeting.

Why does AA appeal to some and not to others? Although AA is described as a "spiritual fellowship" and is not explicitly identified with any specific religious group, many first-timers are put off by the requirement to admit that one is powerless over one's drinking and that only by turning over personal control to a "higher power," recovery is possible. Others are discouraged by the AA doctrine that alcoholism is basically a physical disease that cannot be cured, only "arrested" by total lifelong abstinence from any alcoholic beverages. For those adherents of the disease model, including almost all AA members, there is no possibility of future moderate or controlled drinking. Once an alcoholic, always an alcoholic, according to AA beliefs.

Research has yet to reveal whether it is the specific teachings (theory) associated with AA, or the group support that the meetings provide that is most effective in helping people change their personal habits. Recent evidence indicates the latter is primarily responsible for AA success, which suggests other groups with different theories or beliefs about

alcoholism and recovery can also be effective. In recent years, several new self-help groups for alcoholics have become available, including (1) Rational Recovery, based on rational principles of behavioral change without the need for a "higher power" in order to maintain abstinence; (2) Self Management and Recovery Training (SMART), based on the principles of cognitive-behavioral therapy such as relapse prevention and social skills training; and (3) Women for Sobriety, for women who have problems relating to the mainly masculine flavor of many AA meetings and who could benefit from addressing alcohol problems shared by many women drinkers.

Another alternative to AA is "Moderation Management" self-help groups. After several failed attempts at making AA work for her, Audrey Kishline (1994) developed "Moderation Management," a program of drinking moderation that has been used in many self-help groups in recent years (including some groups that meet on the Internet rather than in person).

Moderate or controlled drinking programs are also known in the addictions treatment field as examples of a "harm-reduction" approach. The goal of harm-reduction programs (such as moderation for heavy drinkers, nicotine replacement therapy for smokers who can't fully kick the habit, etc.) is to reduce the harmful consequences to oneself, one's family, and one's community caused by the drug problem. Although abstinence is accepted as an ideal goal for recovery, any steps toward this goal that reduce

harm are considered steps in the right direction toward enhanced health and the prevention of disease.

Harm-reduction programs have been successful in teaching high-risk college students to drink more safely. Alcohol harm-reduction programs are designed to teach the novice drinker skills about drinking behavior and corresponding levels of intoxication. A recent study of high-risk, first-year college students found those who attended the program showed a significant drop in binge drinking, black-outs, severe hangovers, and acts of vandalism, etc. compared with students in a control group who did not receive this training program. Thus for students who choose to drink and are at risk for experiencing serious drinking problems, harm reduction offers a viable alternative to abstinence (see my article in the August 1998 issue of the *Journal of Consulting and Clinical Psychology*).

In AA, if someone does not accept the requirement of total abstinence, he or she is likely to be told to go away and not to come back until having "hit bottom"—in other words, until the person has experienced such profound negative consequences from drinking that he or she sees no other choice but to go back to AA and pursue total abstinence. But what do we do with those drinkers who have not yet "hit bottom," even though they may be experiencing serious harmful consequences? Harm reduction offers a variety of helpful strategies for this group to get them started on the road to recovery.

ENHANCING MENTAL HEALTH

Aside from seeking professional help, there are many ways in which we can positively influence our own psychological well-being. By monitoring our feelings and behavior, we can determine the kinds of actions and situations that cause us pain or get us into difficulty and, conversely, the kinds that benefit us the most. By trying to analyze our motives and abilities, we can enhance our capacity to make active choices in our lives instead of passively accepting whatever happens. The problems that people face vary greatly, and there are no universal guidelines for staying psychologically healthy. However, a few general suggestions have emerged from the experiences of therapists.

ACCEPT YOUR FEELINGS Anger, sorrow, fear, and a feeling of having fallen short of ideals or goals are all unpleasant emotions, and we may try to escape anxiety by denying these feelings. Sometimes we try to avoid anxiety by facing situations unemotionally, which leads to a false kind of detachment or "cool" that may be destructive. We may try to suppress all emotions, thereby losing the ability to accept as normal the joys and sorrows that are part of our involvement with other people.

Unpleasant emotions are a normal reaction to many situations. There is no reason to be ashamed of feeling homesick, being afraid when learning to ski, or becoming angry at someone who has disappointed us. These emotions are natural, and it is better to recognize them than to deny them. When emotions cannot be expressed directly (for example, it may not be wise to yell at your boss), it helps to find another outlet for releasing tension. Taking a long walk, pounding a tennis ball, or discussing the situation with a friend can dissipate anger. As long as you accept your right to feel emotion, you can express it in indirect or alternative ways when direct channels of expression are blocked.

KNOW YOUR VULNERABILITIES Discovering the kinds of situations that upset you or cause you to overreact may help you guard against stress. Perhaps certain people annoy you. You could avoid them, or you could try to understand just what it is about them that disturbs you. Maybe they seem so poised and confident that they make you feel insecure. Trying to pinpoint the cause of your discomfort may help you see the situation in a new light. Perhaps you become very anxious when you have to speak in class or present a pa-

per. Again, you could try to avoid such situations, or you could gain confidence by taking a course in public speaking. (Many colleges offer courses on controlling speech anxiety.) You could also reinterpret the situation. Instead of thinking, "Everyone is waiting to criticize me as soon as I open my mouth," you could tell yourself, "The class will be interested in what I have to say, and I'm not going to let it worry me if I make a few mistakes."

Many people feel especially anxious when they are under pressure. Careful planning and spacing of work can help you avoid feeling overwhelmed at the last minute. The strategy of purposely allowing more time than you think you need to get to classes or appointments can eliminate one source of stress.

DEVELOP YOUR TALENTS AND INTERESTS People who are bored and unhappy seldom have many interests. Today's college and community programs offer almost unlimited opportunities for people of all ages to explore their talents in many areas, including sports, academic interests, music, art, drama, and crafts. Often, the more you know about a subject, the more interesting it (and life) becomes. In addition, the feeling of competence gained from developing skills can do a great deal to bolster self-esteem.

BECOME INVOLVED WITH OTHER PEOPLE Feelings of isolation and loneliness are at the core of most emotional disorders. We are social beings, and we need the support, comfort, and reassurance provided by other people. Focusing all your attention on your own problems can lead to an unhealthy preoccupation with yourself. Sharing your concerns with others often helps you view your troubles in a clearer perspective. Also, being concerned for the welfare of other people can reinforce your feelings of self-worth.

KNOW WHEN TO SEEK HELP Although these suggestions can help promote emotional well-being, there are limits to self-understanding and self-help. Some problems are difficult to solve alone. Our tendency toward self-deception makes it hard to view problems objectively, and we may not be aware of all the possible solutions. When you feel that you are making little headway toward gaining control over a problem, it is time to seek professional help from a counseling or clinical psychologist, a psychiatrist, or some other trained therapist. Willingness to seek help is a sign of emotional maturity, not weakness; do not wait until you feel overwhelmed. Obtaining psychological help when it is needed should be as accepted a practice as going to a physician for medical problems.

◆ Interim Summary

- Accepting your feelings is the first step to responding effectively to them.

- Knowing your vulnerabilities allows you to avoid triggers for distress and seek help in overcoming certain vulnerabilities.

- Developing your talents gives you multiple sources of self-esteem and joy.

- Seeking out others is a good strategy for distress. Helping others can increase your self-esteem.

- Not all problems can be handled alone; it's important to seek help when you need it.

◆ Critical Thinking Questions

1. In what circumstances do you think self-help books are helpful, and when might they not be helpful?

2. Some people seem never to be overwhelmed by stress and appear able to handle almost anything. What do you think makes such people super-resilient?

CHAPTER SUMMARY

1. Treatment of the mentally ill has progressed from the ancient notion that abnormal behavior resulted from possession by evil spirits that needed to be punished, through custodial care in asylums, to modern mental hospitals and community mental health centers. The policy of deinstitutionalization, despite its good intentions, has added to the number of homeless mentally ill individuals, causing concern about civil rights and adequate care.

2. Psychotherapy is the treatment of mental disorders by psychological means. One type of psychotherapy is psychoanalysis, which was developed by Freud. Through the methods of free association and dream analysis, repressed thoughts and feelings are brought to the patient's awareness. By interpreting these dreams and associations, the analyst helps the patient gain insight into his or her problems. Transference, the tendency to express feelings toward the analyst that the client has for important people in his or her life, provides another source of interpretation.

3. Contemporary psychodynamic therapies are briefer than traditional psychoanalysis and place more emphasis on the client's current interpersonal problems (as opposed to a complete reconstruction of childhood experiences).

4. Behavior therapies apply methods based on learning principles to modify the client's behavior. These methods include systematic desensitization (the individual learns to relax in situations that previously produced anxiety), reinforcement of adaptive behaviors, modeling and rehearsal of appropriate behavior, and techniques for self-regulation of behavior.

5. Cognitive-behavior therapies use behavior modification techniques but also incorporate procedures for changing maladaptive beliefs. The therapist helps the client replace irrational interpretations of events with more realistic ones.

6. Humanistic therapies help clients become aware of their real selves and solve their problems with a minimum of intervention by the therapist. Carl Rogers, who developed client-centered psychotherapy, believed that the therapist must have three characteristics in order to promote the client's growth and self-exploration: empathy, warmth, and genuineness.

7. Sociocultural approaches view individuals as embedded in larger social systems, including families and societies. Group therapy provides an opportunity for clients to explore their attitudes and behavior in interaction with others who have similar problems. Marital therapy and family therapy are specialized forms of group therapy that help couples, or parents and children, learn more effective ways of relating to one another and handling their problems. Community-based programs seek to integrate people with mental disorders back into the community while providing treatment. Several cultures have treatments specific to that culture and based on their own religious and cultural beliefs.

8. Rather than adhering strictly to any single method, many therapists take an eclectic approach, selecting from the different techniques those that are most appropriate for a given client. Some therapists specialize in treating specific problems, such as alcoholism, sexual dysfunction, or depression.

9. The effectiveness of psychotherapy is hard to evaluate because of the difficulty of defining a successful outcome and controlling for spontaneous remission.

Research results indicate that psychotherapy does help but that different approaches do not differ greatly in effectiveness. Factors common to the various psychotherapies—a warm and trustful interpersonal relationship, reassurance and support, desensitization, insight, and reinforcement of adaptive responses—may be more important in producing positive change than the specific therapeutic methods used.

10. Biological therapies include electroconvulsive therapy (ECT) and psychotherapeutic drugs. Of the two, drug therapy is by far the most widely used. Antipsychotic drugs have proved effective in the treatment of schizophrenia, antidepressants help to elevate the mood of depressed patients, and lithium has been effective in treating bipolar disorders. Antianxiety drugs are used to reduce severe anxiety and help clients cope with life crises.

11. African Americans and Native Americans are more likely than members of other ethnic groups to be hospitalized for a psychological disorder or to seek outpatient mental health services for a psychological problem. Hispanics and whites have similar hospitalization rates, but Asian Americans are much less likely than members of other ethnic groups to be hospitalized for psychological problems. These ethnic differences may be caused by differences in attitudes toward hospitalization and in the availability of nonprofessional sources of care. In addition, African Americans may be overdiagnosed with schizophrenia, which leads to their more frequent hospitalization compared with other groups.

Men and women are equally likely to be hospitalized or to seek a mental health professional for psychological problems, but men more frequently seek care for substance abuse and women more frequently seek care for a mood disorder. Women are also more likely than men to talk with their general-practice physician about mental health problems.

12. Some clients may wish to work with a therapist of the same culture or gender, but it is unclear whether matching the therapist and the client is necessary for therapy to be effective. It is important for therapists to be sensitive to the influences of culture and gender on a client's attitudes toward therapy and on the acceptability of different types of solutions to their problems.

CORE CONCEPTS

general paresis
deinstitutionalization
psychotherapy
psychodynamic therapies
free association
dream analysis
transference
interpersonal therapy
behavior therapy
systematic desensitization
in vivo exposure
selective reinforcement

behavioral rehearsal
self-regulation
cognitive-behavior therapy
humanistic therapy
client-centered therapy
group therapy
self-help groups
marital therapy
family therapy
halfway house
phenothiazines
tardive dyskinesia

atypical antipsychotics
antidepressant drugs
monoamine oxidase (MAO)
    inhibitors
tricyclic antidepressants
serotonin reuptake inhibitors
lithium
benzodiazepines
stimulant drugs
electroconvulsive therapy (ECT)

 # WEB RESOURCES

http://psychology.wadsworth.com/
atkinson14e

Take a quiz, try the activities and exercises, and explore web links.

http://www.uea.ac.uk/~wp276/what.htm

Learn more about the antipsychiatry movement on this site.

http://neurosurgery.mgh.harvard.edu/psysurg.htm

Explore the historical background of surgery as a treatment for psychological disorders, and then read about the anatomy and physiology of these controversial procedures.

http://www.npap.org/

This detailed site from the National Psychological Association for Psychoanalysis discusses psychotherapy with an emphasis on psychoanalysis.

 ### InfoTrac Online Library

http://www.infotrac-college.com/
wadsworth

Use InfoTrac College Edition to find popular and scientific articles by using the search terms below or your own relevant terms.

- Behavior therapy
- Cognitive therapy
- Psychoanalysis
- Psychotherapy

CD-ROM LINKS

 ### Psych Odyssey

Check out CD Chapter 17, Psychotherapy
A. Psychotherapies
B. Drug Therapies

 ### Psyk.trek 2.0

Check out CD Unit 11, Abnormal Behavior and Therapy
11d Insight Therapies
11e Behavioral and Biomedical Therapies

SOCIAL INFLUENCE

17

People sometimes do the inexplicable—or what seems inexplicable. Our newspapers and history books provide plenty of examples.

From 1933 to 1945, millions of innocent people—mostly Jews—were forced to live in concentration camps in Nazi Germany. Only after World War II did the world community realize that these camps were in fact high-efficiency death "factories" that systematically slaughtered more than 8 million people. How could this genocide happen? What kind of people could design and operate these death factories? The actions of the Nazi regime seem inexplicable.

On November 18th, 1978, U.S. Congressman Leo Ryan was concluding his visit to Jonestown, a settlement of the People's Temple (formerly of San Francisco) in Guyana, South America. Ryan was investigating Jonestown because reports had come back to the United States that people were being held there against their will. As Ryan boarded his plane to leave Guyana, he and four others were shot and killed by Temple gunmen. Meanwhile, Jim Jones, the leader of the People's Temple, gathered the nearly 1,000 residents of Jonestown and asked them to kill themselves by drinking strawberry-flavored poison. They complied. How could this happen? What kind of people would kill themselves at another person's request? The actions of the members of the People's Temple seem inexplicable.

On September 11, 2001, four U.S. planes were hijacked. Two crashed into New York City's twin World Trade Center towers, one crashed into U.S. military headquarters at the Pentagon, outside Washington, D.C., and the fourth crashed in Pennsylvania, missing its intended target. In addition to the hundreds of people killed on board the airplanes and in the Pentagon, nearly 3,000 people remained in the World Trade Center towers when they collapsed from the impact. How could this happen? What kind of people could take so many innocent lives, as well as their own? The actions of these suicide hijackers seem inexplicable.

Horrific world events often seem completely inexplicable. How could people do these things to themselves and to others? Social psychologists argue that answers that appeal only to personality or character traits overlook the powerful influence that social situations can have in shaping human behavior.

In trying to make sense of these seemingly inexplicable horrors of humanity, our first reaction is often to pin evil (or crazy) actions on evil (or crazy) individuals. "The suicide hijackers were evil terrorists." "Jim Jones's followers were crazy." "The Nazis were evil racists." These sorts of explanations provide some comfort. They distance us "good" and "normal" people, from those "bad" and "crazy" people. To be sure, there is a grain of truth within explanations that attribute evil actions to evil characters. Osama bin Laden, Jim Jones, and Adolf Hitler, for instance, might well be classified as evil leaders. Even so, social psychologists have argued that explanations that attribute the full cause of an action to someone's personality are often wrong—so often wrong that social psychologists identify these explanations as instances of the fundamental attribution error. The **fundamental attribution error** refers to the tendency to explain other people's actions by overestimating the influence of personality or character and underestimating the influence of situations or circumstances. Moreover, we make this fundamental error not only when trying to make sense of unfathomable horrors but also when making sense of the ordinary, everyday actions of our roommates, classmates, and others.

Social psychology is the scientific study of the ways that people's behavior and mental processes are shaped by the real or imagined presence of others. Social psychologists begin with the basic observation that human behavior is a function of both the person and the situation. Each individual brings a unique set of personal attributes to a situation, leading different people to act in different ways in the same situation. But each situation also brings a unique set of forces to bear on an individual, leading him or her to act in different ways in different situations. Research has repeatedly shown that situations are more powerful determinants of behavior than our intuitions lead us to believe. Thus, one of the foremost contributions of social psychology is an understanding of how powerful situations shape people's behavior and mental processes. Our two-chapter discussion of social psychology begins with this focus on the power of situations.

Yet people do not simply react to the objective features of situations but rather to their subjective interpretations of them. As we learned in Chapter 11 on emotions, the person who interprets an offensive act as the product of hostility reacts differently than the person who construes the same act as the product of mental illness. Accordingly, Chapter 18 examines the power that subjective interpretations and people's modes of thinking have in shaping their thoughts, feelings, and social behavior, a topic known as social cognition. We begin, however, with a focus on social influence and the power of situations themselves.

THE PRESENCE OF OTHERS

SOCIAL FACILITATION AND SOCIAL INHIBITION

In 1898, while examining the speed records of bicycle racers, psychologist Norman Triplett noticed that many cyclists achieved better times when they raced against each other than when they raced against the clock. This led him to perform one of social psychology's earliest laboratory experiments. He instructed children to turn a fishing reel as fast as possible for a fixed period. Sometimes two children worked at the same time in the same room, each with his or her own reel. At other times they worked alone. Triplett reported that many children worked faster when someone else doing the same task was present (a situation termed **coaction**) than when they worked alone.

In the more than 100 years since Triplett conducted his experiment, many other studies have demonstrated the facilitating effects of coaction with both human and animal subjects. For example, worker ants in groups dig more than three times as much sand per ant than when alone (Chen, 1937), many animals eat more food if other members of their species are present (Platt, Yaksh, & Darby, 1967), and college students complete more multiplication problems in coaction than when alone (F. H. Allport, 1920, 1924).

Soon after Triplett's experiment on coaction, psychologists discovered that the presence of a passive spectator—an audience rather than a coactor—also facilitates performance. For example, the presence of an

Getty Images/Stone

In 1898 psychologist Norman Triplett noticed that cyclists achieved better times when they raced against other cyclists than when they raced against the clock. This led him to study the phenomenon of social facilitation.

audience had the same facilitating effect on students' multiplication performance as the presence of coactors in the earlier study (Dashiell, 1930). The term **social facilitation** is used to refer to the boosting effects of coactors and audiences on performance.

But this simple case of social influence turned out to be more complicated than social psychologists first thought. For example, researchers found that people made more errors on the multiplication problems when in coaction or in the presence of an audience than when they performed alone (Dashiell, 1930). In other words, accuracy decreased even though speed increased. In many other studies, both the speed and accuracy of performance decreased when others were present. The term **social inhibition** was introduced to refer to the sometimes derailing effects of coactors and audiences on performance.

How can we predict whether the presence of others—either coacting or observing—will improve our performance or impair it? The answer to this question first emerged in the mid-1960s (Zajonc, 1965) and was solidified two decades later in a meta-analysis of 241 studies (Bond & Titus, 1983). The basic finding is that the presence of coactors and audiences improves the speed and accuracy of performance on simple or well-learned tasks but impairs the speed and accuracy of performance on complex or poorly learned tasks.

So social facilitation holds for simple tasks, and social inhibition holds for complex tasks. Despite this useful generalization, this pattern of results still requires explanation. Why does it occur? Social psychologists have offered two competing explanations.

The first explanation, offered by Robert Zajonc (1965), appeals to drive theories of motivation (see Chapter 10). These suggest that high levels of drive or arousal tend to energize the dominant responses of an organism. If the mere presence of another member of the species raises the general arousal or drive level of an organism, the dominant response will be facilitated. For simple or well-learned behaviors, the dominant response is most likely to be the correct response, and performance should be facilitated. For complex behaviors or behaviors that are just being learned, the dominant or most probable response is likely to be incorrect. Consider the multiplication problems discussed earlier. There are many wrong responses but only one correct one. Accurate performance on this complex task should therefore be inhibited.

A number of experiments have confirmed these predictions. For example, people learn simple mazes or easy word lists more quickly but learn complex mazes or difficult word lists more slowly when an audience is present than when it is not (Cottrell, Rittle, & Wack, 1967; Hunt & Hillery, 1973). A study using cockroaches found that, when attempting to escape light, roaches run an easy route more quickly but a difficult route more slowly if other roaches watch from the sidelines (or run with them) than if they run without other roaches present (Zajonc, Heingartner, & Herman, 1969).

The second explanation for social facilitation and social inhibition appeals to attention factors (Baron, 1986; Huguet, Galvaing, Monteil, & Dumas, 1999). The core idea is that the presence of others is often distracting, which can produce a mental overload that results in a narrowed focus of attention. This view can also explain the different effects for simple and complex tasks: Social facilitation should occur when tasks are simple and require that we focus on only a small number of central cues, and social inhibition should occur when tasks are complex and require our attention to a wide range of cues.

Which explanation is correct? In most circumstances, the two explanations make the same predictions and so cannot be tested against one another. A recent study solved this problem, however, by locating a task for which the two views offer different predictions (Huguet et al., 1999). The Stroop task (MacLeod, 1991; Stroop, 1935) is a complex, poorly learned task that involves only a few key stimuli. In this task, a person is asked to identify the ink color in which words or symbols (like "+++") are printed. See Figure 17-1 for an example. People perform this task relatively quickly for symbols but are particularly slowed for words that are incongruent (like the word *red* printed in yellow ink). This phenomenon, called **Stroop interference**, results because word reading is such a dominant and automatic response among skilled readers that it is difficult to follow the instruction to ignore the printed word and name the word's ink color. Because the Stroop task is complex and the automatic response is to name the word (not the ink color),

▌ Figure 17-1
Items From a Stroop Task
Say aloud the color of the inks you see in the top row. Now do the same for the bottom row. Notice how much slower you were to name the ink colors for words versus symbols. This is called *Stroop interference*. Studies show that people perform better on the Stroop task when in the presence of others, a finding that supports the attention explanation for social facilitation.

the dominant-response view predicts that social presence should derail performance, producing social inhibition. At the same time, because the Stroop task involves only two key stimuli—the word and the ink color—and a narrowed focus of attention can reduce attention to the irrelevant information (the word), the attention view, by contrast, predicts that social presence should improve performance, producing social facilitation.

The data from several experiments that have manipulated the presence or absence of an audience or coactors during Stroop performance provide clear support for the attention view and fail to support the dominant-response view: People perform *better* on the Stroop task when in the presence of others (Huguet et al., 1999). These and other studies also identify two key limits to social facilitation effects. First, the mere presence of another person does not produce much social facilitation. If the audience member is reading or blindfolded, for example, social facilitation is greatly reduced (Cottrell, Wack, Sekerak, & Rittle, 1968; Huguet et al., 1999). Second, competition and social comparison with coactors seem to be critical. If coactors perform much worse than participants themselves—that is, if they are no competition—social facilitation is also greatly reduced (Dashiell, 1930; Huguet et al., 1999).

The lineage of studies on social facilitation and social inhibition begins to convey the power of situations. You might have thought that your physical performance (like throwing free throws in basketball) or academic performance (like taking a calculus exam) merely reflected your ability. But the studies described here suggest that whether the performance situation includes others, and what those others are doing (evaluating or providing competition), also critically determines your level of performance. Yet whether the presence of others helps or hurts your performance depends on whether the task at hand is simple or complex for you. A pro basketball player and a student who has mastered the basics of calculus are likely to do better when the situation involves others. For them, the task becomes simple because it is well learned. For a novice basketball player and a student who neglects studying, the situation pulls for much worse.

DEINDIVIDUATION

At about the same time that Triplett was performing his experiment on social facilitation, another observer of human behavior, Gustave LeBon, was also studying the effects of coaction. In *The Crowd* (1895), LeBon complained that "the crowd is always intellectually inferior to the isolated individual." He believed that the aggressive and immoral behaviors shown by lynch mobs (and, in his view, French revolutionaries) spread through a

Audience effects on performance vary depending on whether the task is easy or difficult for them and on how much the person feels that he or she is being evaluated.

mob or crowd by contagion, like a disease, breaking down an individual's moral sense and self-control. Such breakdowns, he argued, caused crowds to commit destructive acts that few individuals would commit when acting alone.

LeBon's early observations of crowd behavior fueled the development of a concept that social psychologists have called *deindividuation*, first introduced in the 1950s (Festinger, Pepitone, & Newcomb, 1952) but revisited and revised in each subsequent decade (in the 1960s by Zimbardo [1969], in the 1970s by Diener [1977, 1980], in the 1980s by Prentice-Dunn & Rogers [1982, 1989], and in the 1990s by Postmes & Spears [1998]). Although the explanations for the phenomenon have shifted over the decades, the core idea within **deindividuation** is that certain group situations can minimize the salience of people's personal identities, reduce their sense of public accountability, and in doing so produce aggressive or unusual behavior (for a meta-analysis of 60 studies, see Postmes & Spears, 1998). Two key characteristics of group situations that contribute to deindivid-

© Peter Turnley/CORBIS

People often behave differently in a crowd than when alone. Some researchers believe that in a situation like a riot, individuals experience deindividuation—a feeling that they have lost their personal identities and merged anonymously into the group.

uation are group size and anonymity. Early explanations for the effects of deindividuation suggested that a reduced sense of public accountability weakened the normal restraints against impulsive and unruly behavior (Diener, 1980; Festinger et al., 1952; Zimbardo, 1969).

In one famous study of deindividuation, groups of four college women were required to deliver electric shocks to another woman who was supposedly participating in a learning experiment. Half of the groups were deindividuated by making them feel anonymous. They were dressed in bulky laboratory coats and hoods that hid their faces, and the experimenter spoke to them only as a group, never referring to any of them by name (see Figure 17-2). The remaining groups were individuated by having them remain in their own clothes and wear large identification tags. In addition, the women in the latter groups were introduced to one another by name. During the experiment, each woman had a shock button in front of her, which she was to push when the learner made an error. Pushing the button appeared to deliver a shock to the learner (in reality, it did not). The results showed that the deindividuated women delivered twice as much shock to the learner as the individuated women (Zimbardo, 1969).

Another study was conducted at several homes on Halloween night. Children out trick-or-treating were greeted at the door by a woman who asked that each child take only one piece of candy. The woman then disappeared into the house briefly, giving the children the opportunity to take more candy. Some

of the children had been asked their names, and others remained anonymous. Children who came in groups or who remained anonymous stole more candy than children who came alone or had given their names to the adult (Diener, Fraser, Beaman, & Kelem, 1976).

These experiments are not definitive, however. For instance, you can see in Figure 17-2 that the laboratory coats and hoods in the first study resembled Ku Klux Klan outfits. Similarly, Halloween costumes often represent witches, monsters, or ghosts. These all carry aggressive or negative connotations. It may be that these costumes did not simply provide anonymity but that they also activated social norms that encouraged aggression. **Social norms** are implicit or explicit rules for acceptable behavior and beliefs. To test whether social norms rather than anonymity produced aggressive behavior, the shock experiment was repeated, but this time each participant wore one of three outfits: a Ku Klux Klan-type costume, a nurse's uniform, or the participant's own clothes. Compared with the group who wore their own clothes, participants wearing Ku Klux Klan-type costumes delivered somewhat more shocks to the learner (but not reliably so). More significantly, participants wearing nurses' uniforms actually gave fewer shocks than participants who wore their own clothes. This study shows that anonymity does not inevitably lead to increased aggression (Johnson & Downing, 1979).

The finding that cues that are specific to the situation (like a nurse's uniform) evoke social norms that

Philip G. Zimbardo, Inc.

▌ Figure 17-2
Anonymity Can Increase Aggression
When women were disguised so that they felt anonymous, they delivered more shock to another person than did nondisguised women.

guide behavior within anonymous groups led to a later reformulation of the mental processes involved in deindividuation. This view holds that situations that reduce public accountability—like group size and anonymity—do not simply reduce the salience of people's personal identities but also simultaneously enhance the salience of people's group identities (like being a nurse, or a member of the People's Temple). Plus, situations that make group identities salient promote behavior that is normative for the salient group (like being less aggressive if you are role-playing a nurse). So whereas earlier explanations of deindividuation suggested that groups and anonymity produce a breakdown of the normal restraints against unruly behavior, this more recent explanation suggests that these same features of group situations promote greater conformity to situation-specific social norms (Lea, Spears, & de Groot, 2001; Postmes & Spears, 1998).

Again, the research on deindividuation conveys the power of situations in determining people's behavior. So the next time you find yourself in a large group situation in which you feel anonymous (not uncommon on a college campus), you may notice yourself getting caught up with the group's behavior. If the group is focused on peaceful activities (like a candlelight vigil for victims of terrorist attacks), you may act more patriotic and reverent than you might on your own. Yet if the group is focused on more raucous activities (like looting or harassing others), watch out!

Bystander Effects

Earlier we noted that people do not react simply to the objective features of a situation but also respond to their subjective interpretations of it. We have seen that even social facilitation, a primitive kind of social influence, depends in part on the individual's interpretation of what other people are doing or thinking. But as we will now see, defining or interpreting the situation is often the very mechanism through which individuals influence one another.

In 1964 a young woman named Kitty Genovese was attacked outside her New York apartment late at night. She fought back for more than half an hour, but in the end she was murdered. At least 38 neighbors heard her screams for help, but nobody came to her aid. No one even called the police.

The American public was horrified by this incident, and social psychologists began to investigate the causes of what came to be called the **bystander effect**, referring to the finding that people are less likely to help when others are present. You might suppose that if you needed help in an emergency, you'd be more likely to receive it if many people witnessed the event. Simple odds should

Although many passers-by have noticed the man lying on the sidewalk, no one has stopped to help—to see if he is asleep, sick, drunk, or dead. Research shows that people are more likely to help if no other bystanders are present.

increase the chances that helpful souls are in the crowd, right? Unfortunately not. Research on bystander effects shows just the reverse: Often it is the very presence of other people that prevents us from taking action. In fact, by 1980 more than 50 studies of bystander effects had been conducted, and most of them showed that people reduced helping when others were present (Latané, Nida, & Wilson, 1981). Latané and Darley (1970) suggest that the presence of others deters an individual from taking action by (1) defining the situation as a nonemergency through the process of pluralistic ignorance and (2) diffusing the responsibility for acting.

DEFINING THE SITUATION Many emergencies begin ambiguously. Is that staggering man ill or simply drunk? Is the woman being threatened by a stranger, or is she arguing with her husband? Is that smoke from a fire or just steam pouring out the window? A common way of dealing with such uncertainties is to postpone action, act as if nothing is wrong, and discreetly glance to see how other people are reacting. What you are likely to see, of course, are other people who, for the same reasons, are also acting as if nothing is wrong. Because people often show blank expressions when confronted with ambiguity, especially if trying to maintain their cool, a state of **pluralistic ignorance** develops—that is, everybody in the group misleads everybody else by defining the situation as a nonemergency. We have all heard about crowds panicking because each person causes everybody else to overreact. The reverse situation–in which a crowd lulls its members into inaction—may be even more common. Several experiments demonstrate this effect.

In one experiment, male college students were invited to an interview. As they sat in a small waiting room completing a questionnaire, what appeared to be smoke began to stream through a wall vent. Some participants were alone in the waiting room when this occurred; others were in groups of three. The experimenters observed them through a one-way window and waited 6 minutes to see if anyone would take action or report the situation. Of the participants who were tested alone, 75% left the room and reported the potential fire. In contrast, less than 13% of the participants who were tested in groups reported the smoke, even though the room was so filled with smoke they had to wave it away to complete their questionnaires. Those who did not report the smoke subsequently reported that they had decided that it must have been steam, air conditioning vapors, or smog— practically anything but a real fire or an emergency. This experiment thus showed that bystanders can define situations as nonemergencies for one another (Latané & Darley, 1968).

But perhaps these participants were simply afraid to appear cowardly. To check on this possibility, a similar study was designed in which the "emergency" did not involve personal danger. Participants waiting in the testing room heard a female experimenter in the next office climb up on a chair to reach a bookcase, fall to the floor, and yell, "Oh my God—my foot. . . . I can't move it. Oh . . . my ankle. . . . I can't get this thing off me." She continued to moan for about a minute longer. The entire incident lasted about 2 minutes. Only a curtain separated the woman's office from the testing room, in which participants waited either alone or in pairs. The results confirmed the findings of the smoke study. Of the participants who were alone, 70% came to the woman's aid, but only 40% of those in two-person groups offered help. Again, those who had not intervened claimed later that they were unsure of what had happened but had decided that it was not serious (Latané & Rodin, 1969). In these experiments, the presence of others produced pluralistic ignorance; each person, observing the calmness of the others, resolved the ambiguity of the situation by deciding that no emergency existed.

Pluralistic ignorance appeared to govern a more recent and disturbing example of the bystander effect. In 1993, near Liverpool, England, two 10-year-old boys kidnapped 2-year-old James Bulger at a local shopping mall. They led the toddler away on a meandering walk, cruelly tortured him along the way, and eventually beat him to death. Over the course of the day, at least 38 adults came across the three boys. Later testimony of these bystanders revealed that they had assumed—or were told—that the three boys were brothers (Levine, 1999). Interpreting aggressive actions as "family squabbles" seemed to define the situation as a nonemergency.

A shopping mall surveillance video shows 2-year-old James Bulger being led away by one of his two 10-year-old kidnappers, who tortured and eventually murdered the toddler. Many adults saw the boys together that day. Yet even though the toddler's head was cut and bruised and his face was tear-streaked, nobody intervened on James Bulger's behalf. Another devastating outcome of pluralistic ignorance.

This is especially troublesome. If the boys were in fact related, would the frightened and injured toddler be in less need of adult intervention? Similarly, is a woman threatened by her boyfriend or husband in less trouble than one threatened by a stranger? Crime statistics suggest not.

DIFFUSION OF RESPONSIBILITY Pluralistic ignorance can lead individuals to define a situation as a nonemergency, but this process does not explain incidents like the Genovese murder, in which the emergency is abundantly clear. Moreover, Kitty Genovese's neighbors could not observe one another behind their curtained windows and could not tell whether others were calm or panicked. The crucial process here was **diffusion of responsibility.** When each individual knows that many others are present, the burden of responsibility does not fall solely on him or her. Each can think, "Someone else must have done something by now; someone else will intervene."

To test this hypothesis, experimenters placed participants in separate booths and told them that they would take part in a group discussion about personal problems faced by college students. To avoid embarrassment, the discussion would be held through an intercom system. Each person would speak for 2 minutes. The microphone would be turned on only in the booth of the person speaking, and the experimenter would not be listening. In reality, all the voices except the participant's were tape recordings. On the first round, one person mentioned that he had problems with seizures. On the second round, this individual sounded as if he were actually starting to have a seizure and begged for help. The experimenters waited to see if the participant would leave the booth to report the emergency and how long it would take. Note that (1) the emergency is not at all ambiguous, (2) the participant could not tell how the bystanders in the other booths were reacting, and (3) the participant knew that the experimenter could not hear the emergency. Some participants were led to believe that the discussion group consisted only of themselves and the seizure victim. Others were told that they were part of a three-person group, and still others that they were part of a six-person group.

Of the participants who thought that they alone knew of the victim's seizure, 85% reported it; of those who thought they were in a three-person group, 62% reported the seizure; and of those who thought they were part of a six-person group, only 31% reported it (see Figure 17-3). Later interviews confirmed that all the participants perceived the situation to be a real emergency. Most were very upset by the conflict between letting the victim suffer and rushing for help. In fact, the participants who did not report the seizure appeared more upset than those who did. Clearly, we cannot interpret their nonintervention as apathy or indifference. Instead, the presence of others diffused the responsibility for acting (Darley & Latané, 1968; Latané & Darley, 1968).

If pluralistic ignorance and diffusion of responsibility are minimized, will people help one another? To find out, three psychologists used the New York City subway system as their laboratory (Piliavin, Rodin, & Piliavin, 1969). Two male and two female experimenters boarded a subway train separately. The female experimenters took seats

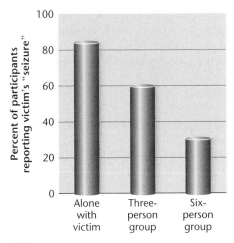

▌Figure 17-3
Diffusion of Responsibility
The percentage of individuals who reported a victim's apparent seizure declined as the number of other people the individual believed were in his or her discussion group increased. (Adapted from M. M. Darley & B. Latané (1968), "Bystander Intervention in Emergencies: Diffusion of Responsibility," in *Journal of Personality and Social Psychology,* 8:377–383. Copyright © 1968 by the American Psychological Association. Adapted with permission.)

and recorded the results, while the two men remained standing. As the train moved along, one of the men staggered forward and collapsed, remaining prone and staring at the ceiling until he received help. If no help came, the other man finally helped him to his feet. Several variations of the study were tried: The victim either carried a cane (so he would appear disabled) or smelled of alcohol (so he would appear drunk). Sometimes the victim was white, sometimes black. There was no ambiguity when the person with a cane fell. Clearly the victim needed help, so pluralistic ignorance was minimized in that case. Diffusion of responsibility was also minimized because each bystander could not continue to assume that someone else was intervening. So if pluralistic ignorance and diffusion of responsibility are the main obstacles to helping, people should help the victim with a cane in this situation.

The results supported this optimistic expectation. The victim with the cane received spontaneous help on more than 95% of the trials, within an average of 5 seconds. The "drunk" victim received help on half of the trials, within an average of 2 minutes. Both black and white cane victims were aided by black and white bystanders. Plus, there was no relationship between the number of bystanders and the speed of help, suggesting that diffusion of responsibility had indeed been minimized.

THE ROLE OF HELPING MODELS In the subway study, as soon as one person moved to help, many others followed. This suggests that just as individuals use other people as models to define a situation as a nonemergency (as in pluralistic ignorance), they also use other people as models to indicate when to be helpful. This possibility was tested by counting the number of drivers who would stop to help a woman who was parked at the side of a road with a flat tire. It was found that significantly more drivers would stop to help if they had seen another woman with car trouble receiving help about a quarter of a mile earlier. Similarly, people are more likely to donate to a person soliciting for charity if they observe others doing so (Bryan & Test, 1967; Macaulay, 1970). These experiments indicate that others not only help us decide when not to act in an emergency but also serve as models to show us how and when to be good Samaritans.

Even role models on television can promote helping. In one study, 6-year-old children were shown an episode of *Lassie* in which a child rescues one of Lassie's pups from a mine shaft. Children in two control groups saw either a scene from *Lassie* that did not show a rescue or a scene from *The Brady Bunch*. Later, while the children were playing a game in which the winner would be given a prize, they were exposed to some whining puppies. Even though helping the puppies would diminish their chances of winning the prize, children who had watched the rescue episode spent more time comforting the puppies than children who had seen the control episodes (Sprafkin, Liebert, & Poulous, 1975). Another study found that children exposed to programs such as *Mister Rogers' Neighborhood* or *Sesame Street* were more likely to behave in giving ways than children who were not exposed to the shows (Forge & Phemister, 1987). These findings reiterate the powerful role that television has in shaping young people's behavior. (Revisit Chapter 11 for a discussion of media violence and aggression.)

THE ROLE OF INFORMATION Now that you have read about the factors that deter bystanders from intervening in an emergency, will you be more likely to act in such a situation? An experiment at the University of Montana suggests that you would. Undergraduates were either given a lecture or shown a film based on the material discussed in this section. Two weeks later, each undergraduate was confronted with a simulated emergency while walking with one other person (a confederate of the experimenters). A person needing aid was sprawled on the floor of a hallway. The confederate was trained to react as if the situation was not an emergency. Those who had heard the lecture or seen the film were significantly more likely than others to offer help (Beaman, Barnes, Klentz, & McQuirk, 1978). This study provides hope: Simply learning about social psychological phenomena—as you are doing now—can begin to lessen the power that situations have to produce unwelcome behavior—at least in this case of intervening in emergencies.

◆ Interim Summary

- Situational forces have tremendous power to shape human behavior, and yet these powerful situational forces are often invisible. People often mistakenly make sense of others' behavior by referring to their personality or character, called the *fundamental attribution error.*

- People perform simple tasks better—and complex tasks worse—when in the presence of coactors or an audience. These social facilitation and social inhibition effects occur because the presence of others narrows people's attention.

- The aggressive behavior sometimes shown by mobs and crowds may be the result of a state of deindividuation, in which individuals feel that they have lost their personal identities and merged into the group. Both anonymity and group size contribute to deindividuation. Deindividuation creates increased sensitivity to situation-specific social norms linked with the group. This can increase aggression when the group's norms are aggressive and reduce aggression when the group norms are benign.

- A bystander to an emergency is less likely to intervene or help if in a group than if alone. Two factors that deter intervention are pluralistic ignorance and diffusion of responsibility. By attempting to appear calm, bystanders may define the situation for one another as a nonemergency, thereby producing a state of pluralistic ignorance. The presence of other people also diffuses responsibility so that no one person feels the necessity to act.

◆ Critical Thinking Questions

1. The presence of others not only alters people's behavior but also alters their mental processes or patterns of thinking. Drawing from studies of (1) social facilitation, (2) deindividuation, and (3) bystander effects, describe three distinct mental processes that are altered by the presence of others in each context.

2. Reconsider the case of the mass suicides at Jonestown described at the opening of this chapter. One thing to know about the members of the People's Temple is that they were devoted to "the Cause," a utopian vision of social equality and racial harmony painted by Jim Jones. They moved to the jungle of Guyana for "the Cause." They signed over their worldly possession, gave up legal custody of their children, and lived separately from their spouses, all for "the Cause." Imagine being in this crowd of followers when Jim Jones asked them to drink the poison. Describe how deindividuation might have played a role in people's compliance to Jim Jones's request.

COMPLIANCE AND OBEDIENCE

CONFORMITY TO A MAJORITY

When we are in a group, we may find ourselves in the minority on some issue. This is a fact of life to which most of us have become accustomed. If we decide that the majority is a more valid source of information than our own experience, we may change our minds and conform to the majority opinion. But imagine yourself in a situation in which you are absolutely sure that your own opinion is correct and that the group is wrong. Would you yield to social pressure and conform under those circumstances? This is the kind of conformity that social psychologist Solomon Asch decided to investigate in a series of classic studies (1952, 1955, 1958).

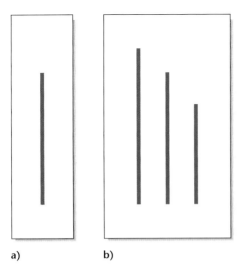

Figure 17-4
A Representative Stimulus in Asch's Study
After viewing display (a), participants were told to pick the matching line from display (b). The displays shown here are typical in that the correct decision is obvious. (After Asch, 1958)

swer that produces the strong forces toward conformity (Ross, Bierbrauer, & Hoffman, 1976). Disagreements in real life typically involve difficult or subjective judgments, such as which economic policy will best prevent recession or which of two paintings is more aesthetically pleasing. In these cases, we expect to disagree with others occasionally. We even know that being a minority of one in an otherwise unanimous group is a plausible, if uncomfortable, possibility.

The situation in Asch's experiments is much more extreme. Here the participant is confronted with unanimous disagreement about a simple physical fact, a bizarre and unprecedented occurrence that appears to have no rational explanation. Participants are clearly puzzled and tense. They rub their eyes in disbelief and jump up to look more closely at the lines. They squirm, mumble, giggle in embarrassment, and look searchingly at other members of the group for some clue to the mystery. After the experiment, they offer halfhearted hypotheses about optical illusions or suggest that perhaps the first person occasionally made a mistake and each

In Asch's standard procedure, a participant was seated at a table with a group of seven to nine others (all confederates of the experimenter). The group was shown a display of three vertical lines of different lengths and asked to judge which line was the same length as a line in another display (see Figure 17-4). Each individual announced his or her decision in turn, and the participant sat in the next-to-last seat. The correct judgments were obvious, and on most trials everyone gave the same response. But on several predetermined trials the confederates had been instructed to each give the wrong answer. Asch then observed the amount of conformity this procedure would elicit from participants.

The results were striking. Even though the correct answer was always obvious, the average participant conformed to the incorrect group consensus about a third of the time; about 75% of the participants conformed at least once. Moreover, the group did not have to be large to produce such conformity. When Asch varied the size of the group from 2 to 16, he found that a group of 3 or 4 confederates was just as effective at producing conformity as larger groups (Asch, 1958).

Why didn't the obviousness of the correct answer provide support for the participant's independence from the majority? Why isn't a person's confidence in his or her ability to make simple sensory judgments a strong force against conformity? According to one line of argument, it is precisely the obviousness of the correct an-

In a study of conformity to majority opinion, (*top*) all of the group members except the man sixth from the left are confederates who have been instructed to give uniformly wrong answers on 12 of the 18 trials. Number 6, who has been told that he is participating in an experiment on visual judgment, therefore finds that he is a lone dissenter when he gives the correct answers. (*bottom left*) The participant, showing the strain of repeated disagreement with the majority, leans forward anxiously to look at the exhibit in question. (*bottom right*) This particular participant persists in his opinion, saying that "he has to call them as he sees them." (The Asch Study of the Resistance of Majority Opinion, from *Scientific American*, November 1995, Vol. 193, No. 5, by Solomon E. Asch)

successive person followed suit because of pressure to conform (Asch, 1952).

Consider what it means to dissent from the majority under these circumstances. Just as the judgments of the group seem incomprehensible to the participant, so the participant believes that his or her dissent will be incomprehensible to the group. Group members will surely judge the dissenter to be incompetent, even out of touch with reality. Similarly, if the participant dissents repeatedly, this would seem to constitute a direct challenge to the group's competence, a challenge that requires enormous courage when one's own perceptual abilities are suddenly and inexplicably called into question. Such a challenge violates a strong social norm against insulting others. This fear of "What will they think of me?" and "What will they think I think of them?" inhibits dissent and generates the strong pressure to conform in Asch's experiments.

If Asch's conformity situation is unlike most situations in real life, why did he use a task in which the correct answer was obvious? The reason is that he wanted to study **compliance, pure public conformity, uncontaminated by the possibility that participants were actually changing their minds** about the correct answers. Several variations of Asch's study have used more difficult or subjective judgments, and although they may reflect conformity in real life more faithfully, they do not permit us to assess the effects of pure pressure to conform to a majority when we are certain that our own minority judgment is correct (Ross et al., 1976).

One of the most important findings from Asch's and later experiments on conformity is that the pressure to conform is far less strong when the group is not unanimous. If even one confederate breaks with the majority, the amount of conformity drops from 32% of the trials to about 6%. In fact, a group of eight containing only one dissenter produces less conformity than a unanimous majority of three (Allen & Levine, 1969; Asch, 1958). Surprisingly, the dissenter does not even have to give the correct answer. Even when the dissenter's answers are more inaccurate than the majority's, the majority influence is broken, and participants are more inclined to give their own correct judgments (Asch, 1955). Nor does it matter who the dissenter is. In a variation that approaches the absurd, conformity was significantly reduced even though the participants thought the dissenter was so visually handicapped that he could not see the stimuli (Allen & Levine, 1971). It seems clear that the presence of just one other dissenter to share the potential disapproval or ridicule of the group permits the participant to dissent without feeling totally isolated.

Here we see the power of situations to shape behavior yet again. A situation in which we face a unanimous majority creates a strong pull for conformity. By contrast, a seemingly minor change in that situation—a simple break in the unanimity—allows us to "be ourselves." Yet whether or not a situation includes a unanimous majority is a central feature of the situation, so perhaps it is not surprising that rates of conformity depend on it. What about subtler background features of situations? Like what newspaper article you just read, or what's playing on the television in the corner of the room? Recent variations on Asch's experiment have explored the influence of such seemingly trivial situational factors by examining how simple exposure to words and pictures can push us conform. The key is whether these words and pictures prime—or activate—ideas about conformity or ideas about nonconformity. In one experiment, some participants were exposed to words like *adhere, comply,* and *conform,* whereas others were exposed to words like *challenge, confront,* and *deviate* (Epley & Gilovich, 1999). In another study, the experimenters primed conformity in some participants by showing them a photo of "Norman, an accountant," whereas they primed nonconformity in others with a photo of "Norman, a punk rocker" (Pendry & Carrick, 2001). In both experiments, participants with prior exposure to the mere idea of conformity actually behaved in more conforming ways when later faced with a unanimous majority. This evidence shows how exquisitely

Simple images can activate the concepts of conformity or nonconformity. Once activated, these concepts can influence people's behavior. Researchers found more conformity among those who saw a picture of "Norman, an accountant" than among those who saw a picture of "Norman, a punk rocker." (After Pendry & Carrick, 2001)

Pluralistic Ignorance and College Drinking

A little knowledge can be a powerful thing. Sometimes, it can even stand up to the power of situational forces and lessen their impact on our behavior. We saw this triumph of knowledge earlier when we discussed the role of information in bystander effects. The study from the University of Montana demonstrated that simply learning about the social psychological factors that deter bystanders from intervening produced more offers to help.

One of the key insights about social influence illustrated in studies of bystander effects is the concept of pluralistic ignorance (Schanck, 1932). When we don't know exactly what to do in a complex or confusing situation, we delay action while we gather information from others around us. Yet rarely do we seek out information directly by going up to others and asking them what they think or feel. Instead, we maintain a calm, cool demeanor—basically pretending that we know what we're doing—and

then slyly check out what others are doing. Suppose everyone does the same? What you get is a group of people who *look* like they know what they're doing, but inside they are each in turmoil, confused and uncertain. This is pluralistic ignorance. Everybody—the plurality—is ignorant of everyone else's true feelings.

This group-level phenomenon characterizes many situations beyond bystanders' reactions to emergencies. You and your classmates have probably experienced it countless times in large lecture courses. Your professor, after presenting some new and complex material, asks the class if they have any questions. Do you raise your hand? Probably not. Why would you want to acknowledge your confusion? You don't want to be known as the one who asks stupid questions. Do your classmates raise their hands? No. They obviously understand the material, which is all the more reason to keep your questions to yourself. Do you see the pluralistic ignorance at work? You and all your classmates are behaving identically—you are all sitting quietly, asking no questions. Even faced with this identical behavior, it's common to interpret your own private feelings as different from those of

others: You alone are confused, whereas others are confident. In this case, pluralistic ignorance can make students feel alienated from their classmates. Imagine how much more at ease you'd feel if the person next to you leaned over and whispered, "I have no idea what she's been saying!" Perhaps you'd even find the courage to raise your hand with your own question!

What does all this have to do with college drinking? As you are no doubt already aware, students' alcohol use is a major concern of parents and college administrators across the United States. Alcohol-related accidents are the number one cause of death among college students, and alcohol use is linked to lower academic performance and higher rates of destructive behavior. Ninety percent of college students, when surveyed, indicate that they've tried alcohol, and about 25% show problems like binge drinking. We know already that peers exert a big influence on students' drinking. The question is how? Do peers cajole each other into drinking and drinking more? Well, sometimes. Other times, pluralistic ignorance is at work. If 90% of students are drinking, it looks like everyone is comfortable with it. Despite this,

responsive to situational factors our behavior can be. Even features of the situation that are in the background—outside our conscious awareness—can exert their power and pull us to conform.

To be sure, we conform to the behavior of others for a number of reasons. Sometimes we find ourselves in ambiguous situations and don't know how to behave. What do you do, for instance, if you don't know which of several forks to use first at a fancy restaurant? You look to see what others do, and conform. This type of conformity is called **informational social influence.** In these cases, we conform because we believe that other people's interpretations of an ambiguous situation are more correct than our own. At other times we find ourselves simply wanting to fit in and be accepted by a group. Perhaps you felt this way when you started college or joined a new high school. This type of conformity is called **nor-**

mative social influence. In these cases, we conform to a group's social norms or typical behaviors to become liked and accepted. We go along to get along. Because the correct line length was not ambiguous in Asch's famous study, we know that normative social influence is what pulled Asch's participants to conform. Luckily, it turns out that age plays an important role in conformity. Although informational social influence continues to produce conformity in old age—suggesting that we still value others' expertise in late life—the pressures to fit in and be liked that fuel normative social influence appear to lessen as people grow older (Pasupathi, 1999).

Sometimes it's easy to tell what the group's norms are because it's evident in the group's behavior. Again, this was true in the Asch study. In real life, however, group norms may be more difficult to identify. In these cases, pluralistic ignorance may promote conformity to imag-

surveys show that many students have clear misgivings about drinking. Perhaps you've nursed a sick roommate, heard about a recent death from binge drinking, or seen that your own hangovers have harmed your academic performance. Even though you have a drink or two at a party, you may not be completely comfortable with the amount of drinking on your campus.

Here again is a pattern of pluralistic ignorance: Everyone's behavior looks basically the same—they all look comfortable as they drink. And yet, even while holding that plastic cup full of beer, many students harbor private misgivings about drinking, while assuming that the group norm is to be unconcerned about drinking. What are the consequences for misperceiving this group norm? Conformity with it—an increase in drinking over time! A series of studies at Princeton University documented this problematic outcome (Prentice & Miller, 1993).

Yet as we've seen, knowledge of social psychology can be a powerful tool. Princeton University also developed and tested a new kind of alcohol education program. First-year students attended a dorm-based discussion about alcohol use that was either peer-oriented, including

information about pluralistic ignorance, or individual-oriented, focusing on decision making in drinking situations. Four to 6 months later, those who learned about the concept of pluralistic ignorance reported drinking less. A little knowledge can be a powerful thing! Moreover, the study's evidence suggested that knowledge of this social psychological principle did not so much change students' perceptions of the group norm but rather lessened the norm's power to induce conformity (Schroeder & Prentice, 1998).

So the next time you find yourself at a party deciding whether you should have a drink (or another drink) and surrounded by nonchalant drinkers, consider basing your choice on your own hunches rather than the apparent beliefs of your companions. Social situations exert powerful pressures toward conformity. But you can fight back with the power of knowledge!

 For more information, go online with InfoTrac College Edition. Use your own term or search:

- Pluralistic Ignorance
- College drinking

When everybody assumes that their peers are comfortable with the amount of drinking on their campus, pluralistic ignorance can, over time, increase alcohol consumption. Fortunately, knowledge of how pluralistic ignorance pulls for conformity can curtail alcohol consumption.

ined social norms rather than actual social norms. Recall that pluralistic ignorance occurs when group members mistakenly believe they know what others think. In the case of bystander effects, people mistakenly believe that other bystanders know that the situation is a nonemergency. Understanding how the concept of pluralistic ignorance fuels conformity can also be used to reduce pressures to conform. See the Cutting-Edge Research box to learn how Princeton University used this social psychological concept to reduce campus alcohol consumption.

MINORITY INFLUENCE

A number of European scholars have been critical of social psychological research in North America because of its preoccupation with conformity and the influence of the majority on the minority. As they correctly point out,

intellectual innovation, social change, and political revolution often occur because an informed and articulate minority begins to convert others to its point of view (Moscovici, 1976). Why not study innovation and the influence that minorities can have on the majority?

To make their point, these European investigators deliberately began their experimental work by setting up a laboratory situation virtually identical to Asch's conformity situation. Participants were asked to make a series of simple perceptual judgments in the face of confederates who consistently gave the incorrect answer. But instead of placing a single participant in the midst of several confederates, these investigators planted two confederates, who consistently gave incorrect responses, in the midst of four real participants. The experimenters found that the minority was able to influence about 32% of the participants to make at least one incorrect judgment. For this to occur, however, the minority had to remain consistent throughout the experiment. If they wavered or showed any inconsistency in their judgments, they were unable to influence the majority (Moscovici, Lage, & Naffrechoux, 1969).

Since this initial demonstration of minority influence, more than 90 related studies have been conducted in both Europe and North America, including several that required groups to debate social and political issues rather than make simple perceptual judgments (Wood, Lundgren, Ouellette, Busceme, & Blackstone, 1994). The general finding of **minority influence** is that minorities can move majorities toward their point of view if they present a consistent position without appearing rigid, dogmatic, or arrogant. Such minorities are perceived to be more confident and, occasionally, more competent than the majority (Maass & Clark, 1984). Minorities are also more effective if they argue a position that is consistent with the developing social norms of the larger society. For example, in two experiments in which feminist issues were discussed, participants were moved significantly more by a minority position that was in line with feminist social norms than by one opposed to feminist norms (Paicheler, 1977).

But the most interesting finding of this research is that the majority members in these studies show a change of private attitude—that is, internalization—not just the public conformity that was found in the Asch experiments. In fact, minorities sometimes cause private attitude change in majority members even when they fail to obtain public conformity.

One investigator has suggested that minorities are able to produce attitude change because they lead majority individuals to rethink the issues. Even when they fail to convince the majority, they broaden the range of acceptable opinions. In contrast, unanimous majorities are rarely prompted to think carefully about their position (Nemeth, 1986).

Another view suggests that minority influence occurs in part because majority members believe that they won't be influenced by the minority but simply extend them the courtesy of hearing them out. That is, simply to show their open-mindedness, those in the majority may thoughtfully consider the minority opinion but don't expect this deliberation to change their own views. Ironically, however, it does change people's minds, because thoughtful deliberation unsettles whole sets of related beliefs, which become more likely to change down the road. This process reflects what psychologists have called an **implicit leniency contract** in the treatment of minority group members, meaning that simply to appear fair, majority members let minority members have their say, but by doing so they unwittingly open the door to minority influence (Crano & Chen, 1998).

These findings remind us that majorities typically have the social power to approve and disapprove, to accept or reject, and it is this power that can produce public compliance or conformity. In contrast, minorities rarely have such social power. But if they have credibility, they have the power to produce genuine attitude change and, hence, innovation, social change, and even revolution.

Social change—such as the end of apartheid in South Africa—is sometimes brought about because a few people manage to persuade the majority in power to change its attitudes.

OBEDIENCE TO AUTHORITY

We opened this chapter with some of the most chilling horrors of humanity—perhaps none is more sobering in sheer magnitude than the systematic genocide undertaken by Nazi Germany during World War II. Think back to all the lives lost (and tears shed) on September 11, 2001, in the terrorist attacks on the United States. Now multiply that by 2,500! You're still below the death count amassed within the Nazi concentration camps. The mastermind of that horror, Adolf Hitler, may well have been a psychopathic monster. But he could not have done it alone. What about the people who ran the day-to-day operations, who built the ovens and gas chambers, filled them with human beings, counted bodies, and did the necessary paperwork? Were they all monsters, too?

Not according to social philosopher Hannah Arendt (1963), who observed the trial of Adolf Eichmann, a Nazi war criminal who was found guilty and executed for causing the murder of millions of Jews. She described him as a dull, ordinary bureaucrat, who saw himself as a little cog in a big machine. The publication of a partial transcript of Eichmann's pretrial interrogation supports Arendt's view. Several psychiatrists found Eichmann to be quite sane, and his personal relationships were quite normal. In fact, he believed that the Jews should have been allowed to emigrate to a separate territory. Moreover, he had a Jewish mistress in secret—a crime for an SS officer—and a Jewish half-cousin whom he arranged to have protected during the war (Von Lang & Sibyll, 1983).

In her book about Eichmann, subtitled *A Report on the Banality of Evil,* Arendt concluded that most of the "evil men" of the Third Reich were just ordinary people following orders from superiors. This suggests that all of us might be capable of such evil and that Nazi Germany was less wildly alien from the normal human condition than we might like to think. As Arendt put it, "In certain circumstances the most ordinary decent person can become a criminal." This is not an easy conclusion to accept because it is more comforting to believe that monstrous evil is done only by monstrous individuals. In fact, our emotional attachment to this explanation of evil was vividly demonstrated by the intensity of the attacks on Arendt and her conclusions.

The problem of obedience to authority arose again in Vietnam in 1968, when a group of American soldiers, claiming that they were simply following orders, killed civilians in the community of My Lai. Again the public was forced to ponder the possibility that ordinary citizens are willing to obey authority, even in violation of their own moral consciences.

This unsettling issue was explored empirically in some of the most important studies in all of social psychology, conducted by Stanley Milgram (1963, 1974) at Yale University. Ordinary men and women were recruited through a newspaper ad that offered $4 for 1 hour's participation in a "study of memory." When they arrived at the laboratory, each participant met another participant (in actuality, a confederate of the experimenter) and was told that one of them would play the role of teacher in the study, and the other would play the learner. The two participants then drew slips of paper out of a hat, and the real participant discovered that he or she would be the teacher. In that role, the participant was to read a list of word pairs to the learner and then test his memory by reading the first word of each pair and asking him to select the correct second word from four alternatives. Each time the learner made an error, the participant was to press a lever that delivered an electric shock to him.

The participant watched while the learner was strapped into a chair and an electrode was attached to his wrist. The participant was then seated in an adjoining room in front of a shock generator whose front panel contained 30 lever switches in a horizontal line (see photos). Each switch was labeled with a voltage rating, ranging in sequence from 15 to 450 volts, and groups of adjacent switches were labeled descriptively, ranging from "Slight Shock" through "Danger: Severe

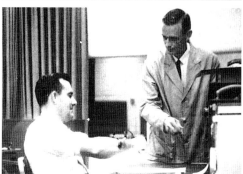

The "shock generator" used in Milgram's experiment on obedience (*top left*). The "learner" is strapped into the "electric chair" (*top right*). A participant receives a sample shock before starting the "teaching session" (*bottom left*). Participant refuses to go on with the experiment (*bottom right*). Most participants became deeply disturbed by the role they were asked to play, whether they remained in the experiment to the end or refused at some point to go on. (From the film *Obedience,* distributed by New York University Film Library, copyright © 1965 by Stanley Milgram, Reprinted by permission of Alexandra Milgram)

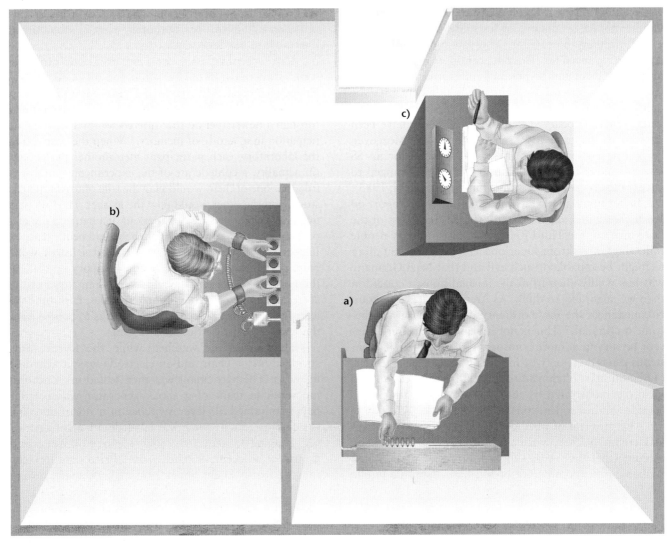

❚ Figure 17-5
Milgram's Experiment on Obedience
The "teacher" (a) was told to give the "learner" (b) a more intense shock after each error. If
the "teacher" objected, the experimenter (c) insisted that it was necessary to go on. (From
Obedience to Authority: An Experimental View by Stanley Milgram. Copyright © 1974 by Stanley Milgram.
Reprinted by permission of Alexandra Milgram.)

Shock" up to the extreme, labeled simply "XXX." When a switch was depressed, an electric buzzer sounded, lights flashed, and the needle on a voltage meter deflected to the right. To illustrate how it worked, the participant was given a sample shock of 45 volts from the generator. As the procedure began, the experimenter instructed the participant to move one level higher on the shock generator after each successive error by the learner (see Figure 17-5).

The learner did not actually receive any shocks. He was a mild-mannered 47-year-old man who had been specially trained for his role. As he began to make errors and the shock levels escalated, he could be heard protest-

ing through the adjoining wall. As the shocks became stronger, he began to shout and curse. At 300 volts, he began to kick the wall, and at the next shock level (marked "Extreme Intensity Shock"), he no longer answered the questions or made any noise. As you might expect, many participants began to object to this excruciating procedure, pleading with the experimenter to call a halt. But the experimenter responded with a sequence of calm prods, using as many as necessary to get the participant to go on: "Please continue," "The experiment requires that you continue," "It is absolutely essential that you continue," and "You have no other choice—you must go on." Obedience to authority was measured by the maximum amount of shock the participant would administer before refusing to continue.

When college students first learn the details of Milgram's procedure and are asked whether they themselves would continue to administer the shocks after the learner begins to pound on the wall, about 99% say that they would not (Aronson, 1995). Milgram himself surveyed psychiatrists at a leading medical school. They predicted that most participants would refuse to go on after reaching 150 volts, that only about 4% would go beyond 300 volts, and that less than 1% would go all the way to 450 volts.

What did Milgram find? That 65% of the participants continued to obey throughout, going all the way to the end of the shock series (450 volts, labeled "XXX"). Not one participant stopped before administering 300 volts, the point at which the learner began to kick the wall (see Figure 17-6).

What makes us so unable to fathom the degree of obedience evident in Milgram's work? The answer ties back to the fundamental attribution error, introduced at the start of the chapter. We assume that people's behavior reflects their inner qualities—their wishes and their personalities. We underestimate—even overlook altogether—the power that situations hold over us. So we put Milgram's procedures together with the knowledge that most people would not wish to inflict severe bodily harm to another innocent person and conclude that few would obey.

It is true that few *wanted* to obey. Most voiced considerable distress and reservations about delivering the shocks. And yet they continued. Somehow their intentions to "do no harm"—although voiced—failed to govern their behavior. In assuming that people's intentions guide their behavior, we've failed to see how subtle features of the situation powerfully pulled for obedience.

How do we know that it's the situation at work here? Maybe these were particularly aggressive or spineless people? Maybe Milgram had unleashed the unconscious aggressive drive that Freud discussed?

We know it's the situation because Milgram conducted many variations on the standard procedure and assigned participants at random to different situations. And each variation in the situation led to drastic changes in the rates of obedience. Four important features of the situation include (1) surveillance, (2) buffers, (3) the presence of role models, and (4) its emerging nature.

SURVEILLANCE One situational comparison varied the degree to which the experimenter supervised the participant. When the experimenter left the room and issued his orders by telephone, the rate of obedience dropped from 65% to 21% (Milgram, 1974). Moreover, several of the participants who continued under these conditions cheated by administering shocks of lower intensity than they were supposed to. So the constant presence or surveillance of the experimenter is one situational factor that pulls for obedience.

BUFFERS Another set of situational comparisons varied the proximity of the teacher and learner. In the standard procedure, the learner was in the next room, out of sight and only heard through the wall. When the learner was in the same room as the participant, the rate of obedience dropped from 65% to 40%. When the participant had to personally ensure that the learner held his hand on a shock plate, obedience declined to 30%. By contrast, when the psychological distance was increased and the learner offered no verbal feedback from the next room, the rate of obedience shot up to 100%. So a second situational factor that pulls for obedience is buffers. Milgram's participants believed that they were committing acts of violence, but there were several buffers that obscured this fact or diluted the immediacy of the experience. The more direct the participants' experience with the victim—the fewer buffers between the person and the consequences of his or her act—the less the participant will obey.

The most common buffer found in warlike situations is the remoteness of the person from the final act of violence. Thus, Eichmann argued that he was not directly responsible for killing Jews; he merely arranged for their deaths. Milgram conducted an analog to this

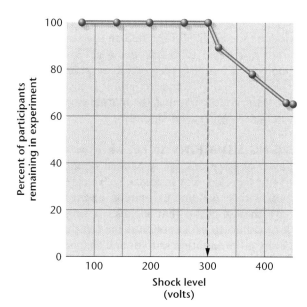

▌ Figure 17-6
Obedience to Authority

The percentage of participants who were willing to administer a punishing shock did not begin to decline until the intensity level of the shock reached 300 volts (the danger level). (Graph based on "Table 2 Distribution of Breakoff Points" in S. Milgram (1963), "Behavioral Study of Obedience," from *Journal of Abnormal and Social Psychology, 67*, p. 376. Used by permission of Alexandra Milgram.)

Modern warfare allows individuals to distance themselves from the actual killing, giving them the feeling that they are not responsible for enemy deaths.

"link-in-the-chain" role by requiring participants only to pull a switch that enabled another teacher (a confederate) to deliver the shocks to the learner. Under these conditions, the rate of obedience soared: A full 93% of the participants continued to the end of the shock series. In this situation, the participant can shift responsibility to the person who actually delivers the shock.

The shock generator itself served as a buffer—an impersonal mechanical agent that actually delivered the shock. Imagine how obedience would have declined if participants were required to hit the learner with their fists. In real life, we have analogous technologies that permit us to destroy distant fellow humans by remote control, thereby removing us from the sight of their suffering. Although we probably would all agree that it is worse to kill thousands of people by pushing a button that releases a guided missile than it is to beat one individual to death with a rock, it is still psychologically easier to push the button. Such are the effects of buffers.

ROLE MODELS One reason Milgram's experiment obtained such high levels of obedience is that the social pressures were directed toward a lone individual. If the participant was not alone, would he or she be less obedient? We have already seen some data to support this possibility: A participant in the Asch conformity situation is less likely to go along with the group's incorrect judgments if there is at least one other dissenter.

A similar thing happens in Milgram's obedience situation. In one variation of the procedure, two additional confederates were employed. They were introduced as participants who would also play teacher roles. Teacher 1 would read the list of word pairs, Teacher 2 would tell the learner if he was right or wrong, and Teacher 3 (the participant) would deliver the shocks. The confederates complied with the instructions through the 150-volt shock, at which point Teacher 1 informed the experimenter that he was quitting. Despite the experimenter's insistence that he continue, Teacher 1 got up from his chair and sat in another part of the room. After the 210-volt shock, Teacher 2 also quit. The experimenter then turned to the participant and ordered him to continue alone. Only 10% of the participants were willing to complete the series in this situation. In a second variation, there were two experimenters rather than two additional teachers. After a few shocks, they began to argue. One of them said that they should stop the experiment; the other said that they should continue. Under these circumstances, not a single participant would continue, despite the orders to do so by the second experimenter (Milgram, 1974).

So role models who disobeyed allow participants to follow their own conscience. But before we congratulate these participants on their autonomy in the face of social pressure, we should consider the implication of these findings more closely. They suggest participants were not choosing between obedience and autonomy but between obedience and conformity: Obey the commanding experimenter or conform to the emerging norm to disobey.

Obeying or conforming may not strike you as a very heroic choice. But these are among the processes that provide the social glue for the human species. One social historian has noted that "disobedience when it is not criminally but morally, religiously, or politically motivated is always a collective act and it is justified by the values of the collectivity and the mutual engagements of its members" (Walzer, 1970, p. 4).

EMERGING SITUATIONS So far, when we've discussed the power of situations, we've painted situations in fairly broad brushstrokes. For instance, we've considered how a group with a unanimous opinion exerts more social pressure than a group that includes a single dissenter. These broad brush strokes obscure the fact that the meaning of any given situation unfolds and changes over time. What begins benignly may insidiously evolve into something horrifying. Yet the emerging nature of situations—just like the power of situations more generally—often eludes us.

For instance, many people who hear about the Milgram study wonder why anyone would ever agree to administer the first shock. Most everyone claims that they themselves wouldn't do it. But that's because people tend to focus on the end of the story—how outrageous the situation ends up, with participants delivering shocks so intense they are beyond description ("XXX") to a man who has presumably lost consciousness. What we need to do is focus on the how the situation started and, more importantly, how it evolved.

The situation began innocuously enough. Participants replied to an advertisement and agreed to participate in a study at Yale University. By doing so they implicitly agreed to cooperate with the experimenter, follow the directions of the person in charge, and see the job through to completion. This is a very strong social norm, and we tend to underestimate how difficult it is to break such an agreement and go back on our implied word to cooperate. And when participants arrived, they found themselves in a fairly straightforward learning experiment. They might have been thinking, "How hard could it be to learn these simple word pairs?" "I bet the threat of shock will speed up the learning process."

Plus, the first shock was just 15 volts—perhaps not even noticeable. And the shock level increased by a mere 15 volts at a time. Although it's abundantly clear that administering 450 volts is not a good thing, the change from innocuous to unfathomable is not so clear. Once participants gave the first shock, there was no longer a natural stopping point. By the time they wanted to quit, they were trapped. The true character of the situation had emerged only slowly over time.

Making matters worse, in order to break off, participants had to suffer the guilt and embarrassment of acknowledging that they were wrong to begin at all. And the longer they put off quitting, the harder it became to admit their misjudgment in going as far as they had. It is often easier to continue with bad behavior than to admit our mistakes.

Perhaps most significantly, Milgram's participants had no time to reflect. They had no time to think about the strange situation they now found themselves in, and what their own conscience would dictate. This effectively prevented them from accessing their own definition of the situation (as "horrifying"). Instead, participants were torn apart by two conflicting definitions of the situations: the authority's definition—"The experiment requires that you continue"—and the victim's definition—"Let me out of here! My heart is starting to bother me!" Most often, in this fast-paced and evolving situation, the participants' behavior reflected other people's definitions of the situation: either the definition offered by the experimenter, which pulled for obedience, or the definitions offered by peers who themselves broke off, which produced disobedience. Participants' own wishes and desires—although voiced—did not steer their behavior. Imagine how much less obedience there would have been if there had been a 15-minute break after 300 volts.

Feature	Experimental Evidence Within Milgram's Studies
Surveillance	Obedience rate drops when experimenter is not physically present.
Buffers	Obedience rates drop when "victim" is moved closer to the participant and increase when the "victim" is never heard.
Role Models	Obedience rates drop when a fellow "teacher" or a second experimenter stops cooperating.
Emerging Situations	Obedience rates seem to depend on the innocuous start to the study, the small rate of change in shock intensity, and the lack of time for the participant to reflect.

IDEOLOGICAL JUSTIFICATION On top of all the situational factors that pull for obedience (see the Concept Review Table for a review) are societal factors. Milgram suggested that the potential for obedience to authority is such a necessary requirement for communal life that it has probably been built into our species by evolution. The division of labor in a society requires that individuals be willing at times to subordinate their own independent actions to serve the goals of the larger social organization. Parents, school systems, and businesses nurture this willingness by reminding the individual of the importance of following the directives of others who "know the larger picture." To understand obedience in a particular situation, then, we need to understand the individual's acceptance of an **ideology**—a set of beliefs and attitudes—that legitimates the authority of the person in charge and justifies following his or her directives. As an example of ideological justification, the Islamic extremists who became suicide hijackers on September 11, 2001, believed that, as martyrs, they would enter infinite paradise if they followed the directives of Osama bin Laden. With eerie similarity, the members of the People's Temple believed that, in drinking the poison, they were "crossing over" into paradise for the sake of "the Cause" that Jim Jones illuminated. Ideologies not only guide the bizarre behaviors of religious extremists but also guide the day-to-day activities of military organizations. Nazi officers believed in the primacy of the German state and hence in the legitimacy of orders issued in its name. Similarly, the American soldiers who followed orders to kill enemy civilians in Vietnam had already

Soldiers follow orders because they believe that national security requires that they do so. This provides an ideological justification for their obedience.

committed themselves to the premise that national security requires strict obedience to military commands.

In the Milgram experiments, "the importance of science" is the ideology that legitimated even extraordinary demands. Some critics have argued that the Milgram experiments were artificial, that the prestige of a scientific experiment led participants to obey without questioning the dubious procedures in which they participated, and that in real life people would never do such a thing (Baumrind, 1964). Indeed, when Milgram repeated his experiment in a rundown set of offices and removed any association with Yale University from the setting, the rate of obedience dropped somewhat from 65% to 48% (Milgram, 1974).

But this criticism misses the major point. The prestige of science is not an irrelevant artificiality but an integral part of Milgram's demonstration. Science serves the same legitimating role in the experiment that the German state served in Nazi Germany and that national security serves in wartime killing. It is precisely their belief in the importance of scientific research that prompts individuals to subordinate their moral autonomy and independence to those who claim to act on behalf of science.

ETHICAL ISSUES Milgram's experiments have been criticized on several grounds. First, critics argue that Milgram's procedures created an unacceptable level of stress in the participants during the experiment itself. In support of this claim, they quote Milgram's own description:

> [Participants] were observed to sweat, tremble, stutter, bite their lips, groan, and dig their fingernails into their flesh. These were characteristic rather than exceptional responses to the experiment. . . . One sign of tension was the

regular occurrence of nervous laughing fits. . . . On one occasion we observed a seizure so violently convulsive that it was necessary to call a halt to the experiment. (Milgram, 1963, p. 375)

Second, critics express concern about the long-term psychological effects on participants of having learned that they would be willing to give potentially lethal shocks to a fellow human being. Third, critics argue that participants are likely to feel foolish and "used" when told the true nature of the experiment, thereby making them less trusting of psychologists in particular and of authority in general.

In response to these and other criticisms, Milgram pointed out that after his experiments he conducted a careful **debriefing;** that is, he explained the reasons for the procedures and reestablished positive rapport with the participant. This included a reassuring chat with the "victim" who the participant had thought was receiving the shocks. After the completion of an experimental series, participants were sent a detailed report of the purposes and results of the experiment. Milgram then conducted a survey, which revealed that 84% of the participants were glad to have taken part in the study; 15% reported neutral feelings; and 1% stated that they were sorry to have participated. These percentages were about the same for those who had obeyed and those who had defied the experimenter. In addition, 74% indicated that they had learned something of personal importance as a result of being in the study.

Milgram also hired a psychiatrist to interview 40 of the participants to determine whether the study had any injurious effects. This follow-up revealed no indications of long-term distress or traumatic reactions (Milgram, 1964).

In Chapter 1 we noted that research guidelines set forth by the U.S. government and the American Psychological Association emphasize two major principles: minimal risk and informed consent. Milgram's studies were conducted in the early 1960s, before these guidelines were in effect. Despite the importance of the research and the precautions that Milgram took, it seems likely that most of the review boards that must now approve federally funded research projects would not permit these experiments to be conducted today.

OBEDIENCE IN EVERYDAY LIFE Because the Milgram experiments have been criticized for being artificial (Orne & Holland, 1968), it is instructive to look at an example of obedience to authority under more ordinary conditions. Researchers investigated whether nurses in public and private hospitals would obey an order that violated hospital rules and professional practice (Hofling, Brotzman, Dalrymple, Graves, & Pierce, 1966). While on regular duty, the participant (a nurse) received a phone call from a doctor whom she knew to be on the staff but had not met: "This is Dr. Smith from Psychiatry calling. I was asked to see Mr. Jones this morning, and I'm going to have to see him again tonight. I'd like him to have had some medication by the time I get to the ward. Will you please check your medicine cabinet and see if you have some Astroten? That's A-S-T-R-O-T-E-N." When the nurse checked the medicine cabinet, she saw a pillbox labeled:

ASTROTEN
5 mg capsules
Usual dose: 5 mg
Maximum daily dose: 10 mg

After she reported that she had found it, the doctor continued, "Now will you please give Mr. Jones a dose of 20 milligrams of Astroten. I'll be up within 10 minutes; I'll sign the order then, but I'd like the drug to have started taking effect." A staff psychiatrist, posted unobtrusively nearby, terminated each trial by disclosing its true nature when the nurse either dispensed the medication (actually a harmless placebo), refused to accept the order, or tried to contact another professional.

This order violated several rules: The dose was clearly excessive. Medication orders may not be given by telephone. The medication was unauthorized—that is, it was not on the ward stock list clearing it for use. Finally, the order was given by an unfamiliar person. Despite all this, 95% of the nurses started to give the medication. Moreover, the telephone calls were all brief, and the nurses put up little or no resistance. None of them insisted on a written order, although several sought reassurance that the doctor would arrive promptly. In interviews after the experiment, all the nurses stated that such orders had been received in the past and that doctors became annoyed if the nurses balked.

Again, these results surprise us. And they surprise professionals as well. When nurses who had not been participants in the study were given a complete description of the situation and asked how they themselves would respond, 83% reported that they would not have given the medication, and most of them thought that a majority of nurses would also refuse. Twenty-one nursing students who were asked the same question all asserted that they would not have given the medication as ordered.

This again portrays the immense power of situational forces, as well as our reluctance to see that power. We make the mistake of assuming that people's behavior reflects their character and their intentions. We make this fundamental attribution error time and again.

◆ Interim Summary

- Asch's classic experiments on conformity found that a unanimous group exerts strong pressure on an individual to conform to the group's judgments—even when those judgments are clearly wrong. Much less conformity was observed if even one person dissented from the group.

- A minority within a larger group can move the majority toward its point of view if it maintains a consistent dissenting position without appearing to be rigid, dogmatic, or arrogant, a process called *minority influence.* Minorities sometimes even obtain private attitude change from majority members, not just public conformity. This is thought to occur through an implicit leniency contract in which majority members agree to let minority members have their say but don't expect to be influenced by them.

- Milgram's classic experiments on obedience to authority demonstrated that ordinary people would obey an experimenter's order to deliver strong electric shocks to an innocent victim. Situational factors conspiring to produce the high obedience rates include (1) surveillance by the experimenter, (2) buffers that distance the person from the consequences of his or her acts, (3) role models, and (4) the emerging properties of situations. An ideology about the importance of science also helped to justify obedience to the experimenter.

- Although Milgram's research is unquestionably important, the ethics of his experiments have generated considerable controversy. It is unclear whether similar research could be conducted today.

◆ Critical Thinking Questions

1. One account of how ordinary individuals are recruited to become suicide terrorists suggests that a charismatic leader indoctrinates a group of people at once, asking them to "please step forward" if they have any doubts about becoming martyrs for the cause. How does this account exploit the concept of pluralistic ignorance?

2. Consider the unsettling message of Milgram's studies: That if a situation is arranged properly and supported by ideological beliefs, ordinary people—like you—can be pulled to act in ways that you find morally reprehensible. How will you fight against the power of such situations in your own life? Can certain other situations pull you to follow your own conscience?

INTERNALIZATION

Most studies of conformity and obedience focus on whether individuals overtly comply with the social influence wielded within the situation. In everyday life, however, those who attempt to influence us usually seek **internalization**; that is, they want to change our private attitudes, not just our public behaviors, and to obtain changes that will be sustained even after they are no longer on the scene. Certainly the major goal of parents, educators, clergy, politicians, and advertisers is internalization, not just compliance. In this section we begin to examine social influence that persuades rather than coerces.

SELF-JUSTIFICATION

When discussing the emerging situational predicament that Milgram's participants found themselves in, we concluded that sometimes it's easier to continue with bad behavior than to admit our mistakes. Why is that? Why is it so difficult for us to come clean and say, "I changed my mind. I no longer think that doing this is right"? Part of the answer is that (at least in Western culture) people hate being inconsistent. The pressure to be consistent can be so strong that often people will justify—or rationalize—past behavior by forming or adjusting their private beliefs to support it.

A classic study of social influence tested the power of this pull to be consistent. To get a sense of the study, imagine that you were to knock on the doors of homeowners in your community, identify yourself as belonging to the Community Committee on Public Safety, and ask those who answered: "Could we install a public service billboard on your front lawn?" Naturally, you'd want to give folks a sense of what the billboard would look like, so you'd show them a photo of an attractive home nearly obscured by a huge, poorly lettered sign that reads "Drive Carefully." Would people agree? Not many. In the early 1960s, a research team found that only 17% said yes (Freedman & Fraser, 1966). Although few could argue with the mission of promoting safe driving, the request was simply too large. There is probably no way that people would hand over the use of their front lawn for this or any other cause. Or is there?

Suppose an associate of yours had approached these homeowners a few weeks earlier with a relatively minor request: "Would you place this sign in your living room window?" Your associate would then show them a small, 3-inch-square sign that reads "Be a Safe Driver." The cause is good and the request so small that nearly everyone says yes. And although the actions taken by

the homeowner are relatively minor, their effects are powerful and lasting. For the next few weeks, every time these people look at their window, they face a salient reminder that they care about public safety, so much so that they took action. When guests ask about the sign, they will find themselves explaining how important the matter of safe driving is to them and why they had to do something about it. Now, 2 weeks later, you drop by with your large request about the billboard. What happens under these circumstances? The study done in the 1960s found that a full 76% said yes (Freedman & Fraser, 1966). Consider how hard it was for these poor homeowners to say no! After all, they're already known to the community and to themselves as the sort of people who care enough about safe driving to take action on the matter, so be it if that action involves a sacrifice.

This study illustrates the social influence tool called the **foot-in-the-door technique**: To get people to say yes to requests that would ordinarily lead to no, one approach is to start with a small request that few would refuse. Ideally, the small request is a miniature version of the larger request that you already have in mind. Once people have publicly complied with this easy request, they'll start reexamining who they are and what they stand for. The result is that their private attitudes will swing more strongly in line with their public behavior, making it harder for them to say no to the larger request.

COGNITIVE DISSONANCE THEORY The foot-in-the-door technique also illustrates that one way to influence people's attitudes is through their behavior. If you can induce people to act in a way that is consistent with the attitude you'd like them to adopt, then they will eventually justify their behavior by adopting the sought-after attitude. The most influential explanation of this sequence of events is Leon Festinger's **cognitive dissonance theory**. This theory assumes that there is a drive toward cognitive consistency, meaning that two cognitions—or thoughts—that are inconsistent will produce discomfort, which will in turn motivate the person to remove the inconsistency and bring the cognitions into harmony. The term *cognitive dissonance* refers to the discomfort produced by inconsistent cognitions (Festinger, 1957).

Although cognitive dissonance theory addresses several kinds of inconsistency, it has been most provocative in predicting the aftermath of behaving in ways that run counter to one's attitudes. One label we have for attitude-behavior discrepancies is hypocrisy. For instance, we call the fundamentalist preacher who frequents strip bars a hypocrite. The sheer negativity of this label offers insight into the discomfort caused by any discrepancies between what we do and what we believe. A core idea within cognitive dissonance theory is that when attitudes and behavior are at odds, we take the easiest route to ridding ourselves of the unpleasant state of dissonance. That is, we create consonance or consistency by changing our attitudes. Past behavior, after all, cannot be changed. And changing a line of action already undertaken—like stopping the shocks in the Milgram experiment or quitting smoking—can produce even more dissonance because it introduces the idea that your initial judgment was poor, a thought that is inconsistent with your generally favorable view of yourself. So, the behavior is maintained or justified by changing or adding new consonant cognitions. **Rationalization** is another term for this process of self-justification. In the case of the Milgram experiment, some participants were likely to tell themselves, "At least I'm following orders, unlike that unruly guy who won't learn these word pairs." If you smoke cigarettes, you may reduce dissonance by telling yourself and others something like, "I know they say smoking is bad for your health, but it relaxes me so much, and that's more important to me."

One of the earliest and most famous studies of cognitive dissonance examined the effects of induced compliance. College students participated one at a time in an experiment in which they worked on a dull, repetitive task: They were asked to turn wooden pegs on a pegboard, over and over again. After completing the boring task, the experimenter asked participants a favor. They were told that the study was really about how people's expectations influence their performance, and that the guy who normally plays the confederate role and tells people what to expect wasn't available. Under this guise, some participants were offered $1 to tell the next participant that the tasks had been fun and interesting. Others were offered $20 to do this. All of the participants complied with the request. Later they were asked how much they had enjoyed the tasks. As shown in Figure 17-7, participants who had been paid only $1 stated that they had in fact enjoyed the tasks. But participants who had been paid $20 did not find them significantly more enjoyable than did members of a control group who never spoke to another participant (Festinger & Carlsmith, 1959). The small incentive for complying with the experimenter's request—but not the large incentive—led participants to believe what they had heard themselves say. Why should this be so?

According to cognitive dissonance theory, being paid $20 provides a very clear and consonant reason for complying with the experimenter's request to talk

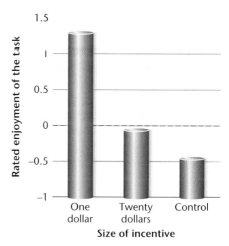

Figure 17-7
An Induced-Compliance Experiment
The smaller incentive for agreeing to say that the tasks were interesting led participants to infer that they had actually enjoyed the tasks. The larger incentive did not. (After Festinger & Carlsmith, 1959)

to the waiting participant, and so the person experiences little or no dissonance. The inconsistency between the person's behavior (telling the next person that the task was interesting) and his or her attitude toward the task (the task was boring) is outweighed by the far greater consistency between the compliance and the huge monetary incentive for complying. (Recall that this study was done in the 1950s, and $20 then was likely to feel more like $100 today!) Accordingly, the participants who were paid $20 did not change their attitudes. Those who were paid $1, however, had no clear or consonant reason for complying. Accordingly, they experienced dissonance, which they reduced by coming to believe that they really did enjoy the tasks. The general conclusion is that dissonance-causing behavior will lead to attitude change in induced-compliance situations when the behavior can be induced with a minimum amount of pressure, whether in the form of reward or punishment.

Experiments with children have confirmed the prediction about minimal punishment. If children obey a very mild request not to play with an attractive toy, they come to believe that the toy is not as attractive as they first thought—a belief that is consistent with their observation that they are not playing with it. But if the children refrain from playing with the toy under a strong threat of punishment, they do not change their liking for the toy (Aronson & Carlsmith, 1963; Freedman, 1965).

Other studies within the tradition of cognitive dissonance theory focused on how people justify their past efforts by valuing their chosen paths more strongly. An illustration of this occurs each year on college campuses: Students often go through elaborate rituals—and sometimes painful and dangerous hazings—to join campus fraternities and sororities. Experiments on cognitive dissonance provide clues as to why these rituals persist. People who go through more effort to join a group end up valuing that group more than those who join with little effort (Aronson & Mills, 1959). We justify our past decisions similarly (Brehm, 1956). Before a decision is made, a number of alternatives may seem equally attractive. Perhaps you had to decide which of several universities to attend. No doubt they each had their good features, but of course, you could only attend one. After you made your decision, cognitive dissonance theory predicts that the simple act of choosing one alternative would create dissonance in you, because it is inconsistent with the good features of the alternatives not chosen. To reduce this unpleasant state, the theory predicts that you will justify your choice by downplaying the good features of the paths not taken and exaggerating the good features of the path you took. Does this prediction fit with your own experience?

SELF-PERCEPTION THEORY Over the years, alternative explanations have been offered for some of the findings of cognitive dissonance theory. For instance, social psychologist Daryl Bem argued that a simpler theory, which he called *self-perception theory*, could explain all results of the classic dissonance experiments without reference to any inner turmoil or dissonance. In brief, self-perception theory proposes that individuals come to know their own attitudes, emotions, and other internal states partially by inferring them from observations of their own behavior and the circumstances in which the behavior occurs. To the extent that internal cues are weak, ambiguous, or uninterpretable, **self-perception theory** states that the individual is like any outside observer who must rely on external cues to infer the individual's inner states (Bem, 1972). Self-perception theory is illustrated by the common remark, "This is my second sandwich; I guess I was hungrier than I thought." Here the speaker has inferred an internal state by observing his or her own behavior. Similarly, the self-observation "I've been biting my nails all day; something must be bugging me" is based on the same external evidence that might lead a friend to remark, "You've been biting your nails all day; something must be bugging you."

With this alternative theory in mind, reconsider the classic peg-turning study (Festinger & Carlsmith,

1959). Recall that participants were induced to tell a waiting participant that a dull peg-turning task had in fact been fun and interesting. Participants who had been paid $20 to do this did not change their attitudes, whereas participants who had been paid only $1 came to believe that the tasks had in fact been enjoyable. Self-perception theory proposes that, just as an observer tries to understand the cause of someone else's behavior, so, too, participants in this experiment looked at their own behavior (telling another participant that the tasks were interesting) and implicitly asked themselves, "Why did I do this?" Self-perception theory further proposes that they sought an answer the same way an outside observer would, by trying to decide whether to explain the behavior with reference to the person (he did it because he really did enjoy the task) or with reference to the situation (he did it for the money). When the individual is paid only $1, the observer is more likely to credit the person: "He wouldn't be willing to say it for only $1, so he must have actually enjoyed the tasks." But if the individual is paid $20, the observer is more likely to credit the situation: "Anyone would have done it for $20, so I can't judge his attitude toward the tasks on the basis of his statement." If the individual follows the same inferential process as this hypothetical outside observer, participants who are paid $1 infer their attitude from their own behavior: "I must think the tasks were enjoyable. Otherwise I would not have said so." But participants who are paid $20 attribute their behavior to the money and therefore express the same attitudes toward the tasks as the control participants who made no statements to another participant.

Importantly, all the participants in the peg-turning study were willing to tell the next participant that the task was enjoyable—even if they were offered only $1 to do so. But the participants themselves did not know this. Thus, when participants who were paid $1 inferred that they must think the tasks are enjoyable because otherwise they would not have said so, they were wrong. They should have inferred that they talked to the next participant because they were paid $1 to do so. In other words, they committed the fundamental attribution error: They overestimated causes due to the person and underestimated causes due to the situation.

The opposite can also happen: People sometimes overestimate causes due to the situation and underestimate causes due to the person. We saw this back in Chapter 1, when we discussed the unexpected effects of rewarding kids with free pizza for meeting monthly reading goals. Kids do read more if reading earns them pizza. But do they enjoy reading? And do they continue reading once the pizza program ends? Dozens of studies, based on the principles of self-perception theory, suggest that rewards can undermine intrinsic interest and motivation. This happens because when people see that their behavior is caused by some external, situational factor—like a free pizza—they discount the input of any internal, personal factors—like their own enjoyment of the activity. So when kids ask themselves why they read, they'll say it's for the pizza. And when there's no more pizza to be had, they'll see no other compelling reason to read. Even though they might have enjoyed reading, the rewards loomed larger. Recall that this undermining effect of rewards is called the **overjustification effect,** whereby people go overboard and explain their own behavior with too much emphasis on salient situational causes and not enough emphasis on personal causes.

So which theory wins? Does cognitive dissonance theory or self-perception theory best explain our tendencies to justify our actions by changing our attitudes? In general, each of the alternative theories has generated data that the other theory cannot explain. Some studies find evidence that participants do experience arousal and discomfort when arguing for positions that are contrary to their true beliefs, a finding that is consistent with cognitive dissonance theory but not with self-perception theory (Elliot & Devine, 1994; Elkin & Leippe, 1986). Others have concluded that each theory may be correct—under slightly different circumstances—and that the focus of research should be on specifying when and where each theory applies (Baumeister & Tice, 1984; Fazio, Zanna, & Cooper, 1977; Paulhus, 1982). Recent experiments actually pose a challenge to both theories. A replication of classic self-justification paradigms used participants who were either amnesiac or under cognitive load (that is, multitasking and therefore having impaired attention and working memory). The results showed just as much attitude change, even when participants couldn't even remember the recent behavior that their newly adopted attitude justified! (Lieberman, Ochsner, Gilbert, & Schacter, 2001). These findings suggest that behavior-induced attitude change can happen automatically, without much conscious thought. So although both cognitive dissonance theory and self-perception theory hold that people "rationalize" their past actions by changing their attitudes, the process may not actually involve the deliberate consonance-seeking or sense-making that either theory has presumed.

These various perspectives on self-justification describe the psychological aftermath of potent social influence techniques. Throughout this chapter, we've seen one core lesson within social psychology illustrated time and again: Situational forces are powerful. A related core lesson within social psychology is that these powerful situational forces are often invisible. When some form of social influence pressures us to behave in a certain way, we often fail to recognize it; and when left to make sense of our actions, we wittingly or unwittingly change our inner attitudes to be in line with our outward behavior. From this perspective, the classic experiments on self-justification can be viewed as social influence techniques in action.

SELF-JUSTIFICATION IN JONESTOWN Knowing how self-justification processes lead people to rationalize their actions by changing their attitudes, think back to the Jonestown case mentioned at the start of the chapter. When the public first learned of the mass suicide, the fundamental attribution error reigned: Jim Jones's followers must have been crazy or weak-willed. Who else would take their own lives at another's request? Later news reports challenged this view by highlighting the diversity of the People's Temple membership. Although some were poor, uneducated, and perhaps more gullible than most, many were educated professionals. Recall that the lesson within the fundamental attribution error is that we underestimate the power of situations. Taking this to heart, a social psychological analysis of the Jonestown tragedy examines followers' paths to Jonestown and the social influence tactics used by Jim Jones (Osherow, 1984).

Oddly enough, we have a window into daily practices within Jonestown because Jim Jones insisted that most events be audiotaped, including the final act of suicide. Reports from former members of the People's Temple also help complete the picture. From this evidence, it becomes clear that Jim Jones was artfully exploiting the foot-in-the-door technique. Jones did not start off by asking would-be members: "Give me your life savings and your children and move with me to the jungle." Rather, he first got prospective members to comply with small requests and then gradually stepped up the level of commitment. Recall that Jim Jones had painted a utopian vision of social equality and racial harmony that became known simply as "the Cause." At first, members were just asked to donate their time to the Cause, later their money, and still later their possessions, legal custody of their children, and so on. Little by little, followers' options became more limited. Step by step, they become motivated to explain or to justify their past behavior in support of the Cause. The easiest way to do that was to become even more committed to the Cause.

Jeanne Mills managed to defect from the People's Temple before the move to Guyana. She became a vocal critic of the group (and was later murdered). In her book, *Six Years With God* (1979), Mills describes the forces of self-justification at work:

> We had to face painful reality. Our life savings were gone. Jim [Jones] had demanded that we sell the life insurance policy and turn the equity over to the church, so that was gone. Our property had all been taken from us. . . . We thought that we had alienated our parents when we told them we were leaving the country. Even the children whom we had left in the care of [others in the church] were openly hostile toward us. Jim had accomplished all this in such a short time! All we had left now was Jim and the Cause, so we decided to buckle under and give our energies to these two. (Mills, 1979, cited in Osherow, 1984).

So, wittingly or unwittingly, Jim Jones used virtually invisible social influence techniques to extract behavioral compliance from his followers. This strategy takes advantage of people's tendencies to self-justify and results in members intensifying their beliefs in Jim Jones and the Cause, while minimizing their assessments of the noxiousness of the costs of membership.

Once in Guyana, Jim Jones continued to escalate the level of commitment he required of members by introducing the idea of the "final ritual" or "revolutionary suicide." He staged events called "White Nights," which were essentially suicide drills. Jones would pass out wine and then announce later that the wine had been poisoned and that they would all soon die. To test his followers' faith, Jones asked them whether they were ready to die for the Cause. One time, the membership was even asked to vote on its own fate. Later in the evening, Jones would announce, "Well, it was a good lesson, I see you're not dead." One ex-member recounted how these White Nights affected him and other followers:

> [Jones] made it sound like we needed the 30 minutes to do very strong, introspective type of thinking. We all felt strongly dedicated, proud of ourselves . . . [Jones] taught that it was a privilege to die for what you believed in. (Winfrey, 1979, cited in Osherow, 1984)

This brief social psychological analysis of the events leading up to the Jonestown mass suicides illustrates social influence in action. It gives a window onto the power that situational forces had to alter the internalized ideologies of Jim Jones's followers.

REFERENCE GROUPS AND IDENTIFICATION

Nearly every group to which we belong has an implicit or explicit set of beliefs, attitudes, and behaviors that it considers correct. Any member of the group who strays from these social norms risks isolation and social disapproval. Through social rewards and punishments, the groups to which we belong obtain compliance from us. Groups may also pull for **identification.** If we respect or admire other individuals or groups, we may obey their norms and adopt their beliefs, attitudes, and behaviors in order to be like them or to identify with them.

Reference groups are groups with which we identify; we refer to them in order to evaluate and regulate our opinions and actions. Reference groups can also serve as a frame of reference by providing us not only with specific beliefs and attitudes but also with a general perspective from which we view the world—an ideology or set of ready-made interpretations of social issues and events. If we eventually adopt these views and integrate the group's ideology into our own value system, the reference group will have produced internalization. The process of identification, then, can provide a bridge between compliance and internalization.

An individual does not necessarily have to be a member of a reference group to be influenced by its values. For example, lower-middle-class individuals often use the middle class as a reference group. An aspiring athlete may use professional athletes as a reference group.

Life would be simple if each of us identified with only one reference group. But most of us identify with several reference groups, which often leads to conflicting pressures. Perhaps the most enduring example of competing reference groups is the conflict that many young people experience between their family reference group

Jim Jones artfully exploited people's tendencies to self-justify.

and their college or peer reference group. The most extensive study of this conflict is Theodore Newcomb's classic Bennington Study—an examination of the political attitudes of the entire population of Bennington College, a small, politically liberal college in Vermont. The dates of the study (1935–1939) are a useful reminder that this is not a new phenomenon.

Today Bennington College tends to attract liberal students, but in 1935 most students came from wealthy conservative families. (It is also coed today, but in 1935 it was a women's college.) More than two-thirds of the parents of Bennington students were affiliated with the Republican Party. Most people at Bennington College were liberal during the 1930s, but this was not the reason that most of the women selected the college.

Newcomb's main finding was that with each year at Bennington, students moved further away from their parents' attitudes and closer to the attitudes of the college community. For example, in the 1936 presidential campaign, about 66% of parents favored the Republican candidate, Alf Landon, over the Democratic candidate, Franklin Roosevelt. Landon was supported by 62% of the Bennington freshmen and 43% of the sophomores, but only 15% of the juniors and seniors.

For most of the women, increasing liberalism reflected a deliberate choice between the two competing reference groups. Two women discussed how they made this choice:

> All my life I've resented the protection of governesses and parents. At college I got away from that, or rather, I guess I should say, I changed it to wanting the intellectual approval of teachers and more advanced students. Then I found that you can't be reactionary and be intellectually respectable.
>
> Becoming radical meant thinking for myself and, figuratively, thumbing my nose at my family. It also meant intellectual identification with the faculty and students that I most wanted to be like. (Newcomb, 1943, pp. 134, 131)

Note that the second woman uses the term *identification* in the sense that we have been using it. Note, too, how the women describe a mixture of change produced by social rewards and punishments (compliance) and change produced by attraction to an admired group that they strive to emulate (identification).

FROM IDENTIFICATION TO INTERNALIZATION As mentioned earlier, reference groups also serve as frames of reference by providing their members with new perspectives on the world. The Bennington community, particularly the faculty, gave students a perspective on the Depression of the 1930s and the threat of World War II that their home environments had not, and this began to move them from identification to internalization: Listen to how two other Bennington women described the process:

> It didn't take me long to see that liberal attitudes had prestige value. . . . I became liberal at first because of its prestige value; I remain so because the problems around which my liberalism centers are important. What I want now is to be effective in solving problems.
>
> Prestige and recognition have always meant everything to me. . . . But I've sweat[ed] blood in trying to be honest with myself, and the result is that I really know what I want my attitudes to be, and I see what their consequences will be in my own life. (Newcomb, 1943, pp. 136–137)

Many of our most important beliefs and attitudes are probably based initially on identification. Whenever we start to identify with a new reference group, we engage in a process of "trying on" a new set of beliefs and attitudes. What we "really believe" may change from day to day. The first year of college often has this effect on students, because many of the views they bring from the family reference group are challenged by students and faculty from very different backgrounds. Students often try on the new beliefs with great intensity and strong conviction, only to discard them for still newer beliefs when the first set does not quite fit. This is a natural process of growth. Although the process never really ends for people who remain open to new experiences, it is greatly accelerated during the college years, before the individual has formed a nucleus of permanent beliefs on which to build more slowly and less radically. The real work of college is to evolve an ideological identity from the numerous beliefs and attitudes that are tested in order to move from identification to internalization.

As noted earlier, one advantage of internalization over compliance is that the changes are self-sustaining. The original source of influence does not have to monitor the individual to maintain the induced changes. The test of internalization, therefore, is the long-term stability of the induced beliefs, attitudes, and behaviors. Was the identification-induced liberalism of Bennington women maintained when the students returned to the "real world"? The answer is yes. Two follow-up studies conducted 25 and 50 years later found the women had remained liberal. For example, in the 1984 presidential election, 73% of Bennington alumnae preferred the Democratic candidate, Walter Mondale, over the Republican candidate, Ronald Reagan, compared with less than 26% of women of the same age and educational level. Moreover, about 60% of Bennington alumnae were politically active, most (66%) within the Democratic Party (Alwin, Cohen, & Newcomb, 1991; Newcomb et al., 1967).

We never outgrow our need for identification with supporting reference groups. The political attitudes of Bennington women remained stable partly because after college they selected new reference groups that supported the attitudes they had developed in college. Those who married more conservative men were more likely to be politically conservative in later life. As Newcomb noted, we often select our reference groups because they share our attitudes, and our reference groups, in turn, help develop and sustain our attitudes. The relationship is circular. The distinction between identification and internalization is a useful one for understanding social influence, but in practice it is not always possible to disentangle them.

◆ Interim Summary

- Cognitive dissonance theory suggests that when people's behavior conflicts with their attitudes it creates an uncomfortable tension that motivates them to change their attitudes to be more in line with their actions. This is one explanation for the process of rationalization, or self-justification.

- Self-perception theory challenged cognitive dissonance theory by stating that inner turmoil does not necessarily occur. To the extent that internal cues are weak, ambiguous, or uninterpretable, people may simply infer their attitudes from their past behavior.

- In the process of identification, we obey the norms and adopt the beliefs, attitudes, and behaviors of groups that we respect and admire. We use such reference groups to evaluate and regulate our opinions and actions. A reference group can regulate our attitudes and behavior by administering social rewards and punishments or providing a frame of reference, a ready-made interpretation of events and social issues.

- Most people identify with more than one reference group, which can lead to conflicting pressures on beliefs, attitudes, and behaviors. College students frequently move away from the views of their family reference group toward the college reference group. These new views are usually sustained in later life because (1) they become internalized and (2) after college we tend to select new reference groups that share our views.

◆ Critical Thinking Questions

1. Rites of passage or initiation rituals are common in young adulthood across many cultures. Explain how these rituals capitalize on people's tendencies to self-justify. What are the outcomes of the self-justification process? How would cognitive dissonance theory and self-perception theory differ in their explanations of the process?

2. Can you identify any changes in your beliefs and attitudes that have come about by being exposed to a new reference group?

GROUP INTERACTIONS

So far in our discussions of social influence and the power of situations we have emphasized the effects of these forces on lone individuals. Among the questions we've addressed are: How and why is an individual's performance affected by the presence of others? How and why is an individual's public behavior shaped by a group's unanimity? How and why do an individual's private attitudes change following social influence? In this section, our focus changes from lone individuals to groups of people. We will look at group interactions more generally to understand the dynamics and outcomes of group processes.

INSTITUTIONAL NORMS

Group interactions are often governed by institutional norms. **Institutional norms** are like social norms—implicit or explicit rules for acceptable behavior and beliefs—except they are applied to entire institutions, or organizations of the same type, like schools, prisons, governments, or commercial businesses. Group interaction patterns within these settings can often become "institutionalized," meaning that behavioral expectations are prescribed for people who occupy particular roles—roles like employee or boss, politician or military officer. Under these circumstances, behavior depends more on particular role expectations than on the individual character of the person who occupies the role. In other words, institutional settings are another potent situation that influences human behavior.

A famous study showing just how potent institutional norms can be is the Stanford Prison Experiment, directed by Philip Zimbardo. Zimbardo and his colleagues were interested in the psychological processes involved in taking the roles of prisoner and prison guard. They created a simulated prison in the basement of the Psychology Department at Stanford University and placed an ad in a local newspaper for participants to take part in a psychological experiment for pay. From the people who responded to the ad, they selected 24 "mature, emotionally stable, normal, intelligent white

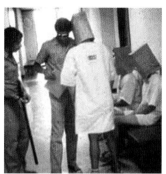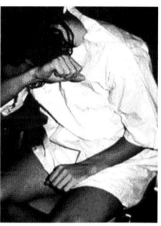

These photos were taken of participants in the now-famous Stanford Prison Experiment. The results demonstrated that group interactions are often shaped by powerful institutional norms. Here we see that prison norms pulled for dehumanizing and violent behavior from guards, and servile and despondent behavior from prisoners.

male college students from middle-class homes throughout the United States and Canada." None had a prison record, and all seemed very similar in their values. By the flip of a coin, half were assigned to be prison guards and half to be prisoners.

The "guards" were instructed about their responsibilities and made aware of the potential danger of the situation and their need to protect themselves. The "prisoners" were unexpectedly picked up at their homes by a mock police car, handcuffed, and taken blindfolded to the improvised jail, where they were searched, deloused, fingerprinted, given numbers, and placed in "cells" with two other prisoners.

The participants had signed up for the sake of the money, and all expected to be in the experiment for about 2 weeks. But by the end of the sixth day the researchers had to abort the experiment because the results were too frightening to allow them to continue. As Zimbardo explained:

> It was no longer apparent to most of the [participants] (or to us) where reality ended and their roles began. The majority had indeed become prisoners or guards, no longer able to clearly differentiate between role playing and self. There were dramatic changes in virtually every aspect of their behavior, thinking, and feeling. In less than a week the experience of imprisonment undid (temporarily) a lifetime of learning; human values were suspended, self-concepts were challenged, and the ugliest, most base, pathological side of human nature surfaced. We were horrified because we saw some boys (guards) treat others as if they were despicable animals, taking pleasure in cruelty, while other boys (prisoners) became servile, dehumanized robots who thought only of escape, of their own individ-

ual survival, and of their mounting hatred for the guards. (1972, p. 243)

Far faster and more thoroughly than the researchers thought possible, "the experiment had become a reality."

The Stanford Prison Experiment is a demonstration of the extraordinary power of situations. It also illustrates the power of institutional norms within prison-like settings. Keep in mind that the participants were randomly assigned to the roles of prisoner and guard. Nothing in their character or backgrounds, then, could explain their behavior. Even though those playing the roles of guard and prisoner were essentially free to interact in any way they wished, the group's interactions tended be negative, hostile, and dehumanizing, a pattern remarkably similar to interactions in actual prisons. These findings suggest that the situation itself—the very institution of prison—is so pathological that it can distort and rechannel the behavior of normal individuals.

It's been more than 30 years since the Stanford Prison Experiment was conducted. Has U.S. prison policy benefited from it? Have institutional norms and practices within U.S. prisons improved? Unfortunately not. Indeed, Zimbardo and one of his original collaborators have argued that U.S. criminal justice policies have turned a blind eye to the lessons of their well-known experiment about the power of situations within prisons (Haney & Zimbardo, 1998). As just one example, they cite the national trend toward "Supermax" prisons, super-maximum security prisons in which the most violent and disruptive prisoners are completely segregated from other prisoners and subjected to extreme social isolation, very limited environmental stimulation, and extraordinary control over their every move. The use of Supermax prisons for so-called problem prisoners ignores the situational roots of prisoners' problematic behavior. Lessons from the Stanford Prison Experiment warn that as "problem prisoners" are removed from the typical prison environment, the continuing pathological prison situation will generate new replacements to assume the roles of those prisoners who have been taken away. Such is the power of institutional norms.

GROUP DECISION MAKING

Many decisions are made not by individuals but by groups. Members of a family jointly decide where to spend their vacation; a jury judges a defendant to be guilty; a city council votes to raise property taxes. How do such decisions compare with those that might have been made by individual decision makers? Are group decisions better or worse, riskier or more cautious? These are the kinds of questions that concern us in this section.

GROUP POLARIZATION In the 1950s, it was widely believed that decisions made by groups were typically cautious and conservative. For example, it was argued that because business decisions were increasingly being made by committees, the bold, innovative risk taking of entrepreneurs like Andrew Carnegie was a thing of the past (Whyte, 1956). James Stoner, then a graduate business student at MIT, decided to test this assumption (1961).

In Stoner's study, participants were asked to consider a number of hypothetical dilemmas. In one, an electrical engineer must decide whether to stick with his present job at a modest but adequate salary or take a job with a new firm offering more money, a possible partnership in the venture if it succeeds, but no long-term security. In another, a man with a severe heart ailment must seriously curtail his customary way of life or else undergo a medical operation that would either cure him completely or prove fatal. Participants were asked to decide how good the odds of success would have to be before they would advise the person to try the riskier course of action. For example, they could recommend that the engineer take the riskier job if the chances that the new venture would succeed were 5 in 10, 3 in 10, or only 1 in 10. By using numerical odds like these, Stoner was able to compare the riskiness of different decisions quantitatively.

Participants first made their decisions alone, as individuals. They then met in groups and arrived at a group decision for each dilemma. After the group discussion, they again considered the dilemmas privately as individuals. When Stoner compared the group's decisions with the average of the individuals' pregroup

Group polarization often occurs in juries, especially when they are required to reach unanimous decisions.

decisions, he found that the group's decisions were riskier than the individuals' initial decisions. Moreover, this shift reflected genuine opinion change on the part of group members, not just public conformity to the group decision: The private individual decisions made after the group discussion were significantly riskier than the initial decisions.

These findings were replicated by other researchers, even in situations that presented real rather than hypothetical risks (Bem, Wallach, & Kogan, 1965; Wallach, Kogan, & Bem, 1962, 1964,). The phenomenon was initially called the *risky shift effect*. This turned out not to be an accurate characterization, however. Even in the early studies, group decisions tended to shift slightly but consistently in the cautious direction on one or two of the hypothetical dilemmas (Wallach, Kogan, & Bem, 1962). The phenomenon is now called the **group polarization effect** because after many more studies it became clear that group discussion leads to decisions that are not necessarily riskier but are more extreme than the individual decisions. If group members are initially inclined to take risks on a particular dilemma, the group's decisions will become riskier; if group members are initially inclined to be cautious, the group will be even more cautious (Myers & Lamm, 1976).

More than 300 studies of the group polarization effect have been conducted, with a dazzling array of variations. For example, in one study, active burglars actually cased houses and then provided individual and group estimates of how easy each would be to burglarize. Compared with the individual estimates, the group estimates were more conservative; that is, they rated the homes to be more difficult to break into successfully (Cromwell, Marks, Olson, & Avary, 1991).

Group polarization extends beyond issues of risk and caution. For example, group discussion caused French students' initially positive attitudes toward the country's premier to become even more positive and their initially negative attitudes toward Americans to become even more negative (Moscovici & Zavalloni, 1969). Jury decisions can be similarly affected, leading to more extreme verdicts (Isozaki, 1984). Polarization in juries is more likely to occur on judgments concerning values and opinions (such as deciding on an appropriate punishment for a guilty defendant) than on judgments concerning matters of fact (such as the defendant's guilt), and they are most likely to show polarization when they are required to reach unanimous decisions (Kaplan & Miller, 1987).

Many explanations for the group polarization effect have been offered over the years, but the two that have stood up best to intensive testing refer to the concepts of informational social influence and normative social influence that we considered earlier in our discussion of conformity to a majority (Isenberg, 1986). Recall that informational social influence occurs when people see others as valid sources of information. During group discussions, members learn new information and hear novel arguments relevant to the decision under discussion. For example, in discussing whether the electrical engineer should go with the new venture—a decision that almost always shifts in the risky direction—it is quite common for someone in the group to argue that riskiness is warranted because electrical engineers can always find good jobs. A shift in the conservative direction occurred in the burglar study after one member of the group noted that it was nearly 3 P.M. and children would soon be returning from school and playing nearby.

The more arguments are raised in support of a position, the more likely it is that the group will move toward that position. And this is where the bias enters: Members of a group are most likely to present points in support of the position they initially favor and to discuss information they already share (Stasser, Taylor, & Hanna, 1989; Stasser & Titus, 1985). Accordingly, the discussion will be biased in favor of the group's initial position, and the group will move toward that position as more of the group members become convinced. Interestingly, the polarization effect still occurs, even when all participants are given an extensive list of arguments before the experiment begins—a finding that casts doubt on explanations based solely on informational social influence (Zuber, Crott, & Werner, 1992).

Normative social influence, you will recall, occurs when people want to be liked and accepted by a group.

Under this type of social influence, people compare their own views with the norms of the group. During the discussion, they may learn that others have similar attitudes or even more extreme views than they themselves do. If they are motivated to be seen positively by the group, they may conform to the group's position or even express a position that is more extreme than the group's. As one researcher noted, "To be virtuous . . . is to be different from the mean—in the right direction and to the right degree" (Brown, 1974, p. 469).

But normative social influence is not simply pressure to conform. Often the group provides a frame of reference for its members, a context within which they can reevaluate their initial positions. This is illustrated by a common and amusing event that frequently occurs in group polarization experiments. For example, in one group a participant began the discussion of the dilemma facing the electrical engineer by confidently announcing, "I feel this guy should really be willing to take a risk here. He should go with the new job even if it has only a 5 in 10 chance of succeeding." Other group members were incredulous: "You think that 5 in 10 is being risky? If he has any guts, he should give it a shot even if there is only 1 chance in 100 of success. I mean, what has he really got to lose?" Eager to reestablish his reputation as a risk taker, the original individual quickly shifted his position further in the risky direction. By redefining "risky," the group moved both its own decision and its members' postdiscussion attitudes further toward the risky extreme of the scale (Wallach, Kogan, & Bem, 1962; from the authors' notes).

As this example illustrates, both informational and normative social influence occur simultaneously in group discussions, and several studies have attempted to untangle them. Some studies have shown that the group polarization effect occurs if participants simply hear the arguments of the group, without knowing the actual positions of other members of the group (Burnstein & Vinokur, 1973, 1977). This demonstrates that informational social influence by itself is sufficient to produce polarization. Other studies have shown that the polarization effect also occurs when people learn others' positions but do not hear any supporting arguments, demonstrating that normative social influence by itself is sufficient (Goethals & Zanna, 1979; Sanders & Baron, 1977). Typically, however, the effect of informational social influence is greater than the effect of normative social influence (Isenberg, 1986).

GROUPTHINK "How could we have been so stupid?" This was President John Kennedy's reaction to the disastrous failure of his administration's attempt to invade Cuba at the Bay of Pigs in 1961 and overthrow the government of Fidel Castro. The plan was badly conceived at many levels. For example, if the initial landing was unsuccessful, the invaders were supposed to retreat into the mountains. But no one in the planning group had studied the map closely enough to realize that no army could have gotten through the 80 miles of swamp that separated the mountains from the landing area. As it turned out, this didn't matter, because other miscalculations caused the invading force to be wiped out long before the retreat would have taken place.

The invasion had been conceived and planned by the president and a small group of advisers. Writing 4 years later, one of these advisers, the historian Arthur Schlesinger Jr., blamed himself

> for having kept so silent during those crucial discussions in the Cabinet Room, though my feelings of guilt were tempered by the knowledge that a course of objection would have accomplished little save to gain me a name as a nuisance. I can only explain my failure to do more than raise a few timid questions by reporting that one's impulse to blow the whistle on this nonsense was simply undone by the circumstances of the discussion. (1965, p. 255)

What were the "circumstances of the discussion" that led the group to pursue such a disastrous course of action? After reading Schlesinger's account, social psychologist Irving Janis introduced the term **groupthink** to describe the phenomenon in which members of a group are led to suppress their own dissent in the interests of group consensus (Janis, 1982). After analyzing several other foreign policy decisions, Janis set forth a broad theory to describe the causes and consequences of groupthink.

Groupthink, according to Janis's theory, is caused by (1) a cohesive group of decision makers, (2) isolation of the group from outside influences, (3) no systematic procedures for considering both the pros and cons of different courses of action, (4) a directive leader who explicitly favors a particular course of action, and (5) high stress, often due to an external threat, recent failures, moral dilemmas, and an apparent lack of viable alternatives. The theory suggests that these conditions foster a strong desire to achieve and maintain group consensus and avoid rocking the boat by dissenting.

Janis argued that the consequences or symptoms of groupthink include (1) shared illusions of invulnerability, morality, and unanimity, (2) direct pressure on dissenters, (3) self-censorship (as Schlesinger's account notes), (4) collective rationalization of a decision rather

than realistically examination of its strengths and weaknesses, and (5) self-appointed mindguards, group members who actively attempt to prevent the group from considering information that would challenge the effectiveness or morality of its decisions. For example, the attorney general (President Kennedy's brother Robert) privately warned Schlesinger, "The President has made his mind up. Don't push it any further." The secretary of state also withheld information that had been provided by intelligence experts who warned against an invasion of Cuba (Janis, 1982). Janis proposed that these symptoms of groupthink combine to produce damaging flaws in the decision-making process—like incomplete information search and failure to develop contingency plans—which in turn lead to bad decisions.

Janis's theory of groupthink has been extremely influential within social psychology, across the social sciences, and within the culture at large (Turner & Pratkanis, 1998b). Yet it has also received sharp criticism (such as Fuller & Aldag, 1998). First, it is based more on historical analysis of select cases than on laboratory experimentation. Plus, the few dozen experiments that have tested the theory have produced only mixed and limited support (Callaway, Marriott, & Esser, 1985; Courtright, 1978; Flowers, 1977; Longley & Pruitt, 1980; McCauley, 1989; Turner, Pratkanis, Probasco, & Lever, 1992). As just one example, Janis's claim that cohesive groups are most likely to succumb to groupthink has not stood up to empirical test. Cohesive groups may, in fact, provide a sense of psychological safety, which has been shown to improve group learning and performance (Edmondson, 1999). One later reformulation of the theory, supported by experimental data, argues that group cohesion yields poor decisions only when combined with threats to the group's positive image of itself. Faced with such threats, group members narrow their focus of attention to the goal of protecting and maintaining their positive group identity, a focus that often comes at the cost of effective decision making (Turner & Pratkanis, 1998a).

Another reformulation of the theory states that the presence or absence of groupthink depends on the specific content of a group's social norms. Recall that social norms are implicit or explicit rules for acceptable behavior and beliefs. In some cases, group norms favor maintaining consensus, and in these cases, the adverse effects of groupthink should take hold, resulting in poor-quality decisions. In other cases, group norms favor critical thinking, and in these cases, group discussion should actually improve decision quality. A recent experiment tested these ideas (Postmes, Spears, &

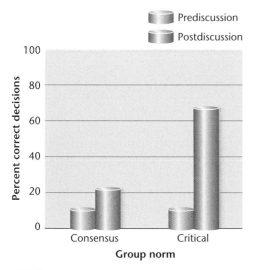

Prediscussion
Postdiscussion

Figure 17-8
Group Norms and the Effectiveness of Group Decisions
Group norms can influence the quality of group decisions. In this experiment, the decisions made by groups with norms for consensus seeking did not benefit from group discussion, whereas those with norms for critical thinking did. (Adapted from Figure 1 on p. 923 in T. Postmes, R. Spears, & S. Cihangir (2001), "Quality of decision making and group norms," in *Journal of Personality and Social Psychology*, 80, 918–930. Copyright © 2001 by the American Psychological Association. Adapted with permission.)

Cihangir, 2001). In it, the researchers manipulated group norms by randomly assigning several groups (of four college students each) to engage either in a task that fostered a norm of consensus seeking (making a poster together) or in a task that fostered a norm of critical thinking (discussing an unpopular policy proposal). Next, all groups participated in an unrelated group decision task. The researchers assessed the quality of decisions both before and after the group discussion. Figure 17-8 portrays the results. Inspection of Figure 17-8 shows that when the group norm favored consensus, group discussion did little to improve decision quality, yet when the group norm favored critical thinking, group discussion improved decision quality dramatically. You might notice that this reformulation of groupthink echoes the reformulation of deindividuation described earlier: In both cases, situation-specific social norms guide behavior more than more general features of the group, like group cohesion or personal anonymity.

This study on group norms spotlights one way to minimize the damaging effects of groupthink: Fostering norms for critical thinking as a college education intends—should produce better group decisions. Other ways to improve group decisions include providing groups with trained facilitators who encourage a full sharing of ideas and alternating private idea-generating sessions with group sessions. Another beneficial strategy is to make the group a heterogeneous mix of people. A diverse group is more likely than a homogeneous group to generate a wide range of ideas (Paulus, 1998). Diversity within groups has other benefits as well. Surveys of college students across the United States have found that students of all ethnic backgrounds—European American, African American, Asian American and Hispanic American—reach higher levels of intellectual engagement and ability when their college classrooms reflect ethnic diversity and when they interact informally with diverse peers outside of class. In addition, ethnic diversity on campus fosters perspective-taking and other skills that aid democracy (Gurin, Dey, Hurtado, & Gurin, in press). Yet despite the evidence that ethnic diversity produces better individual and group outcomes, the value of affirmative action policies continues to be hotly debated. Two social psychological sides of this debate are featured in the Seeing Both Sides section at the end of this chapter. Many of the ideas raised within these essays—like how we decide what caused our own or someone else's success and the self-fulfilling nature of prejudicial stereotypes—will be addressed further in Chapter 18, our second in this two-chapter series on social psychology.

Evidence shows that diversity on college campuses predicts intellectual attainment and skills that foster democracy.

Are the Effects of Affirmative Action Positive or Negative?

NEGATIVE ASPECTS OF AFFIRMATIVE ACTION
Madeline E. Heilman, New York University

Most people would say that rewards should be given according to merit. What happens, then, when people get rewarded not because of their accomplishments but because of who they are or what group they belong to? Many people, perhaps including yourself, react negatively.

This is the heart of the affirmative action dilemma. While created to ensure nondiscriminatory treatment of women and minorities, affirmative action has come to be seen as little more than preferential selection and treatment without regard to merit (Kravitz & Platania, 1993). This, of course, may not depict reality, but it is this *perception* of affirmative action that is so problematic. There are a number of detrimental consequences.

First, affirmative action can stigmatize its intended beneficiaries, causing inferences of incompetence. If you believe that someone has been the beneficiary of preferential selection based on non-merit criteria, then you are likely to "discount" that individual's qualifications. In fact, you are likely to make the assumption that this person would not have been selected without the help of affirmative action.

There has been research linking affirmative action with incompetence inferences (Garcia, Erskine, Hawn, & Casmay, 1981; Heilman, Block, & Lucas, 1992). It has been conducted in the laboratory, where people review employee records, and in the field, where people are asked to evaluate co-workers in their work units. Inferences of incompetence have been found whether the target beneficiary is a woman or a member of a racial minority, and whether the research par-

ticipants are male or female, or students or working people (Heilman, Block, & Stathatos, 1997).

A second negative consequence of affirmative action concerns nonbeneficiaries. When women and minorities are believed to be preferentially selected, those who traditionally would have been selected for jobs often feel they are really the more deserving, and consequently, they feel unfairly bypassed (Nacoste, 1987). This has been suggested as a major reason for the "backlash" against affirmative action.

Evidence indicates that there are indeed unfortunate by-products of feeling unfairly bypassed by affirmative action. In one study, male participants were paired with a female who subsequently was preferentially selected for the more desirable task role on the basis of her gender (Heilman, McCullough, & Gilbert, 1996). Those who believed themselves to be more (or even equally) skilled than the female reported being less motivated, more angry, and less satisfied than those who were told the female was the more skilled and therefore the more deserving of the two.

The third negative consequence of affirmative action concerns its potential effect on the intended beneficiary. When people believe that they have been preferentially selected on the basis of irrelevant criteria there can be a chilling effect on self-view. Ironically, then, affirmative action may sometimes hurt those it was intended to help.

A series of laboratory experiments in which participants were selected for a desired task role (leader) either on the basis of merit or preferentially on the basis of their gender found strong support

for the idea that preferential selection can trigger negative self-regard. In repeated studies, women, but not men, who were preferentially selected were found to rate their performance more negatively, view themselves as more deficient in leadership ability, be more eager to relinquish their desirable leadership role, and shy away from demanding and challenging tasks (see Heilman, 1994, for a review of these studies).

Given these consequences, it appears that affirmative action, as it currently is understood, can undermine its own objectives. The stigma associated with affirmative action is apt to fuel rather than discredit stereotypic thinking and prejudiced attitudes. Depriving individuals of the satisfaction and pride that comes from knowing that they have achieved something on their own merits can be corrosive, decreasing self-efficacy and fostering self-views of inferiority. And the frustration resulting from feeling unfairly bypassed for employment opportunities because one does not fit into the correct demographic niche can aggravate workplace tensions and intergroup hostilities. So, paradoxically, despite its success in expanding employment opportunities for women and minorities, affirmative action may contribute to the very conditions that gave rise to the problems it was designed to remedy.

Madeline E. Heilman

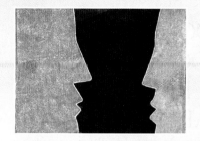

Are the Effects of Affirmative Action Positive or Negative?

THE BENEFITS OF AFFIRMATIVE ACTION
Faye J. Crosby, University of California, Santa Cruz

To assess the effects of affirmative action, you must first know what affirmative action is and what it *is not*. According to the American Psychological Association (APA): "Affirmative action occurs when an organization expends energy to make sure there is no discrimination in employment or education and, instead, equal opportunity exists" (APA, 1995, p. 5). Affirmative action goes beyond reactive policies that passively endorse justice, but waiting until a problem has erupted before enacting measures. Affirmative action requires resources and vigilance. It does not require or endorse quotas, sacrifice standards to diversity, or substitute preference for merit (Turner & Pratkanis, 1994).

For employment, affirmative action law began in earnest in 1965 (Holloway, 1989). Today it applies to all government agencies and most organizations that contract work with the federal government. Chances are that you or someone you know works for an affirmative action employer; one in four employed Americans does (Crosby & Cordova, 1996)! Affirmative action employers monitor themselves to make sure they employ qualified people from the "targeted classes" in proportion to their availability. With the help of the Office of Federal Contract Compliance Programs, any organization can get easy access to well-established methods for calculating availability.

Faye Crosby

How does the system work? Think about your professors as employees of your school. Imagine that 10% of the social science professors in your school are women (utilization 10%). Availability is calculated mostly from the proportion of social science PhDs who are female. If 30% of PhDs in the social sciences are women, while only 10% of the professors are, something is wrong! Detected problems should be corrected. Corrective measures can include flexible goals (not rigid quotas) and realistic timetables.

What are the effects of affirmative action in employment? Economists show that white women and people of color who work for affirmative action employers benefit in terms of hiring, retention, pay, and promotions (Kravitz et al., 1997). Do men of color and women feel stigmatized by affirmative action? Generally not. Do white men feel resentment or fear? Some do, especially if they are racist or sexist or if they equate affirmative action with quotas (Golden, Hinkle, & Crosby, 1998); but, in fact, most do not. Actually, three quarters of Americans endorse affirmative action (Tomasson, Crosby, & Herzberger, 1996).

Many white men—including heads of some huge corporations—endorse affirmative action out of economic realism. When the game is opened to white women and ethnic minorities, it is also opened to talented white men who previously had no inside track. Affirmative action firms appear to be more profitable than other firms (Reskin, 1998). Like effective fire-fighting units where small people squiggle into small spaces while big people maneuver big equipment, diverse business teams seem to enjoy a competitive edge (Leonard, 1986).

In education, affirmative action also entails the two steps of monitoring and correcting. If monitoring reveals, for example, that Hispanics comprise less of the undergraduate student body than expected from high-school graduation rates, corrective steps (e.g., outreach programs) may be undertaken. Affirmative action in education need not entail lowering standards; but it must result in close, sometimes painful, examination of three provocative questions: (1) What traits do we value in individuals? (2) How can we accurately assess these traits? and (3) What kinds of teams of individuals do we want to construct?

One misconception is that white women and students of color feel undermined by affirmative action. Nobody likes to be told that he or she is advancing through unjustified preferential treatment, including quotas, rather than merit (Heilman, 1994). Fortunately, most of the direct beneficiaries do not confuse affirmative action with quotas (Truax, Wood, Wright, Cordova & Crosby, 1998), especially if they feel secure in their ethnic identity (Schmermund, Sellers, Mueller, & Crosby, 1998).

A recent landmark study by the former presidents of Harvard and Princeton has fastidiously documented the positive consequences of considering race in college and university admissions. Bowen and Bok (1998) looked at long-term outcomes for hundreds of black students who had been admitted through affirmative action to 24 elite colleges in 1951, 1976, and 1989. The black students graduated from school and obtained advanced degrees at rates comparable to white students. And even more than white alumni/ae, black graduates became civic leaders—giving back to the society that had nurtured them!

What, then, are the overall effects of well-applied affirmative action in education? They are great. Everyone benefits.

- Institutions have norms that strongly govern the behavior of people who occupy critical roles within the institution. An example of how institutional norms shape group interactions is provided by the Stanford Prison Experiment, in which ordinary young men were randomly assigned roles of "prisoner" and "guard" in a simulated prison.

- When groups make decisions, they often display group polarization: The group decision is in the same direction but is more extreme than the average of the group members' initial positions. This is not just public conformity; group members' private attitudes typically shift in response to the group discussion as well.

- The group polarization effect is due in part to informational social influence, in which group members learn new information and hear novel arguments that are relevant to the decision under discussion. Group polarization is also produced by normative social influence, in which people compare their own initial views with the norms of the group. They may then adjust their position to conform to that of the majority.

- An analysis of disastrous foreign policy decisions led to a proposal that cohesive groups of decision makers can fall into the trap of groupthink, in which members of the group suppress their own dissenting opinions in the interest of group consensus. Later research suggests that group cohesion is not so much the problem, but rather threats to the group's positive identity and group norms of consensus seeking. Evidence suggests that group outcomes can be improved by fostering norms of critical thinking and promoting group diversity.

◆ Critical Thinking Questions

1. How are institutional norms, like those that operated in the Stanford Prison Experiment, communicated to new institutional members? What roles might informational and normative social influence and pluralistic ignorance play in the process of getting new members to conform to institutional norms?

2. Discuss how informational and normative social influence might produce group polarization in a jury's deliberations. How might groupthink operate to affect such deliberations? Can you think of a specific trial in which some of these phenomena appear to have been present?

RECAP: SOCIAL PSYCHOLOGICAL VIEWS OF THE SEEMINGLY INEXPLICABLE

We opened this chapter with several chilling examples—drawn both from recent world events and from history—that portray seemingly inexplicable and horrifying human behavior. How does a hijacker fly a plane into a world-famous skyscraper, killing himself, his passengers, and the thousands of people working in and visiting that building? How does a religious follower decide to drink lethal poison for "the Cause"? How does a military official orchestrate and oversee the deaths of millions of innocent people?

Although we may uncover some clues about the origins of these puzzling actions by looking to the character or personality traits of the people involved, one of the foremost lessons of social psychology is that stopping our inquiry at this level is a mistake, one that goes by the name of the fundamental attribution error. To build a more complete understanding of any form of human social behavior—from the extraordinary to the everyday—we need to also search for clues within situational forces.

In the days, months, and years after September 11, 2001, the world—including many social psychologists—struggles to understand more fully the origins and consequences of that day's tragic events. Knowing that social psychologists have had much to say in the years since the Jonestown massacre and the holocaust of World War II, you can expect social psychologists' analyses of the events on and after September 11 to soon emerge.

These social psychological perspectives will no doubt refer to the power of situations and social influence in shaping people's behavior. As you have seen, social psychologists dissect situations to uncover the particular tools of social influence at work. These tools include, among others, situation-specific social norms, pluralistic ignorance, informational and normative social influence, salient role models, internalized ideologies, and group polarization. Knowing how these and other social psychological concepts operate can help explain behavior that at first seems inexplicable. Many human actions may in fact be inexplicable from the exclusive perspective of personality psychology, but social psychology illuminates a different vantage point altogether.

In Chapter 18, our second in this two-chapter series on social psychology, we take a closer look at the subjective inner workings of people as they make sense of the social world around them. There you will be introduced to the topics and concepts of social cognition.

◆ Critical Thinking Questions

1. Now that you are acquainted with several types of social influence that have been used to explain people's behavior from a social psychological perspective, what sorts of clues about particular situations would you look for to explain the behavior of those who hijacked U.S. planes on September 11, 2001?

2. Think of an example from your own experience when, while trying to explain what caused someone's behavior, you may have committed the fundamental attribution error. What was your initial explanation based on personality or character? What is a possible explanation that makes reference to situational influences?

CHAPTER SUMMARY

1. One of the foremost lessons within social psychology is that situational forces have tremendous power to shape human behavior. A related lesson within social psychology is that these powerful situational forces are often invisible, and we mistakenly make sense of people's behavior by referring to their personality or character. This mistake is so common that social psychologists call it the fundamental attribution error.

2. Both humans and animals respond more quickly when in the presence of other members of their species. This social facilitation occurs whether the others are performing the same task (coactors) or simply watching (an audience). The presence of others appears to narrow people's attention. This facilitates the correct performance of simple responses but hinders the performance of complex ones. For humans, cognitive factors such as concern with evaluation also play a role.

3. The uninhibited aggressive behavior sometimes shown by mobs and crowds may be the result of a state of deindividuation, in which individuals feel that they have lost their personal identities and merged into the group. Both anonymity and group size contribute to deindividuation. A consequence of deindividuation is an increased sensitivity to situation-specific social norms linked with the group. This can increase aggression when the group's norms are aggressive but reduce aggression when the group norms are benign.

4. A bystander to an emergency is less likely to intervene or help if in a group than if alone. Two major factors that deter intervention are defining the situation and diffusion of responsibility. By attempting to appear calm, bystanders may define the situation for one another as a nonemergency, thereby producing a state of pluralistic ignorance. The presence of other people also diffuses responsibility so that no one person feels the necessity to act. Bystanders are more likely to intervene when these factors are minimized, particularly if at least one person begins to help.

5. In a series of classic studies on conformity, Solomon Asch found that a unanimous group exerts strong pressure on an individual to conform to the group's judgments—even when those judgments are clearly wrong. Much less conformity is observed if even one person dissents from the group.

6. A minority within a larger group can move the majority toward its point of view if it maintains a consistent dissenting position without appearing to be rigid, dogmatic, or arrogant. Minorities sometimes obtain private attitude change from majority members even when they fail to obtain public conformity.

7. In a series of classic studies on obedience, Stanley Milgram demonstrated that ordinary people would obey an experimenter's order to deliver strong electric shocks to an innocent victim. Factors conspiring to produce the high obedience rates include surveillance by the experimenter, buffers that distance the person from the consequences of his or her acts, the emerging properties of situations, and the legitimating role of science, which leads people to abandon their autonomy to the experimenter. There has been considerable controversy about the ethics of the experiments themselves.

8. One way that people come to internalize attitudes and beliefs that are consistent with their actions is through the processes of self-justification. Cognitive dissonance theory suggests that when people's behavior conflicts with their attitudes, it creates an uncomfortable tension that motivates them to change their attitudes to be more in line with their actions. Self-perception theory

challenged this view by stating that inner turmoil does not necessarily occur. To the extent that internal cues are weak, ambiguous, or uninterpretable, people may simply infer their attitudes from their past behavior.

9. In the process of identification, we obey the norms and adopt the beliefs, attitudes, and behaviors of groups that we respect and admire. We use such reference groups to evaluate and regulate our opinions and actions. A reference group can regulate our attitudes and behavior by administering social rewards and punishments or providing a frame of reference, a ready-made interpretation of events and social issues.

10. Most people identify with more than one reference group, which can lead to conflicting pressures on beliefs, attitudes, and behaviors. College students frequently move away from the views of their family reference group toward the college reference group. These new views are usually sustained in later life because (1) they become internalized and (2) after college we tend to select new reference groups that share our views.

11. When groups make decisions, they often display group polarization: The group decision is in the same direction but is more extreme than the average of the group members' initial positions. This is not just public conformity; group members' private attitudes typically shift in response to the group discussion as well. The effect is due in part to informational social influence, in which group members learn new information and hear novel arguments that are relevant to the decision under discussion. Group polarization is also produced by normative social influence, in which people compare their own initial views with the norms of the group. They may then adjust their position to conform to that of the majority.

12. An analysis of disastrous foreign policy decisions led to a proposal that cohesive groups of decision makers can fall into the trap of groupthink, in which members of the group suppress their own dissenting opinions in the interest of group consensus. Later research suggests that group cohesion is not so much the problem but rather threats to the group's positive identity and group norms of consensus seeking. Evidence suggests that group outcomes can be improved by fostering norms of critical thinking and promoting group diversity.

CORE CONCEPTS

fundamental attribution error
social psychology
coaction
social facilitation
social inhibition
Stroop interference
deindividuation
social norms
bystander effect
pluralistic ignorance

diffusion of responsibility
compliance
informational social influence
normative social influence
minority influence
implicit leniency contract
ideology
debriefing
internalization
foot-in-the-door technique

cognitive dissonance theory
rationalization
self-perception theory
overjustification effect
identification
reference groups
institutional norms
group polarization effect
groupthink

WEB RESOURCES

http://psychology.wadsworth.com/
atkinson14e

Take a quiz, try the activities and exercises, and explore web links.

http://www.kassiber.de/cults.htm

This site includes a plethora of links to information about different cults. You can research everything from the Freemasons and Hare Krishna to killer cults like the People's Temple and Heaven's Gate.

http://choo.fis.utoronto.ca/FIS/Courses/LIS2149/
Groupthink.html

This online model highlights some of the pitfalls associated with groupthink.

InfoTrac Online Library

http://www.infotrac-college.com/
wadsworth

Use InfoTrac College Edition to find popular and scientific articles by using the search terms below or your own relevant terms.

- Groupthink
- Social influence
- Social psychology

CD-ROM LINKS

Psych Odyssey

Check out CD Chapter 14, Social Psychology: Interpersonal and Group Perspectives

A. Conformity
B. Compliance
C. Prosocial Behavior

Taxi/Getty Images

SOCIAL COGNITION

18

People think about—and judge—other people all the time. For instance, when engaged in casual people-watching on campus, you might surmise that one cluster of people are football players, another are sorority members, and still another a group of library nerds. Another person reminds you of your best friend from grade school, and you smile. And many people—male and female alike—believe that women are, by nature, more emotional than men. More chilling examples of social cognition can be drawn from recent history: Osama bin Laden said in a 2001 televi-sion interview that all Americans were enemies of Islam—or infidels—and so all Americans should be targeted for at-tack. And after the terrorist attacks on the United States of September 2001, people around the world became more aware of their Arab-born neighbors, wondering if they, too, held the anti-American attitudes of bin Laden and his followers.

Our thoughts and judgments about others don't simply help us pass the time. They have consequences. How you categorize your college classmates, for instance, determines whether and how you interact with them and whether they become friends or rivals. As we saw in Chapter 11, endorsing the stereotype that women are more emo-tional than men can shape people's per-ceptions of their own and others' emo-tions. And the generalization made by bin Laden and his followers that all Americans are the enemy led to the deaths of thousands of innocent civil-ians on September 11, 2001, and the subsequent suspicions about Arab-born neighbors has, in some instances, fueled additional prejudice and racially moti-vated hate crimes.

Recall that social psychology concerns the ways that people's behavior and mental processes are shaped by the real or imagined presence of others. In Chapter 17, we saw one of the foremost lessons of social psychology: that social situations—like the presence of others, unanimous majorities, requests from authorities, social norms, and group interactions—have enormous power to influence people's behavior, thoughts, and feelings, power that often goes unrecognized. In this chapter, we will encounter another core lesson of social psychology: that to more fully understand people's social behavior, we need to "get inside their heads." The study of **social cognition** does just that. It examines people's subjective interpretations of their social experiences, as well as their modes of thinking about the social world.

As social psychologists have peered inside people's heads, looking for clues that might illuminate social behavior, they have found evidence for two different modes of thinking, one more automatic and unintentional, often outside conscious awareness, and another more controlled and deliberate, of which we are fully aware. This idea that there are two different modes of thinking should be familiar to you. In Chapter 11, we saw that people's cognitive appraisals—their interpretations of their current circumstances that trigger emotions—can occur at both conscious and unconscious levels. When appraisals are unconscious, people may feel emotions without knowing why. The same can happen for social cognition more generally. Sometimes thinking is automatic and unintended, and other times it is under our conscious control. This is an important discovery because whether thinking is automatic or controlled turns out to influence how and when the contents of mind influence social behavior and social reactions (Chaiken & Trope, 1999). We will see how these two different modes of thinking work as we consider the processes of impression formation, attitudes, and interpersonal attraction.

IMPRESSION FORMATION

When you come across someone new, how do you come to know him or her? How do you form impressions of others? Does the color or apparent age of their skin matter? Their body size and shape? In other words, do your impressions of new people depend on their ethnicity, age, and gender? Do your ulterior motives matter? That is, does it matter whether you simply pass them in the street or whether you are looking for a roommate? Or whether you expect to collaborate with them on an important project? These and other questions guide our discussion of impression formation.

STEREOTYPES

Like many others, social psychologists are invested in social justice—fair treatment for all people. This is why considerable energy within the study of social cognition is devoted to the study of stereotypes. If we can understand why, when, and how stereotypes operate, social psychologists argue, we can be better prepared to limit their adverse effects and treat people more fairly.

Several decades of research on stereotypes tells us that, whether we like it or not, our initial impressions of others are biased by our preexisting expectations. As we saw in previous chapters, this is true of perception more generally. Whenever we perceive any object or event, we implicitly categorize it, comparing the incoming information with our memories of previous encounters with similar objects and events. In earlier chapters, we saw that memories are not usually photograph-like reproductions of the original stimuli but simplified reconstructions of our original perceptions. As noted in Chapter 8, such representations or memory structures are called **schemas;** they are organized beliefs and knowledge about people, objects, events, and situations. The process of searching in memory for the schema that is most consistent with the incoming data is called **schematic processing,** or top-down thinking. Schemas and schematic processing permit us to organize and process enormous and potentially overwhelming amounts of information very efficiently. Instead of having to perceive and remember all the details of each new object or event, we can simply note that it is like one of our preexisting schemas and encode or remember only its most prominent features. For instance, schematic processing is what allows us to readily categorize consumables as either food or drink and then put one on a plate and the other in a glass.

As with objects and events, we also use schemas and schematic processing in our encounters with people. For example, we categorize people into groups based on salient physical attributes—like race, gender, or age—or by their relation to our own social identity—as in "us versus them." Schemas can also be more narrowly defined: When someone tells you that you are about to meet someone who is outgoing, you retrieve your "extravert" schema in anticipation of the coming encounter. The extravert schema is a set of interrelated traits such as sociability, warmth, and possibly loudness and impulsiveness. As mentioned in Chapter 8, **stereotypes** are schemas for classes or subtypes of people. The stereotype of an extravert, a student at a rival school, or an African American is a mini-theory about what particular traits or behaviors go with certain other traits or behaviors. We focus on stereotypes in this section because they are a kind of person schema that has far-reaching consequences for impression formation. You should keep in mind, though, that in addition to schemas for classes of people, we also have schemas for particular individuals, such as the president of the United States or our parents. And as discussed in Chapter 13, we also have a **self-schema** or schema about ourselves—a set of organized self-concepts stored in memory (Markus, 1977). When you see a job advertisement for a peer counselor, for instance, you can evaluate the match between your counselor schema and your self-schema to decide whether you should apply for the job.

AUTOMATIC STEREOTYPE ACTIVATION The associations conveyed within stereotypes—for example, that African Americans are hostile, that women are passive, or that old people are slow—can become overlearned and automatic. We saw in Chapter 6 that through repeated practice driving a car becomes so habitual and automatic that we scarcely need to devote any conscious attention to it. A similar process happens with repeated exposure to stereotypes about people: They, too, can become habitual and automatic, operating outside conscious awareness.

Experiments that demonstrate the automaticity of stereotypes rely on priming techniques. You will recall from Chapter 8 that **priming** refers to the incidental activation of schemas by situational contexts. Beyond effects on memory, we saw in Chapter 17 that priming can also influence social behavior: Simply exposing people to words like *adhere, comply,* and *conform* increased the likelihood that they would later conform to a unanimous majority.

Priming can also activate stereotypes automatically, outside conscious awareness. In one experiment, participants were given a purported test of language ability called the "Scrambled Sentence Test." Each of 30 items on the test consisted of five words. Participants were told to use any four of the five words to construct a grammatically correct sentence as quickly as possible. There were actually two versions of the Scrambled Sentence Test. The critical version primed the elderly stereotype by including words like *old, gray, Florida, retired,* and *bingo*. The other version contained words unrelated to the elderly stereotype (such as *thirsty, clean, private*). Participants took part in the study one at a time. When they finished the Scrambled Sentence Test, the experimenter excused them and directed them toward the elevator. Only after participants left the laboratory did the researchers assess the impact of the elderly stereotype: Those primed with the elderly stereotype actually walked more slowly down the hall to the elevator! Priming the elderly stereotype—which includes the idea that old people are slow—influenced the behavior of young people at a nonconscious level. We know that it's the

Many types of advertising can activate stereotypes of women and trigger sexist behavior.

stereotype at work here because none of the critical words made reference to speed or time directly. We also know that the effect occurred at a nonconscious level because completing the Scrambled Sentence Test does not produce conscious awareness of any theme or stereotype. It is viewed simply as a test of language ability (Bargh, Chen, & Burrows, 1996).

One major source of primed stereotypes is the visual media—television, movies, billboards, and the like. In Chapter 11, we saw that exposure to media violence clearly increases children's aggressive behavior. The same holds for exposure to media stereotypes. By now you've come to recognize that the people you see in the visual mass media are hardly representative of people in the real world. People on television, for instance, are younger, slimmer, and more attractive than people you come across in your hometown. Portrayals of women are especially stereotyped. Many times women are portrayed simply as sex objects valued only for their physical appearance. Although exposure to media stereotypes of women may seem harmless, it does damage. In Chapter 10, we saw how such media promote eating disorders in girls and women. More generally, people who watch a lot of television endorse more sexist attitudes toward women (Gerbner, Gross, Morgan, & Signorielli, 1986). But that's simply a correlation. Maybe television does not cause sexism. An experiment that manipulated television exposure provides the necessary causal evidence. The researchers used television advertisements (drawn from regular U.S. prime-time broadcasts) to prime the stereotype of women as sex objects in one group of men. A separate control group watched other, nonsexist TV ads. All the men were later asked to interview a woman for a job as a research assistant. Compared with men in the control group, those primed by TV ads to think of women in stereotypical terms chose more sexist questions when interviewing the female job candidate and behaved in a more sexualized manner toward her (Rudman & Borgida, 1995).

Stereotypes can also be activated through nonconscious priming. We saw in Chapter 11 that very brief, subliminal exposure to pictures of spiders and snakes (less than 30 milliseconds) can produce physiological arousal and aversive feelings in phobics, even though the phobics could not report having seen anything frightening. The same holds for stereotypes. In one experiment, participants (who were not African American) were shown photographs of young, male faces that were either European American or African American for less than 30 milliseconds, too fast for conscious awareness. These nonconscious, subliminal primes were embedded within a tedious computer task. The computer was rigged so that after participants had spent considerable time on the task, it produced an error message: "F11 error: failure

saving data." It then informed participants that they would need to do the entire computer task over again. Hidden video cameras recorded participants' facial reactions to this news. Those primed with African American faces reacted to the computer error with more hostility. Here, priming the African American stereotype—which includes the idea that African Americans are hostile—automatically generated hostile behavior in unsuspecting participants (Bargh et al., 1996). In fact, people don't even have to personally endorse the stereotype to be affected by it: Stereotypic behavior was activated equally so for those who scored high and low on questionnaire measures of racist attitudes (see also Devine, 1989; Fazio, Jackson, Dunton, & Williams, 1995).

So simply encountering a person can activate a stereotype as we categorize that person by ethnicity, age, or gender, or as "us versus them." But when we categorize others, do we also evaluate them? Experiments suggest that we do. Evidence that automatically activated racial categories carry emotional evaluations comes from a series of studies in which African American and European Americans viewed faces of many ethnic backgrounds, including African American and European American faces. For African Americans, European American faces represent an out-group, whereas the reverse is true for European Americans. The faces were embedded within a word evaluation task in which participants were asked to indicate whether a given adjective (such as *attractive, likeable, annoying,* or *offensive*) was either "good" or "bad" and to make this judgment as quickly and as accurately as possible. Participants made these judgments for dozens of words while the experimenters recorded their reaction times. The results of this study are shown in Figure 18-1. For European American participants, viewing African American faces sped responses to negative words. The opposite was true for African American participants: Viewing European American faces sped responses to negative words (Fazio et al., 1995). These findings suggest that when we categorize others as members of an out-group ("them" as opposed to "us"), we simultaneously and automatically activate negative associations, which facilitates negative responses.

Corroborating evidence comes from a study that used brain imaging (see Chapter 2). Both African American and European American participants viewed photographs of unfamiliar African American and European American faces several times. Imaging data showed that initial exposure to all faces produced activation in the amygdala, an area of the brain that is involved in monitoring

Nonconscious exposure to photographs like these is sufficient to activate stereotypes and influence social behavior.

© Joel Gordon

© Joel Gordon

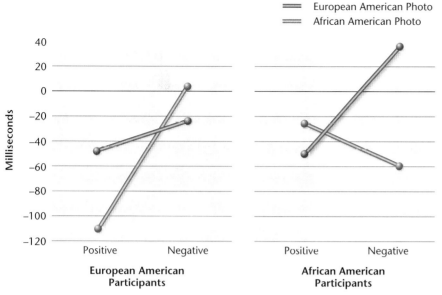

European American Photo
African American Photo

Positive   Negative
**European American
Participants**

Positive   Negative
**African American
Participants**

Milliseconds

❚ Figure 18-1
Automatic Stereotype Activation
These two graphs plot the mean response times for classifying positive and negative adjectives as good or bad when preceded by photos of African American and European American faces. Higher scores indicate faster responses. Notice that for European American participants, the difference in response times for the positive and negative words is greater when preceded by African American faces, with negative judgments made faster. The reverse pattern emerged for African American participants—their negative judgments were facilitated by viewing European American faces. These data indicate that classifying another person as in a racial "out-group" automatically carries with it negative evaluations. (Adaptation of Figure 1 on p. 1018 from R. H. Fazio, J. R. Jackson, B. C. Dunton, & C. J. Williams (1995), "Variability in automatic activation as an unobtrusive measure of racial attitudes: A bona fide pipeline?" in *Journal of Personality and Social Psychology, 69,* 1013–1027. Copyright © 1995 by the American Psychological Association. Adapted with permission.)

emotion-eliciting stimuli at a nonconscious level (see Chapter 11). On reexposure to these same faces, amygdala activation lessened for in-group faces, whereas it remained high for out-group faces (Hart et al., 2000). These data suggest that unfamiliar faces in general, regardless of racial category, are initially perceived as threatening. Over time, however, this threat response abates for those who are "like us" but not for those who are "not like us."

STEREOTYPES AND INFORMATION PROCESSING Research confirms that stereotypes, like schemas more generally, help us process information. For example, if people are explicitly instructed to remember as much information as they can about a person, they actually remember less than if they are simply told to try to form an impression (Hamilton, 1979). This is because the instruction to form an impression induces them to search for relevant schemas or stereotypes that help them organize and recall material better.

Without stereotypes, then, we would be overwhelmed by the information that inundates us. If you had no way to organize or access your expectations about different types of people, you would be extraordinarily slow to form impressions of them. But the price we pay for the efficiency that stereotypes bring are biases in our perceptions and our memories of the information given and in the inferences we make. Consider, for example, the impression you form of Jim from the following observations of his behavior:

Jim left the house to get some stationery. He walked out into the sun-filled street with two of his friends, basking in the sun as he walked. Jim entered the stationery store, which was full of people. Jim talked with an acquaintance while he waited to catch the clerk's eye. On his way out, he stopped to chat with a school friend who was just coming into the store. Leaving the store, he walked toward the school. On his way he met the girl to whom he had been introduced the night before. They talked for a short while, and then Jim left for school. After school, Jim left the classroom alone. Leaving the school, he started on his long walk home. The street was brilliantly filled with sunshine. Jim walked down the street on the shady side. Coming down the street toward him, he saw the pretty girl whom he had met on the previous evening. Jim crossed the street and entered a candy store. The store was crowded with students, and he noticed a few familiar faces. Jim waited quietly until he caught the counterman's eye and then gave his order. Taking his drink, he sat down at a side table. When he had finished his drink, he went home. (Luchins, 1957, pp. 34–35)

What impression do you have of Jim? Do you think of him as friendly and outgoing or as shy and introverted? If you think of him as friendly, you agree with 78% of people who read this description. But examine the description closely; it is actually composed of two very different portraits. Up to the sentence that begins "After school, Jim left," Jim is portrayed in several situations as fairly friendly. After that point, however, a nearly identical set of situations shows him to be much more of a loner. Whereas 95% of the people who are shown only the first half of the description rate Jim as friendly, just 3% of the people who are shown only the second half do so. Thus, in the combined description, Jim's friendliness dominates the overall impression. But when people read the same description with the un-

● Table 18-1
Schematic Processing and the Primacy Effect

Once a schema of Jim has been established, later information is assimilated into it. *(A. Luchens (1957) "Primary Recovery in Impression Formation," in* The Order of Presentation Persuasion, *edited by C. I. Hovland, pp. 34–35. Yale University Press.)*

Conditions	Percentage Rating Jim as Friendly
Friendly description only	95
Friendly first—unfriendly last	78
Unfriendly first—friendly last	18
Unfriendly description only	3

The first information we receive has a greater impact on our overall impressions than later information. This is why people usually wear business suits to interview for a job.

friendly half of the paragraph appearing first, only 18% rate Jim as friendly; his unfriendly behavior leaves the major impression (see Table 18-1). This study illustrates the **primacy effect:** In general, the first information we receive has the greater impact on our overall impressions.

The primacy effect has been found repeatedly in several kinds of studies of impression formation, including studies using real rather than hypothetical individuals (Jones, 1990). For example, people who watched a male student attempt to solve a series of difficult multiple-choice problems were asked to assess his general ability (Jones, Rock, Shaver, Goethals, & Ward, 1968). Although the student always solved exactly 15 of the 30 problems correctly, he was judged more capable if the successes came mostly at the beginning of the series than if they came near the end. Moreover, when asked to recall how many problems the student had solved, participants who had seen the 15 successes bunched at the beginning estimated an average of 21, but participants who had seen the successes at the end estimated an average of 13.

Although several factors contribute to the primacy effect, it appears to be primarily a consequence of schematic processing or top-down thinking. When we are first attempting to form our impressions of a person, we actively search in memory for the schemas or stereotypes that best match the incoming data. At some point we make a preliminary decision: This person is extraverted, or this person is smart (or some such judgment). We then assimilate any further information to that judgment and dismiss discrepant information as not representative of the person we have come to know. For example, when asked to reconcile the apparent contradictions in Jim's behavior, participants sometimes say that Jim is really friendly but was probably tired by the end of the day (Luchins, 1957). Our stereotype of extraverts, activated by Jim's initial behaviors, shapes our perception of all subsequent data about Jim. More generally, our subsequent perceptions become

schema-driven and therefore relatively impervious to new data. There is thus a great deal of truth in the conventional warning that first impressions are important.

Stereotypes also help us make **inferences**, which means to make judgments that go beyond the information given. A classic study by Solomon Asch in 1946 illustrates this effect. To get a sense of the study, form an impression in your mind of Sam, someone described as "intelligent, skillful, industrious, cold, determined, practical, and cautious." Based on the impression you have now formed, do you think that Sam is generous? Could you ask him to lend you his car for the day? If you think not, you agree with the participants in Asch's original study: Only 9% inferred that a person was generous, given these traits. But what if Sam was described as "intelligent, skillful, industrious, warm, determined, practical, and cautious?" Only one trait differs: *Cold* is replaced by *warm*. Now would you think that Sam is generous? Probably so. A full 91% of those in Asch's original study inferred generosity from the same trait constellation that included *warm* instead of *cold*. So although no information is given about Sam's likely generosity, we can use our expectations or stereotypes about warm or cold people to go beyond what's given and make an inference. Studies like Asch's have also been done with real rather than hypothetical individuals. For instance, students told that an upcoming guest lecturer was "rather cold" came to evaluate him quite negatively, whereas other students told that this same guest lecturer was "rather warm" came to evaluate him quite favorably, even though they observed the same lecturer behaving in the same way (Kelley, 1950). The bottom line here is that advance reputations are hard to shake!

Stereotypes about race and gender have also been found to shape our interpretations of other people's behavior. Suppose you learn that someone performed exceptionally well on a math test. Studies show that if that someone is male, most people think he's smart, whereas if she's female, they think she got lucky by studying the right material (Deaux, 1984; Swim & Sanna, 1996). Likewise, when European Americans hear that an African American man punched someone, they tend to conclude that he's aggressive, but if they learn that a European American man punched someone, they tend to wonder what provoked him (Hewstone, 1990; Pettigrew, 1979). In these examples, we see that information consistent with a stereotype is taken as diagnostic of that person's underlying ability or personality, whereas information inconsistent with a stereotype is dismissed as not characteristic of them.

Similar evidence comes from the experiment, described earlier, in which one group of men was primed by viewing TV ads with stereotypic images of women. In a later word-recognition task (disguised as a separate study), primed men, compared with men who were not primed, were faster to recognize sexist words (like *babe* and *bimbo*) and slower to recognize nonsexist words (like *mother* and *sister*) (Rudman & Borgida, 1995). Simply through media exposure, these men were primed to see the world through the lens of the activated gender stereotype.

To sum, stereotypes (like top-down, schematic processing more generally) determine how we perceive, recall, and interpret information about people. So, as we form impressions of others, we don't simply take in the available information about them and process it in an unbiased manner. Instead, we filter incoming information through our preexisting stereotypes and actively construct our perceptions, memories, and inferences. Making matters worse, the effects of stereotypes on perception and thinking often remain invisible to us: We often take our constructions to be direct and unbiased representations of reality! In other words, we rarely see the role of stereotypes in shaping our interpretations but instead believe that we simply "call it like it is." You can begin to see how entrenched and persistent stereotypes

can be: Even if initially incorrect, people can come to believe that a stereotype is "true" because they construct—and see—a world in which it is.

SELF-FULFILLING STEREOTYPES Stereotypes can also be like omens—they can predict the future. But this is not because stereotypes are necessarily true. Rather, once activated, stereotypes can set in motion a chain of behavioral processes that serve to draw out from others behavior that confirms the initial stereotype, an effect called the **self-fulfilling prophecy** (Jussim, 1991; Rosenthal & Jacobson, 1968; Snyder, Tanke, & Berscheid, 1977). This works because stereotypes don't just reside in our heads. They leak out in our actions. To get feel for this, suppose that women who attend your rival university have the reputation for being snobs. In actuality, most are quite friendly, but your sources tell you differently. How will you act toward a student from that university when you cross paths with her before a football game? Most likely you'll look away. Why should you bother to smile and say hello to a snob? And how will she act? Now that you've given her the cold shoulder, she'll probably do the same. And now that you see her cold, aloof manner, you'll take that as proof positive that she *is* a snob and fail to see your own role in producing this evidence! So your stereotype of women from the rival school, although initially wrongly applied to the woman you met, shaped your own behavior, which in turn shaped her behavior, which in turn provided behavioral confirmation for your initially erroneous stereotype. Beliefs have a way of becoming reality.

In a classic study illustrating this process, investigators first noted that European American job interviewers displayed a less friendly manner when interviewing African American applicants than when interviewing European American applicants. They hypothesized that this could cause African American applicants to come off less well in the interviews. To test this hypothesis, they trained interviewers to reproduce both the less friendly and the more friendly interviewing styles. Applicants (all European Americans) were then videotaped while being interviewed by an interviewer using one of these two styles. Judges who viewed the videotapes rated applicants who had been interviewed in a less friendly manner much lower on their interview performance compared with those who had been interviewed in the friendlier manner (Word, Zanna, & Cooper, 1974). The study thus confirmed the hypothesis that people who hold stereotypes can interact in ways that actually evoke the stereotyped behaviors that sustain their biased beliefs.

Self-fulfilling prophecies can occur completely outside conscious awareness. Earlier we saw that when people's stereotypes about African Americans were primed through brief, subliminal exposure to young African

American male faces, they were more likely to act in a hostile manner. Is this hostile behavior potent enough to draw out hostility from others? Another experiment tested this possibility. The same priming procedure was used for one person in a pair before the two played a potentially frustrating game with each other. Replicating the first study, those who had been primed with African American faces showed greater hostility than those primed with European American faces. Plus, as the self-fulfilling prophecy predicts, the partners of those primed with African American faces (who were *not* themselves primed) also showed greater hostility than those whose partners were primed with European American faces. Moreover, the primed participants saw their partners as hostile but did not see their own role in drawing that hostility out (Chen & Bargh, 1997). These data suggest that the mere presence of a stereotyped person can activate stereotypes that soon become self-fulfilling.

Stereotypes that we hold about our own group can also be self-fulfilling. When college students are primed with racial stereotypes—which include the idea that African Americans are intellectually inferior—African Americans perform worse than European Americans on difficult academic tests. But when no racial stereotype is activated, African Americans perform equal to European Americans (Steele & Aronson, 1995). The same holds for the stereotype that women are bad at math: When the stereotype is activated, women perform worse than men on difficult math tests. When it is not activated, women perform equal to men (Spencer, Steele, & Quinn, 1999). Stereotypes about the elderly can be similarly self-fulfilling. When a negative stereotype is activated by brief, subliminal exposure to words like *senile*, elderly participants perform worse on a later memory test. By contrast, elderly participants who are subliminally primed with positive stereotypes about their group (such as *wise*) perform better on the same memory task (Levy, 1996).

The dominant explanation for the self-fulfilling nature of self-stereotypes appeals to a concept called **stereotype threat,** which suggests that the mere threat of being identified with a stereotype can raise an individual's anxiety level, which in turn degrades his or her performance (Steele, 1997). Other explanations downplay the role of experienced threat and appeal more to simple mental representations of the behaviors associated with the activated stereotypes. Through a principle called **ideomotor action,** mentally activating these behavioral representations—simply thinking about them—can make actual corresponding behaviors more likely. For example, if the stereotype of African Americans—which includes the trait of "laziness"—is activated in a testing situation, it can automatically yield "lazy" behavior, like guessing or failing to read test items carefully (Dijksterhuis & Bargh, 2001;

Wheeler & Petty, 2001). The ideomotor perspective predicts that stereotypes don't have to target one's own group to harm performance in testing situations, and some experiments have shown this to be the case (Wheeler, Jarvis, & Petty, 2001; for a review, see Wheeler & Petty, 2001).

INDIVIDUATION

As we've seen, stereotypes can be activated automatically, simply by seeing someone's face. Plus, once activated, stereotypes can influence our thinking and behavior in ways that actually draw out stereotype-confirming behaviors from ourselves and from others. (For a review of the various cognitive and behavioral effects of stereotypes, see the Concept Review Table.) If the effects of stereotypes are so automatic and far-reaching, can we ever truly come to know another person accurately? In the 1960s, Martin Luther King Jr. expressed a similar yearning to be free from the pernicious effects of stereotypes. In his famous speech entitled "I Have a Dream," King voiced his hope that African American children might "one day live in a nation where they will not be judged by the color of their skin, but by the content of their character." Dr. King was actually describing a process that social psychologists call **individuation,** which means assessing an individual's personal qualities on a person-by-person basis. Fortunately, Martin Luther King Jr.'s dream can come true: We can sometimes override the effects of stereotypes and form more accurate and personalized impressions of others through individuation. But typically, this more accurate impression formation requires a more thoughtful and controlled mode of thinking.

CONCEPT REVIEW TABLE
Summary of the Effects of Stereotypes

Cognitive Effects

1. Automatic evaluation
2. Biased perceptions of incoming information
3. Biased memories
4. Biased inferences and interpretations

Behavioral Effects

1. Automatic emotion expression
2. Automatic behavioral tendencies
3. Self-fulfilling prophecies

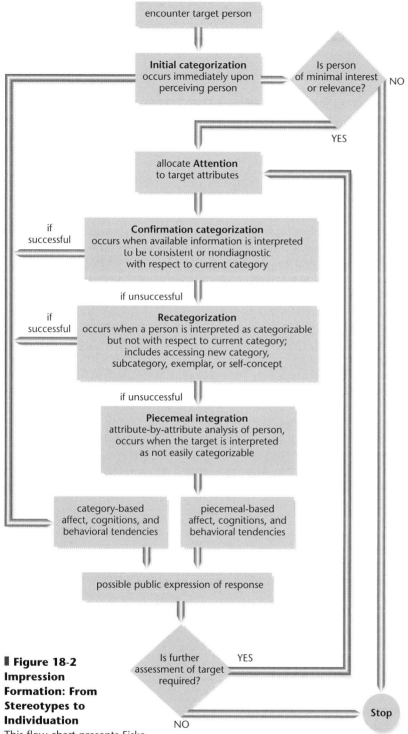

**Figure 18-2
Impression
Formation: From
Stereotypes to
Individuation**
This flow chart presents Fiske
and Neuberg's continuum model of impression formation. It shows the
continuum of impression formation processes ranging from stereotyping to individuation as a function of attention and interpretation. Here the most individuating stage
is called "piecemeal integration." The information available about the person perceived and the perceivers' motivational goals determine how attention and interpretations combine to shape the process of impression formation. (From S. T. Fiske, M. Lin,
& S. L. Neuberg (1999). "The continuum model: Ten years later," in S. Chaiken & Y. Trope (eds.), *Dual-process Theories in Social Psychology*, pp. 231–254. New York: Guilford Press.)

TRIGGERS OF INDIVIDUATION When and how do we move beyond stereotyping to individuation? One influential model of impression formation, called the **continuum model,** describes the full continuum of processes from stereotyping to individuation (Fiske, Lin, & Neuberg, 1999). The model is described by the flow chart shown in Figure 18-2. You can see in this flow chart that the automatic stereotyping that we've discussed so far is the first psychological process set in motion when we first encounter a person (called "initial categorization" in Figure 18-2). Within milliseconds of an initial encounter, we have already automatically and nonconsciously categorized the person in terms of gender, ethnicity, and age. These categories are used first because they (1) apply to most people, (2) are available immediately and physically (in face-to-face encounters), and (3) often have important cultural meanings relevant to our interaction goals. Whether we move beyond simple stereotyping depends on whether the person we've encountered has any personal relevance to us. If, for instance, you are deciding whether to share an apartment with this new person, you most certainly will devote more attention to forming your impression.

As Figure 18-2 shows, the first thing that we do once we move into this more thoughtful process of impression formation is try to confirm our initial categorization. Return to that potential roommate. You might want to know whether the young man you've just met is a "typical 20-year-old guy." Will he be interested in loud parties, fast cars, and frequent dates? Or is he more of a loner, truly engaged with his studies? You notice that his backpack is overflowing with texts for the most advanced courses, and he tells you that he spends most evenings at the library. So the available information suggests that the initial categorization won't do. Now you find another, narrower category for him: A studious nerd. This is called "recategorization" in Figure 18-2. Because you are also engaged with your studies most evenings, you suspect that you'd be compatible roommates. You decide to share the apartment.

Over time, and as you learn more about your new roommate, you come to recognize that being a studious nerd is just one facet of his character. He also plays the saxophone, competes in triathlons, and has traveled extensively across South America. Only now do you recognize that he doesn't fit any one category fully, so instead you form an impression of him by piecing together and integrating all the different things you know about him, a process called "piecemeal integration" in Figure 18-2. So, when ample information about someone becomes available, and when we are motivated and able to pay close attention to that information, we eventually judge people "by the content of their character." And that's individuation. The most important thing to note, however, is how slowly we move away from stereotyping and categorization toward individuation. In fact, many social psychologists would argue that we never fully abandon categorizing people, however well intentioned we are, because doing so provides a wealth of information with little mental effort. Even so, when others become personally relevant to us—that is, if our future outcomes depend on them in some way—we become motivated to make more thoughtful, accurate, and individuated impressions of them.

STRUCTURES THAT PROMOTE INDIVIDUATION The importance of personal relevance carries a lesson for those who aim to reduce stereotyping in their schools, businesses, or other organizations. Studies show that structured cooperative contact between members of different social groups reduces stereotyping and fosters individuation. In one study, participants met another student who was identified as a former mental patient. At first, participants expected this new acquaintance to be somewhat depressed, fearful, and insecure, traits that fit the stereotype of a former mental patient. Next, the experimenters randomly assigned participants to either cooperate with this new acquaintance to jointly learn new material on an assigned topic or to simply study that new material independently but in the same room as the new acquaintance. Compared with those who didn't cooperate on the learning task, those who did cooperate moved away from their initial stereotyped impressions and judged the new acquaintance more positively, presumably because the cooperative structure of the task provided the opportunity to individuate. Perhaps more importantly, participants extended their favorable impressions of their learning partner to former mental patients in general (Desforges et al., 1991). So if you find yourself teaching or leading a group of others who seem to be divided by their stereotyped impressions of one another, remember that you can greatly reduce the harmful effects of stereotyping by structuring in the need to cooperate or share consequential information. Cooperation, of course, has other benefits as well. It can also produce more successful individual and group outcomes (Aronson & Thibodeau, 1992).

CONTROLLING STEREOTYPES As we've seen, sometimes we are drawn toward the individuation end of the impression formation continuum because we are motivated to get to know other people personally and accurately and have ample time to do so. Other times, we may not so much be drawn to individuate as we are motivated to avoid being prejudiced by the biasing effects of stereotypes. In fact, simply knowing that stereotypes can produce biases in our judgments and actions (as you now know) can create a strong desire to override stereotypic responses and apply more egalitarian responses instead. Luckily, laboratory studies have shown that we can consciously override the influence of stereotypes, but only if certain conditions are met: (1) being aware of the potential negative influence of stereotypes, (2) being motivated to reduce prejudice, and (3) having sufficient attentional resources to engage in controlled and deliberate thinking. Although researchers continue to debate how and how often such conditions can be met in day-to-day life (Bargh, 1999), studies show that certain people, through mental effort, can overcome the harmful effects of stereotypes, even in brief encounters (Bodenhausen, Macrea & Sherman, 1999; Devine & Monteith, 1999). Recent studies even show that people who are highly identified with the goal of being nonprejudiced can also overcome the automatic activation of stereotypes, like that shown in Figure 18-1 (Devine, Plant, Amodio, Harmon-Jones, & Vance, 2002). These findings are important. They tell us that we need not be slaves to automatically activated social stereotypes. Instead, with the proper combination of motivation and controlled thought, we can learn to treat people justly, based on "the content of their character," a manner in which we all deserve to be treated.

ATTRIBUTIONS

Another process through which we form impressions of others involves understanding the causes of their behavior. Suppose, for example, that a famous athlete endorses a particular brand of athletic shoes on television. Why does he do it? Does he really like those shoes, or is he doing it for the money? You see a woman give a $5 donation to Planned Parenthood. Why? Is she altruistic? Was she being pressured? Did she need a tax write-off? Does she believe in the work of the organization?

Each of these cases creates an attribution problem. We witness some behavior and must decide to which of many possible causes the action should be attributed.

Is this woman giving money to the Salvation Army because she supports its work, because she feels pressured, or because she is generally altruistic?

Attribution refers to our intuitive attempts to infer the causes of behavior. It has long been a central topic in social psychology and continues to be today (Heider, 1958; Kelley, 1967; Malle, 1999; Trope & Gaunt, 1999).

THE FUNDAMENTAL ATTRIBUTION ERROR REVISITED

As the two preceding examples illustrate, one of the major attribution tasks we face is deciding whether an observed behavior reflects something about the person or something about the situation in which we observed the person. The former option is called an internal or **dispositional attribution.** We infer that something about the person is primarily responsible for the behavior (for instance, the athlete really loves those shoes). Here, *disposition* here refers to a person's beliefs, attitudes, and personality characteristics. The alternative choice is called an external or **situational attribution.** We infer that some external cause is primarily

responsible for the behavior (for instance, money, social norms, threats).

Fritz Heider, the founder of attribution theory, noted that an individual's behavior is so compelling to us that we take it as a face value representation of a person and give insufficient weight to the circumstances surrounding it (1958). Research has confirmed Heider's observation. We underestimate the situational causes of behavior, jumping too easily to conclusions about the person's disposition. If we observe someone behaving aggressively, we too readily assume that he or she has an aggressive personality, rather than concluding that the situation might have provoked similar aggression in anyone. To put it another way, we have a schema of cause and effect for human behavior that gives too much weight to the person and too little to the situation. In Chapter 17, you learned one of the foremost lessons of social psychology: that situations are, in fact, powerful causes of people's social behavior. You also learned a corollary lesson: that in our everyday reasoning, we often overlook the causal power of situations. And you will recall that this corollary lesson has a name of its own: the fundamental attribution error. Formally stated, the **fundamental attribution error** occurs when we underestimate the situational influences on behavior and assume that some personal characteristic of the individual is responsible (Ross, 1977).

In the classic early studies that revealed this bias, participants read a debater's speech that either supported or attacked Cuban leader Fidel Castro. The participants were explicitly told that the debate coach had assigned each debater one side of the issue or the other; the debater had no choice as to which side to argue. Despite this knowledge, when asked to estimate the debater's actual attitude toward Castro, participants inferred a position close to the one argued in the debate. In other words, the participants made a dispositional attribution, even though situational forces were fully sufficient to account for the behavior (Jones & Harris, 1967). This effect is quite powerful. Even when the participants themselves designate which side of the issue a speaker is to argue, they still tend to see him or her as actually holding that opinion (Gilbert & Jones, 1986). The effect occurs even if the presentations are deliberately designed to be drab and unenthusiastic and the speaker simply reads a transcribed version of the speech in a monotone and uses no gestures (Schneider & Miller, 1975).

An experiment designed as a quiz game illustrates how both participants and observers make the same fundamental attribution error in the same setting. Pairs of male or female participants were recruited to take part in a question-and-answer game testing general knowledge. One member of the pair was randomly assigned to be the questioner and to make up 10 difficult questions to which he or she knew the answers (such as "What is the world's largest glacier?"). The other participant acted as the contestant and attempted to answer the questions. When the contestant was unable to answer a question, the questioner gave the answer. In a reenactment of the study, observers watched the contest. After the game, both participants and observers were asked to rate the level of general knowledge possessed by the questioner and the contestant, relative to that possessed by the "average student." Note that participants and observers all knew that the roles of questioner and contestant had been assigned randomly.

As Figure 18-3 shows, questioners judged both themselves and the contestant to be about average in level of general knowledge. But contestants rated the questioner as superior and themselves as inferior to the average student. They attributed the outcome of the game to their (and the questioner's) level of knowledge rather than taking into account the overwhelming situational advantage enjoyed by the questioner, who was able to decide which questions to ask and to omit any questions to which he or she did not know the answer. Observers, aware that the questioner could ask questions that neither they nor the contestant could answer, rated the questioner's level of knowledge even higher. In other words, both contestants and observers gave too much weight to disposition and too little to the situation—

the fundamental attribution error (Ross, Amabile, & Steinmetz, 1977).

One implication of this study is that people who select the topics discussed in a conversation will be seen as more knowledgeable than those who passively let others set the agenda, even if everyone is aware of the differential roles being played. This, in turn, has implications for contemporary sex roles. Research has shown that men talk more than women in mixed-sex interactions (Henley, Hamilton, & Thorne, 1985), they interrupt more (West & Zimmerman, 1983), and they are more likely to raise the topics discussed (Fishman, 1983). The questioner-contestant study implies that one consequence of these sex-role patterns is that women leave most mixed-sex interactions thinking themselves less knowledgeable than the men, with bystanders of both sexes sharing this illusion. The take-home message is clear: The fundamental attribution error can work for or against you. If you want to appear knowledgeable both to yourself and to others, learn how to structure the situation so that you control the choice of topics discussed. Be the questioner, not the contestant!

Causal attributions, like other aspects of impression formation, have also been found to be governed by two different modes of thinking, one more automatic and unintentional, and another more controlled and deliberate. This turns out to influence how frequently the fundamental attribution error occurs. To understand why, it's helpful to break the attribution process down into stages. One framework divides the process of causal attribution into at least two parts. The first step is a dispositional inference (what trait does this action imply?), and the second is situational correction (what situational constraints might have caused that action?). Experiments suggest that the first step of dispositional inference is more automatic than the second step of situational correction (Gilbert & Malone, 1995; Gilbert, Pelham, & Krull, 1988) This suggests that we make the fundamental attribution error so often because it is an overlearned, automatic process that frequently occurs outside conscious awareness. Only when we have the cognitive resources to think deliberately and carefully can we correct our initial, automatic dispositional attributions with reference to plausible situational causes. Although it may seem encouraging that effortful thinking can override the fundamental attribution error, we need to recognize that most often, as we're forming our impressions of others, we are cognitively busy, thinking about many things at once, like planning our next move, anticipating the other's reaction, and managing the impression that others form of us. All this "cognitive busyness" means that we will continue to commit the fundamental attribution error time and again (Gilbert & Malone, 1995).

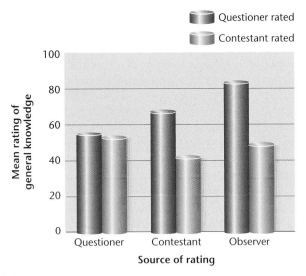

▌Figure 18-3
The Fundamental Attribution Error
Ratings of questioners and contestants after they had participated in a quiz game. The questioner is rated as superior by both the contestant and observers even though the questioner had an overwhelming situational advantage. Both contestants and observers gave too much weight to dispositional causes and too little to situational causes. (After Ross, Amabile, & Steinmetz, 1977)

CUTTING-EDGE RESEARCH
Culture and Cognition

For centuries, Western philosophers and psychologists have discussed cognitive processes—or modes of thinking—as if they were the same for all normal adults. In fact, much of the research and thinking on social cognition conveyed within this very chapter has made a similar assumption: that the cognitive processes described are universal, characteristic of humans everywhere. Although it's obvious that different cultures practice different social customs, these were thought to be irrelevant to "basic" cognitive processes like categorization and causal reasoning. Cutting-edge research in social cognition shatters this assumption and argues that divergent social systems in fact create and reinforce distinct systems of thought (Nisbett, Peng, Choi, & Norenzayan, 2001).

The first evidence that aspects of social cognition might not be universal after all took aim at the fundamental attribution error itself. Early studies showed that whereas Americans have long been shown to explain other people's behavior in terms of dispositional attributions, Hindu Indians and Chinese people preferred to explain similar behavior in terms of situational attributions (Miller, 1984, Morris & Peng, 1994; Norenzayan & Nisbett, 2000).

In addition, the classic study in which participants read a speech that another person had been assigned to produce (such as supporting or denouncing Cuban leader Fidel Castro) was replicated with both Korean and American students (Choi, Nisbett, & Norenzayan, 1999). Here the speechwriter had no choice of topics, so it is a mistake to conclude that his or her attitude corresponds to the arguments within the speech. Even so, like Americans, Koreans inferred that the speechwriter held the position he or she was advocating, a dispositional inference that reflects the fundamental attribution error. Yet Americans and Koreans responded quite differently if they had the opportunity to "walk in the shoes" of the speechwriter before making their judgments. In a variation of the classic study,

they were each first assigned to prepare a speech themselves using a set of arguments given by the experimenter, an experience that should highlight the strong situational constraints on attitude expression. With this personal experience salient, Koreans no longer made dispositional inferences, whereas Americans continued to do so just the same. From this and other studies, the authors conclude that East-West differences in the commission of the fundamental attribution error do not so much reflect cultural differences in the propensity to make dispositional attributions. Indeed, both Koreans and Americans made the dispositional error in the standard condition. Instead, cultural differences in attribution reflect a greater sensitivity to contexts and situational constraints among East Asians when those situational constraints are salient (Choi et al., 1999).

Evidence continues to mount that East Asians, more than Westerners, pay more attention to contexts and situations (Masuda & Nisbett, 2001) and are more influenced by them (Ji, Peng, & Nisbett, 2000). These and countless other East-West differences in styles of thinking are now taken as evidence that East Asians engage in more holistic thinking, whereas Westerners engage in more analytic thinking (Nisbett et al., 2001). **Holistic thought** is defined as an orientation toward the entire context or field and assigning causality to it, making relatively little use of categories and formal logic, and relying instead on dialectical reasoning, which involves recognizing and transcending apparent contradictions. By contrast, **analytic thought** is defined as an orientation toward objects, detached from their contexts, with much use of categories and formal logic and the avoidance of contradiction.

How did such wide-scale differences in thinking styles emerge? From long-standing different social practices, leading researchers say. In Chapter 1, we introduced the distinction between collectivist and individualist cultures. Collectivist cultures, you will recall, emphasize the fundamental connectedness and interdependence among people, whereas individualist cultures emphasize the fundamental separateness and independence of indi-

viduals. Indeed, we saw in Chapter 11 that the very emotions people experience and express reflect their cultural upbringing.

Collectivist tendencies can be traced back to the ancient Chinese focus on social harmony and collective agency, whereas individualist tendencies can be traced back to the ancient Greek focus on personal agency. These quite divergent views of human agency not only infused East-West differences in social practices but also shaped their respective advances in science, mathematics, and philosophy. The legacy of these distinct ancient orientations toward the locus of causality includes the cultural differences in cognition that we find evidence of today: that contemporary East Asians are more holistic in their thinking, whereas contemporary Westerners are more analytical (Nisbett et al., 2001). The ways we use our brains, then, are not universal or dictated by biology. Rather, our styles of thinking are malleable, shaped by those in our culture who came millennia before us, and reinforced by contemporary social practices.

These recent advances in the understanding of culture and cognition undermine all prior claims of universality made within the study of cognition and social cognition. Indeed, one of the most influential texts on social cognition in the 1980s was written by one of the scholars who now leads the foray into culture and cognition. Listen to what he says about his past work:

Two decades ago, [I] wrote a book with Lee Ross entitled, modestly, *Human Inference* (Nisbett & Ross, 1980). Roy D'Andrade, a distinguished cognitive anthropologist, read the book and told [me] he thought it was a "good ethnography." [I] was shocked and dismayed. But [I] now wholeheartedly agree with D'Andrade's contention about the limits of research conducted in a single culture. Psychologists who choose not to do cross-cultural psychology may have chosen to be ethnographers instead. (Nisbett et al., 2001, p. 306)

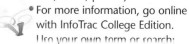 For more information, go online with InfoTrac College Edition. Use your own term or search:

- Attribution error
- Situational constraints

◆ Interim Summary

- Through schematic processing, we perceive and interpret incoming information in terms of simplified memory structures called *schemas*. Schemas are mini-theories about everyday objects and events that allow us to process information efficiently. Stereotypes are schemas about groups of people.

- Through repeated exposure, stereotypes can become habitual and automatic, operating outside conscious awareness.

- Because schemas and stereotypes simplify reality, schematic processing produces biases and errors in our processing of social information. In forming impressions of other people, for example, we are prone to the primacy effect: The first information we receive evokes an initial schema and, hence, becomes more powerful in determining our impression than does later information. Schemas and stereotypes also govern our inferences.

- Once activated, stereotypes can set in motion a chain of behavioral processes that serve to draw out from ourselves and others behavior that confirms the initial stereotype, an effect called the *self-fulfilling prophecy*. This behavioral sequence can occur completely outside conscious awareness.

- Individuation is the process of forming impressions of others by assessing their personal qualities on a person-by-person basis. The continuum model of impression formation, presented in Figure 18-2, details when and how people come to individuate others. Cooperative activities can promote individuation.

- Although stereotypes are activated automatically, under the right conditions they can also be controlled through effortful thinking.

- Attribution is the process by which we interpret and explain the behavior of other people. One major attribution task is to decide whether someone's action should be attributed to dispositional causes (the person's personality or attitudes) or to situational causes (social forces or other external circumstances). We tend to give too much weight to dispositional factors and too little to situational factors, a bias called the *fundamental attribution error*.

◆ Critical Thinking Questions

1. Suppose you perform badly on an exam. You know it's because you hardly studied at all, but your professor has made the fundamental attribution error and comes to conclude that you're not too bright. Some social psychologists have claimed that the fundamental attribution error is self-erasing—that, over time, it ceases to be an error. Building on the example of your bad test performance, use the concepts of the self-fulfilling prophecy and stereotype threat to explain the logic of this claim.

2. Think of someone you have come to know well over the past few months or years. Did your initial impressions of this person match your current impressions? If not, can you see how stereotypes and categorizations might have influenced your initial impressions? Can you trace your increasing individuation of this person through the continuum model, presented in Figure 18-2?

ATTITUDES

So far our discussion of social cognition has focused on the processes of perceiving, thinking, and impression formation. With the concept of attitude, we take a broader look at how feelings and opinions influence social cognition and social behavior.

Attitudes are likes and dislikes—favorable or unfavorable evaluations of and reactions to objects, people, situations, or other aspects of the world, including abstract ideas and social policies. We often express our attitudes in statements of opinion: "I love grapefruit" or "I can't stand liberals." But even though attitudes express feelings, they are often linked to cognitions—specifically, to beliefs about the attitude objects ("Grapefruit contain lots of vitamins" or "Liberals just want to tax and spend"). Moreover, attitudes are sometimes linked to the actions we take with respect to the attitude objects ("I eat a grapefruit every morning" or "I never vote for liberal candidates").

Accordingly, social psychologists usually conceive of attitudes as comprising a cognitive component, an affective component, and a behavioral component. For example, in studying negative attitudes toward groups, social psychologists often distinguish between negative stereotypes (negative beliefs and perceptions about a group—the cognitive component), prejudice (negative feelings toward the group—the affective component), and discrimination (negative actions against members of the group—the behavioral component). Some theorists prefer to define an attitude as only the cognitive and affective components; others include only the affective component. But despite differing definitions, all share a concern with the interrelationships among the pertinent beliefs, feelings, and behaviors.

Research on attitudes has kept social psychologists busy for decades. As early as the 1950s, attitudes were dubbed "the primary building stone in the edifice of social psychology" (Allport, 1954). But why exactly are attitudes so important? Two reasons are most critical. The first reason is that, at least in democratic societies, people talk about their attitudes a lot. They also ask about others' attitudes a lot. When we leave the movie theater, for instance, the first thing we ask our companion is "Did you like it?" After we've introduced our new heart-throb to our friends, we ask, "What do you think?" Facing a critical election, we ask respected others, "Who will you vote for?" Marketing and scientific polls turn such queries into formal assessments of public opinion, predicting everything from the box office success of Hollywood movies to the outcomes of presidential elections, and describing everything from month-by-month ratings of public support for a country's elected officials to the public's attitude toward teaching evolutionary theory in elementary schools.

The second reason attitudes have been so central to social psychology and cause for so much talk and polling is a key underlying assumption: that people's attitudes predict their behavior. This assumption is so widely accepted that it has served as the base for psychology's neighboring behavioral science of economics and underlies other rational views of human nature. This assumption can be decomposed into three parts: First, human behavior is intentional and reflects individual preferences. This is the heart of utility theory within economics and the notion of free will within philosophy. Second, attitudes represent preferences. And third, to predict behavior, we can simply look at attitudes. A corollary to this logic is that if we wish to change people's behaviors, we should start by changing their attitudes.

A long-standing agenda among social psychologists, then, has been to find ways to change people's attitudes. You will recall from Chapter 17 that one way this agenda has been pursued is through social influence techniques. In particular, research on self-justification shows that we can sometimes change people's attitudes by slyly inducing them to engage in some hypocritical (counterattitudinal) action, like telling another person that a boring task was fun. Reference groups can also play a role in changing people's attitudes, as was illustrated in the study of Bennington College students. Here we take up more direct approaches to attitude change, those undertaken through persuasive communication, like political speeches, advertisements, sermons, and other forms of formal or informal lobbying.

PERSUASIVE COMMUNICATION

Just as the practices of Nazi Germany under Hitler created interest in obedience to authority (see Chapter 17), so did wartime propaganda efforts prompt the study of persuasive communication. Intensive research began in the late 1940s at Yale University, where investigators sought to determine the characteristics of successful persuasive communicators, successful communications, and the kinds of people who are most easily persuaded (Hovland, Janis, & Kelley, 1953). As research on these topics continued over the years, a number of interesting phenomena were discovered, but few general principles emerged. The results became increasingly complex and difficult to summarize, and every conclusion seemed to require several "it depends" qualifications. Beginning in the 1980s, however, interest in the two modes of cogni-

Priests and politicians are among those who seek to present persuasive messages that will change the attitudes and behavior of their audiences.

tive processing that we've been discussing—one more automatic and effortless and the other more controlled and effortful—gave rise to new theories of persuasion that provided a more unified framework for analyzing persuasive communication (Chaiken, 1987; Chen & Chaiken, 1999; Petty & Cacioppo, 1981; 1986; Petty & Wegener, 1999).

THE ELABORATION LIKELIHOOD MODEL The elaboration likelihood model is one of the more prominent dual-process theories of persuasion (Petty & Cacioppo, 1981, 1986; Petty & Wegener, 1999). It aims to predict when certain aspects of a persuasive communication—like argument strength and source credibility—will matter and when they won't. A key idea within this model is that people experience a continuum of elaboration likelihood. In simple terms, this means that sometimes we are motivated and able to pay attention, think, and elaborate on the persuasive message, and other times we are not. Which end of this continuum we're on at any given moment determines the cognitive processes that govern persuasion. So, according to the **elaboration likelihood model,** if we're at the high end of the continuum—willing and able to think deeply— then persuasion is said to follow a central route, relying on controlled and effortful thinking; if we're at the low end of the continuum—for whatever reasons, not willing or able to think deeply—then persuasion is said to follow a peripheral route, relying on automatic and effortless thinking.

THE CENTRAL ROUTE TO PERSUASION Persuasion is said to follow the **central route** when an individual mentally responds to—and elaborates on—the persuasive communication. The central route to persuasion is taken only when the individual is motivated to generate thoughts in response to the substantive content of a communication and has the ability and opportunity to do so. These thoughts can be about the content of the communication itself or about other aspects of the situation, such as the credibility of the communicator. If the communication evokes thoughts that support the position being advocated, the individual will move toward that position; if the communication evokes unsupportive thoughts (such as counterarguments or disparaging thoughts about the communicator), the individual will remain unconvinced or even shift away from the position being advocated (Greenwald, 1968; Petty, Ostrom, & Brock, 1981).

A number of studies provide evidence that effortful thought accounts for the central route to persuasion. In one, each participant read a communication containing arguments about a controversial issue and wrote a one-sentence reaction to each argument. One week later, the participants were unexpectedly given a memory test ask-ing them to recall both the arguments in the communication and their written reactions to those arguments. Participants' opinions on the issue were assessed before receiving the communication and again at the time of the memory test. The results showed that the amount of opinion change produced by the communication was significantly correlated with both the supportiveness of participants' reactions to the communication and with their later recall of those reactions, but it was not significantly correlated with their recall of the arguments themselves (Love & Greenwald, 1978). This experiment not only supports the central route to persuasion but also explains what had previously been a puzzling observation: that the persistence of opinion change is often unrelated to an individual's memory of the arguments that produced that change.

In a sense, then, the central route to persuasion can be considered self-persuasion produced by the thoughts that the person generates while reading, listening to, or even just anticipating the communication. Those thoughts turn out to be more influential than the communication itself.

THE PERIPHERAL ROUTE TO PERSUASION Persuasion is said to follow the **peripheral route** when the individual responds to non-content cues in a communication (such as the sheer number of arguments it contains) or to the context of the communication (such as the credibility of the communicator or the pleasantness of the surroundings). The peripheral route is taken when the individual is—for whatever reason—unable or unwilling to do the cognitive work required to carefully evaluate the content of the communication.

Classical conditioning (which you learned about in Chapter 7) is one of the most primitive means of changing attitudes through the peripheral route. Advertisers use classical conditioning quite a lot, by repeatedly pairing their initially neutral or unknown product with images or ideas that are known to produce positive feelings, like attractive people or beautiful scenery. Through classical conditioning—a peripheral route to persuasion— viewers should come to hold positive attitudes toward the new product as well.

Another peripheral route to persuasion relies on heuristics, or rules of thumb (discussed in Chapter 9) to infer the validity of persuasive messages. Examples of such rules might include "Messages with many arguments are more likely to be valid than messages with few arguments," "Politicians always lie," and "College professors know what they are talking about" (Chaiken, 1980, 1987; Eagly & Chaiken, 1984). Communications that follow these rules of thumb can be persuasive—even if their substantive content is unconvincing—to the extent that listeners are unlikely to elaborate on the information given.

CENTRAL OR PERIPHERAL? Several factors can influence which route—central or peripheral—will be taken. One such factor is personal involvement. If a communication addresses an issue in which the individual has a personal stake, he or she is more likely to attend carefully to the arguments. In such a case, the individual is also likely to have a rich store of prior information and opinions on the issue. On the other hand, if an issue has no personal relevance for the individual, he or she is not likely to make much of an effort either to support or refute arguments about it. What happens then?

The elaboration likelihood model has been tested in several studies. In one rather complex study, college undergraduates read an essay allegedly written by the chairperson of a university committee charged with advising the chancellor on changes in academic policy. The essay proposed that the university institute a comprehensive examination that every undergraduate would have to pass before being permitted to graduate. To manipulate the students' involvement in the issue, half of them were told that any policy changes adopted by the chancellor would be instituted the next year (high involvement), and the other half were told that any changes would take effect in 10 years (low involvement). Different forms of the essay were also used. Some contained strong arguments, others weak ones. Some contained only three arguments, others nine.

The post-communication attitudes of students in the high-involvement conditions are shown in Figure 18-4a. It can be seen that strong arguments produced more favorable attitudes overall than did weak arguments. But more important, nine strong arguments produced greater agreement with the essay than did three strong arguments, whereas nine weak arguments produced less agreement than did three weak arguments. How can we make sense of these patterns?

The elaboration likelihood model predicts that students in the high-involvement conditions will be motivated to process the essay's substantive arguments and thus generate topic-relevant cognitive responses. This is the central route of persuasion, which holds that strong arguments will evoke more supportive cognitive responses and fewer counterarguments than will weak arguments and hence will produce more agreement with the essay—as, indeed, they did. Moreover, nine strong arguments should be more persuasive than three strong arguments because the more strong arguments the individual encounters, the more supportive cognitive responses he or she will generate. In contrast, nine weak arguments should be less persuasive than three weak arguments because the more weak arguments the individual encounters, the more counterarguments he or she will generate. These predictions are in accordance with the findings displayed in Figure 18-4a.

As shown in Figure 18-4b, a different pattern emerges for students in the low-involvement conditions. Here the elaboration likelihood model predicts that students in the low-involvement conditions will not be motivated to scrutinize the essay's arguments closely and will instead rely on simple heuristics to evaluate its merits and form their attitudes. This is the peripheral route, which holds that an individual in this setting will not even bother to determine whether the arguments are strong or weak but will simply invoke the

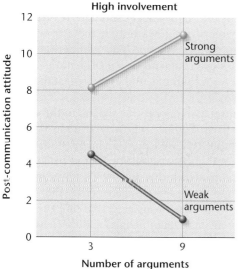

a) **Post-communication attitudes through the central route.** When individuals have high involvement in the issue, nine strong arguments produce more agreement than three strong arguments, but nine weak arguments produce less agreement than three weak arguments.

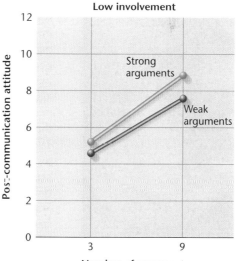

b) **Post-communication attitudes through the peripheral route.** When individuals have low involvement in the issue, nine arguments produce more agreement than three arguments, regardless of whether the arguments are strong or weak.

▍**Figure 18-4**
A Test of the Elaboration Likelihood Model
(R. E. Petty & J. T. Cacioppo (1984), "The effects of involvement on responses to arguments quantity and quality, central and peripheral routes to persuasion," in *Journal of Personality & Social Psychology,* 46:6–81. Copyright © 1984 by the American Psychological Association. Adapted with permission.)

heuristic rule "Messages with many arguments are more likely to be valid than messages with few arguments." Thus, strong arguments will be no more effective than weak arguments, and nine arguments will be more persuasive than three arguments—regardless of whether they are strong or weak. This is precisely the pattern shown in Figure 18-4b: Overall, there were no significant differences between strong and weak arguments, but nine arguments were more effective than three arguments in both conditions (Petty & Cacioppo, 1984).

An experiment that varied the expertise of the communicator rather than the number of arguments found similar results: Participants in the high-involvement conditions were more influenced by the strength of the arguments, but participants in the low-involvement conditions relied more on the heuristic "Arguments made by an expert are more valid than arguments made by a non-expert" (Petty, Cacioppo, & Goldman, 1981).

Although much research on persuasion has been conducted in laboratories, there has always been an interest in the practical applications of the findings. An example is an educational program designed to inoculate junior high school students against peer pressure to smoke. High school students conducted sessions in which they taught seventh-graders how to generate counterarguments. For example, in role-playing sessions they were taught to respond to being called "chicken" for not taking a cigarette by saying things like "I'd be a real chicken if I smoked just to impress you." They were also taught to respond to advertisements implying that liberated women smoke by saying, "She's not really liberated if she is hooked on tobacco." Several inoculation sessions were held during seventh and eighth grades, and records were kept of how many of the students smoked from the beginning of the study through the ninth grade. The results showed that inoculated students were half as likely to smoke as students at a matched junior high school that used a more typical smoking education program (McAlister, Perry, Killen, Slinkard, & Maccoby, 1980). Similar programs have been designed to inoculate elementary school children against being taken in by deceptive television commercials (Cohen, 1980; Feshbach, 1980).

ATTITUDES AND BEHAVIOR

As we've said, a major reason for studying attitudes is the expectation that they will enable us to predict a person's future behavior. A political candidate is interested in a survey of voters' opinions only if the attitudes expressed relate to voting behavior. The assumption that a person's attitudes determine his or her behavior is deeply ingrained in Western thinking, and in many instances the assumption holds.

But this central assumption was shaken to the core in the late 1960s by a scathing scholarly critique (Wicker, 1969). The critique reviewed more than 40 studies that tested the relationship between attitudes and behavior. A classic study conducted during the 1930s illustrated the problem. A white professor traveled across the United States with a young Chinese couple. At that time there was strong prejudice against Asian people, and there were no laws against racial discrimination in public accommodations. The three travelers stopped at more than 200 hotels, motels, and restaurants and were served at all the restaurants and all but one of the hotels and motels without a problem. Later, a letter was sent to all of the restaurants and hotels asking them whether they would accept a Chinese couple as guests. Of the 128 replies received, 92% said that they would not. In other words, these proprietors expressed attitudes that were much more prejudiced than their actual behavior (LaPiere, 1934). Drawing on this and many other studies, critics argued that attitudes did not predict behavior at all. Some even recommended that social psychologists abandon the attitude concept altogether

Whether an ad like this coaxes a girl to smoke Newport cigarettes depends on the thoughts that the ad prompts in her. If she thinks the woman is attractive, she is more likely to begin smoking. But if she thinks the ad exploits women, she is less likely to begin smoking.

and focus instead on the situational determinants of behavior. The logic of this recommendation, you will see, parallels the fundamental attribution error: that even social psychologists had overestimated the causal force of dispositional factors—like attitudes—on determining behavior and underestimated the causal force of situations.

Certainly people's behavior is determined by many factors other than their attitudes. One obvious factor is the degree of constraint in the situation: We must often act in ways that are not consistent with what we feel or believe. As children, we ate vegetables that we detested, and as adults we attend lectures and dinner parties that we consider boring. In Chapter 17, we saw the power of situations time and again. In the Asch study, participants conformed to the majority, even when they knew the majority was wrong. In the Milgram study, participants delivered shocks even when doing so went against their consciences. And in the racial discrimination study just described, the prejudiced proprietors may have found it difficult to act on their prejudices when actually faced with the Chinese couple seeking service.

Peer pressure can exert similar influences on behavior. For example, a teenager's attitude toward marijuana is moderately correlated with his or her actual use of marijuana, but the number of marijuana-using friends the teenager has is an even better predictor of his or her marijuana use (Andrews & Kandel, 1979). Can you see a similarity here to the classic Asch study?

Far from ending research on attitudes, this critical challenge to the assumption that attitudes predict behavior served to kindle a new generation of research on attitudes that aimed to specify the special conditions under which attitudes do in fact predict behavior. In general, attitudes have been found to predict behavior best when (1) they are strong and consistent, (2) they are specifically related to the behavior being predicted, (3) they are based on the person's direct experience, and (4) the individual is aware of his or her attitudes. We will look briefly at each of these factors.

STRONG AND CONSISTENT ATTITUDES
Strong and consistent attitudes predict behavior better than weak or ambivalent ones. Many voters experience ambivalence because they are under pressure from friends and associates who do not agree with one another. For example, a Jewish businessperson belongs to an ethnic group that generally holds liberal political positions, but she also belongs to a business community that frequently holds conservative political positions, particularly on economic issues. When it comes time to vote, she is subjected to conflicting pressures.

Ambivalence and conflict can arise from within the person as well. When the affective and cognitive components of an attitude are not consistent—for example, when we like something that we know is bad for us—it is often difficult to predict behavior (Norman, 1975). In general, when the components of an attitude are clear and consistent, they better predict behavior (Millar & Tesser, 1989).

ATTITUDES SPECIFICALLY RELATED TO BEHAVIOR
Another finding is that attitudes that are specifically related to the behavior being assessed predict the behavior better than attitudes that are only generally related to it. For example, in one study students in the United States, Britain, and Sweden were asked both about their general attitudes toward nuclear war and about their specific attitudes toward nuclear war, nuclear weapons, and nuclear power plants. Specific attitudes were much better predictors of activist behaviors (such as writing a letter to a newspaper or signing a petition) than more general attitudes (Newcomb, Rabow, & Hernandez, 1992).

ATTITUDES BASED ON DIRECT EXPERIENCE
Attitudes based on direct experience predict behavior better than attitudes formed from reading or hearing about an issue (Fazio, 1990). For example, during a housing shortage at a university, many freshmen had to spend the first few weeks of the term in crowded temporary housing. Researchers measured students' attitudes toward the housing crisis and their willingness to sign and distribute petitions or join committees to study it. For students who actually had to live in the temporary housing, there was a high correlation between their attitude toward the crisis and their willingness to take action to solve it. But for students who had not directly experienced the temporary housing, no such correlation existed (Regan & Fazio, 1977).

AWARENESS
Finally, there is evidence that people who are more aware of their attitudes are more likely to behave in ways that are consistent with those attitudes. This is true of people who are generally more focused on their thoughts and feelings as part of their personalities (Scheier, Buss, & Buss, 1978), as well as of people who are placed in situations designed to make them more aware, such as in front of a mirror or video camera (Carver & Scheier, 1981; Hutton & Baumeister, 1992; Pryor et al., 1977).

◆ Interim Summary

- Attitudes are likes and dislikes—favorable or unfavorable evaluations of and reactions to objects, people, events, or ideas. Attitudes have a cognitive component, an affective component, and a behavioral component.

- The elaboration likelihood model states that persuasion can take two routes in producing belief and attitude change: the central route, in which the individual responds to the substantive arguments of a communication, and the peripheral route, in which the individual responds to non-content cues in a communication (such as the number of arguments) or to context cues (such as the credibility of the communicator or the pleasantness of the surroundings).

- A communication about an issue of personal relevance is more likely to generate thoughts in response to the communication's substantive arguments. When an issue is of little personal relevance or people are unwilling or unable to respond to the substantive content of a communication, they tend to use simple heuristics—rules of thumb—to judge the merits of the communication.

- Attitudes tend to predict behavior best when they are (1) strong and consistent, (2) specifically related to the behavior being predicted, and (3) based on the person's direct experience, as well as (4) when the individual is aware of his or her attitudes.

◆ Critical Thinking Questions

1. Suppose you are running for political office. What sort of television ad should you design if you suspect that your audience will be distracted? What sort of ad should you design if you suspect that your audience will be motivated to think deeply? Can you appeal to both audiences in the same ad?

2. Many young people are addicted to shopping at the expense of other interests. Based on what you now know about attitude change and the links between attitudes and behavior, identify at least two ways that you could prevent your younger sister from spending all of her time and money shopping for the latest advertised fashions.

INTERPERSONAL ATTRACTION

In our discussion of attitudes, we distinguished between the cognitive and affective components—thinking and feeling. There is, however, no area of human behavior in which cognitions and affects are intertwined in a more complex way than in interpersonal attraction: liking, loving, and sexual desire. Research in these areas has often confirmed common knowledge, but it has also produced a number of surprises and contradictions. We begin with liking—namely, friendship and the early stages of more intimate relationships.

LIKING AND ATTRACTION

We cannot all be beautiful film stars, but when two such people become a couple, they do illustrate several of the determinants of interpersonal attraction that apply even to us ordinary mortals: physical attractiveness, proximity, familiarity, and similarity. As the high divorce rate among contemporary couples also illustrates, however, these factors are not always sufficient to sustain a long-term relationship.

PHYSICAL ATTRACTIVENESS To most of us, there is something mildly undemocratic about the possibility that a person's physical appearance is a determinant of how well others like him or her. Unlike character and personality, physical appearance is a factor over which we seemingly have little control, and so it seems unfair to use it as a criterion for liking someone. In fact, surveys conducted over a span of several decades have shown that people do not rank physical attractiveness as very important in their liking of other people (Buss & Barnes, 1986; Hudson & Hoyt, 1981; Perrin, 1921; Tesser & Brodie, 1971).

But research on actual behavior shows otherwise (Brehm, 1992). One group of psychologists set up a "computer dance" in which college men and women were randomly paired. At intermission, everyone filled out an anonymous questionnaire evaluating his or her date. In addition, the experimenters obtained several personality test scores for each person, as well as an independent estimate of his or her physical attractiveness. The results showed that only physical attractiveness played a role in how much the person was liked by his or her partner. None of the measures of intelligence, social skills, or personality was related to the partners' liking for each other (Walster, Aronson, Abrahams, & Rottman, 1966). This experiment has been replicated many times, and in each case the results have been similar to those just described. Moreover, the importance of physical attractiveness has been found to operate not only on first dates but on subsequent dates (Mathes, 1975) and in marriages (Margolin & White, 1987) as well.

Why is physical attractiveness so important? Part of the reason is that our social standing and self-esteem are enhanced when we are seen with physically attractive companions. Both men and women are rated more favorably when they are with an attractive romantic partner or friend than when they are with an unattractive companion (Sheposh, Deming, & Young, 1977; Sigall & Landy, 1973). But there is an interesting twist to this: Both men and women are rated less favorably when they are seen with a stranger who is physically more attractive than they are (Kernis & Wheeler, 1981). Apparently they suffer by comparison with the other person. This effect has been found in other studies. For example, male college students who had just watched a television show starring beautiful young women gave lower attractiveness ratings to a photograph of a more typical-looking woman (Kendrick & Gutierres, 1980).

Fortunately, there is hope for the unbeautiful among us. First of all, physical attractiveness appears to decline in importance when a permanent partner is being chosen (Stroebe, Insko, Thompson, & Layton, 1971). And, as we will see, several other factors can work in our favor.

PROXIMITY An examination of 5,000 marriage license applications in Philadelphia in the 1930s found that one-third of the couples lived within five blocks of each other (Rubin, 1973). Research shows that the best single predictor of whether two people are friends is **proximity,** or how far apart they live. In a study of friendship patterns in apartment houses, residents were asked to name the three people they saw socially most often. Residents mentioned 41% of neighbors who lived in the apartment next door, 22% of those who lived two doors away (about 30 feet), and only 10% of those who lived at the other end of the hall (Festinger, Schachter, & Back, 1950). Studies of college dormitories show the same effect. After a full academic year, roommates were twice as likely as floormates to be friends, and floormates were more than twice as likely as dormitory residents in general to be friends (Priest & Sawyer, 1967).

There are cases, of course, in which neighbors and roommates hate one another, and the major exception to the friendship-promoting effect of proximity seems to occur when there are initial antagonisms. In a test of this, a participant waited in a laboratory with a female confederate who treated the participant pleasantly or unpleasantly. When she was pleasant, the closer she sat to the participant, the better she was liked; when she was unpleasant, the closer she sat to the participant, the less she was liked. Proximity simply increased the intensity of the initial reaction (Schiffenbauer & Schiavo, 1976). But because most initial encounters probably range from neutral to pleasant, the most frequent result of sustained proximity is friendship.

Those who believe in miracles when it comes to matters of the heart may believe that there is a perfect mate chosen for each of us waiting to be discovered somewhere in the world. But if this is true, the far greater miracle is the frequency with which fate conspires to place this person within walking distance.

FAMILIARITY One of the major reasons that proximity creates liking is that it increases familiarity, and there is now abundant evidence for what is called the **mere exposure effect,** the finding that familiarity all by itself increases

These neighbors are likely to form a friendship simply because of proximity.

liking (Zajonc, 1968). This familiarity-breeds-liking effect is a very general phenomenon. For example, rats repeatedly exposed to the music of either Mozart or Schoenberg enhance their liking for the composer they have heard, and humans repeatedly exposed to selected nonsense syllables or Chinese characters come to prefer those they have seen most often. The effect occurs even when individuals are unaware that they have been previously exposed to the stimuli (Bornstein, 1992; Bornstein & D'Agostino, 1992; Moreland & Zajonc, 1979; Wilson, 1979). More germane to the present discussion is a study in which participants were exposed to pictures of faces and then asked how much they thought they would like the person shown. The more frequently they had seen a particular face, the more they said they liked it and thought they would like the person (Zajonc, 1968) (see Figure 18-5). Similar results are obtained when individuals are exposed to one another in real life (Moreland & Beach, 1992).

In one clever demonstration of the mere exposure effect, the investigators took photographs of college women and then prepared prints of both the original face and its mirror image. These prints were then shown to the women themselves, their female friends, and their lovers. The

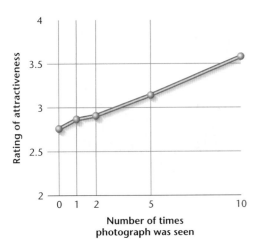

Figure 18-5
Familiarity Breeds Liking
People were asked to rate photographs of unknown faces according to how much they thought they would like the person. The lowest ratings of liking were made by those who had never seen the photograph before; the highest ratings of liking were made by those who had seen the photograph most often. This illustrates the mere exposure effect. (After Zajonc, 1968)

women themselves preferred the mirror-image prints by a margin of 68% to 32%, but the friends and lovers preferred the nonreversed prints by a margin of 61% to 39% (Mita, Dermer, & Knight, 1977). Can you guess why?

The take-home message is clear. If you are not beautiful or you find your admiration of someone unreciprocated, be persistent and hang around. Proximity and familiarity are your most powerful weapons.

SIMILARITY An old saying declares that opposites attract, and lovers are fond of recounting how different they are from each other: "I love boating, but she prefers mountain climbing." "I'm in engineering, but he's a history major." What such lovers overlook is that they both like outdoor activities; they are both preprofessionals; they are both Democrats; they are both the same nationality, the same religion, the same social class, and the same educational level; and they are within 3 years of each other in age and within 5 IQ points of each other in intelligence. In short, the old saying is mostly false.

Research dating all the way back to 1870 supports this conclusion. More than 95% of the married couples in the United States are of the same race, and most are of the same religion. Moreover, statistical surveys show that husbands and wives are significantly similar to each other not only in sociological characteristics—such as age, race, religion, education, and socioeconomic class—but also with respect to psychological characteristics like intelligence and physical characteristics such as height and eye color (Rubin, 1973). A study of dating couples finds the same patterns, in addition to finding that cou-

ples were also similar in their attitudes about sexual behavior and sex roles. Moreover, couples who were most similar in background at the beginning of the study were most likely to be together a year later (Hill, Rubin, & Peplau, 1976). Of particular pertinence to our earlier discussion is the finding that couples are closely matched on physical attractiveness as well (Feingold, 1988).

For example, in one study, judges rated photographs of each partner of 99 couples for physical attractiveness without knowing who was paired with whom. The physical attractiveness ratings of the couples matched each other significantly more closely than did the ratings of photographs that were randomly paired into couples (Murstein, 1972). Similar results were obtained in a real-life field study in which separate observers rated the physical attractiveness of members of couples in bars and theater lobbies and at social events (Silverman, 1971).

This matching of couples on physical attractiveness appears to come about because we weigh a potential partner's attractiveness against the probability that the person would be willing to pair up with us. Put bluntly, less attractive people seek less attractive partners because they expect to be rejected by someone more attractive than themselves. A study of a video dating service found that both men and women were most likely to pursue a relationship with someone who matched them in physical attractiveness. Only the most attractive people sought dates with the most attractive partners (Folkes, 1982). The overall result of this process is attractiveness similarity: Most of us end up with partners who are about as attractive as we are.

But similarities on dimensions other than physical attractiveness are probably even more important over the long-term course of a relationship. A longitudinal study of 135 married couples found that spouses who were more similar to each other in personality also resembled each other more in terms of how much they enjoyed similar daily activities like visiting friends, going out for dinner, and participating in community activities and professional meetings. These couples also reported less marital conflict and greater closeness, friendliness, and marital satisfaction than less similar spouses (Caspi & Herbener, 1990).

In an ambitious study of similarity and friendship, male students received free room for the year in a large house at the University of Michigan in exchange for their participation. On the basis of information from tests and questionnaires, some men were assigned roommates who were quite similar to them, and others were assigned roommates who were quite dissimilar. The investigator observed the friendship patterns that developed over the course of the year and obtained more questionnaire and attitude data from the participants at regular intervals. In all other respects, the men lived as they would in any dormitory.

Partners in successful long-term relationships tend to be similar to each other in characteristics such as age, race, and education, as well as in their interests, personality traits, and even physical attractiveness.

Roommates who were initially similar generally liked each other and ended up as better friends than those who were dissimilar. When the study was repeated with a new group of men the next year, however, the familiarity-breeds-liking effect turned out to be even more powerful than similarity. Regardless of whether low or high similarity had been the basis for room assignments, roommates came to like each other (Newcomb, 1961).

One possible reason that similarity produces liking is that people value their own opinions and preferences and enjoy being with others who validate their choices, boosting their self-esteem in the process. But perhaps the major reason that similarity produces liking is that both social norms and situational circumstances throw us together with people who are like us. Most religious groups prefer (or insist) that their members date and mate within the religion, and cultural norms regulate what is considered acceptable in terms of race and age matches—a couple comprising an older woman and a younger man is still viewed as inappropriate. Situational circumstances also play an important role. Many couples meet in college or graduate school, thus ensuring that they will be similar in educational level, general intelligence, and professional aspirations, and probably in age and socioeconomic status. Moreover, tennis players will have met on the tennis courts, political liberals at a pro-choice rally, and gay people at a gay pride parade or a meeting of the Lesbian, Gay, and Bisexual Task Force.

Despite all this, it is often suggested that the saying that opposites attract may still apply to certain comple-mentary personality traits (Winch, Ktsanes, & Ktsanes, 1954). To take the most obvious example, one partner may be quite dominant and therefore require someone who is relatively more submissive. A person with strong preferences may do best with someone who is very flexible or even wishy-washy. But despite the plausibility of this complementarity hypothesis, there is not much evidence for it (Levinger, Senn, & Jorgensen, 1970). In one study, marital adjustment among couples who had been married for up to 5 years was found to depend more on similarity than on complementarity (Meyer & Pepper, 1977). Attempts to identify the pairs of personality traits that bring about complementarity have not been very successful (Strong et al., 1988).

TRANSFERENCE In Chapter 16, you learned about transference, or the tendency for clients to transfer their feelings and assumptions about a particular significant other—like their parent or spouse—onto their therapist. Recent work from a social cognitive perspective applies the concept of **transference** more generally, arguing that any time we encounter someone new who reminds us of someone who has been important to us in our past, that sense of recognition influences our perceptions—and indeed our liking—of the new person (Chen & Andersen, 1999). The approach follows the tradition of social cognition because it holds that simply being reminded of someone who has been significant to us in the past automatically activates stored knowledge—or schemas—about that significant other. This, in turn, leads us to process information about the newly encountered person in ways consistent with the activated schema.

Laboratory experiments have tested the influence of transference on interpersonal liking. In one study, participants were tested twice. In a pretest session, they identified two of their significant others—one whom they felt good about and one they disliked—and provided several short descriptions of them ("Terry is sincere" or "Pat likes to go dancing"). More than 2 weeks later, these same participants were tested again. This time, they learned about a new person—supposedly seated next door—with whom they would soon interact. The descriptions of this new person were rigged to resemble participants' significant others by mirroring some of the descriptions gathered in the pretest phase. For one experimental group, the new person resembled a liked significant other. For another experimental group, the new person resembled a disliked significant other. To control for the valence of the descriptions used, each was given to another participant as well. For these control groups, the description of the new person resembled somebody else's significant other, not their own. The results are shown in Figure 18-6. When a new person resembled a significant other, he or she is liked or disliked, depending on the participant's attitude toward the significant other—participants even smiled more when the new

person resembled their significant other! Additional experiments using this same procedure confirm that this effect of transference on liking is carried by activated schemas. As we learned at the start of this chapter (and in Chapter 8), schemas can be activated (or primed) automatically and, once activated, they influence various aspects of information processing, including memory and inferences. Our schemas for significant others, when triggered by new acquaintances who in some way resemble them, produce all the cognitive and behavioral effects that social psychologists have come to expect (Chen & Andersen, 1999).

The take-home message here is that if you want to forge a new friendship or relationship, and not merely recycle an old one, you need to start with a new acquaintance who is like no other. And you should be cautious when someone approaches you and says, "You remind me of someone."

LOVING AND MATING

Love is more than just strong liking. Most of us know people we like very much but do not love, and some of us have felt passionate attraction for someone we did not particularly like. Research confirms these everyday observations. One of the first researchers to study romantic love compiled a number of statements that people thought reflected liking and loving and then constructed separate scales to measure each (Rubin, 1973). Items on the liking scale tap the degree to which the other person is regarded as likable, respected, admired, and having maturity and good judgment. Items on the love scale tap three main themes: a sense of attachment ("It would be hard for me to get along without _____"), a sense of caring for the other person ("I would do almost anything for _____"), and a sense of trust ("I feel that I can confide in _____ about virtually everything"). The two scales are only moderately correlated: .56 for men and .36 for women.

LOVE AND MARRIAGE The concept of romantic love is an old one, but the belief that it has much to do with marriage is more recent and far from universal. In some non-Western cultures, marriage is still considered to be a contractual or financial arrangement that has nothing to do with love. In the United States, the link between love and marriage has actually become stronger over the past 30 years. In 1967, U.S. college students were asked, "If a man (woman) had all the other qualities you desired, would you marry this person if you were not in love with him (her)?" About 65% of the men said no, but only 24% of the women said no (only 4% actually said yes; the majority of the women were undecided) (Kephart, 1967). The women's movement had just begun at that time, and it may be that women were more likely than they are now to consider marriage necessary for financial security.

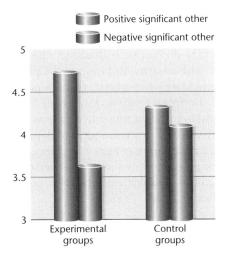

■ Figure 18-6
Transference in Interpersonal Attraction
How much participants liked a new acquaintance depended on whether that new person shared characteristics with the participants' significant others and whether they held positive or negative attitudes about those significant others. Notice that evaluations were more extreme when new acquaintances resembled a participant's own significant other (the experimental groups) than when they resembled someone else's significant other (the control groups). (From S. Chen & S. M. Andersen (1999), "Relationships from the past in the present: significant-other representations and transference in interpersonal life," in *Advances in Experimental Social Psychology, 31,* 123–190. Copyright © 1999, Elsevier Science (USA), reproduced by permission of the publisher.)

When the survey was repeated in 1984, 85% of both men and women said that they would refuse to marry without being in love (Simpson, Campbell, & Berscheid, 1986).

LOVE AND SELF-EXPANSION Why do people fall in love? Why do they forge close, loving relationships? At one level, the answer is obvious—because love feels good! But then you could ask, why does love feel good? Some social psychologists have suggested that a primary motivation for falling in love lies in the urge to expand the self (Aron, Norman, & Aron, 1998). Close relationships are said to produce **self-expansion**—or *increase our potential abilities and resources*—in multiple ways. As we become close to another person, we gain access to that person's resources, perspectives, and identities—this might include someone's circle of friends, cooking skills, views on politics or religion, or popularity more generally—each of which can help us to achieve our own goals. People are motivated to expand the self, the reasoning continues, not only to become more able themselves but also because self-expansion, particularly rapid expanding, is exhilarating. So falling in love feels good, this logic suggests, because it produces rapid self-expansion.

The researchers tested the association between falling in love and self-expansion by targeting a large group of first-year college students over the fall semester. Every 2 weeks for 10 weeks, these students answered the question, "Who are you today?" by listing as many self-descriptive words or phrases as came to mind in a 3-minute period. They also answered a number of other questions, including whether they had fallen in love since the last testing session. First-year college students, it so happens, have a very high chance of falling in love in their first semester—a full one-third of them do! (Aron, 2002). This large sample of those "lucky in love" enabled the researchers to compare self-descriptions made just prior to falling in love to those made just after. The comparisons provided clear evidence of self-expansion: The diversity of self-descriptions increased significantly after falling in love, an effect that could not be attributed to positive mood. (The self-descriptions of those unlucky in love provided an additional comparison for the degree of change that might be expected in the absence of love; Aron, Norman, & Aron, 1998.)

A corollary to the notion that love produces self-expansion is the claim that within close relationships, people tend to think about their beloved in the same manner in which they think of the self. That is, the close other becomes fused—even confused—with the self. One study tested the idea that we "include the other in the self" by asking married participants to choose as quickly and accurately as possible whether each of a large set of personality traits was "me" or "not me." Based on prior testing, the researchers knew that some of those traits were true of the participant's self but not true of their spouse, or true of the spouse but not true of the self. As expected, participants were slower to respond—and made more errors—for traits on which they and their spouse differed (Aron, Aron, Tudor, & Nelson, 1991). So, for instance, if you are not particularly gracious, but your beloved is, when faced with deciding whether the term *gracious* describes you, you get confused. It takes you a moment to sort out that even though you benefit from your beloved's graciousness, you are not actually gracious yourself! But this confusion is a good thing. Other research has shown that the extent to which couples "include the other in the self" on a simple pictorial measure (see Figure 18-7) predicts how long they will stay together (Aron, Aron, & Smollen, 1992).

PASSIONATE AND COMPANIONATE LOVE Several social scientists have attempted to distinguish among different kinds of love. One of the most widely accepted distinctions is between passionate and companionate love (Hatfield, 1988; Peele, 1988).

Passionate love is defined as an intensely emotional state in which "tender and sexual feelings, elation and pain, anxiety and relief, altruism and jealousy coexist in a confusion of feelings" (Berscheid & Walster, 1974, p. 177). It has been suggested that the experience of passionate love combines physiological arousal with the perception that the arousal is evoked by the beloved (Berscheid & Walster, 1974).

In contrast, **companionate love** is defined as "the affection we feel for those with whom our lives are deeply

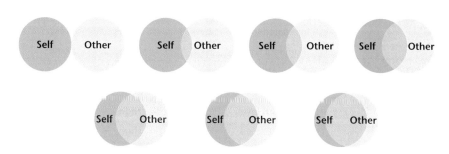

❚ Figure 18-7
Including the Other in the Self
People are asked to circle the picture that best describes their relationship. Research has found that the degree to which people include the other in the self predicts how long a relationship will last. (Fig. 1, p. 597, from A. Aron, E. N. Aron, & D. Smollan (1992), "Inclusion of other in the self scale and the structure of interpersonal closeness," in *Journal of Personality and Social Psychology, 63,* 596–612. Copyright © 1992 by the American Psychological Association. Reprinted with permission.)

intertwined" (Hatfield, 1988, p. 205). The characteristics of companionate love are trust, caring, tolerance of the partner's flaws and idiosyncrasies, and an emotional tone of warmth and affection rather than high-pitched emotional passion. As a relationship continues over time, interdependence grows, and the potential for strong emotion actually increases. This can be seen when long-time partners experience intense feelings of loneliness and desire when temporarily separated or in the emotional devastation typically experienced by someone who loses a long-time partner. But, paradoxically, because companionate couples become so compatible and coordinated in their daily routines, the actual frequency of strong emotions is usually fairly low (Berscheid, 1983).

Many of the young men and women in the survey cited earlier stated that if love disappears from a marriage, that is sufficient reason to end it. Those who equate love with passionate love, however, are likely to be disappointed. Most successful long-term couples emphasize the companionate elements of their relationship, and both theory and research suggest that the intense feelings that characterize passionate love are unlikely to persist over time (Berscheid, 1983; Solomon & Corbit, 1974). As the 16th-century writer Giraldi put it, "The history of a love affair is in some sense the drama of its fight against time."

This point is illustrated in a study that compared long-term marriages in the United States—where couples claim to marry for love—with marriages in Japan that had been arranged by the couples' parents. As expected, the American marriages started out with a higher level of expressed love and sexual interest than the Japanese marriages. But the amount of love expressed decreased in both groups until after 10 years there were no differences between the two groups. Nevertheless, many couples in this study reported quite gratifying marriages, marriages that had evolved into a deep companionate love characterized by communication between the partners, an equitable division of labor, and equality of decision-making power (Blood, 1967).

In later life the passionate component of romantic love tends to become less important than the companionate component.

The take-home message is that passionate love might be terrific for starters, but the sustaining forces of a good long-term relationship are less exciting, require more work, and have more to do with equality than with passion. In fact, as we will see shortly, there may even be a built-in incompatibility between passionate and companionate love.

THE TRIANGULAR THEORY OF LOVE Other researchers find the strategy of dichotomizing love into two kinds—passionate and companionate—to be too simplistic. One of the more differentiated classifications offered is the **triangular theory of love**. It divides love into three components: intimacy, passion, and commitment (Sternberg, 1986). **Intimacy** is the emotional component and involves closeness and sharing of feelings. **Passion**, the motivational component, consists of sexual attraction and the romantic feeling of being "in love." **Commitment** is the cognitive component; it reflects the intention to remain in the relationship. Combining these three components in different ways yields the eight kinds of relationships shown in Table 18-2. As can be seen, in this scheme passionate love is split into two types: infatuated love and romantic love. Both are characterized by high passion and low commitment, but infatuated love is low in intimacy whereas romantic love is high in intimacy. Companionate love is characterized by high intimacy and commitment but low passion.

PAIR BONDING AND MATING STRATEGIES One of the newest approaches to romantic and sexual attraction is also one of the oldest: Darwin's theory of evolution. As noted in Chapter 1, evolutionary psychology is concerned with the origins of psychological mechanisms. The key idea is that, just like biological mechanisms, psy-

● **Table 18-2**
The Triangular Theory of Love

The three dimensions of love combine to produce eight types of love relationships. *(R. Sternberg (1986), "Triangular Theory of Love," in* Psychological Review, *93:119–135. Copyright © 1986 by the American Psychological Association. Adapted by permission.)*

	Intimacy	Passion	Commitment
Nonlove	Low	Low	Low
Liking	High	Low	Low
Infatuated love	Low	High	Low
Romantic love	High	High	Low
Empty love	Low	Low	High
Companionate love	High	Low	High
Fatuous love	Low	High	High
Consummate love	High	High	High

chological mechanisms must have evolved over millions of years through a process of natural selection. They therefore have a genetic basis and have proved useful to the human species in the past for solving some problems of survival or increasing the chances of reproducing.

The renewed interest in evolution among social psychologists has led to a (sometimes controversial) reexamination of several behavioral phenomena. Among these are pair bonding in humans and differences between men and women in sexual behavior and mating strategies.

From an evolutionary perspective, men and women mate to produce offspring who will pass their genes along to future generations. To do this, individuals must solve several problems, including (1) winning out over competitors in gaining access to fertile members of the other sex, (2) selecting mates with the greatest reproductive potential, (3) engaging in the necessary social and sexual behavior to achieve conception, (4) preventing the mate from defecting or deserting, and (5) ensuring the survival and reproductive success of one's offspring (Buss, 1994). According to evolutionary psychologists, humans have evolved to form intense, long-term bonds with a partner to ensure that human offspring survive to reproductive age. As noted in Chapter 3, the more complex an organism's nervous system, the longer the time required to reach maturity. A chimpanzee will be a functioning adult member of its species years before a human of the same age is ready to fend for itself. Accordingly, in the history of our species it has been important to have both parents stick around to defend, provide for, and help rear the young. In contrast to humans, both male and female chimpanzees are quite promiscuous, and males have little or no involvement in rearing the young.

Evolutionary psychology further argues that because men and women play different roles in reproduction, the mating tactics and strategies used by the two sexes might also have evolved to be different as well. Because it is theoretically possible for a man to father hundreds of children, it is to his evolutionary advantage to impregnate as many women as possible in order to pass along the greatest number of his own genes. The woman, however, must invest a great deal of time and energy in each birth and can have only a limited number of offspring. It is to her advantage to select a mate who is most willing and best able to assist in protecting and raising her children, thereby maximizing the likelihood of passing her genes along to future generations. This reasoning suggests that evolution would have made men more promiscuous and less discriminating in their choice of sexual partners than women. In fact, it has been documented repeatedly that in most societies men are more promiscuous than women, and societies that permit one man to mate with more than one woman far outnumber those in which one woman may mate with many different men (Wilson, 1978).

Evolutionary psychology also predicts that a man should prefer to mate with the most fertile young women available because they are most likely to bear his children. A woman should prefer to mate with a man of high social status and solid material resources, one who can give the children the best chance of surviving to adulthood and reproducing in their turn. As a result, evolutionary psychologists predict that men will prefer younger women (with many more fertile years ahead of them), whereas women will prefer older men (who have more resources). This sex difference in mate preference was strongly confirmed in a study of 37 different cultures (Buss, 1989), and is summarized one of the Seeing Both Sides essays at the end of this chapter.

Evolutionary psychology has not gone unchallenged. (See the other Seeing Both Sides essay!) Some critics argue that even if a behavioral pattern appears across many or all cultures, it does not necessarily follow that it is programmed into the genes. For example, some universal cross-cultural sex differences may have arisen simply because women had less upper body strength than men and—until very recently in technological societies—were pregnant or nursing during most of their adult lives. This created sex-based divisions of labor in virtually all societies, which placed political power and decision making in the hands of men and confined women to the domestic sphere (Bem, 1993). Greater sexual freedom for men could easily emerge from such power differences.

It is often instructive to ask whether evolutionary reasoning could also have predicted a different or opposite outcome. For example, we have seen the argument that a male's ability to produce many hundreds of offspring would create an evolutionary push toward male promiscuity. But the need to ensure that one's offspring survive to reproductive age—the same need that presumably gave rise to human pair bonding in the first place—would provide an opposing evolutionary push toward monogamy. In other words, evolutionary theory could be invoked to explain either male promiscuity or male sexual fidelity.

Despite these criticisms, there is no doubt that evolutionary thinking has reinvigorated both personality and social psychology. There is probably no other single principle in the behavioral sciences with as much potential explanatory power as the principle of evolution. Moreover, the emergence of evolutionary psychology shows once again the important role of biological evidence in contemporary psychology. Even social psychologists who study the processes of social cognition now theorize about how and why our strategies for processing social information might have evolved (Nisbett & Ross, 1980; see also Buss & Kenrick, 1998).

Are the Origins of Gender Differences in Mate Selection Primarily Due to Evolution or Social Learning?

EVOLUTIONARY ORIGINS OF SEX DIFFERENCES IN MATE PREFERENCES

David M. Buss, University of Texas at Austin

Evolutionary psychology provides a powerful theoretical guide to identifying both commonalities and differences between men and women. The logic stems from understanding the *adaptive problems* the sexes have faced over the long course of human evolutionary history—problems of survival and reproduction. Both sexes have faced many similar survival problems—the need to select food, combat diseases, and fend off predators. Where men and women have confronted similar adaptive problems, evolutionary psychologists predict the sexes will be similar. Both sexes, for example, have similar taste preferences (e.g., sugar, protein, and fat) and similar fears (e.g., snakes).

In reproduction, however, the sexes have faced fundamentally different adaptive problems, and here we expect sex differences in adaptive solutions. Women, for example, bear the burdens and joys of a nine-month minimum obligatory investment (pregnancy) to produce a single child; men's minimum investment is as low as a few hours, a few minutes, or a few seconds.

Much evidence, emerging from varied data sources—self-reports, behavioral studies, and laboratory studies—confirms several sex differences predicted in advance by evolutionary psychologists. One pertains to choosiness. When approached by an opposite-sex stranger, 50% of women agreed to a date, 6% agreed to go back to his apartment, and 0% agreed to sex. In contrast, of the men approached by women, 50% agreed to a date, 69% agreed to go back to her apartment, and 75% agreed to sex (Clarke & Hatfield, 1989). This is one among hundreds of studies that document that women are more selective and discriminating in short-term mating contexts (Buss, 2003). This psychological sex difference stems from a long evolutionary history of an asymmetry between the sexes in parental investment.

Humans, unlike most other primates, also pursue long-term mating. Because of women's heavy parental investment, they are predicted to value mates who are able and willing to invest resources in them and their children. In my study of 10,047 individuals in 37 cultures located on six continents and five islands, from coastal Australia to the Zulu tribe in South Africa, this prediction was soundly supported. Women placed a greater premium on a mate's financial resources, ambition, and industriousness. Women also desired spouses who were roughly three years older.

Sometimes an alternative explanation is proposed—women do not have an evolved desire for resourceful men, but rather are forced to prefer such men because they have been excluded from other means to economic resources (Buss & Barnes, 1986). Although reasonable, the available evidence fails to support it. Women living in more economically equal cultures, such as Sweden and Norway, show just as strong a desire for mates with resources as women in more economically unequal cultures such as Japan or Iran (Buss, 1989). Furthermore, women in the United States who are economically successful place even more emphasis on a man's resources. Although more tests are needed, the available evidence supports the hypothesis that women have an evolved desire for resourceful mates.

Another key sex difference stems from ovulation. Unlike most other primate females, who experience estrus cycles with large red genital swellings, women's ovulation evolved to be cryptic or concealed. This posed a unique adaptive problem for ancestral men—how to identify fertile women in the absence of obvious estrus cues. According to one evolutionary hypothesis, men evolved to value certain features of physical appearance because appearance provides a wealth of cues to a woman's age and health, and hence to her fertility. The 37-culture study supports this explanation. Men worldwide, from Zambia to Austria, value women who are young and physically attractive, precisely as predicted.

Although these findings and their evolutionary explanations are upsetting to some people, there are three important qualifications. First, discoveries that men and women have evolved psychological differences does not justify discrimination based on sex, nor does it excuse behavior some consider immoral, such as sexual infidelity. Second, neither men nor women can be considered superior or inferior; each sex has evolved adaptations to solve its own unique problems. Third, in most psychological domains, the sexes are similar since both sexes have faced similar adaptive problems, such as identifying who will be a good long-term cooperator. Both sexes equally value a potential mate's intelligence, kindness, dependability, creativity, and adaptability. And both sexes in all 37 cultures place a premium on love and mutual attraction, which may be evolution's way of bringing the sexes together over the long term to transcend whatever differences they display.

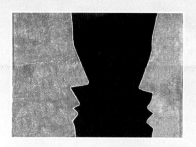

Are the Origins of Gender Differences in Mate Selection Primarily Due to Evolution or Social Learning?

THE INFLUENCE OF SOCIAL LEARNING AND SOCIAL ROLES ON MATE SELECTION

Janet S. Hyde, University of Wisconsin, Madison

A man's attraction to a woman is, on average, powerfully determined by her physical appearance. Women, too, are attracted to good-looking men but, on average, physical appearance is less important to women (Feingold, 1990). Women are more likely to take other characteristics of men—such as success—into account in their attractions. Furthermore, men prefer women who are younger than themselves, and women prefer men who are slightly older than they are. Why do these differences occur?

The answer lies in social roles and social learning. Let's first consider social roles, specifically gender roles (Eagly & Wood, 1999). One key feature of gender roles in American society, as in most other societies around the world, is that women have less power and status than men. In the United States, women earn only 75 cents for every dollar that men earn. Women are sparsely represented in the seats of power such as the U.S. Senate and House of Representatives. In a study of *Fortune 500* companies, only 12 percent of corporate officers and fewer than 1 percent of CEOs were women (Wellington & Giscombe,

Janet Hyde

2001). A second key feature of gender roles in American society is the gendered division of labor, both in paid work and in home work. Most occupations are highly gender segregated. For example, only 3.4 percent of airline pilots are women, as are 1.2 percent of carpenters,

Only 2.9 percent of childcare workers are men, as are only 1.9 percent of dental assistants (Costello & Stone, 2001). Women and men, even today, occupy quite different roles. Given the wage gap and women's lesser access to high-paid, high-status occupations, is it any wonder that women, on average, are attracted to men who are successful and earn more? They literally can't afford to do otherwise. Or is it any wonder that men do not take into account women's occupational success or earnings?

A key aspect of the female role is beauty and heterosexual attractiveness. Women's beauty is highly visible in American society and is used to sell everything from mattresses to sportscars. Girls quickly learn that they should be beautiful, and boys learn that they should be associated with beautiful girls. Gender roles also specify that certain age pairings are acceptable. When ads or TV programs show silver-haired men, they are often paired with romantic partners who are much younger than they are. Have you ever seen the reverse pairing?

How and why does each new generation of children generally adopt behaviors that are consistent with gender roles? The answer lies in social learning, particularly reinforcement, punishment, and modeling (Bussey & Bandura, 1999). Gender-role violations typically receive severe punishments, particularly in adolescent culture. Suppose that Ernie, a high school sophomore, invites Ellen, who is pleasant and friendly, to the class dance. Because she is not good looking, Ernie's friends tease him mercilessly for dating a "dog." Ernie won't make that mistake again. Justin, one of Ernie's friends, observed what happened and Justin will be careful to invite only good looking girls to dances in the fu-

ture. According to cognitive social learning theory, Justin only needed to observe Ernie's punishment to learn that boys shouldn't date unattractive girls.

Any good psychological theory should be able to specify the processes or mechanisms that produce the behaviors it seeks to explain. One of the problems with evolutionary psychology is that it does not specify mechanisms. The theory simply says there was evolutionary selection for a predisposition to this behavior and that is why it is present in modern culture. But evolution affects behavior only if genetic factors influence the behavior. Evolution acts through genes. Genes, in turn, have their effect by directing the synthesis of various biochemicals in the body, such as hormones and neurotransmitters. None of this is specified in evolutionary psychology. In contrast, social learning theory tells us exactly the processes that produce human behavior that conforms to gender roles.

A problem with the evidence from evolutionary psychologists is that, although they may have data from many different cultures, all of those cultures have a gender-based division of labor, and the division of labor is generally quite similar to the one in the United States (Eagly & Wood, 1999)—that is, women have more responsibility for caring for the home and children, and men occupy positions of power. Therefore, in regard to gender roles, the other cultures may not be as different from ours as they at first appear.

Gender differences in attraction to romantic partners are quite clearly shaped by gender roles through the process of social learning by reinforcements, punishments, and modeling.

◆ Interim Summary

- Many factors influence whether we will be attracted to a particular individual. The most important are physical attractiveness, proximity, familiarity, similarity, and transference.

- Theorists have suggested that one reason people fall in love is that doing so expands the self.

- There have been several attempts to classify types of love. Passionate love is characterized by intense and often conflicting emotions, whereas companionate love is characterized by trust, caring, tolerance of the partner's flaws, and an emotional tone of warmth and affection. Another classification of love divides it into the components of intimacy, passion, and commitment.

- Evolutionary psychology suggests that humans have evolved to form long-term bonds with a partner because historically such pair bonds operated to ensure the survival of offspring to reproductive age. A more controversial hypothesis from evolutionary psychology is that men and women have evolved to pursue different mating strategies, with men evolving to be more promiscuous and seek out younger women.

◆ Critical Thinking Questions

1. Proximity most often leads to liking because proximity creates familiarity. But why does familiarity—or mere exposure—lead to liking? Provide some possible explanations.

2. Which of the three components of love featured in Sternberg's triangular theory of love is most likely to be associated with self-expansion? Justify your choice.

RECAP: A TALE OF TWO MODES OF SOCIAL COGNITION

The major lesson of this chapter is that, in addition to understanding the power of social situations (the major lesson of Chapter 17), to more fully understand people's social behavior we also need to "get inside their heads" and examine how they think about others. The field of social cognition takes this task on. It examines the processes by which stereotypes and other social schemas become activated and affect people's thinking and behavior. It also examines the processes by which people can get beyond stereotypes to more accurately know one another. And it examines the processes by which people are persuaded to change their minds and even fall in love.

Across these many domains of study, social psychologists have repeatedly found that social cognition—or thinking about others—happens in two modes: One mode is more automatic and outside of conscious awareness, and the other is more effortful and deliberate. This recognition has produced a range of "dual-process theories" within social psychology. Two theories that received the spotlight in this chapter—the continuum model of impression formation (see Figure 18-2) and the elaboration likelihood model of persuasion (see pages 660–662)—illustrate dual-process perspectives, but there are many other renditions (see Chaiken & Trope, 1999). Recognizing these two modes of thinking helps us better understand and even alter social outcomes. To the extent that we are able and willing to engage in effortful thinking, we can curb stereotyping, avert peripheral routes to persuasion, and minimize transference. But when, for whatever reasons, we are unable engage in effortful thought—perhaps because we're busy carrying on a conversation, conducting an interview, or trying to manage the impression others form of us—we are more susceptible to various forms of automatic social cognition and behavior.

◆ Critical Thinking Questions

1. We all succumb to stereotyping others at times. Identify a time when you stereotyped someone. Now examine the circumstances. Were there situational forces that pulled for automatic thinking? What conditions would have been required for you to engage in effortful thinking?

2. Think of a time when someone tried to persuade you to her or his opinion, but you resisted. Considering the persuasion attempt, was that person expecting you to be in an automatic or deliberate mode of thinking? In actuality, was your thinking automatic or deliberate?

1. Social cognition is the study of people's subjective interpretations of their social experiences, as well as their modes of thinking about the social world. Two different modes of thinking have been found to be critical within social cognition: one more automatic and unintentional, often outside conscious awareness, and another more controlled and deliberate, of which we are fully aware.

2. Schematic processing is the perceiving and interpreting of incoming information in terms of simplified memory structures called *schemas*. Schemas are mini-theories about everyday objects and events. They allow us to process social information efficiently by permitting us to encode and remember only the unique or most prominent features of a new object or event. Stereotypes are schemas about groups of people.

3. Through repeated exposure, stereotypes can become habitual and automatic, operating outside conscious awareness.

4. Because schemas and stereotypes simplify reality, schematic processing produces biases and errors in our processing of social information. In forming impressions of other people, for example, we are prone to the primacy effect: The first information we receive evokes an initial schema and, hence, becomes more powerful in determining our impression than does later information. Schemas and stereotypes also govern our inferences.

5. Once activated, stereotypes can set in motion a chain of behavioral processes that serve to draw out from others behavior that confirms the initial stereotype, an effect called the *self-fulfilling prophecy*. This behavioral sequence can occur completely outside conscious awareness.

6. Stereotypes about the self can be self-fulfilling as well. Two explanations for the phenomenon have been offered: One refers to stereotype threat, the other to the principle of ideomotor action.

7. Individuation is the process of forming impressions of others by assessing their personal qualities on a person-by-person basis. The continuum model of impression formation details when and how people come to individuate others. Cooperative activities can promote individuation.

8. Although stereotypes are activated automatically, under the right conditions they can also be controlled through effortful thinking.

9. Attribution is the process by which we attempt to interpret and explain the behavior of other people— that is, to discern the causes of their actions. One major attribution task is to decide whether someone's action should be attributed to dispositional causes (the person's personality or attitudes) or to situational causes (social forces or other external circumstances). We tend to give too much weight to dispositional factors and too little to situational factors. This bias has been called the *fundamental attribution error*.

10. Ancient cultural practices and beliefs about the locus of causality are believed to have shaped contemporary cultural differences in styles of thinking. Research has shown repeatedly that East Asians think more holistically, whereas Westerners think analytically. This work challenges all claims to universality made about human cognition, both basic and social.

11. Attitudes are likes and dislikes—favorable or unfavorable evaluations of and reactions to objects, people, events, or ideas. Attitudes have a cognitive component, an affective component, and a behavioral component.

12. The elaboration likelihood model states that persuasion can take two routes in producing belief and attitude change: the central route, in which the individual responds to the substantive arguments of a communication, and the peripheral route, in which the individual responds to non-content cues in a communication (such as the number of arguments) or to context cues (such as the credibility of the communicator or the pleasantness of the surroundings). A communication about an issue of personal relevance is more likely to generate thoughts in response to the communication's substantive arguments. When an issue is of little personal relevance or people are unwilling or unable to respond to the substantive content of a communication, they tend to use simple heuristics—rules of thumb—to judge the merits of the communication.

13. Attitudes tend to predict behavior best when they are (1) strong and consistent, (2) specifically related to the behavior being predicted, and (3) based on the per-

son's direct experience, as well as (4) when the individual is aware of his or her attitudes.

14. Many factors influence whether we will be attracted to a particular individual. The most important are physical attractiveness, proximity, familiarity, similarity, and transference.

15. Theorists have suggested that one reason people fall in love is that doing so expands the self.

16. There have been several attempts to classify types of love. Passionate love is characterized by intense and often conflicting emotions, whereas companionate love is characterized by trust, caring, tolerance of the partner's flaws, and an emotional tone of warmth and affection. Even though passionate love decreases over time in long-term relationships, the potential for strong emotion actually increases. But because companionate couples become so compatible in their daily routines, the actual frequency of strong emotions is fairly low. Another classification of love divides it into the components of intimacy, passion, and commitment.

17. Evolutionary psychology suggests that humans have evolved to form long-term bonds with a partner because historically such pair bonds operated to ensure the survival of offspring to reproductive age. A more controversial hypothesis from evolutionary psychology is that men and women have evolved to pursue different mating strategies, with men evolving to be more promiscuous and seek out younger women.

CORE CONCEPTS

social cognition
schemas
schematic processing
stereotypes
self-schema
priming
primacy effect
inferences
self-fulfilling prophecy
stereotype threat
ideomotor action

individuation
continuum model
attribution
dispositional attribution
situational attribution
fundamental attribution error
holistic thought
analytic thought
attitudes
elaboration likelihood model
central route

peripheral route
proximity
mere exposure effect
transference
self-expansion
passionate love
companionate love
triangular theory of love
intimacy
passion
commitment

WEB RESOURCES

http://psychology.wadsworth.com/
atkinson14e

Take a quiz, try the activities and exercises, and explore web links.

http://www.socialpsychology.org/

Everything you ever wanted to know about social psychology and more! This huge warehouse of information offers a wide array of direct links, as well as a search engine to help you find exactly what you are looking for.

http://www.apa.org/pi/oema/racism/contents.html

This site from the American Psychological Association offers a frank discussion of racism and stereotypes.

 InfoTrac Online Library

http://www.infotrac-college.com/
wadsworth

Use InfoTrac College Edition to find popular and scientific articles by using the search terms below or your own relevant terms.

- Attribution
- Stereotype
- Transference

CD-ROM LINKS

 Psych Odyssey

Check out CD Chapter 13, Social Psychology: Personal Perspectives

A. Attribution Theory
B. Attraction, Liking, and Loving
C. Sternberg's Triangular Theory of Love

 Psyk.trek 2.0

Check out CD Unit 12, Social Psychology
12a Attribution Processes
12b Theories of Love
12c Attitude Change
12d Prejudice

APPENDIX

STATISTICAL METHODS AND MEASUREMENT

Much of the work of psychologists calls for making measurements—either in the laboratory or under field conditions. This work may involve measuring the eye movements of infants when first exposed to a novel stimulus, recording the galvanic skin response of people under stress, counting the number of trials required to condition a monkey that has a prefrontal lobotomy, determining achievement test scores for students using computer-assisted learning, or counting the number of patients who show improvement following a particular type of psychotherapy. In all these examples, the *measurement operation* yields numbers; the psychologist's problem is to interpret them and to arrive at some general conclusions. Basic to this task is statistics—the discipline that deals with collecting numerical data and with making inferences from such data. The purpose of this appendix is to review certain statistical methods that play an important role in psychology.

This appendix is written on the assumption that the problems students have with statistics are essentially problems of clear thinking about data. An introductory acquaintance with statistics is not beyond the scope of anyone who understands enough algebra to use plus and minus signs and to substitute numbers for letters in equations.

DESCRIPTIVE STATISTICS

Statistics serves, first of all, to provide a shorthand description of large amounts of data. Suppose that we want to study the college entrance examination scores of 5,000 students recorded on cards in the registrar's office. These scores are the raw data. Thumbing through the cards will give us some impressions of the students' scores, but it will be impossible for us to keep all of them in mind. So we make some kind of summary of the data, possibly averaging all the scores or finding the highest and lowest scores. These statistical summaries make it easier to remember and to think about the data. Such summarizing statements are called *descriptive statistics*.

FREQUENCY DISTRIBUTIONS

Items of raw data become comprehensible when they are grouped in a *frequency distribution*. To group data, we must first divide the scale along which they are measured into intervals and then count the number of items that fall into each interval. An interval in which scores are grouped is called a *class interval*. The decision of how many class intervals the data are to be grouped into is not fixed by any rules but is based on the judgment of the investigator.

Table 1 provides a sample of raw data representing college entrance examination scores for 15 students. The scores are listed in the order in which the students were tested (the first student tested had a score of 84; the second, 61; and so on). Table 2 shows these data arranged in a frequency distribution for which the class interval has been set at 10. One score falls in the interval from 50 to 59, three scores fall in the interval from 60 to 69, and so on. Note that most scores fall in the interval from 70 to 79 and that no scores fall below the 50 to 59 interval or above the 90 to 99 interval.

A frequency distribution is often easier to understand if it is presented graphically. The most widely used graph form is the *frequency histogram*; an example is

● **Table 1**
Raw Scores

College entrance examination scores for 15 students, listed in the order in which they were tested.

84	75	91
61	75	67
72	87	79
75	79	83
77	51	69

● **Table 2**
A Frequency Distribution

Scores from Table 1, accumulated by class intervals.

Class Interval	Number of Persons in Class
50–59	1
60–69	3
70–79	7
80–89	3
90–99	1

shown in the top panel of Figure 1. Histograms are constructed by drawing bars, the bases of which are given by the class intervals and the heights of which are determined by the corresponding class frequencies. An alternative way of presenting frequency distributions in graph form is to use a *frequency polygon*, an example of which is shown in the bottom panel of Figure 1. Frequency polygons are constructed by plotting the class frequencies at the center of the class interval and connecting the points obtained by straight lines. To complete the picture, one extra class is added at each end of the distribution; since these classes have zero frequencies, both ends of the figure will touch the horizontal axis. The frequency polygon gives the same information as the frequency histogram but by means of a set of connected lines rather than bars.

In practice, we would obtain a much greater number of items than those plotted in Figure 1, but a minimum amount of data is shown in all of the illustrations in this appendix so that you can easily check the steps in tabulating and plotting.

MEASURES OF CENTRAL TENDENCY

A *measure of central tendency* is simply a representative point on our scale—a central point that summarizes important information about the data. Three such measures are commonly used: the *mean*, the *median*, and the *mode*.

The mean is the familiar arithmetic average obtained by adding the scores and dividing by the number of scores. The sum of the raw scores in Table 1 is 1,125. If we divide this by 15 (the number of students' scores), the mean turns out to be 75.

The median is the score of the middle item, which is obtained by arranging the scores in order and then counting into the middle from either end. When the 15 scores in Table 1 are placed in order from highest to lowest, the eighth score from either end turns out to be 75.

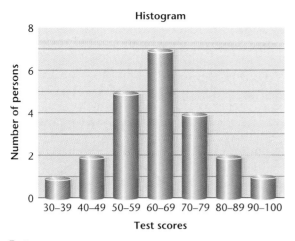

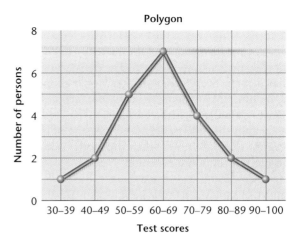

Figure 1
Frequency Diagrams
The data from Table 2 are plotted here. A frequency histogram is on the left, a frequency polygon on the right.

If the number of cases is even, we simply average the two cases on each side of the middle.

The mode is the most frequent score in a given distribution. In Table 1, the most frequent score is 75; hence, the mode of the distribution is 75.

In a *normal distribution*, in which the scores are distributed evenly on either side of the middle (as in Figure 1), the mean, median, and mode all fall together. This is not true for distributions that are *skewed*, or unbalanced. Suppose we want to analyze the departure times of a morning train. The train usually leaves on time; occasionally it leaves late, but it never leaves early. For a train with a scheduled departure time of 8:00 AM, one week's record might be as follows:

M	8:00	Mean = 8:07
Tu	8:04	Median = 8:02
W	8:02	Mode = 8:00
Th	8:19	
F	8:22	
Sat	8:00	
Sun	8:00	

The distribution of departure times in this example is skewed because of the two late departures; they raise the mean departure time but do not have much effect on the median or the mode.

Skewness is important because, unless it is understood, the differences between the median and the mean may sometimes be misleading (see Figure 2). If, for example, company executives and the company's union are arguing about the prosperity of the company's workforce, it is possible for the mean and median incomes to move in opposite directions. Suppose that a company raises the

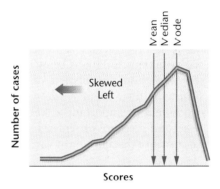

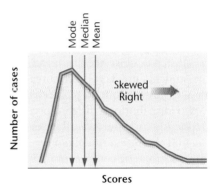

Figure 2
Skewed Distribution Curves
Note that skewed distributions are designated by the direction in which the tail falls. Also note that the mean, median, and mode are not identical for a skewed distribution; the median commonly falls between the mode and the mean.

wages of most of its employees, but cuts the wages of its top executives, who were at the extremely high end of the pay scale. The median income of the company might have gone up while the mean went down. The party wanting to show that incomes were getting higher would choose the median, and the party wanting to show that incomes were getting lower would choose the mean.

The mean is the most widely used measure of central tendency, but there are times when the mode or the median is a more meaningful measure.

MEASURES OF VARIATION

Usually more information is needed about a distribution than can be obtained from a measure of central tendency. For example, we need a measure to tell us whether scores cluster closely around their average or whether they scatter widely. A measure of the spread of scores around the average is called a *measure of variation.*

Measures of variation are useful in at least two ways. First, they tell us how representative the average is. If the variation is small, we know that individual scores are close to it. If the variation is large, we cannot use the mean as a representative value with as much assurance. Suppose that clothing is being designed for a group of people without the benefit of precise measurements. Knowing their average size would be helpful, but it also would be important to know the spread of sizes. The second measure provides a yardstick that we can use to measure the amount of variability among the sizes.

To illustrate, consider the data in Figure 3, which show frequency distributions of entrance examination scores for two classes of 30 students. Both classes have the same mean of 75, but they exhibit clearly different degrees of variation. The scores of all the students in Class I are clustered close to the mean, whereas the scores of the students in Class II are spread over a wide range. Some measure is required to specify more exactly how these two distributions differ. Three measures of variation frequently used by psychologists are the *range*, the *variance*, and the *standard deviation*.

To simplify arithmetic computation, we will suppose that five students from each class seek entrance to college and that their entrance examination scores are as follows:

Student scores from Class I:
73, 74, 75, 76, 77 (mean = 75)

Student scores from Class II:
60, 65, 75, 85, 90 (mean = 75)

We will now compute the measures of variation for these two samples. The range is the spread between the highest score and the lowest score. The range of scores

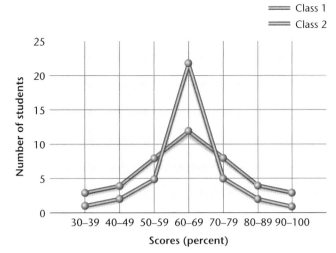

▌Figure 3
Distributions Differing in Variation
It is easy to see that the scores for Class I cluster closer to the mean than the scores for Class II, even though the means of the two classes are identical (75). For Class I, all the scores fall between 60 and 89, with most of the scores falling in the interval from 70 through 79. For Class II, the scores are distributed fairly uniformly over a wide range from 40 through 109. This difference in variability between the two distributions can be measured using the standard deviation, which is smaller for Class I than for Class II.

for the five students from Class I is 4 (from 73 to 77); the range of scores from Class II is 30 (from 60 to 90).

The range is easy to compute, but the variance and standard deviation are more frequently used. They are more sensitive measures of variation because they account for every score, not just extreme values as the range does. The variance measures how far the scores making up a distribution depart from that distribution's mean. To compute the variance, first compute the deviation *d* of each score from the mean of the distribution by subtracting each score from the mean (see Table 3). Then, each of the deviations is squared to get rid of negative numbers. Finally, the deviations are added together and divided by the total number of deviations to obtain the average deviation. This average deviation is the variance. When this is done for the data in Figure 3, we find that the variance for Class I is 2.0 and the variance for Class II is 130. Obviously, Class II has much more variability in its scores than Class I.

One disadvantage of the variance is that it is expressed in squared units of measurement. Thus, to say that Class I has a variance of 2 does not indicate that, on average, scores varied an average of 2 points from the mean. Instead, it indicates that 2 is the average of the squared number of points that scores varied from the

● Table 3
Computation of the Variance and Standard Deviation

Class I Scores (Mean = 75)	d	d²
77 − 75 =	2	4
76 − 75 =	1	1
75 − 75 =	0	0
74 − 75 =	−1	1
73 − 75 =	−2	4
		10

Sum of d^2 = 10
Variance = mean of d^2 = 10/5 = 2.0
Standard Deviation (σ) = $\sqrt{2.0}$ = 1.4

Class II Scores (Mean = 75)	d	d²
90−75 =	15	225
85−75 =	10	100
75−75 =	0	0
65−75 =	−10	100
60−75 =	−15	225
		650

Sum of d^2 = 650
Variance = mean of d^2 = 650/5 = 130
Standard Deviation (σ) = $\sqrt{130}$ = 11.4

mean. In order to obtain a measure of variability that is expressed in the original units of measurement (in this case, points on an exam), simply take the square root of the variance. This is known as the standard deviation. The standard deviation is denoted by the lowercase Greek letter *sigma*, σ, which also is used in several other statistical calculations, as we will discuss shortly. The formula for the standard deviation is:

$$\sigma = \sqrt{\frac{\text{sum of } d^2}{N}}$$

The scores for the samples from the two classes are arranged in Table 3 for easy computation of the standard deviation. The first step involves subtracting the mean from each score (the mean is 75 for both classes). This operation yields positive d values for scores above the mean and negative d values for scores below the mean. The minus signs disappear when the d values are squared in the next column. The squared deviations are

added and then divided by N, the number of cases in the sample; in our example, N = 5. Taking the square root yields the standard deviation.*

STATISTICAL INFERENCE

Now that we have become familiar with statistics as a way of describing data, we are ready to turn to the processes of interpretation—to the making of inferences from data.

POPULATIONS AND SAMPLES

First, it is necessary to distinguish between a *population* and a *sample* drawn from that population. The United States Census Bureau attempts to describe the whole population by obtaining descriptive material on age, marital status, and so on from everyone in the country. The word *population* is appropriate to the census because it represents *all* the people living in the United States.

In statistics, the word "population" is not limited to people or animals or things. The population may be all of the temperatures registered on a thermometer during the last decade, all of the words in the English language, or all of any other specified supply of data. Often we do not have access to the total population, and so we try to represent it by a sample drawn in a *random* (unbiased) fashion. We may ask some questions of a random fraction of the people, as the Census Bureau has done as part of recent censuses; we may derive average temperatures by reading the thermometer at specified times, without taking a continuous record; we may estimate the number of words in the encyclopedia by counting the words on random pages. These illustrations all involve the selection of a sample from the population. If any of these processes are repeated, we will obtain slightly different results due to the fact that a sample does not fully represent the whole population and therefore contains *errors of sampling*. This is where statistical inference enters.

A sample of data is collected from a population in order to make inferences about that population. A sam-

---

* For this introductory treatment, we will use sigma (σ) throughout. However, in the scientific literature, the lowercase letter s is used to denote the standard deviation of a sample and s is used to denote the standard deviation of the population. Moreover, in computing the standard deviation of a sample s, the sum of d^2 is divided by $N - 1$ rather than by N. For reasonably large samples, however, the actual value of the standard deviation is only slightly affected whether we divide by $N - 1$ or N. To simplify this presentation, we will not distinguish between the standard deviation of a sample and that of a population; instead, we will use the same formula to compute both. For a discussion of this point, see Phillips (1992).

ple of census data may be examined to see whether the population is getting older, for example, or whether there is a trend of migration to the suburbs. Similarly, experimental results are studied to determine what effects experimental manipulations have had on behavior—whether the threshold for pitch is affected by loudness, whether child-rearing practices have detectable effects later in life. To make *statistical inferences*, we have to evaluate the relationships revealed by the sample data. These inferences are always made under some degree of uncertainty due to sampling errors. If the statistical tests indicate that the magnitude of the effect found in the sample is fairly large (relative to the estimate of the sampling error), then we can be confident that the effect observed in the sample holds for the population at large.

Thus, statistical inference deals with the problem of making an inference or judgment about a feature of a population based solely on information obtained from a sample of that population. As an introduction to statistical inference, we will consider the normal distribution and its use in interpreting standard deviations.

THE NORMAL DISTRIBUTION

When large amounts of data are collected, tabulated, and plotted as a histogram or polygon, they often fall into a roughly bell-shaped symmetrical distribution known as the *normal distribution*. Most items fall near the mean (the high point of the bell), and the bell tapers off sharply at very high and very low scores. This form of curve is of special interest because it also arises when the outcome of a process is based on a large number of *chance* events all occurring independently. The demonstration device displayed in Figure 4 illustrates how a sequence of chance events gives rise to a normal distribution. The chance factor of whether a steel ball will fall to the left or right each time it encounters a point where the channel branches results in a symmetrical distribution: More balls fall straight down the middle, but occasionally one reaches one of the end compartments. This is a useful way of visualizing what is meant by a chance distribution closely approximating the normal distribution.

The normal distribution (Figure 5) is the mathematical representation of the idealized distribution approximated by the device shown in Figure 4. The normal distribution represents the likelihood that items within a normally distributed population will depart from the mean by any stated amount. The percentages shown in Figure 5 represent the *percentage of the area* lying under the curve between the indicated scale values; the total area under the curve represents the whole population. Roughly two thirds of the cases (68%) will fall between plus and minus one standard deviation from

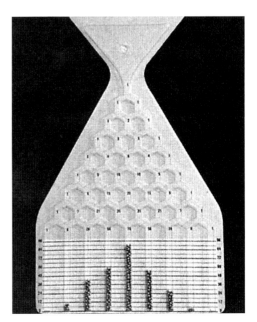

Figure 4
A Device to Demonstrate a Chance Distribution
The board is held upside down until all the steel balls fall into the reservoir. Then the board is turned over and held vertically until the balls fall into the nine columns. The precise number of balls falling into each column will vary from one demonstration to the next. On average, however, the heights of the columns of balls will approximate a normal distribution, with the greatest height in the center column and gradually decreasing heights in the outer columns.

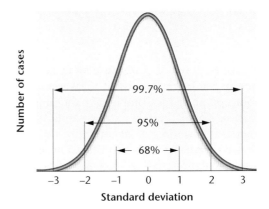

Figure 5
The Normal Distribution
The normal distribution curve can be constructed using the mean and the standard deviation. The area under the curve below -3σ and above $+3\sigma$ is negligible.

the mean ($\pm 1\sigma$); 95% of the cases within $\pm 2\sigma$ and virtually all cases (99.7%) within $\pm 3\sigma$. A more detailed listing of areas under portions of the normal curve is given in Table 4.

● Table 4
The Area of the Normal Distribution as a Proportion of Total Area

Standard Deviation	(1) Area to the Left of This Value	(2) Area to the Right of This Value	(3) Area Between This Value and Mean
-3.0σ	.001	.999	.499
-2.5σ	.006	.994	.494
-2.0σ	.023	.977	.477
-1.5σ	.067	.933	.433
-1.0σ	.159	.841	.341
-0.5σ	.309	.691	.191
0.0σ	.500	.500	.000
$+0.5\sigma$	.691	.309	.191
$+1.0\sigma$	.841	.159	.341
$+1.5\sigma$	.933	.067	.433
$+2.0\sigma$	.977	.023	.477
$+2.5\sigma$	.994	.006	.494
$+3.0\sigma$	.999	.001	.499

Using Table 4, let us trace how the 68% and 95% values in Figure 5 are derived. We find from Column 3 of Table 4 that between -1σ and the mean lies .341 of the total area and between $+1\sigma$ and the mean also lies .341 of the area. Adding these values gives us .682, which is expressed in Figure 5 as 68%. Similarly, the area between -2σ and $+2\sigma$ is $2 \times 477 = .954$, which is expressed as 95%.

These percentages have several uses. One is in connection with the interpretation of standard scores, to which we turn next. Another is in connection with tests of significance.

SCALING OF DATA

In order to interpret a score, we often need to know whether it is high or low in relation to other scores. If a person taking a driver's test requires .500 seconds to brake after a danger signal, how can we tell whether the performance is fast or slow? Does a student who scores 60 on a physics examination pass the course? To answer questions of this kind, we have to derive a scale against which the scores can be compared.

RANKED DATA By placing scores in rank order from high to low, we derive one kind of scale. An individual score is interpreted on the basis of where it ranks among the group of scores. For example, the graduates of West Point know where they stand in their class—perhaps 35th or 125th in a class of 400.

STANDARD SCORES The standard deviation is a convenient unit to use in scaling because we can interpret how far away 1σ or 2σ is from the mean (see Table 4). A score based on a multiple of the standard deviation is known as a *standard score*. Many scales used in psychological measurement are based on the principle of standard scores.

Table 1 presented college entrance scores for 15 students. Without more information, we do not know whether these scores are representative of the population of all college applicants. On this examination, however, we will assume that the population mean is 75 and the standard deviation is 10.

What, then, is the standard score for a student who had 90 on the examination? We must express how far this score lies above the mean in multiples of the standard deviation.

Standard score for grade of 90:

$$\frac{90 - 75}{10} = \frac{15}{10} = 1.5\sigma$$

As a second example, consider a student with a score of 53.

Standard score for grade of 53:

$$\frac{53 - 75}{10} = \frac{-22}{10} = -2.2\sigma$$

In this case, the minus sign tells us that the student's score is below the mean by 2.2 standard deviations. Thus, the sign of the standard score ($+$ or $-$) indicates whether the score is above or below the mean, and its value indicates how far from the mean the score lies in standard deviations.

How Representative Is a Mean?

How useful is the mean of a sample in estimating the population mean? If we measure the height of a random sample of 100 college students, how well does the sample mean predict the true population mean (that is, the mean height of *all* college students)? These questions raise the issue of making an *inference* about a population based on information from a sample.

The accuracy of such inferences depends on *errors of sampling*. Suppose we were to select two random samples from the same population and compute the mean for each sample. What differences between the first and the second mean could be expected to occur by chance?

Successive random samples drawn from the same population will have different means, forming a distribution of *sample means* around the *true mean* of the population. These sample means are themselves numbers for which the standard deviation can be computed. We call this standard deviation the standard error of the mean, or σ_M, and can estimate it on the basis of the following formula:

$$\sigma_M = \frac{\sigma}{\sqrt{N}}$$

where σ is the standard deviation of the sample and N is the number of cases from which each sample mean is computed.

According to the formula, the size of the standard error of the mean decreases as the sample size increases; thus, a mean based on a large sample is more trustworthy (more likely to be close to the actual population mean) than a mean based on a smaller sample. Common sense would lead us to expect this. Computations of the standard error of the mean permit us to make clear assertions about the degree of uncertainty in our computed mean. The more cases in the sample, the more uncertainty has been reduced.

The Significance of a Difference

In many psychological experiments, data are collected on two groups of subjects; one group is exposed to certain specified experimental conditions, and the other serves as a control group. The question is whether there is a difference in the mean performance of the two groups, and if such a difference is observed, whether it holds for the population from which these groups of subjects have been sampled. Basically, we are asking whether a difference between two sample means reflects a true difference or whether this difference is simply the result of sampling error.

As an example, we will compare the scores on a reading test for a sample of first-grade boys with the scores for a sample of first-grade girls. The boys score lower than the girls as far as mean performances are concerned, but there is a great deal of overlap; some boys do extremely well, and some girls do very poorly. Thus, we cannot accept the obtained difference in means without making a test of its *statistical significance*. Only then can we decide whether the observed differences in sample means reflect true differences in the population or are due to sampling error. If some of the brighter girls and some of the duller boys are sampled by sheer luck, the difference could be due to sampling error.

As another example, suppose that we have set up an experiment to compare the grip strength of right-handed and left-handed men. The top panel of Table 5 presents hypothetical data from such an experiment. A sample of five right-handed men averaged 8 kilograms stronger than a sample of five left-handed men. In general, what can we infer from these data about left-handed and right-handed men? Can we argue that right-handed men are stronger than left-handed men? Obviously not, because the averages derived from most of the right-handed men would not differ from those from the left-handed men; the one markedly deviant score of 100 tells us we are dealing with an uncertain situation.

Now suppose that the results of the experiment were those shown in the bottom panel of Table 5. Again, we find the same mean difference of 8 kilograms, but we are now inclined to have greater confidence in the results, because the left-handed men scored consistently lower than the right-handed men. Statistics provides a precise way of taking into account the reliability of the mean differences so that we do not have to depend solely on intuition to determine that one difference is more reliable than another.

These examples suggest that the significance of a difference will depend on both the size of the obtained difference and the variability of the means being compared. From the standard error of the means, we can compute the *standard error of the difference between two means*, $\sigma\Delta_M$. We can then evaluate the obtained difference by using a *critical ratio*—the ratio of the obtained difference between the means D_M to the standard error of the difference:

$$\text{Critical Ratio} = \frac{D_M}{\sigma D_M}$$

This ratio helps us evaluate the significance of the difference between the two means. As a rule of thumb, a critical ratio should be 2.0 or larger for the difference between means to be accepted as significant. Throughout

● Table 5
The Significance of a Difference

Two examples that compare the difference between means are shown. The difference between means is the same (8 kilograms) in both the top and bottom panel. However, the data in the bottom panel indicate a more reliable difference between means than do the data in the top panel.

Strength of Grip in Kilograms, Right-Handed Men	Strength of Grip in Kilograms, Left-Handed Men
40	40
45	45
50	50
55	55
100	60
Sum 290	Sum 250
Mean 58	Mean 50

Strength of Grip in Kilograms, Right-Handed Men	Strength of Grip in Kilograms, Left-Handed Men
56	48
57	49
58	50
59	51
60	52
Sum 290	Sum 250
Mean 58	Mean 50

this rule, we will make fewer than 5 errors in 100 decisions by concluding on the basis of sample data that a difference in means exists when in fact there is none. The 5% level need not always be used; a higher level of significance may be appropriate in certain experiments, depending on how willing we are to make an occasional error in inference.

The computation of the critical ratio calls for finding the *standard error of the difference between two means*, which is given by the following formula:

$$\sigma_{\Delta_M} = \sqrt{(\sigma M_1)^2 + (\sigma M_2)^2}$$

In this formula, σM_1, and σM_2 are the standard errors of the two means being compared.

As an illustration, suppose we wanted to compare reading achievement test scores for first-grade boys and girls in the United States. A random sample of boys and girls would be identified and given the test. We will assume that the mean score for the boys was 70 with a standard error of .40 and that the mean score for the girls was 72 with a standard error of .30. On the basis of these samples, we want to decide whether there is a real difference between the reading achievement of boys and girls in the population as a whole. The sample data suggest that girls do achieve better reading scores than boys, but can we infer that this would have been the case if we had tested all the girls and all the boys in the United States? The critical ratio helps us make this decision.

$$\sigma D_M = \sqrt{(\sigma M_1)^2 + (\sigma M_2)^2}$$
$$= \sqrt{.16 + .09} = \sqrt{.25}$$
$$= .5$$

$$\text{Critical Ratio} = \frac{D_M}{\sigma D_M} = \frac{72 - 70}{.5} = \frac{2.0}{.5} = 4.0$$

Because the critical ratio is well above 2.0, we may assert that the observed mean difference is statistically significant at the 5% level. Thus, we can conclude that there is a reliable difference in performance on the reading test between boys and girls. Note that the sign of the critical ratio could be positive or negative, depending on which mean is subtracted from which; when the critical ratio is interpreted, only its magnitude (not its sign) is considered.

this book, statements that the difference between means is "statistically significant" indicate that the critical ratio is at least that large.

Why is a critical ratio of 2.0 selected as statistically significant? Simply because a value this large or larger can occur by chance only 5 out of 100 times. Where do we get the 5 out of 100? We can treat the critical ratio as a standard score because it is merely the difference between two means, expressed as a multiple of its standard error. Referring to Column 2 in Table 4, we note that the likelihood is .023 that a standard deviation as high as or higher than +2.0 will occur by chance. Because the chance of deviating in the opposite direction is also .023, the total probability is .046. This means that 46 times out of 1,000, or about 5 times out of 100, a critical ratio as large as 2.0 would be found by chance if the population means were identical.

The rule of thumb that says a critical ratio should be at least 2.0 is just that—an arbitrary but convenient rule that defines the "5% level of significance." Following

THE COEFFICIENT OF CORRELATION

Correlation refers to the parallel variation of two measures. Suppose that a test is designed to predict success in college. If it is a good test, high scores on it will be related to high performance in college and low scores will be related to poor performance. The *coefficient of correlation* gives us a way of stating the degree of relationship more precisely.

PRODUCT-MOMENT CORRELATION

The most frequently used method of determining the coefficient of correlation is the *product-moment method*, which yields the index conventionally designated by the lowercase letter *r*. The product-moment coefficient *r* varies between perfect positive correlation ($r = +1.00$) and perfect negative correlation ($r = -1.00$). Lack of any relationship yields $r = .00$.

The formula for computing the product-moment correlation is:

$$r = \frac{\text{Sum } (dx)(dy)}{N\sigma_x\sigma_y}$$

Here, one of the paired measures has been labeled the *x*-score; the other, the *y*-score. The *dx* and *dy* refer to the deviations of each score from its mean, *N* is the number of paired measures, and σ_x and σ_y are the standard deviations of the *x*-scores and the *y*-scores.

The computation of the coefficient of correlation requires the determination of the sum of the (*dx*)(*dy*) products. This sum, in addition to the computed standard deviations for the *x*-scores and *y*-scores, can then be entered into the formula.

Suppose that we have collected the data shown in Table 6. For each subject, we have obtained two scores—the first being a score on a college entrance test

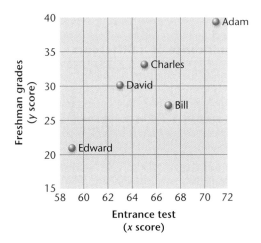

▌Figure 6
A Scatter Design
Each point represents the *x*- and *y*-scores for a particular student. The letters next to the points identify the students in the data table (A = Adam, B = Bill, and so on).

(to be labeled arbitrarily the *x*-score) and the second being freshman grades (the *y*-score).

Figure 6 is a *scatter diagram* of these data. Each point represents the *x*-score and *y*-score for a given subject; for example, the uppermost right-hand point is for Adam (labeled A). Looking at these data, we can easily detect that there is some positive correlation between the *x*-scores and the *y*-scores. Adam attained the highest score on the entrance test and also earned the highest freshman grades; Edward received the lowest scores on both. The other students' test scores and grades are a lit-

● Table 6
Computation of a Product-Moment Correlation

Student	Entrance Test (*x*-score)	Freshman Grades (*y*-score)	(*dx*)	(*dy*)	(*dx*)(*dy*)
Adam	71	39	6	9	+54
Bill	67	27	2	−3	−6
Charles	65	33	0	3	0
David	63	30	−2	0	0
Edward	59	21	−6	−9	+54
Sum	325	150	0	0	+102
Mean	65	30			

$$\sigma_x = 4$$
$$\sigma_y = 6$$

$$r = \frac{\text{Sum } (dx)(dy)}{N\sigma_x\sigma_y} = \frac{+102}{5 \times 4 \times 6} = +.85$$

tle irregular, so we know that the correlation is not perfect; hence, r is less than 1.00.

We will compute the correlation to illustrate the method, although no researcher would consent, in practice, to determining a correlation for so few cases. The details are given in Table 6. Following the procedure outlined in Table 3, we compute the standard deviation of the x-scores and then the standard deviation of the y-scores. Next, we compute the $(dx)(dy)$ products for each subject and total the five cases. Entering these results in our equation yields an r of $+.85$.

INTERPRETING A CORRELATION COEFFICIENT

We can use correlations in making predictions. For example, if we know from experience that a certain entrance test correlates with freshman grades, we can predict the freshman grades for beginning college students who have taken the test. If the correlation were perfect, we could predict their grades without error. But r is usually less than 1.00, and some errors in prediction will be made; the closer r is to 0, the greater the sizes of the errors in prediction.

Although we cannot go into the technical problems of predicting freshman grades from entrance examinations or of making other similar predictions, we can consider the meanings of correlation coefficients of different sizes. It is evident that with a correlation of 0 between x and y, knowledge of x will not help to predict y. If weight is unrelated to intelligence, it does us no good to know a subject's weight when we are trying to predict his or her intelligence. At the other extreme, a perfect correlation would mean 100% predictive efficiency—knowing x, we can predict y perfectly. What about intermediate values of r? Some appreciation of the meaning of correlations of intermediate sizes can be gained by examining the scatter diagrams in Figure 7.

In the preceding discussion, we did not emphasize the sign of the correlation coefficient, since this has no bearing on the strength of a relationship. The only distinction between a correlation of $r = +.70$ and $r = -.70$ is that increases in x are accompanied by increases in y for the former, and increases in x are accompanied by decreases in y for the latter.

Although the correlation coefficient is one of the most widely used statistics in psychology, it is also one of the most widely misused procedures. Those who use it sometimes overlook the fact that r does not imply a

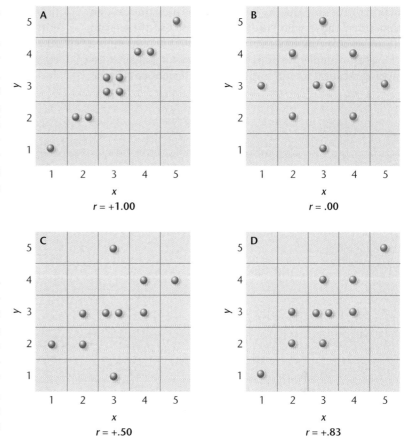

▌ Figure 7
Scatter Diagrams Illustrating Correlations of Various Sizes
Each dot represents one individual's score on two tests, x and y. In A, all cases fall on the diagonal and the correlation is perfect ($r = +1.00$); if we know a subject's score on x, we know that it will be the same on y. In B, the correlation is 0; knowing a subject's score on x, we cannot predict whether it will be at, above, or below the mean on y. In both C and D, there is a diagonal trend to the scores, so that a high score on x is associated with a high score on y and a low score on x with a low score on y, but the relationship is imperfect.

cause-and-effect relationship between x and y. When two sets of scores are correlated, we may suspect that they have some causal factors in common, but we cannot conclude that one of them causes the other.

Correlations sometimes appear paradoxical. For example, the correlation between study time and college grades has been found to be slightly negative (about $-.10$). If a causal interpretation were assumed, we might conclude that the best way to raise grades would be to stop studying. The negative correlation arises because some students have advantages over others in grade making (possibly due to better college preparation), so that often those who study the hardest are those who have difficulty earning the best grades.

This example provides sufficient warning against assigning a causal interpretation to a coefficient of correlation. It is possible, however, that when two variables are correlated, one may be the cause of the other. The search for causes is a logical one, and correlations can help us by providing leads to experiments that can verify cause-and-effect relationships.

GLOSSARY

The glossary defines the technical words that appear in the text and some common words that have special meanings when used in psychology. No attempt is made to give the range of meanings beyond those used in the text. For fuller definitions and other shades of meaning, consult any standard dictionary of psychology.

A

abnormal. Away from the norm.

absolute threshold. The minimum magnitude of a stimulus that can be reliably discriminated from no stimulus at all.

abstractions. Properties that characterize sets of instances rather than just single instances.

accommodation. (1) The process by which the lens of the eye varies its focus. (2) In Piaget's theory of cognitive development, the process by which an infant modifies a pre-existing schema in order to include a novel object or event.

action potential. An electrochemical impulse that travels from the dendritic area down to the end of the axon.

activation model. In memory, the proposal that retrieval of an item depends on the activation of that item reaching a critical level.

actualizing tendency. A tendency toward fulfillment or actualization of all the capacities of the organism.

addiction. A pattern of compulsive and destructive drug-taking behavior.

adolescence. The period of transition from childhood to adulthood.

adolescent growth spurt. A period of rapid physical growth that accompanies the onset of puberty.

affect. Emotions and feelings.

affective neuroscience. The study of how emotional phenomena are executed in the brain.

aggression. Behavior that is intended to injure another person (physically or verbally) or to destroy property.

agnosia. The general term for breakdowns or disorders in recognition.

agonists. A drug that binds to receptors and activates them in much the same way that another drug does.

agoraphobia. Fear of places where one might be trapped or unable to receive help in an emergency.

alliesthesia. An interaction between incentive and drive theories of motivation which states that any external stimulus that corrects an internal trouble is experienced as pleasurable.

altered states of consciousness. A change from an ordinary pattern of mental functioning to a state that seems different to the person experiencing the change.

alternative form reliability. The consistency between two or more versions of the same test when given to the same person.

American College Test (ACT). An example of a group-administered general-ability test.

American Law Institute. "A person is not responsible for criminal conduct if at the time of such conduct, as a result of mental disease or defect, he lacks substantial capacity either to appreciate the wrongfulness of his conduct or to conform his conduct to the requirements of the law."

amnesia. Partial loss of memory.

amphetamines. Central nervous system stimulants that produce restlessness, irritability, anxiety, and rapid heart rate. Dexedrine sulfate ("speed") and methamphetamine ("meth") are two types of amphetamines.

amplitude (of a tone). The difference in pressure between the peak and the trough.

amygdala. A brain structure located below the cerebral cortex that is involved in consolidation of emotional memories.

anal stage. The second stage in Freud's psychoanalytic theory of psychosexual development, following the oral stage. The sources of gratification and conflict have to do with the expulsion and retention of feces.

analytic thought. An orientation toward objects, detached from their contexts, with much use of categories and formal logic and the avoidance of contradiction.

Anderson's theory of intelligence. The theory that differences in intelligence result from differences in the "basic processing mechanism" that implements thinking, which in turn yields knowledge. Individuals vary in the speed at which basic processing occurs.

androgenization. Influence of androgen on anatomy and brain development.

anhedonia. The loss of the ability to experience joy, even in response to the most joyous occasions.

anomic aphasic. Patients who primarily have problems in retrieving and recognizing words (as a result of some brain damage).

anorexia nervosa. Self-imposed weight loss—at least 15 percent of the individual's minimum normal weight.

antagonists. A drug that locks onto receptors but in a way that does not activate them; the drug serves to "block" the receptors so that another drug cannot gain access to them.

anterior system (for attention). Designed to control when and how the perceptual features of an object (location in space, shape, color) will be used for selection. See also posterior system (for attention).

anterograde amnesia. Loss of memory for events and experiences occurring subsequent to an amnesia-causing trauma; the patient is unable to acquire new information, although recall of information learned prior to the onset may be largely unaffected.

antidepressant. Drug used to elevate the mood of depressed individuals, presumably by increasing the availability of the neurotransmitters norepinephrine and/or serotonin. Examples are imipramine (Tofranil), isocarboxazid (Marplan), and fluoxetine (Prozac).

antisocial personality. A type of personality disorder marked by impulsivity, inability to abide by the customs and laws of society, and lack of anxiety or guilt regarding behavior (syn. sociopathic personality, psychopathic personality).

antisocial personality disorder. A disorder characterized by deficits in normal emotional responding—especially for shame, guilt, and fear—as well as deficits in empathy for the emotions of others.

anxiety. A state of apprehension, tension, and worry. Synonymous with fear for some theorists, although others view the object of anxiety (such as a vague danger or foreboding) as less specific than the object of a fear (such as a vicious animal).

anxiety disorders. A group of mental disorders characterized by intense anxiety or by maladaptive behavior designed to relieve anxiety. Includes generalized anxiety and panic disorders, phobic and obsessive-compulsive disorders. Major category of DSM-IV covering most of the disorders formerly called neuroses.

aphasia. Language deficits caused by brain damage.

apnea. The individual stops breathing while asleep.

assimilation. In Piaget's theory of cognitive development, the process by which an infant comprehends a novel object or event in terms of a pre-existing schema.

associationist psychology. The view that the mind is filled with ideas that enter by way of the senses and then become associated through principles such as similarity and contrast.

associative learning. Learning that certain contingencies (or relations) exist between events; learning that one event is associated with another.

ataque de nervios. Trembling, feelings of out of control, sudden crying, screaming uncontrollably, verbal and physical aggression, and sometimes seizure-like or fainting episodes and suicidal gestures.

Atkinson-Shiffrin theory (of memory). The basis for the distinction between different memories corresponding to different time intervals.

attachment. An infant's tendency to seek closeness to particular people and to feel more secure in their presence.

attention. The ability to select some information for more detailed inspection, while ignoring other information.

attitudes. Favorable or unfavorable evaluations of and reactions to objects, people, situations, or other aspects of the world.

attribution. The process by which we attempt to explain the behavior of other people. Attribution theory deals with the rules people use to infer the causes of observed behavior.

attributional styles. Styles of making attributions for the events in one's life.

atypical antipsychotics. Reduce symptoms of schizophrenia without causing so many side effects.

auditory cue. A sound cue that is presented immediately after the array.

auditory system. The ears, parts of the brain, and the various connecting neural pathways.

augmented network. A network that includes inhibitory as well as excitatory connections.

autism. A mental disorder, first evident during early childhood, in which the child shows significant deficits in communication, social interaction, and bonding and play activities, and engages in repetitive stereotyped behaviors and self-damaging acts.

automaticity. The habituation of responses that initially requires conscious attention.

autonomic nervous system. The division of the peripheral nervous system that regulates smooth muscle (organ and glandular) activities. It is divided into the sympathetic and parasympathetic divisions.

autonomic system. Connects with the internal organs and glands.

autonomy. A child's independence from caretakers.

available wavelengths. The wavelengths of the light that is reflected off the paper reaching your eyes.

axon. That portion of a neuron that transmits impulses to other neurons.

B

back projections. Activities that modify the way sensory input is processed.

backward masking. A method used in psychological testing. The participant is shown a picture for only 30 milliseconds, which is then masked by a neutral picture so that participants are unaware of the picture's content.

basic level. In a hierarchy of concepts, the level at which one first categorizes an object.

basilar membrane. A membrane of the ear within the coils of the cochlea supporting the organ of Corti. Movements of the basilar membrane stimulate the hair cells of the organ of Corti, producing the neural effects of auditory stimulation.

behavior genetics. Combines the methods of genetics and psychology to study the inheritance of behavioral characteristics.

behavior therapy. A method of psychotherapy based on learning principles. It uses such techniques as counterconditioning, reinforcement, and shaping to modify behavior (syn. behavior modification).

behavioral medicine. The study of how social, psychological, and biological factors interact to contribute to physical illness (syn. health psychology).

behavioral perspective. An approach to psychology that focuses only on observable behavior, and tries to explain it in terms of its relation to environmental events.

behavioral rehearsal. Role-playing.

behaviorism. A school or system of psychology associated with the name of John B. Watson; it defined psychology as the study of behavior and limited the data of psychology to observable activities. In its classical form it was more restrictive than the contemporary behavioral viewpoint in psychology.

behaviorist approach (to personality). Emphasizes the importance of environmental, or situational, determinants of behavior.

benzodiazepines. A class of drugs with similar chemical structures that are effective in reducing anxiety. Examples are diazepam (Valium) and alprazolam (Xanax).

bias. A criterion, set by the observer, for making a particular response.

"Big Five." Five trait dimensions capture most of what we mean by personality. They are Openness to experience, Conscientiousness, Extraversion, Agreeableness, and Neuroticism.

binding problem. How activity in different parts of the brain, corresponding to different primitives such as color and shape, are combined into a coherent perception of an object.

binocular disparity (as a depth cue). The difference in the views seen by each eye.

biofeedback. Receiving information (feedback) about an aspect of one's physiological state and then attempting to alter that state.

biological perspective. An approach to psychology that tries to explain behavior in terms of electrical and chemical events taking place inside the body, particularly within the brain and nervous system.

biological psychologist. A psychologist concerned with the relationship between biological processes and behavior.

bipolar disorders. Alternating between periods of depression and periods of mania. (syn. manic-depression).

blocking. A phenomenon in classical conditioning: if one conditioned stimulus reliably predicts an unconditioned stimulus, and another conditioned stimulus is added, the relation between the added conditioned stimulus and the unconditioned stimulus will not be learned.

borderline personality disorder. A mental disorder in which the individual has manifested unstable moods, relationships with others, and self-perceptions chronically since adolescence or childhood.

bottom-up processes. Processes in perception, learning, memory, and comprehension that are driven solely by the information input, and that do not involve the organism's prior knowledge and expectations.

brain imaging. Techniques such as event-related potentials (ERPs), positron emission tomography (PET), and functional magnetic resonance imaging (fMRI).

brain's dopamine system. The neurons of this system lie in the upper brain stem and send their axons through the nucleus accumbens and up to the prefrontal cortex. As their name implies, these neurons use the neurotransmitter dopamine to convey their message.

brightness. How much light appears to be reflected from a colored surface.

broaden-and-build theory. The theory that positive emotions broaden our typical ways of thinking and acting and, in turn, build our lasting personal resources.

Broca's aphasia. Disrupted language caused by damage to Broca's area, that portion of the left cerebral hemisphere involved in the control of speech. Individuals with damage in this area have difficulty enunciating words correctly and speak in a slow and labored way; their speech often makes sense, but it includes only key words.

bulimia. Recurrent episodes of binge eating (rapid consumption of a large amount of food in a discrete period of time), followed by attempts to purge the excess by means of vomiting or laxatives.

bystander effect. The rule that people are less likely to help when others are present.

C

cannabis. The hemp plant from which marijuana is obtained.

case histories. Biographies designed for scientific use.

categorization. The process of assigning an object to a concept.

catharsis. Purging an emotion by experiencing it intensely.

cathartic effect. The hypothesized reduction of aggression that follows the vicarious expression of it.

causality heuristic. The use of the strength of the causal connections between the events in a claim to estimate the probability of that claim.

Ceci's bioecological theory. This theory proposes "multiple cognitive potentials," rather than a single underlying general intelligence. These multiple abilities are biologically based and place limits on mental processes and their emergence is shaped by the challenges and opportunities in the individual's environment, or context.

central core. The most central portion of the brain, including structures that regulate basic life processes.

central nervous system. All the neurons in the brain and spinal cord.

central route. When an individual mentally responds to and elaborates on the persuasive communication.

cerebellum. Lobed structure attached to the rear of the brain stem that regulates muscle tone and coordination of intricate movements.

cerebral cortex. The surface layer of the cerebral hemispheres in higher animals, including humans, commonly called gray matter.

cerebrum. The brain's two cerebral hemispheres.

childhood amnesia. The inability to recall events from the first years of one's life.

chromosomes. Structures found in the nucleus of each cell in the body.

chunking. Recoding new material into larger, more meaningful units and storing those units in working memory.

circadian rhythm. Rhythms of the body that occur approximately every 24 hours.

classical conditioning. A learning process in which a previously neutral stimulus becomes associated with another stimulus through repeated pairing with that stimulus.

client-centered therapy. A method of psychotherapy developed by Carl Rogers in which the therapist is nondirective and reflective and does not interpret or advise. The operating assumption is that the client is the best expert on his or her problems and can work them out in a nonjudgmental, accepting atmosphere (syn. nondirective counseling).

clinical psychologist. A psychologist, usually with a Ph.D. or Psy.D. degree, trained in the diagnosis and treatment of emotional or behavioral problems and mental disorders.

clock-dependent alerting process. The process in the brain that arouses us at a particular time each day.

coaction. The interaction between individuals performing the same task.

cocaine. A central nervous system stimulant derived from leaves of the coca plant. Increases energy, produces euphoria, and in large doses causes paranoia.

cochlea. The portion of the inner ear containing the receptors for hearing.

cognitive appraisal. The interpretation of an event or situation with respect to one's goals and well-being. The cognitive appraisal of an event influences both the quality and intensity of the emotion experienced and the degree of perceived threat.

cognitive approach (to personality). A general empirical approach and a set of topics related to how people process information about themselves and the world.

cognitive behavior therapy. A therapy that attempts to help people identify the kinds of stressful situations that produce their physiological or emotional symptoms and alter the way they cope with these situations.

cognitive dissonance theory. This theory assumes that there is a drive toward cognitive consistency, meaning that two cognitions or thoughts—that are inconsistent will produce discomfort, which will in turn motivate the person to remove the inconsistency and bring the cognitions into harmony.

cognitive map. A hypothetical structure in memory that preserves and organizes information about the various events that occur in a learning situation; a mental picture of the learning situation.

cognitive neuroscience. An interdisciplinary approach that combines aspects of cognitive psychology and neuroscience to study how mental activities are executed in the brain.

cognitive perspective. An approach to psychology that focuses on mental processes such as perceiving, remembering, reasoning, deciding, and problem solving, and tries to explain behavior in terms of these mental processes.

collective unconscious. A part of the mind that is common to all humans and consisting of primordial images or archetypes inherited from our ancestors.

collectivism. Refers to cultures that emphasize the fundamental connectedness and interdependence among people.

color constancy. The tendency to see a familiar object as of the same color, regardless of changes in illumination on it that alter its stimulus properties.

color-matching experiment. An experiment that measures an observer's inclination to see two physically different lights as having the same color.

commitment. The cognitive component of love that reflects the intention to remain in the relationship.

companionate love. Contrasted with passionate love. The affection we feel for those with whom our lives are deeply intertwined.

complex cell. A cell in the visual cortex that responds to a bar of light or straight edge of a particular orientation located anywhere in the visual field.

compliance. We comply with the wishes of the influencer but do not necessarily change our beliefs or attitudes.

comprehension of language. Understanding language by hearing sounds, attaching meanings to the sounds in the form of words, combining the words to create a sentence, and then somehow extracting meaning from it.

compulsion. Irresistible urges to carry out certain acts or rituals that reduce anxiety.

concept. The set of properties that we associate with a particular class.

concrete operational stage. Piaget's third stage of cognitive development (ages 7 to 11 years) during which children become capable of logical thought and conservation.

conditioned aversion. Learning that occurs when negative associative memories cause something (often food) to subsequently be experienced as unpleasant.

conditioned reinforcer. A stimulus that has become reinforcing through prior association with a reinforcing stimulus (syn. secondary reinforcer).

conditioned response (CR). The learned or acquired response to a stimulus that did not evoke the response originally (i.e., a conditioned stimulus).

conditioned satiety. The idea that the fullness we feel after a meal is at least in part a product of learning.

conditioned stimulus (CS). A previously neutral stimulus that comes to elicit a conditioned response through association with an unconditioned stimulus.

cone. In the eye, a specialized cell of the retina found predominantly in the fovea and more sparsely throughout the retina. The cones mediate both chromatic and achromatic sensations.

connectionist models. Models of cognitive processes (like perception) that incorporate a network of nodes, with excitatory and inhibitory connections between them.

conscious. Our current awareness.

consciousness. (a) Monitoring ourselves and our environment so that percepts, memories, and thoughts are represented in awareness. (b) Controlling ourselves and our environment so that we are able to initiate and terminate behavioral and cognitive activities.

conservation. The understanding that the amount of a substance remains the same even when its form is changed.

constancy. The brain's ability to maintain a perception of the underlying physical characteristics of an object, such as shape, size or color, even when the sensory manifestations of these objects change drastically.

construct validity. The ability of a test or assessment instrument to confirm predictions of the theory underlying some theoretical concept or construct. Confirming results validate both the concept and the assessment instrument simultaneously.

constructive perception. What is perceived forms the basis for the initial memory; therefore, if what is originally perceived differs systematically from the objective world, the perceiver's initial memory of what happened will likewise be distorted.

constructive processes. The processes by which perception is based on prior knowledge and inference in addition to the objective data from the environment.

continuum model. This model describes the full continuum of processes from stereotyping to individuation.

contrast acuity. The ability to see differences in brightness.

control group. In an experiment, the group in which the condition under study is absent.

controllability. The degree to which we can stop an event or bring it about.

controlled stimulation. Conditions in which the perceptual experiences of an organism are systematically varied in order to determine the effect on subsequent performance. For example, rearing kittens in an environment where they see only vertical stripes for the first few months of life.

conventional level of moral development. Level of moral development in which children evaluate actions in terms of other people's opinions.

coping. The process by which a person attempts to manage stressful demands.

core. The part of a concept that contains the properties that are more essential for determining membership in the concept.

core relational theme. The personal meaning that results from a particular pattern of appraisals about a specific person-environment relationship.

coronary heart disease. The narrowing or closing of the blood vessels that supply the heart muscles by the gradual buildup of a hard, fatty substance called plaque, blocking the flow of oxygen and nutrients to the heart.

correlation coefficient. An estimate of the degree to which two variables are related.

counseling psychologist. A trained psychologist, usually with a Ph.D. or Psy.D. degree, who deals with personal problems not classified as illness, such as academic, social, or vocational problems of students. He or she has skills similar to those of the clinical psychologist but usually works in a nonmedical setting.

criterion problem in assessment. The difficulty that arises in validating a test or assessment instrument when there is no criterion behavior the investigator is willing to accept as the "true" measure of the concept being evaluated.

criterion validity. The ability of a test or assessment instrument to predict the behavior it is designed to predict (syn. empirical validity).

critical periods. Crucial time periods in a person's life during which specific events occur if development is to proceed normally.

cue. A directing stimulus such as a small arrow that directs the subject to attend either to the left or to the right.

cultural perspective (of abnormality). The view that mental disorders are not situated in the brain or mind of the individual but in the social context in which the individual lives.

cultural psychology. An interdisciplinary approach involving psychologists, anthropologists, sociologists, and other social scientists that is concerned with how an individual's culture influences his or her mental representations and psychological processes.

cultural relativist perspective (for acceptable behavior). This perspective follows that people should respect each culture's definitions of abnormality for the members of that culture.

D

dark adaptation. The increased sensitivity to light when the subject has been continuously in the dark or under conditions of reduced illumination.

dark-adaptation curve. The absolute threshold decreases with the length of time the person is in darkness.

data-driven learning. A kind of associative learning in which people have no prior beliefs about the relation that has to be learned; learning is driven only by the input or data.

debriefing. The meeting between researcher and participant following a study in which the researcher tells the participant the reasons for keeping them in ignorance—or deceiving them—about the procedures or hypotheses. The researcher also deals with any of the participants' residual emotional reactions so that participants leave with their dignity intact and their appreciation for the research enhanced.

decibel scale. A logarithmic scale of loudness. A change of 10 decibels corresponds to a change in sound power of 10 times; 20 decibels, a change of 100 times; and so forth.

deductive validity. It is impossible for the conclusion of the argument to be false if its premises are true.

deductive validity (of an argument). According to logicians, an argument in which it is impossible for the conclusion of the argument to be false if its premises are true.

defense mechanisms. Strategies that people use to deal with anxiety, which are largely unconscious.

degradation. The process in which enzymes in the membrane of a receiving neuron react with a neurotransmitter to break it up chemically and make it inactive; one method (in addition to reuptake) of terminating a neurotransmitter's action.

deindividuation. A feeling that one has lost his or her personal identity and merged anonymously into a group.

deinstitutionalization. The movement toward discharge of institutionalized mental patients to community-based services.

delusions. Beliefs that most people would view as misinterpretations of reality.

dendrite. The specialized portion of the neuron that (together with the cell body) receives impulses from other neurons.

denial. A defense mechanism by which unacceptable impulses or ideas are not perceived or allowed into full awareness.

dependent variable. A variable that is hypothesized to depend on the value of the independent variable.

depressants. Drugs that depress the central nervous system.

depressive disorders. Having one or more periods of depression without a history of manic episodes.

depth cues. Different kinds of visual information that, logically or mathematically, provide information about some object's depth.

developmental psychologist. A psychologist whose research interest lies in studying the changes that occur as a function of the growth and development of the organism, in particular the relationship between early and later behavior.

***Diagnostic and Statistical Manual of Mental Disorders*, 4th edition.** The classification of mental disorders used by most mental health professionals in the United States.

dichromatism. Color blindness in which either the red-green or the blue-yellow system is lacking. The red-green form is relatively common; the blue-yellow form is the rarest of all forms of color blindness.

difference reduction. A problem-solving strategy in which one sets up subgoals that, when obtained, put one in a state closer to the goal.

difficult temperament. Term used to describe a child who is irritable, has irregular sleeping and eating patterns, and responds intensely and negatively to new situations.

diffusion of responsibility. The tendency for persons in a group situation to fail to take action (as in an emergency) because others are present, thus diffusing the responsibility for acting. A major factor in inhibiting bystanders from intervening in emergencies.

digit-span task. An experiment in which the observer is shown various sequences of unrelated items (digits, letters, or words) and is then asked to recall the items in order.

dimensional appraisal theories. A group of appraisal theories that identify a range of appraisal dimensions thought to be sufficient to account for differences among emotions.

direct observation. The observation of a particular phenomenon under study as it occurs naturally.

discrimination. A reaction to differences.

disorganized. Term used to describe a child who exhibits contradictory behaviors related to attachment to his or her caretaker.

displacement. (a) A defense mechanism whereby a motive that may not be directly expressed (such as sex or aggression) appears in a more acceptable form. (b) The principle of loss of items from short-term memory as too many new items are added.

display rules. A culture's rules for the types of emotions people should experience in certain situations, and the behaviors (including facial expressions) appropriate for each emotion.

dispositional attribution. Attributing a person's actions to internal dispositions (attitudes, traits, motives), as opposed to situational factors.

dissociation. Under certain conditions some thoughts and actions become split off, or dissociated, from the rest of consciousness and function outside of awareness.

dissociative identity disorder. The existence in a single individual of two or more distinct identities or personalities that alternate in controlling behavior. Formerly called multiple personality disorder.

distress. Feelings of anxiety, depression, or agitation, or experiences such as insomnia, loss of appetite, or numerous aches and pains.

dream analysis. Talking about the content of one's dreams and then free associating to that content.

dreaming. An altered state of consciousness in which remembered images and fantasies are temporarily confused with external reality.

drive theories. Theories of motivation that emphasize the role of internal factors.

drug abuse. Continued use of a drug by a person who is not dependent on it (that is, shows no signs of tolerance, withdrawal, or compulsive craving), despite serious consequences.

drug dependence. A pattern of compulsive drug use usually characterized by tolerance (the need to take more and more of the drug to achieve the same effect), withdrawal (unpleasant physical and psychological reactions if the drug is discontinued), and compulsive use (taking more of the drug than intended, being unable to control drug use, or spending a great deal of time trying to obtain the drug).

dynamic control theory. Instead of an early, hard-wired system sensitive to a small number of visual primitives, there is a malleable system whose components can be quickly reconfigured to perform different tasks at different times.

E

eardrum. The membrane at the inner end of the auditory canal, leading to the middle ear.

easy temperament. Term used to describe a child who is playful, regular in his or her sleeping and eating patterns, and adapts readily to new situations.

eclectic approach. An approach to looking at topics within psychology using multiple psychological perspectives.

educational psychologist. A psychologist whose research interest lies in the application of psychological principles to the education of children and adults in schools.

ego. The executive of the personality.

egocentrism. The condition of being unaware of perspectives other than one's own and believing that everyone perceives the environment in the same way.

elaboration. A memory process wherein one expands verbal material so as to increase the number of ways to retrieve the material.

elaboration likelihood model. According to this model, if a person is at the high end of the continuum—willing and able to think deeply—then persuasion is said to follow a central route, relying on controlled and effortful thinking; if a person is at the low end of the continuum—for whatever reasons not willing or able to think deeply—then persuasion is said to follow a peripheral route, relying on automatic and effortless thinking.

electroconvulsive therapy (ECT). A mild electric current is applied to the brain to produce a seizure similar to an epileptic convulsion. Also known as electroshock therapy.

emergent features. Features that owe their existence to the configuration of other features.

emotion. A complex condition that arises in response to certain affectively toned experiences.

emotion-focused coping. Ways of reducing anxiety or stress that do not deal directly with the emotion-producing situation; defense mechanisms are a form of emotion-focused coping.

emotion regulation. People's responses to their own emotions.

encoding stage. Occurs when environmental information is translated into and stored as a meaningful entity.

engineering psychologist. A psychologist who specializes in the relationship between people and machines, seeking, for example, to design machines that minimize human error.

episodic memory. A type of memory that stores facts about personal episodes. The fact or episode is encoded with respect to the memorizer, and often with respect to the specific time and place as well.

evocative interaction. The interaction between individuals and their environments that arises because the behavior of different individuals evokes different responses from others.

evolutionary psychology. An area of research that studies how psychological processes have evolved by means of natural selection; those behaviors that aided survival or increased the chance of reproduction have tended to persist through the course of evolutionary history.

excitatory conditioning. The ability of a CS to increase the probability or magnitude of a given behavior.

excitatory connections. Connections between two nodes in a connectionist network that are positive: An increase in one leads to an increase in the other.

exotic-becomes-erotic. A theory about the determinants of sexual orientation that integrates nature and nurture views.

experiment. The strongest test of hypotheses about cause and effect in which an investigator carefully controls conditions and takes measurements to discover the causal relationships among variables.

experimental group. In an experiment, the group of subjects given the treatment whose effect is under investigation.

experimental psychologist. A psychologist who uses experimental methods to study how people (and other animals) react to sensory stimuli, perceive the world, learn and remember, reason and respond emotionally.

explicit memory. The kind of memory that underlies a conscious recollection of something in the past.

exponent (of a power function). A unique number that characterizes the function of each sensory modality.

extinction. (a) The experimental procedure, following classical or operant conditioning, of presenting the conditioned stimulus without the usual reinforcement. (b) The reduction in response that results from this procedure.

extracellular thirst. The psychological manifestation of the need for water that occurs when our bodies lose water because we have gone without drinking or have exercised intensively.

F

facial expressions. The muscle actions that move facial landmarks in particular ways.

facial feedback hypothesis. The hypothesis that people's subjective experience of an emotion is determined by feedback from the physiological arousal caused by engaging in specific facial expressions.

facial preference. In infants, an inborn, unlearned preference for faces.

factor analysis. A statistical method used in test construction and in interpreting scores from batteries of tests. The method enables the investigator to compute the minimum number of determiners (factors) required to account for the intercorrelations among the scores on the tests making up the battery.

false-alarm rate. The proportion of false alarms over all the trials in an experiment.

false alarms. The response of incorrectly responding yes when only noise is present.

family therapy. Psychotherapy with the family members as a group rather than treatment of the patient alone.

feature-integration theory. A cornerstone of understanding object perception that was initially proposed by Anne Treisman.

fetal alcohol syndrome. Mental retardation and multiple deformities of the infant's face and mouth due to exposure to alcohol in the womb.

fight-or-flight response. A pattern of bodily responses that prepares the organism for an emergency. Includes increases in pupil size, heart rate, blood pressure, respiration, muscle tension, and the secretion of epinephrine, norepinephrine, ACTH and other hormones; decreases in saliva, mucous, digestive activity, and the size of blood vessels.

figure. The objects of interest, which appear more solid than the ground and appear in front of it. The figure and ground regions are the two most elementary forms of perceptual organization.

fixation. In Freud's psychoanalytic theory, arrested development through failure to pass beyond one of the earlier stages of psychosexual development or to change the objects of attachment (such as fixation at the oral stage or fixation on the mother).

fixed interval schedule. The organism is reinforced for its first response after a certain amount of time has passed since its last reinforcement.

fixed ratio schedule (FR). The number of responses that has to be made before reinforcement is fixed at a particular value.

flashbulb memory. A vivid and relatively permanent record of the circumstances in which one learned of an emotionally charged, significant event.

foot-in-the-door technique. To get people to say "yes" to requests that would ordinarily lead to "no," this technique suggests beginning with a small request that few would refuse.

forebrain. The structures located in the front, or anterior, part of the brain.

formal operational stage. Piaget's fourth stage of cognitive development in which the child becomes able to use abstract rules.

fovea. In the eye, a small area in the central part of the retina, packed with cones; the most sensitive part of the retina for detail vision and color vision in daylight.

free association. A patient is instructed to say everything that comes to mind, regardless of how trivial or embarrassing it may seem.

frequency. The number of cycles per second.

Freudian slip. In psychoanalytic theory, a mistake or substitution of words in speaking or writing that is contrary to the speaker's conscious intention and presumably expresses wishes or thoughts repressed to the unconscious.

frustration-aggression hypothesis. The hypothesis that frustration (thwarting a person's goal-directed efforts) induces an aggressive drive, which, in turn, motivates aggressive behavior.

functional fixedness. When a person has difficulty with a problem, presumably because they represent components of the problem as having a different function than that needed to solve the problem.

functional magnetic imaging (fMRI). A brain imaging technique that measures and records brain activity while participants are engaged in tasks.

functionalism. Studying how the mind works so that an organism can adapt to and function in its environment.

fundamental attribution error. The tendency to underestimate situational influences on behavior and assume that some personal characteristic of the individual is responsible.

G

g. General intelligence factor.

ganglia (sing. ganglion). A group of neuronal cell bodies found outside the brain and spinal cord.

ganzfeld procedure. Tests for telepathic communication between a participant who serves as the "receiver" and another participant who serves as the "sender."

Gardner's theory of multiple intelligences. The theory that there are seven distinct kinds of intelligence that are independent of one another, each operating as a separate system (or module) in the brain according to its own rules. These are (1) linguistic, (2) musical, (3) logical-mathematical, (4) spatial, (5) bodily-kinesthetic, (6) intrapersonal, and (7) interpersonal.

gate control theory of pain. According to this theory, the sensation of pain requires not only that pain receptors be activated, but also that a neural gate in the spinal cord allow these signals to continue to the brain. Pressure stimulation tends to close the gate; this is why rubbing a hurt area can relieve pain. Attitudes, suggestions, and drugs may act to close the gate.

gender identity. A firm sense of oneself as either male or female.

gender schema. A mental structure that organizes the person's perceptual and conceptual world into gender categories (male-female, masculine-feminine).

gene. A segment of a deoxyribonucleic acid molecule.

general adaptation syndrome. A set of responses that is displayed by all organisms in response to stress.

general paresis. A gradual decline in mental and physical functioning, marked changes in personality, and delusions and hallucinations.

generalization. (a) In learning, the detection of a characteristic or principle common to a class of objects or events. (b) In conditioning, the principle that once a conditioned response has been established to a given stimulus, similar stimuli will also evoke that response.

generalized anxiety disorder. A constant sense of tension and dread.

genital stage. In Freud's psychoanalytic theory, the final stage of psychosexual development, beginning at puberty and culminating in mature adult sexuality.

geon. In perception, geometric forms (such as cylinders, cones, blocks, and wedges) that comprise the features of objects. Recognition of an object is good to the extent that the geons of the object can be recovered.

Gestalt. A German word meaning "form" or "configuration." Gestalt psychologists are interested primarily in perception and believe that perceptual experiences depend on the patterns formed by stimuli and on the organization of experience.

glia cells. Supporting cells (not neurons) composing a substantial portion of brain tissue; recent speculation suggests that they may play a role in neural conduction.

grain size. A limiting feature in both imaginal and perceptual processing. It can be thought of as our images are occurring in a mental medium whose grain limits the amount of detail we can detect in an image.

grammatical morpheme. A morpheme that is not a word, including what are commonly referred to as articles and prepositions.

ground. The region that appears to be behind the figure. The figure and ground regions are the two most elementary forms of perceptual organization.

group polarization effect. The tendency of groups to arrive at decisions that are in the same direction but are more extreme than the mean of the pre-discussion decisions of the individuals in the group.

group therapy. A group discussion or other group activity with a therapeutic purpose participated in by more than one client or patient at a time.

grouping by proximity. If the vertical distance between dots is reduced columns will most likely be seen.

grouping by similarity. Grouping like with like.

groupthink. A phenomenon in which members of a group are led to suppress their own dissent in the interests of group consensus.

guilty but mentally ill. A defendant is found to have a substantial disorder of thought or mood that afflicted him at the time of the crime and significantly impaired his judgment, behavior, capacity to recognize reality, or ability to cope with the ordinary demands of life.

H

habit. A learned stimulus-response sequence.

habituation. The reduction in the strength of a response to a repeated stimulus.

habituation method. A technique used to study perception in infants. It is based on the fact that while infants look directly at novel objects they soon tire of doing so (habituation). Hence one can determine the degree to which an infant perceives an object as novel by measuring the time spent looking at it.

hair cells. In audition, hairlike receptors in the cochlea that bend due to vibration of the basilar membrane and then send electrical impulses to the brain.

halfway house. A place where patients who have been hospitalized can live while making the transition back to independent living in the community.

hallucinations. Sensory experiences in the absence of relevant or adequate external stimulation.

hallucinogens. Drugs whose main effect is to change perceptual experience (syn. psychedelic drugs).

hardiness. Resistance to becoming physically or emotionally impaired even in the face of major stressful events.

hashish. A form of cannabis commonly used in the Middle East.

hemispheres. Structures on the left and right sides of the brain that are connected by the corpus callosum.

heritability. The percentage of the variance in any trait that is accounted for by genetic differences among the individuals in a population.

heroin. An extremely addictive central nervous system depressant derived from opium.

hertz (Hz). The unit used to measure the frequency of a sound wave, specifically the number of cycles per second.

heuristic. A short-cut procedure that is relatively easy to apply and can often yield the correct answer, but not inevitably so.

hidden observer. A part of the mind that is not within awareness seems to be watching the person's experience as a whole.

hierarchy of needs. Maslow's way of classifying needs and motives, from the basic biological needs to the more complex psychological motivations that become important only after the basic needs have been satisfied.

hindbrain. All the structures located in the hind, or posterior, part of the brain, closest to the spinal cord.

hippocampus. A brain structure located below the cerebral cortex that is involved in the consolidation of new memories; its role seems to be that of a cross-referencing system, linking together aspects of a particular memory that are stored in separate parts of the brain.

hit rate. The proportion of hits over all the trials in an experiment.

hits. The response of correctly responding "yes" when a signal is present.

holistic thought. An orientation toward the entire context or field and assigning causality to it, making relatively little use of categories and formal logic, and relying instead on dialectical reasoning, which involves recognizing and transcending apparent contradictions.

homeostasis. The normal level of functioning that is characteristic of the healthy organism (Chapter 2); a constant internal state (Chapter 10).

homeostatic sleep drive. A physiological process that strives to obtain the amount of sleep required for a stable level of daytime alertness.

hormones. Chemicals secreted by the endocrine glands into the bloodstream and transported to other parts of the body, where they have specific effects on cells that recognize their message.

hue. The quality best described by the color's name.

humanistic therapies. A general term for approaches to psychotherapy that emphasize the individual's subjective experiences, free will, and ability to solve his or her own problems. Client-centered therapy and Gestalt therapy are examples.

hypercomplex cell. A cell in the visual cortex that responds to a particular orientation and length.

hypnosis. A willing and cooperative individual relinquishes some control over his or her behavior to the hypnotist and accepts some distortion of reality.

hypothalamus. A small but very important structure located just above the brain stem and just below the thalamus. Considered a part of the central core of the brain, it includes centers that govern motivated behavior such as eating, drinking, sex, and emotions; it also regulates endocrine activity and maintains body homeostasis.

hypothesis. A statement that can be tested.

I

id. The most primitive part of the personality and the part from which the ego and the superego later develop.

identification. Respecting or admiring other individuals or groups and obeying their norms and adopting their beliefs, attitudes, and behaviors in order to be like them and identify with them.

identity confusion. Occurs when a person has no consistent sense of self or set of internal standards for evaluating his or her self-worth in major areas of life.

identity crisis. In Erikson's theory of psychosocial development, a period of self-doubt and active questioning about one's definition of self ("Who am I?" "Where am I going?") which typically takes place during adolescence.

ideology. A set of beliefs and attitudes.

ideomotor action. Mentally activating (thinking about) behavioral representations can make actual corresponding behaviors more likely.

illusion. A percept that is false or distorted.

illusory conjunction. An incorrect combination of two separate attributes of an object.

imaginal thought. Images, particularly visual ones, that we can "see" in our mind.

implicit leniency contract. To appear fair, majority members let minority members have their say, but by doing so they unwittingly open the door to minority influence.

implicit memory. The kind of memory that underlies perceptual and cognitive skills. It is often expressed as an improvement on some perceptual or cognitive task without any conscious recollection of the experiences that led to the improvement.

imprinting. A type of early learning in which a newborn forms an attachment with some kind of model (normally, a parent).

in vivo exposure. A method of therapy highly similar to systematic desensitization that requires the client to actually experience the anxiety-producing situations.

incentive motivation. Wanting something.

incentive salience. Objects and events that have become linked with anticipated affect, which serves to grab attention and steer seeking behavior.

incentive theory. A theory of motivation that emphasizes the importance of negative and positive incentives in determining behavior; internal drives are not the sole instigators of activity.

incus. One of three small bones located in the middle ear.

independent variable. A variable that is independent of what the participant does.

individualism. Refers to cultures that emphasize the fundamental separateness and independence of individuals.

individuation. Assessing an individual's personal qualities on a person-by-person basis.

inductive reasoning. Reasoning about arguments in which it is improbable that the conclusion is false if the premises are true.

inductive strength. It is improbable that the conclusion is false if the premises are true.

inferences. (a) A perceptual or memorial process based on what is believed to be true rather than what necessarily is true. (b) Judgments that go beyond the information given.

information-processing model. In general, a model based on assumptions regarding the flow of information through a system; usually best realized in the form of a computer program. In cognitive psychology, theories of how the mind functions are often represented in the form of an information-processing model. By simulating the model on a computer, one can study the properties and implications of the theory.

information-processing skills. Skills that help one gather and analyze information from the environment.

informational social influence. We conform because we believe that other people's interpretations of an ambiguous situation are more correct than our own.

informed consent. The participants must enter a study voluntarily and be permitted to withdraw from it at any time without penalty if they so desire.

inhibitory conditioning. The ability of a CS to decrease the probability or magnitude of a behavioral response.

inhibitory connections. Connections between two nodes in a connectionist network that are negative: An increase in one leads to a decrease in the other.

insecurely attached. Term used to describe a child who is ambivalent and/or shows resistance to his or her caretaker during a reunion episode.

insomnia. Dissatisfaction with the amount or quality of one's sleep.

institutional norms. Like social norms—implicit or explicit rules for acceptable behavior and beliefs—except they are applied to entire institutions, or organizations of the same type.

instrumental conditioning. Certain responses that are learned because they operate on, or affect, the environment.

intellectualization. A defense mechanism whereby a person tries to gain detachment from an emotionally threatening situation by dealing with it in abstract, intellectual terms.

intelligence. (a) That which a properly standardized intelligence test measures. (b) The ability to learn from experience, think in abstract terms, and deal effectively with one's environment.

intelligence quotient (IQ). A ratio of mental age to chronological age.

intensity. How strong a particular stimulus is.

interference. A factor that can impair retrieval from long-term memory. It arises when different items are associated with the same retrieval cue; attempted retrieval of one of these items can be blocked by the inadvertent retrieval of the other item.

interjudge reliability. The consistency achieved by two or more observers when assessing or rating some behavior (for example, in rating the aggressiveness of nursery-school children). Also called interrater agreement.

internal conflicts. Unresolved issues that may be either conscious or unconscious.

internal consistency. A form of test reliability. Specifically, the homogeneity of a set of items on a test, the degree to which they are all measuring the same variable.

internalization. We are convinced that the influencer is correct and change our beliefs and attitudes.

interpersonal therapy. A style of therapy that tends to be more structured and short-term than traditional psychoanalysis.

interposition (as a depth cue). If one object is positioned so that it obstructs the view of the other, the viewer perceives the overlapping object as being nearer.

interrater agreement. See interjudge reliability.

interval schedules. Reinforcement is available only after a certain time interval has elapsed.

intimacy. The emotional component of love which involves closeness and sharing of feelings.

intracellular thirst. The psychological manifestation of the need for water that is caused by osmosis—the tendency of water to move from zones where it is plentiful to zones where it is relatively rare.

introspection. The observation and recording of one's own perceptions, thoughts, and feelings.

introversion–extraversion. The personality dimension first identified by Carl Jung that refers to the degree to which a person's basic orientation is turned inward toward the self or outward toward the external world. At the introversion end are shy individuals who tend to withdraw into themselves; at the extraversion end are sociable individuals who prefer to be with others.

ion channel. A specialized protein molecule that permits specific ions to enter or leave cells. Some ion channels open or close in response to appropriate neurotransmitter molecules; others open or close in response to voltage changes across the cell membrane. This process regulates depolarization and the firing of nerve impulses.

J

James, William. The author of the very first psychology textbook, published in 1890.

James–Lange theory. A classical theory of emotion, named for the two men who independently proposed it. The theory states that the stimulus first leads to bodily responses, and then the awareness of these responses constitutes the experience of emotion.

just noticeable difference (jnd). The minimum difference in stimulus magnitude necessary to tell two stimuli apart.

K

knowledge. According to knowledge acquisition approaches to development, the child's understanding of how facts in a particular domain are organized.

L

language. A multilevel system for relating thoughts to speech by means of word and sentence units.

latency period. In Freud's psychoanalytic theory, a period in middle childhood, roughly the years 6–12, when both sexual and aggressive impulses are said to be in a quiescent state.

lateral hypothalamic syndrome. An apparent total lack of hunger caused by the destruction of the lateral hypothalamus.

law of effect. The principle that any behavior that is followed by reinforcement is strengthened; from the infinite pool of possible responses, those that lead to reinforcement are repeated, whereas those that do not are extinguished.

learned helplessness. A condition of apathy or helplessness created experimentally by subjecting an organism to unavoidable trauma (such as shock, heat, or cold). Being unable to avoid or escape an aversive situation produces a feeling of helplessness that generalizes to subsequent situations.

learning. A relatively permanent change in behavior that occurs as the result of practice.

libido. (Latin for "lust.") In Freud's psychoanalytic theory, the psychic energy of the id.

liking. Friendship and the early stages of more intimate relationships.

limbic system. A set of structures that are closely interconnected with the hypothalamus and appear to impose additional controls over some of the instinctive behaviors regulated by the hypothalamus and the brain stem.

literature review. A scholarly summary of the existing body of research on a given topic.

lobes. Large regions of the cerebral cortex that perform diverse functions.

long-term depression. A long-lasting decrease in synaptic transmission at synapses in the cerebellar cortex.

long-term potentiation. A phenomenon concerning the neural bases of learning. Once stimulated, neurons will show an increase in their rate of activity when subsequently stimulated (at least up to a period of months).

long-term store. The large repository of information where we maintain all information that is generally available to us.

loosening of associations. Occurs when the individual's ideas shift from one topic to another in ways that appear unrelated.

loudness. An intensity dimension of hearing correlated with the amplitude of the sound waves that constitute the stimulus. Greater amplitudes yield greater loudnesses.

LSD. A potent drug that produces hallucinations at very low doses. See also hallucinogen.

lucid dream. A dream in which events seem so normal (lacking the bizarre and illogical character of most dreams) that the dreamer believes he or she is awake and conscious.

M

magnetic resonance imaging (MRI). A computer-based scanning procedure that uses strong magnetic fields and radio-frequency pulses to generate a picture of a cross section of the brain or body. Provides greater precision than the CT scanner.

maladaptive. Having adverse effects on the individual or on society.

malleus. One of three small bones located in the middle ear.

manic episodes. An episode in which an individual is energetic, enthusiastic, full of self-confidence, talks continually, rushes from one activity to another with little need for sleep, and makes grandiose plans, paying little attention to their practicality.

marijuana. The dried leaves of the hemp plant (cannabis); also known as hashish, "pot," or "grass." Hashish is actually an extract of the plant material and, hence, is usually stronger than marijuana. Intake may enhance sensory experiences and produce a state of euphoria.

marital therapy. Psychotherapy with both members of a couple aimed at resolving problems in their relationship (syn. couples therapy).

maturation. An innately determined sequence of growth and change that is relatively independent of external events.

McGurk effect. Results from conflicting auditory and visual information.

mean. The technical term for an arithmetic average.

meaning. The concept named by a word.

means-ends analysis. A problem-solving strategy in which one compares one's current state to the goal state in order to find the most important difference between them; eliminating this difference then becomes the main subgoal.

measurement. A system for assigning numbers to variables.

meditation. Achieving an altered state of consciousness by performing certain rituals and exercises.

medulla. The lowest section of the brainstem, a slight enlargement of the spinal cord as it enters the skull; the point at which the major nerve tracts cross over so that the right cerebral hemisphere controls the left side of the body, and the left cerebral hemisphere controls the right side.

melatonin. A hormone that induces sleep.

menarche. The first menstrual period.

mental imagery. Mental representations that are picture-like. Not the same as eidetic imagery.

mental model. A concrete mental representation of a problem situation that may be useful in solving the problem.

mental rotation. The notion that a mental image of an object can be rotated in the mind in fashion analogous to rotating the real object.

mere exposure effect. The finding that familiarity all by itself increases liking.

meta-analysis. A form of literature review in which authors use statistical techniques to combine and draw conclusions about studies previously conducted.

metacognition. Thinking about thinking.

metamers. A pair of such matching lights—that is, two lights with different physical makeups that appear identical.

methadone. An agonist drug used in treating heroin-dependent individuals.

method of loci. An aid to serial memory. Verbal material is transformed into mental images, which are then located at successive positions along a visualized route, such as an imaged walk through the house or down a familiar street.

midbrain. The middle of the brain.

middle ear. The part of the ear that transmits sound waves from the eardrum to the oval window of the inner ear by means of three tiny connecting bones (malleus, incus, and stapes).

minimal risk. The principle that risks anticipated in the research should be no greater than those ordinarily encountered in daily life.

minimalist appraisal theories. A group of appraisal theories that are based on reducing the number of appraisal dimensions to minimum, often based on fundamental themes.

Minnesota Multiphasic Personality Inventory (MMPI). A pencil-and-paper version of a psychiatric interview that consists of more than 550 statements concerning attitudes, emotional reactions, physical and psychological symptoms, and experiences. Test takers respond to each statement by answering, "True," "False," or "Cannot say."

minority influence. Minorities can move majorities toward their point of view if they present a consistent position without appearing rigid, dogmatic, or arrogant.

misattribution of arousal. Lingering physiological arousal can be mistakenly attributed to subsequent circumstances and intensify our emotional reactions to those circumstances.

M'Naghten Rule. A defendant may be found not guilty by reason of insanity only if he was so severely disturbed at the time of his act that he did not know what he was doing, or if he did know what he was doing, did not know that it was wrong.

model of the environment. A representation of the world within our brains that we use to consciously perceive, make decisions, and behave.

monoamine oxidase (MAO). One of the enzymes responsible for the breakdown of a group of neurotransmitters called biogenic amines (norepinephrine, dopamine, and serotonin are examples); believed to be important in the regulation of emotion. Drugs that inhibit the action of this enzyme (MAO inhibitors) are used in treating depression.

monoamine oxidase inhibitor (MAOI). A class of drugs used to treat depression; the drug inhibits the action of an enzyme (monoamine oxidase) that breaks down certain neurotransmitters (such as dopamine, norepinephrine, and serotonin), thereby prolonging the action of these neurotransmitters.

monochromatism. Total color blindness, the visual system being achromatic. A rare disorder.

mood disorder. A mental disorder characterized by disturbances of mood. Depression, mania (exaggerated excitement), and bipolar disorders in which the individual experiences both extremes of mood are examples.

moods. Free-floating and diffuse affective states.

moral judgment. Children's understanding of moral rules and social conventions.

morpheme. Any small linguistic unit that carries meaning.

motivation. A condition that energizes behavior and gives it direction.

multimodal attention. Attention can move within a modality, such as from one visual stimulus to another, or between modalities.

multivariate experiment. A type of experiment that involves the simultaneous manipulation of several independent variables.

Munsell system. A scheme for specifying colored surfaces by assigning them one of 10 hue names and two numbers, one indicating saturation and the other brightness.

N

naïve realism. People's tendency to take their constructed, subjective realities to be faithful renderings of an objective world.

naltrexone. An antagonist drug that blocks the action of heroin because it has a greater affinity for the opioid receptors than does heroin itself.

narcolepsy. Recurring, irresistible attacks of drowsiness with the likelihood of falling asleep at any time.

narrative review. A form of literature review in which authors use words to describe studies previously conducted and to discuss the strength of the available psychological evidence.

nature view. The view that human beings enter the world with an inborn store of knowledge and understanding of reality.

nature-nurture issue. The problem of determining the relative importance of heredity (nature) and the result of upbringing in a particular environment (nurture) on behavior.

negative hallucinations. In a hypnotic state, when a person does not perceive something that normally would be perceived.

negative reinforcement. Reinforcing a response by the removal of an aversive stimulus.

negatively correlated. As the value of one variable increases, the value of another decreases.

nerve. A bundle of elongated axons belonging to hundreds or thousands of neurons.

neural sensitization. Potentially permanent changes in the brain that follow drug addition whereby dopamine neurons are activated more highly by drugs and drug-related stimuli.

neuron. A specialized cell that transmits neural impulses or messages to other neurons, glands, and muscles.

neurosis (pl. neuroses). A mental disorder in which the individual is unable to cope with anxieties and conflicts and develops symptoms that he or she finds distressing, such as obsessions, compulsions, phobias, or anxiety attacks. In Freud's psychoanalytic theory, neurosis results from the use of defense mechanisms to ward off anxiety caused by unconscious conflicts. No longer a diagnostic category of DSM-IV.

neurotic anxiety. Fear that is out of proportion to the actual danger posed (such as stage fright).

neuroticism. The name of the emotional instability–stability dimension in Eysenck's factor-analytic theory of personality. Moody, anxious, and maladjusted individuals are at the neurotic or unstable end; calm, well-adjusted individuals are at the other.

neurotransmitter. A chemical that diffuses across the synaptic gap and stimulates the next neuron.

noise. Anything in the environment irrelevant to what the observer is trying to detect.

nonassociative learning. Learning about a single stimulus.

non-REM sleep (or NREM sleep). Refers to the other four sleep stages (besides REM) in which eye movements are virtually absent, heart and breathing rates decrease markedly, the muscles are relaxed, and the brain's metabolic rate decreases 25 to 30 percent compared to wakefulness.

normality. Appropriate perception of reality, ability to exercise voluntary control over behavior, self-esteem and acceptance, ability to form affectionate relationships, and productivity.

normative social influence. We conform to a group's social norms or typical behaviors to become liked and accepted.

noun phrase. A phrase that centers on a noun and specifies the subject of an underlying proposition.

nuclei (sing. nucleus). A collection of nerve cell bodies grouped in the brain or spinal cord.

nurture view. The view that human knowledge is acquired through experiences and interactions with the world.

O

obese. Being 30% or more above the weight level that would be appropriate for a person's body structure and height.

object permanence. The awareness that an object continues to exist even when it is not present.

object relations theory. An outgrowth of psychoanalytic theory that deals with the person's attachments to others over the course of development. Emphasizes ego functioning more than did classical psychoanalytic theory.

objectification theory. A sociocultural account of how being raised in a culture that sexually objectifies the female body fundamentally alters girls' and women's self-views and well-being.

objective anxiety. Fear that is proportionate to the danger posed.

observational learning. People can learn by observing the actions of others and noting the consequences of those actions.

obsessions. Persistent intrusions of unwelcome thoughts, images, or impulses that elicit anxiety.

obsessive-compulsive disorder. An anxiety disorder taking one of three forms: (a) persistent intrusions of unwelcome thoughts, images, or impulses that elicit anxiety (obsessions); (b) irresistible urges to carry out certain acts or rituals that reduce anxiety (compulsions); (c) both of these in combination.

Oedipal conflict. In Freud's psychoanalytic theory, the conflict that arises during the phallic stage of psychosexual development in which the individual is sexually attracted to the parent of the opposite sex and perceives the same-sex parent as a rival.

olfactory bulb. A region of the brain involved in olfaction (smell); it is a way station between the receptors in the nasal passage and the olfactory cortex.

olfactory cortex. The area in the brain responsible for the sense of smell. Located on the inside of the temporal lobes.

olfactory system. The receptors in the nasal passage, certain regions of the brain, and interconnecting neural pathways.

omission training. Behavior that prevents an appetitive stimulus.

operant conditioning. Certain responses are learned because they operate on, or affect, the environment.

operation. A mental routine for separating, combining, and otherwise transforming information in a logical manner.

opiates. Drugs that diminish physical sensation and the capacity to respond to stimuli by depressing the central nervous system.

opponent-color theory. A theory of color perception that postulates two types of color-sensitive units that respond in opposite ways to the two colors of an opponent pair. One type of unit responds to red or green, the other to blue or yellow. Since a unit cannot respond in two ways at once, reddish-greens and yellowish-blues cannot occur.

opponent-process model of sleep and wakefulness. A theory that states that the brain possesses two opponent processes that govern the tendency to fall asleep or remain awake: the homeostatic sleep drive and the clock-dependent alerting process.

oral stage. In Freud's psychoanalytic theory, the first stage of psychosexual development; pleasure derives from the lips and mouth, as in sucking at the mother's breast.

organizational psychologist. A psychologist concerned with selecting people who are most suitable for particular jobs or designing structures that facilitate collaboration and teamwork.

outer ear. The external ear and auditory canal, whose purpose is to funnel sound waves towards the inner ear.

oval window. A membrane on the cochlea of the inner ear that receives vibrations from the ear drum via three connecting bones (malleus, incus, and stapes). Vibrations at the oval window set up similar vibrations in the internal fluid of the cochlea, ultimately activating the hair cells that serve as auditory receptors.

overextension. Tendency to apply a new word too widely.

overjustification effect. Explaining one's own behavior with too much emphasis on salient situational causes and not enough emphasis on personal causes, like intrinsic interest.

P

panic attack. An episode of acute and overwhelming apprehension or terror.

panic disorder. An anxiety disorder in which the individual has sudden and inexplicable episodes of terror and feelings of impending doom accompanied by physiological symptoms of fear (such as heart palpitations, shortness of breath, muscle tremors, faintness).

paranoid. An individual who has delusions of persecution.

parapsychology. Phenomena that are "beside psychology," including telepathy, clairvoyance, precognition, psychokinesis.

parasympathetic nervous system. A division of the automatic nervous system, the nerve fibers of which originate in the cranial and sacral portions of the spinal cord. Active in relaxed or quiescent states of the body and to some extent antagonistic to the sympathetic division, or system.

partial-report condition. After viewing an array of letters in Sperling's partial-report procedure an observer is asked to report only one, randomly chosen row of letters.

partial-report procedure. An experiment devised by George Sperling in which a varied array of letters is flashed to observers for a brief period.

passion. The motivational component of love which consists of sexual attraction and the romantic feeling of being "in love."

passionate love. Contrasted with companionate love. An intensely emotional state in which tender and sexual feelings, elation and pain, anxiety and relief, altruism and jealousy coexist in a confusion of feelings.

PCP. Sold as a hallucinogen (under such street names as "angel dust," "Shermans," and "superacid"), this drug is technically a dissociative anesthetic.

peak experiences. Transient moments of self-actualization.

perceptual interference. The finding that objects had to eventually be more focused for the observers to recognize them in the very-out-of-focus condition than in the moderately-out-of-focus condition.

periaqueductal gray. A section of the brain in which neurons are connected to other neurons that inhibit cells that would normally carry the pain signals arising in the pain receptors. This area appears to be the main place where strong painkillers such as morphine affect neural processing.

peripheral nervous system. The nerves connecting the brain and spinal cord to other parts of the body.

peripheral route. When an individual responds to noncontent cues in a communication or to the context of a communication.

personal construct. The dimensions that individuals themselves use to interpret themselves and their social worlds.

personality. The distinctive and characteristic patterns of thought, emotion, and behavior that define an individual's personal style of interacting with the physical and social environment.

personality disorders. Ingrained habitual, and rigid patterns of behavior or character that severely limit the individual's adaptive potential; often society sees the behavior as maladaptive whereas the individual does not.

personality inventory. An inventory for self-appraisal, consisting of many statements or questions about personal characteristics and behavior that the person judges to apply or not to apply to him or her.

personality psychologist. A psychologist whose area of interest focuses on classifying individuals and studying the differences between them. This specialty overlaps both developmental and social psychologists to some extent.

person-environment relationship. The objective situation in which a person finds herself.

perspective (as a depth cue). When parallel lines in a scene appear to converge in the im-

age, they are perceived as vanishing in the distance.

phallic stage. In Freud's psychoanalytic theory, the third stage of psychosexual development in which gratification is associated with stimulation of the sex organs and sexual attachment is to the parent of the opposite sex.

phasic pain. The kind of sharp pain experienced immediately upon suffering an injury; usually brief with a rapid increase in intensity followed by a decrease.

phenothiazines. A group of antipsychotic drugs that relieve the symptoms of schizophrenia by blocking the access of the neurotransmitter dopamine to its receptors. Chlorpromazine (Thorazine) and fluphenazine (Prolixin) are examples.

pheromones. Chemicals that float through the air to be sniffed by other members of the species.

phobia. Intense fear of a stimulus or situation that most people do not consider particularly dangerous.

phoneme. Discrete speech categories.

phonological buffer. One of the two distinct stores of working memory that briefly stores information in an acoustic code.

phonological code. Memory encoding that is based on the sounds of the names of the digits.

photon. The smallest unit of light energy.

physical description (of an object). A listing of all the information necessary to completely reproduce the object.

physiology. The study of the functions of the living organism and its parts.

pitch. A sensation based on the frequency of sound.

place theory of pitch perception. A theory of hearing that associates pitch with the place on the basilar membrane where activation occurs.

pluralistic ignorance. The phenomenon in which everybody in a group misleads everybody else by defining an ambiguous situation as a nonemergency.

positive hallucinations. In a hypnotic state, when a person sees objects or hears voices that are not actually present.

positive psychology. The study of how positive experiences, emotions, and personality traits promote human flourishing.

positive reinforcement. Reinforcing a response by the presentation of a positive stimulus.

positively correlated. The values of two variables either increase together or decrease together.

positron emission tomography (PET). A computer-based scanning procedure that measures regional changes in blood flow to map the neural activities of the brain.

postconventional level of moral development. Level of moral development in which children evaluate actions in terms of higher-order ethical principles.

posterior system (for attention). Represents the perceptual features of an object, such as its location in space, shape, and color, responsible for selecting one object among many on the basis of the features associated with that object.

post-event memory construction. During memory formation, we may add new information that is suggested to us by others.

posthypnotic amnesia. A particular form of posthypnotic suggestion in which the hypnotized person forgets what has happened during the hypnosis until signaled to remember.

posthypnotic response. A response that occurs when a subject who has been roused from hypnosis responds with movement to a prearranged signal by the hypnotist.

post-traumatic stress disorder. An anxiety disorder in which a stressful event that is outside the range of usual human experience, such as military combat or a natural disaster, brings in its aftermath such symptoms as a re-experiencing of the trauma and avoidance of stimuli associated with it, a feeling of estrangement, a tendency to be easily startled, nightmares, recurrent dreams, and disturbed sleep.

power function. The relation between Ψ and Φ, which is (basically) $\Psi = \phi^\Gamma$.

pragmatic rules. Rules used in deductive reasoning that are less abstract than logical rules, but still applicable to many different domains of life. An example is the permission rule.

precognitive emotions. Emotions that are not based on appraisal.

preconscious. All the information that is not currently "on our mind" but that we could bring into consciousness if called upon to do so.

preconscious memories. Memories that are accessible to consciousness.

preconventional level of moral development. Level of moral development in which children evaluate actions are as right or wrong on the basis of anticipated punishment.

predictability. The degree to which we know if and when an event will occur.

preferential looking method. A method of examining infants' perceptual preferences by presenting them two stimuli simultaneously and noting the amount of time the infants gaze at each object.

prefrontal lobes. The lobes just behind the forehead.

preoperational stage. Piaget's second stage of cognitive development. The children think in terms of symbols, but does not yet comprehend certain rules or operations.

primacy effect. The tendency for first information we receive to have a greater impact on our overall impressions.

primary reinforcer. A reinforcer that is able to act as a reward independently of prior learning.

sexual selection. A special case of natural selection that yields traits that promote reproductive success in the sex with the greater potential reproductive rate.

shading and shadows (as a depth cue). The configuration of shading and shadows provides information about an object's depth.

shadowing. Repeating back one auditory message.

sham feeding. A result of a surgical procedure so that whenever something is eaten, it will fall out of the body rather than be digested.

shaping. Reinforcing only variations in response that deviate in the direction desired by the experimenter.

short-term store. The second repository of information (after the sensory store), into which attended information from sensory store is placed.

signal. What the observer is trying to detect in an experiment.

signal detection theory. A theory of the sensory and decision processes involved in psychophysical judgments, with special reference to the problem of detecting weak signals in noise.

similarity heuristic. The use of similarity—to a specific case or to a prototype—to estimate the probability of an event.

simple cell. A cell in the visual cortex that responds to a bar of light or straight edge of a particular orientation and location in the visual field.

simple phobia. Excessive fear of a specific object, animal, or situation in the absence of real danger.

situational attribution. Attributing a person's actions to factors in the situation or environment, as opposed to internal attitudes and motives.

sleep disorder. When inability to sleep well produces impaired daytime functioning or excessive sleepiness.

slow to warm up temperament. Term used to describe a child who is relatively inactive, tends to withdraw from new situations in a mild way, and requires more time than easy infants to adapt to new situations.

Snellen acuity. Acuity measured relative to a viewer who does not need to wear glasses.

social cognition. The examination of people's subjective interpretations of their social experiences, as well as their modes of thinking about the social world.

social cognitive neuroscience. The study of how stereotyping, attitudes, person perception, and self-knowledge are executed in the brain.

social desirability effects. A particular form of bias that can occur during a survey when some people try to present themselves in a favorable light.

social facilitation. The effects of coaction and the presence of an audience.

social inhibition. The sometimes derailing effects of coactors and audiences on performance.

social norms. Implicit rules and expectations that dictate what we ought to think and how we ought to behave.

social phobia. Extreme insecurity in social situations accompanied by an exaggerated fear of embarrassing oneself.

social psychologist. A psychologist who studies social interaction and the ways in which individuals influence one another.

social psychology. The study of how people think and feel about their social world and how they interact and influence one another.

social stereotype. Personality traits or physical attributes given to a whole class of people.

social-cognitive theory (to personality). Reciprocal determinism, in which external determinants of behavior (such as rewards and punishments) and internal determinants (such as beliefs, thoughts, and expectations) are part of a system of interacting influences that affect both behavior and other parts of the system.

social-learning theory. The application of learning theory to the problems of personal and social behavior (syn. social behavior theory).

sociocultural approach to development. An approach that characterizes the child not as a physical scientist seeking "true" knowledge but as a newcomer to a culture who seeks to become a native by learning how to look at social reality through the lens of that culture.

somatic system. Carries messages to and from the sense receptors, muscles, and the surface of the body.

sound wave. A wave defined by periodically varying air pressure over time.

source wavelengths. Wavelengths coming from some light source.

span of apprehension. The number of immediately recallable items.

spontaneous recovery. A phenomenon in classical conditioning discovered by Pavlov. When an organism undergoes execution of a conditioned response and is then moved to a new context, the conditioned response may reappear.

stages of development. Developmental periods, usually following a progressive sequence, that appear to represent qualitative changes in either the structure or the function of the organism (such as Freud's psychosexual stages, Piaget's cognitive stages).

standard. An arbitrary level of stimulus intensity against which other intensities are judged.

Stanford-Binet Intelligence Scale. Stanford revision of the Binet test which measures the kinds of changes in intelligence ordinarily associated with growing older.

stapes. One of three small bones located in the middle ear.

statistical significance. The trustworthiness of an obtained statistical measure as a state-

ment about reality; for example, the probability that the population mean falls within the limits determined from a sample. The expression refers to the reliability of the statistical finding and not to its importance.

statistics. The discipline that deals with sampling data from a population of individuals and then drawing inferences about the population from those data.

stereotype. A set of inferences about the personality traits or physical attributes of a whole class of people; schemas of classes of people.

stereotype threat. The mere threat of being identified with a stereotype can raise an individual's anxiety level, which in turn degrades his or her performance.

Sternberg memory-scanning task. Type of experiment introduced by Sternberg in which during each trial a participant is shown a set of digits that he or she must temporarily maintain in the working memory.

Sternberg's triarchic theory. This theory has three parts or subtheories. The componential subtheory, which deals with thought processes; the experiential subtheory, which deals with the effects of experience on intelligence; and the contextual subtheory, which considers the effects of the individual's environment and culture.

stimulants. Drugs that increase alertness and general arousal.

storage stage. The maintenance of stored information over time.

stress. Experiencing events that are perceived as endangering one's physical or psychological well-being.

stress responses. Reactions to events an individual perceives as endangering his or her well-being. These may include bodily changes that prepare for emergency (the fight-or-flight response) as well as such psychological reactions as anxiety, anger and aggression, apathy and depression, and cognitive impairment.

stressors. Events that an individual perceives as endangering his or her physical or psychological well-being.

stroboscopic motion. An illusion of motion resulting from the successive presentation of discrete stimulus patterns arranged in a progression corresponding to movement, such as motion pictures.

Stroop interference. Results because word reading is such a dominant and automatic response among skilled readers it is difficult for them to ignore a printed word and name the word's ink color when the word is a color that is different from the color of the ink.

structuralism. The analysis of mental structures.

subjective experience. The affective state or feeling tone.

subjectivist perspective. An orientation toward understanding behavior and mental processes in terms of the subjective realities people actively construct.

superego. The part of personality that judges whether actions are right or wrong.

suprathreshold conditions. Conditions in which stimulus intensity is above threshold.

survey method. A method of obtaining information by questioning a large sample of people.

symbol. Anything that stands for or refers to something other than itself.

sympathetic nervous system. A division of the autonomic nervous system, characterized by a chain of ganglia on either side of the spinal cord, with nerve fibers originating in the thoracic and lumbar portions of the spinal cord. Active in emotional excitement and to some extent antagonistic to the parasympathetic division.

synapse. The close functional connection between the axon of one neuron and the dendrites or cell body of another neuron.

synaptic plasticity. Changes in the morphology and/or physiology of synapses involved in learning and memory.

syntax. A specification of the relationships between words in phrases and sentences.

systematic desensitization. A behavior therapy technique in which hierarchies of anxiety-producing situations are imagined (or sometimes confronted in reality) while the person is in a state of deep relaxation. Gradually the situations become dissociated from the anxiety response.

T

tabula rasa. Latin, meaning "blank slate." The term refers to the view that human beings are born without any innate knowledge or ideas; all knowledge is acquired through learning and experience. Proposed by the 17th- and 18th-century British empiricists (Locke, Hume, Berkeley, Hartley).

tardive dyskinesia. Involuntary movements of the tongue, face, mouth, or jaw.

taste receptors. Receptors for taste located in clusters on the tongue and around the mouth. Also called taste buds.

temperament. Mood-related personality characteristics.

temporal-integration paradigm. An experiment in which 24 dots are presented in 24 of the 25 squares of an imaginary 55 array, and the observer's task is to report the location of the missing dot.

temporal pattern. The spacing sequence of electrical impulses.

temporal theory of sound. A theory of pitch perception which assumes that the frequency of neural impulses traveling up the auditory nerve correspond to the frequency of a tone.

test. Presents a uniform situation to a group of people who vary in a particular trait.

thalamus. Two groups of nerve cell nuclei located just above the brain stem and inside

the cerebral hemispheres. Considered a part of the central core of the brain. One area acts as a sensory relay station, the other plays a role in sleep and waking; this portion is considered part of the limbic system.

Thematic Apperception Test (TAT). A participant is shown up to 20 ambiguous pictures of persons and scenes and asked to make up a story about each picture.

theory. An interrelated set of propositions about a particular phenomenon.

theory of ecological optics. The information from the environment—or more specifically, its two-dimensional representation on our retina—is all that is really necessary to live a normal life.

theory of mind. The child's understanding of basic mental states, such as desires, percepts, beliefs, knowledge, thoughts, intentions, and feelings.

thirst. The psychological manifestation of the need for water.

thought and action tendencies. Urges to think and act in certain ways.

timbre. Our experience of the complexity of a sound.

tolerance. The need for a greater amount of a drug to achieve the same euphoria.

tonic pain. The kind of steady, long-lasting pain experienced after an injury has occurred; usually produced by swelling and tissue damage. In contrast to phasic pain.

top-down feedback connections. Connections that go from the higher levels to the lower levels.

top-down processes. Processes in perception, learning, memory, and comprehension that are driven by the organism's prior knowledge and expectations, rather than by the input.

transduction. Translate physical energy into electrical signals that can make their way to the brain.

transference. The tendency for the client to make the therapist the object of emotional responses.

traumatic events. Situations of extreme danger that are outside the range of usual human experience.

triangular theory of love. This theory divides love into three components: intimacy, passion, and commitment.

trichromatic theory. A theory of color perception that postulates three basic color receptors (cones), a "red" receptor, a "green" receptor, and a "blue" receptor. The theory explains color blindness by the absence of one or more receptor types (syn. Young-Helmholtz theory).

tricyclic antidepressant. A class of antidepressants that relieve the symptoms of depression by preventing the reuptake of the neurotransmitters serotonin and norepinephrine, thereby prolonging their action. Imipramine (brand names, Tofranil and Elavil) is one drug commonly prescribed.

two-factor theory. The theory that emotions result from the combination of two factors—an initial state of unexplained arousal plus a cognitive explanation (or appraisal) for that arousal.

type A pattern. A behavior pattern discovered in studies of coronary heart disease. Type As are people who have a sense of time urgency, find it difficult to relax, and become impatient and angry when confronted with delays or with people whom they view as incompetent. Type As are at risk for heart disease.

U

unconditional positive regard. Feeling that oneself is valued by parents and others even when their feelings, attitudes, and behaviors are less than ideal.

unconditioned response (UCR). In classical conditioning, the response given originally to the unconditioned stimulus used as the basis for establishing a conditioned response to a previously neutral stimulus.

unconditioned stimulus (UCS). In classical conditioning, a stimulus that automatically elicits a response, typically via a reflex, without prior conditioning.

unconscious. The thoughts, attitudes, impulses, wishes, motivations, and emotions of which we are unaware (Chapter 1); contains some memories, impulses, and desires that are not accessible to consciousness (Chapter 6); impulses, wishes, and inaccessible memories that affect our thoughts and behavior (Chapter 13).

undoing effect of positive emotions. Positive emotions may be particularly suited for helping people recover from any lingering arousal that follows negative emotions.

V

validity. Measuring what is intended to be measured.

variable. Something that can occur with different values.

variable interval schedule. Reinforcement still depends on a certain interval having elapsed, but the interval's duration varies unpredictably.

variable ratio schedule. The organism is reinforced only after making a certain number of responses, but that number varies unpredictably.

ventromedial hypothalamic syndrome. Extreme appetites caused by lesions of the ventromedial hypothalamus.

verb phrase. The section of a sentence that gives the predicate of the proposition.

vicarious learning. Learning by observing the behavior of others and noting the consequences of that behavior (syn. observational learning).

visceral perception. Our perception of our own arousal.

visual acuity. The eye's ability to resolve details.

visual code. A mental picture of digits.

visual cortex. The part of the brain that is concerned with vision.

visual field. The total visual array acting on the eye when it is directed toward a fixation point.

visual neglect. A patient who, although not blind, ignores everything on one side of their visual field (usually the left side).

visual search task. A task in which the observer is asked to determine whether some target object is present in a cluttered display.

visual-spatial sketchpad. One of the two distinct stores of working memory that briefly stores information in a visual or spatial code.

vulnerability-stress model. An interactive model of physical or mental disorders that proposes that an individual will develop a disorder only when he or she has both some constitutional vulnerability (predisposition) and experiences stressful circumstances. Same as diathesis-stress model.

W

wanting. The anticipation of pleasure, as in cravings.

weapon focus. Rapt attention on a weapon in the scene.

Weber fraction. The constant of proportionality.

Wechsler Adult Intelligence Scale. A verbal scale and a performance scale that yield separate scores as well as a full-scale IQ.

Wernicke's aphasia. A language defect caused by damage to Wernicke's area, that portion of the left cerebral hemisphere involved in language understanding. Individuals with damage in this area are not able to comprehend words; they can hear words, but they do not know their meanings.

whole-report condition. After viewing an array of letters for a brief period of time, the observer is asked to report as many letters as possible.

withdrawal. The intensely aversive reaction to the cessation of drug use.

withdrawal symptoms. Unpleasant physiological and psychological reactions that occur when a person suddenly stops taking an addictive drug; these range from nausea, anxiety, mild tremors, and difficulty sleeping at low levels of dependence to vomiting, cramps, hallucinations, agitation, and severe tremors or seizures at higher levels.

word salad. Unrelated words and phrases and idiosyncratic word associations.

working backwards. A problem-solving strategy in which one works backwards from the goal towards the current state.

working memory. Memories that are stored for only a few seconds.

REFERENCES

ABBOTT, B. B., SCHOEN, L. S., & BADIA, P. (1984). Predictable and unpredictable shock: Behavioral measures of aversion and physiological measures of stress. *Psychological Bulletin, 96,* 45–71.

ABELSON, R. P. (1968). Computers, polls, and public opinion—Some puzzles and paradoxes. *Transaction, 5,* 20–27.

ABRAMSON, L. Y., ALLOY, L. B., HOGAN, M. E., WHITEHOUSE, W. G., DONOVAN, P., ROSE, D., PANZARELLA, C., & RANIERE, D. (1999). Cognitive vulnerability to depression: Theory and evidence. *Journal of Cognitive Psychotherapy: An International Quarterly, 13,* 5–20.

ABRAMSON, L. Y., METALSKY, G. I., & ALLOY, L. B. (1989). Hopelessness depression: A theory-based subtype of depression. *Psychological Review, 96,* 358–372.

ABRAMSON, L. Y., SELIGMAN, M. E. P., & TEASDALE, J. (1978). Learned helplessness in humans: Critique and reformulation. *Journal of Abnormal Psychology, 87,* 49–74.

ADAMS, J. L. (1974). *Conceptual blockbusting.* Stanford, CA: Stanford Alumni Association.

ADAMS, M., & COLLINS, A. (1979). A schema-theoretic view of reading. In R. O. Freedle (Ed.), *New Directions Discourse Processing,* Vol. 12. Norwood, NJ: Ablex.

ADER, R. (2001). Psychoneuroimmunology. *Current Directions in Psychological Science, 10,* 94–98.

ADKINS-REGAN, E. (1988). Sex hormones and sexual orientation in animals. *Psychobiology, 16,* 335–347.

ADORNO, T. W., FRENKEL-BRUNSWIK, E., LEVINSON, D. J., & SANFORD, R. N. (1950). *The authoritarian personality.* New York: Harper.

AFFLECK, G., & TENNEN, H. (1996). Construing benefits from adversity: Adaptational significance and dispositional underpinnings. *Journal of Personality, 64,* 899–922.

AFFLECK, G., TENNEN, H., CROOG, S., & LEVINE, S. (1987a). Causal attribution, perceived benefits and morbidity after a heart attack: An eight-year study. *Journal of Consulting and Clinical Psychology, 55,* 29–55.

AFFLECK, G., TENNEN, H., CROOG, S., & LEVINE, S. (1987b). Causal attribution, perceived control, and recovery from a heart attack. *Journal of Social and Clinical Psychology, 5,* 339–355.

AGRAS, W. S. (1993). Short term psychological treatments for binge eating. In C. G. Fairburn & G. T. Wilson (Eds.), *Binge eating: Nature, assessment, and treatment.* New York: Guilford.

AINSWORTH, M. D. S., BLEHAR, M. C., WALTERS, E., & WALL, S. (1978). *Patterns of attachment: A psychological study of the strange situation.* Hillsdale, NJ: Erlbaum.

AKERS, C. (1984). Methodological criticisms of parapsychology. In S. Krippner (Ed.), *Advances in parapsychological research* (Vol. 4). Jefferson, NC: McFarland.

AKHTAR, S., WIG, N. N., VARMA, V. K., PERSHARD, D., & VERMA, S. K. (1975). A phenomenological analysis of symptoms in the obsessive-compulsive neurosis. *British Journal of Psychiatry, 127,* 342–348.

ALBERTS, B., BRAY, D., LEWIS, J., RAFF, M., ROBERTS, K., & WATSON, J. D. (1994). *Molecular biology of the cell* (3rd ed.). New York: Garland.

ALDAG, R. J., & FULLER, S. R. (1993). Beyond fiasco: A reappraisal of the groupthink phenomenon and a new model of group decision processes. *Psychological Bulletin, 113,* 533–552.

ALLEN, J. B., KENRICK, D. T., LINDER, D. E., & MCCALL, A. M. (1989). Arousal and attraction: A response-facilitation alternative to misattribution and negative-reinforcement models. *Journal of Personality and Social Psychology, 57,* 261–270.

ALLEN, V. L., & LEVINE, J. M. (1969). Consensus and conformity. *Journal of Experimental Social Psychology, 5,* 389–399.

ALLEN, V. L., & LEVINE, J. M. (1971). Social support and conformity: The role of independent assessment of reality. *Journal of Experimental Social Psychology, 7,* 48–58.

ALLOY, L., & ABRAMSON, L. Y. (1997, May). *The cognitive vulnerability to depression project.* Paper presented to the Midwestern Psychological Association, Chicago.

ALLOY, L. B., & ABRAMSON, L. Y. (1979). Judgment of contingency in depressed and nondepressed students: Sadder but wiser? *Journal of Experimental Psychology: General, 108,* 441–485.

ALLOY, L. B., ABRAMSON, L. Y., SAFFORD, S. M., & GIBB, B. E. (in press). The Cognitive Vulnerability to Depression (CVD) Project: Current findings and future directions. In L. B. Alloy & J. H. Riskind (Eds.), *Cognitive vulnerability to emotional disorders.* Hillsdale, NJ: Erlbaum.

ALLOY, L. B., ABRAMSON, L. Y., WHITEHOUSE, W. G., HOGAN, M. E., PANZARELLA, C., ROBINSON, M. S., ROSE, D. T., & DONOVAN, P. (2001). *Prospective incidence of Axis I disorders in individuals at high and low cognitive risk for depression.* Manuscript in preparation, Temple University.

ALLOY, L. B., ABRAMSON, L. Y., WHITEHOUSE, W. G., HOGAN, M. E., TASHMAN, N., STEINBERG, D., ROSE, D. T., & DONOVAN, P. (1999). Depressogenic cognitive styles: Predictive validity, information processing and personality characteristics, and developmental origins. *Behaviour Research and Therapy, 37,* 503–531.

ALLOY, L. B., & TABACHNIK, N. (1984). Assessment of covariation by animals and humans: Influence of prior expectations and current situational information. *Psychological Review, 91,* 112–149.

ALLPORT, F. H. (1920). The influence of the group upon association and thought. *Journal of Experimental Psychology, 3,* 159–182.

ALLPORT, F. H. (1924). *Social psychology.* Boston: Houghton Mifflin.

ALLPORT, G. H. (1954). *The nature of prejudice.* Reading, MA: Addison Wesley.

ALLPORT, G. W., & ODBERT, H. S. (1936). Trait-names: A psycholexical study. *Psychological Monographs, 47* (1, Whole No. 211).

ALTEMEYER, B. (1988). *Enemies of freedom: Understanding right-wing authoritarianism.* San Francisco: Jossey-Bass.

ALWIN, D. F., COHEN, R. L., & NEWCOMB, T. M. (1991). *Personality and social change: Attitude persistence and changes over the lifespan.* Madison: University of Wisconsin Press.

AMERICAN ACADEMY OF PAIN MEDICINE AND AMERICAN PAIN SOCIETY CONSENSUS STATEMENT. (1997). The use of opioids for the treatment of chronic pain. *Pain Forum, 6,* 77–79.

AMERICAN ACADEMY OF PEDIATRICS. (2001). Clinical practice guideline: Treatment of school-aged children with attention-deficit/hyperactivity disorder. *Pediatrics, 108,* 1033–1045.

AMERICAN PSYCHIATRIC ASSOCIATION. (1994). *Diagnostic and statistical manual of mental disorders* (4th ed.). Washington, DC: American Psychiatric Association.

AMERICAN PSYCHOLOGICAL ASSOCIATION. (1996). *Affirmative action: Who benefits?* Washington, DC: Author.

AMERICAN PSYCHIATRIC ASSOCIATION. (2000). *Diagnostic and Statistical Manual of Mental Disorders* (4th ed., text revision). Washington, DC: American Psychiatric Association Press.

AMERICAN PSYCHOLOGICAL ASSOCIATION. (1990). Ethical principles of psychologists. *American Psychologist, 45,* 390–395.

ANCH, M. A., BROWMAN, C. P., MITLER, M. M., & WALSH, J. K. (1988). Sleep: A scientific perspective. Englewood Cliffs, NJ: Prentice-Hall.

ANCOLI-ISRAEL, S., KRIPKE, D. F., & MASON, W. (1987). Characteristics of obstructive and central sleep apnea in the elderly: An interim report. *Biological Psychiatry, 22,* 741–750.

ANDERSEN, S. M., & GLASSMAN, N. S. (1996). Responding to significant others when they are not there: Effects on interpersonal inference, motivation, and affect. In R. M. Sorrentino & E. T. Higgins (Eds.), *Handbook of motivation and cognition* (Vol. 3, pp. 262–321). New York: Guilford.

ANDERSON, C. A., & BUSHMAN, B. J. (2001). Effects of violent video games on aggressive behavior, aggressive cognition, aggressive affect, physiological arousal, and prosocial behavior: A meta-analytic review of the scientific literature. *Psychological Science, 12*, 353–359.

ANDERSON, J. R. (1983). *The architecture of cognition*. Cambridge, MA: Harvard University Press.

ANDERSON, J. R. (1987). Skill acquisition: Compilation of weak-method problem solutions. *Psychological Review, 94*, 192–210.

ANDERSON, J. R. (1990). *Cognitive psychology and its implications* (3rd ed.). New York: Freeman.

ANDERSON, J. R. (1991). The adaptive nature of human categorization. *Psychological Review, 98*, 409–429.

ANDERSON, M. (1992). *Intelligence and development: A cognitive theory*. Oxford: Blackwell.

ANDERSSON, B. E. (1992). Effects of day-care on cognitive and socioemotional competence of thirteen-year-old Swedish schoolchildren. *Child Development, 63*, 20–36.

ANDREASEN, N. C. (1988). Brain imaging: Applications in psychiatry. *Science, 239*, 1381–1388.

ANDREASEN, N. C., FLAUM, M., SCHULTZ, S., DUZYUREK, S., & MILLER, D. (1997). Diagnosis, methodology, and subtypes of schizophrenia. *Neuropsychobiology, 35*, 61–63.

ANDREASEN, N. C., FLAUM, M., SWAYZE, V. W., TYRRELL, G., & ARNDT, S. (1990). Positive and negative symptoms in schizophrenia: A critical reappraisal. *Archives of General Psychiatry, 47*, 615–621.

ANDREWS, K. H., & KANDEL, D. B. (1979). Attitude and behavior. *American Sociological Review, 44*, 298–310.

ANGHOFF, W. H., & JOHNSON, E. G. (1988). *A study of the differential impact of curriculum on aptitude test scores. Research report 88-46.* Princeton, NJ: Educational Testing Service.

ANGOFF, W. H. (1988). The nature-nurture debate, aptitudes, and group differences. *American Psychologist, 43*, 713–720.

ANTROBUS, J. (1983). REM and NREM sleep reports: Comparisons of word frequencies by cognitive classes. *Psychophysiology, 20*, 562–568.

ANTROBUS, J. (1991). Dreaming: Cognitive processes during cortical activation and high afferent thresholds. *Psychological Review, 98*, 96–121.

ANTROBUS, J. (1993). Dreaming: Could we do without it? In A. Moffitt, M. Kramer, & R. Hoffman (Eds.), *The functions of dreaming*. Albany: State University of New York Press.

APOINTE, J. F., RIVERS, R. Y., & WOHL, J. (1995). *Psychological interventions and cultural diversity*. Boston: Allyn & Bacon.

ARCHER, D., & McDANIEL, P. (1995). Violence and gender: Differences and similarities across societies. In R. B. Ruback & N. A. Weiner (Eds.), *Interpersonal violent behaviors: Social and cultural aspects* (pp. 63–87). New York: Springer.

ARDREY, R. (1966). *The territorial imperative*. New York: Dell.

ARENDT, H. (1963). *Eichmann in Jerusalem: A report on the banality of evil*. New York: Viking Press.

ARMOR, D. A., & TAYLOR, S. E. (1998). Situated optimism: Specific outcome expectancies and self-regulation. In M. P. Zanna (Ed.), *Advances in experimental social psychology* (vol. 30, pp. 309–379). New York: Academic Press.

ARMSTRONG, S. L., GLEITMAN, L. R., & GLEITMAN, H. (1983). What some concepts might not be. *Cognition, 13*, 263–308.

ARNOLD, M. (1949). A demonstrational analysis of the TAT in a clinical setting. *Journal of Abnormal and Social Psychology, 44*, 97–111.

ARNTZ, A., DRESSON, L., & DE JONG, P. (1994). The influence of anxiety on pain: Attentional and attributional mediators. *Pain, 56*, 307–314.

ARON, A. (2002, January). Self-expansion as a motivational basis for positive psychology. In M. Green & T. McLaughlin-Volpe (Chairs), *Positive Relationships*, Symposium presented at the first annual pre-conference on Positive Psychology, Savannah, GA: Society for Personality and Social Psychology.

ARON, A., ARON, E. N., & SMOLLAN, D. (1992). Inclusion of other in the self scale and the structure of interpersonal closeness. *Journal of Personality and Social Psychology, 63*, 596–612.

ARON, A., ARON, E. N., TUDOR, M., & NELSON, G. (1991). Close relationships as including other in the self. *Journal of Personality and Social Psychology, 60*, 241–253.

ARON, A., NORMAN, C. C., & ARON, E. N. (1998). The self-expansion model and motivation. *Representative Research in Social Psychology, 22*, 1–13.

ARONSON, E. (1995). *The social animal* (7th ed.). San Francisco: Freeman.

ARONSON, E., & CARLSMITH, J. M. (1963). The effect of the severity of threat on the devaluation of forbidden behavior. *Journal of Abnormal and Social Psychology, 66*, 584–588.

ARONSON, E., & MILLS, J. (1959). The effect of severity of initiation on liking for a group. *Journal of Abnormal and Social Psychology, 59*, 177–181.

ARONSON, E., & THIBODEAU, R. (1992). The jigsaw classroom: A cooperative strategy for reducing prejudice. In J. Lynch, C. Modgil, & S. Modgil (Eds.), *Cultural diversity in the schools*. London: Falmer Press.

ARRIGO, J. M., & PEZDEK, K. (1997). Lessons from the study of psychogenic amnesia. *Current Directions in Psychological Science, 6*, 148–152.

ARTMAN, L., & CAHAN, S. (1993). Schooling and the development of transitive inference. *Developmental Psychology, 29*, 753–759.

ASCH, S. E. (1946). Forming impressions of personality. *Journal of Abnormal and Social Psychology, 41*, 258–290.

ASCH, S. E. (1952). *Social psychology*. Englewood Cliffs, NJ: Prentice-Hall.

ASCH, S. E. (1955). Opinions and social pressures. *Scientific American, 193*, 31–35.

ASCH, S. E. (1958). Effects of group pressure upon modification and distortion of judgments. In E. E. Maccoby, T. M. Newcomb, & E. L. Hartley (Eds.), *Readings in social psychology* (3rd ed.). New York: Holt, Rinehart & Winston.

ASHMEAD, D. H., DAVIS, D. L., WHALEN, T., & ODOM, R. D. (1991). Sound localization and sensitivity to interaural time differences in human infants. *Child Development, 62*, 1211–1226.

ASLIN, R. N. (1987). Visual and auditory development in infancy. In J. D. Osofsky (Ed.), *Handbook of infant development* (2nd ed.). New York: Wiley.

ASLIN, R. N., & BANKS, M. S. (1978). Early visual experience in humans: Evidence for a critical period in the development of binocular vision. In S. Schneider, H. Liebowitz, H. Pick, & H. Stevenson (Eds.), *Psychology: From basic research to practice*. New York: Plenum.

ASLIN, R. N., PISONI, D. V., & JUSCZYK, P. W. (1983). Auditory development and speech perception in infancy. In P. H. Mussen (Ed.), *Handbook of child psychology* (Vol. 2). New York: Wiley.

ASPINWALL, L. G., & BRUNHART, S. M. (1996). Distinguishing optimism from denial: Optimistic beliefs predict attention to health threats. *Personality and Social Psychology Bulletin, 22*, 993–1003.

ASSAD, G., & SHAPIRO, B. (1986). Hallucinations: Theoretical and clinical overview. *American Journal of Psychiatry, 143*, 1088–1097.

ATKINSON, D. (1983). Ethnic similarity in counseling psychology: A review of the research. *Counseling Psychologist, 11*, 79–92.

ATKINSON, D., MARUYAMA, M., & MATSUI, S. (1978). The effects of counselor race and counseling approach on Asian Americans' perceptions of counselor credibility and utility. *Journal of Counseling Psychology, 25*, 76–83.

ATKINSON, D. R., & HACKETT, G. (1998). *Counseling diverse populations*. Boston: McGraw-Hill.

ATKINSON, R. C. (1975). Mnemotechnics in second-language learning. *American Psychologist, 30*, 821–828.

ATKINSON, R. C., HERRNSTEIN, R. J., LINDZEY, G., & LUCE, R. D. (Eds.). (1988). *Stevens' handbook of experimental psychology* (Vols. 1 and 2). New York: Wiley.

ATKINSON, R. C., & SHIFFRIN, R. M. (1971a). The control of short-term memory. *Scientific American, 225*, 82–90.

ATKINSON, R. C., & SHIFFRIN, R. M. (1971b). Human memory: A proposed system and its control processes. In K. W. Spence (Ed.), *The psychology of learning and motivation: Advances in research and theory* (pp. 89–195). New York: Academic Press.

AULD, F., & HYMAN, M. (1991). *Resolution of inner conflict: An introduction to psychoanalytic therapy*. Washington, DC: American Psychological Association.

AVERILL, J. R. (1983). Studies on anger and aggression: Implications for theories of emotion. *American Psychologist, 38*, 1145–1160.

AWAYA, S., MIYAKE, Y., IMAYUMI, Y., SHIOSE, Y., KNADA, T., & KOMURO, K. (1973). Amblyopia. *Japanese Journal of Ophthalmology, 17*, 69–82.

AX, A. (1953). The physiological differentiation between fear and anger in humans. *Psychosomatic Medicine, 15*, 433–442.

BAARS, B. J. (1988). *A cognitive theory of consciousness*. New York: Cambridge University Press.

BACHMAN, J. G., JOHNSTON, L. D., & O'MALLEY, M. (1998). Explaining recent increase in students' marijuana use: Impacts of perceived risks and disapproval, 1976 through 1996. *American Journal of Public Health, 88*, 887–892.

BADDELEY, A. D. (1986). *Working memory*. Oxford: Clarendon.

BADDELEY, A. D. (1990). *Human memory: Theory and practice*. Boston: Allyn and Bacon.

BADDELEY, A. D., & HITCH, G. J. (1974). Working memory. In G. H. Bower (Ed.), *The psychology of learning and motivation* (Vol. 8). New York: Academic Press.

BADDELEY, A. D., THOMPSON, N., & BUCHANAN, M. (1975). Word length and the structure of short-term memory. *Journal of Verbal Learning and Verbal Behavior, 14*, 575–589.

BAER, P. E., & FUHRER, M. J. (1968). Cognitive processes during differential trace and delayed conditioning of the G. S. R. *Journal of Experimental Psychology, 78*, 81–88.

BAHRICK, H. P., & PHELPS, E. (1987). Retention of Spanish vocabulary over eight years. *Journal of Experimental Psychology: Learning, Memory and Cognition, 13*, 344–349.

BAILEY, J. M., & MARTIN, N. G. (1995, September). *A twin registry study of sexual orientation*. Paper presented at the twenty-first annual meeting of the International Academy of Sex Research, Provincetown, MA.

BAILEY, J. M., & PILLARD, R. C. (1991). A genetic study of male sexual orientation. *Archives of General Psychiatry, 48,* 1089–1096.

BAILEY, J. M., & PILLARD, R. C. (1995). Genetics of human sexual orientation. *Annual Review of Sex Research, 6,* 126–150.

BAILEY, J. M., PILLARD, R. C., NEALE, M. C., & AGYEI, Y. (1993). Heritable factors influence sexual orientation in women. *Archives of General Psychiatry, 50,* 217–223.

BAILEY, J. M., & ZUCKER, K. J. (1995). Childhood sex-typed behavior and sexual orientation: A conceptual analysis and quantitative review. *Developmental Psychology, 31,* 43–45.

BAILLARGEON, R. (1987). Object permanence in 3½- and 4½-month-old infants. *Developmental Psychology, 23,* 655–664.

BAILLARGEON, R., & DEVOS, J. (1991). Object permanence in young infants: Further evidence. *Child Development, 62,* 1227–1246.

BAILLARGEON, R., SPELKE, E. S., & WASSERMAN, S. (1985). Object permanence in five-month-old infants. *Cognition, 20,* 191–208.

BANDURA, A. (1969). *Principles of behavior modification.* New York: Holt, Rinehart and Winston.

BANDURA, A. (1973). *Aggression: A social learning analysis.* Englewood Cliffs, NJ: Prentice-Hall.

BANDURA, A. (1977). *Social learning theory.* Englewood Cliffs, NJ: Prentice-Hall.

BANDURA, A. (1986). *Social foundations of thought and action: A social cognitive theory.* Englewood Cliffs, NJ: Prentice-Hall.

BANDURA, A. (1995). *Self-efficacy in changing societies.* New York: Cambridge University Press.

BANDURA, A. (2001). Social cognitive theory: An agentic perspective. *Annual Review of Psychology, 52,* 1–26.

BANDURA, A., BLANCHARD, E. B., & RITTER, B. (1969). The relative efficacy of desensitization and modeling approaches for inducing behavioral, affective, and attitudinal changes. *Journal of Personality and Social Psychology, 13,* 173–199.

BANKS, W. P., & PRINTZMETAL, W. (1976). Configurational effects in visual information processing. *Perception and Psychophysics, 19,* 361–367.

BANKS, W. P., & SALAPATEK, P. (1983). Infant visual perception. In P. H. Mussen (Ed.), *Handbook of child psychology* (Vol. 2). New York: Wiley.

BANYAI, E. I., & HILGARD, E. R. (1976). A comparison of active-alert hypnotic induction with traditional relaxation induction. *Journal of Abnormal Psychology, 85,* 218–224.

BAREFOOT, J. C., DODGE, K. A., PETERSON, B. L., DAHLSTROM, W. G., WILLIAMS, R. B., Jr. (1989). The Cook-Medley Hostility scale: Item content and ability to predict survival. *Psychosomatic Medicine, 51,* 46–57.

BAREFOOT, J. C., WILLIAMS, R. B., & DAHLSTROM, W. G. (1983). Hostility, CHD incidence and total mortality: A 25-year follow-up study of 255 physicians. *Psychosomatic Medicine, 45,* 59–63.

BARGH, J. A. (1997). The automaticity of everyday life. In R. S. Wyer Jr. (Ed.), *Advances in social cognition* (Vol. 10). Mahway, NJ: Erlbaum.

BARGH, J. A. (1999). The cognitive monster: The case against the controllability of automatic stereotype effects. In S. Chaiken & Y. Trope (Eds.), *Dual-process theories in social psychology* (pp. 361–382). New York: Guilford.

BARGH, J. A., CHEN, M., & BURROWS, L. (1996). Automaticity of social behavior: Direct effects of trait construct and stereotype activation on action. *Journal of Personality and Social Psychology, 71,* 230–244.

BARKOW, J., COSMIDES, L., & TOOBY, J. (1990). *The adapted mind: Evolutionary psychology and the generation of culture.* New York: Oxford University Press.

BARLOW, D. H. (1988). *Anxiety and its disorders: The nature and treatment of anxiety and panic.* New York: Guilford.

BARLOW, H. B., & MOLLON, J. D. (1982). *The senses.* Cambridge, England: Cambridge University Press.

BARON, R. S. (1986). Distraction-conflict theory: Progress and problems. In L. Berkowitz (Ed.), *Advances in experimental social psychology* (Vol. 19). New York: Academic Press.

BARRERA, M. E., & MAURER, D. (1981). Recognition of mother's photographed face by the three-month-old infant. *Child Development, 52,* 714–716.

BARRERA, M. E., & MAURER, D. (1981). Discrimination of strangers by the three-month-old. *Child Development, 52,* 558–563.

BARSALOU, L. W. (1985). Ideals, central tendency, and frequency of instantiation as determinants of graded structure in categories. *Journal of Experimental Psychology: Learning, Memory, and Cognition, 11,* 629–654.

BARSALOU, L. W. (1992). *Cognitive psychology: An overview for cognitive scientists.* Hillsdale, NJ: Erlbaum.

BARTLETT, F. C. (1932). *Remembering: A study in experimental and social psychology.* Cambridge, England: Cambridge University Press.

BARTOSHUK, L. M. (1979). Bitter taste of saccharin: Related to the genetic ability to taste the bitter substance propylthiourial (PROP). *Science, 205,* 934–935.

BARTOSHUK, L. M. (1993). Genetic and pathological taste variation: What can we learn from animal models and human disease? *Ciba Foundation Symposium (D7X), 179,* 251–262.

BARTOSHUK, L. M. (2000). Psychophysical advances aid the study of genetic variation in taste. *Appetite, 34,* 105.

BARTSCH, K., & WELLMAN, H. M. (1995). *Children talk about the mind.* New York: Oxford University Press.

BASOGLU, M. (Ed.). (1992). *Torture and its consequences: Current treatment approaches.* Cambridge, England: Cambridge University Press.

BASOGLU, M., & MINECKA, S. (1992). The role of uncontrollable and unpredictable stress in posttraumatic stress responses in torture survivors. In M. Basoglu (Ed.), *Torture and its consequences: Current treatment approaches.* (pp. 182–225). New York: Cambridge University Press.

BASOGLU, M., MINEKA, S., PAKER, M., AKER, T., LIVANOU, M., & GOEK, S. (1997). Psychological preparedness for trauma as a protective factor in survivors of torture. *Psychological Medicine, 27,* 1421–1433.

BATESON, P. (1978). Sexual imprinting and optimal outbreeding. *Nature, 273,* 659–660.

BATSON, C. D. (1991). *The altruism question: Toward a social-psychological answer.* Hillsdale, NJ: Erlbaum.

BAUCOM, D. H., EPSTEIN, N., & GORDON, K. C. (2000). Marital therapy: Theory, practice, and empirical status. In C. R. Snyder & R. Ingram (Eds.), *Handbook of psychological change* (pp. 280–308). New York: Wiley.

BAUCOM, D. H., SHOHAM, V., MUESSER, K. T., DAIUTO, A. D., & STICKLE, T. R. (1998). Empirically supported couple and family interventions for marital distress and adult mental health problems. *Journal of Consulting and Clinical Psychology, 66,* 53–88.

BAUM, A., & POSLUSZNY, D. M. (1999). Health psychology: Mapping biobehavioral contributions to health and illness. *Annual Reviews of Psychology, 50,* 147–163.

BAUMEISTER, R. F., & TICE, D. M. (1984). Role of self-presentation and choice in cognitive dissonance under forced compliance: Necessary or sufficient causes? *Journal of Personality and Social Psychology, 43,* 838–852.

BAUMRIND, D. (1964). Some thoughts on ethics of research: After reading Milgram's "Behavioral study of obedience." *American Psychologist, 19,* 421–423.

BAUMRIND, D. (1971). Current patterns of parental authority. *Developmental Psychology Monographs, 1,* 1–103.

BAUMRIND, D. (1980). New directions in socialization research. *American Psychologist, 35,* 639–652.

BAXTER, L., SCHWARTZ, J., BERGMAN, K., & SZUBA, M. (1992). Caudate glucose metabolic rate changes with both drug and behavior therapy for obsessive-compulsive disorder. *Archives of General Psychiatry, 49,* 681–689.

BAXTER, L. R., SCHWARTZ, J. M., GUZE, B. H., & BERGMAN, K. (1990). PET imaging in obsessive compulsive disorder with and without depression. *Journal of Clinical Psychiatry, 51(suppl.),* 61–69.

BAYLEY, J. (1999). *Elegy for Iris.* New York: St. Martin's Press.

BEAMAN, A. L., BARNES, P. J., KLENTZ, B., & MCQUIRK, B. (1978). Increasing helping rates through information dissemination: Teaching pays. *Personality and Social Psychology Bulletin, 4,* 406–411.

BEAUBRUN, G., & GRAY, G. E. (2000). A review of herbal medicines for psychiatric disorders. *Psychiatric Services, 51,* 11301–134.

BECHARA, A., TRANEL, D., DAMASIO, H., ADOLPHS, R., ROCKLAND, C., & DAMASIO, A. R. (1995). Double dissociation of conditioning and declarative knowledge relative to the amygdala and hippocampus in humans. *Science, 269,* 1115–1118.

BECHARA, A., TRANEL, D., DAMASIO, H., & DAMASIO, A. R. (1996). Failure to respond autonomically to anticipated future outcomes following damage to prefrontal cortex. *Cerebral Cortex, 6,* 215–225.

BECK, A. T. (1976). *Cognitive therapy and the emotional disorder.* New York: International Universities Press.

BECK, A. T., RUSH, A. J., SHAW, B. F., & EMERY, G. (1979). *Cognitive therapy of depression.* New York: Guilford.

BECK, J. G. (1995). Hypoactive sexual desire: An overview. *Journal of Consulting and Clinical Psychology, 42,* 861–865.

BEECHER, H. K. (1961). Surgery as placebo. *Journal of the American Medical Association, 176,* 1102–1107.

BEHRMANN, M., & HAIMSON, C. (1999). The cognitive neuroscience of visual attention. *Current Opinion in Neurobiology, 9,* 158–163.

BÉKÉSY, G. VON (1960). *Experiments in hearing* (E. G. Weaver, Trans). New York: McGraw-Hill.

BELL, A. P. (1982). Sexual preference: A postscript. *Siecus Report, 11,* 1–3.

BELL, A. P., & WEINBERG, M. S. (1978). *Homosexualities: A study of diversity among men and women.* New York: Simon & Schuster.

BELL, A. P., WEINBERG, M. S., & HAMMER-SMITH, S. K. (1981a). *Sexual preference: Its development in men and women.* Bloomington: Indiana University Press.

BELL, A. P., WEINBERG, M. S., & HAMMER-SMITH, S. K. (1981b). *Sexual preference: Its development in men and women. Statistical appendix.* Bloomington: Indiana University Press.

BELL, C. J., & NUTT, D. J. (1998). Serotonin and panic. *British Journal of Psychiatry, 172,* 465–471.

BELL, S. M., & AINSWORTH, M. D. (1972). Infant crying and maternal responsiveness. *Child Development, 43,* 1171–1190.

BELOFF, H. (1957). The structure and origin of the anal character. *Genetic Psychology Monographs, 55,* 141–172.

BELSKY, J. (1986). Infant day care: A cause for concern? *Zero to Three, 7,* 1–7.

BELSKY, J., FISH, M., & ISABELLA, R. A. (1991). Continuity and discontinuity in infant negative and positive emotionality: Family antecedents and attachment consequences. *Developmental Psychology, 27,* 421–431.

BELSKY, J., & ROVINE, M. J. (1987). Temperament and attachment security in the strange situation: An empirical rapprochement. *Child Development, 58,* 787–795.

BELSKY, J., & ROVINE, M. J. (1988). Nonmaternal care in the first year of life and the security of infant-parent attachment. *Child Development, 59,* 157–167.

BELSKY, J., WOODWORTH, S., & CRNIC, K. (1996). Trouble in the second year: Three questions about family interactions. *Child Development, 60,* 649–662.

BEM, D. J. (1972). Self-perception theory. In L. Berkowitz (Ed.), *Advances in experimental social psychology* (Vol. 6). New York: Academic Press.

BEM, D. J. (1995). *Exotic becomes erotic: A developmental theory of sexual orientation.* Unpublished manuscript, Cornell University, Ithaca, New York.

BEM, D. J. (1996). Exotic becomes erotic: A developmental theory of sexual orientation. *Psychological Review, 103,* 320–335.

BEM, D. J. (2000). Exotic becomes erotic: Interpreting the biological correlates of sexual orientation. *Archives of Sexual Behavior, 29,* 531–548.

BEM, D. J., & HONORTON, C. (1994). Does psi exist? Replicable evidence for an anomalous process if information transfer. *Psychological Bulletin, 115,* 4–18.

BEM, D. J., PLAMER, J., & BROUGHTON, R. S. (2001). Updating the ganzfeld database: A victim of its own success? *Journal of Parapsychology, 65,* 207–218.

BEM, D. J., WALLACH, M. A., & KOGAN, N. (1965). Group decision-making under risk of aversive consequences. *Journal of Personality and Social Psychology, 1,* 453–460.

BEM, S. L. (1975). Sex role adaptability: One consequence of psychological androgyny. *Journal of Personality and Social Psychology, 31,* 634–643.

BEM, S. L. (1981). Gender schema theory: A cognitive account of sex typing. *Psychological Review, 88,* 354–364.

BEM, S. L. (1985). Androgyny and gender schema theory: A conceptual and empirical integration. In T. B. Sonderegger (Ed.), *Nebraska symposium on motivation 1984: Psychology and gender* (pp. 179–226). Lincoln: University of Nebraska Press.

BEM, S. L. (1987). Gender schema theory and the romantic tradition. In P. Shaver & C. Hendrick (Eds.), *Review of personality and social psychology* (Vol. 7, pp. 251–271). Newbury Park, CA: Sage.

BEM, S. L. (1989). Genital knowledge and gender constancy in preschool children. *Child Development, 60,* 649–662.

BEM, S. L. (1993). *The lenses of gender: Transforming the debate on sexual inequality.* New Haven, CT: Yale University Press.

BENJAMIN, J., LI, L., PATTERSON, C., GREENBERG, B. D., MURPHY, D. L., & HAMER, D. H. Population and familial association between the D4 dopamine receptor gene and measures of novelty seeking. *Nature Genetics, 12,* 81–84.

BENOTSCH, E. G., CHRISTENSEN, A. J., & MCKELVEY, L. (1997). Hostility, social support, and ambulatory cardiovascular activity. *Journal of Behavioral Medicine, 20,* 163–176.

BENSON, D. F. (1985). Aphasia. In K. M. Heilman & E. Valenstein (Eds.), *Clinical neuropsychology* (2nd ed., pp. 17–47). New York: Oxford University Press.

BERENT, I. (2001). Can connectionist models of phonology assembly account for phonology? *Psychonomic Bulletin and Review, 8,* 661–676.

BERGER, T. W. (1984). Long-term potentiation of hippocampal synaptic transmission affects rate of behavioral learning. *Science, 224,* 627–630.

BERGIN, A. E., & LAMBERT, M. J. (1978). The evaluation of therapeutic outcomes. In S. L. Garfield & A. E. Bergin (Eds.), *Handbook of psychotherapy and behavior change* (2nd ed.). New York: Wiley.

BERGIN, A. E., & LAMBERT, M. J. (1979). Counseling the researcher. *Counseling Psychologist, 8,* 53–56.

BERK, L. E. (1997). *Child development* (4th ed.). Needham Heights, MA: Allyn and Bacon.

BERKOWITZ, L. (1965). The concept of aggressive drive. In L. Berkowitz (Ed.), *Advances in experimental social psychology* (Vol. 2). New York: Academic Press.

BERKOWITZ, L. (1981). On the difference between internal and external reactions to legitimate and illegitimate frustration: A demonstration. *Aggressive Behavior, 7,* 83–96.

BERLIN, B., & KAY, P. (1969). *Basic color terms: Their universality and evolution.* Los Angeles: University of California Press.

BERMAN, A. L., & JOBES, D. A. (1991). *Adolescent suicide assessment and intervention.* Washington, DC: American Psychological Association.

BERMAN, K. F., TORREY, E. F., DANIEL, D. G., & WEINBERGER, D. R. (1992). Regional cerebral blood flow in monozygotic twins discordant and concordant for schizophrenia. *Archives of General Psychiatry, 49,* 927–934.

BERMAN, M. E., KAVOUSSI, R. J., & COCCARO, E. F. (1997). Neurotransmitter correlates of human aggression. In D. M. Stoff, J. Breiling, & J. D. Maser (Eds.), *Handbook of antisocial personality disorder* (pp. 305–314). New York: Wiley.

BERNHEIM, K. F. (1997). *The Lanahan cases and readings in abnormal behavior.* Baltimore: Lanahan.

BERNSTEIN, I. L. (1978). Learned taste aversions in children receiving chemotherapy. *Science, 200,* 1302–1303.

BERRIDGE, K. C., & VALENSTEIN, E. S. (1991). What psychological process mediates feeding evoked by electrical stimulation of the lateral hypothalamus? *Behavioral Neuroscience, 105,* 3–14.

BERSCHEID, E. (1983). Emotion. In H. H. Kelley, E. Berscheid, A. Christensen, J. H. Harvey, T. L. Huston, G. Levinger, E. McClintock, L. A. Peplau, & D. R. Peterson (Eds.), *Close relationships* (pp. 110–168). New York: Freeman.

BERSCHEID, E., & WALSTER, E. H. (1974). A little bit about love. In T. Huston (Ed.), *Foundation of interpersonal attraction.* New York: Academic Press.

BEST, J. B. (1992). *Cognitive psychology.* New York: West.

BIBRING, E. (1953). The mechanism of depression. In P. Greenacre (Ed.), *Affective disorders* (pp. 13–48). New York: International Universities Press.

BIEDERMAN, I. (1987). Recognition by components: A theory of human image understanding. *Psychological Review, 94,* 115–1947.

BIEDERMAN, I. (1990). Higher-level vision. In D. N. Osherson, S. M. Kossyln, & J. M. Hollerbach (Eds.). *An invitation to cognitive science: Visual cognition and action* (Vol. 2). Cambridge, MA: MIT Press.

BIEDERMAN, I., & JU, G. (1988). Surface versus edge-based determinants of visual recognition. *Cognitive Psychology, 20,* 38–64.

BIERBRAUER, G. (1973). *Attribution and perspective: Effects of time, set, and role on interpersonal inference.* Unpublished Ph.D. dissertation, Stanford University.

BILLINGS, A. G., & MOOS, R. H. (1984). Coping, stress, and social resources among adults with unipolar depression. *Journal of Personality and Social Psychology, 46,* 887–891.

BINET, A., & SIMON, T. (1905). New methods for the diagnosis of the intellectual level of subnormals. *Annals of Psychology, 11,* 191.

BINNS, K. E., & SALT, T. E. (1997). Post eye-opening maturation of visual receptive field diameters in the superior colliculus of normal- and dark-reared rats. *Brain Research: Developmental Brain Research, 99,* 263–266.

BISIACH, E., & LUZZATI, C. (1978). Unilateral neglect of representational space. *Cortex, 14,* 129–133.

BLAGROVE, M. (1992). Dreams as a reflection of our waking concerns and abilities: A critique of the problem-solving paradigm in dream research. *Dreaming, 2,* 205–220.

BLAGROVE, M. (1996). Problems with the cognitive psychological modeling of dreaming. *Journal of Mind and Behavior, 17,* 99–134.

BLAGROVE, M., & AKEURST, L. (2000). *In search of the light: The adventures of a parapsychologist.* Amherst, NY: Prometheus Books.

BLAKE, P., PINCUS, J., & BUCKNER, C. (1995). Neurologic abnormalities in murderers. *Neurology, 45,* 1641–1657.

BLAKE, R. (1981). Strategies for assessing visual deficits in animals with selective neural deficits. In R. N. Aslin, J. R. Alberts, & M. R. Petersen (Eds.), *Development of perception*: Vol. 2. *The visual system* (pp. 95–110). New York: Academic Press.

BLAKESLEE, S. (1998, October 13). Placebos prove so powerful even experts are surprised. *New York Times,* pp. F1, F4.

BLAMEY, P. J., DOWELL, R. C., BROWN, A. M., CLARK, G. M., & SELIGMAN, P. M. (1987). Vowel and consonant recognition of cochlear implant patients using formant-estimating speech processors. *Journal of the Acoustical Society of America, 82,* 48–57.

BLANCK, G. (1990). Vygotsky: The man and his cause. In L. C. Moll (Ed.), *Vygotsky and education.* New York: Cambridge University Press.

BLATT, S. J. (1974). Levels of object representation in anaclitic and introjective depression. *Psychoanalytic Study of the Child, 29,* 107–159.

BLAZER, D. G., GEORGE, L., & HUGHES, D. (1991). The epidemiology of anxiety disorders. In C. Salzman & B. Liebowitz (Eds.), *Anxiety disor-*

ders in the elderly (pp. 17–30). New York: Springer-Verlag.

BLISS, E. L. (1980). Multiple personalities: Report of fourteen cases with implications for schizophrenia and hysteria. *Archives of General Psychiatry, 37*, 1388–1397.

BLISS, T. V. P., & LMO, T. (1973). Long-lasting potentiation of synaptic transmission in the dentate area of the anesthetized rabbit following stimulation of the preforant path. *Journal of Physiology, 232*, 331–356.

BLOCK, J. (1961/1978). *The Q-sort method in personality assessment and psychiatric research.* Palo Alto: Consulting Psychologists Press.

BLOOD, R. O. (1967). *Love match and arranged marriage.* New York: Free Press.

Bloom, P. (2000). *How children learn the meaning of words.* Cambridge, MA: MIT Press.

BLUM, G. S. (1953). *Psychoanalytic theories of personality.* New York: McGraw-Hill.

BLUM, K., CULL, J. G., BRAVERMAN, E. R., & COMINGS, D. E. (1996). Reward deficiency syndrome. *American Scientist, 84*, 132–145.

BLUMENTHAL, J. A., EMERY, C. F., MADDEN, D. J., SCHNIEBOLK, S., WALSH-RIDDLE, M., GEORGE, L. K., MCKEE, D. C., HIGGINBOTHAM, M. B., COBB, F. R., & COLEMAN, R. E. (1991). Long term effects of exercise on psychological functioning in older men and women. *Journal of Gerontology, 46*, 352–361.

BODENHAUSEN, G. V., MACRAE, C. N., & SHERMAN, J. W. (1999). On the dialectics of discrimination: Dual processes in social stereotyping. In S. Chaiken & Y. Trope (Eds.), *Dual-process theories in social psychology* (pp. 271–290). New York: Guilford.

BOFF, K. R., KAUFMAN, L., & THOMAS, J. P. (Eds.). (1986). *Handbook of perception and human performance* (Vol. 1). New York: Wiley.

BOLLES, R. C. (1970). Species-specific defense reactions and avoidance learning. *Psychological Review, 77*, 32–48.

BONANNO, G. A., & SINGER, J. L. (1990). Repressive personality style: Theoretical and methodological implications for health and pathology. In J. L. Singer (Ed.), *Repression and dissociation* (pp. 435–465). Chicago: University of Chicago Press.

BOND, C. F. (1982). Social facilitation: A self-presentational view. *Journal of Personality and Social Psychology, 42*, 1042–1050.

BOND, C. F., & TITUS, L. J. (1983). Social facilitation: A meta-analysis of 241 studies. *Psychological Bulletin, 94*, 265–292.

BOON, S., & DRAIJER, N. (1993). Multiple personality disorder in The Netherlands: A clinical investigation of 71 patients. *American Journal of Psychiatry, 150*, 489–494.

BOOTH, A., SHELLEY, G., MAZUR, A., THARP, G., & KITTOK, R. (1989). Testosterone and winning and losing in human competition. *Hormones and Behavior, 23*, 556–571.

BOOTH, D. (1990). Learned role of tastes in eating motivation. In E. D. Capaldi et al. (Eds.), *Taste, experience, and feeding* (pp. 179–194). Washington, DC: American Psychological Association.

BOOTH, D. A. (1987). Cognitive experimental psychology of appetite. In R. A. Boakes (Ed.), *Eating habits: Food, physiology, and learned behavior* (pp. 175–209). New York: Wiley.

BOOTH, D. A. (1991). Learned ingestive motivation and the pleasures of the palate. In R. C. Bolles (Ed.), *The hedonics of taste* (pp. 29–58). Hillsdale, NJ: Erlbaum.

BOOTH-KEWLEY, S., & FRIEDMAN, H. S. (1987). Psychological predictors of heart disease: A quantitative review. *Psychological Bulletin, 101*, 343–362.

BOOTZIN, R. R., KIHLSTROM, J. F., & SCHACTER, D. L. (Eds.). (1990). *Sleep and cognition.* Washington, DC: American Psychological Association.

BORGIDA, E., & NISBETT, R. E. (1977). The differential impact of abstract vs. concrete information on decisions. *Journal of Applied Social Psychology, 7*, 258–271.

BORING, E. G. (1930). A new ambiguous figure. *American Journal of Psychology, 42*, 444–445.

BORNSTEIN, R. F. (1992). Subliminal mere exposure effects. In R. F. Bornstein & T. S. Pittman (Eds.), *Perception without awareness: Cognitive, clinical and social perspectives* (pp. 191–210). New York: Guilford.

BORNSTEIN, R. F., & D'AGOSTINO, P. R. (1992). Stimulus recognition and the mere exposure effect. *Journal of Personality and Social Psychology, 63*, 545–552.

BOTMAN, H., & CROVITZ, H. (1992). Dream reports and autobiographical memory. *Imagination, Cognition and Personality, 9*, 213–214.

BOUCHARD, C., TREMBLAY, A., DESPRES, J. P., NADEAU, A., LUPIEN, P. J., THERIAULT, G., DUSSAULT, J., MOORJANI, S., PINAULT, S., & FOURNIER, G. (1990). The response to long-term overeating in identical twins. *New England Journal of Medicine, 322*, 1477–1482.

BOUCHARD, T. J., & MCGUE, M. (1981). Familial studies of intelligence: A review. *Science, 212*, 1055–1059.

BOUCHARD, T. J., JR. (1984). Twins reared apart and together: What they tell us about human diversity. In S. Fox (Ed.), *The chemical and biological bases of individuality.* New York: Plenum.

BOUCHARD, T. J., JR. (1995). *Nature's twice-told tale: Identical twins reared apart—What they tell us about human individuality.* Paper presented at the annual meeting of the Western Psychological Association, Los Angeles.

BOUCHARD, T. J., JR., LYKKEN, D. T., MCGUE, M., SEGAL, N. L., & TELLEGEN, A. (1990). Sources of human psychological differences: The Minnesota study of twins reared apart. *Science, 250*, 223–228.

BOURIN, M., BAKER, G. B., & BRADWEJN, J. (1998). Neurobiology of panic disorder. *Journal of Psychosomatic Research, 44*, 163–180.

BOURNE, L. E. (1966). *Human conceptual behavior.* Boston: Allyn and Bacon.

BOUTON, M. E., MINEKA, S., & BARLOW, D. H. (2001). A modern learning theory perspective on the etiology of panic disorder. *Psychological Review, 108*, 4–32.

BOWDEN, C. L. (2000). Efficacy of lithium in mania and maintenance therapy of bipolar disorder. *Journal of Clinical Psychiatry, 61*, 35–40.

BOWEN, W. G., & BOK, D. (1998). *The shape of the river: Long-term consequences of considering race in college and university admissions.* Princeton, NJ: Princeton University Press.

BOWER, G. H. (1981). Mood and memory. *American Psychologist, 6*, 129–148.

BOWER, G. H., BLACK, J. B., & TURNER, T. R. (1979). Scripts in memory for text. *Cognitive Psychology, 11*, 177–220.

BOWER, G. H., & CLARK, M. C. (1969). Narrative stories as mediators for serial learning. *Psychonomic Science, 14*, 181–182.

BOWER, G. H., CLARK, M. C., WINZENZ, D., & LESGOLD, A. (1969). Hierarchical retrieval schemes in recall of categorized word lists. *Journal of Verbal Learning and Verbal Behavior, 8*, 323–343.

BOWER, G. H., & SPRINGSTON, F. (1970). Pauses as recoding points in letter series. *Journal of Experimental Psychology, 83*, 421–430.

BOWER, J. E., KEMENY, M. E., TAYLOR, S. E., & FAHEY, J. L. (1998). Cognitive processing, discovery of meaning, CD 4 decline, and AIDS-related mortality among bereaved HIV-seropositive men. *Journal of Consulting and Clinical Psychology, 66*, 979–986.

BOWER, J. E., TAYLOR, S. E., & FAHEY, J. L. (1998). Cognitive processing, discovery of meaning, CD4 decline, and AIDS-related mortality among HIV-seropositive men. *Journal of Consulting and Clinical Psychology, 66*, 979–986.

BOWLBY, J. (1969). *Attachment and loss,* Vol. 1: *Attachment.* New York: Basic Books.

BOWLBY, J. (1973). *Attachment and loss: Separation, anxiety and anger* (Vol. 2). London: Hogarth Press.

BOYNTON, R. M. (1979). *Human color vision.* New York: Holt, Rinehart & Winston.

BOZZA, T. C., & MOMBAERTS, P. (2001). Olfactory coding: Revealing intrinsic representations of odors. *Current Biology, 11*, R687–R690.

BRADLEY, S. J., OLIVER, G. D., CHERNICK, A. B., & Zucker, K. J. (1998). Experiment of nurture: ablatio penis at 2 months, sex reassignment at 7 months, and a psychosexual follow-up in young adulthood. *Pediatrics, 102*, 9.

BRADSHAW, G. L., & ANDERSON, J. R. (1982). Elaborative encoding as an explanation of levels of processing. *Journal of Verbal Learning and Verbal Behavior, 21*, 165–174.

BRAINARD, D. H. (1999). Color Vision. In R. Wilson & F. Keil (Eds.), *MIT Encyclopedia of the Cognitive Sciences.* Cambridge, MA: MIT Press.

BRANSFORD, J. D., & JOHNSON, M. K. (1973). Considerations of some problems of comprehension. In W. G. Chase (Ed.), *Visual information processing.* New York: Academic Press.

BRAUN, B. G. (1986). *Treatment of multiple personality disorder.* Washington, DC: American Psychiatric Press.

BRAZELTON, T. B. (1978). The remarkable talents of the newborn. *Birth and Family Journal, 5*, 4–10.

BREEDLOVE, S. M. (1994). Sexual differentiation of the human nervous system. *Annual Review of Psychology, 45*, 389–418.

BREGGIN, P. R. (1994). *Talking back to Prozac.* New York: St. Martin's Press.

BREGMAN, A. S. (1990). *Auditory scene analysis.* Cambridge, MA: MIT Press.

BREHM, J. W. (1956). Postdecision changes in the desirability of alternatives. *Journal of Abnormal and Social Psychology, 52*, 384–389.

BREHM, S. S. (1992). *Intimate relationships* (2nd ed.). New York: McGraw-Hill.

BREIER, A., SCHREIBER, J. L., DYER, J., & PICKAR, D. (1992). Course of illness and predictors of outcome in chronic schizophrenia: Implications for pathophysiology. *British Journal of Psychiatry, 161*, 38–43.

BRELAND, K., & BRELAND, M. (1966). *Animal behavior.* New York: Macmillan.

BREMNER, J. D. (1998). Neuroimaging of posttraumatic stress disorder. *Psychiatric Annals, 28*, 445–455.

BRENNER, C. (1980). A psychoanalytic theory of affects. In R. Plutchik & H. Kellerman (Eds.), *Emotion: Theory, research, and experience* (Vol. 1). New York: Academic Press.

BREVOORT, P. (1998). The booming U.S. botanical market: A new overview. *HerbalGram, 44,* 33–46.

BREWIN, C. R., MACCARTHY, B., DUDA, K., & VAUGHN, C. E. (1991). Attribution and expressed emotion in the relatives of patients with schizophrenia. *Journal of Abnormal Psychology, 100,* 546–554.

BRIDGER, W. H. (1961). Sensory habituation and discrimination in the human neonate. *American Journal of Psychiatry, 117,* 991–996.

BRITT, T. W., ADLER, A. B., & BARTONE, P. T. (2001). Deriving benefits from stressful events: The role of engagement in meaningful work and hardiness. *Journal of Occupational Health Psychology, 6,* 53–63.

BROADBENT, D. E. (1958). *Perception and communication.* London: Pergamon.

BROMAN, C. L. (1987). Race differences in professional help seeking. *American Journal of Community Psychology, 15,* 473–489.

BROOKS-GUNN, J., & RUBLE, D. N. (1983). The experience of menarche from a developmental perspective. In J. Brooks-Gunn & A. C. Petersen (Eds.), *Girls at puberty: Biological and psychological perspectives.* New York: Plenum.

BROWN, A. E. (1936). Dreams in which the dreamer knows he is asleep. *Journal of Abnormal Psychology, 31,* 59–66.

BROWN, D. P. (1977). A model for the levels of concentrative mediation. *International Journal of Clinical and Experimental Hypnosis, 25,* 236–273.

BROWN, E. L., & DEFFENBACHER, K. (1979). *Perception and the senses.* Oxford: Oxford University Press.

BROWN, G. W., BIRLEY, J. L., & WING, J. K. (1972). Influence of family life on the course of schizophrenic disorders: A replication. *British Journal of Psychiatry, 121,* 241–258.

BROWN, J. (1991). Staying fit and staying well: Physical fitness as a moderator of life stress. *Journal of Personality and Social Psychology, 60,* 555–561.

BROWN, J. D. (1986). Evaluations of self and others: Self-enhancement biases in social judgments. *Social Cognition, 4,* 353–376.

BROWN, L. L., TOMKARKEN, A. J., ORTH, D. N., LOOSEN, P. T., KALIN, N. H., & DAVIDSON, R. J. (1996). Individual differences in repressive-defensiveness predict basal salivary cortisol levels. *Journal of Personality and Social Psychology, 70,* 362–371.

BROWN, R. (1973). *A first language: The early stages.* Cambridge, MA: Harvard University Press.

BROWN, R. (1974). Further comment on the risky shift. *American Psychologist, 29,* 468–470.

BROWN, R. (1986). *Social psychology: The second edition.* New York: Free Press.

BROWN, R., & KULIK, J. (1977). Flashbulb memories. *Cognition, 5,* 73–99.

BROWN, R., CAZDEN, C. B., & BELLUGI, U. (1969). The child's grammar from 1 to 3. In J. P. Hill (Ed.), *Minnesota symposium on child psychology* (Vol. 2). Minneapolis: University of Minnesota Press.

BROWN, R. W., & MCNEILL, D. (1966). The "tip-of-the-tongue" phenomenon. *Journal of Verbal Learning and Verbal Behavior, 5,* 325–337.

BROWNELL, K. (1988, January). Yo-yo dieting. *Psychology Today, 22,* 20–23.

BROWNELL, K. D., & RODIN, J. (1994). The dieting maelstrom: Is it possible and advisable to lose weight? *American Psychologist, 49,* 781–791.

BRUCH, H. (1973). *Eating disorders: Obesity, anorexia nervosa, and the person within.* New York: Basic Books.

BRUNER, J., PARHOFER, K. G., SCHWANDT, P., & BRONISCH, T. (2002). Cholesterol, essential fatty acids, and suicide. *Pharmacopsychiatry, 35,* 1–5.

BRUNER, J. S. (1957). Going beyond the information given. In *Contemporary approaches to cognition: A symposium held at the University of Colorado.* Cambridge, MA: Harvard University Press.

BRUNER, J. S., GOODNOW, J. J., & AUSTIN, G. A. (1956). *A study of thinking.* New York: Wiley.

BRUNER, J. S., OLVER, R. R., GREENFIELD, P. M., & Collaborators. (1966). *Studies in cognitive growth.* New York: Wiley.

BRUNER, J. S., & POTTER, M. C. (1964). Interference in visual search. *Science, 144,* 424–425.

BRUYER, R., LATERRE, C., SERON, X., & Collaborators. (1983). A case of prosopagnosia with some preserved covert remembrance of familiar faces. *Brain and Cognition, 2,* 257–284.

BRYAN, J. H., & TEST, M. A. (1967). Models and helping: Naturalistic studies in aiding behavior. *Journal of Personality and Social Psychology, 6,* 400–407.

BUB, D., BLACKS, S., & HOWELL, J. (1989). Word recognition and orthographic context effects in a letter-by-letter reader. *Brain and Language, 36,* 357–376.

BUCHANAN, C. M., ECCLES, J. S., & BECKER, J. B. (1992). Are adolescents the victims of raging hormones? Evidence for activational effects of hormones on moods and behavior at adolescence. *Psychological Bulletin, 111,* 62–107.

BUCHSBAUM, M. S., HAIER, R. J., POTKIN, S. G., & NUECHTERLEIN, K. (1992). Fronostriatal disorder of cerebral metabolism in never-medicated schizophrenics. *Archives of General Psychiatry, 49,* 935–942.

BUCHSBAUM, M. S., SOMEYA, T., WU, J. C., TANG, C. Y., & BUNNEY, W. E. (1997). Neuroimaging bipolar illness with positron emission tomography and magnetic resonance imaging. *Psychiatric Annals, 27,* 489–495.

BUCK, L., & AXEL, R. (1991). A novel multigene family may encode odorant receptors: A molecular basis for odor recognition. *Cell, 65,* 175–187.

BURNAM, M. A., STEIN, J. A., GOLDING, J. M., SIEGEL, J. M., SORENSON, S. B., FORSYTHE, A. B., & TELLES, C. A. (1988). Sexual assault and mental disorders in a community population. *Journal of Consulting and Clinical Psychology, 56,* 843–850.

BURNSTEIN, E., & VINOKUR, A. (1973). Testing two classes of theories about group-induced shifts in individual choice. *Journal of Experimental Social Psychology, 9,* 123–137.

BURNSTEIN, E., & VINOKUR, A. (1977). Persuasive arguments and social comparison as determinants of attitude polarization. *Journal of Experimental Social Psychology, 13,* 315–332.

BUSBY, P. A., TONG, Y. C., & CLARK, G. M. (1993). Electrode position, repetition rate, and speech perception by early- and late-deafened cochlear implant patients. *Journal of the Acoustical Society of America, 93,* 1058–1067.

BUSEY, T. A., TUNNICLIFF, J., LOFTUS, G. R., & LOFTUS, E. F. (2000). Accounts of the confidence-accuracy relation in recognition memory. *Psychonomic Bulletin and Review, 7,* 26–48.

BUSS, A. H., & PLOMIN, R. (1975). *A temperament theory of personality development.* New York: Wiley.

BUSS, D. (1999). *Evolutionary psychology: The new science of the mind.* Needham Heights, MA: Allyn & Bacon.

BUSS, D. (2000). *The dangerous passion: Why jealousy is as necessary as love and sex.* New York: Free Press.

BUSS, D., SHACKELFORD, T. K., KIRKPATRICK, L. A., CHOE, J. C., LIM, H. K., HASEGAWA, M., HASEGAWA, T., & BENNETT, K. (1999). Jealousy and the nature of beliefs about infidelity: Tests of competing hypotheses about sex differences in the United States, Korea, and Japan. *Personal Relationships, 61,* 125–150.

BUSS, D. M. (1988). The evolution of human intrasexual competition: Tactics of mate attraction. *Journal of Personality and Social Psychology, 54,* 616–628.

BUSS, D. M. (1989). Sex differences in human mate preferences: Evolutionary hypotheses testing in 37 cultures. *Behavioral and Brain Sciences, 12,* 1–49.

BUSS, D. M. (1991). Evolutionary personality psychology. *Annual Review of Psychology, 42,* 459–491.

BUSS, D. M. (1994a). *The evolution of desire: Strategies of human mating.* New York: Basic Books.

BUSS, D. M. (1994b). Personality evoked: The evolutionary psychology of stability and change. In T. F. Heatherton & J. Weinberger (Eds.), *Can personality change?* Washington DC: APA Press.

BUSS, D. M. (2003). *The evolution of desire: Strategies of human mating* (rev. ed.). New York: Basic Books.

BUSS, D. M., & BARNES, M. (1986). Preferences in human mate selection. *Journal of Personality and Social Psychology, 50,* 559–570.

BUSS, D. M., & KENRICK, D. T. (1998). Evolutionary social psychology. In D. T. Gilbert, S. T. Fiske, & G. Lindzey (Eds.), *Handbook of social psychology,* Vol 2 (4th ed., pp. 982–1026). Boston: McGraw-Hill.

BUSS, D. M., LARSEN, R. J., WESTERN, D., & SEMMELROTH, J. (1992). Sex differences in jealousy: Evolution, physiology, and psychology. *Psychological Science, 3,* 251–255.

BUSS, D. M., & SCHMIDT, D. P. (1993). Sexual strategies theory: An evolutionary perspective on human mating. *Psychological Review, 100,* 204–232.

BUSS, D. M., & SHACKELFORD, T. K. (1997). Human aggression in evolutionary psychological perspective. *Clinical Psychology Reviews, 17,* 605–619.

BUTLER, J. M., & HAIGH, G. V. (1954). Changes in the relation between self-concepts and ideal concepts consequent upon client centered counseling. In C. R. Rogers & R. F. Dymond (Eds.), *Psychotherapy and personality change: Coordinated studies in the client-centered approach* (pp. 55–76). Chicago: University of Chicago Press.

BUTTERFIELD, E. L., & SIPERSTEIN, G. N. (1972). Influence of contingent auditory stimulation on nonnutritional sucking. In J. Bosma (Ed.), *Oral sensation and perception: The mouth of the infant.* Springfield, IL: Charles B. Thomas.

CABANAC, M. (1979). Sensory pleasure. *Quarterly Review of Biology, 54,* 1–29.

CABANAC, M. (1992). Pleasure: The common currency. *Journal of Theoretical Biology, 155,* 173–200.

CACIOPPO, J. T., BERNTSON, G. G., LARSEN, J. T., POEHLMANN, K. M., & ITO, T. A. (2000). The psychophysiology of emotion. In M. Lewis & J. M. Haviland-Jones (Eds.), *Handbook of emotions* (2nd ed., pp. 173–191). New York: Guilford.

CACIOPPO, J. T., KLEIN, D. J., BEMSTON, G. G., & HATFIELD, E. (1993). The psychophysiology of emotion. In M. Lewis & J. M. Haviland (Eds.), *The handbook of emotions.* New York: Guilford.

CADORET, R. J., & CAIN, C. A. (1980). Sex differences in predictors of antisocial behavior in adoptees. *Archives of General Psychiatry, 37,* 1171–1175.

CAHILL, L., BABINSKY, R., MARKOWITSCH, H. J., & MCGAUGH, J. L. (1996). The amygdala and emotional memory. *Nature, 377,* 295–296.

CAHILL, L., PRINS, B., WEBER, M., & MCGAUGH, J. L. (1994). Adrenergic activation and memory for emotional events. *Nature, 371,* 702–704.

CAIN, W. S. (1988). Olfaction. In R. C. Atkinson, R. J. Hernstein, G. Lindzey, & R. D. Luce (Eds.), *Stevens' handbook of experimental psychology* (Vol. 1, pp. 409–459). New York: Wiley.

CALLAWAY, M. R., MARRIOTT, R. G., & ESSER, J. K. (1985). Effects of dominance on group decision making: Toward a stress-reduction explanation of group-think. *Journal of Personality and Social Psychology, 49,* 949–952.

CAMPOS, J. J., BARRETT, K. C., LAMB, M. E., GOLDSMITH, H. H., & STENBERG, C. (1983). Socioemotional development. In P. Mussen (Ed.), *Handbook of child psychology* (Vol. 1, pp. 1–101). New York: Wiley.

CANINO G. J., BURNAM, A., & CAETANO, R. (1992). The prevalence of alcohol abuse and/or dependence in two Hispanic Communities. In J. E. Helzer & G. J. Canino (Eds.), *Alcoholism in North America, Europe & Asia* (pp. 131–155). New York: Oxford University Press.

CANNON, W. B. (1927). The James-Lange theory of emotions: A critical examination and an alternative theory. *American Journal of Psychology, 39,* 106–124.

CAPLAN, D., & WATERS, G. (2002). Working memory and connectionist models of parsing: A reply to MacDonald and Christiansen. *Psychological-Review, 109,* 66–74.

CARAMAZZA, A. (2000). The organization of conceptual knowledge in the brain. In M. S. Gazzaniga (Ed.), *The new cognitive neurosciences.* Cambridge: MIT Press.

CARAMAZZA, A., & ZURIF, E. B. (1976). Dissociation of algorithmic and heuristic processes in language comprehension: Evidence from aphasia. *Brain and Language, 3,* 572–582.

CARDNO, A. G., O'DONOVAN, M. C., & OWEN, M. J. (2000). Genetic risk factors for depression. *International Journal of Mental Health, 29,* 13 38.

CARDON, L. R., FULKER, D. W., DEFRIES, J. C., & PLOMIN, R. (1992). Continuity and change in general cognitive ability from 1 to 7 years of age. *Developmental Psychology, 28,* 64–73.

CARDOZO, B. L., VERGARA, A., AGAIN, F., & COTWAY, C. A. (2000). Mental health, social functioning, and attitudes of Kosovar Albanians following the war in Kosovo. *Journal of the American Medical Association, 284,* 569–577.

CAREY, G. & GOLDMAN, D. (1997). The genetics of antisocial behavior. In D. M. Stoff, J. Breiling, & J. D. Maser (Eds.), *Handbook of Antisocial Personality Disorder* (pp. 243–254). New York: Wiley.

CARLSON, N. R. (1994). *Physiology of behavior* (5th ed.). Boston: Allyn and Bacon.

CARLSON, N. R. (1998). *Foundations of physiological psychology* (4th ed.). Boston: Allyn and Bacon.

CARLSON, N. R. (2001). *Physiology of behavior* (7th ed.). Boston: Allyn and Bacon.

CARLSON, R. (1971). Where is the person in personality research? *Psychological Bulletin, 75,* 203–219.

CARLSON, W. R. (1986). *Physiology of behavior* (3rd ed.). Boston: Allyn and Bacon.

CARMICHAEL, L., HOGAN, H. P., & WALTER, A. A. (1932). An experimental study of the effect of language on the reproduction of visually perceived form. *Journal of Experimental Psychology, 15,* 73–86.

CARPENTER, P. A., JUST, M. A., & SHELL, P. (1990). What one intelligence test measures: A theoretical account of the processing in the Raven Progressive Matrices Test. *Psychological Review, 97,* 404–431.

CARROLL, D. W. (1985). *Psychology of language.* Monterey, CA: Brooks/Cole.

CARROLL, J. B. (1988). Individual differences in cognitive functioning. In R. C. Atkinson, R. J. Herrnstein, G. Lindzey, & R. D. Luce (Eds.), *Stevens' handbook of experimental psychology* (Vol. 2). New York: Wiley.

CARROLL, J. B. (1993). *Human cognitive abilities: A survey of factor-analytic studies.* New York: Cambridge University Press.

CARSKADON, M. A., MITLER, M. M., & DEMENT, W. C. (1974). A comparison of insomniacs and normals: Total sleep time and sleep latency. *Sleep Research, 3,* 130.

CARTER, M. M., HOLLON, S. D., CARON, R. S., & SHELTON, R. C. (1995). Effects of a safe person on induced distress following a biological challenge in panic disorder with agoraphobia. *Journal of Abnormal Psychology, 104,* 156–163.

CARTERETTE, E. C., & FRIEDMAN, M. P. (Eds.). (1974–1978). *Handbook of perception* (Vols. 1–11). New York: Academic Press.

CARTWRIGHT, R. (1978, December). Happy endings for our dreams. *Psychology Today,* pp. 66–67.

CARTWRIGHT, R. (1992). Masochism in dreaming and its relation to depression. *Dreaming, 2,* 79–84.

CARTWRIGHT, R. (1996). Dreams and adaptation to divorce. In D. Barrett (Ed.), *Trauma and dreams.* Cambridge, MA: Harvard University Press.

CARTWRIGHT, R. D. (1974). The influence of a conscious wish on dreams. A methodological study of dream meaning and function. *Journal of Abnormal Psychology, 83,* 387–393.

CARVER, C. S., & SCHEIER, M. F. (1981). *Attention and self-regulation: A control-theory approach to human behavior.* New York: Springer-Verlag.

CARVER, C. S., & SCHEIER, M. F. (2000). *Perspectives on personality.* Boston: Allyn & Bacon.

CASE, R. (1985). *Intellectual development: A systematic reinterpretation.* New York: Academic Press.

CASE, R., & OKAMOTO, Y. (1996). The role of central conceptual structures in the development of children's thoughts. *Nomographs of the Society for Research in Child Development, 61,* 1–265.

CASE, R. B., HELLER, S. S., CASE, N. B., & MOSS, A. J. (1985). Type A behavior and survival after acute myocardial infarction. *New England Journal of Medicine, 312,* 737.

CASPI, A., & HERBENER, E. S. (1990). Continuity and change: Assortative marriage and the consistency of personality in adulthood. *Journal of Personality and Social Psychology, 58,* 250–258.

CASPI, A., & MOFFIT, T. E. (1991). Individual differences are accentuated during periods of social change: The sample case of girls at puberty. *Journal of Personality and Social Psychology, 61,* 157–168.

CATTELL, R. B. (1957). *Personality and motivation structure and measurement.* Yonkers-on-Hudson, NY: World.

CATTELL, R. B. (1966). *The scientific analysis of personality.* Chicago: Aldine.

CATTERALL, W. A. (2000). From ionic currents to molecular mechanisms: the structure and function of voltage-gated sodium channels. *Neuron, 26,* 13–25.

CAVALLERO, C., CICOGNA, P., NATALE, V., & OCCIONERO, M. (1992). Slow wave sleep dreaming. *Sleep, 15,* 562–566.

CECI, S. J. (1990). *On intelligence . . . more or less: A bio-ecological treatise on intellectual development.* Englewood Cliffs, NJ: Prentice-Hall.

CECI, S. J. (1996). *On intelligence: A bioecological treatise.* Cambridge, MA: Harvard University Press.

CECI, S. J., & BRUCK, M. (1993). The suggestibility of the child witness: A historical review and synthesis. *Psychological Bulletin, 113,* 403–409.

CECI, S. J., & ROAZZI, A. (1994). The effect of context on cognition: Postcards from Brazil. In R. J. Sternberg & R. K. Wagner (Eds.), *Mind in context: Interactionist perspectives on human intelligence.* Cambridge, England: Cambridge University Press.

CENTERS FOR DISEASE CONTROL. (1988). Health status of Vietnam veterans: Psychosocial characteristics. *Journal of the American Medical Association, 259,* 2701–2707.

CERNOCH, J. M., & PORTER, R. H. (1985). Recognition of maternal axillary odors by infants. *Child Development, 56,* 1593–1598.

CHAIKEN, S. (1980). Heuristic versus systematic information processing and the use of source versus message cues in persuasion. *Journal of Personality and Social Psychology, 39,* 752–766.

CHAIKEN, S. (1987). The heuristic model of persuasion. In M. P. Zanna, J. N. Olson, & C. P. Herman (Eds.), *Social influence: The Ontario symposium* (Vol. 5, pp. 3–39). Hillsdale, NJ: Erlbaum.

CHAIKEN, S., & TROPE, Y. (1999). *Dual-process theories in social psychology.* New York: Guilford.

CHAMBLESS, D. L., & HOLLON, S. D. (1998). Defining empirically supported therapies. *Journal of Consulting and Clinical Psychology, 66,* 7–18.

CHAMBLESS, D. L., & OLLENDECK, T. H. (2001). Empirically supported psychological interventions. *Annual Reviews of Psychology, 52,* 685–716.

CHAPMAN, L. J., & CHAPMAN, J. P. (1969). Illusory correlation as an obstacle to the use of valid psychodiagnostic signs. *Journal of Abnormal Psychology, 74,* 271–280.

CHARNEY, D. S., SOUTHWICK, S. M., KRYSTAL, J. H., DEUTCH, A. Y., MURBURG, M. M., & DAVIS, M. (1994). Neurobiological mechanisms of PTSD. In M. M. Murburg (Ed.), *Catecholamine function in posttraumatic stress disorder: Emerging concepts* (pp. 131–158). Washington DC: American Psychiatric Press.

CHASE, W. G., & SIMON, H. A. (1973a). The mind's eye in chess. In W. G. Chase (Ed.), *Visual information processing.* New York: Academic Press.

CHASE, W. G., & SIMON, H. A. (1973b). Perception in chess. *Cognitive Psychology, 4,* 55–81.

CHAUDURI, H. (1965). *Philosophy of meditation.* New York: Philosophical Library.

CHELAZZI, L., DUNCAN, J., MILLER, E. K., & DESIMONE, R. (1998). Responses of neurons in inferior temporal cortex during memory guided visual search. *Journal of Neurophysiology, 80,* 2818–2940.

CHEN, M., & BARGH, J. A. (1997). Nonconscious behavioral confirmation processes: The self-fulfilling consequences of automatic stereotype activation. *Journal of Experimental Social Psychology, 33,* 541–560.

CHEN, S., & ANDERSEN, S. M. (1999). Relationships from the past in the present: Significant-other representations and transference in interpersonal life. *Advances in Experimental Social Psychology, 31,* 123–190.

CHEN, S., & CHAIKEN, S. (1999). The heuristic-systematic model in its broader context. In S. Chaiken & Y. Trope (Eds.), *Dual-process theories in social psychology* (pp. 73–96). New York: Guilford.

CHEN, S. C. (1937). Social modification of the activity of ants in nest-building. *Physiological Zoology, 10,* 420–436.

CHEN, X. H., GELLER, E. B., & ADLER, M. W. (1996). Electrical stimulation at traditional acupuncture sites in periphery produces brain opioid-receptor-mediated antinociception in rats. *Journal of Pharmacology and Experimental Therapy, 277,* 654–660.

CHENG, P. W., HOLYOAK, K. J., NISBETT, R. E., & OLIVER, L. (1986). Pragmatic versus syntactic approaches to training deductive reasoning. *Cognitive Psychology, 18,* 293–328.

CHERNISS, C. (2000). Social and emotional competence in the workplace. In R. Bar-On & J. D. A. Parker (Eds.), *The handbook of emotional intelligence.* San Francisco: Jossey-Bass.

CHERRY, E. C. (1953). Some experiments on the recognition of speech with one and with two ears. *Journal of the Acoustical Society, 25,* 975–979.

CHESS, S., & THOMAS, A. (1984). *Origins and evolution of behavior disorders: Infancy to early adult life.* New York: Brunner/Mazel.

CHI, M. (1978). Knowledge structures and memory development. In R. S. Siegler (Ed.), *Children's thinking: What develops?* Hillsdale, NJ: Erlbaum.

CHI, M., GLASER, R., & REES, E. (1982). Expertise in problem solving. In R. Sternberg (Ed.), *Advances in the psychology of human intelligence* (Vol. 1). Hillsdale, NJ: Erlbaum.

CHOCOLLE, R. (1940). Variations des temps de réaction auditifs en fonction de l'intensité à diverses fréquences. *Année Psychologique, 41,* 65–124.

CHOI, I., NISBETT, R. E., & NORENZAYAN, A. (1999). Causal attribution across cultures: Variation and universality. *Psychological Bulletin, 125,* 47–63.

CHOMSKY, N. (1957). *Syntactic structures.* Hague: Mouton.

CHOMSKY, N. (1965). *Aspects of the theory of syntax.* Cambridge, MA: MIT Press.

CHOMSKY, N. (1972). *Language and mind* (2nd ed.). New York: Harcourt Brace Jovanovich.

CHOMSKY, N. (1980). *Rules and representations.* New York: Columbia University Press.

CHOMSKY, N. (1991, March). Quoted in Discover.

CHORNEY, M. J., CHORNEY, K., SEESE, N., OWEN, M. J., DANIELS, J., MCGUFFIN, P., THOMPSON, L. A., DETTERMAN, D. K., BENBOW, C., LUBINSKI, D., ELEY, T., & PLOMIN, R. (1998). A quantitative trait locus associated with cognitive ability in children. *Psychological Science, 13,* 159–166.

CHRISTIE, R., & JOHODA, M. (Eds.). (1954). *Studies in the scope and method of "the authoritarian personality."* New York: Free Press.

CHURCHLAND, P. M. (1995) *The engine of reason, the seat of the soul.* Cambridge, MA: MIT Press.

CHURCHLAND, P. S., & SEJNOWSKI, T. J. (1988). Perspectives on cognitive neuroscience. *Science, 242,* 741–745.

CLARK, D. A., & DESILVA, P. (1985). The nature of depressive and anxious, intrusive thoughts: Distinct or uniform phenomena? *Behaviour Research and Therapy, 23,* 383–393.

CLARK, D. A., & PURDON, C. (1993). New perspectives for a cognitive theory of obsessions. *Australian Psychologist, 28,* 161–167.

CLARK, D. M. (1988). A cognitive model of panic attacks. In S. Rachman & J. D. Maser (Eds.), *Panic: Psychological perspectives.* Hillsdale, NJ: Erlbaum.

CLARK, D. M., SALKOVSKIS, P. M., HACKMANN, A., MIDDLETON, H., & collaborators. (1994). A comparison of cognitive therapy, applied relaxation, and imipramine in the treatment of panic disorder. *British Journal of Psychiatry, 164,* 759–769.

CLARK, E. V. (1983). Meanings and concepts. In P. H. Mussen (Ed.), *Handbook of child psychology* (Vol. 3). New York: Wiley.

CLARK, H. H. (1984). Language use and language users. In G. Lindzey & E. Aronson (Eds.), *The handbook of social psychology* (Vol. 2, 3rd ed.). New York: Harper & Row.

CLARK, H. H., & CLARK, E. V. (1977). *Psychology and language: An introduction to psycholinguistics.* New York: Harcourt Brace Jovanovich.

CLARK, R. D., & HATFIELD, E. (1989). Gender differences in receptivity to sexual offers. *Journal of Psychology and Human Sexuality, 2,* 39–55.

CLARKE-STEWART, K. A. (1973). Interactions between mothers and their young children: Characteristics and consequences. *Monographs of the Society for Research in Child Development, 38* (6 & 7, Serial No. 153).

CLARKE-STEWART, K. A. (1989). Infant day care: Maligned or malignant? *American Psychologist, 44,* 266–273.

CLONINGER, C. R., & GOTTESMAN, I. I. (1987). Genetic and environmental factors in antisocial behavior disorders. In S. A. Mednick, T. E. Moffitt, & S. A. Stack (Eds.), *The causes of crime: New biological approaches* (pp. 92–109). New York: Cambridge University Press.

CLONINGER, C. R., SYRAKIC, D. M., & PRZYBECK, T. R. (1993). A psychobiological model of temperament and character. *Archives of General Psychiatry, 50,* 975–990.

CLORE, G. L., GASPER, K., & GARVIN, E. (2001). Affect as information. In J. P. Forgas (Ed.), *Handbook of affect and social cognition* (pp. 121–144). Mahwah, NJ: Erlbaum.

COHEN, C. E. (1981). Person categories and social perception: Testing some boundaries of the processing effects of prior knowledge. *Journal of Personality and Social Psychology, 40,* 441–452.

COHEN, D., & NISBETT, R. E. (1994). Self-protection and culture of honor: Explaining Southern violence. *Personality and Social Psychology Bulletin, 20,* 551–567.

COHEN, J. D., AARCH, D. M., CARTER, C., & SERVAN SCHREIBER, D. (1999). Context processing deficits in schizophrenia: Converging evidence from three theoretically motivated cognitive tasks. *Journal of Abnormal Psychology, 108,* 120–133.

COHEN, N. J., & SQUIRE, L. R. (1980). Preserved learning and retention of pattern analyzing skill in amnesia: Dissociation of knowing how and knowing that. *Science, 210,* 207–209.

COHEN, S. (1980, September). *Training to understand TV advertising: Effects and some policy implications.* Paper presented at the American Psychological Association convention, Montreal.

COHEN, S. (1996). Psychological stress, immunity, and upper respiratory infections. *Current Directions in Psychological Science, 5,* 86–90.

COHEN, S., & EDWARDS, J. R. (1989). Personality characteristics as moderators of the relationship between stress and disorder. In R. J. Neufeld (Ed.), *Advances in the investigation of psychological stress* (pp. 235–283). New York: Wiley.

COHEN, S., TYRRELL, D. A. J., & SMITH, A. P. (1991). Psychological stress and susceptibility to the common cold. *New England Journal of Medicine, 325,* 606–612.

COLAS, E. (1998). *Just checking: Scenes from the life of an obsessive-compulsive.* New York: Pocket Books.

COLBY, A., KOHLBERG, L., GIBBS, J., & LIEBERMAN, M. A. (1983). A longitudinal study of moral judgment. *Monographs of the Society for Research in Child Development, 48,* 1–2.

COLBY, C. L., & GOLDBERG, M. E. (1999). Space and attention in parietal cortex. *Annual Review of Neuroscience, 22,* 319–349.

COLE, M., & COLE, S. R. (1993). *The development of children* (2nd ed.) New York: Scientific American Books.

COLE, M., & COLE, S. R. (2001). *The development of children.* New York: Worth.

COLE, P. M., ZAHN-WAXLER, C., & SMITH, K. D. (1994). Expressive control during a disappointment: Variations related to preschoolers' behavior problems. *Developmental Psychology, 30,* 835–846.

COLE, S. W., KEMENY, M. E., TAYLOR, S. E., VISSCHER, B. R., & FAHEY, J. L. (1995). Accelerated course of human immunodeficiency virus infection in gay men who conceal their homosexual identity. *Psychosomatic Medicine, 58,* 219–238.

COLE, S. W., KEMENY, M. E., TAYLOR, S. E., & VISSCHER, B. R. (1996). Elevated physical health risk among gay men who conceal their homosexual identity. *Health Psychology, 15,* 243–251.

COLEGROVE, F. W. (1899). Individual memories. *American Journal of Psychology, 10,* 228–255.

COLLINS, A. M., & LOFTUS, E. G. (1975). A spreading-activation theory of semantic processing. *Psychological Review, 82,* 407–428.

COLTHEART, M. (1980). Iconic memory and visible persistence. *Perception and Psychophysics, 27,* 183–228.

COMREY, A. L., & LEE, H. B. (1992). *A first course in factor analysis* (2nd ed.). Hillsdale, NJ: Erlbaum.

CONKLIN, H. M. & IACONO, W. G. (2002). Schizophrenia: A neurodevelopmental perspective. *Current directions in Psychological Science, 11,* 33–37.

CONRAD, R. (1964). Acoustic confusions in immediate memory. *British Journal of Psychology, 55,* 75–84.

COOPER, L. A., & SHEPARD, R. N. (1973). Chronometric studies of the rotation of mental images. In W. G. Chase (Ed.), *Visual information processing.* New York: Academic Press.

COOPER, L. M. (1979). Hypnotic amnesia. In E. Fromm & R. E. Shor (Eds.), *Hypnosis: Developments in research and new perspectives* (Rev. Ed.). New York: Aldine.

CORBETTA, M., MIEZIN, F. M., DOBMEYER, S., SCHULMAN, G. L., & PETERSON, S. E. (1990). Attentional modulation of neural processing of shape, color, and velocity in humans. *Science, 248,* 1556–1559.

CORBETTA, M., MIEZIN, F. M., SHULMAN, G. I., & PETERSEN, S. E. (1991). Selective attention modulates extrastriate visual regions in humans during visual feature discrimination and recognition. In D. J. Chadwick & J. Whelan (Eds.), *Ciba Foundation symposium 163: Exploring brain functional anatomy with positron tomography* (pp. 165–180). Chichester, England: Wiley.

CORBETTA, M., MIEZIN, F. M., SHULMAN, G. I., & PETERSEN, S. E. (1993). A PET study of visuospatial attention. *Journal of Neuroscience, 13,* 1202–1226.

COREN, S. (1992). The moon illusion: A different view through the legs. *Perceptual and Motor Skills, 75,* 827–831.

COREN, S., & GIRGUS, J. S. (1980). Principles of perceptual organization and spatial distortion: The gestalt illusions. *Journal of Experimental Psychology: Human Perception and Performance, 6,* 404–412.

COREN, S., WARD, L. M., & ENNS, J. T. *Sensation and perception* (5th ed.). Fort Worth: Harcourt Brace.

COSCINA, D. V., & DIXON, L. M. (1983). Body weight regulation in anorexia nervosa: Insights from an animal model. In F. L. Darby, P. E. Garfinkel, D. M. Garner, & D. V. COSCINA (Eds.),

Anorexia nervosa: Recent developments. New York: Allan R. Liss.

COSMIDES, L. (1989). The logic of social exchange: Has natural selection shaped how we reason? *Cognition, 31,* 187–276.

COSMIDES, L., & TOOBY, J. (1989). Evolutionary psychology and the generation of culture, part II. *Ethology and Sociobiology, 10,* 51–97.

COSTELLO, C., & STONE, A. (Eds.). (2001). *The American Woman, 2001–02.* New York: Norton.

COTT, J. M., & FUGH-BERMAN, A. (1998). Is St. John's wort (*Hypericum perforatum*) an effective antidepressant? *Journal of Nervous and Mental Disease, 186,* 500–501.

COTTRELL, N. B. (1972). Social facilitation. In C. G. McClintock (Ed.), *Experimental social psychology.* New York: Holt, Rinehart & Winston.

COTTRELL, N. B., RITTLE, R. H., & WACK, D. L. (1967). Presence of an audience and list type (competitional or noncompetitional) as joint determinants of performance in paired-associates learning. *Journal of Personality, 25,* 425–434.

COTTRELL, N. B., WACK, D. L., SEKERAK, G. J., & RITTLE, R. H. (1968). Social facilitation of dominant responses by the presence of an audience and the mere presence of others. *Journal of Personality and Social Psychology, 9,* 245–250.

COURAGE, M. L., & ADAMS, R. J. (1990a). Visual acuity assessment from birth to three years using the acuity card procedures: Cross-sectional and longitudinal samples. *Optometry and Vision Science, 67,* 713–718.

COURAGE, M. L., & ADAMS, R. J. (1990b). The early development of visual acuity in the binocular and monocular peripheral fields. *Infant Behavioral Development, 13,* 123–128.

COURTRIGHT, J. A. (1978). A laboratory investigation of groupthink. *Communications Monographs, 43,* 229–246.

COUSINS, S. D. (1989). Culture and self-perception in Japan and the U.S. *Journal of Personality and Social Psychology, 56,* 124–131.

CRAIGHEAD, L. W., STUNKARD, A. J., & O'BRIEN, R. M. (1981). Behavior therapy and pharmacotherapy for obesity. *Archives of General Psychiatry, 38,* 763–768.

CRAIK, F. I. M., & TULVING, E. (1975). Depth of processing and the retention of words in episodic memory. *Journal of Experimental Psychology: General, 104,* 268–294.

CRANO, W. D., & CHEN, X. (1998). The leniency contract and persistence of majority and minority influence. *Journal of Personality and Social Psychology, 74,* 1437–1450.

CRARY, W. G. (1966). Reactions to incongruent self experiences. *Journal of Consulting Psychology, 30,* 246–252.

CRASILNECK, H. B., & HALL, J. A. (1985). *Clinical hypnosis: Principles and applications* (2nd ed.). Orlando, FL: Grune & Stratton.

CRASKE, M. G., & BARLOW, D. H. (2001). Panic disorder and agoraphobia. *Clinical handbook of psychological disorders: a step-by-step treatment manual* (3rd ed., pp. 1–59). New York: Guilford.

CREWS, F. C. (Ed.). (1998). *Unauthorized Freud: Doubters confront a legend.* New York: Viking.

CRICK, F. (1994). *The astonishing hypothesis: The scientific search for the soul.* New York: Macmillan.

CRICK, F., & MITCHINSON, G. (1983). The function of dream sleep. *Nature, 304,* 111–114.

CRICK, N. R., & DODGE, K. A. (1994). A review and reformulation of social information-processing mechanisms in children's social adjustment. *Psychological Bulletin, 115,* 74–101.

CRITS-CHRISTOPH, P., COOPER, A., & LUBORSKY, L. (1990). The measurement of accuracy of interpretations. In L. Luborsky & P. Crits-Christoph (Eds.), *Understanding transference: The CCRT method* (pp. 173–188). New York: Basic Books.

CROMWELL, P. F., MARKS, A., OLSON, J. N., & AVARY, D. W. (1991). Group effects on decision-making by burglars. *Psychological Reports, 69,* 579–588.

CROSBY, A. E., CHELTENHAM, M. P., & SACKS, J. J. (1999). Incidence of suicidal ideation and behavior in the United States, 1994. *Suicide and Life-Threatening Behavior, 29,* 131–140.

CROSBY, F., & CORDOVA, D. I. (1996). Words worth of wisdom. *Journal of Social Issues, 52,* 33–49.

CROSS, S. E., & MARKUS, H. R. (1999). The cultural constitution of personality. In L. A. Pervin & O. P. John (Eds.), *Handbook of personality: theory and research* (pp. 378–398). New York: Guilford Press.

CROYLE, R. T., SUN, Y., & HART, M. (1997). Processing risk factor information: Defensive biases in health-related cognitions. In J. A. Petrie & J. A. Weinman (Eds.), *Perceptions of health and illness: Current research and applications* (pp. 267–290). Singapore: Harwood Academic.

CURCI, A., LUMINET, O., FINKENAUER, C., & GISLE, L. (2001). Flashbulb memories in social groups: A comparative test-retest study of the memory of French President Mitterrand's death in a French and a Belgian group. *Memory, 9,* 81–101.

CURTISS, S. (1977). *Genie: A psycholinguistic study of a modern-day "wild child."* New York: Academic Press.

CURTISS, S. (1989). The independence and task-specificity of language. In M. H. Bornstein & J. S. Bruner (Eds.), *Interaction in human development.* Hillsdale, NJ: Erlbaum.

CUTLER, W. B., PRETI, G., KRIEGER, A., HUGGINS, G. R., GARCIA, C. R., & LAWLEY, H. J. (1986). Human axillary secretions influence women's menstrual cycles: The role of donor extract from men. *Hormones and Behavior, 20,* 463–473.

CUTTING, J. E. (1986). *Perception with an eye for motion.* Cambridge, MA: MIT Press.

CYANDER, M., TIMNEY, B. N., & MITCHELL, D. E. (1980). Period of susceptibility of kitten visual cortex to the effects of monocular deprivation extends beyond 6 months of age. *Brain Research, 191,* 545–550.

DABBS, J. M., & MORRIS, R., JR. (1990). Testosterone, social class, and antisocial behavior in a sample of 4,462 men. *Psychological Science, 1,* 209–211.

DALE, A. J. D. (1975). Organic brain syndromes associated with infections. In A. M., Freeman, H. I. Kaplan, & B. J. Sadock (Eds.), *Comprehensive textbook of psychiatry* (Vol. 2, pp. 1121–1130). Baltimore, MD: Williams & Wilkins.

DALY, M., & WILSON, M. I. (1990). Killing the competition: Female/female and male/male homicide. *Human Nature, 1,* 81–107.

DAMASIO, A. R. (1985). Disorders of complex visual processing: Agnosia, achromatopsia, Balint's syndrome, and related difficulties of orientation and construction. In M. M. Mesulam (Ed.), *Principles of behavioral neurology* (pp. 259–288). Philadelphia: F. A. Davis.

DAMASIO, A. R. (1990). Category related recognition defects as a clue to the neural substrates of knowledge. *Trends in Neurosciences, 13,* 95–98.

DAMASIO, A. R. (1994). *Descartes' error.* New York: Putnam.

DAMASIO, H., GRABOWSKI, T., FRANK, R., GALABURDA, A. M., & DAMASIO, A. R. (1994). The return of Phineas Gage: Clues about the brain from the skull of a famous patient. *Science, 264,* 1102–1105.

DAMON, W. (1977). *The social world of the child.* San Francisco: Jossey-Bass.

DAMON, W. (1983). *Social and personality development.* New York: Norton.

DANEMAN, M., & CARPENTER, P. A. (1980). Individual differences in working memory and reading. *Journal of Verbal Learning and Verbal Behavior, 19,* 450–466.

DANNER, D. D., SNOWDON, D. A., & FRIESEN, W. V. (2001). Positive emotions in early life and longevity: Findings from the nun study. *Journal of Personality and Social Psychology, 80,* 804–813.

DARIAN-SMITH, I. (Ed.). (1984). *Handbook of physiology: The nervous system:* Section 1, Vol. 3. *Sensory processes.* Bethesda, MD: American Physiological Society.

DARLEY, C. F., TINKLENBERG, J. R., ROTH, W. T., HOLLISTER, L. E., & ATKINSON, R. C. (1973a). Influence of marijuana on storage and retrieval processes in memory. *Memory and Cognition, 1,* 196–200.

DARLEY, C. F., TINKLENBERG, J. R., ROTH, W. T., HOLLISTER, L. E., & ATKINSON, R. C. (1973b). Marijuana and retrieval from short-term memory. *Psychopharmacologia, 29,* 231–238.

DARLEY, C. F., TINKLENBERG, J. R., ROTH, W. T., VERNON, S., & KOPELL, B. S. (1977). Marijuana effects on long-term memory assessment and retrieval. *Psychopharmacology, 52,* 239–241.

DARLEY, J. M., & LATANÉ, B. (1968). Bystander intervention in emergencies: Diffusion of responsibility. *Journal of Personality and Social Psychology, 8,* 377–383.

DARWIN, C. (1872/1998). *The expression of the emotions in man and animals.* New York: Oxford University Press.

DARWIN, C. (1859). *On the origin of the species.* London: Murray.

DARWIN, C. (1872). *The expression of emotion in man and animals.* New York: Philosophical Library.

DASHIELL, J. F. (1930). An experimental analysis of some group effects. *Journal of Abnormal and Social Psychology, 25,* 190–199.

DASHIELL, J. F. (1935). Experimental studies of the influence of social situations on the behavior of individual human adults. In C. Murchison (Ed.), *Handbook of social psychology.* Worcester, MA: Clark University.

DAVIDSON, J. (1989). Sexual emotions, hormones, and behavior. *Advances, 6,* 56–58.

DAVIDSON, K., & PRKACHIN, K. (1997). Optimism and unrealistic optimism have an interacting effort on health-promoting behavior and knowledge changes. *Personality and Social Psychology Bulletin, 23,* 617–625.

DAVIDSON, R. J., PUTNAM, K. M., & LARSON, C. L. (2000). Dysfunction in the neural circuitry of emotion regulation—A possible prelude to violence. *Science, 289,* 591–594.

DAVIS, C. G., NOLEN-HOEKSEMA, S., & LARSON, J. (1998). Making sense of loss and benefiting from the experience: Two construals of meaning. *Journal of Personality and Social Psychology, 75,* 561–574.

DAVIS, K. L., KAHN, R. S., KO, G., & DAVIDSON, M. (1991). Dopamine in schizophrenia: A review and conceptualization. *American Journal of Psychiatry, 148,* 1474–1486.

DE WAAL, F. B. M. (1996). *Good natured: The origins of right and wrong in humans and other animals.* Cambridge, MA: Harvard University Press.

DE WIT, H., KIRK, J. M., & JUSTICE, A. (1998). Behavioral pharmacology of cannabinoids. In R. E. Tarter (Ed.), *Handbook of substance abuse: Neurobehavioral pharmacology.* (pp. 131–146). New York: Plenum.

DEAKIN, J. W., & GRAEFF, F. G. (1991). 5-HT and mechanisms of defense. *Journal of Psychopharmacology, 5,* 305–315.

DEARY, I. (1992). Multiple minds. *Science, 259,* 28.

DEARY, I. J., WHALLEY, L. J., LEMMON, H., CRAWFORD, J. R., & STARR, J. M. (2000). The stability of individual differences in mental ability from childhood to old age: Follow-up of the 1932 Scottish Mental Survey. *Intelligence, 28,* 49–55.

DEAUX, K. (1984). From individual differences to social categories: Analysis of a decade's research on gender. *American Psychologist, 39,* 105–116.

DECASPER, A. J., & FIFER, W. P. (1980). Of human bonding: Newborns prefer their mothers' voices. *Science, 208,* 1174–1176.

DECASPER, A. J., & PRESCOTT, P. A. (1984). Human newborns' perception of male voices: Preference, discrimination and reinforcing value. *Developmental Psychobiology, 17,* 481–491.

DECASPER, A. J., & SPENCE, M. J. (1986). Prenatal maternal speech influences newborns' perception of speech sounds. *Infant Behavior and Development, 9,* 133–150.

DEFFENBACHER, K. (1980). Eyewitness accuracy and confidence: Can we infer anything about their relationship? *Law and Human Behavior, 4,* 243–260.

DEHART, G. B., SROUFE, L. A., & COOPER, R. G. (2000). *Child Development: Its Nature and Course.* Boston: McGraw Hill.

DEIKMAN, A. J. (1963). Experimental meditation. *Journal of Nervous and Mental Disease, 136,* 329–373.

DEMBROSKI, T. M., MACDOUGALL, J. M., WILLIAMS, B., & HANEY, T. L. (1985). Components of type A hostility and anger: Relationship to angiographic findings. *Psychosomatic Medicine, 47,* 219–233.

DEMENT, W. C., & KLEITMAN, N. (1957). The relation of eye movements during sleep to dream activity: An objective method for the study of dreaming. *Journal of Experimental Psychology, 53,* 339–346.

DEMENT, W. C., & WOLPERT, E. (1958). The relation of eye movements, bodily mobility, and external stimuli to dream content. *Journal of Experimental Psychology, 55,* 543–553.

DENNIS, W., & DENNIS, M. (1940). The effects of cradling practices upon the onset of walking in Hopi children. *Journal of Genetic Psychology, 56,* 77–86.

DEPUE, R. A., & COLLINS, P. F. (1999). Neurobiology of the structure of personality: Dopamine, facilitation of incentive motivation and extraversion. *Behavioral and Brain Sciences, 22,* 491–569.

DERRYBERRY, D., & TUCKER, D. M. (1994). Motivating the focus of attention. In P. M. Neidenthal & S. Kitayama (Eds.), *The heart's eye: Emotional influences in perception and attention* (pp. 167–196). San Diego: Academic Press.

DERUBEIS, R. J., & CRITS-CHRISTOPH, P. (1998). Empirically supported individual and group psychological treatments for adult mental disorders. *Journal of Abnormal Psychology, 101,* 371–382.

DESFORGES, D. M., LORD, C. G., RAMSEY, S. L., MASON, J. A., VAN LEEUWEN, M. D., WEST, S. C., & LEPPER, M. R. (1991). Effects of structured cooperative contact on changing negative attitudes toward stigmatized social groups. *Journal of Personality and Social Psychology, 60,* 531–544.

DEVALOIS, R. L., & DEVALOIS, K. K. (1980). Spatial vision. *Annual Review of Psychology, 31,* 309–341.

DEVALOIS, R. L., & JACOBS, G. H. (1984). Neural mechanisms of color vision. In I. Darian-Smith (Ed.), *Handbook of physiology* (Vol. 3). Bethesda, MD: American Physiological Society.

DEVINE, P. G. (1989). Stereotypes and prejudice: Their automatic and controlled components. *Journal of Personality and Social Psychology, 56,* 5–18.

DEVINE, P. G., & MONTEITH, M. J. (1999). Automaticity and control in stereotyping. In S. Chaiken & Y. Trope (Eds.), *Dual-process theories in social psychology* (pp. 339–360). New York: Guilford.

DEVINE, P. G., PLANT, E. A., AMODIO, D. M., HARMON-JONES, E., & VANCE, S. L. (2002). The regulation of explicit and implicit race bias: The role of motivations to respond without prejudice. *Journal of Personality and Social Psychology, 82,* 835–848.

DIJKSTERHUIS, A., & BARGH, J. A. (2002). The perception-behavior expressway: Automatic effects of social perception on social behavior. In M. Zanna (Ed.), *Advances in Experimental Social Psychology, 33,* 1–40.

DI LOLLO, V. (1980). Temporal Integration in Visual Memory. *Journal of Experimental Psychology: General, 109,* 75–97.

DI LOLLO, V., KAWAHARA J., ZUVIC, S. M., & VISSER, T. A. W. (2001) The preattentive emperor has no clothes: A dynamic redressing. *Journal of Experimental Psychology: General, 130,* 479–492.

DIAMOND, M. (1982). Sexual identity, monozygotic twins reared in discordant sex roles and a BBC follow-up. *Archives of Sexual Behavior, 11,* 181–186.

DIAMOND, M., (1996). Prenatal predisposition and the clinical management of some pediatric conditions. *Journal of Sex and Marital Therapy, 22,* 139–147.

DIAMOND, M., & SIGMUNDSON, K. (1997). Sex reassignment at birth: Long-term review and clinical implications. *Archives of Pediatric Medicine, 151,* 298.

DIENER, E. (1977). Deindividuation: Causes and consequences. *Social Behavior and Personality, 5,* 143–155.

DIENER, E. (1979). Deindividuation, self-awareness, and disinhibition. *Journal of Personality and Social Psychology, 37,* 1160–1171.

DIENER, E. (1980). Deindividuation: The absence of self-awareness and self-regulation in group members. In P. B. Paulus (Ed.), *The psychology of group influence.* Hillsdale, NJ: Erlbaum.

DIENER, E., FRASER, S. C., BEAMAN, A. L., & KELEM, R. T. (1976). Effects of deindividuation variables on stealing among Halloween trick-or-treaters. *Journal of Personality and Social Psychology, 33,* 178–183.

DIENSTBIER, R. A. (1989). Arousal and physiological toughness: Implications for mental and physical health. *Psychological Review, 96,* 84–100.

DIGMAN, J. M., & INOUYE, J. (1986). Further specification of the five robust factors of personality. *Journal of Personality and Social Psychology, 50,* 116–123.

DILLBECK, M. C., & ORME-JOHNSON, D. W. (1987). Physiological differences between transcendental meditation and rest. *American Psychologist, 42,* 879–881.

DINGES, D. F., & BROUGHTON, R. J. (Eds.). (1989). *Sleep and alertness: Chronobiological, behavioral, and medical aspects of napping.* New York: Raven.

DIPIETRO, J. A. (2001). Fetal neurobehavioral assessment. In L. T. Singer (Ed.), *Biobehavioral assessment of the infant.* (pp. 43–80). New York: Guilford.

DISHION, T. J., & PATTERSON, G. R. (1997). The timing and severity of antisocial behavior: Three hypotheses within an ecological framework. In D. M. Stoff, J. Breiling, & J. D. Maser (Eds.), *Handbook of antisocial personality disorder* (pp. 205–217). New York: Wiley.

DIXON, J. F., & HOKIN, L. E. (1998). Lithium acutely inhibits and chronically up-regulates and stabilizes glutamate uptake by presynaptic nerve endings in mouse cerebral cortex. *Neurobiology, 95,* 8363–8368.

DOBB, E. (1995, November–December). The scents around us. *The Sciences, 29,* 46–53.

DOBELLE, W. H., MEADEJOVSKY, M. G., & GIRVIN, J. P. (1974). Artificial vision for the blind: Electrical stimulation of visual cortex offers hope for a functional prosthesis. *Science, 183,* 440–444.

DOLLARD, J., DOOB, L. W., MILLER, N. E., MOWRER, O. H., & SEARS, R. R. (1939). *Frustration and aggression.* New Haven, CT: Yale University Press.

DOMHOFF, G. W. (1985). *The mystique of dreams.* Berkeley: University of California Press.

DOMHOFF, G. W. (1996). *Finding meaning in dreams: A quantitative approach.* New York: Plenum.

DOMHOFF, G. W., & SCHNEIDER, A. (1998). *The quantitative study of dreams.* http://zzyx.ucsc.edu?~dreams/.

DOMJAN, M., & BURKHARD, B. (1986). *The principles of learning and behavior.* Monterey, CA: Brooks/Cole.

DOWLING, J. E., & BOYCOTT, B. B. (1966). Organization of the primate retina. *Proceedings of the Royal Society of London, Series b, 166,* 80–111.

DOYLE, A. C. (1892/1981). *The original illustrated Sherlock Holmes.* Secaucus, NJ: Castle Books. (Originally published in America by Harper & Bros. in McClure's Magazine, 1893).

DUCLAUX, R., & KENSHALO, D. R. (1980). Response characteristics of cutaneous warm fibers in the monkey. *Journal of Neurophysiology, 43,* 1–15.

DREVETS, W. C. (2000). Neuroimaging studies of mood disorders. *Biological Psychiatry, 48,* 813–829.

DREVETS, W. C., BURTON, H., VIDEEN, T. O., SNYDER, A. Z., SIMPSON, J. R., & RAICHLE, M. E. (1995). Blood flow changes in human somatosensory cortex during anticipated stimulation. *Nature, 373,* 249–252.

DREVETS, W. C., VIDEEN, T. O., PRICE, J. L., PRESKORN, S. H., CARMICHAEL, S. T., & RAICHLE, M. E. (1992). A functional anatomical study of unipolar depression. *Journal of Neuroscience, 12,* 3628–3641.

DRONKERS, N. F., REDFERN, B. B., & KNIGHT, R. T. (2000). The neural architecture of language disorders. In: M. S. Gazzaniga (Ed.), *The new cognitive neuroscience* (2nd ed., pp. 949–958). Cambridge, MA: MIT Press.

DUBOIS, D. L., BULL, C. A., SHERMAN, M. D., & ROBERTS, M. (1998). Self-esteem and adjustment in early adolescence: A social-contextual perspective. *Journal of Youth and Adolescence, 27,* 557–583.

DUJARDIN, K., GUERRIEN, A., & LECONTE, P. (1990). Sleep, brain activation and cognition. *Physiology and Behavior, 47,* 1271–1278.

DUNCAN, J., & HUMPHREYS, G. W. (1989). Visual search and stimulus similarity. *Psychological Review, 96,* 433–458.

DUNCAN, P. D., and collaborators. (1985). The effects of pubertal timing on body image, school behavior, and deviance. *Journal of Youth and Adolescence, 14,* 227–235.

DUNCAN, R. D., SAUNDERS, B. E., KILPATRICK, D. G., HANSON, R. F., & RESNICK, H. S. (1996). Childhood physical assault as a risk factor for PTSD, depression, and substance abuse: Findings from a national survey. *American Journal of Orthopsychiatry, 66,* 437–448.

DUTTON, D. G., & ARON, A. P. (1974). Some evidence for heightened sexual attraction under conditions of high anxiety. *Journal of Personality and Social Psychology, 30,* 510–517.

EAGLY, A. H., & CHAIKEN, S. (1984). Cognitive theories of persuasion. In L. Berkowitz (Ed.), *Advances in experimental social psychology* (Vol. 17, pp. 267–359). New York: Academic Press.

EAGLY, A. H., & WOOD, W. (1999). The origins of sex differences in human behavior: Evolved dispositions versus social roles. *American Psychologist, 54,* 408–423.

EATON, W. W., MOORTENSENK, P. B., HERRMAN, H., & FREEMAN, H. (1992). Long-term course of hospitalization for schizophrenia: risk for rehospitalization. *Schizophrenia Bulletin, 18,* 217–228.

EATON, W. W., THARA, R., FEDERMAN, E., & THIEN, A. (1998). Remission and relapse in schizophrenia: the Madras longitudinal study. *The Journal of Nervous and Mental Disease, 186,* 357–363.

EBBESEN, E., DUNCAN, B., & KONECNI, V. (1975). Effects of content of verbal aggression on future verbal aggression: A field experiment. *Journal of Experimental Psychology, 11,* 192–204.

EBBINGHAUS, H. (1885). *Uber das gedachthis.* Leipzig: Dunckes and Humbolt.

EDGAR, D. M., & DEMENT, W. C. (1992). Evidence for opponent processes in sleep/wake regulation. *Sleep Research, 20A,* 2.

EDMONDSON, A. (1999). Psychological safety and learning behavior in work teams. *Administrative Science Quarterly, 44,* 350–383.

EHLERS, A. (1995). A 1-year prospective study of panic attacks: Clinical course and factors associated with maintenance. *Journal of Abnormal Psychology, 104,* 164–172.

EHLERS, A., & BREUER, P. (1992). Increased cardiac awareness in panic disorder. *Journal of Abnormal Psychology, 101,* 371–382.

EHRHARDT, A. A., MEYER-BAHLBURG, H. F., ROSEN, L. R., FELDMAN, J. F., VERIDIANO, N. P., ELKIN, E. J., & MCEWEN, B. S. (1989). The development of gender-related behavior in females following prenatal exposure to diethylstibestrol (DES). *Hormones and Behavior, 23,* 526–541.

EIBL-EIBESFELDT, I. (1970). *Ethology: The biology of behavior* (E. Klinghammer, Trans.). New York: Holt, Rinehart & Winston.

EICH, J. E. (1980). The cue-dependent nature of state-dependent retrieval. *Memory and Cognition, 8,* 157–173.

EICHENBAUM, H. (2000). A cortical-hippocampal system for declarative memory. *Nature Reviews Neuroscience, 1,* 41–50.

EIMAS, P. D. (1975). Speech perception in early infancy. In L. B. Cohen & P. Salapatek (Eds.), *Infant perception: From sensation to cognition* (Vol. 2). New York: Academic Press.

EIMAS, P. D. (1985). The perception of speech in early infancy. *Scientific American, 252,* 46–52.

EISENBERG, N., CUMBERLAND, A., & SPINRAD, T. L. (1998). Parental socialization of emotion. *Psychological Inquiry, 9,* 241–273.

EKMAN, P. (1972). Universals and cultural differences in facial expressions of emotion. In J. Cole (Ed.), *Nebraska symposium on motivation, 1971*

(pp. 207–283). Lincoln: University of Nebraska Press.

EKMAN, P. (1982). *Emotion in the human face* (2nd ed.). New York: Cambridge University Press.

EKSTROM, R. B., FRENCH, J. W., & HARMAN, H. H. (1979). *Cognitive factors: Their identification and replication. Multivariate behavioral research monographs.* Fort Worth: Society for Multivariate Experimental Psychology.

EKSTROM, R. B., FRENCH, J. W., HARMAN, H. H., & DERMAN, D. (1976). *Manual for kit of factor-referenced cognitive tests, 1976.* Princeton, NJ: Educational Testing Service.

ELKIN, I. SHEA, T., WATKINS, J. T., IMBER, S. D., SOTSKY, S. M., COLLINS, J. F., GLASS, D. R., PILKONIS, P. A., LEBER, W. R., DOCHERTY, J. P., FIESTER, S. J., & PARLOFF, M. B. (1989). National Institute of Mental Health treatment of depression collaborative research program: General effectiveness of treatments. *Archives of General Psychiatry, 46,* 971–982.

ELKIN, R. A., & LEIPPE, M. R. (1986). Physiological arousal, dissonance, and attitude change: Evidence of a dissonance-arousal link and a "don't remind me" effect. *Journal of Personality and Social Psychology, 51,* 55–65.

ELLASON, J. W., ROSS, C. A., FUCHS, D. L. (1996). Lifetime Axis I and II comorbidity and childhood trauma history in dissociative identity disorder. *Psychiatry: Interpersonal & Biological Processes, 59,* 255–266.

ELLIOT, A. J., & DEVINE, P. G. (1994). On the motivational nature of cognitive dissonance: Dissonance as psychological discomfort. *Journal of Personality and Social Psychology, 67,* 382–394.

ELLIS, L., & AMES, M. A. (1987). Neurohormonal functioning and sexual orientation: A theory of homosexuality-heterosexuality. *Psychological Bulletin, 2,* 233–258.

ELLISON, C. G., & LEVIN, J. S. (1998). The religion-health connection: Evidence, theory, and future directions. *Health Education and Behavior, 25,* 700–720.

ELLISON, L. F., & MORRISON, H. I. (2001). Low serum cholesterol concentration and risk of suicide. *Epidemiology, 12,* 168–172.

ELLSWORTH, P. (1991). Some implications of cognitive appraisals on theories of emotion. In K. T. Strongman (Ed.), *International review of studies on emotion* (Vol. 1). New York: Wiley.

ELMES, D. G., KANTOWITZ, B. H., & ROEDIGER, H. L. (1989). *Research methods in psychology* (3rd ed.). St. Paul, MN: West.

EMMELKAMP, P. M. G. (1994). Behavior therapy with adults. In A. E. Bergin & S. L. Garfield (Eds.), *Handbook of psychotherapy and behavior change* (4th ed., pp. 379–427). New York: Wiley.

EMMELKAMP, P., & KUIPERS, A. (1979). Agoraphobia: A follow-up study four years after treatment. *British Journal of Psychiatry, 134,* 352–355.

ENGEN, T. (1982). *The perception of odors.* New York: Academic Press.

ENNS, J. T., & GIRGUS, J. S. (1985). Perceptual grouping and spatial distortion: A developmental study. *Developmental Psychology, 21,* 241–246.

ENNS, J. T., & PRINZMETAL, W. (1984). The role of redundancy in the object-line effect. *Perception and Psychophysics, 35,* 22–32.

ENNS, J. T., & RENSINK, R. A. (1990). Sensitivity to three-dimensional orientation in visual search. *Psychological Science, 1,* 323–326.

EPLEY, N., & GILOVICH, T. (1999). Just going along: Nonconscious priming and conformity to social pressure. *Journal of Experimental Social Psychology, 35,* 578–589.

EPSTEIN, S., & MEIER, P. (1989). Constructive thinking: A broad coping variable with specific components. *Journal of Personality and Social Psychology, 57,* 332–350.

ERDELYI, M. H. (1985). *Psychoanalysis: Freud's cognitive psychology.* New York: Freeman.

ERICSSON, K. A., CHASE, W. G., & FALOON, S. (1980). Acquisition of a memory skill. *Science, 208,* 1181–1182.

ERICSSON, K. A., & SIMON, H. A. (1993). *Protocol analysis: Verbal reports as data* (Rev. Ed.). Cambridge, MA: MIT Press.

ERIKSEN, C. W., & COLLINS, J. F. (1967). Some temporal characteristics of visual pattern perception. *Journal of Experimental Psychology, 74,* 476–484.

ERIKSON, E. H. (1963). *Childhood and society* (2nd ed.). New York: Norton.

ERIKSON, E. H. (1968). *Identity: Youth and crisis.* New York: Norton.

ERON, L. D. (1987). The development of aggressive behavior from the perspective of a developing behaviorism. *American Psychologist, 42,* 435–442.

ERON, L. D., HUESMANN, L. R., LEFKOWITZ, M. M., & WALDER, L. O. (1972). Does television violence cause aggression? *American Psychologist, 27,* 253–263.

ERVIN-TRIPP, S. (1964). Imitation and structural change in children's language. In E. H. Lenneberg (Ed.), *New directions in the study of language.* Cambridge, MA: MIT Press.

ESCOBAR, J. I. (1993). Psychiatric epidemiology. In A. C. Gaw (Ed.), *Culture, ethnicity and mental illness* (pp. 43–73). Washington, DC: American Psychiatric Press.

ESTERSON, A. (1993). *Seductive mirage: An exploration of the work of Sigmund Freud.* Chicago: Open Court.

ESTES, W. K. (1972). An associative basis for coding and organization in memory. In A. W. Melton & E. Martin (Eds.), *Coding processes in human memory.* Washington, DC: Winston.

ESTES, W. K. (Ed.). (1975–1979). *Handbook of learning and cognitive processes* (Vols. 1–6). Hillsdale, NJ: Erlbaum.

ESTES, W. K. (1994). *Classification and cognition.* New York: Oxford University Press.

ETCOFF, N. L. (1985). The neuropsychology of emotional expression. In G. Goldstein & R. E. Tarter (Eds.), *Advances in clinical neuropsychology* (Vol. 3). New York: Plenum.

EVANS, C. (1984). *Landscapes of the night: How and why we dream.* New York: Viking.

EXNER, J. (1986). *The Rorschach: A comprehensive system* (2nd ed., Vol. 1). New York: Wiley.

EXNER, J. E., & WEINER, I. B. (1995). *The Rorschach: A comprehensive system. Volume 3: Assessment of children and adolescents* (2nd ed.). New York: Wiley.

EYLER ZORRILLA, L. T., CANNON, T. D., KRONENBERG, S., MEDNICK, S. A., SCHULSINGER, F., PARNAS, J., PRAESTHOLM, J., BESTERGAARD, A. (1997). Structural brain abnormalities in schizophrenia: a family study. *Biological Psychiatry, 42,* 1080–1086.

EYSENCK, H. J. (1953). *The structure of human personality.* New York: Wiley.

EYSENCK, H. J., & KAMIN, L. (1981). *The intelligence controversy.* New York: Wiley.

EYSENCK, J. H., & RACHMAN, S. (1973). The future of clinical psychology. *Bulletin of the British Psychological Society, 26,* 113–116.

FABREGA, H., ULRICH, R., PILKONIS, P., & MEZZICH, J. (1991). On the homogeneity of personality disorder clusters. *Comprehensive Psychiatry, 32,* 373–386.

FAGOT, B. I. (1978). The influence of sex of child on parental reactions to toddler children. *Child Development, 49,* 459–465.

FAIKKONEN, K., MATTHEWS, K. A., FLORY, J. D., OWENS, J. F., & GUMP, B. B. (1999). Effects of optimism, pessimism, and trait anxiety on ambulatory blood pressure and mood during everyday life. *Journal of Personality and Social Psychology, 76,* 104–113.

FAIRBURN, C. G., & HAY, P. J. (1992). Treatment of bulimia nervosa. *Annals of Medicine, 24,* 297–302.

FAIRBURN, C. G., NORMAN, P. A., WELCH, S. L., O'CONNOR, M. E., DOLL, H. A., & PEVELER, R. C. (1995). A prospective study of outcome in bulimia nervosa and the long-term effects of three psychological treatments. *Archives of General Psychiatry, 52,* 304–312.

FAIRBURN, C. G., WELCH, S. L., & HAY, P. J. (1993). The classification of recurrent overeating: The "binge eating disorder" proposal. Fifth International Conference on Eating Disorders (1992, New York). *International Journal of Eating Disorders, 13,* 155–159.

FALS-STEWART, W. M., & ALLEN, P. J. (1993). A comparison of behavioral group therapy and individual behavior therapy in treating obsessive-compulsive disorder. *Journal of Nervous and Mental Disease, 18,* 189–193.

FANSELOW, M. S. (1997). Species-specific defense reactions: Retrospect and prospect. In M. E. Bouton & M. S. Fanselow (Eds.), *Learning, motivation, and cognition: The functional behaviorism of Robert C. Bolles* (pp. 321–341). Washington, DC: American Psychological Association.

FANTZ, R. L. (1961). The origin of form perception. *Science, 204,* 66–72.

FANTZ, R. L. (1970). Visual perception and experience in infancy: Issues and approaches. In National Academy of Science, *Early experience and visual information processing in perceptual and reading disorders* (pp. 351–381). New York: National Academy of Science.

FARAH, M., HAMMOND, K. M., & LEVINE, D. N. (1988). Visual and spatial mental imagery: Dissociable systems of representation. *Cognitive Psychology, 20,* 439–462.

FARAH, M. J. (1990). *Visual agnosia: Disorders of object recognition and what they tell us about normal vision.* Cambridge, MA: MIT Press.

FARAH, M. J. (2000). *The cognitive neuroscience of vision.* Malden, MA: Blackwell.

FARAH, M. J., & MCCLELLAND, J. L. (1991). A computational model of semantic memory impairment. *Journal of Experimental Psychology: General, 120,* 339–357.

FARAONE, S. V., and collaborators. (1990). Genetic transmission of major affective disorders: Quantitative models and linkage analyses. *Psychological Bulletin, 108,* 109–127.

FARBER, E. W., SCHWARTZ, J. A. J., SCHAPER, P. E., MOONEN, D. J., & MCDANIEL, J. S. (2000). Resilience factors associated with adaptation to HIV disease. *Psychosomatics, 41,* 140–146.

FARRINGTON, D. P. (1995). The challenge of teenager antisocial behavior. In M. Rutter (Ed.), *Psychosocial disturbances in young people: Challenges for prevention.* (pp. 83–130). New York: Cambridge University Press.

FARTHING, G. W. (1992). *The psychology of consciousness.* Englewood Cliffs, NJ: Prentice Hall.

FAUST, I. M. (1984). Role of the fat cell in energy balance physiology. In A. T. Stunkard & E. Stellar (Eds.), *Eating and its disorders.* New York: Raven Press.

FAVA, M., COPELAND, P. M., SCHWEIGER, U., & HERZOG, D. B. (1989). Neurochemical abnormalities of anorexia nervosa and bulimia nervosa. *American Journal of Psychiatry, 146,* 963–971.

FAWCETT, J., BUSCH, K. A., JACOBS, D., KRAVITZ, H. M., & FOGG, L. (1997). Suicide: A four-pathway clinical-biochemical model. *Annals of the New York Academy of Sciences, 836,* 288–301.

FAZIO, R., ZANNA, M. P., & COOPER, J. (1977). Dissonance and self-perception: An integrative view of each theory's proper domain of application. *Journal of Experimental Social Psychology, 13,* 464–479.

FAZIO, R. H. (1990). Multiple processes by which attitudes guide behavior: The MODE model as an integrative framework. In M. P. Zanna (Ed.), *Advances in experimental social psychology* (Vol. 23). San Diego: Academic Press.

FAZIO, R. H., JACKSON, J. R., DUNTON, B. C., & WILLIAMS, C. J. (1995). Variability in automatic activation as an unobtrusive measure of racial attitudes: A bona fide pipeline? *Journal of Personality and Social Psychology, 69,* 1013–1027.

FECHNER, G. T. (1860/1966). *Elements of psychophysics* (H. E. Adler, Trans.). New York: Holt, Rinehart & Winston.

FEINGOLD, A. (1988). Cognitive gender differences are disappearing. *American Psychologist, 43,* 95–103.

FELDMAN, H., GOLDIN-MEADOW, S., & GLEITMAN, L. R. (1978). Beyond Herodotus: The creation of language by linguistically deprived children. In A. Lock (Ed.), *Action, gesture, and symbol: The emergence of language.* London: Academic Press.

FELDMAN, H., MEYER, J.S. & QUENZER, L. S. (1997). *Principles of neuropsychopharmacology.* New York: Sinauer.

FELDMAN BARRETT, L., ROBIN, L., PIETROMONACO, P. R., & EYSSELL, K. M. (1998). Are women the "more emotional" sex? Evidence from emotional experiences in social context. *Cognition and Emotion, 12,* 555–578.

FENWICK, P. (1987). Meditation and the EEG. In M. A. West (Ed.), *The psychology of meditation.* Oxford, England: Oxford University Press.

FERGUSON, M. L., & KATKIN, E. S. (1996). Visceral perception, anhedonia, and emotion. *Biological Psychology, 42,* 131–145.

FERRIS, C. F., & DE VRIES, G. J. (1997). Ethological models for examining the neurobiology of aggressive and affiliative behaviors. In D. M. Stoff, J. Breiling, & J. D. Maser (Eds.) *Handbook of antisocial personality disorder* (pp. 255–268). New York: Wiley.

FESHBACH, N. D. (1980, September). *The child as psychologist and economist: Two curricula.* Paper presented at the American Psychological Association convention. Montreal.

FESTINGER, L. (1957). *A theory of cognitive dissonance.* Stanford: Stanford University Press.

FESTINGER, L., & CARLSMITH, J. M. (1959). Cognitive consequences of forced compliance. *Journal of Abnormal and Social Psychology, 58,* 203–210.

FESTINGER, L., PEPITONE, A., & NEWCOMB, T. M. (1952). Some consequences of deindividuation in a group. *Journal of Abnormal and Social Psychology, 47,* 383–389.

FESTINGER, L., SCHACHTER, S., & BACK, K. (1950). *Social pressures in informal groups: A study of human factors in housing.* New York: Harper & Row.

FIELD, J. (1987). The development of auditory-visual localization in infancy. In B. E. McKenzie & R. H. Day (Eds.), *Perceptual development in early infancy.* Hillsdale, NJ: Erlbaum.

FIELD, T. (1991). Quality infant day care and grade school behavior and performance. *Child Development, 62,* 863–870.

FIELD, T. (1998). Massage therapy effects. *American Psychologist, 53,* 1270–1281.

FIELD, T. (2001). Massage therapy facilitates weight gain in preterm infants. *Current Directions in Psychological Science, 10,* 51–53.

FIELD, T., GRIZZLE, N., SCAFIDI, F., ABRAMS, S., & RICHARDSON, S. (1996). Massage therapy for infants of depressed mothers. *Infant Behavior and Development, 19,* 109–114.

FIELD, T., HENTELEFF, T., HERNANDEZ-REIF, M., MARTINEZ, E., MAVUNDA, K., KUHN, C., & SCHANBERG, S. (1998). Children with asthma have improved pulmonary function after massage therapy. *Journal of Pediatrics, 132,* 854–858.

FIELD, T., HERNANDEZ-REIF, M., SELIGMAN, S., KRASNEGOR, J., SUNSHINE, W., RIVAS-CHACON, R., SCHANBERG, S., & KUHN, C. (1997). Juvenile rheumatoid arthritis: Benefits from massage therapy. *Journal of Pediatric Psychology, 22,* 607–617.

FIELD, T., HERNANDEZ-REIF, M., SHAW, K. H., LA GRECA, A., SCHANBERG, S., & KUHN, C. (1997). Glucose levels decreased after giving massage therapy to children with diabetes mellitus. *Diabetes Spectrum, 10,* 23–25.

FIELD, T., SCHANBERG, S. M., SCAFIDI, F., BAUER, C. R., VEGA-LAHR, N., GARCIA, R., NYSTROM, J., & KUHN, C. (1986). Tactile/kinesthetic stimulation effects on preterm neonates. *Pediatrics, 77,* 654–658.

FINCK, H. T. (1887). *Romantic love and personal beauty: Their development, causal relations, historic and national pecularities.* London: Macmillan.

FINKE, R. A. (1985). Theories relating mental imagery to perception. *Psychological Bulletin, 98,* 236–259.

FISCHER, A. H. (2000). *Gender and emotion: Social psychological perspectives.* New York: Cambridge University Press.

FISCHER, A. H., MANSTEAD, A. S. R., & MOSQUERA, P. M. R. (1999). The role of honour-related vs. individualistic values in conceptualizing pride, shame, and anger: Spanish and Dutch cultural prototypes. *Cognition and Emotion, 13,* 149–179.

FISHBEIN, M., TRIANDIS, H. C., KANFER, F. H., BECKER, M., MIDDLESTADT, S. E., & EICHLER, A. (1998). Factors influencing behavior and behavior change. *Handbook of Health Psychology.* In press.

FISHER, G. H. (1967). Preparation of ambiguous stimulus materials. *Perception and Psychophysics, 2,* 421–422.

FISHER, P. J., TURIC, D., WILLIAMS, N. M., MCGUFFIN, P., ASHERSON, P., BALL, D., CRAIG, I., ELEY, T., HILL, L., CHURNEY, K., CHURNEY, M. J., BENBOW, C. P., LUBINSKI, D., PLUMIN, R., OWEN, M. J. (1999). DNA pooling identifies QTLs on chromosome 4 for general cognitive ability in children. *Human Molecular Genetics, 8,* 915–922.

FISHER, R. A. (1958). *The cancer controversy.* London: Oliver & Boyd.

FISHER, S., & GREENBERG, R. (1977). *The scientific credibility of Freud's theories and therapy.* New York: Basic Books.

FISHER, S., & GREENBERG, R. (1996). *Freud scientifically appraised.* New York: Wiley.

FISHMAN, P. (1983). Interaction: The work women do. In B. Thorne, C. Kramarae, & N. Henley

(Eds.), *Language, gender, and society*. Rowley, MA: Newbury House.

FISKE, S. T. (1993). Social cognition and social perception. *Annual Review of Psychology, 44*, 155–194.

FISKE, S. T., & TAYLOR, S. E. (1991). *Social cognition* (2nd ed.). New York: McGraw-Hill.

FISKE, S. T., LIN, M., & NEUBERG, S. L. (1999). The continuum model: Ten years later. In S. Chaiken & Y. Trope (Eds.), *Dual-process theories in social psychology* (pp. 231–254). New York: Guilford.

FITZSIMONS, J. T. (1969). The role of a renal thirst factor in drinking induced by extra cellular stimuli. *Journal of Physiology, London, 201*, 349–368.

FITZSIMONS, J. T. (1990). Thirst and sodium appetite. In E. M. Stricker (Ed.), *Neurobiology of food and fluid intake* (pp. 23–44). New York: Plenum.

FIVUSH, R., & BUCKNER, J. P. (2000). Gender, sadness, and depression: The development of emotional focus through gendered discourse. In A. H. Fischer (Ed.), *Gender and emotion: Social psychological perspectives* (pp. 232–253). New York: Cambridge University Press.

FIVUSH, R., & HAMOND, N. R. (1991). Autobiographical memory across the preschool years: Toward reconceptualizing childhood memory. In R. Fivush & N. R. Hamond (Eds.), *Knowing and remembering in young children*. New York: Cambridge University Press.

FIXSEN, D. L., PHILLIPS, E. L., PHILLIPS, E. A., & WOLF, M. M. (1976). The teaching-family model of group home treatment. In W. E. Craighead, A. E. Kazdin, & M. J. Mahoney (Eds.), *Behavior modification: Principles, issues, and applications*. Boston: Houghton Mifflin.

FLAVELL, J. H. (1992). *Cognitive development* (3rd ed.). Englewood Cliffs, NJ: Prentice Hall.

FLAVELL, J. H. (1999). Cognitive development: Children's knowledge about the mind. *Annual Review of Psychology, 50*, 21–45.

FLEMING, J., & DARLEY, J. M. (1986). *Perceiving intention in constrained behavior: The role of purposeful and constrained action cues in correspondence bias effects*. Unpublished manuscript, Princeton University.

FLODERUS-MYRED, B., PETERSEN, N., & RASMUSON, I. (1980). Assessment of heritability for personality based on a short form of the Eysenck Personality Inventory. *Behavior Genetics, 10*, 153–161.

FLOR, H., FYDRICH, T., & TURK, D. C. (1992). Efficacy of multidisciplinary pain treatment: A meta-analytic review. *Pain, 49*, 221–230.

FLOWERS, M. L. (1977). A laboratory test of some implications of Janis's groupthink hypothesis. *Journal of Personality and Social Psychology, 35*, 888–896.

FLUOXETINE BULIMIA NERVOSA STUDY GROUP (1992). Fluoxetine in the treatment of bulimia nervosa: A multi-center, placebo-controlled, double-blind trial. *Archives of General Psychiatry, 49*, 156–162.

FLYNN, J. R. (1987). Massive IQ gains in 14 nations: What IQ tests really measure. *Psychological Bulletin, 101*, 171–191.

FOA, E., & STEKETEE, G. (1989). Obsessive-compulsive disorder. In C. Lindemann (Ed.), *Handbook of phobia therapy*. Northvale, NJ: Jason Aronson.

FOA, E. B., & FRANKLIN, M. E. (2001). Obsessive-compulsive disorder. *Clinical handbook of psychological disorders: a step-by-step treatment manual* (3rd ed., pp. 209–263). New York: Guilford.

FOA, E. D., & RIGGS, D. S. (1995). Posttraumatic stress disorder following assault: Theoretical considerations and empirical findings. *Current Directions in Psychological Science, 4*, 61–65.

FODOR, J. A., BEVER, T. G., & GARRETT, M. F. (1974). *The psychology of language: An introduction to psycholinguistics and generative grammar*. New York: McGraw-Hill.

FOLEY, D. L., PICKLES, A., MAES, H. H., SILBERG, J. L., HEWITT, J. K., & EAVES, L. J. (2001). Parental concordance and comorbidity for psychiatric disorder and associate risks for current psychiatric symptoms and disorders in a community sample of juvenile twins. *Journal of Child Psychology and Psychiatry & Allied Disciplines, 42*, 381–394.

FOLKES, V. S. (1982). Forming relationships and the matching hypothesis. *Personality and Social Psychology Bulletin, 8*, 631–636.

FOLLETTE, W. C., & HAYES, S. C. (2000). Contemporary behavior therapy. In C. R. Snyder & R. Ingram (Eds.), *Handbook of psychological change* (pp. 381–408). New York: Wiley.

FORDYCE, W. E. (1976). *Behavioral methods for chronic pain and illness*. St. Louis, MO: C. V. Mosby.

FORGE, K. L., & PHEMISTER, S. (1987). The effect of prosocial cartoons on preschool children. *Child Development Journal, 17*, 83–88.

FORSYTH, D. R., & CORAZZINI, J. G. (2000). Groups as change agents. In C. R. Snyder & R. Ingram (Eds.), *Handbook of psychological change* (pp. 309–336). New York: Wiley.

FOSS, D. J., & HAKES, D. T. (1978). *Psycholinguistics: An introduction to the psychology of language*. Englewood Cliffs, NJ: Prentice-Hall.

FOULKES, D. (1985). *Dreaming: A cognitive psychological analysis*. Hillsdale, NJ: Erlbaum.

FOULKES, D. (1993). Data constraints on theorizing about dream function. In A. Moffitt, M. Kramer, & R. Hoffman (Eds.), *The functions of dreaming*. Albany: State University of New York Press.

FOULKES, D (1999). *Children's dreaming and the development of consciousness*. Cambridge, MA: Harvard University Press.

FOULKES, D., & SCHMIDT, M. (1983). Temporal sequence and unit comparison composition in dream reports from different stages of sleep. *Sleep, 6*, 265–280.

FRABLE, D. E. (1989). Sex typing and gender ideology: Two facets of the individual's gender psychology that go together. *Journal of Personality and Social Psychology, 56*, 95–108.

FRANK, J. D., & FRANK, J. B. (1991). *Persuasion and healing: A comparative study of psychotherapy* (3rd edition). Baltimore: Johns Hopkins University Press.

FRANKENHAEUSER, M. (1983). The sympathetic-adrenal and pituitary-adrenal response to challenge: Comparison between the sexes. In T. M. Dembroski, T. H. Schmidt, & G. Blumchen (Eds.), *Biobehavioral bases of coronary heart disease*. Basel: Karger.

FRANKLIN, J. (1987). *Molecules of the mind*. New York: Atheneum.

FRANTZ, R. L. (1966). Pattern discrimination and selective attention as determinants of perceptual development from birth. In A. H. Kikk & J. F. Rivoire (Eds.), *Development of perception: Vol. 2, The visual system* (pp. 143–173). New York: International University Press.

FRAZIER, K. (1987). Psychic's imagined year fizzles (again). *Skeptical Inquirer, 11*, 335–336.

FREDRICKSON, B. L. (1998). What good are positive emotions? *Review of General Psychology, 2*, 300–319.

FREDRICKSON, B. L. (2000). Cultivating positive emotions to optimize health and well-being. *Prevention and Treatment*. Available on the World Wide Web: http://journals.apa.org/prevention.

FREDRICKSON, B. L. (2001). The role of positive emotions in positive psychology: The broaden-and-build theory of positive emotions. *American Psychologist, 56*, 218–226.

FREDRICKSON, B. L. (2002). Positive emotions. In C. R. Snyder & S. J. Lopez (Eds.), *Handbook of positive psychology* (pp. 120–134). New York: Oxford University Press.

FREDRICKSON, B. L., & BRANIGAN, C. (2001). Positive emotions. In T. J. Mayne & G. A. Bonnano (Eds.), *Emotion: Current issues and future developments* (pp. 123–151). New York: Guilford.

FREDRICKSON, B. L., & BRANIGAN, C. (2002). *Positive emotions broaden the scope of attention and thought-action repertoires*. Manuscript under review.

FREDRICKSON, B. L., & JOINER, T. (2002). Positive emotions trigger upward spirals toward emotional well-being. *Psychological Science, 13*, 172–175.

FREDRICKSON, B. L., & LEVENSON, R. W. (1998). Positive emotions speed recovery from the cardiovascular sequelae of negative emotions. *Cognition and Emotion, 12*, 191–220.

FREDRICKSON, B. L., MANCUSO, R. A., BRANIGAN, C., & TUGADE, M. M. (2000). The undoing effect of positive emotions. *Motivation and Emotion, 24*, 237–258.

FREE, L. A., & CANTRIL, H. (1967). *The political beliefs of Americans*. New Brunswick, NJ: Rutgers University Press.

FREEDMAN, J. L. (1965). Long-term behavioral effects of cognitive dissonance. *Journal of Experimental Social Psychology, 1*, 145–155.

FREEDMAN, J. L., & FRASER, S. C. (1966). Compliance without pressure: The foot-in-the-door technique. *Journal of Personality and Social Psychology, 4*, 195–203.

FREESTON, M. H., LADOUCEUR, R., THIBODEAU, N., & GAGNON, F. (1992). Cognitive intrusions in a non-clinical population: II. Associations with depressive, anxious, and compulsive symptoms. *Behaviour Research and Therapy, 30*, 263–271.

FREUD, A. (1946/1967). *The ego and the mechanisms of defense* (Rev. Ed.). New York: International Universities Press.

FREUD, A. (1958). Adolescence. *The Psychoanalytic Study of the Child, 13*, 255–278.

FREUD, S. (1885). *Ueber coca*. Vienna: Moritz Perles. (Translated in Freud, 1974)

FREUD, S. (1885/1974). *Cocaine papers* (edited and introduction by R. Byck; notes by A. Freud). New York: Stonehill.

FREUD, S. (1900/1953). *The interpretation of dreams* (Reprint ed., Vols. 4, 5). London: Hogarth Press.

FREUD, S. (1901/1960). *Psychopathology of everyday life* (Standard ed., Vol. 6). London: Hogarth Press.

FREUD, S. (1905/1962). *Three contributions to theory of sex* (4th ed.; A. A. Brill, Trans.). New York: Nervous and Mental Disease Monograph.

FREUD, S. (1915/1976). Repression. In J. Strachey (Ed. and Trans.), *The complete psychological works: Standard edition* (Vol. 14). London: Hogarth Press.

FREUD, S. (1920/1975). *Beyond the pleasure principle*. New York: Norton.

FREUD, S. (1925/1961). Some psychical consequences of the anatomical distinctions between the sexes. In J. Strachey (Ed. and Trans.), *The complete psychological works: Standard edition* (Vol. 18). London: Hogarth Press.

FREUD, S. (1933/1964). *New introductory lectures on psychoanalysis* (J. Strachey, Ed. and Trans.). New York: Norton.

FREUD, S. (1933/1965). Revision of the theory of dreams. In J. Strachey (Ed. and Trans.), *New introductory lectures on psychoanalysis* (Vol. 22, Lect. 29). New York: Norton.

FREUD, S. (1940). An outline of psychoanalysis. *International Journal of Psychoanalysis, 21*, 27–84.

FRIEDMAN, M., & ROSENMAN, R. H. (1974). *Type A behavior.* New York: Knopf.

FRIEDMAN, M., THORESEN, C. E., GILL, J. J., ULMER, D., POWELL, L. H., PRICE, V., BROWN, B., THOMPSON, L., RABIN, D. D., and collaborators. (1994). Alteration of Type A behavior and its effect on cardiac recurrences in post myocardial infarction patients: Summary results of the recurrent coronary prevention project. In A. Steptoe (Ed.), *Psychosocial processes and health: A reader.* Cambridge, England: Cambridge University Press.

FRIEDMAN, M. I. (1990). Making sense out of calories. In E. M. Stricker (Ed.), *Neurobiology of food and fluid intake* (pp. 513–528). New York: Plenum.

FRIJDA, N. H. (1986). *The emotions.* Cambridge, England: Cambridge University Press.

FRISCHHOLZ, E. J. (1985). The relationship between dissociation, hypnosis, and child abuse in the development of multiple personality disorder. In R. P. Kluft (Ed.), *Childhood antecedents of multiple personality.* Washington, DC: American Psychiatric Press.

FRODI, A., & THOMPSON, R. (1985). Infants' affective responses in the strange situation: Effects of prematurity and of quality of attachment. *Child Development, 56*, 1280–1290.

FUGH-BERMAN, A., & COTT, J. M. (1999). Dietary supplements and natural products as psychotherapeutic agents. *Psychosomatic Medicine, 61*, 712–728.

FULLER, S. R., & ALDAG, R. J. (1998). Organizational Tonypandy: Lessons from a quarter century of groupthink phenomenon. *Organizational Behavior and Human Decision Processes, 73*, 163–184.

FUNDER, D. C. (2001). Personality. *Annual Reviews of Psychology, 52*, 197–221.

FUNKENSTEIN, D. (1955). The physiology of fear and anger. *Scientific American, 192*, 74–80.

FYER, A. J., MANNUZZA, S., CHAPMAN, T. F., & LIEBOWITZ, M. R. (1993). A direct interview family study of social phobia. *Archives of General Psychiatry, 50*, 286–293.

FYER, A. J., MANNUZZA, S., GALLOPS, M. S., & MARTIN, L. Y. (1990). Familial transmission of simple phobias and fears: A preliminary report. *Archives of General Psychiatry, 47*, 252–256.

GADOW, K. D. (1991). Clinical issues in child and adolescent psychopharmacology. *Journal of Consulting and Clinical Psychology, 59*, 842–852.

GADOW, K. D. (1992). Pediatric psychopharmacotherapy: A review of recent research. *Journal of Child Psychology and Psychiatry, 33*, 153–195.

GALANTER, E. (1962). Contemporary psychophysics. In R. Brown & collaborators (Eds.), *New directions in psychology* (Vol. 1). New York: Holt, Rinehart & Winston.

GALDERISI, S., VITA, A., ROSSI, A., STRATTA, P., LEONARDI, A., & INVERNIZZI, G. (2000). Qualitative MRI findings in patients with schizophrenia: A controlled study. *Psychiatry Research, 98*, 117–126.

GALINSKY, E., HOWES, C., KONTOS, S., & SHINN, M. (1994). *The study of children in family child care and relative care: Highlights of findings.* New York: Families and Work Institute.

GALLANT, J. L., SHUOP, R. E., & MAZER, J. A. (2000) A human extrastriate area functionally homologous to macaque V4. *Neuron, 27*, 227–235.

GALLUP ORGANIZATION (1995). *Sleep in America: A national survey of U.S. adults.* Poll conducted for the National Sleep Foundation. Princeton, NJ: National Sleep Foundation.

GALOTTI, K. M. (1989). Approaches to studying formal and everyday reasoning. *Psychological Bulletin, 105*, 331–351.

GAMSON, W. B., FIREMAN, B., & RYTINA, S. (1982). *Encounters with unjust authority.* Homewood, IL: Dorsey Press.

GANELLEN, R. J., & CARVER, C. S. (1985). Why does self-reference promote incidental encoding? *Journal of Personality and Social Psychology, 21*, 284–300.

GARCIA, J., & KOELLING, R. A. (1966). The relation of cue to consequence in avoiding learning. *Psychonomic Science, 4*, 123–124.

GARCIA, L. T., ERSKINE, N., HAWN, K., & CASMAY, S. R. (1981). The effect of affirmative action on attributions about minority group members. *Journal of Personality, 49*, 427–437.

GARDNER, B. T., & GARDNER, R. A. (1972). Two-way communication with an infant chimpanzee. In A. M. Schrier & F. Stollnitz (Eds.), *Behavior of nonhuman primates* (Vol. 4). New York: Academic Press.

GARDNER, E. L. (1992). Brain reward mechanisms. In J. H. Lowinson, P. Ruiz, & R. B. Millman (Eds.), *Substance abuse: A comprehensive textbook* (2nd ed.). Baltimore, MD: Williams & Wilkins.

GARDNER, H. (1975). *The shattered mind.* New York: Knopf.

GARDNER, H. (1985). *The mind's new science: A history of the cognitive revolution.* New York: Basic Books.

GARDNER, H. (1993a). *Frames of mind: The theory of multiple intelligences.* New York: Basic Books.

GARDNER, H. (1993b). *Multiple intelligences: The theory in practice.* New York: Basic Books.

Gardner, H. (1999) *Intelligence reframed: Multiple intelligences for the 21st century.* New York: Basic Books.

GARDNER, H., KORNHABER, M. L., & WAKE, W. K. (1996). *Intelligence: Multiple perspectives.* Fort Worth: Harcourt Brace.

GARDNER, M. (1981). *Science: Good, bad, and bogus.* New York: Prometheus.

GARDNER, W., LIDZ, C. W., MULVEY, E. P., & SHAW, E. C. (1996). Clinical versus actuarial predictions of violence in patients with mental illnesses. *Journal of Consulting and Clinical Psychology, 64*, 602–609.

GARFIELD, S. L. (1994a). Research on client variables in psychotherapy. In S. L. Garfield & A. E. Bergen (Eds.), *Handbook of psychotherapy and behavior change* (pp. 190–228). New York: Wiley.

GARFIELD, S. L. (1994b). Research on client variables in psychotherapy. In A. E. Bergin (Ed.), *Handbook of psychotherapy integration* (pp. 190–228), New York: Wiley.

GARNER, D. M., & GARFINKEL, P. E. (1980). Socio-cultural factors in the development of anorexia nervosa. *Psychological Medicine, 10*, 647–656.

GARRETT, M. (1997). The effects of infant child care on infant-mother attachment security: Results of the NICHD Study of Early Child Care. *Child Development, 68*, 860–879.

GARRETT, M. F. (1990). Sentence processing. In D. N. Osherson & H. Lasnik (Eds.), *An invitation to cognitive science: Language* (Vol. 1). Cambridge, MA: MIT Press.

GARRISON, C. Z., BRYANT, E. S., ADDY, C. L., SPURRIER, P. G., FREEDY, J. R., & KILPATRICK, D. G. (1995). Posttraumatic stress disorder in adolescents after Hurricane Andrew. *Journal of the American Academy of Child and Adolescent Psychiatry, 34*, 1193–1201.

GARROD, S. C., & PICKERING, M. J. (1999). *Language processing of words.* Hove, UK: Psychology Press.

GARRY, M., MANNING, C., LOFTUS, E. F., & SHERMAN, S. J. (1996) Imagination inflation. *Psychonomic Bulletin & Review, 3*, 208–214.

GATES, A. I. (1917). Recitation as a factor in memorizing. *Archives of Psychology, 40*.

GAW, A. (1993). *Culture, ethnicity, and mental illness.* Washington, DC: American Psychiatric Press.

GAZZANIGA, M. S. (1985). *The social brain: Discovering the networks of mind.* New York: Basic Books.

GE, X., CONGER, R. D., & ELDER, G. H., Jr. (1996). Coming of age too early: Pubertal influences on girls' vulnerability to psychological distress. *Child Development, 67*, 3386–3400.

GEEN, R. G. (1990). *Human aggression.* Pacific Grove, CA: Brooks/Cole.

GEER, J. H., & MAISEL, E. (1972). Evaluating the effects of the prediction-control confound. *Journal of Personality & Social Psychology, 23*, 314–319.

GELLATLY, A. R. H. (1987). Acquisition of a concept of logical necessity. *Human Development, 30*, 32–47.

GENTER, D., & STEVENS, A. L. (1983). *Mental models.* Hillsdale, NJ: Erlbaum.

GERBNER, G., GROSS, L., MORGAN, M., & SIGNORIELLI, N. (1986). Living with television: The dynamics of the cultivation process. In J. Bryant & D. Zillmann (Eds.), *Perspectives on media effects.* Hillsdale, NJ: Erlbaum.

GERSHON, E. S. (1990). Genetics. In F. K. Goodwin & K. R. Jamison (Eds.), *Manic-depressive illness* (pp. 373–401). New York: Oxford University Press.

GESCHWIND, N. (1972). Language and the brain. *Scientific American, 226*, 76–83.

GESCHWIND, N. (1979). Specializations of the human brain. *Scientific American, 241*, 180–199.

GESELL, A., & THOMPSON, H. (1929). Learning and growth in identical twins: An experimental study by the method of co-twin control. *Genetic Psychology Monographs, 6*, 1–123.

GHEORGHIU, V. A., NETTER, P., EYSENCK, H. J., & ROSENTHAL, R. (Eds.). (1989). *Suggestion and suggestibility: Theory and research.* New York: Springer-Verlag.

GIANOULAKIS, C., KRISHNAN, B., & THAVUNDAYIL, J. (1996). Enhanced sensitivity of pituitary β-endorphin to ethanol in subjects at high risk of alcoholism. *Archives of General Psychiatry, 53*, 250–257.

GIBSON, E. J., & WALK, R. D. (1960). The "visual cliff." *Scientific American, 202*, 64–71.

GIGERENZER, G., & GOLDSTEIN, D. G. (1996). Reasoning the fast and frugal way: Models of bounded rationality. *Psychological Review, 103*, 650–669.

GILBERT, D. T., & JONES, E. E. (1986). Perceiver-induced constraint: Interpretations of self-generated reality. *Journal of Personality and Social Psychology, 50*, 269–280.

GILBERT, D. T., & MALONE, P. S. (1995). The correspondence bias. *Psychological Bulletin, 117*, 21–38.

GILBERT, D. T., PELHAM, B. W., & KRULL, D. S. (1988). On cognitive busyness: When person perceivers meet persons perceived. *Journal of Personality and Social Psychology, 54*, 733–740.

GILCHRIST, A. L. (1988). Lightness contrast and failures of constancy: A common explanation. *Perception and Psychophysics, 43,* 415–424.

GILLIGAN, C. (1982). *In a different voice.* Cambridge, MA: Harvard University Press.

GILLIN, J. C. (1985). Sleep and dreams. In G. L. Klerman, M. M. Weissman, P. S. Applebaum, & L. H. Roth (Eds.), *Psychiatry* (Vol. 3). Philadelphia: Lippincott.

GINSBERG, A. (1983). *Contrast perception in the human infant.* Unpublished manuscript.

GLANZER, M. (1972). Storage mechanisms in recall. In G. H. Bower & J. T. Spence (Eds.), *The psychology of learning and motivation* (Vol. 5). New York: Academic Press.

GLASER, R., RICE, J., SPEICHER, C. E., STOUT, J. C., & KIECOLT-GLASER, J. K. (1986). Stress depresses interferon production by leukocytes concomitant with a decrease in natural killer cell activity. *Behavioral Neuroscience, 100,* 675–678.

GLASS, D. C., & SINGER, J. E. (1972). *Urban stress: Experiments on noise and social stressors.* New York: Academic Press.

GLASS, G. V., MCGAW, B., & SMITH, M. L. (1981). *Meta-analysis in social research.* Beverly Hills, CA: Sage.

GLEITMAN, H. (1986). *Psychology* (2nd ed.). New York: Norton.

GLEITMAN, L. R. (1986). Biological predispositions to learn language. In P. Marler & H. S. Terrace (Eds.), *The biology of learning.* New York: Springer-Verlag.

GODDEN, D., & BADDELEY, A. D. (1975). Context dependent memory in two natural environments: On land and under water. *British Journal of Psychology, 66,* 325–331.

GOEL, V., GOLD, B., KAPUR, S., & HOULE, S. (1998). Neuroanatomical correlates of human reasoning. *Journal of Cognitive Neuroscience, 10,* 293–302.

GOETHALS, G. P., & ZANNA, M. P. (1979). The role of social comparison in choice shifts. *Journal of Personality and Social Psychology, 37,* 1469–1476.

GOLDEN, H., HINKLE, S., & CROSBY, F. J. (1998). *Affirmative action: Semantics and substance.* Ann Arbor: University of Michigan.

GOLDIN-MEADOW, S. (1982). The resilience of recursion: A structure within a conventional model. In E. Wanner & L. R. Gleitman (Eds.), *Language acquisition: The state of the art.* Cambridge, England: Cambridge University Press.

GOLDMAN-RAKIC, P. S. (1987). Circuitry of primate prefrontal cortex and regulation of behavior by representational memory. In F. Plum (Ed.), *Handbook of physiology: The nervous system.* Bethesda, MD: American Physiology Society.

GOLDMAN-RAKIC, P. S. (1996). Regional and cellular fractionation of working memory. *Proceedings of the National Academy of Science of the United States of America, 93,* 13473–13480.

GOLDSTEIN, A. (1994). *Addiction: From biology to drug policy.* New York: Freeman.

GOLDSTEIN, E. B. (1989). *Sensation and perception* (3rd ed.). Belmont, CA: Wadsworth.

GOLDSTEIN, M. (1987). Family interaction patterns that antedate the onset of schizophrenia and related disorders: A further analysis of data from a longitudinal prospective study. In K. Hahlweg & M. Goldstein (Eds.), *Understanding major mental disorders: The contribution of family interaction research* (pp. 11–32). New York: Family Process Press.

GOLDSTEIN, M. J., TALOVIC, S. A., NUECHTERLEIN, K. H., & FOGELSON, D. L. (1992).

Family interaction versus individual psychopathology: Do they indicate the same processes in the families of schizophrenia? *British Journal of Psychiatry, 161,* 97–102.

GOLEMAN, D. (1995, May 2). Biologists find the site of working memory. *New York Times.*

GOLEMAN, D. J. (1988, October 18). Chemistry of sexual desire yields its elusive secret. *New York Times.*

GOODALL, J. (1978). Chimp killings: Is it the man in them? *Science News, 113,* 276.

GOODGLASS, H., & BUTTERS, N. (1988). Psychobiology of cognitive processes. In R. C. Atkinson, R. J. Hernstein, G. Lindzey, & R. D. Luce (Eds.), *Stevens' handbook of experimental psychology* (Vol. 2). New York: Wiley.

GOODWIN, F. K., & JAMISON, K. R. (1990). *Manic-depressive illness.* New York: Oxford University Press.

GORDON, W. (1989). *Learning & memory.* Pacific Grove, CA: Brooks/Cole.

GOTTESMAN, I. I. (1991). *Schizophrenia genesis: The origins of madness.* New York: W. H. Freeman.

GOTTESMAN, I. I., & SHIELDS, J. (1982). *Schizophrenia, the epigenetic puzzle.* New York: Cambridge University Press.

GOTTFRIED, A. E., FLEMING, J. S., & GOTTFRIED, A. W. (1998). The role of cognitively stimulating home environment on children's academic intrinsic motivation. *Child Development, 69,* 1448–1460.

GOTTLIEB, G. (2000). Environmental and behavioral influences on gene activity. *Current Directions in Psychological Science, 9,* 93–97.

GOULD, E., BEYLIN, A., TANAPAT, P., REEVES, A., & SHORS, T. J. (1999). Learning enhances adult neurogenesis in the hippocampal formation. *Nature Neuroscience, 2,* 260–265.

GOY, R. W. (1968). Organizing effect of androgen on the behavior of rhesus monkeys. In R. F. Michael (Ed.), *Endocrinology of human behaviour.* London: Oxford University Press.

GRACZYK, P. A., WEISSBERG, R. P., PAYTON, J. W., ELIAS, M. J., GREENBERG, M. T., & ZINS, J. E. (2000). Criteria for evaluating the quality of school-based social and emotional learning programs. In R. Bar-On & J. D. A. Parker (Eds.), *The handbook of emotional intelligence,* San Francisco: Jossey-Bass.

GRADY, C. L., HAXBY, J. V., HORWITZ, B., SCHAPIRO, M. B., RAPOPORT, S. I., UNGERLEIDER, L. G., MISHKIN, M., CARSON, R. E., & HERSCOVITCH, P. (1992). Dissociation of object and spatial vision in human extrastriate cortex: Age-related changes in activation of regional cerebral blood flow measured with [^{15}O] water and positron emission tomography. *Journal of Cognitive Neuroscience, 4,* 23–34.

GRAF, P., & MANDLER, G. (1984). Activation makes words more accessible, but not necessarily more retrievable. *Journal of Verbal Learning and Verbal Behavior, 23,* 553–568.

GRAF, P., & MASSON, M. E. J. (Eds.). (1993). *Implicit memory: New directions in cognition, development, and neuropsychology.* Hillsdale, NJ: Erlbaum.

GRAHAM, J. R. (1990). *The MMPI-2: Assessing personality and psychopathology.* New York: Oxford University Press.

GRANDIN, T. (1995). *Thinking in pictures and other reports from my life with autism.* New York: Vintage Books.

GRANRUD, C. E. (1986). Binocular vision and spatial perception in 4- and 5-month-old infants. *Jour-*

nal of Experimental Psychology: Human Perception and Performance, 12, 36–49.

GRAY, E., & COSGROVE, J. (1985). Ethnocentric perception of childbearing practices in protective services. *Child Abuse and Neglect, 9,* 389–396.

GRAY, J. (1982). Precis of the neuropsychology of anxiety: An enquiry into the functions of the septohippocampal system. *Behavioural and Brain Sciences, 5,* 469–534.

GRAY, J. (1992). *Men are from Mars, women are from Venus: A practical guide for improving communication and getting what you want in your relationships.* New York: HarperCollins.

GRAY, J. A. (1987). *The psychology of fear and stress* (2nd ed.). Cambridge, England: Cambridge University Press.

GRAY, J. A. (1994) Personality dimensions and emotion systems. In P. Ekman & R. J. Davidson (Eds.), *The nature of emotion: Fundamental questions* (pp. 329–331). New York: Oxford University Press.

GRAY-LITTLE, B., & HAFDAHL, A. R. (2000). Factors influencing racial comparisons of self-esteem: A quantitative review. *Psychological Bulletin, 126,* 26–54.

GRAY-LITTLE, B. & KAPLAN, D. (2000). Race and ethnicity in psychotherapy research. In C. R. Snyder & R. E. Ingram (Eds.), *Handbook of psychological change: Psychotherapy processes and practices for the 21st century* (pp. 592–613). New York: Wiley.

GRAZZANI-GAVAZZI, I., & OATLEY, K. (1999). The experience of emotions of interdependence and independence following interpersonal errors in Italy and Anglophone Canada. *Cognition and Emotion, 13,* 49–63.

GREEN, B. L., LINDY, J. D., GRACE, M. C., & LEONARD, A. C. (1992). Chronic post-traumatic stress disorder and diagnostic comorbidity in a disaster sample. *Journal of Nervous and Mental Disease, 180,* 760–766.

GREEN, D. M., & WIER, C. C. (1984). Auditory perception. In I. Darian-Smith (Ed.), *Handbook of physiology* (Vol. 3). Bethesda, MD: American Physiological Society.

GREEN, J. G., FOX, N. A., & LEWIS, M. (1983). The relationship between neonatal characteristics and three-month mother-infant interaction in high-risk infants. *Child Development, 54,* 1286–1296.

GREEN, R. (1987). *The "sissy boy syndrome" and the development of homosexuality.* New Haven, CT: Yale University Press.

GREENFIELD, P. M., & SAVAGE-RUMBAUGH, S. (1990). Grammatical combination in *Pan Paniscus:* Processes of learning and invention in the evolution and development of language. In S. Parker & K. Gibson (Eds.), *"Language" and intelligence in monkeys and apes: Comparative developmental perspectives.* New York: Cambridge University Press.

GREENWALD, A. G. (1968). Cognitive learning, cognitive response to persuasion, and attitude change. In A. G. Greenwald, T. C. Brock, & T. M. Ostrom (Eds.), *Psychological foundations of attitudes.* New York: Academic Press.

GREENWALD, A. G. (1992). Unconscious cognition reclaimed. *American Psychologist, 47,* 766–779.

GRICE, H. P. (1975). Logic and conversation. In G. Harman & D. Davidson (Eds.), *The logic of grammar.* Encino, CA: Dickinson.

GRIGGS, R. A., & COX, J. R. (1982). The elusive thematic-materials effect in Watson's selection task. *British Journal of Psychology, 73,* 407–420.

GRILL, H. J., & KAPLAN, J. M. (1990). Caudal brainstem participates in the distributed neural control of feeding. In E. M. Stricker (Eds.), *Neurobiology of food and fluid intake* (pp. 125–149). New York: Plenum Press.

GRODZINSKY, Y. (1984). The syntactic characterization of agrammatism. *Cognition, 16,* 99–120.

GROSS, J. J. (2001). Emotion regulation in adulthood: Timing is everything. *Current Directions in Psychological Science, 10,* 214–219.

GROSS, J. J., & LEVENSON, R. W. (1997). Hiding feelings: The acute effects of inhibiting positive and negative emotions. *Journal of Abnormal Psychology, 106,* 95–103.

GROSS-ISSEROFF, R., BIEGON, A., VOET, H., & WEIZMAN, A. (1998) The suicide brain: A review of postmortem receptor/transporter binding studies. *Neuroscience and Biobehavioral Reviews, 22,* 653–661.

GROSSMAN, M., & WOOD, W. (1993). Sex differences in intensity of emotional experience: A social role interpretation. *Journal of Personality and Social Psychology, 65,* 1010–1022.

GROVES, P. M., & REBEC, G. V. (1992). *Introduction to biological psychology* (4th ed.). Dubuque, IA: Brown.

GRÜNBAUM, A. (1984). *The foundations of psychoanalysis.* Berkeley, CA: University of California Press.

GUARNACCIA, P. J., CANINO, G., RUBIO-STIPEC, M., & BRAVO, M. (1993). The prevalence of ataques de nervios in the Puerto Rico Disaster Study: The role of culture in psychiatric epidemiology. *Journal of Nervous and Mental Disease, 181,* 157–165.

GUARNACCIA, P. J., GUEVARA-RAMOS, L. M., GONZALES, G., CANINO, G. J., & BIRD, H. (1992). Cross-cultural aspects of psychiatric symptoms in Puerto Rico. *Community and Mental Health, 7,* 99–110.

GUARNACCIA, P. J., RIVERA, M., FRANCO, F., NEIGHBORS, C., & ALLENDE-RAMOS, C. (1996). The experiences of ataques de nervios: Toward an anthropology of emotions in Puerto Rico. *Culture, Medicine and Psychiatry, 15,* 139–165.

GUILFORD, J. P. (1982). Cognitive psychology's ambiguities: Some suggested remedies. *Psychological Review, 89,* 48–49.

GUMPERZ, J. J., & LEVINSON, S. C. (Eds.). (1996). *Rethinking linguistic relativity.* Cambridge: Cambridge University Press.

GURIN, P., DEY, E. L., HURTADO, S., & GURIN, G. (in press). Diversity and higher education: Theory and impact on educational outcomes. *Harvard Educational Review.*

GURNEY, R. (1936). The hereditary factor in obesity. *Archives of Internal Medicine, 57,* 557–561.

HAAGA, D. A. F., DYCK, M. J., & ERNST, D. (1991). Empirical status of cognitive theory of depression. *Psychological Bulletin, 110,* 215–236.

HAAGA, D. F., & STILES, W. B. (2000). Randomized clinical trials in psychotherapy research: Methodology, design and evaluation. In C. R. Snyder & R. Ingram (Eds.), *Handbook of psychological change* (pp. 14–39) New York: Wiley.

HABER, R. N. (1969). Eidetic images. *Scientific American, 220,* 36–55.

HABER, R. N. (1979). Twenty years of haunting edetic imagery: Where's the ghost? *Behavioral and Brain Sciences, 24,* 583–629.

HABERLANDT, K. (1993). *Cognitive psychology.* Boston, MA: Allyn and Bacon.

HAITH, M. M. (1998). Who put the cog in infant cognition: Is the rich interpretation too costly? *Infant Behaviour and Development, 21,* 167–180.

HAITH, M. M., BERGMAN, T., & MOORE, M. J. (1977). Eye contact and face scanning in early infancy. *Science, 198,* 853–855.

HALL, C., & VAN DE CASTLE, R. (1966). *The content analysis of dreams.* New York: Appleton-Century-Crofts.

HALL, C. S. (1947). Diagnosing personality by the analysis of dreams. *Journal of Abnormal and Social Psychology, 42,* 68–79.

HALL, C. S. (1953). A cognitive theory of dreams. *Journal of General Psychology, 48,* 169–186.

HAMER, D., & COPELAND, P. (1994). *The science of desire: The search for the gay gene and the biology of behavior.* New York: Simon & Schuster.

HAMER, D. H., HU, S., MAGNUSON, V. L., HU, N., & PATTATUCCI, A. M. L. (1993). A linkage between DNA markers on the X chromosome and male sexual orientation. *Science, 261,* 321–327.

HAMILTON, D. L. (1979). A cognitive-attributional analysis of stereotyping. In L. Berkowitz (Ed.), *Advances in experimental social psychology* (Vol. 12). New York: Academic Press.

HAMILTON, D. L., & GIFFORD, R. K. (1976). Illusory correlation in interpersonal perception: A cognitive basis of stereotypic judgments. *Journal of Experimental Social Psychology, 12,* 392–407.

HAMILTON, D. L., & SHERMAN, S. J. (1989). Illusory correlations: Implications for stereotype theory and research. In D. Bar-Tal, C. F. Gravmann, A. W. Kruglanski, & W. Stroebe (Eds.), *Stereotypes and prejudice: Changing conceptions.* New York: Springer-Verlag.

HANEY, C., & ZIMBARDO, P. (1998). The past and the future of U.S. prison policy: Twenty-five years after the Stanford Prison Experiment. *American Psychologist, 53,* 709–727.

HANNIGAN, S. L., & REINITZ, M. T. (2001). A demonstration and comparison of two types of inference-based memory errors. *Journal of Experimental Psychology: Learning, Memory, and Cognition, 37,* 931–940.

HARDIN, C. L., & MAFFI, L. (Eds.). (1997). Color categories in thought and language. *Contemporary Psychology, 3,* 684.

HARE, R. D. (1980). A research scale for the assessment of psychopathy in criminal populations. *Personality and Individual Differences, 1,* 111–119.

HARE, R. D. (1999). *Without conscience: The disturbing world of the psychopaths among us.* New York: Guilford.

HARLOW, H. F. (1971). *Learning to love.* San Francisco: Albion.

HARLOW, H. F., & HARLOW, M. K. (1969). Effects of various mother-infant relationships on rhesus monkey behaviors. In B. M. Foss (Ed.), *Determinants of infant behavior* (Vol. 4). London: Methuen.

HARLOW, J. M. (1868). Recovery from passage of an iron bar through the head. *Boston Medical and Surgical Journal, 39,* 389–393.

HARRIS, J. R. (1995). Where is the child's environment? A group socialization theory of development. *Psychological Review, 102,* 458–489.

HARRIS, M. J., & ROSENTHAL, R. (1988). *Interpersonal expectancy effects and human performance research.* Washington, DC: National Academy Press.

HARRIS, P. R. (1996). Sufficient grounds for optimism? The relationship between perceived controllability and optimistic bias. *Journal of Social and Clinical Psychology, 15,* 9–52.

HART, A. J., WHALEN, P. J., SHIN, L. M., MCINERNEY, S. C., FISCHER, H., & RAUCH, S. L. (2000). Differential response in the human amygdala to racial outgroup vs. ingroup face stimuli. *Neuroreport, 11,* 2351–2355.

HARTER, S. (1998). The development of self-representation. In N. Eisenberg (Ed.), *Handbook of child psychology* (5th ed.), Vol 3: Social, emotional, and personality development (pp. 553–617). New York: Wiley.

HARTMANN, E. (1968). The day residue: Time distribution of waking events. *Psychophysiology, 5,* 222.

HATFIELD, E. (1988). Passionate and companionate love. In R. J. Sternberg & M. L. Barnes (Eds.), *The psychology of love* (pp. 191–217). New Haven, CT: Yale University Press.

HATHAWAY, S. R., & MCKINLEY, J. C. (1943). *Manual for the Minnesota Multiphasic Personality Inventory.* New York: Psychological Corporation.

HAWKINS, R. D., & KANDEL, E. R. (1984). Is there a cell-biological alphabet for simple forms of learning? *Psychological Review, 91,* 375–391.

HAXBY, J. V., GRADY, C. L., HORWIZ, B., UNGERLEIDER, L. G., MISHKIN, M., CARSON, R. E., HERSCOVITCH, P., SCHAPIRO, M. B., & RAPOPORT, S. I. (1990). Dissociation of object and spatial visual processing pathways in human extrastriate cortex. *Neurobiology, 88,* 1621–1625.

HAYDON, P. G. (2001). GLIA: listening and talking to the synapse. *Nature Reviews Neuroscience, 2,* 185–193.

HAYES, J. R. (1989). *The complete problem solver* (2nd ed.). Hillsdale, NJ: Erlbaum.

HAYES, L. A., & WATSON, J. S. (1981). Neonatal imitation: Fact or artifact. *Developmental Psychology, 17,* 655–660.

HAYNE, H., ROVEE-COLLIER, C., & BORZA, M. A. (1991). Infant memory for place information. *Memory and Cognition, 19,* 378–386.

HAYNES, S. G., & FEINLEIB, M. (1980). Women, work, and coronary heart disease: Prospective findings from the Framingham heart study. *American Journal of Public Health, 70,* 133–141.

HAYNES, S. G., FEINLEIB, M., & KANNEL, W. B. (1980). The relationship of psychosocial factors to coronary heart disease in the Framingham study: Pt. 3. Eight-year incidence of coronary heart disease. *American Journal of Epidemiology, 111,* 37–58.

HE, Z. J., & NAKAYAMA, K. (1992). Surfaces versus features in visual search. *Nature, 359,* 231–233.

HEATH, R. G. (1972). Pleasure and brain activity in man. Deep and surface electroencephalograms during orgasm. *Journal of Nervous and Mental Disease, 154,* 3–18.

HEBB, D. O. (1982). Understanding psychological man: A state-of-the-science report. *Psychology Today, 16,* 52–53.

HECHT, S., SHALER, S., & PIREENE, M. H. (1942). Energy, quanta, and vision. *Journal of General Physiology, 25,* 819–840.

HEIDER, F. (1958). *The psychology of interpersonal relations.* New York: Wiley.

HEILBRUN, K. S. (1982). Silverman's subliminal psychodynamic activation: A failure to replicate. *Journal of Abnormal Psychology, 89,* 560–566.

HEILMAN, M. E. (1994). Affirmative action: Some unintended consequences for working women. In B. Staw & L. L. Cummings (Eds.), *Research in organizational behavior* (vol. 16, pp. 125–169). Greenwich, CT: JAI Press.

HEILMAN, M. E., BLOCK, C. J., & LUCAS, J. A. (1992). Presumed incompetent? Stigmatization and affirmative action efforts. *Journal of Applied Psychology, 77,* 536–544.

HEILMAN, M. E., BLOCK, C. J., & STATHATOS, P. (1987). The affirmative action stigma of incompetence: Effects of performance information ambiguity. *Academy of Management Journal, 40,* 603–625.

HEILMAN, M. E., McCULLOUGH, S. E., & GILBERT, D. (1996). The other side of affirmative action. Reactions of non-beneficiaries to sex-based preferential selection. *Journal of Applied Psychology, 81,* 346–357.

HELBURN, S. W. (Ed.). (1995). *Cost, quality and child outcomes in child care centers.* Denver: University of Colorado.

HELD, R. (1965). Plasticity in sensory motor systems. *Scientific American, 21,* 84–94.

HELD, R., & HEIN, A. (1963). Movement produced stimulation in the development of visually guided behavior. *Journal of Comparative and Physiological Psychology, 56,* 872–876.

HELLIGE, J. B. (1990). Hemispheric asymmetry. *Annual Review of Psychology, 41,* 55–80.

HELLIGE, J. B. (1993). Unity of thought and action: Varieties of interaction between left and right hemispheres. *Current Directions in Psychological Science, 2,* 21 25.

HELZER, J. E., & CANINO, G. J. (1992). *Alcoholism in North America, Europe, and Asia.* New York: Oxford University Press.

HELZER, J. E., BUCHOLZ, K., & ROBINS, L. N. (1992). Five communities in the United States: Results of the Epidemiologic Catchment Area Survey. In J. E. Helzer & G. J. Canino (Eds.). *Alcoholism in North America, Europe & Asia.* New York: Oxford University Press.

HEMMI, T. (1969). How we have handled the problem of drug abuse in Japan. In F. Sjoqvist & M. Tottie (Eds.), *Abuse of central stimulants.* New York: Raven Press.

HENCHY, T., & GLASS, D. C. (1968). Evaluation apprehension and social facilitation of dominant and subordinate responses. *Journal of Personality and Social Psychology, 10,* 445–454.

HENDERSON, J. M., WEEKS, P. A. JR., & HOLLINGWORTH, A. (1999). The effects of semantic consistency on eye movements during complex scene viewing. *Journal of Experimental Psychology: Human Perception and Performance, 25,* 210–228.

HENLEY, N., HAMILTON, M., & THORNE, B. (1985). Womanspeak and manspeak: Sex differences and sexism in communication, verbal and nonverbal. In A. G. Sargent (Ed.), *Beyond sex roles.* St. Paul, MN: West.

HENRY, B., & MOFFITT, T. E. (1997). Neuropsychological and neuroimaging studies of juvenile delinquency and adult criminal behavior. In D. M. Stoff, J. Breiling, & J. D. Maser (Eds.) *Handbook of antisocial personality disorder* (pp. 280–288). New York: Wiley.

HENSEL, H. (1973). Cutaneous thermoreceptors. In A. Iggo (Ed.), *Handbook of sensory physiology* (Vol. 2). Berlin: Springer-Verlag.

HERDT, G. H. (Ed.) (1984). *Ritualized homosexuality in Melanesia.* Berkeley: University of California Press.

HEREK, G. M. (1986). The instrumentality of attitudes: Toward a neofunctional theory. *Journal of Social Issues, 42,* 99–114.

HEREK, G. M. (1987). Can functions be measured? A new perspective on the functional approach to attitudes. *Social Psychology Quarterly, 50,* 285–303.

HERING, E. (1878). *Outlines of a theory of the light sense* (L. M. Hurvich & D. Jameson, Trans.). Cambridge, MA: Harvard University Press.

HERING, E. (1920). Memory as a universal function of organized matter. In S. Butler (Ed.), *Unconscious memory.* London: Jonathon Cape.

HERMAN, C. P., & MACK, D. (1975). Restrained and unrestrained eating. *Journal of Personality, 43,* 647–660.

HERMAN, C. P., & POLIVY, J. (1980). Restrained eating. In A. J. Stunkard (Ed.), *Obesity.* Philadelphia: Saunders.

HERRNSTEIN, R. J., & MURRAY, C. (1994). *The bell curve: Intelligence and class structure in American life.* New York: Free Press.

HESS, E. H. (1972). "Imprinting" in a natural laboratory. *Scientific American, 227,* 24–31.

HETHERINGON, E. M., & BRACKBILL, Y. (1963). Etiology and covariation of obstinacy, orderliness, and parsimony in young children. *Child Development, 34,* 919–943.

HETTEMA, J. M., NEALE, M. C., & KENDLER, K. S. (2001). A review and meta-analysis of the genetic epidemiology of anxiety disorders. *American Journal of Psychiatry, 158,* 1568–1578.

HEWLETT, W. A. (2000). Benzodiazepines in the treatment of obsessive-compulsive disorder. *Obsessive-compulsive disorder: contemporary issues in treatment* (pp. 405–429). Mahwah, NJ: Lawrence Erlbaum Associates, Inc.

HEWSTONE, M. (1990). The "ultimate attribution error"? A review of the literature on intergroup causal attribution. *European Journal of Social Psychology, 20,* 311–335.

HIGGINS, E. T. (1987). Self-discrepancy: A theory relating self and affect. *Psychological Review, 94,* 319–340.

HILGARD, E. R. (1965). *Hypnotic susceptibility.* New York: Harcourt Brace Jovanovich.

HILGARD, E. R. (1968). *The experience of hypnosis.* New York: Harcourt Brace Jovanovich.

HILGARD, E. R. (1986). *Divided consciousness: Multiple controls in human thought and action.* New York: Wiley-Interscience.

HILGARD, E. R. (1987). *Psychology in America: A historical survey.* San Diego: Harcourt Brace Javanovich.

HILGARD, E. R., & HILGARD, J. R. (1975). *Hypnosis in the relief of pain.* Los Altos, CA: Kaufmann.

HILGARD, E. R., HILGARD, J. R., MACDONALD, H., MORGAN, A. H., & JOHNSON, L. S. (1978). Covert pain in hypnotic analgesia: Its reality as tested by the real-simulator design. *Journal of Abnormal Psychology, 87,* 655–663.

HILL, C., RUBIN, Z., & PEPLAU, L. A. (1976). Breakups before marriage: The end of 103 affairs. *Journal of Social Issues, 32,* 147–168.

HILLIER, L., HEWITT, K. L., & MORRONGIELTO, B. A. (1992). Infants' perception of illusions in sound localization: Reaching to sounds in the dark. *Journal of Experimental Child Psychology, 53,* 159–179.

HILLYARD, S. A. (1985). Electrophysiology of human selective attention. *Trends in Neuroscience, 8,* 400–406.

HILLYARD, S. A., VOGEL, E. K., & LUCK, S. J. (1998). Sensory gain control (amplification) as a mechanism of selective attention: Electrophysiological and neuroimaging evidence. *Philosophical Transactions of the Royal Society: Biological Science, 353,* 1257–1270.

HINDE, R. (1982). *Ethology: Its nature and relations with other sciences.* New York: Oxford University Press.

HINSHAW, S. P. (1994). *Attention deficits and hyperactivity in children.* Thousand Oaks, CA: Sage.

HIRSCH, J., & BATCHELOR, B. R. (1976). Adipose tissue cellularity and human obesity. *Clinical Endocrinology and Metabolism, 5,* 299–311.

HIRSCH, S. M., & BOLLES, R. C. (1980). On the ability of prey to recognize predators. *Zeitschrift für Tierpsychologie, 54,* 71–84.

HOBSON, J. A. (1988). *The dreaming brain.* New York: Basic Books.

HOBSON, J. A. (1989). *Sleep.* New York: Freeman.

HOBSON, J. A. (1994). *The chemistry of conscious states, how the brain changes its mind.* New York: Little, Brown.

HOBSON, J. A. (1997). Dreaming as delirium: A mental status analysis of our nightly madness. *Seminars in Neurology, 1,* 121–128.

HOEBEL, B. G., & TEITELBAUM, P. (1966). Effects of force-feeding and starvation on food intake and body weight on a rat with ventromedial hypothalamic lesions. *Journal of Comparative and Physiological Psychology, 61,* 189–193.

HOFFMAN, H. G., DOCTOR, J. N., PATTERSON, D. R., CARROUGHER, G. J., & FURNESS, T. A. III. (2000). Use of virtual reality for adjunctive treatment of adolescent burn pain during wound care: A case report. *Pain, 85,* 305–309.

HOFFMAN, H. G, PATTERSON, D. R., & CARROUGHER, G. J. (2000). Use of virtual reality for adjunctive treatment of adult burn pain during physical therapy: A controlled study. *Clinical Journal of Pain, 16,* 244–250.

HOFLING, C. K., BROTZMAN, E., DALRYMPLE, S., GRAVES, N., & PIERCE, C. M. (1966). An experimental study in nurse-physician relationships. *Journal of Nervous and Mental Disease, 143,* 171–180.

HOGARTY, G. E. (1986). Family psychoeducation, social skills training, and maintenance chemotherapy in the aftercare treatment of schizophrenia: I. One-year effects of a controlled study on relapse and expressed emotion. *Archives of General Psychiatry, 43,* 633–642.

HOGARTY, G. E., SCHOOLER, N. R., ULRICH, R., MUSSARE, F., FERRO, P., & HERRON, E. (1979). Fluphenazine and social therapy in the after care of schizophrenic patients. *Archives of General Psychiatry, 36,* 1283–1294.

HOGBEN, J. H., & DI LOLLO, V. (1974). Perceptual integration and perceptual segregation of brief visual stimuli. *Vision Research, 14,* 1059–1069.

HOHMANN, G. W. (1962). Some effects of spinal cord lesions on experienced emotional feelings. *Psychophysiology, 3,* 143–156.

HOLLAND, J. H., HOLYOAK, K. J., NISBETT, R. E., & THAGARD, P. R. (1986). *Induction: Processes of inference, learning, and discovery.* Cambridge, MA: MIT Press.

HOLLINGWORTH, A., & HENDERSON, J. M. (2000). Semantic informativeness mediates the detection of changes in natural scenes. *Visual Cognition, 7,* 213–235.

HOLLOWAY, F. A. (1989). What is affirmative action? In F. A. Blanchard & F. J. Crosby (Eds.), *Affirmative action in perspective* (pp. 9–19). New York: Springer Verlag.

HOLMES, D. S. (1974). Investigations of repression: Differential recall of material experimentally or naturally associated with ego threat. *Psychological Bulletin, 81,* 632–653.

HOLMES, D. S. (1984). Meditation and somatic arousal reduction: A review of the experimental evidence. *American Psychologist, 39,* 1–10.

HOLMES, D. S. (1985a). To meditate or rest? The answer is rest. *American Psychologist, 40,* 728–731.

HOLMES, D. S. (1985b). Self-control of somatic arousal: An examination of the effects of meditation and feedback. *American Behavioral Scientist, 28,* 486–496.

HOLMES, T. H., & RAHE, R. H. (1967). The social readjustment rating scale. *Journal of Psychosomatic Research, 11,* 213–218.

HOLROYD, K. A., APPEL, M. A., & ANDRASIK, F. (1983). A cognitive behavioral approach to psychophysiological disorders. In D. Meichenbaum & M. E. Jaremko (Eds.), *Stress reduction and prevention.* New York: Plenum.

HONIG, W. K., & STADDON, J. E. R. (Eds.). (1977). *Handbook of operant behavior.* Englewood Cliffs, NJ: Prentice-Hall.

HONORTON, C. (1985). Meta-analysis of psi ganzfeld research: A response to Hyman. *Journal of Parapsychology, 49,* 51–91.

HOOLEY, J. M., RICHTERS, J. E., WEINTRAUB, S., & NEALE, J. M. (1987). Psychopathology and marital distress: The positive side of positive symptoms. *Journal of Abnormal Psychology, 96,* 27–33.

HOON, P. W., WINCZE, J. P., & HOON, E. F. (1977). A test of reciprocal inhibition: Are anxiety and sexual arousal in women mutually inhibitory? *Journal of Abnormal Psychology, 86,* 65–74.

HOPKINS, J. R. (1977). Sexual behavior in adolescence. *Journal of Social Issues, 33,* 67–85.

HORM, J., & ANDERSON, K. (1993). Who in America is trying to lose weight? *Annals of Internal Medicine, 119,* 672–676.

HORNE, J. A., & MCGRATH, M. J. (1984). The consolidation hypothesis for REM sleep function: Stress and other confounding factors—A review. *Biological Psychology, 18,* 165–184.

HOROWITZ, F. D. (1974). Visual attention, auditory stimulation, and language stimulation in young infants. *Monographs of the Society for Research in Child Development, 31,* Serial No. 158.

HOROWITZ, M. (1986). Stress-response syndromes: A review of postraumatic and adjustment disorders. *Hospital and Community Psychiatry, 37,* 241–249.

HOVLAND, C., JANIS, I., & KELLEY, H. H. (1953). *Communication and persuasion.* New Haven, CT: Yale University Press.

HOWES, C. (1990). Can the age of entry into child care and the quality of child care predict adjustment in kindergarten? *Developmental Psychology, 26,* 292–303.

HOWES, C., PHILLIPS, D. A., & WHITEBOOK, M. (1992). Thresholds of quality: Implications for the social development of children in center-based child care. *Child Development, 63,* 449–460.

HSER, Y. I., ANGLIN, D., & POWERS, K. (1993). A 24-year follow-up of California narcotics addicts. *Archives of General Psychiatry, 50,* 577–584.

HU, S., PATTATUCCI, A. M., PATTERSON, C., LI, L., FULKER, D. W., CHERNY, S. S., KRUGLYAK, L., HAMER, D. H. (1995). Linkage between sexual orientation and chromosome Xq28 in males but not in females. *Nature Genetics, 11,* 248–256.

HUBEL, D. H., & WIESEL, T. N. (1963). Receptive fields of cells in striate cortex of very young visually inexperienced kittens. *Journal of Neurophysiology, 26,* 994–1002.

HUBEL, D. H., & WIESEL, T. N. (1968). Receptive fields and functional architecture of monkey striate cortex. *Journal of Physiology, 195,* 215–243.

HUDSON, J. L., & RAPEE, R. M. (2000). The origins of social phobia. *Behavior Modification, 24,* 102–129.

HUDSON, J. W., & HOYT, L. L. (1981). Personal characteristics important in mate preference among college students. *Social Behavior and Personality, 9,* 93–96.

HUESMANN, L. R., ERON, L. D., LEFKOWITZ, M. M., & WALDER, L. O. (1984). The stability of aggression over time and generations. *Developmental Psychology, 20,* 1120–1134.

HUGHES, J. R. (1986). Genetics of smoking: A review. *Behavior Therapy, 17,* 335–345.

HUGUET, P., GALVAING, M. P., MONTEIL, J. M., & DUMAS, F. (1999). Social presence effects in the Stroop task: Further evidence for an attentional view of social facilitation. *Journal of Personality and Social Psychology, 77,* 1011–1025.

HUMMEL, J. E., & BIEDERMAN, I. (1992). Dynamic binding in a neutral network for shape recognition. *Psychological Review, 99,* 480–517.

HUNT, E. (1990). A modern arsenal for mental assessment. *Educational Psychologist, 25,* 223–241.

HUNT, E. (1996). *Will we be smart enough?* New York: Russell Sage.

HUNT, M. (1974). *Sexual behavior in the 1970's.* Chicago: Playboy Press.

HUNT, P. J., & HILLERY, J. M. (1973). *Social facilitation at different stages in learning.* Paper presented at the Midwestern Psychological Association Meetings, Cleveland.

HUNTER, I. M. L. (1974). *Memory.* Baltimore: Penguin.

HURVICH, L. M., & JAMESON, D. (1974). Opponent processes as a model of neural organizations. *American Psychologist, 29,* 88–102.

HUSELID, R. F., & COOPER, M. L. (1992). Gender roles as mediators of sex difference in adolescent alcohol use and abuse. *Journal of Health and Social Behavior, 33,* 348–362.

HUTTON, D. C., & BAUMEISTER, R. F. (1992). Self-awareness and attitude change: Seeing oneself on the central route to persuasion. *Personality and Social Psychology Bulletin, 18,* 68–75.

HYMAN, I. E., HUSBAND, T. H., & BILLINGS, F. G. (1995). False memories of childhood experiences. *Applied Cognitive Psychology, 9,* 181–197.

HYMAN, R. (1985). The ganzfield psi experiment: A critical appraisal. *Journal of Parapsychology, 49,* 3–49.

HYMAN, R. (1994). Anomaly or Artifact? Comments on Bem and Honorton. *Psychological Bulletin, 115,* 19–24.

HYMAN, R., & HONORTON, C. (1986). A joint communiqué: The psi ganzfeld controversy. *Journal of Parapsychology, 50,* 351–364.

IMPERATO-MCGINLEY, J., PETERSON, R. E., GAUTIER, T., & STURLA, E. (1979). Androgens and the evolution of male gender identity among male pseudohermaphrodites with 5 alpha reductase deficiency. *New England Journal of Medicine, 300,* 1233–1237.

INGRAM, R. E., HAYES, A., & SCOTT, W. (2000). Empirically supported treatments: A critical analysis. In C. R. Snyder & R. Ingram (Eds.), *Handbook of psychological change* (pp. 40–60). New York: Wiley.

INSEL, T. R. (Ed.). (1984) *New findings in obsessive-compulsive disorder.* Washington, DC: American Psychiatric Press.

INSTITUTE OF MEDICINE. (1982). *Marijuana and health.* Washington, DC: National Academy Press.

INTERNATIONAL NARCOTICS CONTROL BOARD (1998). *Psychotropic substances: Statistics for 1996.* New York: United Nations.

INTRAUB, H, & RICHARDSON, M. (1989) Wide-angle memories of close-up scenes. *Journal of Experimental Psychology: Learning, Memory, and Cognition, 15,* 179–187.

IRONSON, G., WYNINGS, C., SCHNEIDERMAN, N., BAUM, A., RODRIGUEZ, M. GREENWOOD, D., BENIGHT, C., ANTONI, M., LAPERRIER, A., HUANG, H. S., KLIMAS, N., & FLETCHER, M. A. (1997). Posttraumatic stress symptoms, intrusive thoughts, loss and immune function after Hurricane Andrew. *Psychosomatic Medicine, 59,* 128–141.

ISABELLA, R. A., & BELSKY, J. (1991). Interactional synchrony and the origins of infant-mother attachment: A replication study. *Child Development, 62,* 373–384.

ISEN, A. M. (2002). A role for neuropsychology in understanding the facilitating effects of positive affect on social behavior and cognitive processes. In C. R. Snyder & S. J. Lopez (Eds.), *Handbook of positive psychology* (pp. 528–540). Oxford: Oxford University Press.

ISEN, P. M. (1985). The asymmetry of happiness and sadness in effects on memory in normal college students. *Journal of Experimental Psychology: General, 114,* 388–391.

ISEN, P. M., SHALKER, T. E., CLARK, M., & KARP, L. (1978). Affect, accessibility of material in memory, and behavior: A cognitive loop? *Journal of Personality and Social Psychology, 36,* 1–12.

ISENBERG, D. J. (1986). Group polarization: A critical review and meta-analysis. *Journal of Personality and Social Psychology, 50,* 1141–1151.

ISOZAKI, M. (1984). The effect of discussion on polarization of judgments. *Japanese Psychological Research, 26,* 187–193.

JABLENSKY, A. (1989). Epidemiology and cross-cultural aspects of schizophrenia. *Psychiatric Annals, 19,* 516–524.

JABLENSKY, A. (2000). Epidemiology of schizophrenia: The global burden of disease and disability. *European Archives of Clinical Psychiatry and Neuroscience, 250,* 274–285.

JACKENDOFF, R. (1990). *Consciousness and the computational mind.* Cambridge, MA: MIT Press.

JACOBS, D., BLACKBURN, H., HIGGINS, M., REED, D., ISO, H., MCMILLAN, G., NEATON, J., NELSON, J., POTTER, J., RIFKIND, B., ROSSOUW, J., SHEKELLE, R., & YUSUF, S. (1992). Report of the conference on low blood cholesterol: Mortality associations. *Circulation, 86,* 1046–1060.

JACOBS, W. J., & NADEL, W. (1985). Stress-induced recovery of fears and phobias. *Psychological Review, 92,* 512–531.

JACOBSON, A. L., FRIED, C., & HOROWITZ, S. D. (1967). Classical conditioning, pseudoconditioning, or sensitization in the planarian. *Journal of Comparative and Physiological Psychology, 64,* 73–79.

JACOBSON, N. S., DOBSON, K. S., TRUAX, P. A., ADDIS, M. E., KOERNER, K., GOLLAN, J. K., GORTNER, E., & PRINCE, S. E. (1996). A component analysis of cognitive-behavioral treatment for depression. *Journal of Consulting and Clinical Psychology, 64,* 295–304.

JACOBSON, N. S., & HOLLON, S. D. (1996). Cognitive-behavior therapy versus pharmacotherapy: Now that the jury's returned its verdict, it's time to present the rest of the evidence. *Journal of Consulting and Clinical Psychology, 64,* 74–80.

JAMES, W. (1884). What is an emotion? *Mind, 9,* 188–205.

JAMES, W. (1890/1950). *Principles of psychology,* Vol. 2. New York: Dover.

JAMISON, K. R. (1995, February). Manic-depressive illness and creativity. *Scientific American* 46–51.

JAMISON, K. R. (1995). *An unquiet mind.* New York: Knopf.

JAMISON, K. R. (1999). *Night falls fast: understanding suicide.* New York: Knopf.

JAMISON, R. N. (1976). *Mastering chronic pain: A professional's guide to behavioral treatment.* Sarasota, FL: Professional Resource Press.

JAMISON, R. N., RAYMOND, S. A., SLAWSBY, E. A. NEDELJKOVIC, S. S., & KATZ, N. P. (1998). Opioid therapy for noncancer back pain: A randomized prospective study. *Spine, 23,* 2591–2600.

JANET, P. (1889). *L'automisme psychologigue*. Paris: Félix Alcan.

JANIS, I. L. (1982). *Groupthink: Psychological studies of policy decisions and fiascoes* (2nd ed.). Boston: Houghton Mifflin.

JANIS, I. L. (1985). Sources of error in strategic decision making. In J. M. Pennings (Ed.), *Organizational strategy and change*. San Francisco: Jossey-Bass.

JANOFF-BULMAN, R. (1992). *Shattered assumptions: Toward a new psychology of trauma*. New York: Maxwell Macmillan International.

JANOF-BULMAN, R., & MCPHERSON FRANTZ, C. (1997). The impact of trauma on meaning: From meaningless world to meaningful life. In M. Power & C. R. Brewin (Eds.), *The transformation of meaning in psychological therapies: Integrating theory and practice* (pp. 245–266). New York: Wiley.

JASMOS, T. M., & HAKMILLER, K. L. (1975). Some effects of lesion level and emotional cues on affective expression in spinal cord patients. *Psychological Reports, 37*, 859–870.

JEMMOTT, J. B., III, BORYSENKO, M., MCCELLAND, D. C., CHAPMAN, R., MEYER, D., & BENSON, H. (1985). Academic stress, power motivation, and decrease in salivary secretory immunoglobulin: A secretion rate. *Lancet, 1*, 1400–1402.

JENNINGS, D., AMABILE, T. M., & ROSS, L. (1982). Informal covariation assessment: Data-based vs. theory-based judgments. In A. Tversky, D. Kahneman, & P. Slovic (Eds.), *Judgment under uncertainty: Heuristics and biases*. New York: Cambridge University Press.

JI, L., PENG, K., & NISBETT, R. E. (2000). Culture, control, and perception of relationship in the environment. *Journal of Personality and Social Psychology, 78*, 943–955.

JOHANSSON, G., & FRANKENHAEUSER, J. (1973). Temporal factors in sympatho-adrenomedullary activity following acute behavioral activation. *Biological Psychology, 1*, 63–73.

JOHANSSON, G., VON HOFSTEN, C., & JANSON, G. (1980). Event perception. *Annual Review of Psychology, 31*, 27–63.

JOHN, O. P. (1990). The "Big Five" factor taxonomy: Dimension of personality in the natural language and in questionnaires. In L. A. Pervin (Ed.), *Handbook of personality: Theory and research* (pp. 66–100). New York: Guilford.

JOHNSON, E. J., & TVERSKY, A. (1983). Affect, generalization, and the perception of risk. *Journal of Personality and Social Psychology, 45*, 20–31.

JOHNSON, M. H. (1997). *Developmental cognitive neuroscience: An introduction*. Oxford, England: Blackwell.

JOHNSON, R. D., & DOWNING, L. L. (1979). Deindividuation and valence of cues: Effect on prosocial and antisocial behavior. *Journal of Personality and Social Psychology, 37*, 1532–1538.

JOHNSON-LAIRD, P. N. (1985). The deductive reasoning ability. In R. J. Sternberg (Ed.), *Human abilities: An information processing approach*. New York: Freeman.

JOHNSON-LAIRD, P. (1988a). A computational analysis of consciousness. In A. J. Marcel & E. Bisiach (Eds.), *Consciousness in contemporary science*. New York: Oxford University Press.

JOHNSON-LAIRD, P. N. (1988b). *The computer and the mind: An introduction to cognitive science*. Cambridge, MA: Harvard University Press.

JOHNSON-LAIRD, P. N. (1989). Mental models. In M. I. Posner (Ed.), *Foundations of cognitive science*. Cambridge, MA: MIT Press.

JOHNSON-LAIRD, P. N., & BYRNE, R. M. J. (1991). *Deduction*. Hillsdale, NJ: Erlbaum.

JOHNSON-LAIRD, P. N., LEGRENZI, P., GIROTTO, V., LEGRENZI, M. S., & CAVERNI, J. P. (1999). Naïve probability: A mental model theory of extensional reasoning. *Psychological Review, 106*, 62–88.

JOHNSTON, L. D., O'MALLEY, P. M., & BACHMAN, J. G. (1995). *National survey results on drug use*. Rockville, MD: National Institute on Drug Abuse.

JONES, E. E. (1978). Effects of race on psychotherapy process and outcome: An exploratory investigation. *Psychotherapy: Theory, Research, and Practice, 15*, 226–236.

JONES, E. E. (1990). *Interpersonal perception*. New York: Freeman.

JONES, E. E., & HARRIS, V. A. (1967). The attribution of attitudes. *Journal of Experimental Social Psychology, 3*, 1–24.

JONES, E. E., ROCK, L., SHAVER, K. G., GOETHALS, G. R., & WARD, L. M. (1968). Pattern of performance and ability attribution: An unexpected primacy effect. *Journal of Personality and Social Psychology, 9*, 317–340.

JONES, H. C., & LOVINGER, P. W. (1985). *The marijuana question and science's search for an answer*. New York: Dodd, Mead.

JUDD, L., AKISKAL, H., MASER, J., ZELLER, P. J., ENDICOTT, J., CORYELL, W., PAULUS, M., KUNOVAC, J., LEON, A., MUELLER, T., RICE, J., & KELLER, M. (1998). A prospective 12-year study of subsyndromal and syndromal depressive symptoms in unipolar major depressive disorders. *Archives of General Psychiatry, 55*, 694–700.

JULIEN, R. M. (1988). *Drugs and the body*. New York: Freeman.

JULIEN, R. M. (1992). *A primer of drug action: A concise, nontechnical guide to the actions, uses, and side effects of psychoactive drugs* (6th ed.). New York: Freeman.

JUSSIM, L. (1991). Social perception and social reality: A reflection-construction model. *Psychological Review, 98*, 54–73.

JUST, M. A., & CARPENTER, P. A. (1980). A theory of reading: From eye fixations to comprehension. *Psychological Review, 87*, 329–354.

JUST, M. A., & CARPENTER, P. A. (1992). A capacity theory of comprehension: Individual differences in working memory. *Psychological Review, 99*, 122.

KAGAN, J. (1979). Overview: Perspectives on human infancy. In J. D. Osofsky (Ed.), *Handbook of infant development*. New York: Wiley-Interscience.

KAGAN, J. (1998). *Three seductive ideas*. Cambridge, MA: Harvard University Press.

KAGAN, J., KEARSLEY, R. B., & ZELAZO, P. (1978). *Infancy: Its place in human development*. Cambridge, MA: Harvard University Press.

KAGAN, J., & SNIDMAN, N. (1991). Temperamental factors in human development. *American Psychologist, 46*, 856–862.

KAGAN, N. (1984). *The nature of the child*. New York: Basic Books.

KAGAN, N., & MOSS, H. A. (1962). *Birth to maturity*. New York: Wiley.

KAHNEMAN, D., SLOVIC, P., & TVERSKY, A. (Eds.). (1982). *Judgment under uncertainty: Heuristics and biases*. New York: Cambridge University Press.

KAHNEMAN, D., & TVERSKY, A. (1996). On the reality of cognitive illusions. *Psychological Review, 103*, 582–591.

KAIL, R. (1989). *The development of memory in children* (3rd ed.). New York: Freeman.

KALAT, P. W. (2001). *Biological psychology* (7th ed.). Belmont, CA: Wadsworth/Thomson Learning.

KAMEN-SIEGEL, L., RODIN, J., SELIGMAN, M. E., & DWYER, J. (1991). Explanatory style and cell-mediated immunity in elderly men and women. *Health Psychology, 10*, 229–235.

KAMIN, L. J. (1974). *The science and politics of IQ*. Hillsdale, NJ: Erlbaum.

KANDEL, E. R., SCHWARTZ, J. H., & JESSELL, T. M. (Eds.). (1991). *Principles of neural science* (3rd ed.). New York: Elsevier.

KAPLAN, J. R., & KAUFMANN, P. (1993). Low or lowered cholesterol and risk of death from suicide and trauma. *Metabolism, 42 (supp. 1)*, 45–56.

KAPLAN, J. R., MULDOON, M. F., MANUCK, S. B., & MANN, J. J. (1997). Assessing the observed relationship between low cholesterol and violence-related mortality: Implications for suicide risk. In Stoff, D. M. (Ed.), *The neurobiology of suicide: From the bench to the clinic* (pp. 57–85), New York: New York Academy of Sciences.

KAPLAN, M. R., & MILLER, C. E. (1987). Group decision making and normative versus informational influence: Effects of type of issue and assigned decision rule. *Journal of Personality and Social Psychology, 53*, 306–313.

KARASEK, R., BAKER, D., MARXER, F., AHLBOM, A., & THEORELL, T. (1981). Job decision latitude, job demands, and cardiovascular disease: A prospective study of Swedish men. *American Journal of Public Health, 71*, 694–705.

KARASEK, R. A., THEORELL, T. G., SCHWARTZ, J., PIEPER, C., & ALFREDSSON, L. (1982). Job, psychological factors and coronary heart disease: Swedish prospective findings and U.S. prevalence findings using a new occupation inference method. *Advances in Cardiology, 29*, 62–67.

KARNI, A., TANNE, D., RUBENSTEIN, B. S., ASKENASY, J. J. M., & SAGI, D. (1994). Dependence on REM sleep of overnight improvement of a perceptual skill. *Science, 265*, 679–682.

KARNO, M., & GOLDING, J. M. (1991). Obsessive compulsive disorder. In L. R. Robins & D. A. Regier (Eds.), *Psychiatric disorders in America: The epidemiologic catchment area study*. New York: Maxwell Macmillan International.

KARNO, M., HOUGH, R., BURNAM, A., ESCOBAR, J. I., TIMBERS, D. M., SANTANA, F., & BOYD, J. H. (1987). Lifetime prevalence of specific psychiatric disorders among Mexican-Americans and non-Hispanic whites in Los Angeles. *Archives of General Psychiatry, 44*, 695–701.

KARNO, M., & JENKINS, J. H. (1993). Cross-cultural issues in the course and treatment of schizophrenia. *Psychiatric Clinics of North America, 16*, 339–350.

KARYLOWSKI, J. J. (1990). Social reference points and accessibility of trait-related information in self-other similarity judgments. *Journal of Personality and Social Psychology, 58*, 975–983.

KASSIN, S.M. (1997). The psychology of confession evidence. *American Psychologist, 52*, 221–233.

KASTNER, S., DE WEERD, P., DESIMONE, R., & UNGERLEIDER, L. G. (1998). Mechanisms of directed attention in the human extrastriate cortex as revealed by functional MRI. *Science, 282*, 108–111.

KASTNER, S., & UNGERLEIDER, L. G. (2000). Mechanisms of visual attention in the human cortex. *Annual Review of Neuroscience, 23*, 315–341.

KATZ, D. (1960). The functional approach to the study of attitudes. *Public Opinion Quarterly, 24*, 163–204.

KATZ, L. C., & SHATZ, C. J. (1996). Synaptic activity and the construction of cortical circuits. *Science, 274*, 1133.

KATZ, R., & WYKES, T. (1985). The psychological difference between temporally predictable and unpredictable stressful events: Evidence for information control theories. *Journal of Personality and Social Psychology, 48*, 781–790.

KAUFMAN, G. (1995, November). *Methylphenidate findings from New York's triplicate prescription data.* Presented at the annual conference of the National Association of State Controlled Substances Authorities.

KAUFMAN, L., & ROCK, I. (1989). The moon illusion thirty years later. In M. Hershenson (Ed.), *The moon illusion* (pp. 193–234). Hillsdale, NJ: Erlbaum.

KAZDIN, A. E. (1982). Symptom substitution, generalization, and response covariation: Implications for psychotherapy outcome. *Psychological Bulletin, 91*, 349–365.

KAZDIN, A. E., & WEISZ, J. R. (1998). Identifying and developing empirically supported child and adolescent treatments. *Journal of Consulting and Clinical Psychology, 66*, 19–36.

KEIL, F. C. (1989). *Concepts, kinds, and cognitive development.* Cambridge, MA: MIT Press.

KEIL, F. C., & BATTERMAN, N. A. (1984). Characteristic-to-defining shift in the development of word meaning. *Journal of Verbal Learning and Verbal Behavior, 23*, 221–236.

KELLER, M. B., & BAKER, L. A. (1991). Bipolar disorder: Epidemiology, course, diagnosis, and treatment. *Bulletin of the Menninger Clinic, 55*, 172–181.

KELLEY, H. H. (1950). The warm-cold variable in first impressions of persons. *Journal of Personality, 18*, 431–439.

KELLEY, H. H. (1967). Attribution theory in social psychology. In D. Levine (Ed.), *Nebraska symposium on motivation* (Vol. 15). Lincoln: University of Nebraska Press.

KELLMAN, P. J. (1984). Perception of three-dimensional form by human infants. *Perception and Psychophysics, 36*, 353–358.

KELLY, G. A. (1955). *The psychology of personal constructs.* New York: Norton.

KELTNER, D., ELLSWORTH, P. C., & EDWARDS, K. (1993). Beyond simple pessimism: Effects of sadness and anger on social perception. *Journal of Personality and Social Psychology, 64*, 740–752.

KENDLER, K. S., NEALE, M. C., KESSLER, R. C., & HEATH, A. C. (1992). Major depression and generalized anxiety disorder: Same genes, (partly) different environments? *Archives of General Psychiatry, 49*, 716–722.

KENDLER, K. S., NEALE, M. C., KESSLER, R. C., & HEATH, A. C. (1993). Panic disorder in women: A population-based twin study. *Psychological Medicine, 23*, 397–406.

KENDLER, K. S., NEALE, M. C., KESSLER, R. C., HEATH, A. C., & EAVES, L. J. (1992). The genetic epidemiology of phobias in women. *Archives of General Psychiatry, 49*, 273–281.

KENRICK, D. T. (2001). Evolutionary psychology, cognitive science, and dynamical systems: Building an integrative paradigm. *Current Directions in Psychological Science, 10*, 13–17.

KENRICK, D. T., & GUTIERRES, S. E. (1980). Contrast effects and judgments of physical attractiveness: When beauty becomes a social problem. *Journal of Personality and Social Psychology, 38*, 131–140.

KENRICK, D. T., & KEEFE, R. C. (1992). Age preferences in mates reflect sex differences in human reproductive strategies. *Behavioral and Brain Sciences, 15*, 75–91.

KENRICK, D. T., SADALLA, E. K., GROTCH, G., & TROST, M. R. (1990). Evolution, traits and the stages of human courtship: Qualifying the parental

investment model. *Journal of Personality, 58*, 97–116.

KENSHALO, D. R., NAFE, J. P., & BROOKS, B. (1961). Variations in thermal sensitivity. *Science, 134*, 104–105.

KEPHART, W. M. (1967). Some correlates of romantic love. *Journal of Marriage and the Family, 29*, 470–474.

KERNBERG, P. F. (1979). Psychoanalytic profile of the borderline adolescent. *Adolescent Psychiatry, 7*, 234–256.

KERNIS, M. H., & WHEELER, L. (1981). Beautiful friends and ugly strangers: Radiation and contrast effects in perception of same-sex pairs. *Journal of Personality and Social Psychology, 7*, 617–620.

KESSLER, R. C., BROWN, R. L., & BROMAN, C. L. (1981). Sex differences in psychiatric help-seeking: Evidence from four large-scale surveys. *Journal of Health and Social Behavior, 22*, 49–64.

KESSLER, R. C., DAVIS, C. G., & KENDLER, K. S. (1997). Childhood adversity and adult psychiatric disorder in the US National Comorbidity Survey. *Psychological Medicine, 27*, 1101–1119.

KESSLER, R. C., MCGONAGLE, K. A., ZHAO, S., NELSON, C., HUGHES, M., ESHLEMAN, S., WITTCHEN, H., & KENDLER, K. (1994). Lifetime and 12-month prevalence of DSM-III-R psychiatric disorders in the United States. *Archives of General Psychiatry, 51*, 8–19.

KESSLER, R. C., STEIN, M. B., & BERGLUND, P. (1998). Social phobia subtypes in the National Comorbidity Survey. *American Journal of Psychiatry, 155*, 613–619.

KIECOLT-GLASER, J. K., and collaborators. (1985). Psychosocial enhancement of immunocompetence in a geriatric population. *Health Psychology, 4*, 25–41.

KIECOLT-GLASER, J. K., GLASER, R., CACIOPPO, J. T., & MALARKEY, W. B. (1998). Marital stress: Immunologic, neuroendocrine, and autonomic correlates. *Annals of the New York Academy of Sciences, 840*, 656–663.

KIECOLT-GLASER, J. K., KENNEDY, S., MALKOFF, S., FISHER, L., SPEICHER, C. E., & GLASER, R. (1988). Marital discord and immunity in males. *Psychosomatic Medicine, 50*, 213–229.

KIECOLT-GLASER, J. K., MCGUIRE, L., ROBLES, T. F., & GLASER, R. (2002). Emotions, morbidity, and mortality: New perspectives from psychoneuroimmunology. *Annual Review of Psychology, 53*, 83–107.

KIECOLT-GLASER, J. K., PAGE, G. G., MARUCHA, P. T., MACCALLUM, R. C., & GLASER, R. (1998). Psychological influences on surgical recovery. *American Psychologist, 53*, 1209–1218.

KIEHL, K. A., SMITH, A. M., HARE, R. D., MENDREK, A., FORSTER, B. B., BRINK, J., & LIDDLE, P. F. (2001). Limbic abnormalities in affective processing by criminal psychopaths as revealed by functional magnetic resonance imaging. *Biological Psychiatry, 50*, 677–684.

KIESLER, C. A., & SIBULKIN, A. E. (1987). *Mental hospitalization: Myths and facts about a national crisis.* Newbury Park, CA: Sage.

KIHLSTROM, J. F. (1984). Conscious, subconscious, unconscious: A cognitive view. In K. S. Bowers & D. Meichenbaum (Eds.), *The unconscious: Reconsidered.* New York: Wiley.

KIHLSTROM, J. F. (1985). Hypnosis. *Annual Review of Psychology, 36*, 385–235.

KIHLSTROM, J. F. (1987). The cognitive unconscious. *Science, 237*, 1445–1452.

KIHLSTROM, J. F. (1994). Psychodynamics and social cognition: Notes on the fusion of psychoanalysis and psychology. *Journal of Personality, 62*, 681–696.

KIHLSTROM, J. F. (1999). The psychological unconscious. In L. R. Pervin & O. John (Eds.), *Handbook of personality* (2nd ed., pp. 424–442). New York: Guilford.

KIHLSTROM, J. F., GLISKY, M. L., & ANGIULO, M. J. (1994). Dissociative tendencies and dissociative disorders. *Journal of Abnormal Psychology, 103*, 117–124.

KIM, L. I. C. (1993). Psychiatric care of Korean-Americans. In A. C. Gaw (Ed.). *Culture, ethnicity and mental illness* (pp. 347–345). Washington, DC: Government Printing Office.

KIMMEL, D. C., & WEINER, I. B. (1985). *Adolescence: A developmental transition.* Hillsdale, NJ: Erlbaum.

KINDER, D. R., & SEARS, D. O. (1985). Public opinion and political action. In G. Lindzey & E. Aronson, (Eds.), *The handbook of social psychology* (3rd ed., Vol. 2). New York: Random House.

KING, N. J., GULLONE, E, TONGE, B. J., & OLLENDICK, T. H. (1993). Self-reports of panic attacks and manifest anxiety in adolescents. *Behavior Research and Therapy, 31*, 111–116.

KINSEY, A. C., POMEROY, W. B., & MARTIN, C. E. (1948). *Sexual behavior in the human male.* Philadelphia: Saunders.

KINSEY, A. C., POMEROY, W. B., MARTIN, C. E., & GEBHARD, P. H. (1953). *Sexual behavior in the human female.* Philadelphia: Saunders.

KIRSCH, I., & LYNN, S. J. (1998). Dissociation theories of hypnosis. *Psychological Bulletin, 123*, 100–115.

KISHLINE, A. (1994). *Moderate drinking.* New York: Three Rivers Press.

KITAYAMA, S., MARKUS, H. R., & KUROKAWA, M. (2000). Culture, emotion, and well-being: Good feelings in Japan and the United States. *Cognition and Emotion, 14*, 93–124.

KLAHR, D. (1982). Nonmonotone assessment of monotone development: An information processing analysis. In S. Strauss (Ed.), *U-shaped behavioral growth.* New York: Academic Press.

KLATZKY, R. L., LEDERMAN, S. J., & METZGER, V. A. (1985). Identifying objects by touch: An expert system. *Perception and Psychophysics, 37*, 299–302.

KLEIN, S. B., & LOFTUS, J. (1988). The nature of self-referent encoding: The contributions of elaborative and organizational processes. *Journal of Personality and Social Psychology, 55*, 5–11.

KLEIN, S. B., LOFTUS, J., & BURTON, H. A. (1989). Two self-reference effects: The importance of distinguishing between self-descriptiveness judgments and autobiographical retrieval in self-referent encoding. *Journal of Personality and Social Psychology, 56*, 853–865.

KLERMAN, G. L., WEISSMAN, M. M., ROUNSAVILLE, B., & CHEVRON, E. (1984). *Interpersonal psychotherapy of depression.* New York: Basic Books.

KLINE, P. (1972). *Fact and fancy in Freudian theory.* London: Methuen.

KLINEBERG, O. (1938). Emotional expression in Chinese literature. *Journal of Abnormal and Social Psychology, 33*, 517–520.

KLING, K. C., HYDE, J. S., SHOWERS, C. J., & BUSWELL, B. N. (1999). Gender differences in self-esteem: A meta-analysis. *Psychological Bulletin, 125*, 70–500.

KLÜVER, H., & BUCY, P. C. (1937). "Psychic blindness" and other symptoms following temporal lobectomy in rhesus monkeys. *American Journal of Physiology, 119*, 352–353.

KNITTLE, J. L., & HIRSCH, J. (1968). Effect of early nutrition on the development of rat epididymal fat pads: Cellularity and metabolism. *Journal of Clinical Investigation, 47,* 2091.

KNOBLICH, G., & KING, R. (1992). Biological correlates of criminal behavior. In I. McCord (Ed.), *Advances in criminological theory: Facts, frameworks, and forecasts* (pp. 1–21). New Brunswick, NJ: Transaction.

KNUTSON, B., WOLKOWITZ, O. M., COLE, S. W., CHAN, T., MOORE, E. A., JOHSON, R. C., TERPSTRA, J., TURNER, R. A., & REUS, V. I. (1998). Selective alteration of personality and social behavior by serotonergic intervention. *American Journal of Psychiatry, 155,* 373–379.

KOBASA, S. C. (1979). Stressful life events, personality, and health: An inquiry into hardiness. *Journal of Personality and Social Psychology, 37,* 1–11.

KOBASA, S. C., MADDI, S. R., & KAHN, S. (1982). Hardiness and health: A prospective study. *Journal of Personality and Social Psychology, 42,* 168–177.

KOENIG, H. G., HAYS, J. C., GEORGE, L. K., BLAZER, D. G., LARSON, D. B., & LANDERMAN, L. R. (1997). Modeling the cross-sectional relationships between religion, physical health, social support and depressive symptoms. *American Journal of Geriatric Psychology, 5,* 131–144.

KOHLBERG, L. (1966). A cognitive-developmental analysis of children's sex role concepts and attitudes. In E. E. Maccoby (Ed.), *The development of sex differences* (pp. 82–173). Stanford, CA: Stanford University Press.

KOHLBERG, L. (1969). Stage and sequence: The cognitive-developmental approach to socialization. In D. A. Goslin (Ed.), *Handbook of socialization theory and research.* Chicago: Rand McNally.

KOHLBERG, L. (1976). Moral stages and moralization: The cognitive-developmental approach. In T. Lickong (Ed.), *Moral development and behavior.* New York: Holt, Rinehart & Winston.

KOHLER, W. (1925). *The mentality of apes.* New York: Harcourt Brace. (Reprint ed., 1976. New York: Liveright.)

KOHNSTAMM, G. A., BATES, J. E., & ROTHBART, M. K. (Eds.) (1989). *Temperament in childhood.* Chichester: Wiley.

Kolata, G. (2002, May). Runner's High? Endorphins? Fiction, Some Scientists Say. *New York Times.*

KOLB, B., & WHISHAW, I. Q. (1985). *Fundamentals of human neuropsychology* (2nd ed.). San Francisco: Freeman.

KOLODNY, J. A., (1994). Memory processes in classification learning. *Psychological Science, 5,* 164–169.

KOOB, G. F., & BLOOM, F. E. (1988). Cellular and molecular mechanisms of drug dependence. *Science, 242,* 715–723.

KORNER, A. F. (1973). Individual differences at birth: Implications for early experience and later development. In J. C. Westman (Ed.), *Individual differences in children.* New York: Wiley.

KORNHABER, M., & GARDNER, H. (1991). Critical thinking across multiple intelligences. In S. Maclure & P. Davies (Eds.), *Learning to think: Thinking to learn.* Oxford, England: Pergamon.

KORNHABER, M., KRECHEVSKY, M., & GARDNER, H. (1990). Engaging intelligence. *Educational Psychologist, 25,* 177–199.

KORNITZER, M., MAGOTTEAU, V., DEGRE, C., KITTEL, F., STRUYVEN, J., & VAN THIEL, E. (1982). Angiographic findings and the type A pattern assessed by means of the Bortner Scale. *Journal of Behavioral Medicine, 5,* 313–320.

KOSAMBI, D. D. (1967). Living prehistory in India. *Scientific American, 215,* 105.

KOSS, M., & BOESCHEN, L. (1998). Rape. In *Encyclopedia of Mental Health,* (Vol. 3). New York: Academic Press.

KOSS-CHIONO, J. D. (1995). Traditional and folk approaches among ethnic minorities. In J. F. Aponte (Ed.), *Psychological interventions and cultural diversity* (pp. 145–163). Boston: Allyn & Bacon.

KOSSLYN, S. M. (1980). *Image and mind.* Cambridge, MA: Harvard University Press.

KOSSLYN, S. M. (1983). *Ghosts in the mind's machine.* New York: Norton.

KOSSLYN, S. M. (1988). Aspects of a cognitive neuroscience of mental imagery: *Science, 240,* 1621–1626.

KOSSLYN, S. M. (1994). *The resolution of the imagery debate.* Cambridge, MA: MIT Press.

KOSSLYN, S. M., ALPERT, N. M., THOMPSON, W. L., MALJKOVIC, V., WEISE, S. B., CHABRIS, C. F., HAMILTON, S. E., RAUCH, S. L., & BUONANNO, F. S. (1993). Visual mental imagery activates topographically organized visual cortex. *Journal of Cognitive Neuroscience, 5,* 263–287.

KOSSLYN, S. M., BALL, T. M., & REISER, B. J. (1978). Visual images preserve metric spatial information: Evidence from studies of image scanning. *Journal of Experimental Psychology: Human Perception and Performance, 4,* 47–60.

KOSSLYN, S. M., & KOENIG, O. (1992). *Wet mind: The new cognitive neuroscience.* New York: Free Press.

KOULACK, D., & GOODENOUGH, D. R. (1976). Dream recall and dream recall failure: An arousal-retrieval model. *Psychological Bulletin, 83,* 975–984.

KRAMER, P. D. (1993). *Listening to Prozac.* New York: Viking.

KRAUS, G., & REYNOLDS, D. J. (2001). The "A-B-C's" of the cluster B's: Identifying, understanding and treating cluster B personality disorders. *Clinical Psychology Review, 21,* 345–373.

KRAUT, R. E. (1982). Social presence, facial feedback, and emotion. *Journal of Personality and Social Psychology, 42,* 853–863.

KRAVITZ, D., & PLATANIA, J. (1993). Attitudes and beliefs about affirmative action: Effects of target and/or respondent sex and ethnicity. *Journal of Applied Psychology, 78,* 928–938.

KRAVITZ, D. A., HARRISON, D. A., TURNER, M. E., LEVINE, E. L., CHAVES, W., BRANNICK, M. T., DENNING, D. L., RUSSELL, C. J., & CONARD, M. A. (1997). *Affirmative action: A review of psychological and behavioral research.* Bowling Green, OH: Society for Industrial and Organizational Psychology.

KRING, A. (2000). Gender and anger. In A. H. Fischer (Ed.), *Gender and emotion: Social psychological perspectives* (pp. 211–231). New York: Cambridge University Press.

KRIPKE, D. F. (1985). Biological rhythms. In L. L. Klerman, M. M. Weissman, P. S. Applebaum, & L. H. Roth (Eds.), *Psychiatry* (Vol. 3). Philadelphia: Lippincott.

KRIPKE, D. F., & GILLIN, J. C. (1985). Sleep disorders. In G. L. Klerman, M. M. Weissman, P. S. Applebaum, & L. N. Roth (Eds.), *Psychiatry* (Vol. 3). Philadelphia: Lippincott.

KRYGER, M. H., ROTH, T., & DEMENT, W. C. (Eds.). (1994). *Principles and practice of sleep medicine.* Philadelphia: Saunders.

KUCH, K., & COX, B. J. (1992). Symptoms of PTSD in 124 survivors of the Holocaust. *American Journal of Psychiatry, 149,* 337–340.

KUHL, P. K., WILLIAMS, K. A., LACERDA, F., STEVENS, K. N., & LINDBLOM, B. (1992). Linguistic experience alters phonetic perception in infants by 6 months of age. *Science, 255,* 606–608.

KUHN, C., SWARTZWELDER, S., & WILSON, W. (1998). *Buzzed: The straight facts about the most used and abused drugs.* New York: Norton.

KUIPER, N. A., MACDONALD, M. R., & DERRY, P. A. (1983). Parameters of a depressive self-schema. In J. Suls & A. G. Greenwald (Eds.), *Psychological perspectives on the self* (Vol. 2) Hillsdale, NJ: Erlbaum.

KUIPER, N. A., OLINGER, L. J., MACDONALD, M. R., & SHAW, B. F. (1985). Self-schema processing of depressed and nondepressed content: The effects of vulnerability on depression. *Social Cognition, 3,* 77–93.

KUIPER, N. A., & ROGERS, T. B. (1979). Encoding of personal information: Self-other differences. *Journal of Personality and Social Psychology, 37,* 499–514.

KUJAWA, M. J., & NEMEROFF, C. B. (2000). The biology of bipolar disorder. In A. Marneros & J. Angst (Eds.), *Bipolar disorders: 100 years after manic-depressive insanity* (pp. 281–314). Great Britain: Kluwer Academic Publishers.

KUMAN, I. G., FEDROV, C. N., & NOVIKOVA, L. A. (1983). Investigation of the sensitive period in the development of the human visual system. *Journal of Higher Nervous Activity, 33,* 434–441.

KURTINES, W., & GREIF, E. B. (1974). The development of moral thought: Review and evaluation of Kohlberg's approach. *Psychological Bulletin, 81,* 453–470.

LA BERGE, D. (1995). *Attentional processing: The brain's art of mindfulness.* Cambridge, MA: Harvard University Press.

LAFROMBOISE, T. D., TRIMBLE, J. E., & MOHATT, G. V. (1998). Counseling intervention and American Indian tradition: An integrative approach. In D. R. Atkinson (Ed.), *Counseling American minorities* (5th Ed.) Boston: McGraw-Hill.

LAGERSPETZ, K., VIEMERO, V., & AKADEMI, A. (1986). Television and aggressive behavior among Finnish children. In L. R. Huesmann & L. D. Eron (Eds.), *Television and the aggressive child.* New York: Erlbaum.

LAGRECA, A. M., SLIVERMAN, W. K., VERNBERG, E. M., & PRINSTEIN, M. J. (1996). Symptoms of posttraumatic stress in children after Hurricane Andrew: A prospective study. *Journal of the American Academy of the Child and Adolescent Psychiatry, 27,* 330–335.

LAKOFF, G. (1987). *Women, fire, and dangerous things.* Chicago: University of Chicago Press.

LAMB, M. E., & BORNSTEIN, M. H. (1987). *Development in infancy: An introduction* (2nd ed.). New York: Random House.

LAMBERT, M. J., & BERGIN, A. E. (1994). The effectiveness of psychotherapy. In A. Bergin (Ed.), *Handbook of psychotherapy and behavior change* (4th ed., pp. 143–189). New York: Wiley.

LAND, E. H. (1977). The retinex theory of color vision. *Scientific American, 237,* 108–128.

LAND, E. H. (1986). Recent advances in retinex theory. *Vision Research, 26,* 7–21.

LANGLOIS, J. H., & DOWNS, A. C. (1980). Mothers, fathers, and peers as socialization agents of sex-typed play behaviors in young children. *Child Development, 51,* 1237–1247.

LAPIERE, R. (1934). Attitudes versus actions. *Social Forces, 13,* 230–237.

LARKIN, J. H., MCDERMOTT, J., SIMON, D. P., & SIMON, H. A. (1980). Expert and novice performance in solving physics problems. *Science, 208,* 1335–1342.

LARSEN, R. J., & SEIDMAN, E. (1986). Gender schema theory and sex role inventories: Some conceptual and psychometric considerations. *Journal of Personality and Social Psychology, 50,* 205–211.

LARSON, R., & RICHARDS, M. H. (1991). Daily companionship in late childhood and early adolescence: Changing developmental contexts. *Child Development, 62,* 284–300.

LATANÉ, B., & DARLEY, J. M. (1968). Group inhibition of bystander intervention in emergencies. *Journal of Personality and Social Psychology, 10,* 215–221.

LATANÉ, B., & DARLEY, J. M. (1970). *The unresponsive bystander: Why doesn't he help?* New York: Appleton-Century-Crofts.

LATANÉ, B., NIDA, S. A., & WILSON, D. W. (1981). The effects of group size on helping behavior. In J. P. Rushton & R. M. Sorrentino (Eds.), *Altruism and helping behavior: Social personality, and developmental perspectives.* Hillsdale, NJ: Erlbaum.

LATANÉ, B., & RODIN, J. (1969). A lady in distress: Inhibiting effects of friends and strangers on bystander intervention. *Journal of Experimental and Social Psychology, 5,* 189–202.

LAUDENSLAGER, M. L., RYAN, S. M., DRUGAN, R. C., HYSON, R. L., & MAIER, S. F. (1983). Coping and immunosuppression: Inescapable but not escapable shock suppresses lymphocyte proliferation. *Science, 221,* 568–570.

LAUMANN, E. O., GAGNON, J. H. MICHAEL, R. T., & MICHAELS, S. (1994). *The social organization of sexuality: Sexual practices in the United States.* Chicago: University of Chicago Press.

LAZARUS, R. S. (1991a). Cognition and motivation in emotion. *American Psychologist, 46,* 352–367.

LAZARUS, R. S. (1991b). *Emotion and adaptation.* New York: Oxford University Press.

LAZARUS, R. S., & FOLKMAN, S. (1984). *Stress, appraisal, and coping.* New York: Springer.

LAZARUS, R. S., KANNER, A. D., & FOLKMAN, S. (1980). Emotions: A cognitive-phenomenological analysis. In R. Plutchik & H. Kellerman (Eds.), *Emotion: Theory, research, and experience* (Vol. 1). New York: Academic Press.

LE BARS, P. L., KATZ, M. M., BERMAN, N., ITIL, T. M., FREEDMAN, A. M., & SCHATZBERG, A. F. (1997a). *A placebo-controlled, double-blind, randomized trial of an extract of ginkgo biloba for dementia.* Tarrytown: New York Institute for Medical Research.

LE BARS, P. L., KATZ, M. M., BERMAN, N., ITIL, T. M., FREEDMAN, A. M., & SCHATZBERG, A. F. (1997b). A placebo-controlled, double-blind randomized trial of an extract of ginkgo biloba for dementia. *Journal of the American Medical Association, 278,* 1327–1332.

LE BON, G. (1895). *The crowd.* London: Ernest Benn.

LE DEOX, J. E. (1989). Cognitive-emotional interactions in the brain. *Cognition and Emotion, 3,* 267–289.

LE DOUX, J. E., & PHELPS, E. A. (2000). Emotional networks in the brain. In M. Lewis & J. M. Haviland-Jones (Eds.), *Handbook of emotions* (2nd ed., pp. 157–172). New York: Guilford.

LEA, M., SPEARS, R., & DE GROOT, D. (2001). Knowing me knowing you: Anonymity effects on social identity processes within groups. *Personality and Social Psychology Bulletin, 27,* 526–537.

LEEDHAM, B., MEYEROWITZ, B. E., MUIRHEAD, J., & FRIST, M. H. (1995). Positive expectations predict health after heart transplantation. *Health Psychology, 14,* 74–79.

LEFF, J. P., & VAUGHN, C. E. (1981). The role of maintenance therapy and relatives' expressed emotion in relapse of schizophrenia: A two-year follow-up. *British Journal of Psychiatry, 139,* 102–104.

LEIPPE, M. R. (1980). Effects of integrative memorial and cognitive processes on the correspondence

of eyewitness accuracy and confidence. *Law and Human Behavior, 4,* 261–274.

LENNEBERG, E. H. (1967). *Biological foundations of language.* New York: Wiley.

LENNON, M. C., & ROSENFIELD, S. (1992). Women and mental health: The interaction of job and family conditions. *Journal of Health and Social Behavior, 33,* 316–327.

LEO, R. (1996). Miranda's revenge: Police interrogation as a confidence game. *Law and Society Review, 30,* 259–288.

LEONARD, J. S. (1986). The effectiveness of equal employment law and affirmative action regulation. In R. G. Ehrenberg (Ed.), *Research in labor economics* (vol. 8, pp. 319–350). Greenwich, CT: JAI Press.

LERMAN, C., CAPORASO, N. E., AUDRAIN, J., MAIN, D., BOWMAN, E. D., LOCKSHIN, B., BOYD, N. R., & SHIELDS, P. G. (1999). Evidence suggesting the role of specific genetic factors in cigarette smoking. *Health Psychology, 18,* 14–20.

LERNER, B. (1972). *Therapy in the ghetto: Political impotence and personal disintegration.* Baltimore: Johns Hopkins University Press.

LERNER, J. S., & KELTNER, D. (2001). Fear, anger, and risk. *Journal of Personality and Social Psychology, 81,* 146–159.

LESHNER, A. I. (1997). Addiction is a brain disease, and it matters. *Science, 278,* 45–47.

LEVAV, I., FRIEDLANDER, Y., KARK, J. D., & PERITZ, E. (1988). An epidemiologic study of mortality among bereaved parents. *New England Journal of Medicine, 319,* 457–461.

LEVAY, S. (1991). A difference in hypothalamic structure between heterosexual and homosexual men. *Science, 253,* 1034–1037.

LEVAY, S. (1996). *Queer science: The use and abuse of research into homosexuality.* Cambridge, MA: MIT Press.

LEVENSON, R. W. (1992). Autonomic nervous system differences among emotions. *Psychological Science, 3,* 23–27.

LEVENSON, R. W. (1994). Human emotions: A functional view. In P. Ekman & R. Davidson, (Eds.). *The nature of emotion: Fundamental questions* (pp. 123–126). New York: Oxford University Press.

LEVENSON, R. W., EKMAN, P., & FRIESEN, W. V. (1990). Voluntary facial action generates emotion-specific nervous system activity. *Psychophysiology, 27,* 363–384.

LEVENSON, R. W., EKMAN, P., HEIDER, K., & FRIESEN, W. V. (1992). Emotion and autonomic nervous system activity in an Indonesian culture. *Journal of Personality and Social Psychology, 62,* 927–988.

LEVINE, M. (1999). Rethinking bystander nonintervention. Social categorization and the evidence of witnesses at the James Bulger murder trial. *Human Relations, 52,* 1133–1155.

LEVINE, S. (1960). Stimulation in infancy. *Scientific American, 202,* 80–86.

LEVINGER, G., SENN, D. J., & JORGENSEN, B. W. (1970). Progress toward permanence in courtship: A test of the Kerckhoff-Davis hypotheses. *Sociometry, 33,* 427–443.

LEVY, B. (1996). Improving memory in old age through implicit stereotyping. *Journal of Personality and Social Psychology, 71,* 1092–1107.

LEVY, J. (1985). Right brain, left brain: Facts and fiction. *Psychology Today, 19,* 38–44.

LEVY, S. M., & HEIDEN, I., (1991). Depression, distress and immunity: Risk factors for infectious disease. *Stress Medicine, 7,* 45–51.

LEVY, S., HERBERMAN, R., WHITESIDE, T., SANZO, K., LEE, J., & KIRKWOOD, J. (1990).

Perceived social support and tumor estrogen/progesterone receptor status as predictors of natural killer cell activity in breast cancer patients. *Psychosomatic Medicine, 52,* 73–85.

LEWINSOHN, P. M., MISCHEL, W., CHAPLIN, W., & BARTON, R. (1980). Social competence and depression: The role of illusory self-perceptions. *Journal of Abnormal Psychology, 89,* 203–212.

LEWINSOHN, P. M., ROHDE, P., & SEELEY, J. R. (1996). Alcohol consumption in high school adolescents: Frequency of use and dimensional structure of associated problems. *Addiction, 91,* 375–390.

LEY, R. G., & BRYDEN, M. P. (1982). A dissociation of right and left hemispheric effects for recognizing emotional tone and verbal content. *Brain and Cognition, 1,* 3–9.

LIBERMAN, A. M., COOPER, F., SHANKWEILER, D., & STUDERT-KENNEDY, M. (1967). Perception of the speech code. *Psychological Review, 74,* 431–459.

LICHTERMAN, D., KARBE, E., & MAIER, W. (2000). The genetic epidemiology of schizophrenia and of schizophrenia spectrum disorders. *European Archives of Clinical Psychiatry and Neuroscience, 250,* 304–310.

LICKEY, M. E., & GORDON, B. (1991). *Medicine and mental illness.* New York: Freeman.

LIDZ, C. W., MULVEY, E. P., & GARDNER, W. (1993). The accuracy of predictions of violence to others. *Journal of the American Medical Association, 269,* 1007–1011.

LIEBERMAN, L. R., & DUNLAP, J. T. (1979). O'Leary and Borkovec's conceptualization of placebo: The placebo paradox. *American Psychologist, 34,* 553–554.

LIEBERMAN, M. D., OCHSNER, K. N., GILBERT, D. T., & SCHACTER, D. L. (2001). Attitude change in amnesia and under cognitive load. *Psychological Science, 12,* 135–140.

LIGHT, P., & PERRETT-CLERMONT, A. (1989). Social context effects in learning and testing. In A. R. H. Gellatly, D. Rogers, & J. Sloboda (Eds.), *Cognition and social worlds.* Oxford: Clarendon Press.

LILIENFELD, S. O., WOOD, J. W., & GARB, H. N. (2000). The scientific status of projective techniques. *Psychological science in the public interest, 1,* 27–66.

LINDE, K., RAMIREZ, G., MULROW, C. D., PAULS, A., WEIDENHAMMER, W., & MELCHART, D. (1996). St. John's wort for depression: An overview and meta-analysis of randomized clinical trials. *British Medical Journal, 313,* 253–258.

LINDSAY, M., CRINO, R., & ANDREWS, G. (1997) Controlled trial of exposure and response prevention in obsessive-compulsive disorder. *British Journal of Psychiatry, 171,* 135–139.

LINE, L. (1998, August–September). Leader of the flock. *National Wildlife,* pp. 20–27.

LINN, R. L. (1982). Ability testing: Individual differences, prediction, and differential prediction. In A. Wigdor & W. Gardner (Eds.), *Ability testing: Uses, consequences, and controversies.* Washington, DC: National Academy Press.

LINNOILA, N., VIRKUNNEN, M., SCHEININ, M., NUTTILA, A., RIMON, R., & GOODWIN, F. (1983). Low cerebrospinal fluid 5-hydroxyindoleacetic acid concentration differentiates impulsive from nonimpulsive violent behavior. *Life Sciences, 33,* 2609–2624.

LINNOILA, V. M., & VIRKKUNEN, M. (1992). Aggression, suicidality, and serotonin. *Journal of Clinical Psychiatry, 53,* 46–51.

LIOTTI, M., & MAYBERG, H. S. (2001). The role of functional neuroimaging in the neuropsychology of depression. *Journal of Clinical and Experimental Neuropsychology, 23,* 121–136.

LIPPERT, W. W., & SENTER, R. J. (1966). Electrodermal responses in the sociopath. *Psychonomic Science, 4,* 25–26.

LIVINGSTONE, M., & HUBEL, D. (1988). Segregation of form, color, movement, and depth: Anatomy, physiology, and perception. *Science, 240,* 740–750.

LOFTUS, E., & KETCHAM, K. (1994). *The myth of repressed memory.* New York: St. Martin's Press.

LOFTUS, E. F. (1997). Creating false memories. *Scientific American, 277,* 70–75.

LOFTUS, E. F., COAN, J. A., & PICKRELL, J. E. (1996). Manufacturing false memories using bits of reality. In L. Reder (Ed.) *Implicit memory and metacognition* (pp. 195–220). Mahwah, NJ: Erlbaum.

LOFTUS, E. F., & LOFTUS, G. R. (1980). On the permanence of stored information in the human brain. *American Psychologist, 35,* 409–420.

LOFTUS, E. F., LOFTUS, G. R., & MESSO, J. (1987). Some facts about "weapon focus." *Law and Human Behavior, 11,* 55–62.

LOFTUS, E. F., & PALMER, J. C. (1974). Reconstruction of automobile destruction. *Journal of Verbal Learning and Verbal Behavior, 13,* 585–589.

LOFTUS, E. F., & PICKRELL, J. E. (1995). The formation of false memories. *Psychiatric Annals, 25,* 720–725.

LOFTUS, E. F., SCHOOLER, J. W., & WAGENAAR, W. A. (1985). The fate of memory: Comment on McCloskey and Zaragoza. *Journal of Experimental Psychology: General, 114,* 375–380.

LOFTUS, G. R. (1972). Eye fixations and recognition memory for pictures. *Cognitive Psychology, 3,* 525–551.

LOFTUS, G. R., & IRWIN, D. E. (1998). On the relations among different measures of visible and informational persistence. *Cognitive Psychology, 35,* 135–199.

LOFTUS, G. R., & MACKWORTH, N. H. (1978). Cognitive determinants of fixation location during picture viewing. *Journal of Experimental Psychology: Human Perception and Performance, 4,* 565–572.

LOGUE, A. W. (1991). *The psychology of eating and drinking: An introduction* (2nd ed.). New York: Freeman.

LONG, P. W. (1996). *Internet mental health.* http://www.mentalhealth.com/

LONGLEY, J., & PRUITT, D. G. (1980). Groupthink: A critique of Janis's theory. In L. Wheeler (Ed.), *Review of personality and social psychology* (Vol. 1). Beverly Hills, CA: Sage.

LOOMIS, A. L., HARVEY, E. N., & HOBART, G. A. (1937). Cerebral states during sleep as studied by human potentials. *Journal of Experimental Psychology, 21,* 127–144.

LOPEZ, A., ATRAN, S., MEDIN, D. L., COOLEY, J., & SMITH, E. E. (1997). The tree of life: Universals of folk biological taxonomies and inductions. *Cognitive Psychology, 32,* 251–295.

LOPEZ, S. R., & GUARNACCIA, P. J. (2000). Cultural psychopathology: Uncovering the social world of mental illness. *Annual Review of Psychology, 51,* 571–598.

LORD, C. G. (1980). Schemas and images as memory aids: Two modes of processing social information. *Journal of Personality and Social Psychology, 38,* 257–269.

LORD, C. G., ROSS, L., & LEPPER, M. R. (1979). Biased assimilation and attitude polarization: The effects of prior theories on subsequently considered evidence. *Journal of Personality and Social Psychology, 37,* 2098–2109.

LORENZ, K. (1966). *On aggression.* New York: Harcourt Brace Jovanovich.

LOVE, R. E., & GREENWALD, A. C. (1978). Cognitive responses to persuasion as mediators of opinion change. *Journal of Social Psychology, 104,* 231–241.

LOVIBOND, P. F., SIDDLE, D. A. T., & BOND, N. W. (1993). Resistance to extinction of fear-relevant stimuli: Preparedness or selective sensitization? *Journal of Experimental Psychology: General, 122,* 449–461.

LUBINSKI, D. (2000). Scientific and social significance of assessing individual differences: "Sinking shafts at a few critical points." *Annual Reviews of Psychology, 51,* 405–444.

LUBORSKY, L. L., MCLELLAN, A. T., WOODY, G. E., O'BRIEN, E. P., & AUERBACH, A. (1985). Therapist success and its determinants. *Archives of General Psychiatry, 42,* 602–611.

LUBORSKY, L. L., SINGER, B., & LUBORSKY, L. (1975). Comparative studies of psychotherapies: Is it true that "everyone has won and all must have prizes"? *Archives of General Psychiatry, 32,* 995–1008.

LUCHINS, A. (1957). Primacy-recency in impression formation. In C. L. Hovland (Ed.), *The order of presentation in persuasion.* New Haven: Yale University Press.

LUNDIN, R. W. (1985). *Theories and systems of psychology* (3rd ed.). Lexington, MA: Heath.

LURIA, Z., & RUBIN, J. Z. (1974). The eye of the beholder: Parents' views on sex of newborns. *American Journal of Orthopsychiatry, 44,* 512–519.

LYKKEN, D. T. (1980). *Tremor in the blood: Uses and abuses of the lie detector.* New York: McGraw-Hill.

LYKKEN, D. T. (1982). Research with twins: The concept of emergenesis. *The Society for Psychophysiological Research, 19,* 361–373.

LYKKEN, D. T. (1984). Polygraphic interrogation. *Nature, 307,* 681–684.

LYKKEN, D. T., MCGUE, M., TELLEGEN, A., & BOUCHARD, T. J., Jr. (1992). Emergenesis: Genetic traits that may not run in families. *American Psychologist, 47,* 1565–1577.

LYNN, S. J., KIRSCH, I., BARABASZ, A., CARDENA, E., & PATTERSON, D. (1999). Hypnosis as an empirically supported clinical intervention: The state of the evidence and a look to the future. *International Journal of Clinical and Experimental Hypnosis, 48,* 239–259.

LYNN, S. J., KIRSCH, I., BARABASZ, A., CARDENA, E., & PATTERSON, D. (1999). Hypnosis as an empirically supported clinical intervention: The state of the evidence and a look to the future. *International Journal of Clinical and Experimental Hypnosis, 48,* 239–259.

LYUBOMIRSKY, S., & NOLEN HOEKSEMA, S. (1995). Effects of self focused rumination on negative thinking and interpersonal problem solving. *Journal of Personality and Social Psychology, 69,* 176–190.

MAAS, J. B. (1998). *Power sleep: The revolutionary program that prepares your mind for peak performance.* New York: HarperCollins.

MAASS, A., & CLARK, R. D., III (1984). Hidden impact of minorities: Fifteen years of minority influence research. *Psychological Bulletin, 95,* 428–450.

MACAULAY, J. (1970). A shill for charity. In J. Macaulay & L. Berkowitz (Eds.), *Altruism and helping behavior* (pp. 43–59). New York: Academic Press.

MACCOBY, E. (1998). *The two sexes.* Cambridge, MA: Harvard University Press.

MACCOBY, E. E. (1980). *Social development: Psychological growth and the parent-child relationship.* New York: Harcourt Brace Jovanovich.

MACCOBY, E. E., & JACKLIN, C. N. (1974). *The psychology of sex differences.* Stanford, CA: Stanford University Press.

MACKINNON, D., JAMISON, R., & DEPAULO, J. R. (1997). Genetics of manic depressive illness. *Annual Review of Neuroscience, 20,* 355–373.

MACLEAN, P. D. (1973). *A triune concept of the brain and behavior.* Toronto: Toronto University Press.

MACLEOD, C. M. (1991). Half a century of research on the Stroop effect: An integrative review. *Psychological Bulletin, 109,* 163–203.

MACMILLAN, M. B. (1996). *Freud evaluated: The completed arc.* Cambridge, MA: MIT Press.

MADDEN, D. R. (2002). The structure and function of glutamate receptor ion channels. *Nature Reviews Neuroscience, 3,* 91–101.

MAHER, B. A. (1966). *Principles of psychotherapy: An experimental approach.* New York: McGraw-Hill.

MAIER, S. F., & SELIGMAN, M. E. P. (1976). Learned helplessness: Theory and evidence. *Journal of Experimental Psychology: General, 105,* 3–46.

MAIN, M., & CASSIDY, J. (1988). Categories of response to reunion with parents at age 6: Predictable from infant attachment classifications and stable over a 1-month period. *Developmental Psychology, 24,* 415–426.

MAIN, M., & SOLOMON, J. (1986). Discovery of an insecure-disorganized/disoriented attachment pattern: Procedures, findings and implications for the classification of behavior. In T. B. Brazelton, & M. Yogman (Eds.), *Affective development in infancy* (pp. 95–124). Norwood, NJ: Ablex.

MAJ, M., PIROZZI, R., MAGLIANO, L., & BARTOLI, L. (1998). Long-term outcome of lithium prophylaxis in bipolar disorder: A 5-year prospective study of 402 patients at a lithium clinic. *American Journal of Psychiatry, 155,* 30–35.

MALINOW, R., OTMAKHOV, N., BLUM, K. I., & LISMAN, J. (1994). Visualizing hippocampal synaptic function by optical detection of $Ca2+$ entry through the N-methyl-D-aspartate channel. *Proceedings of the National Academy of Sciences of the United States of America, 91,* 8170–8174.

MALLE, B. F. (1999). How people explain behavior: A new theoretical framework. *Personality and Social Psychology Review, 3,* 23–48.

MALOF, M., & LOTT, A. J. (1962). Ethnocentrism and the acceptance of Negro support in a group pressure situation. *Journal of Abnormal and Social Psychology, 65,* 254–258.

MALONE, K., & MANN, J. J. (1993). Serotonin and major depression. In J. J. Mann & D. J. Kupfer (Eds.), *Biology of depressive disorders: Part A. A systems perspective* (pp. 29–49). New York: Plenum Press.

MALONEY, L. T., & WANDELL, B. A. (1986). Color constancy: A method for recovering surface spectral reflectance. *Journal of the Optical Society of America, 3,* 29–33.

MANDLER, J. (1983). Representation. In P. H. Mussen (Ed.), *Handbook of child psychology* (Vol. 3). New York: Wiley.

MANN, J. J., & ARANGO, V. (1999). The neurobiology of suicidal behavior. In D. G. Jacobs (Ed.), *The Harvard Medical School guide to suicide assessment and intervention.* San Francisco: Jossey-Bass.

MANN, J. J., BRENT, D. A., & ARANGO, V. (2001). The neurobiology and genetics of suicide and attempted suicide: a focus on the serotonergic system. *Neuropsychopharmacology, 24,* 467–477.

MANSON, S., BEALS, J., O'NELL, T., PIASECKI, J., BECHTOLD, D., KEANE, E., & JONES, M. (1996). Wounded spirits, ailing hearts: PTSD and related disorders among American Indians. In A. J. Marsella, M. J. Friedman, E. T. Gerrity, & R. M. Scurfield (Eds.), *Ethnocultural aspects of posttraumatic stress disorder* (pp. 255–283). Washington, DC: American Psychiatric Press.

MANSON, S. M., SHORE, J. H., BARON, A. E., ACKERSON, L., & NELIGH, G. (1992). Alcohol abuse and dependence among American Indians. In J. E. Helzer & G. J. Canino (Eds.), *Alcoholism in North America, Europe, and Asia* (pp. 113–127). New York: Oxford University Press.

MANUCK, S. B., KAPLAN, J. R., & MATTHEWS, K. A. (1986). Behavioral antecedents of coronary heart disease and atherosclerosis. *Arteriosclerosis, 6*, 1–14.

MAO, J., PRICE, D. D., & MAYER, D. J. (1995). Mechanism of hyperalgesia and morphine tolerance. Current review of their possible interactions. *Pain, 62*, 259–274.

MARBLY, N. (1987). But you weren't there. In T. Williams (Ed.), *Posttraumatic stress disorders: A handbook for clinicians.* Cincinnati, OH: Disabled American Veterans.

MARCIA, J. E. (1966). Development and validation of ego identify status. *Journal of Personality and Social Psychology, 3*, 551–558.

MARCIA, J. E. (1980). Identity in adolescence. In J. Adelson (Ed.), *Handbook of adolescent psychology.* New York: Wiley.

MARCUS, G. F. (1996). Why do children say "breaked"? *Current Directions in Psychological Science, 5*, 81–85.

MAREN, S. (2001). Neurobiology of Pavlovian fear conditioning, *Annual Review of Neuroscience, 24*, 897–931.

MAREN, S., & FANSELOW, M. S. (1996). The amygdala and fear conditioning: Has the nut been cracked? *Neuron, 16*, 237–240.

MARGOLIN, L., & WHITE, L. (1987). The continuing role of physical attractiveness in marriage. *Journal of Marriage and the Family, 49*, 21–27.

MARGRAF, J., BARLOW, D. H., CLARK, D. M., & TELCH, M. J. (1993). Psychological treatment of panic: Work in progress on outcome, active ingredients, and follow-up. *Behaviour Research & Therapy, 31*, 1–8.

MARKMAN, E. M. (1979). Classes and collections: Conceptual organization and numerical abilities. *Cognitive Psychology, 11*, 395–411.

MARKMAN, E. M. (1987). How children constrain the possible meanings of words. In U. Neisser (Ed.), *Concepts and conceptual development: Ecological and intellectual factors in categorizations.* New York: Cambridge University Press.

MARKOWITZ, J. C., & WEISSMAN, M. M. (1995). Interpersonal psychotherapy. In E. E. Beckham & W. R. Leber (Eds.), *Handbook of depression* (2nd ed.). New York: Guilford.

MARKUS, H. (1977). Self-schemata and processing information about the self. *Journal of Personality and Social Psychology, 35*, 63–78.

MARKUS, H., & NURIUS, P. (1986). Possible selves. *American Psychologist, 41*, 954–969.

MARKUS, H., & SENTIS, K. (1982). The self in social information processing. In J. Suls (Ed.), *Psychological perspectives on the self* (Vol. 1). Hillsdale, NJ: Erlbaum.

MARKUS, H., & SMITH, J. (1981). The influence of self-schema on the perception of others. In N. Cantor & J. F. Kihlstrom (Eds.), *Personality, cognition, and social interaction.* Hillsdale, NJ: Erlbaum.

MARKUS, H. R., & KITAYAMA, S. (1991). Culture and the self: Implication for cognition, emotion, and motivation. *Psychological Review, 98*, 224–253.

MARLATT, G. A., LARIMER, M. E., BAER, J. S., & QUIGLEY, L. A. (1993). Harm reduction for alcohol problems: Moving beyond the controlled drinking economy. *Behavior Therapy, 24*, 461–503.

MARR, D. (1982). *Vision.* San Francisco: Freeman.

MARSHALL, D. A., BLUMER, L., & MOULTON, D. G. (1981). Odor detection curves for n-pentanoic acid in dogs and humans. *Chemical Senses, 6*, 445–453.

MARSHALL, G., & ZIMBARDO, P. G. (1979). Affective consequences of inadequately explained physiological arousal. *Journal of Personality and Social Psychology, 37*, 970–988.

MARTIN, A., UNGERLEIDER, L., & HAXBY, J. V. (2000). Category specificity and the brain: The sensory/motor model of semantic representations of objects. In M. S. Gazzaniga (Ed.), *The new cognitive neurosciences* (pp. 1023–1036). Cambridge, MA: MIT Press.

MARTIN, N., BOOMSMA, D., & MACHIN, G. (1997). A twin-pronged attack on complex traits. *Nature Genetics, 17*, 387–392.

MARTINEZ, C. (1993). Psychiatric care of Mexican-Americans. In A. C. Gaw (Ed.), *Culture, ethnicity, and mental illness* (pp. 431–466). Washington, DC: American Psychiatric Association Press.

MARTINEZ-TABOAS, A. (1989). Preliminary observations on MPD in Puerto Rico. *Dissociation: Progress in the Dissociative Disorders, 2*, 128–131.

MARUCHA, P. T., KICOLT-GLASER, J. K., & FAVAGEHI, M. (1998). Mucosal wound healing is impaired by examination stress. *Psychosomatic Medicine, 60*, 362–365.

MASLACH, C. (1979). The emotional consequences of arousal without reason. In Izard, C. E. (Ed.), *Emotion in personality and psychopathology.* New York: Plenum.

MASLACH, C., SCHAUFELI, W. B., & LEITER, M. P. (2001). Job burnout. *Annual Reviews of Psychology, 52*, 397–422.

MASLOW, A. H. (1970). *Motivation and personality* (2nd ed.). New York: Harper and Row.

MASSARO, D., & LOFTUS, G. R. (1996). Sensory storage: Icons and echoes. In E. L. Bjork & R. A. Bjork (Eds.), *Handbook of perception and cognition* (Vol. 10, pp. 68–101). New York: Academic Press.

MASSON, J. M. (1984). *The assault on truth.* New York: Farrar, Straus & Giroux.

MASTERS, W. H., & JOHNSON, V. E. (1966). *Human sexual response.* Boston: Little, Brown.

MASUDA, M., & HOLMES, T. H. (1978). Life events: Perceptions and frequencies. *Psychosomatic Medicine, 40*, 236–261.

MASUDA, T., & NISBETT, R. E. (2001). Attending holistically versus analytically: Comparing the context sensitivity of Japanese and Americans. *Journal of Personality and Social Psychology, 81*, 922–934.

MATAS, L., AREND, R. A., & SROUFE, L. A. (1978). Continuity of adaption in the second year: The relationship between quality of attachment and later competence. *Child Development, 49*, 547–556.

MATHES, E. W. (1975). The effects of physical attractiveness and anxiety on heterosexual attraction over a series of five encounters. *Journal of Marriage and the Family, 37*, 769–773.

MATTHEWS, D. F. (1972). Response patterns of single neurons in the tortoise olfactory epithelium and olfactory bulb. *Journal of General Physiology, 60*, 166–180.

MAYER, J. D., & SALOVEY, P. (1997). What is emotional? In P. Savoley & D. Sluyter (Eds.), *Emotional development and emotional intelligence: Implications for educators* (pp. 3–31.) New York: Basic Books.

MAYER, J. D., SALOVEY, P., & CARUSO, D. (2000). Models of emotional intelligence. In *Handbook of intelligence,* (pp. 396–420). Cambridge: Cambridge University Press.

MAYER, R. E. (1983). *Thinking, problem solving and cognition.* New York: Freeman.

MAZZONI, G., & LOFTUS, E. (1998). Dreaming, believing, and remembering. In J. de Rivera & T. R. Sarbin (Eds.), *Believed-in imaginings: The narrative construction of reality* (pp. 145–156). American Psychological Association. Washington, DC: American Psychological Association Press.

MCALISTER, A., PERRY, C., KILLEN, J., SLINKARD, L. A., & MACCOBY, N. (1980). Pilot study of smoking, alcohol and drug abuse prevention. *American Journal of Public Health, 70*, 719–721.

MCBRIDE, P., BROWN, R. P., DEMEO, M., & KEILP, J. (1994). The relationship of platelet 5-HT-sub-2 receptor indices to major depressive disorder, personality traits, and suicidal behavior. *Biological Psychiatry, 35*, 295–308.

MCBURNEY, D. H. (1978). Psychological dimensions and the perceptual analysis of taste. In E. C. Carterette & M. P. Friedman (Eds.), *Handbook of perception* (Vol. 6). New York: Academic Press.

MCCARTHY, R. A., & WARRINGTON, E. K. (1990). *Cognitive neuropsychology: A clinical introduction.* New York: Academic Press.

MCCAULEY, C. (1989). The nature of social influence in groupthink: Compliance and internalization. *Journal of Personality and Social Psychology, 57*, 250–260.

MCCLANAHAN, K. K., GOLD, J. A., LENNEY, E., RYCKMAN, R. M., & KULBERG, G. E. (1990). Infatuation and attraction to a dissimilar other: Why is love blind? *Journal of Social Psychology, 130*, 433–445.

MCCLELLAND, D. C. (1987). *Human motivation.* New York: Cambridge University Press.

MCCLELLAND, J. L., & RUMELHART, D. E. (1981). An interactive model of context effects in letter perception: Pt. 1. An account of basic findings. *Psychological Review, 88*, 375–407.

MCCLINTOCK, M. K. (1971). Menstrual synchrony and suppression. *Nature, 229*, 244–245.

MCCOLSKEY, M., WIBLE, C. G., & COHEN, N. J. (1988). Is there a flashbulb-memory system? *Journal of Experimental Psychology, 117*, 171–181.

MCCONAGHY, M. J. (1979). Gender permanence and the genital basis of gender. Stages in the development of constancy of gender identity. *Child Development, 50*, 1223–1226.

MCCRAE, R. R., & COSTA, P. T., JR. (1987). Validation of the five-factor model of personality across instruments and observers. *Journal of Personality and Social Psychology, 52*, 81–90.

MCCRAE, R. R., & COSTA, P. T., Jr. (1999). A five-factor theory of personality. In L. A. Pervin (Ed.), *Handbook of Personality: Theory and Research.* New York: Guilford.

MCDOUGALL, W. (1908). *Social psychology.* New York: Putnam.

MCELREE, B. DOSHER, B. A. (1989). Serial position and set size in short-term memory. The time course of recognition. *Journal of Experimental Psychology: General, 118*, 346–373.

MCEWEN, B. S. (1999). Allostasis and allostatic load: Implications for neuropsychopharmacology. *Neuropsychopharmacology, 22*, 108–124.

MCFARLAND, S. G., AGEYEV, V. S., & ABALAKINA-PAAP, M. A. (1992). Authoritarianism in the former Soviet Union. *Journal of Personality and Social Psychology, 63,* 1004–1010.

MCGHIE, A., & CHAPMAN, J. (1961). Disorders of attention and perception in early schizophrenia. *British Journal of Medical Psychology, 34,* 103–116.

MCGLASHAN, T. H. Omnipotence, helplessness, and control with the borderline patient. *American Journal of Psychotherapy, 37,* 49–61.

MCGRATH, E., KEITA, G. P., STRICKLAND, B. R., & RUSSO, N. F. (1990). *Women and depression: Risk factors and treatment issues.* Washington, DC: American Psychological Association.

MCGRAW, M. B. (1975). *Growth: A study of Johnny and Jimmy.* New York: Acno Press. (Originally published 1935).

MCGUFFIN, P. (2001). Toward behavioral genomics. *Science, 291,* 1232–1249.

MCGUFFIN, P., KATZ, R., & RUTHERFORD, J. (1991). Nature, nurture and depression: A twin study. *Psychological Medicine, 21,* 329–335.

MCGURK, H., & MACDONALD, J. (1976). Hearing lips and seeing voices. *Nature, 264,* 746–748.

MCHUGH, P. R. (1990). Clinical issues in food ingestion and body weight maintenance. In E. M. Stricker (Ed.), *Neurobiology of food and fluid intake* (pp. 531–547). New York: Plenum.

MCINTOSH, D. N., SILVER, R. C., & WORTMAN, C. B. (1993). Religion's role in adjustment to a negative life event: Coping with the loss of a child. *Journal of Personality and Social Psychology, 65,* 812–821.

MCINTOSH, J. L. (1991). Epidemiology of suicide in the United States. In A. A. Leenaars (Ed.), *Life span perspectives of suicide: Time-lines in the suicide process.* New York: Plenum.

MCKENNA, R. J. (1972). Some effects of anxiety level and food cues on the eating behavior of obese and normal subjects. *Journal of Personality and Social Psychology, 22,* 311–319.

MCNALLY, R. J. (1994). Choking phobia: A review of the literature. *Comprehensive Psychiatry, 35,* 83–89.

MCNALLY, R. J. (2001). The cognitive psychology of repressed and recovered memories of childhood sexual abuse: clinical implications. *Psychiatric Annals, 31,* 509–514.

MCNALLY, R. J. (2001). Vulnerability to anxiety disorders in adulthood. In *Vulnerability to psychopathology: Risk across the lifespan* (pp. 304–321). New York: Guilford.

MCNALLY, R. J., & REISS, S. (1984). The preparedness theory of phobias: The effects of initial fear level on safety signal conditioning to fear-relevant stimuli. *Psychophysiology, 21,* 647–652.

MCNEILL, D. (1966). Developmental psycholinguistics. In F. Smith & G. A. Miller (Eds.), *The genesis of language: A psycholinguistic approach.* Cambridge, MA: MIT Press.

MEANEY, M. J., AITKENS, D. H., BERKEL, C., BHATNAGAR, S., SARRIEAU, A., & SAPOLSKY, R. M. (1987). *Post-natal handling attenuates age-related changes in the adrenocortical stress response and spatial memory deficits in the rat.* Paper presented at the 17th Annual Meeting of the Society of Neuroscience, New Orleans.

MECHANIC, D. (1962). *Students under stress.* New York: Free Press.

MEDCOF, J., & ROTH, J. (Eds.). (1988). *Approaches to psychology.* Philadelphia: Open University Press, Milton Keynes.

MEDIN, D. L., & ROSS, B. H. (1992). *Cognitive psychology.* Fort Worth: Harcourt Brace.

MEDNICK, B., REZNICK, C., HOCEVAR, D., & BAKER, R. (1987). Long-term effects of parental divorce on young adult male crime. *Journal of Youth and Adolescence, 16,* 31–45.

MEDNICK, S. A., GABRIELLI, W. F., & HUTCHINGS, B. (1984). Genetic influences in criminal convictions: Evidence from an adoption cohort. *Science, 224,* 891–894.

MEEHL, P. E., & DAHLSTROM, W. G. (1960). Objective configural rules for discriminating psychotic from neurotic MMPI profiles. *Journal of Consulting Psychology, 24,* 375–387.

MEGARGEE, E. I. (1972). *The California psychological inventory handbook.* San Francisco: Jossey-Bass.

MEIER, R. P. (1991). Language acquisition by deaf children. *American Scientist, 79,* 60–76.

MELAMED, B. G., & SIEGEL, L. J. (1975). Reduction of anxiety in children facing hospitalization and surgery by use of filmed modeling. *Journal of Consulting and Clinical Psychiatry, 43,* 511–521.

MELTON, A. W. (1963). Implications of short-term memory for a general theory of memory. *Journal of Verbal Learning and Verbal Behavior, 1,* 1–21.

MELZAK, R. (1973). *The puzzle of pain.* New York: Basic Books.

MELZAK, R. (1990). The tragedy of needless pain. *Scientific American, 262,* 27–33.

MELZAK, R., & WALL, P. D. (1982, 1988). *The challenge of pain.* New York: Basic Books.

MENDOLA, R., TENNEN, H., AFFLECK, G., MCCANN, L., & FITZGERALD, R. (1990). Appraisal and adaptation among women with impaired fertility. *Cognitive Therapy and Research, 14,* 79–93.

MERVIS, C. B., & PANI, J. R. (1981). Acquisition of basic object categories. *Cognitive Psychology, 12,* 496–522.

MERVIS, C. B., & ROSCH, E. (1981). Categorization of natural objects. In M. R. Rosenz & L. W. Porter (Eds.), *Annual review of psychology* (Vol. 21). Palo Alto, CA: Annual Reviews.

MESQUITA, B. (2001). Emotions in collectivist and individualist contexts. *Journal of Personality and Social Psychology, 80,* 68–74.

MESQUITA, B., & FRIJDA, N. H. (1992). Cultural variations in emotions: A review. *Psychological Bulletin, 112,* 179–204.

MESSICK, S. (1992). Multiple intelligences or multilevel intelligence? Selective emphasis on distinctive properties of hierarchy: On Gardner's Frames of mind and Sternberg's Beyond IQ in the context of theory and research on the structure of human abilities. *Journal of Psychological Inquiry, 1,* 305–384.

METALSKY, G. I., HALBERSTADT, L. J., & ABRAMSON, L. Y. (1987). Vulnerability to depressive mood reactions: Toward a more powerful test of the diathesis-stress and causal meditation components of the reformulated theory of depression. *Journal of Personality and Social Psychology, 52,* 386–393.

METZNER, R. J. (1994, March 14). Prozac is medicine, not a miracle. *Los Angeles Times,* p. B7.

MEYER, J. P., & PEPPER, S. (1977). Need compatibility and marital adjustment in young married couples. *Journal of Personality and Social Psychology, 8,* 331–342.

MEZZACAPPA, E. S., KATKIN, E. S., & PALMER, S. N. (1999). Epinephrine, arousal, and emotion: A new look at two-factor theory. *Cognition and Emotion, 13,* 181–199.

MIDDLETON, F. A., & STRICK, P. L. (1994). Anatomic evidence for cerebellar and basal ganglia involvement in higher cognitive function. *Science, 266,* 458–463.

MIGNAULT, A (2001). Connectionist models of the perception of facial expressions of emotion. *Dissertation Abstracts International: Section B: The Sciences and Engineering, 61,* 6743.

MIGNOT, E. (1998). Genetic and familial aspects of narcolepsy. *Neurology, 50,* 16–22.

MILGRAM, S. (1963). Behavioral study of obedience. *Journal of Abnormal and Social Psychology, 67,* 371–378.

MILGRAM, S. (1974). *Obedience to authority: An experimental view.* New York: Harper & Row.

MILLAR, M. G., & TESSER, A. (1989). The effects of affective-cognitive consistency and thought on the attitude-behavior relation. *Journal of Experimental Social Psychology, 25,* 189–202.

MILLER, D. T., & ROSS, M. (1975). Self-serving biases in attribution of causality: Fact or fiction? *Psychological Bulletin, 82,* 213–225.

MILLER, E. K., & COHEN, J. D. (2001) An integrative theory of prefrontal cortex function. *Annual Review of Neuroscience, 24,* 167–202.

MILLER, G. A. (1956). The magical number seven plus or minus two: Some limits on our capacity for processing information. *Psychological Review, 63,* 81–97.

MILLER, G. A., & GILDEA, P. M. (1987). How children learn words. *Scientific American, 257,* 94–99.

MILLER, J. G. (1984). Culture and the development of everyday social explanation. *Journal of Personality and Social Psychology, 46,* 961–978.

MILLER, J. M., & SPELMAN, F. A. (1990). *Cochlear implants: Models of the electrically stimulated ear.* New York: Springer-Verlag.

MILLER, N. E., & KESSEN, M. L. (1952). Reward effects of food via stomach fistula compared with those of food via mouth. *Journal of Comparative and Physiological Psychology, 45,* 555–564.

MILLER, P. A., & EISENBERG, N. (1988). The relation of empathy to aggressive and externalizing/antisocial behavior. *Psychological Bulletin, 103,* 324–344.

MILLER, P. H. (1993). *Theories of developmental psychology* (3rd ed.). New York: Freeman.

MILLON, T. (1981). *Disorders of personality: DSM-III.* New York: Wiley.

MILLS, J. (1979). *Six years with God.* New York: A & W Publishers.

MILNER, B. (1970). Memory and the medial temporal regions of the brain. In K. H. Pribram & D. E. Broadbent (Eds.), *Biology of memory.* New York: Academic Press.

MILNER, B., CORKIN, S., & TEUBER, H. L. (1968). Further analysis of the hippocampal amnesic syndrome: 14-year follow-up study of H. M. *Neuropsychologia, 6,* 215–234.

MINARD, R. D. (1952). Race relations in the Pocahontas coal field. *Journal of Social Issues, 8,* 29–44.

MINEKA, S. (1987). A primate model of phobic fears. In H. Eysenck & I. Martin (Eds.), *Theoretical foundation of behavior therapy* (pp. 81–111). New York: Plenum.

MINEKA, S., DAVIDSON, M., COOK, M., & KEIR, R. (1984). Observational conditioning of snake fear in rhesus monkeys. *Journal of Abnormal Psychology, 93,* 355–372.

MINTZ, L. I., LIEBERMAN, R. P., MIKLOWITZ, D. J., & MINTZ, J. (1987). Expressed emotion: A call for partnership among relatives, patients, and professionals. *Schizophrenia Bulletin, 13,* 227–235.

MINUCHIN, S., ROSMAN, B. L., & BAKER, L. (1978). *Psychosomatic families: Anorexia nervosa in context.* Cambridge, MA: Harvard University Press.

MISCHEL, W. (1966). A social learning view of sex differences in behavior. In E. E. Maccoby (Ed.), *The development of sex differences*. Stanford, CA: Stanford University Press.

MISCHEL, W. (1973). Toward a cognitive social learning reconceptualization of personality. *Psychological Review, 80*, 272–283.

MISCHEL, W. (1993). *Introduction to personality* (5th ed.). Fort Worth: Harcourt Brace Jovanovich.

MISCHEL, W. (1999). Personality coherence and dispositions in a cognitive-affective personality (CAPS) approach. In *The coherence of personality: Social-cognitive bases of consistency, variability, and organization* (pp. 37–60). New York: Guilford.

MISCHEL, W., & SHODA, Y. (1999). Integrating dispositions and processing dynamics within a unified theory of personality: The cognitive-affective personality system. In *Handbook of personality: Theory and research* (2nd ed.; pp. 197–218.). New York: Guilford.

MISHKIN, M., UNGERLEIDER, L. G., & MACKO, K. A. (1983). Object vision and spatial vision: Two cortical pathways. *Trends in Neuroscience, 6*, 414–417.

MITA, T. H., DERMER, M., & KNIGHT, J. (1977). Reversed facial images and the mere-exposure hypotheses. *Journal of Personality and Social Psychology, 35*, 597–601.

MITCHELL, J. E., & DEZWAAN, M. (1993). Pharmacological treatments of binge eating. In C. F. Fairburn & G. T. Wilson (Eds.), *Binge eating: Nature, assessment, and treatment*. New York: Guilford.

MIYAHARA, E., POKORNY, J., & SMITH, V. C. (1996). Increment threshold and purity discrimination spectral sensitivities of x chromosome linked color defective observers culprit. *Vision Research, 36*, 1597–1613.

MOFFITT, T. E. (1990). Juvenile delinquency and attention deficit disorder: Boys' development trajectories from age 3 to age 15. *Child Development, 61*, 893–910.

MOFFITT, T. E. (1993). The neuropsychology of conduct disorder. *Development and Psychopathology, 5*, 135–151.

MOFFITT, T. E., BRAMMER, G. L., CASPI, A., FAWCET, J. P., RALEIGH, M., YUWILER, A, & SILVA, P. A. (1998). Whole blood serotonin relates to violence in an epidemiological study. *Biological Psychiatry, 43*, 446–457.

MONAHAN, J. (1992). Mental disorder and violent behavior: Perceptions and evidence. *American Psychologist, 47*, 511–521.

MONAHAN, J. (2001). Major mental disorder and violence: Epidemiology and risk assessment. In G. Pinard & L. Pagani (Eds.) *Clinical assessment of dangerousness*. New York: Cambridge University Press.

MONAHAN, J., & WALKER, L. (1990). *Social science in law: Cases and materials*. Westbury, NY: Foundation Press.

MONEY, J. (1980). Endocrine influences and psychosexual status spanning the life cycle. In H. M. Van Praag (Ed.), *Handbook of biological psychiatry* (Part 3). New York: Marcel Dekker.

MONEY, J. (1987). Sin, sickness, or status? Homosexual gender identity and psychoneuroendocrinology. *American Psychologist, 42*, 384–400.

MONEY, J. (1988). *Gay, straight, and in-between: The sexology of erotic orientation*. New York: Oxford University Press.

MONEY, J., & EHRHARDT, A. A. (1972). *Man and woman, boy and girl: The differentiation and dimorphism of gender identity from conception to maturity*. Baltimore: Johns Hopkins University Press.

MONEY, J., SCHWARTZ, M., & LEWIS, V. G. (1984). Adult heterosexual status and fetal hormonal masculinization and demasculinization: 46, XX congenital virilizing adrenal hyperplasia and 46, XY androgen-insensitivity syndrome compared. *Psychoneuroendocrinology, 9*, 405–414.

MONEY, J., WEIDEKING, C., WALKER, P. A., & GAIN, D. (1976). Combined antiandrogenic and counseling programs for treatment for 46 XY and 47 XXY sex offenders. In E. Sacher (Ed.), *Hormones, behavior and psychopathology*. New York: Raven Press.

MONMANEY, T. (1998, August 31). Labels' potency claims often inaccurate, analysis finds. *Los Angeles Times*, p. A10.

MONSELL, S. (1979). Recency, immediate recognition memory, and reaction time. *Cognitive Psychology, 10*, 465–501.

MOORE, B. C. J. (1982). *An introduction to the psychology of hearing* (2nd ed.). New York: Academic Press.

MOOS, R. H. (1988). *Coping responses inventory manual*. Palo Alto, CA: Social Ecology Laboratory, Department of Psychiatry, Stanford University and Veterans Administration Medical Centers.

MORAN, J., & DESIMONE, R. (1985). Selective attention gates visual processing in the extrastriate cortex. *Science, 229*, 782–784.

MORAY, N. (1969a). Attention in dichotic listening: Affective cues and the influence of attention. *Quarterly Journal of Experimental Psychology, 11*, 56–60.

MORAY, N. (1969b). *Attention: Selective processes in vision and hearing*. London: Hutchinson.

MORELAND, R. L., & BEACH, S. R. (1992). Exposure effects in the classroom: The development of affinity among students. *Journal of Experimental Social Psychology, 28*, 255–276.

MORELAND, R. L., & ZAJONC, R. B. (1979). Exposure effects may not depend on stimulus recognition. *Journal of Personality and Social Psychology, 37*, 1085–1089.

MOREY, L. C. (1993). Psychological correlates of personality disorder. *Journal of Personality Disorders (suppl.)*, 149–166.

MORGENSTERN, H., & GLAZER, W. M. (1993). Identifying risk factors for tardive dyskinesia among long-term outpatients maintained with neuroleptic medications: Results of the Yale tardive dyskinesia study. *Archives of General Psychiatry, 50*, 723–733.

MORRIS, M. W., & PENG, K. (1994). Culture and cause: American and Chinese attributions for social and physical events. *Journal of Personality and Social Psychology, 67*, 949–971.

MOSCOVICI, S. (1976). *Social influence and social change*. London: Academic Press.

MOSCOVICI, S., LAGE, E., & NAFFRECHOUX, M. (1969). Influence of a consistent minority on the responses of a majority in a color perception task. *Sociometry, 32*, 365–379.

MOSCOVICI, S., & ZAVALLONI, M. (1969). The group as a polarizer of attitudes. *Journal of Personality and Social Psychology, 12*, 125–135.

MOSKOWITZ, H. R., KUMRAICH, V., SHARMA, H., JACOBS, L., & SHARMA, S. D. (1975). Cross-cultural difference in simple taste preference. *Science, 190*, 1217–1218.

MOVSHON, J. A., & VAN SLUYTERS, R. C. (1981). Visual neural development. *Annual Review of Psychology, 32*, 477–522.

MOWRER, O. H. (1947). On the dual nature of learning: A reinterpretation of "conditioning" and "problem-solving." *Harvard Educational Review, 17*, 102–148.

MOYER, K. E. (1976). *The psychobiology of aggression*. New York: Harper & Row.

MUKHERJEE, S., SHUKLA, S., WOODLE, J., ROSEN, A. M., & OLARTE, S. (1983). Misdiagnosis of schizophrenia in bipolar patients: A multiethnic comparison. *American Journal of Psychiatry, 140*, 1571–1574.

MUKHOPADHYAY, P., & TURNER, R. M. (1997). Biofeedback treatment of essential hypertension. *Social Science International, 13*, 1–9.

MURAVEN, M., TICE, D. M., & BAUMEISTER, R. F. (1998). Self-control as a limited resource: Regulatory depletion patterns. *Journal of Personality and Social Psychology, 74*, 774–789.

MURDOCK, B. B., JR. (1962). The serial position effect in free recall. *Journal of Experimental Psychology, 64*, 482–488.

MURPHY, G. L., & BROWNELL, H. H. (1985). Category differentiation in object recognition: Typicality constraints on the basic category advantage. *Journal of Experimental Psychology, 11*, 70.

MURSTEIN, B. I. (1972). Physical attractiveness and marital choice. *Journal of Personality and Social Psychology, 22*, 8–12.

MUSSEN, P. H. (Ed.) (1983). *Handbook of child psychology* (4th ed.). New York: Wiley.

MYERS, D. G. (1993). *Social psychology* (4th ed.). New York: McGraw-Hill.

MYERS, D. G., & LAMM, H. (1976). The group polarization phenomenon. *Psychological Bulletin, 83*, 602–627.

NACOSTE, R. W. (1987). But do they care about fairness? The dynamics of preferential treatment and minority interest. *Basic and Applied Social Psychology, 8*, 117–191.

NARROW, W. E., REGIER, D. A., RAE, D., MANDERSCHEID, R. W., & LOCKE, B. Z. (1993). Use of services by persons with mental and addictive disorders. *Archives of General Psychiatry, 50*, 95–107.

NASAR, S. (1998). *A beautiful mind*. New York: Simon & Schuster.

NATHANS, J. (1987). Molecular biology of visual pigments. *Annual Review of Neuroscience, 10*, 163–164.

NATIONAL INSTITUTE OF MENTAL HEALTH. (2000). *Suicide facts*. Washington DC: Author. Retrieved January 26, 2000 from the World Wide Web: http://www.nimh.nih.gov/genpop/su_fact.htm.

NATIONAL INSTITUTE ON DRUG ABUSE. (2002). 2001 *Monitoring the future survey released*. www.nida.nih.gov/MedAQdv/00/HHS12-14.html.

NEISSER, U. (Ed.). (1982). *Memory observed: Remembering in natural contexts*. New York: Freeman.

NEISSER, U., & HARSCH, N. (1993). Phantom flashbulbs: False recollections of hearing the news about *Challenger*. In E. Winograd & U. Neisser (Eds.), *Affect and accuracy in recall: Studies of "flashbulb" memories* (pp. 9–31). Cambridge: Cambridge University Press.

NELSON, C. B., & WITTCHEN, H. (1998). DSM-IV alcohol disorders in a general population sample of adolescents and young adults. *Addiction, 93*, 1065–1077.

NELSON, R. J., & CHIAVEGATTO, S. (2001). Molecular basis of aggression. *Trends in Neurosciences, 24*, 713–719.

NEMETH, C. (1986). Differential contributions of majority and minority influence. *Psychological Review, 93*, 23–32.

NESTADT, G., SAMUELS, J., RIDDLE, M., BIENVENU, J., LABUDA, M., GRADOS, M., &

HOEHN-SARIC, R. (2000). A family study of obsessive-compulsive disorder. *Archives of General Psychiatry, 57,* 358–363.

NEW YORK TIMES/CBS NEWS POLL. (1999, October 20). Teen-ager's concerns. *New York Times,* A1.

NEUMANN, R. (2000). The causal influence of attributions on emotions. A procedural priming approach. *Psychological Science, 11,* 179–182.

NEWCOMB, M. D., RABOW, J., & HERNANDEZ, A. C. R. (1992). A cross-national study of nuclear attitudes, normative support, and activist behavior: Additive and interactive effects. *Journal of Applied Social Psychology, 22,* 780–200.

NEWCOMB, T. M. (1943). *Personality and social change.* New York: Dryden Press.

NEWCOMB, T. M. (1961). *The acquaintance process.* New York: Holt, Rinehart & Winston.

NEWCOMB, T. M., KOENING, K. E., FLACKS, R., & WARWICK, D. P. (1967). *Persistence and change: Bennington College and its students after twenty-five years.* New York: Wiley.

NEWELL, A., & SIMON, H. A. (1972). *Human problem solving.* Englewood Cliffs, NJ: Prentice-Hall.

NEWMAN, D. L., TELLEGEN, A., & BOUCHARD, T. J., Jr. (1998). Individual differences in adult ego development: Sources of influence in twins reared apart. *Journal of Personality and Social Psychology, 74,* 985–995.

NEWPORT, E. L. (1990). Maturational constraints on language learning. *Cognitive Science, 14,* 11–28.

NEZU, A. M., NEZU, C. M., & PERRI, M. G. (1989). *Problem-solving therapy for depression: Theory, research, and clinical guidelines.* New York: Wiley.

NICHD Early Child Care Research Network. (1996). Characteristics of infant child care: Factors contributing to positive caregiving. *Early Childhood Research Quarterly, 11,* 296–307.

NICHD Early Child Care Research Network. (1997). Familial factors associated with the characteristics of nonmaternal care for infants. *Journal of Marriage and the Family, 59,* 389–408.

NICHD Early Child Care Research Network. (1998). Early child-parent self-control, compliance, and problem behavior at 24 to 36 months. *Child Development, 69,* 1145–1170.

NIELSON, T., & POWELL, R. (1992). The day-residue and dream-lag effect. *Dreaming, 2,* 67–77.

NILSON, D. C., NILSON, L. B., OLSON, R. S., & MCALLISTER, B. H. (1981). *The planning environment report for the Southern California Earthquake Safety Advisory Board.* Redlands, CA: Social Research Advisory & Policy Research Center.

NISAN, M., & KOHLBERG, L. (1982). Universality and variation in moral judgment: A longitudinal and cross-sectional study in Turkey. *Child Development, 53,* 865–876.

NISBETT, R. E., & ROSS, L. (1980). *Human inference: Strategies and shortcomings of social judgment.* Englewood Cliffs, NJ: Prentice-Hall.

NISBETT, R. E., & WILSON, T. D. (1977). Telling more than we can know: Verbal reports on mental processes. *Psychological Review, 84,* 231–259.

NISBETT, R. E., KRANZ, D. H., JEPSON, D., & KUNDA, Z. (1983). The use of statistical heuristics in everyday inductive reasoning. *Psychological Review, 90,* 339–363.

NISBETT, R. E., PENG, K., CHOI, I., & NOREN-ZAYAN, A. (2001). Culture and systems of thought: Holistic versus analytic cognition. *Psychology Review, 108,* 291–310.

NOLEN-HOEKSEMA, S. (1991). Responses to depression and their effects on the duration of depressive episodes. *Journal of Abnormal Psychology, 100,* 569–582.

NOLEN-HOEKSEMA, S. (2002). Gender differences in depression. In I. H. Gotlib & C. L. Hammen (Eds.), *Handbook of depression.* New York: Guilford.

NOLEN-HOEKSEMA, S., & LARSON, J. (1999). *Coping with loss.* Mahwah, NJ: Erlbaum.

NOLEN-HOEKSEMA, S., & MORROW, J. (1991). A prospective study of depression and distress following a natural disaster: The 1989 Loma Prieta earthquake. *Journal of Personality and Social Psychology, 61,* 105–121.

NORENZAYAN, A., & NISBETT, R. E. (2000). Culture and causal cognition. *Current Directions in Psychological Science, 9,* 132–135.

NORMAN, R. (1975). Affective-cognitive consistency, attitudes, conformity, and behavior. *Journal of Personality and Social Psychology, 32,* 83–91.

NORTH, C. (1987). *Welcome silence.* New York: Simon and Schuster.

NOSOFSKY, R. M., & JOHANSEN, M. K. (2000). Exemplar-based accounts of "multiple-system" phenomena in perceptual categorization. *Psychonomic Bulletin and Review, 7,* 375–402.

NUCCLI, L. (1981). The development of personal concepts: A domain distinct from moral or societal concepts. *Child Development, 52,* 114–121.

OATLEY, K., & JENKINS, J. M. (1996). *Understanding emotions.* Cambridge, MA: Blackwell.

OFFIR, C. (1982). *Human sexuality.* San Diego: Harcourt Brace Jovanovich.

OFSHE, R. (1992). Inadvertent hypnosis during interrogation: False confessions to dissociative state; misidentified multiple personality and the satanic cult hypothesis. *International Journal of Clinical and Experimental Hypnosis, 40,* 125–156.

OFSHE, R., & WATTERS, E. (1994). *Making monsters: false memories, psychotherapy, and sexual hysteria.* New York: Charles Scribner's Sons.

OHMAN, A. (1986). Face the beast and fear the face: Animal and social fears as prototypes for evolutionary analyses of emotion. *Psychophysiology, 23,* 123–145.

OHMAN, A. (2000). Fear and anxiety: Evolutionary, cognitive, and clinical perspectives. In M. Lewis & J. M. Haviland-Jones (Eds.), *Handbook of emotions* (2nd ed., pp. 573–593). New York: Guilford.

OJEMANN, G. (1983). Brain organization for language from the perspective of electrical stimulation mapping. *Behavioral and Brain Sciences, 6,* 189–230.

OLLENDICK, T. H., & KING, N. J. (1998). Empirically validated treatments in clinical psychology. *Australian Psychologist, 33,* 89–95.

OLLENDICK, T. H., & KING, N. J. (2000). Empirically supported treatments for children and adolescents. In *Child & adolescent therapy: Cognitive-behavioral procedures* (2nd ed.), New York: Guilford.

OLSEN, G., & SHERMAN, T. (1983). Attention, learning and memory in infants. In P. H. Mussen (Series Ed.), M. M. Haith & J. J. Campos (Eds.), *Handbook of child psychology:* Vol. 2. *Infancy and developmental psychobiology* (4th ed., pp. 1001–1080). New York: Wiley.

OLSHO, L. W. et al. (1982). Auditory frequency discrimination in infancy. *Developmental Psychology, 18,* 721–726.

OLTON, D. S. (1978). Characteristics of spatial memory. In S. H. Hulse, H. F. Fowler, & W. K. Honig (Eds.), *Cognitive processes in animal behavior.* Hillsdale, NJ: Erlbaum.

OLTON, D. S. (1979). Mazes, maps, and memory. *American Psychologist, 34,* 583–596.

OLWEUS, D. (1969). *Prediction of aggression.* Stockholm: Scandinavian Test Corporation.

OLWEUS, D., MATTSSON, A., SCHALLING, D., & LOW, H. (1988). Circulating testosterone levels and aggression in adolescent males: A causal analysis. *Psychosomatic Medicine, 50,* 261–272.

OMAN, D., & REED, D. (1998). Religion and mortality among the community dwelling elderly. *American Journal of Public Health, 88,* 1469–1475.

ORLINSKY, D. E., & HOWARD, K. I. (1987). A generic model of psychotherapy. *Journal of Integrative and Eclectic Psychotherapy, 6,* 6–27.

ORNE, M. T., & HOLLAND, C. C. (1968). On the ecological validity of laboratory deceptions. *International Journal of Psychiatry, 6,* 282–293.

OSHEROW, N. (1984). Making sense of the nonsensical: An analysis of Jonestown. In E. Aronson (Ed.), *Readings about the social animal* (4th ed., pp. 68–86). New York: Freeman.

OSHERSON, D., PERANI, D., CAPPA, S., SCHNUR, T., GRASSI, F., & FAZIO, F. (1998). Distinct brain loci in deductive versus probabilistic reasoning. *Neuropsychologia, 36,* 369–376.

OSHERSON, D. N., KOSLYN, S. M., & HOLLERBACH, J. M. (1990). *An invitation to cognitive science* (Vol. 2). Cambridge, MA: MIT Press.

OSHERSON, D. N., & LASNIK, H. (1990). *An invitation to cognitive science* (Vol. 1). Cambridge, MA: MIT Press.

OSHERSON, D. N., & SMITH, E. E. (1990). *An invitation to cognitive science* (Vol. 3). Cambridge, MA: MIT Press.

OSHERSON, D. N., SMITH, E. E., WILKIE, O., LOPEZ, A., & SHAFIR, E. B. (1990). Category based induction. *Psychological Review, 97,* 185–200.

OSOFSKY, J. D. (Ed.) (1987). *Handbook of infant development* (2nd ed.). New York: Wiley.

OVERMEIER, J. B., & SELIGMAN, M. E. P. (1967). Effects of inescapable shock upon subsequent escape and avoidance responding. *Journal of Comparative and Physiological Psychology, 63,* 28.

OVERMIER, J. B., & MURRISON, R. (1998). Animal models reveal the "psych" in the psychosomatics of peptic ulcers. *Current Directions I Psychological Science, 6,* 180–184.

OZER, D. J., & REISE, S. P. (1994). Personality assessment. *Annual Review of Psychology, 45,* 357–388.

PAFFENBERGER, R. S., HYDE, R. T., WING, A. L., & HSIEH, C. (1986). Physical activity, all-cause mortality, and longevity of college alumni. *New England Journal of Medicine, 314,* 605–613.

PAICHELER, G. (1977). Norms and attitude change: Pt. 1. Polarization and styles of behavior. *European Journal of Social Psychology, 7,* 5–14.

PALLIS, C. A. (1955). Impaired identification of faces and places with agnosia for colors. *Journal of Neurology, Neurosurgery, and Psychiatry, 18,* 218–224.

PALMER, J., VERGHESE, P., & PAVEL, M. (2000). The psychophysics of visual search. *Vision Research, 40,* 1227–1268.

PALMER, S. E. (1975). The effect of contextual scenes on the identification of objects. *Memory and Cognition, 3,* 519–526.

PANKSEPP, J. (1998). *Affective neuroscience: The foundations of human and animal emotions.* New York: Oxford University Press.

PARKER, G., & HADZZI-PAVLOVIC, D. (1990). Expressed emotion as a predictor of schizophrenic relapse: An analysis of aggregated data. *Psychological Medicine, 20,* 961–965.

PARKER, G., JOHNSTON, P., & HAYWARD, L. (1988). Parental "expressed emotion" as a predictor of schizophrenic relapse. *Archives of General Psychiatry, 45,* 806–813.

PARKINSON, B., & MANSTEAD, A. S. R. (1992). Appraisal as the cause of emotion. In M. S. Clark (Ed.), *Review of personality and social psychology* (Vol. 13, pp. 122–149). Newbury Park, CA: Sage.

PARKINSON, B., & TOTTERDELL, P. (1999). Classifying affect-regulation strategies. *Cognition and Emotion, 13,* 277–303.

PASHLER, H. (2001). *Semantic oddities draw early saccades.* Talk presented at the meetings of the Psychonomics Society, Orlando.

PASUPATHI, M. (1999). Age differences in responses to conformity pressure for emotional and nonemotional material. *Psychology and Aging, 14,* 170–174.

PASZTOR, A. (1996, July 1). An air-safety battle brews over the issue of pilots' rest time. *Wall Street Journal.*

PATALANO, A. L., SMITH, E. E., JONIDES, J., & KOEPPE, R. A. (2002). PET evidence for multiple strategies of categorization. *Cognitive, Affective, and Behavioral Neuroscience, 1,* 360–370.

PATEL, V. L., & GROEN, G. J. (1986). Knowledge based solution strategies in medical reasoning. *Cognitive Science, 10,* 91.

PATTERSON, F. G. (1978). The gestures of a gorilla: Language acquisition in another pongid. *Brain and Language, 5,* 72–97.

PATTERSON, F. G., & LINDEN, E. (1981). *The education of Koko.* New York: Holt, Rinehart & Winston.

PATTERSON, G. (1974). Intervention for boys with conduct problems: Multiple settings, treatment, and criteria. *Journal of Consulting and Clinical Psychology, 42,* 471–483.

PATTERSON, G. R., DEBARSHYE, B. D., & RAMSEY, E. (1989). A developmental perspective on antisocial behavior. *American Psychologist, 44,* 329–335.

PATTERSON, G. R., LITTMAN, R. A., & BRICKER, W. A. (1967). Assertive behavior in children: A step toward a theory of aggression. *Monographs of the Society for Research in Child Development* (Serial No. 113), 5.

PATTERSON, G. R., REID, J. B., & DISHION, T. J. (1992). *Antisocial boys.* Eugene, OR: Castalia Press.

PAUL, G. L. (1967). Insight versus desensitization in psychotherapy two years after termination. *Journal of Consulting Psychology, 31,* 333–348.

PAUL, G. L., & LENTZ, R. J. (1977). *Psycho-social treatment of chronic mental patients: milieu versus social learning programs.* Cambridge, MA: Harvard University Press.

PAULHUS, D. (1982). Individual differences, self-presentation, and cognitive dissonance: Their concurrent operation in forced compliance. *Journal of Personality and Social Psychology, 43,* 838–852.

PAULUS, P. B. (1998). Developing consensus about groupthink after all these years. *Organizational Behavior and Human Decision Processes, 73,* 362–374.

PAULUS, P. B., & MURDOCK, P. (1971). Anticipated evaluation and audience presence in the enhancement of dominant responses. *Journal of Experimental Social Psychology, 7,* 280–291.

PAVLOV, I. P. (1927). *Conditioned reflexes.* New York: Oxford University Press.

PECHURA, C. M., & MARTIN, J. B. (Eds.). (1991). *Mapping the brain and its functions.* Washington, DC: National Academy Press.

PEDERSEN, N. L., PLOMIN, R., MCCLEARN, G. E., & FRIBERG, L. (1988). Neuroticism, extraversion and related traits in adult twins reared apart and reared together. *Journal of Personality and Social Psychology, 55,* 905–957.

PEELE, S. (1988). Fools for love: The romantic ideal, psychological theory, and addictive love. In R. J. Sternberg & M. L. Barnes (Eds.), *The psychology of love* (pp. 159–188). New Haven, CT: Yale University Press.

PELHAM, W. E., & BENDER, M. E. (1982). Peer relationships in hyperactive children. In K. Gadow & I. Bialer (Eds.), *Advances in learning and behavioral disabilities* (vol. 1, pp. 365–436). Greenwich, CT: JAI Press.

PELLEGRINO, J. W. (1985). Inductive reasoning ability. In R. J. Sternberg (Ed.), *Human abilities: An information-processing approach.* New York: Freeman.

PENDRY, L., & CARRICK, R. (2001). Doing what the mob do: Priming effects on conformity. *European Journal of Social Psychology, 31,* 83–92.

PENG, K., & NISBETT, R. E. (1999). Naive dialecticism and its effects on reasoning and judgment about contradiction. *American Psychologist, 54,* 741–754.

PENNEBAKER, J. W. (1990). *Opening up: The healing power of confiding in others.* New York: William Morrow.

PENNEBAKER, J. W. (1997a). *Opening up: The healing power of expressing emotions* (rev. ed.). New York: Guilford.

PENNEBAKER, J. W. (1997b). Writing about emotional experiences as a therapeutic process. *Psychological Science, 8,* 162–167.

PENNEBAKER, J. W., KIECOLT-GLASER, J. K., & GLASER, R. (1988). Disclosure of traumas and immune function: Health implications for psychotherapy. *Journal of Consulting and Clinical Psychology, 56,* 239–245.

PENNEBAKER, J. W., & O'HEERON, R. C. (1984). Confiding in others and illness rates among spouses of suicide and accidental-death victims. *Journal of Abnormal Psychology, 93,* 473–476.

PENROD, S., & CUTLER, B. (1995). Witness confidence and witness accuracy: Assessing their forensic relation. Special Issue: Witness memory and law. *Psychology, Public Policy, & Law, 1,* 817–845.

PEPLAU, L. A., RUBIN, Z., & HILL, C. T. (1977). Sexual intimacy in dating relationships. *Journal of Social Issues, 33,* 86–109.

PERKINS, K. A., & STITZER, M. (1998). Behavioral pharmacology of nicotine. In R. E. Tarter (Ed.), *Handbook of substance abuse: Neurobehavioral pharmacology.* (pp. 299–317). New York: Plenum.

PERRIN, F. A. C. (1921). Physical attractiveness and repulsiveness. *Journal of Experimental Psychology, 4,* 203–217.

PERRY, D. G., & BUSSEY, K. (1984). *Social development.* Englewood Cliffs, NJ: Prentice-Hall.

PERRY, D. G., PERRY, L. C., & BOLDIZAR, J. P. (1990). Learning of aggression. In M. Lewis & S. Miller (Eds.), *Handbook of developmental psychopathology* (pp. 135–146). New York: Plenum.

PERRY, J. C. (1993). Longitudinal studies of personality disorders. *Journal of Personality Disorders, 1* (Suppl.), 63–85.

PETERSEN, A. C. (1989). Adolescent development. In M. R. Rosenzweig & L. W. Porter (Eds.), *Annual review of psychology* (Vol. 39). Palo Alto, CA: Annual Reviews.

PETERSON, C. (1995). *Explanatory style.* Hillsdale, NJ: Erlbaum.

PETERSON, C., & BOSSIO, L. M. (2001). Optimism and physical well-being. In *Optimism and pessimism: Implications for theory, research and practice.* Washington, DC: American Psychological Association.

PETERSON, C., & SELIGMAN, M. E. P. (1984). Causal explanations as a risk factor for depression: Theory and evidence. *Psychological Review, 91,* 347–374.

PETERSON, C., SELIGMAN, M. E., VAILLANT, G. E. (1988). Pessimistic explanatory style is a risk factor for physical illness: A thirty-five-year longitudinal study. *Journal of Personality & Social Psychology, 55,* 23–27.

PETRIE, K. J., BOOTH, R. J., & PENNEBAKER, J. W. (1998). The immunological effects of thought suppression. *Journal of Personality and Social Psychology, 75,* 1264–1272.

PETTIGREW, T. F. (1959). Regional differences in anti-Negro prejudice. *Journal of Abnormal and Social Psychology, 59,* 28–36.

PETTIGREW, T. F. (1979). The ultimate attribution error: Extending Allport's cognitive analysis of prejudice. *Personality and Social Psychology Bulletin, 5,* 461–476.

PETTY, R. E., & CACIOPPO, J. T. (1981). *Attitudes and persuasion: Classic and contemporary approaches.* Dubuque, IA: Wm. C. Brown.

PETTY, R. E., & CACIOPPO, J. T. (1984). The effects of involvement on responses to argument quantity and quality: Central and peripheral routes to persuasion. *Journal of Personality and Social Psychology, 46,* 69–81.

PETTY, R. E., & CACIOPPO, J. T. (1986). Elaboration likelihood model of persuasion. In L. Berkowitz (Ed.), *Advances in experimental social psychology* (Vol. 19, pp. 123–205). New York: Academic Press.

PETTY, R. E., CACIOPPO, J. T., & GOLDMAN, R. (1981). Personal involvement as a determinant of argument-based persuasion. *Journal of Personality and Social Psychology, 41,* 847–855.

PETTY, R. E., OSTROM, T. M., & BROCK, T. C. (1981). Historical foundations of the cognitive response approach to attitudes and persuasion. In R. E. Petty, T. M. Ostrom, & T. C. Brock (Eds.), *Cognitive responses in persuasion.* Hillsdale, NJ: Erlbaum.

PETTY, R. E., & WEGENER, D. T. (1999). The elaboration likelihood model: Current status and controversies. In S. Chaiken & Y. Trope (Eds.), *Dual-process theories in social psychology* (pp. 41–72). New York: Guilford.

PEZDEK, K., FINGER, K., & HODGE, D. (1997). Planting false childhood memories: The role of event plausibility. *Psychological Science, 8,* 437–441.

PHILLIPS, D. A., MCCARTNEY, K., & SCARR, S. (1987). Child-care quality and children's social development. *Developmental Psychology, 23,* 537–543.

PHILLIPS, D. A., VORAN, M., KISKER, E., HOWES, C., & WHITEBROOK, M. (1994). Child care for children in poverty: Opportunity or inequity? *Child Development, 65,* 472–492.

PHILLIPS, J. L., JR. (1981). *Piaget's theory: A primer.* San Francisco: Freeman.

PHILLIPS, J. L., JR. (1992). *How to think about statistics* (rev. ed.). New York: Freeman.

PHINNEY, J. S., & ALIPURIA, L. L. (1990). Ethnic identity in college students form four ethnic groups. *Journal of Adolescence, 13,* 171–183.

PHOENIX, C. H., GOY, R. H., & RESKO, J. A. (1968). Psychosexual differentiation as a function of androgenic stimulation. In M. Diamond (Ed.), *Reproduction and sexual behavior.* Bloomington: Indiana University Press.

PIAGET, J. (1932/1965). *The moral judgment of the child.* New York: Free Press.

PIAGET, J. (1950a). *The origins of intelligence in children.* New York: International Universities Press.

PIAGET, J. (1950b). *The psychology of intelligence.* New York: International Universities Press.

PIAGET, J., & INHELDER, B. (1956). *The child's conception of space.* London: Routledge & Kegan Paul. (originally published 1948)

PIAGET, J., & INHELDER, B. (1969). *The psychology of the child.* New York: Basic Books.

PICCIONE, C., HILGARD, E. R., & ZIMBARDO, P. G. (1989). On the degree of stability of measured hypnotizability over a 25-year period. *Journal of Personality and Social Psychology, 56,* 289–295.

PICCIOTTO, M. R., ZOLI, M., RIMONDI, R., LENA, C., MARUBIO, L. M., PICH, E. M., FUXE, K., & CHAGENEUX, J. P. (1998). Acetylcholine receptors containing the B2 subunit are involved in the reinforcing properties of nicotine. *Nature, 391,* 173–177.

PICKEL, K. L. (1998). Unusualness and threat as possible causes of "weapon focus." *Memory, 6,* 277–295.

PICKERING, T. G., DEVEREUX, R. B., JAMES, G. D., GERIN, W., LANDSBERGIS, P., SCHNALL, P. L., & SCHWARTZ, J. E. (1996). Environmental influences on blood pressure and the role of job strain. *Journal of Hypertension, 14* (Suppl.), S179–S185.

PILIAVIN, I. M., RODIN, J., & PILIAVIN, J. A. (1969). Good Samaritanism: An underground phenomenon? *Journal of Personality and Social Psychology, 13,* 289–299.

PINKER, S. (1984). *Language learnability and language development.* Cambridge, MA: Harvard University Press.

PINKER, S. (1991). Rules of language. *Science, 253,* 530–555.

PINKER, S. (1994). *The language instinct.* New York: Morrow.

PINKER, S. (1997). *How the mind works.* New York: Norton

PINKER, S., & PRINCE, A. (1988). On language and connectionism: Analysis of a parallel distributed processing model of language acquisition. *Cognition, 28,* 71–193.

PINNELL, C. M., & COVINO, N. A. (2000). Empirical findings on the use of hypnosis in medicine: A critical review. *International Journal of Clinical and Experimental Hypnosis, 48,* 170–194.

PION, G. M. (1991). Psychologists wanted: Employment trends over the past decade. In R. R. Kilburg (Ed.), *How to manage your career in psychology.* Washington, DC: American Psychological Association

PLANT, A. E., HYDE, J. S., KELTNER, D., & DEVINE, P. G. (2000). The gender stereotyping of emotions. *Psychology of Women Quarterly, 24,* 81–92.

PLATT, J. J., YAKSH, T., & DARBY, C. L. (1967). Social facilitation of eating behavior in armadillos. *Psychological Reports, 20,* 1136.

PLOMIN, R. (1989). Environment and genes: Determinants of behavior. *American Psychologist, 44,* 105–111.

PLOMIN, R. (1994). *Genetics and experience.* Thousand Oaks, CA: Sage.

PLOMIN, R., & DANLIES, D. (1987). Why are children in the same family so different from one another? *Behavioral and Brain Sciences, 10,* 1–60.

PLOMIN, R., DEFRIES, J. C., & LOEHLIN, J. C. (1977). Genotype-environment interaction and correlation in the analysis of human behavior. *Psychological Bulletin, 84,* 309–322.

PLOMIN, R., FULKER, D. W., CORLEY, R., & DEFRIES, J. C. (1997). Nature, nurture, and cognitive development from 1 to 16 years: A parent-offspring adoption study. *Psychological Science, 8,* 442–447.

PLOMIN, R., & KOSSLYN, S. M. (2001). Genes, brain and cognition. *Nature Neuroscience, 4,* 1153–1154.

PLOMIN, R., OWEN, M. J., & MCGUFFIN, P. (1994) The genetic basis of complex human behaviors. *Science, 264,* 1733–1739.

POLIVY, J., & HERMAN, C. P. (1985). Dieting and bingeing: A causal analysis. *American Psychologist, 40,* 193–201.

POLIVY, J., & HERMAN, C. P. (1993). Etiology of binge eating: Psychological mechanisms. In C. E. Fairburn & G. T. Wilson (Eds.), *Binge eating: Nature, assessment, and treatment.* New York: Guilford.

POMERLEAU, O., & KARDIA, S. (1999). Introduction to the featured section: research on smoking. *Health Psychology, 18,* 3–6.

PORTENOY, R. K. (1990). Chronic opioid therapy in nonmalignant pain. *Journal of Pain and Symptom Management, 5,* S46–S62.

PORTENOY, R. K., & FOLEY, K. M. (1986). Chronic use of opioid analgesics in non-malignant pain: Report of 38 cases. *Pain, 25,* 171–186.

PORTER, R. H., MAKIN, J. W., DAVIS, L. B., & CHRISTENSEN, K. M. (1992). An assessment of the salient olfactory environment of formula-fed infants. *Physiology and Behavior, 50,* 907–911.

PORTER, S., YUILLE, J. C., & LEHMAN, D. R. (1999). The nature of real, implanted, and fabricated memories for emotional childhood events: Implications for the recovered memory debate. *Law and Human Behavior, 23,* 517–537.

POSNER, M. I. (1988). Structures and functions of selective attention. In T. Boll & B. K. Bryant (Eds.), *Clinical neuropsychology and brain function: Research, measurement, and practice.* Washington, DC: American Psychological Association.

POSNER, M. I. (1993). Seeing the mind. *Science, 262,* 673–674.

POSNER, M. I., & DEHAENE, S. (1994). Attentional networks. *Trends in Neuroscience, 17,* 75–79.

POSNER, M. I., & RAICHLE, M. E. (1994). *Images of mind.* New York: Scientific American Library.

POST, R. FRYE, M., DENICOFF, K., LEVERICH, G., KIMBRELL, T., & DUNN, R. (1998). Beyond lithium in the treatment of mental illness. *Neuropsychopharmacology, 19,* 206–219.

POSTMES, T., & SPEARS, R. (1998). Deindividuation and antinormative behavior: A meta-analysis. *Psychological Bulletin, 123,* 238–259.

POSTMES, T., SPEARS, R., & CIHANGIR, S. (2001). Quality of decision making and group norms. *Journal of Personality and Social Psychology, 80,* 918–930.

POWELL, R. A., & BOER, D. P. (1994). Did Freud mislead patients to confabulate memories of abuse? *Psychological Reports, 74,* 1283–1298.

PREMACK, D. (1971). Language in chimpanzees? *Science, 172,* 808–822.

PREMACK, D. (1985). "Gavagi!" Or the future history of the animal language controversy. *Cognition, 19,* 207–296.

PREMACK, D., & PREMACK, A. J. (1983). *The mind of an ape.* New York: Norton.

PRENTICE, D. A., & MILLER, D. T. (1993). Pluralistic ignorance and alcohol use on campus: Some consequences of misperceiving the social norm. *Journal of Personality and Social Psychology, 64,* 243–256.

PRENTICE-DUNN, S., & ROGERS, R. W. (1982). Effect of public and private self-awareness on deindividuation and aggression. *Journal of Personality and Social Psychology, 43,* 503–513.

PRENTICE-DUNN, S., & ROGERS, R. W. (1989). Deindividuation and the self-regulation of behavior. In P. B. Paulus (Ed.), *The psychology of group influence* (2nd ed., pp. 86–109). Hillsdale, NJ: Erlbaum.

PRESSLEY, M., LEVIN, J. R., & DELANEY, H. D. (1982) The mnemonic keyword method. *Review of Educational Research, 52,* 61–91.

PRETI, G., CUTLER, W. B., GARCIA, C. R., HUGGINS, G. R., and collaborators. (1986). Human axillary secretions influence women's menstrual cycles: The role of donor extract of females. *Hormones and Behavior, 20,* 474–482.

PRICE, D. D. (2000). Psychological and neural mechanisms of the affective dimensions of pain. *Science, 288,* 1769–1772.

PRIEST, R. F., & SAWYER, J. (1967). Proximity and peership: Bases of balance in interpersonal attraction. *American Journal of Sociology, 72,* 633–649.

PRINZMETAL, W. (1981). Principles of feature integration in visual perception. *Perception and Psychophysics, 30,* 330–340.

PROTHRO, E. T. (1952). Ethnocentrism and anti-Negro attitudes in the deep South. *Journal of Abnormal and Social Pathology, 47,* 105–108.

PRYOR, J. B. (1977). Self-focused attention and self-report validity. *Journal of Personality, 45,* 513–527.

PUTNAM, F. W. (1991). Recent research on multiple personality disorder. *Psychiatric Clinics of North America, 14,* 489–502.

QUIRK, G. J., REPA, C., & LEDOUX, J. E. (1995). *Neuron, 15,* 1029–1039.

RAAIJMAKERS, J. G., & SHIFFRIN, R. M. (1981). Search of associative memory. *Psychological Review, 88,* 93–134.

RAAIJMAKERS, J. G., & SHIFFRIN, R. M. (1992). Models for recall and recognition. *Annual Review of Psychology, 43,* 205–234.

RACHMAN, S. (1993). Obsessions, responsibility and guilt. *Behaviour Research and Therapy, 31,* 149–154.

RACHMAN, S. J., & HODGSON, R. J. (1980). *Obsessions and compulsions.* Englewood Cliffs, NJ: Prentice-Hall.

RACHMAN, S. J., & WILSON, G. T. (1980). *The effects of psychological therapy* (2nd ed.). Elmsford, NY: Pergamon Press.

RAEIKKOENEN, K., MATTHEWS, K. A., FLORY, J. D., & OWENS, J. F. (1999). Effects of hostility on ambulatory blood pressure and mood during daily living in healthy adults. *Health Psychology, 18,* 44–53.

RAGSDALE, D. S., MCPHEE, J. C., SCHEUER, T., & CATTERALL, W. A. (1994). Molecular determinants of state-dependent block of Na channels by local anesthetics. *Science, 265,* 1724–1728.

RAICHLE, M. E. (1994). Images of the mind: Studies with modern imaging techniques. *Annual Review of Psychology, 45,* 333–356.

RAINE, A. (1997). Antisocial behavior and psychophysiology: A biological perspective. In D. M. Stoff, J. Breiling, & J. D. Maser (Eds.) *Handbook of antisocial personality disorder* (pp. 289–304). New York: Wiley.

RAMACHANDRAN, V. S., & BLAKESLEE, S. (1998). *Phantoms in the brain.* New York: William Morrow.

RAMACHANDRAN, V. S., & GREGORY, R. L. (1991). Perceptual filling in of artificially induced scotomas in human vision. *Nature, 350,* 699–702.

RAMACHANDRAN, V. S., LEVI, L., STONE, L., ROGERS-RAMACHANDRAN, D., and collaborators. (1996). Illusions of body image: What they reveal about human nature. In R. R. Llinas & P. S. Churchland (Eds.), *The mind brain continuum. Sensory processes* (pp. 29–60). Cambridge, MA: MIT Press.

RANDI, J. (1982). *Flim-flam! Psychics, ESP, unicorns and other delusions.* Buffalo: Prometheus Books.

RAPAPORT, D. (1942). *Emotions and memory.* Baltimore: Williams & Wilkins.

RAPAPORT, J. L. (1989). The biology of obsessions and compulsions. *Scientific American, March,* 83–89.

RAPAPORT, J. L. (1990). *The boy who couldn't stop washing.* New York: Plume.

RAPAPORT, J. L. (1991). Recent advances in obsessive-compulsive disorder. *Neuropsychopharmacology, 5,* 1–10.

RAPEE, R. M., BROWN, T. A., ANTONY, M. M., & BARLOW, D. H. (1992). Response to hyperventilation and inhalation of 5.5% carbon dioxide-enriched air across the DSM III-R anxiety disorders. *Journal of Abnormal Psychology, 101,* 538–552.

RASMUSSEN, S. A., & EISEN, J. L. (1990). Epidemiology of obsessive compulsive disorder. *Journal of Clinical Psychiatry, 51* (suppl.), 10–13.

RATHBUN, C., DI VIRGILIO, L., & WALDFOGEL, S. (1958). A restitutive process in children following radical separation from family and culture. *American Journal of Orthopsychiatry, 28,* 408–415.

RAVENS, J. C. (1965). *Advanced progressive matrices, sets II and II.* London: H. K. Lewis.

RAVUSSIN, E., and collaborators. (1988). Reduced rate of energy expenditure as a risk factor for body-weight gain. *New England Journal of Medicine, 318,* 467–472.

RAY, O., & KSIR, C. (1993). *Drugs, society, and human behavior.* St. Louis: Mosby.

RAY, W. J., & RAVIZZA, R. (1988). *Methods toward a science of behavior and experience* (3rd ed.). Belmont, CA: Wadsworth.

RAYNER, K. (1978). Eye movements, reading and information processing. *Psychological Bulletin, 6,* 618–660.

REDER, L. M., & ANDERSON, J. R. (1980). A comparison of texts and their summaries: Memorial consequences. *Journal of Verbal Learning and Verbal Behavior, 19,* 121–134.

REED, G. M., KEMENY, M. E., TAYLOR, S. E., WANG, H.-Y. J., & VISSCHER, B. R. (1994). "Realistic acceptance" as a predictor of decreased survival time in gay men with AIDS. *Health Psychology, 13,* 299–307.

REGAN, D., BEVERLEY, K. I., & CYNADER, M. (1979). The visual perception of motion depth. *Scientific American, 241,* 136–151.

REGAN, D. T., & FAZIO, R. (1977). On the consistency between attitudes and behavior: Look to the method of attitude information. *Journal of Experimental Social Psychology, 13,* 28–45.

REICHER, G. M. (1969). Perceptual recognition as a function of the meaningfulness of the material. *Journal of Experimental Psychology, 81,* 275–280.

REIMAN, E. M., LANE, R. D., AHERN, G. L., SCHWARTZ, G. E., & DAVIDSON, R. J. (2000). Positron emission tomography in the study of emotion, anxiety, and anxiety disorders. In *Cognitive neuroscience of emotion.* New York: Oxford University Press.

REINISCH, J. M. (1981). Prenatal exposure to synthetic progestins increases potential for aggression in humans. *Science, 211,* 1171–1173.

REISENZEIN, R. (1983). The Schachter theory of emotion: Two decades later. *Psychological Bulletin, 94,* 239–264.

RESCORLA, R. A. (1967). Pavlovian conditioning and its proper control procedures. *Psychological Review, 74,* 71–80.

RESCORLA, R. A. (1972). Informational variables in Pavlovian conditioning. In G. H. Bower (Ed.), *Psychology of learning and motivation* (Vol. 6). New York: Academic Press.

RESCORLA, R. A. (1980). Overextension in early language development. *Journal of Child Language, 7,* 321–335.

RESCORLA, R. A. (1987). A Pavlovian analysis of goal-directed behavior. *American Psychologist, 42,* 119–129.

RESCORLA, R. A., & SOLOMON, R. L. (1967). Two-process learning theory: Relations between Pavlovian conditioning and instrumental learning. *Psychological Review, 74,* 151–182.

RESKIN, B. (1998). *The realities of affirmative action in employment.* Washington, DC: American Sociological Association.

RESNICK, H. S., KILPATRICK, D. G., DANSKY, B. S., & SAUNDERS, B. E. (1993). Prevalence of civilian trauma and posttraumatic stress disorder in a representative national sample of women. *Journal of Consulting and Clinical Psychology, 61,* 984–991.

RESNICK, H. S., YEHUDA, R., PITMAN, R. K., & FOY, D. W. (1995). Effect of previous trauma on acute plasma cortisol level following rape. *American Journal of Psychiatry, 152,* 1675–1677.

REUBENS, A. B., & BENSON, D. F. (1971). Associative visual agnosia. *Archives of Neurology, 24,* 305–316.

REYNOLDS, D. V. (1969). Surgery in the rat during electrical analgesia induced by focal brain stimulation. *Science, 164,* 444–445.

RHEINGOLD, H. F., & COOK, K. V. (1975). The content of boys' and girls' rooms as an index of parent behavior. *Child Development, 46,* 459–463.

RICE, B. (1978). The new truth machine. *Psychology Today, 12,* 61–78.

RICHARDS, J. M., & GROSS, J. J. (2000). Emotion regulation and memory: The cognitive costs of keeping one's cool. *Journal of Personality and Social Psychology, 79,* 410–424.

RICHARDSON, J. L., SHELTON, D. R., KRAILO, M., & LEVINE, A. M. (1990). The effect of compliance with treatment in survival among patients with hematologic malignancies. *Journal of Clinical Oncology, 8,* 356.

RICHARDSON, K. (1986). Theory? Or tools for social selection? *Behavioral and Brain Sciences, 9,* 579–581.

RIESEN, A. H. (1947). The development of visual perception in man and chimpanzee. *Science, 106,* 107–108.

RIMM-KAUFMAN, S., & KAGAN, J. (1996). The psychological significance of changes in skin temperature. *Motivation and Emotion, 20,* 63–78.

RIPS, L. J. (1983). Cognitive processes in propositional reasoning. *Psychological Review, 90,* 38–71.

RIPS, L. J. (1994). *The psychology of proof.* Cambridge, MA: MIT Press.

ROBERT, M. (1989). Reduction of demand characteristics in the measurement of certainty during modeled conservation. *Journal of Experimental Child Psychology, 47,* 451–466.

ROBERTS, M. C., VERNBERG, E., & JACKSON, Y. (2000). Psychotherapy with children and families. In C. R. Snyder,., & R. Ingram (Eds.) *Handbook of psychological change* (pp. 500–519). New York: Wiley.

ROBINS, L. N., HELZER, J. E., WEISSMAN, M. M., ORVASCHEL, H., GRUENBERG. E., BURKE, J. D., & REIGIER, D. A. (1984). Lifetime prevalence of specific psychiatric disorders in three sites. *Archives of General Psychiatry, 41,* 949–958.

ROBINSON, M. D. (1998). Running from William James' bear: A review of preattentive mechanisms and their contributions to emotional experience. *Cognition and Emotion, 12,* 667–696.

ROBINSON, T. E., & BERRIDGE, K. C. (1993). The neural basis of drug craving: An incentive-sensitization theory of addiction. *Brain Research Review, 18,* 247–291.

RODIN, J. (1981). Current status of the internal-external hypothesis of obesity: What went wrong? *American Psychologist, 36,* 361–372.

ROFFWARG, H. P., HERMAN, J. H., BOWER-ANDERS, C., & TAUBER, E. S. (1978). The effects of sustained alterations of waking visual input on dream content. In A. M. Arkin, J. S. Antrobus, & S. J. Ellman (Eds.), *The mind in sleep.* Hillsdale, NJ: Erlbaum.

ROGERS, C. R. (1951). *Client-centered therapy.* Boston: Houghton Mifflin.

ROGERS, C. R. (1959). A theory of therapy, personality, and interpersonal relationships as developed in the client-centered framework. In S. Koch (Ed.), *Psychology: A study of a science*: Vol. 3. *Formulations of the person and the social context.* New York: McGraw-Hill.

ROGERS, C. R. (1963). The actualizing tendency in relation to motives and to consciousness. In M. Jones (Ed.), *Nebraska symposium on motivation* (pp. 1–24). Lincoln: University of Nebraska Press.

ROGERS, C. R. (1970). *On becoming a person: A therapist's view of psychotherapy.* Boston: Houghton Mifflin.

ROGERS, T. B., KUIPER, N. A., & KIRKER, W. S. (1977). Self-reference and the encoding of personal information. *Journal of Personality and Social Psychology, 35,* 677–688.

ROGOFF, B. (1990). *Apprenticeship in thinking.* New York: Oxford University Press.

ROGOFF, B. (2000). *Culture and development.* New York: Oxford University Press.

ROITBLAT, H. L. (1986). *Introduction to comparative cognition.* New York: Freeman.

ROLAND, P. E., & FRIBERG, L. (1985). Localization of cortical areas activated by thinking. *Journal of Neurophysiology, 53,* 1219–1243.

ROLLIN, H. R. (1980). *Coping with schizophrenia.* London: Burnnet Books.

ROLLS, E. T. (2000) Hippocampo cortical and cortico cortical back-projections. *Hippocampus, 10,* 380–388.

ROOK, K. (1984). The negative side of social interaction: Impact on psychological well-being. *Journal of Personality and Social Psychology, 46,* 1097–1108.

ROSCH, E. (1974). Linguistic relativity. In A. Silverstein (Ed.), *Human communication: Theoretical perspectives.* New York: Halsted Press.

ROSCH, E. (1978). Principles of categorization. In E. Rosch & B. L. Lloyd (Eds.), *Cognition and categorization.* Hillsdale, NJ: Erlbaum.

ROSCH, E. (1997). Transformation of the wolf man. In J Pickering (Ed.), *The authority of experience.* London: Curzon.

ROSE, J. E., BRUGGE, J. F., ANDERSON, D. J., & HIND, J. E. (1967). Phase-locked response to lower frequency tones in single auditory nerve fibers of the squirrel monkey. *Journal of Neurophysiology, 390,* 769–793.

ROSEMAN, I. J. (1984). Cognitive determinants of emotion: A structural theory. *Review of Personality and Social Psychology, 5,* 11–36.

ROSEN, R. C., & LEIBLUM, S. R. (1995). Treatment of sexual disorders in the 1990s: An integrated approach. *Journal of Consulting and Clinical Psychology, 63,* 877–890.

ROSENBERG, E. L. (1998). Levels of analysis and the organization of affect. *Review of General Psychology, 2,* 247–270.

ROSENBLITH, J. F. (1992). *In the beginning: Development from conception to age two years* (2nd ed.). Newbury Park, CA: Sage.

ROSENBLOOM, P. S., LAIRD, J. E., NEWELL, A., & MCCARL, R. (1991). A preliminary analysis of the foundations of Soar. *Artificial Intelligence, 47,* 289–325.

ROSENMAN, R. H., BRAND, R. J., JENKINS, C. D., FRIEDMAN, M., STRAUS, R., & WRUM, M. (1976). Coronary heart disease in the Western Collaborative Group Study: Final follow-up experience of 8½ years. *Journal of the American Medical Association, 233,* 878–877.

ROSENTHAL, R. (1984). *Meta-analytic procedures for social research.* Beverly Hills, CA: Sage.

ROSENTHAL, R., & JACOBSON, L. (1968). *Pygmalion in the classroom: Teacher expectation and student intellectual development.* New York: Holt, Rinehart, & Winston.

ROSENZWEIG, M. R., BREEDLOVE, S. M., & LEIMAN, A. L. (2001). *Biological psychology* (3rd ed.). Sunderland, MA: Sinauer Press.

ROSENZWEIG, M. R., & LEIMAN, A. L. (1989). *Physiological psychology* (2nd ed.). Lexington, MA: Heath.

ROSS, B. H. (1984). Reminders and their effects in learning a cognitive skill. *Cognitive Psychology, 16,* 371–416.

ROSS, C. A. (1989). *Multiple personality disorder: diagnosis, clinical features, and treatment.* New York: Wiley.

ROSS, C. A. (1997). *Dissociative identity disorder: diagnosis, clinical features, and treatment of multiple personality.* Toronto: Wiley.

ROSS, L. (1977). The intuitive psychologist and his shortcomings: Distortions in the attribution process. In L. Berkowitz, (Ed.), *Advances in experimental social psychology* (Vol. 10). New York: Academic Press.

ROSS, L., AMABILE, T. M., & STEINMETZ, J. L. (1977). Social roles, social control, and biases in social-perception processes. *Journal of Personality and Social Psychology, 35,* 485–494.

ROSS, L., BIERBRAUER, G., & HOFFMAN, S. (1976). The role of attribution processes in conformity and dissent. Revisiting the Asch situation. *American Psychologist, 31,* 148–157.

ROSS, L., LEPPER, M. R., & HUBBARD, M. (1975). Perseverance in self perception and social perception: Biased attributional processes in the debriefing paradigm. *Journal of Personality and Social Psychology, 32,* 880–892.

ROSS, L., LEPPER, M. R., STRACK, F., & STEINMETZ, J. L. (1977). Social explanation and social expectation: The effects of real and hypothetical explanations upon subjective likelihood. *Journal of Personality and Social Psychology, 35,* 817–829.

ROSS, L., & NISBETT, R. E. (1991). *The person and the situation: Perspectives of social psychology.* New York: McGraw-Hill.

ROSSI, P. (1990). The old homelessness and the new homelessness in historical perspective. *American Psychologist, 45,* 954–959.

ROTH, A., FONAGY, P., PARRY, G., TARGET, M., and collaborators. (1996). *What works for whom? A critical review of psychotherapy research.* New York: Guilford.

ROTH, M. (1998). *Freud: Conflict and culture.* New York: Knopf.

ROTHBART, M., & BATES, J. (1998). Temperament. In W. Damon (Series Ed.) and N. Eisenberg (Vol. Ed.), Handbook of child psychology: Vol. 3. *Social, emotional and personality development* (5th ed., pp. 105–176.). New York: Wiley.

ROTTER, J. B. (1954). *Social learning and clinical psychology.* Englewood Cliffs, NJ: Prentice-Hall.

ROTTER, J. B. (1982). *The development and applications of social learning theory. Selected papers.* New York: Praeger.

ROVEE-COLLIER, C. (1999). The development of infant memory. *Current Directions in Psychological Science, 8,* 80–85.

ROVEE-COLLIER, C., & HAYNE, H. (1987). Reactivation of infant memory: Implications for cognitive development. In H. W. Reese (Ed.), *Advances in child development and behavior* (Vol. 20). New York: Academic Press.

ROWLAND, N. E., & ANTELMAN, S. M. (1976). Stress-induced hyperphagia and obesity in rats: A possible model for understanding human obesity. *Science, 191,* 310–312.

ROY, A. (1992). Genetics, biology, and suicide in the family. In R. W. Maris, A. L. Berman, J. T. Maltsberger, & R. I. Yufit (Eds.), *Assessment and prediction of suicide* (pp. 574–588). New York: Guilford.

ROYCE, J. R., & MOS, L. P. (Eds.). (1981). *Humanistic psychology: Concepts and criticisms.* New York: Plenum.

ROZIN, P. N., & SCHULKIN, J. (1990). Food selection. In E. M. Stricker (Ed.), *Neurobiology of food and fluid intake* (pp. 297–328). New York: Plenum.

RUBIN, Z. (1973). *Liking and loving.* New York: Holt, Rinehart & Winston.

RUCH, J. C. (1975). Self-hypnosis: The result of heterohypnosis or vice versa? *International Journal of Clinical and Experimental Hypnosis, 23,* 282–304.

RUCH, J. C., MORGAN, A. H., & HILGARD, E. R. (1973). Behavioral predictions from hypnotic responsiveness scores when obtained with and without prior induction procedures. *Journal of Abnormal Psychology, 82,* 543–546.

RUDERMAN, A. J. (1986). Dietary restraint: A theoretical and empirical review. *Psychological Bulletin, 99,* 247–262.

RUDMAN, L. A., & BORGIDA, E. (1995). The afterglow of construct accessibility: The behavioral consequences of priming men to view women as sexual objects. *Journal of Experimental Social Psychology, 31,* 493–517.

RUMELHART, D. E., & MCCLELLAND, J. L. (1987). Learning the past tenses of English verbs: Implicit rules or parallel distributed processing? In B. MacWhinney (Ed.), *Mechanisms of language acquisition.* Hillsdale, NJ: Erlbaum.

RUMELHART, D. E., MCCLELLAND, J. L., & THE PDP RESEARCH GROUP. (1986). *Parallel distributed processing: Explorations in the microstructure of cognition.* Volume 1: *Foundations.* Cambridge, MA: Bradford Books/MIT Press.

RUSSELL, J. A., & FELDMAN BARRETT, L. (1999). Core affect, prototypical emotional episodes, and other things called emotion: Dissecting the elephant. *Journal of Personality and Social Psychology, 76,* 805–819.

RUSSELL, M. J. (1976). Human olfactory communication. *Nature, 260,* 520–522.

RUSSELL, M. J., SWITZ, G. M., & THOMPSON, K. (1980). Olfactory influence on the human menstrual cycle. *Pharmacology, Biochemistry and Behavior, 13,* 737–738.

RUSSO, N. F., & SOBEL, S. B. (1981). Sex differences in the utilization of mental health facilities. *Professional Psychology, 12,* 7–19.

RUTTER, M. (1997). Antisocial behavior: Developmental psychopathology perspectives. In D. M. Stoff, J. Breiling, & J. D. Maser (Eds.), *Handbook of antisocial personality disorder* (pp. 115–124). New York: Wiley.

RUTTER, M., MACDONALD, H., CONTEUR, A. L., HARRINGTON, R., BOLTON, P., & BAILEY, A. (1990). Genetic factors in child psychiatric disorders: II. Empirical findings *Journal of Child Psychology and Psychiatry, 31,* 39–83.

RUTTER, M., QUINTON, D., & HILL, J. (1990). Adult outcome of institution-reared children: Males and females compared. In L. Robins (Ed.), *Straight and devious pathways from childhood to adulthood* (pp. 135–157). Cambridge, England: Cambridge University Press.

RYMER, R. (1992a, April 13). A silent childhood. *New Yorker,* pp. 41–53.

RYMER, R. (1992b, April 20). A silent childhood, pt. II. *New Yorker,* pp. 43–47.

SABOL, S. Z., NELSON, M. L., FISHER, C., GUNZERATH, L., BRODY, C. L., HU, S., SIROTA, L. A., MARCUS, S. E., GREENBERG, B. D., LUCAS, F. R., BENJAMIN, J., MURPHY, D. L., & HAMER, D. H. (1999). A genetic association for cigarette smoking behavior. *Health Psychology, 18,* 7–13.

SACHS, J. D. S. (1967). Recognition memory for syntactic and semantic aspects of connected discourse. *Perception and Psychophysics, 2,* 437–442.

SACKS, O. (1985). *The man who mistook his wife for a hat and other clinical tales.* New York: Harper Perennial.

SACKS, O. W. (1983). *Awakenings.* New York: Dutton.

SAFER, D. J., ZITO, J. M., & FINE, E. M. (1996). Increased methylphenidate usage for attention deficit disorder in the 1990s. *Pediatrics, 98,* 1084–1088.

SALAMY, J. (1970). Instrumental responding to internal cues associated with REM sleep. *Psychonomic Science, 18,* 342–343.

SALAPATEK, P. (1975). Pattern perception in early infancy. In L. B. Cohen & P. Salapatek (Eds.), *Infant perception: From sensation to cognition* (Vol. 1). New York: Academic Press.

SALKOVSKIS, P. M. (1989). Cognitive-behavioral factors and the persistence of intrusive thoughts in obsessional problems. *Behaviour Research & Therapy, 27,* 677–682.

SANDERS, G. S. (1984). Self-presentation and drive in social facilitation. *Journal of Experimental Social Psychology, 20,* 312–322.

SANDERS, G. S., & BARON, R. S. (1975). The motivating effects of distraction on task performance. *Journal of Personality and Social Psychology, 32,* 956–963.

SANDERS, G. S., & BARON, R. S. (1977). Is social comparison irrelevant for producing choice shifts? *Journal of Experimental Social Psychology, 13,* 303–314.

SANDERSON, W. C., RAPEE, R. M., & BARLOW, D. H. (1989). The influence of illusion of control on panic attacks induced via inhalation of 5.5% carbon dioxide-enriched air. *Archives of General Psychology, 46,* 157–162.

SAPOLSKY, R. M. (1990). Stress in the wild. *Scientific American, 262,* 116–123.

SATINOFF, E. (1964). Behavioral thermoregulation in response to local cooling of the rat brain. *American Journal of Physiology, 206,* 1389–1394.

SATINOFF, E. (1983). A reevaluation of the concept of the homeostatic organization of temperature regulation. In E. Satinoff & P. Teitelbaum (Eds.), *Motivation* (pp. 443–474). New York: Plenum Press.

SAUNDERS, D. R. (1985). On Hyman's factor analyses. *Journal of Parapsychology, 49,* 86–88.

SAXE, L., DOUGHERTY, D., & CROSS, T. (1985). The validity of polygraph testing. *American Psychologist, 40,* 355–366.

SAXENA, S., BRODY, A. L., SCHWARTZ, J. M., & BAXTER, L. R. (1998). Neuroimaging and frontal-subcortical circuitry in obsessive-compulsive disorder. *British Journal of Psychiatry, 173,* 26–37.

SCAFIDI, F., & FIELD, T. (1986). Massage therapy improves behavior in neonates born to HIV positive mothers. *Journal of Pediatric Psychology, 21,* 889–898.

SCAFIDI, F., FIELD, T., SCHANBERG, S., BAUER, C., TUCCI, K., ROBERTS, J., MORROW, C., & KUHN, C. M. (1990). Massage stimulates growth in preterm infants: A replication. *Infant Behavior and Development, 13,* 167–168.

SCARR, S. (1985). An author's frame of mind: Review of Frames of mind, by Howard Gardner. *New Ideas in Psychology, 3,* 95–100.

SCARR, S. (1988). How genotypes and environments combine: Development and individual differences. In N. Bolger, A. Caspi, G. Downey, & M. Moorehouse (Eds.), *Persons in context: Developmental processes* (pp. 217–244). New York: Cambridge University Press.

SCARR, S. (1992). Developmental theories for the 1990s: Development and individual differences. *Child Development, 63,* 1–19.

SCARR, S. (1996). How people make their own environments: Implications for parents and policy makers. *Psychology, Public Policy, and Law, 2,* 204–228.

SCARR, S., & EISENBERG, M. (1993). Child care research: Issues, perspectives, and results. *Annual Review of Psychology, 44,* 613–644.

SCARR, S., & MCCARTNEY, K. (1983). How people make their own environments: A theory of genotype-environment effects. *Child Development, 54,* 424–435.

SCARR, S., PHILLIPS, D., MCCARTNEY, K., & ABBOTT-SHIM, M. (1993). Quality of child care as an aspect of family and child care policy in the United States. *Pediatrics, 91,* 182–188.

SCARR, S., WEINBERG, R. A., & LEVINE, A. (1986). *Understanding development.* San Diego: Harcourt Brace Jovanovich.

SCHACHTEL, E. G. (1982). On memory and childhood amnesia. In U. Neisser (Ed.), *Memory observed: Remembering in natural contexts.* San Francisco: Freeman.

SCHACHTER, S. (1964). The interaction of cognitive and physiological determinants of emotional state. In L. Berkowitz (Ed.), *Advances in experimental social psychology* (pp. 49–80). New York: Academic Press.

SCHACHTER, S., & SINGER, J. E. (1962). Cognitive, social and physiological determinants of emotional state. *Psychological Review, 69,* 379–399.

SCHACTER, D. L. (1989). Memory. In M. Posner (Ed.), *Foundations of cognitive science.* Cambridge, MA: MIT Press.

SCHAFER, R. (1976). *A new language for psychoanalysis.* New Haven, CT: Yale University Press.

SCHANCK, R. L. (1932). A study of a community and its groups and institutions conceived of as behaviors of individuals. *Psychological Monographs, 43,* 1–133.

SCHARNBERG, M. (1993). *The nonauthentic nature of Freud's observations:* Vol. 1. *The seduction theory.* Philadelphia: Coronet.

SCHATZBERG, A. F. (2000). New indications for antidepressants. *Journal of Clinical Psychiatry, 61,* 9–17.

SCHEIER, M. F., BUSS, A. H., & BUSS, D. M. (1978). Self-consciousness, self-reports of aggressiveness, and aggressions. *Journal of Research in Personality, 12,* 133–140.

SCHEIER, M. F., & CARVER, C. S. (1992). Effects of optimism on psychological and physical well-being: Theoretical overview and empirical update. *Cognitive Therapy and Research, 16,* 201–228.

SCHEIER, M. F., MATTHEWS, K. A., OWENS, J. F., MAGOVERN, G. J., LEFEBYRE, R. C., ABBOTT, R. A., & CARVER, C. S. (1989). Dispositional optimism and recovery from coronary artery bypass surgery: The beneficial effects on physical and psychological well-being. *Journal of Personality and Social Psychology, 57,* 1024–1040.

SCHERRER, J. F., XIAN, H., LYONS, M. J., EISEN, S. A., GOLDBERG, J., LIN, N., & TSUANG, M. T. (2000). Evidence for genetic influences common and specific to symptoms of generalized anxiety and panic. *Journal of Affective Disorders, 57,* 25–35.

SCHIFF, W., & FOULKE, E. (Eds.). (1982). *Tactual perception: A sourcebook.* Cambridge, England: Cambridge University Press.

SCHIFFENBAUER, A., & SCHIAVO, R. S. (1976). Physical distance and attraction: An intensification effect. *Journal of Experimental Social Psychology, 12,* 274–282.

SCHINDLER, R. A., & MERZENICH, M. M. (Eds.). (1985). *Cochlear implants.* New York: Raven Press.

SCHLEIDT, M., HOLD, B., & ATTILI, G. (1981). A cross-cultural study on the attitude toward personal odors. *Journal of Chemical Ecology, 7,* 19–31.

SCHLEIFER, S. J., KELLER, S. E., MCKEGNEY, F. P., & STEIN, M. (1979, March). *The influence of stress and other psychosocial factors on human immunity.* Paper presented at the 36th Annual Meeting of the Psychosomatic Society, Dallas.

SCHLENGER, W. E., KULKA, R. A., FAIRBANK, J. A., & HOUGH, R. L. (1992). The prevalence of post-traumatic stress disorder in the Vietnam generation: A multi-method multi-source assessment of psychiatric disorders. *Journal of Traumatic Stress, 5,* 333–363.

SCHLESINGER, A. M., JR. (1965). *A thousand days.* Boston: Houghton Mifflin.

SCHMERMUND, A., SELLERS, R., MUELLER, B., & CROSBY, F. (2001). Attitudes toward affirmative action as a function of racial identity among black college students. *Political Psychology 22,* 759–774.

SCHMIDT, D. P., & BUSS, D. M. (1996). Strategic self-promotion and competitor derogation: Sex and context effects on the perceived effectiveness of mate attraction tactics. *Journal of Personality and Social Psychology, 70,* 1185–1204.

SCHMITT, B. H., GILOVICH, T., GOORE, N., & JOSEPH, L. (1986). Mere presence and social facilitation: One more time. *Journal of Experimental Social Psychology, 22,* 242–248.

SCHMOLCK, H., BUFFALO, E. A., & SQUIRE, L. (2000). Memory distortions develop over time: Recollections of the O. J. Simpson trial verdict after 15 and 32 months. *Psychological Science, 11,* 39–45.

SCHNEIDER, A. M., & TARSHIS, B. (1986). *An introduction to physiological psychology* (3rd ed.). New York: Random House.

SCHNEIDER, D. J., & MILLER, R. S. (1975). The effects of enthusiasm and quality of arguments on attitude attribution. *Journal of Personality, 43,* 693–708.

SCHNEIDER, F., R., JOHNSON, J., HORNIG, C. D., & LIEBOWITZ, M. R. (1992). Social phobia: Comorbity in an epidemiologic sample. *Archives of General Psychiatry, 49,* 282–288.

SCHNEIDERMAN, N., ANTONI, M. H., SAAB, P. G., & IRONSON, G. (2001). Health psychology: Psychosocial and biobehavioral aspects of chronic disease management. *Annual Reviews of Psychology, 52,* 555–580.

SCHNEIER, F. R., JOHNSON, J., HORNIG, C. D., & LIEBOWITZ, M. R. (1992). Social phobia: Comorbidity and morbidity in an epidemiologic sample. *Archives of General Psychiatry, 49,* 282–288.

SCHROEDER, C. M., & PRENTICE, D. A. (1998). Exposing pluralistic ignorance to reduce alcohol use among college students. *Journal of Applied Social Psychology, 28,* 2150–2180.

SCHULTZ, D. (2000). *A history of modern psychology* (7th ed.). Fort Worth: Harcourt.

SCHULZ, R., BOOKWALA, J., KNAPP, J. E., SCHEIER, M., & WILLIAMSON, G. (1996). Pessimism, age, and cancer mortality. *Psychology and Aging, 11,* 304–309.

SCHULTZ, S. K., O'LEARY, D. S., BOLES PONTO, L. L., ARNDT, S., MAGNOTTA, V., WATKINS, G. L., HICHWA, R. D., & ANDREASEN, N. C. (2002). Age and regional cerebral blood flow in schizophrenia: Age effects in anterior cingulate, frontal, and parietal cortex. *Journal of Neuropsychiatry and Clinical Neuroscience, 14,* 19–24.

SCHUR, E. M. (1971). *Labeling deviant behavior: Its sociological implications.* New York: Harper & Row.

SCHWARTZ, B. (1989). *Psychology of learning and behavior* (3rd ed.). New York: Norton.

SCHWARTZ, B., & REISBERG, D. (1991). *Learning and memory.* New York: Norton.

SCHWARTZ, B., SNIDMAN, N., & KAGAN, J. (1996). Early childhood temperament as a determinant of externalizing behavior in adolescence. *Development and Psychopathology, 8,* 527–537.

SCHWARTZ, J., STOESSEL, P. W., BAXTER, L. R., MARTIN, K. M., & PHELPS, M. C. (1996). Systemic changes in cerebral glucose metabolic rate after successful behavior modification treatment of obsessive compulsive disorder. *Archives of General Psychiatry, 53,* 109–113.

SCHWARTZBERG, S. S. (1993). Struggling for meaning: How HIV-positive gay men make sense of AIDS. *Professional Psychology: Research and Practice, 24,* 483–490.

SCOTT, T. R., & MARK, G. P. (1986). Feeding and taste. *Progress in Neurobiology, 27,* 293–317.

SEARS, R. R. (1943). *Survey of objective studies of psychoanalytic concepts.* Social Science Research Council Bulletin, No. 51.

SEARS, R. R. (1944). Experimental analyses of psychoanalytic phenomena. In J. Hunt (Ed.), *Personality and the behavior disorders* (Vol. 1, pp. 306–332). New York: Ronald.

SEARS, R. R., MACCOBY, E. E., & LEVIN, H. (1957) *Patterns of child rearing.* New York: Harper & Row.

SEGERSTROM, S. C., SOLOMON, G. F., KEMENY, M. E., & FAHEY, J. L. (1998). Relationship of worry to immune sequelae of the Northridge earthquake. *Journal of Behavioral Medicine, 21,* 433–450.

SEGERSTROM, S. C., TAYLOR, S. E., KEMENY, M. E., & FAHEY, J. L. (1998). Optimism is associated with mood, coping, and immune change in response to stress. *Journal of Personality and Social Psychology, 74,* 1646–1655.

SEGERSTROM, S. C., TAYLOR, S. E., KEMENY, M. E., REED, G. M., & VISSCHER, B. R. (1996). Causal attributions predict rate of immune decline in HIV-seropositive gay men. *Health Psychology,* *15,* 485–493.

SEIFERT, C. M., ROBERTSON, S. P., & BLACK, J. B. (1985). Types of inferences generated during reading. *Journal of Memory and Language, 24,* 405–422.

SEKULER, R. (1975). Visual motion perception. In E. C. Carterette & M. Friedman (Eds.), *Handbook of perception* (Vol. 5, pp. 387–433). New York: Academic Press.

SEKULER, R., & BLAKE, R. (1985). *Perception.* New York: Knopf.

SELIGMAN, M. E. P. (1975). *Helplessness.* San Francisco: Freeman.

SELIGMAN, M. E. P. (1996). The effectiveness of psychotherapy: The *Consumer Reports* study. *American Psychologist, 50,* 965–974.

SELIGMAN, M. E. P., & BINIK, Y. M. (1977). The safety signal hypothesis. In H. Davis & H. Hurwitz (Eds.), *Pavlovian operant interactions.* Hillsdale, NJ: Erlbaum.

SELLERS, R. M., SMITH, J. A., SHELTON, J. N., ROWLEY, S. A. J., & CHAVOUS, T. M. (1998). Multidimensional model of racial identity: A reconceptualization of African American racial identity. *Personality and Social Psychology Review, 2,* 18–39.

SELYE, H. (1978). *The stress of life.* New York: McGraw-Hill.

SEWELL, W. H., & MUSSEN, P. H. (1952). The effects of feeding, weaning, and scheduling procedures on childhood adjustment and the formation of oral symptoms. *Child Development, 23,* 185–191.

SHALLICE, T. (1988). *From neuropsychology to mental structure.* Cambridge, England: Cambridge University Press.

SHALLICE, T., FLETCHER, P., FRITH, C. D., GRASBY, P., FRACKOWIAK, R. S. J., & DOLAN, R. J. (1994). Brain regions associated with acquisition and retrieval of verbal episodic memory. *Nature, 368,* 633–635.

SHANKS, D. R., & DICKINSON, A., (1987). Associative accounts of causality judgment. *Psychology of Learning and Motivation, 21,* 229–261.

SHANNON, R. V., & OTTO, S. R. (1990). Psychophysical measures from electrical stimulation of the human cochlear nucleus. *Hearing Research, 47,* 159–168.

SHAPIRO, A. K., & MORRIS, L. A. (1978). The placebo effect in medical and psychological therapies. In S. L. Garfield & A. E. Bergin (Eds.), *Handbook of psychotherapy and behavior change* (2nd ed.). New York: Wiley.

SHAPIRO, D. A., & SHAPIRO, D. (1982). Meta-analysis of comparative therapy outcome studies: A replication and refinement. *Psychological Bulletin, 92,* 581–604.

SHAPLEY, R., & LENNIE, P. (1985). Spatial frequency analysis in the visual system. *Annual Review of Neurosciences, 8,* 547–583.

SHAW, D. W., & THORESEN, C. E. (1974). Effects of modeling and desensitization in reducing dentist phobia. *Journal of Counseling Psychology, 21,* 415–420.

SHEDLER, J., MAYMAN, M., & MANIS, M. (1993). The illusion of mental health. *American Psychologist, 48,* 1117–1131.

SHEINGOLD, K., & TENNEY, Y. J. (1982). Memory for a salient childhood event. In U. Neisser (Ed.), *Memory observed: Remembering in natural contexts.* San Francisco: Freeman.

SHEKELLE, R., NEATON, J. D., JACOBS, D., HULLEY, S., & BLACKBURN, H. (1983). Type A be-

havior pattern in MRFIT. A paper presented to the American Heart Association Council on Epidemiology Meetings, San Diego.

SHELTON, R. C., KELLER, M. B., GELENBERG, A., DUNNER, D. L., HIRSCHFIELD, R., THASE, M. E., RUSSEL, J., LYDIARD, L., CRITS-CRISTOPH, P., GALLOP, R., TODD, L., HELLERSTEIN, D., GOODNICK, P., KEITNER, G., STAHL, S. M., & HALBRIECH, U. (2001). Effectiveness of St. John's wort in major depression: A randomized controlled-trial. *JAMA, 285,* 1978–1993.

SHEPARD, R. N., & COOPER, L. A. (1982). *Mental images and their transformations.* Cambridge, MA: MIT Press, Bradford Books.

SHEPHER, J. (1971). Mate selection among second generation kibbutz adolescents and adults: Incest avoidance and negative imprinting. *Archives of Sexual Behavior, 1,* 293–307.

SHEPOSH, J. P., DEMING, M., & YOUNG, L. E. (1977, April). *The radiating effects of status and attractiveness of a male upon evaluating his female partner.* Paper presented at the annual meeting of the Western Psychological Association, Seattle.

SHERWIN, B. (1988). A comparative analysis of the role of androgen in human male and female sexual behavior: Behavioral specificity, critical thresholds, and sensitivity. *Psychobiology, 16,* 416–425.

SHIN, L. M., KOSSLYN, S. M., MCNALLY, R. J., ALPERT, N. M., THOMPSON, W. L., RAUCH, S. L., MACKLIN, M. L., & PITMAN, R. K. (1997). Visual imagery and perception in posttraumatic stress disorder: A positron emission tomographic investigation. *Archives of General Psychiatry, 54,* 233–241.

SHORS, T. J., MIESEGAES, G., BEYLIN, A., ZHAO, M., RYDEL, T., & GOULD, E. (2001). Neurogenesis in the adult is involved in the formation of trace memories. *Nature, 410,* 372–376.

SHRESTHA, N. M., SHARMA, B., VAN OM-MEREN, M., REGMI, S., MAKAJU, R., KOMPROE, I., SHRESTHA, G. B., & DE JONG, J. T. V. M. (1998). Impact of torture on refugees displaced within the developing world. *Journal of the American Medical Association, 280,* 443–448.

SHWEDER, R. A. (1984). Anthropology's romantic rebellion against the enlightenment, or there's more to thinking than reason and evidence. In R. A. Shweder & R. A. LeVine (Eds.), *Culture theory: Essays on mind, self, and emotion* (pp. 27–66). Cambridge, England: Cambridge University Press.

SIEGEL, P., & WEINBERGER, J. (1998). Capturing the "MOMMY AND I ARE ONE" merger fantasy: The oneness motive. In R. F. Bornstein & J. M. Masling (Eds.), *Empirical perspectives on the psychoanalytic unconscious* (pp. 71–98). Washington, DC: APA Press.

SIEGLER, R. S. (1991). *Children's thinking* (2nd ed.). Englewood Cliffs: NJ: Prentice-Hall.

SIEMER, M. (2001). Mood-specific effects on appraisal and emotion judgments. *Cognition and Emotion, 15,* 453–485.

SIERRA, M., & BERRIOS, G. (2000). Flashbulb and flashback memories. In G. Berrios & J. R. Hodges (Ed.), *Memory disorders in psychiatric practice* (pp. 369–383). Cambridge: Cambridge University Press.

SIGALL, H., & LANDY, D. (1973). Radiating beauty: The effects of having a physically attractive partner on person perception. *Journal of Personality and Social Psychology, 31,* 410–414.

SILVERBERG, S. B., & STEINBERG, L. (1990). Psychological well-being of parents with early adoles-

cent children. *Developmental Psychology, 26,* 658–666.

SILVERMAN, I. (1964). Self-esteem and differential responsiveness to success and failure. *Journal of Abnormal and Social Psychology, 69,* 115–119.

SILVERMAN, I. (1971). Physical attractiveness and courtship. *Sexual Behavior, 1,* 22–25.

SIMMONS, J. V. (1981). *Project sea hunt: A report on prototype development and tests.* Technical Report 746, Naval Ocean Systems Center, San Diego.

SIMMONS, R. G., & BLYTH, D. A. (1988). *Moving into adolescence: The impact of pubertal change and school context.* Hawthorne, NY: Aldine.

SIMON, H. A. (1985, June). Using cognitive science to solve human problems. Paper presented at Science and Public Policy Seminar, Federation of Behavioral, Psychological, and Cognitive Sciences.

SIMON, H. A., & GILMARTIN, K. (1973). A simulation of memory for chess positions. *Cognitive Psychology, 5,* 29–46.

SIMPSON, J. A., CAMPBELL, B., & BERSCHEID, E. (1986). The association between romantic love and marriage: Kephart (1967) twice revisited. *Personality and Social Psychology Bulletin, 12,* 363–372.

SINGER, J. L., & SINGER, D. G. (1981). *Television, imagination and aggression.* Hillsdale, NJ: Erlbaum.

SINGH, M., & HOFFMAN, D. M. (2001). Part-based representations of visual shape and implications for visual cognition. In B. K. Shipley, F. Thomas, & P. J. Kellman (Eds.), *From fragments to objects: Segmentation and grouping in vision. Advances in Psychology* (pp. 401–459). New York: Elsevier Science.

SIQUELAND, E. R., & LIPSITT, J. P. (1966). Conditioned head-turning in human newborns. *Journal of Experimental Child Psychology, 3,* 356–376.

SIZEMORE, C. C., & PITTILLO, E. S. (1977). *I'm Eve.* Garden City, NY: Doubleday.

SKINNER, B. F. (1938). *The behavior of organisms.* New York: Appleton-Century-Crofts.

SKINNER, B. F. (1948). "Superstition" in the pigeon. *Journal of Experimental Psychology, 38,* 168–172.

SKINNER, B. F. (1971). *Beyond freedom and dignity.* New York: Knopf.

SKINNER, B. F. (1981). Selection by consequences. *Science, 213,* 501–504.

SKYRMS, B. (1986). *Choice and chance: An introduction to inductive logic.* Belmont, CA: Dickenson.

SLOBIN, D. I. (1971). Cognitive prerequisites for the acquisition of grammar. In C. A. Ferguson & D. I. Slobin (Eds.), *Studies of child language developments.* New York: Holt, Rinehart & Winston.

SLOBIN, D. I. (1979). *Psycholinguistics* (2nd. ed.). Glenville, IL: Scott, Foresman.

SLOBIN, D. I. (Ed.). (1985). *The cross-linguistic study of language acquisition.* Hillsdale, NJ: Erlbaum.

SLOBIN, D. I. (1996). From "thought and language" to "thinking to speaking." In J. J. Gumperz & S. C. Levinson (Eds.), *Rethinking linguistic relativity* (pp. 70–96). Cambridge, England: Cambridge University Press.

SMITH, A. (1937). *A theory of moral sentiments.* New York: Modern Library. (Originally published 1759).

SMITH, C. A., & ELLSWORTH, P. C. (1985). Patterns of cognitive appraisal in emotion. *Journal of Personality and Social Psychology, 48,* 813–848.

SMITH, C. A., & ELLSWORTH, P. C. (1987). Patterns of appraisal and emotion related to taking an exam. *Journal of Personality and Social Psychology, 52,* 475–488.

SMITH, D., KING, M., & HOEBEL, B. G. (1970). Lateral hypothalamic control of killing: Evidence for a cholinoceptive mechanism. *Science, 167,* 900–901.

SMITH, E. E. (1989). Concepts and induction. In M. I. Posner (Ed.), *Foundations of cognitive science.* Cambridge, MA: MIT Press.

SMITH, E. E. (1995). Concepts and categorization. In E. E. Smith & D. Osherson (Eds.), *Invitation to cognitive science,* Vol. 3, *Thinking* (2nd ed.). Cambridge, MA: MIT Press.

SMITH, E. E., & JONIDES, J. (1994). Neuropsychological studies of working memory. In M. Gazzaniga (Ed.), *The cognitive neurosciences.* Cambridge, MA: MIT Press. SMITH, E. E., JONIDES, J., & KOEPPE, R. A. (1996). Dissociating verbal and spatial working memory using PET. *Cerebral Cortex, 6,* 11–20.

SMITH, E. E., & MEDIN, D. L. (1981). *Categories and concepts.* Cambridge, MA: Harvard University Press.

SMITH, E. E., PATALANO, A. L., & JONIDES, J. (1998). Alternative strategies of categorization. *Cognition, 65,* 167–196.

SMITH, G. P., & GIBBS, J. (1994). Satiating effect of cholecystokinin. *Annals of the New York Academy of Sciences, 713,* 236–241.

SMITH, M. B., BRUNER, J. S., & WHITE, R. W. (1956). *Opinions and personality.* New York: Wiley.

SMITH, M. L., GLASS, G. V., & MILLER, T. I. (1980). *The benefits of psychotherapy.* Baltimore: Johns Hopkins University Press.

SMITH, V. C., & POKORNY, J. (1975). Spectral sensitivity of the foveal cones between 400 and 500 nm. *Vision Research, 15,* 161.

SMUTS, B. B. (1986). Gender, aggression, and influence. In B. Smuts, D. Cheney, R. Seyfarth, R. Wrangham, & T. Struhsaker (Eds.), *Primate societies.* Chicago: University of Chicago Press.

SNAITH, P. (1998). Meditation and psychotherapy. *British Journal of Psychiatry, 173,* 193–195.

SNODGRASS, J. G., LEVY-BERGER, G., & HAYDON, M. (1985). *Human experimental psychology.* New York: Oxford University Press.

SNOW, C. (1987). Relevance of the notion of a critical period to language acquisition. In M. H. Bornstein (Ed.), *Sensitive periods in development: Interdisciplinary perspectives.* Hillsdale, NJ: Erlbaum.

SNOWDEN, L. R. (1988). Ethnicity and utilization of mental health services: An overview of current findings. In *Oklahoma Mental Health Research Institute, 1988 professional symposium* (pp. 227–238). Oklahoma City: Oklahoma Mental Health Research Institute.

SNOWDEN, L., & CHEUNG, F. (1990, March). Use of inpatient mental health services by members of ethnic minority groups. *American Psychologist, 45,* 347–355.

SNYDER, C. R., ILARDI, S., MICHAEL, S. T., & CHEAVENS, J. (2000). Hope theory: Updating a common process for psychological change. In C. R. Snyder & R. E. Ingram (Eds.), *Handbook of psychological change: Psychotherapy processes and practices for the 21st Century.* New York: Wiley.

SNYDER, C. R., & INGRAM, R. E.(2000). *Handbook of psychological change: Psychotherapy processes and practices for the 21st century.* New York: Wiley.

SNYDER, M., TANKE, E. D., & BERSCHEID, E. (1977). Social perception and interpersonal behavior: On the self-fulfilling nature of stereotypes.

Journal of Personality and Social Psychology, 35, 656–666.

SOLMS, M. (1997). The neuropsychology of dreams: A clinico-anatomical study. Mahwah, NJ: Erlbaum.

SOLOMON, G. F., SEGERSTROM, S. C., GROHR, P., KEMENY, M., & FAHEY, J., (1997). Shaking up immunity: Psychological and immunologic changes following a natural disaster. *Psychosomatic Medicine, 59,* 114–127.

SOLOMON, R. L., & CORBIT, J. D. (1974). An opponent-process theory of motivation: I. Temporal dynamics of affect. *Psychological Review, 81,* 119–145.

SONTHEIMER, H. (1995). Glial neuronal interactions: A physiological perspective. *The Neuroscientist, 1,* 328–337.

SORCE, J. F., EMDE, R. N., CAMPOS, J., & KLINNERT, M. D. (1985). Maternal emotional signaling: Its effect on the visual cliff behavior of 1-year-olds. *Developmental Psychiatry, 21,* 195–200.

SOUTHWICK, S. M., YEHUDA, R., & WANG, S. (1998). Neuroendocrine alterations in posttraumatic stress disorder. *Psychiatric Annals, 28,* 436–442.

SPANOS, B. (1996, December). Quotas, ARCOs, UN report, and statistics. In G. Feussner (Moderator), *Prevalence of ADHD and psychostimulant utilization for treatment.* Symposium conducted at Drug Enforcement Administration meeting on stimulant use in the treatment of ADHD.

SPANOS, N. P. (1986). Hypnotic behavior: A social-psychological interpretation of amnesia, analgesia, and "trance logic." *Behavioral and Brain Sciences, 9,* 449–502.

SPANOS, N. P., & HEWITT, E. C. (1980). The hidden observer in hypnotic analgesia: Discovery or experimental creation? *Journal of Personality and Social Psychology, 39,* 1201–1214.

SPEARMAN, C. (1904). "General intelligence" objectively determined and measured. *American Journal of Psychology, 15,* 201–293.

SPECA, M., CARLSON, L. E., GOODEY, E., & ANGEN, M. (2000). A randomized wait-list controlled clinical trial: The effect of a mindfulness meditation-based stress reduction program on mood and symptoms of stress in cancer patients. *Psychosomatic Medicine, 62,* 613–622.

SPEIGEL, J. M., & BRAINARD, D. H. (1999). Predicting color from gray: The relationship between achromatic adjustment and asymmetric matching, *Journal of the Optical Society of America, 16,* 2370–2376.

SPELKE, E. S. (1998). Nativism, empiricism, and the origins of knowledge. *Infant Behaviour and Development, 21,* 181–200.

SPENCER, S., STEELE, C. M., & QUINN, D. (1997). *Under suspicion of inability: Stereotype threat and women's math performance.* Unpublished manuscript, Stanford University.

SPENCER, S., STEELE, C. M., & QUINN, D. M. (1999). Stereotype threat and women's math performance. *Journal of Experimental Social Psychology, 35,* 4–28.

SPERLING, G. (1960). The information available in brief visual presentations. *Psychological Monographs, 74,* 329.

SPERLING, G. (1967). Successive approximations to a model for short term memory. *Acta Psychologica, 27,* 285–292.

SPERRY, R. W. (1968). Perception in the absence of neocortical commissures. In Association for Research in Nervous and Mental Disease, *Perception and its disorders.* New York: Williams & Wilkins.

SPERRY, R. W. (1970). Perception in the absence of the neocortical commissures. *Research Publications—Association for Research in Nervous and Mental Disease, 48,* 123–128.

SPIEGEL, D. (1991). Mind matters: Effects of group support on cancer patients. *Journal of NIH Research, 3,* 61–63.

SPIEGEL, D., BLOOM, J. R., KRAEMER, H. C., & GOTTHEIL, E. (1989). Psychological support for cancer patients. *Lancet, 2,* 1447.

SPIELBERGER, C. D., JOHNSON, E. H., RUSSELL, S. F., CRANE, R. S., JACOBS, G. A., & WORDEN, T. J. (1985). The experience and expression of anger: Construction and validation of an anger expression scale. In M. A. Chesney & R. H. Rosenman (Eds.), *Anger and hostility in cardiovascular and behavioral disorders.* New York: Hemisphere/McGraw-Hill.

SPIVEY, C. B., & PRENTICE-DUNN, S. (1990). Assessing the directionality of deindividuated behavior: Effects of deindividuation, modeling, and private self-consciousness on aggressive and prosocial responses. *Basic and Applied Social Psychology, 11,* 387–403.

SPRAFKIN, J. N., LIEBERT, R. M., & POULOUS, R. W. (1975). Effects of a prosocial televised example on children's helping. *Journal of Personality and Social Psychology, 48,* 35–46.

SPRINGER, S. P., & DEUTSCH, G. (1989). *Left brain, right brain* (3rd ed.). San Francisco: Freeman.

SQUIER, L. H., & DOMHOFF, G. W. (1998). *The presentation of dreaming and dreams in introductory psychology textbooks: A critical examination.* Unpublished paper.

SQUIRE, L. R. (1987). *Memory and brain.* New York: Oxford University Press.

SQUIRE, L. R. (1992). Memory and the hippocampus: A synthesis from findings with rats, monkeys, and humans. *Psychological Review, 99,* 195–231.

SQUIRE, L. R., & BUTTERS, N. (Eds.). (1984). *The neuropsychology of memory.* New York: Guilford.

SQUIRE, L. R., & FOX, M. M. (1980). Assessment of remote memory: Validation of the television test by repeated testing during a seven-day period. *Behavioral Research Methods and Instrumentation, 12,* 583–586.

SQUIRE, L. R., & KANDEL, E. R. (2000). *Memory: From mind to molecules.* New York: Scientific American Library.

SQUIRE, L. R., & KNOWLTON, B. J. (1995). Learning about categories in the absence of memory. *Proceedings of the National Academy of Sciences, USA, 92,* 12470–12474.

SQUIRE, L. R., KNOWLTON, B., & MUSEN, G. (1993). The structure and organization of memory. *Annual Review of Psychology, 44,* 453–495.

SQUIRE, L. R., OJEMANN, J. G., MIEZIN, F. M., PETERSEN, S. E., VIDEEN, T. O., & RAICHLE, M. E. (1992). Activation of the hippocampus in normal humans: A functional anatomical study of memory. *Proceedings of the National Academy of Science, 89,* 1837–1841.

SQUIRE, L. R., & ZOLA, S. M. (1996). Ischemic brain damage and memory impairment: A commentary. *Hippocampus, 6,* 546–552.

SQUIRE, L. R., ZOLA-MORGAN, S., CAVE, C. B., HAIST, F., MUSEN, G., & SUZUKI, W. A. (1990). Memory: Organization of brain systems and cognition. In *Symposium on quantitative biology, the brain* (Vol. 55). Cold Spring Harbor, NY: Cold Spring Harbor Laboratory.

STAATS, A. W. (1968). *Language, learning, and cognition.* New York: Holt, Rinehart & Winston.

STANGOR, C., & MCMILLAN, D. (1992). Memory for expectancy-congruent and expectancy-incongruent information: A review of the social and social developmental literature. *Psychological Bulletin, 111*, 42–61.

STASSER, G., & TITUS, W. (1985). Pooling of unshared information in group decision making: Biased information sampling during discussion. *Journal of Personality and Social Psychology, 48*, 1467–1478.

STATHAM, D. J., HEATCH, A. C., MADDEN, P., BUCHOLZ, K., BIERUT, L., DINWIDDIE, S. H., SLUTSKE, W. S., DUNNE, M. P., & MARTIN, N. G. (1998). Suicidal behavior: An epidemiological study. *Psychological Medicine, 28*, 839–855.

STATTIN, H., & MAGNUSSON, D. (1990). *Pubertal maturation in female development*. Hillsdale, NJ: Erlbaum.

STAYTON, D. J. (1973, March). *Infant responses to brief everyday separations: Distress, following, and greeting*. Paper presented at the meeting of the Society for Research in Child Development.

STEADMAN, H. J., MULVEY, E. P., MONAHAN, J., ROBBINS, P. C., APPLEBAUM, P. S., GRISSO, T., ROTH, L., & SILVER, E. (1998). Violence by people discharged from acute psychiatric inpatient facilities and by others in the same neighborhoods. *Archives of General Psychiatry, 55*, 393–401.

STEBLAY, N. M (1992). A meta-analytic review of the weapon focus effect. *Law and Human Behavior, 16*, 413–424.

STEELE, C. M. (1997). A threat in the air: How stereotypes shape intellectual identify and performance. *American Psychologist, 52*, 613–629.

STEELE, C. M., & ARONSON, J. (1995). Stereotype threat and the intellectual test performance of African Americans. *Journal of Personality and Social Psychology, 69*, 797–811.

STEIN, D. J. (Ed.). (1997). *Cognitive science and the unconscious*. Washington, DC: American Psychiatric Press.

STEINBERG, L. (1996). *Adolescence* (4th ed.). New York: Knopf.

STEINBERG, L., & MORRIS, A. S. (2001). Adolescent development. *Annual Reviews of Psychology, 52*, 83–110.

STEINER, J. E. (1979). Human facial expressions in response to taste and smell stimulation. *Advances in Child Development and Behavior, 13*, 257–295.

STEKETEE, G., & WHITE, K. (1990). *When once is not enough*. Oakland, CA: New Harbinger.

STELLAR, J. R., & STELLAR, E. (1985). *The neurobiology of motivation and reward*. New York: Springer-Verlag.

STERN, R. S., & COBB, J. P. (1978). Phenomenology of obsessive-compulsive neurosis. *British Journal of Psychiatry, 132*, 233–239.

STERNBERG, R. (2000). *Handbook of intelligence*. New York: Cambridge University Press.

STERNBERG, R., & GRIGORENKO, E. (2001). *Environmental effects on cognitive abilities*. Mahwah, NJ: Erlbaum.

STERNBERG, R., GRIGORENKO, E., & BUNDY, D. (2001) The predictive value of IQ. *Merrill-Palmer Quarterly, 47*, 1–41.

STERNBERG, R., GRIGORENKO, E., CASTEJON, J. L., PRIETO, M. D., & HAUTAMEKI, J. (2001). Confirmatory factor analysis of the Sternberg Triarchic Abilities Test in three international samples: An empirical test of the triarchic theory of intelligence. *European Journal of Psychological Assessment, 17*, 1–16.

STERNBERG, R. J. (1985). *Beyond IQ: A triarchic theory of human intelligence*. Cambridge, England: Cambridge University Press.

STERNBERG, R. J. (1986). *Intelligence applied: Understanding and increasing your intellectual skills*. San Diego: Harcourt Brace Jovanovich.

STERNBERG, R. J. (1988). *The triarchic mind: A new theory of human intelligence*. New York: Viking.

STERNBERG, R. J. (2000). The concept of intelligence. In *Handbook of intelligence* (pp. 3–16). Cambridge, England: Cambridge University Press.

STERNBERG, R. J., & KAUFMAN, J. C. (1998). Human abilities. *Annual Reviews of Psychology, 49*, 479–502.

STERNBERG, R. J., & WILLIAMS, W. M. (1997). Does the Graduate Record Examination predict meaningful success in the graduate training of psychologists? A case study. *American Psychologist, 52*, 630–651.

STERNBERG, S. (1966). Highspeed scanning in human memory. *Science, 153*, 652–654.

STERNBERG, S. (1975). Memory scanning: New findings and current controversies. *Quarterly Journal of Experimental Psychology, 27*, 1–32.

STEUER, F. B., APPLEFIELD, J. M., & SMITH, R. (1971). Televised aggression and the interpersonal aggression of preschool children. *Journal of Experimental Child Psychology, 11*, 422–447.

STEVENSON, H. W., LEE, S., & GRAHAM, T. (1993). Chinese and Japanese kindergartens: Case study in comparative research. In B. Spodek (Ed.), *Handbook of research on the education of young children*. New York: Macmillan.

STILES, W. B., SHAPIRO, D. A., & ELLIOTT, R. (1986). Are all psychotherapies equivalent? *American Psychologist, 41*, 165–180.

STOLL, A. L., RENSHAW, P. F., YURGELUN-TODD, D., & COHEN, B. M. (2000). Neuroimaging in bipolar disorder: What have we learned? *Biological Psychiatry, 48*, 505–517.

STONER, J. A. F. (1961). *A comparison of individual and group decisions involving risk*. Unpublished master's thesis, Massachusetts Institute of Technology.

STOWERS, L., HOLY, T. E., MEISTER, M., DULAC, C., & KOENTEGES, G. (2002). Loss of sex discrimination and male-male aggression in mice deficient for TRP2. *Science, 295*, 1493–1500.

STRACK, F., MARTIN, L. L., & STEPPER, S. (1988). Inhibiting and facilitating conditions of the human smile: A non-obtrusive test of the facial feedback hypothesis. *Journal of Personality and Social Psychology, 54*, 768–777.

STREISSGUTH, A. P., BARR, H. M., BOOKSTEIN, F. L., SAMPSON, P. D., & OLSON, H. C. (1999). The long-term neurocognitive consequences of prenatal alcohol exposure: A 14-year study. *Psychological Science, 10*, 186–190.

STREISSGUTH, A. P., CLARREN, S. K., & JONES, K. L. (1985). Natural history of the fetal alcohol syndrome: A 10-year follow-up of eleven patients. *Lancet, 2*, 85–91.

STROEBE, W., INSKO, C. A., THOMPSON, V. D., & LAYTON, B. D. (1971). Effects of physical attractiveness, attitude similarity and sex on various aspects of interpersonal attraction. *Journal of Personality and Social Psychology, 18*, 79–91.

STRONG, S. R., HILLS, H. J., KILMARTIN, C. T., DEVRIES, H., LANIER, A. K., NELSON, B. N., STRICKLAND, D., & MEYER, C. W., III (1988). The dynamic relations among interpersonal behaviors: A test of complementarity and anti-complementarity. *Journal of Personality and Social Psychology, 54*, 798–810.

STROOP, J. R. (1935). Studies of interference in serial-verbal reaction. *Journal of Experimental Psychology, 18*, 643–662.

STUNKARD, A. J. (1982). Obesity. In M. Hersen, A. Bellack, & A. Kazdin (Eds.), *International handbook of behavior modification and therapy*. New York: Plenum.

STUNKARD, A. J. (1996). *The origins and consequences of obesity*. Chichester, England: Wiley.

STUNKARD, A. J., HARRIS, J. R., PEDERSEN, N. L., & MCCLEARN, G. E. (1990). A separated twin study of the body mass index. *New England Journal of Medicine, 322*, 1483–1487.

STYRON, W. (1990). *Darkness visible*. New York: Vintage Books.

SUAREZ, E. C., KUHN, C. M., SCHANBERG, S. M., WILLIAMS, R. B., JR., & ZIMMERMAN, E. A. (1998). Neuroendocrine, cardiovascular, and emotional responses of hostile men: The role of interpersonal challenge. *Psychosomatic Medicine, 60*, 78–88.

SUE, D. W. & SUE, D. (1999). Counseling the culturally different: Theory and practice (3rd ed.). New York: Wiley.

SUE, S., ALLEN, D., & CONAWAY, L. (1978). The responsiveness and equality of mental health care to Chicanos and Native Americans. *American Journal of Community Psychology, 6*, 137–146.

SUE, S., & ZANE, N. (1987). The role of culture and cultural techniques in psychotherapy: A critique and reformulation. *American Psychologist, 42*, 37–51.

SULLIVAN, H. S. (1953). *The interpersonal theory of psychiatry*. New York: Norton.

SULLIVAN, P. F., NEALE, M. C., & KENDLER, K. S. (2000). Genetic epidemiology of major depression: Review and meta-analysis. *American Journal of Psychiatry, 157*, 1552–1562.

SUTKER, P. B., DAVIS, J. M., UDDO, M., & DITTA, S. R. (1995). Assessment of psychological distress in Persian Gulf troops: Ethnicity and gender comparisons. *Journal of Personality Assessment, 64*, 415–427.

SVENSON, O. (1981). Are we all less risky and more skillful than our fellow drivers? *Acta Psychologica, 47*, 143–148.

SWARTZ, C. (1995). Setting the ECT stimulus. *Psychiatric times, 12*, 6 (Reprint addition)

SWARTZ, M., BLAZER, D., GEORGE, L., & WINFIELD, I. (1990). Estimating the prevalence of borderline personality disorder in the community. *Journal of Personality Disorders, 4*, 257–272.

SWEDO, S. PIETRINI, P., & LEONARD, H. (1992). Cerebral glucose metabolism in childhood-onset obsessive-compulsive disorder. *Archives of General Psychiatry, 49*, 690–694.

SWETS, J. A., & BJORK, R. A. (1990). Enhancing human performance: An evaluation of "new age" techniques considered by the U.S. Army. *Psychological Science, 1*, 85–96.

SWIM, J. K., & SANNA, L. J. (1996). He's skilled, she's lucky: A meta-analysis of observer's attributions for women's and men's successes and failures. *Personality and Social Psychology Bulletin, 22*, 507–519.

SWINNEY, D. A. (1979). Lexical access during sentence comprehension: Consideration of context effects. *Journal of Verbal Learning and Verbal Behavior, 18*, 645–659.

SYMONS, D. (1992). On the use and misuse of Darwinism in the study of human behavior. In J. H. Barkow & L. Cosmides (Eds.), *The adapted mind: Evolutionary psychology and the generation of cul-*

ture (pp. 137–159). New York: Oxford University Press.

SZASZ, T. S. (1971). The sane slave: An historical note on the use of medical diagnosis as justificatory rhetoric. *American Journal of Psychotherapy, 25,* 228–239.

SZKRYBALO, J., & RUBLE, D. N. (1999). "God made me a girl": Sex-category constancy and judgments and explanations revisited. *Developmental Psychology, 35,* 392–402.

TABER, K. H., LEWIS, D. A., & HURLEY, R. A. (2001). Schizophrenia: What's under the microscope. *Journal of Clinical Neuropsychiatry, 13,* 1–4.

TANENHAUS, M. G., LEIMAN, J., & SEIDENBERG, M. (1979). Evidence for multiple stages in the processing of ambiguous words in syntactic contexts. *Journal of Verbal Learning and Verbal Behavior, 18,* 427–441.

TANNEN, D. (1990). *You just don't understand: Women and men in conversation.* New York: Ballantine Books.

TANNEN, D. (1998). *The argument culture.* New York: Random House.

TARTTER, V. C. (1986). *Language processes.* New York: Holt, Rinehart & Winston.

TATEYAMA, M, & KASPER, S. (1998). Transcultural study of schizophrenic delusions: Tokyo versus Vienna versus Tuebingen (Germany). *Psychopathology, 31,* 59–68.

TAVRIS, C., & SADD, S. (1977). *The Redbook report on female sexuality.* New York: Dell.

TAYLOR, S. (1999). *Health psychology* (4th ed.). Boston: McGraw-Hill.

TAYLOR, S., KEMENY, M., ASPINWALL, L., SCHNEIDER, S., RODRIGUEZ, R., & HERBERT, M. (1992). Optimism, coping, psychological distress, and high-risk sexual behavior among men at risk for acquired immunodeficiency syndrome (AIDS). *Journal of Personality and Social Psychology, 63,* 460–473.

TAYLOR, S., KEMENY, M. E., REED, G. M., BOWER, J. E., & GRUENWALD, T. L. (2000). Psychological resources, positive illusions, and health. *American Psychologist, 55,* 99–109.

TAYLOR, S. E., & BROWN, J. D. (1988). Illusion and well-being: A social psychological perspective on mental health. *Psychological Bulletin, 103,* 193–210.

TAYLOR, S. E., KEMENY, M., ASPINWALL, L. G., SCHNEIDER, S. G., RODRIGUEZ, R., & HERBERT, M. (1992). Optimism, coping, psychological distress, and high-risk sexual behavior among men at risk for AIDS. *Journal of Personality and Social Psychology, 63,* 460–473.

TAYLOR, S. E., & THOMPSON, S. C. (1982). Stalking the elusive "vividness" effect. *Psychological Review, 89,* 155–181.

TEASDALE, J. D., SEGAL, Z. V., WILLIAMS, J. M. G., RIDGEWAY, V. A., SOULSBY, J. M., & LAU, M. A. (2000). Prevention of relapse/recurrence in major depression by mindfulness-based cognitive therapy. *Journal of Consulting and Clinical Psychology, 68,* 615–523.

TEITELBAUM, P., & EPSTEIN, A. N. (1962). The lateral hypothalamic syndrome: Recovery of feeding and drinking after lateral hypothalamic lesions. *Psychological Review, 69,* 74–90.

TELLEGEN, A., BOUCHARD, T. J., WILCOX, K. J., SEGAL, N. L., LYKKEN, D. T., & RICH, S. (1988). *Journal of Personality and Social Psychology, 54,* 1031–1039.

TELLEGEN, A., LYKKEN, D. T., BOUCHARD, T. J., JR., WILCOX, K. J., SEGAL, N. L., & RICH, S.

(1988). Personality similarity in twins reared apart and together. *Journal of Personality and Social Psychology, 54,* 1031–1039.

TELLER, D. Y. (1979). The forced-choice preferential looking procedure: A psychophysical technique for use with human infants. *Infant Behavior and Development, 2,* 135–153.

TELLER, D. Y., & MOVSHON, J. A. (1986). Visual development. *Vision Research, 26,* 1483–1506.

TEMPLIN, M. C. (1957). *Certain language skills in children: Their development and interrelationships.* Minneapolis: University of Minnesota Press.

TENNEN, H., & AFFLECK, G. (1999). Finding benefits in adversity. In C. R. Snyder (Ed), *Coping: The psychology of what works* (pp. 279–304). New York: Oxford University Press.

TERMAN, L. M., & ODEN, M. H. (1959). *Genetic studies of genius,* Vol. IV: *The gifted group at midlife.* Stanford, CA: Stanford University Press.

TERRACE, H. S., PETITTO, L. A., SANDERS, D. J., & BEVER, T. G. (1979). Can an ape create a sentence? *Science, 206,* 891–902.

TESSER, A., & BRODIE, M. (1971). A note on the evaluation of a "computer date." *Psychonomic Science, 23,* 300.

THASE, M., JINDAL, & HOWLAND. (2002). Biological aspects of depression. In I. H. Gotlib & C. L. Hammen (Eds.), *Handbook of depression.* New York: Guilford.

THIGPEN, C. H., & CLECKLEY, H. (1957). *The three faces of Eve.* New York: McGraw-Hill.

THOMAS, A., & CHESS, S. (1977). *Temperament and development.* New York: Brunner/Mazel.

THOMAS, A., & CHESS, S. (1986). The New York longitudinal study: From infancy to early adult life. In R. Plomin & J. Dunn (Eds.), *The study of temperament: Changes, continuities and challenges* (pp. 39–52). Hillsdale, NJ: Erlbaum.

THOMAS, A., CHESS, S., BIRCH, H., HERTZIG, M., & KORN, S. (1963). *Behavioral individuality in early childhood.* New York: New York University Press.

THOMAS, E. L., & ROBINSON, H. A. (1982). *Improving reading in every class.* Boston: Allyn and Bacon.

THOMPSON, P. M., CANNON, T. D., NARR, K. L., VAN ERP, T., POUTANEN, V. P., HUTTUNEN, M., LONNQVIST, J., STANDERTSKJOLD-NORDENSTAM, C. G., KAPRIO, J., KHALEDY, M., DAIL, R., ZOUMALAN, C. I., & TOGA, A. W. (2001). Genetic influences on brain structure. *Nature Neuroscience, 4,* 1253–1258.

THOMPSON, R. A., LAMB, M., & ESTES, D. (1982). Stability of infant-mother attachment and its relationship to changing life circumstances in an unselected middle-class sample. *Child Development, 53,* 144–148.

THOMPSON, S. C. (1991). The search for meaning following a stroke. *Basic and Applied Social Psychology, 12,* 81–96.

THOMPSON, S. K. (1975). Gender labels and early sex role development. *Child Development, 46,* 339–347.

THOMPSON, W. R. (1954). The inheritance and development of intelligence. *Proceedings of the Association for Research on Nervous and Mental Disease, 33,* 209–231.

THORESEN, C. E., TELCH, M. J., & EAGLESTON, J. R. (1981). Altering type A behavior. *Psychosomatics, 8,* 472–482.

THORNDIKE, E. L. (1898). Animal intelligence: An experimental study of the associative processes in animals. *Psychological Monographs, 2,* 8.

THORPE, G. L., & OLSON, S. L. (1997). *Behavior therapy: Concepts, procedures, and applications* (2nd ed.). Boston: Allyn and Bacon.

THURSTONE, L. L. (1938). *Primary mental abilities.* Psychometric Monographs, No. 1. Chicago: University of Chicago Press.

TIMMERS, M., FISCHER, A. H., & MANSTEAD, A. S. R. (1998). Gender differences in motives for regulating emotions. *Personality and Social Psychology Bulletin, 24,* 974–985.

TIZARD, B., & REES, J. (1975). The effect of early institutional rearing on the behavioural problems and affectional relationships of four-year-old children. *Journal of Child Psychology and Psychiatry, 16,* 61–73.

TOATES, F. (1986). *Motivational systems.* Cambridge, England: Cambridge University Press.

TOLMAN, E. C. (1932). *Purpose behavior in animals and men.* New York: Appleton-Century-Crofts. (Reprinted 1967. New York: Irvington)

TOMASSON, R. F., CROSBY, F. J., & HERZBERGER, S. D. (1996). *Affirmative action: the pros and cons of policy and practice.* Washington, DC: American University Press.

TOMPKINS, S. S. (1962). *Affect, imagery, consciousness:* Vol. 1. *The positive affects.* New York: Springer.

TOMPKINS, S. S. (1980). Affect as amplification: Some modifications in theory. In R. Plutchik & H. Kellerman (Eds.), *Emotion: Theory, research and experience* (Vol. 1). New York: Academic Press.

TONAY, V. (1993). Personality correlates of dreams. *Dreaming, 3,* 1–8.

TONG, F., & ENGEL, S. A. (2001). Interocular rivalry revealed in the human cortical blind spot representation. *Nature, 411,* 195–199.

TOOBY, J., & COSMIDES, L. (1990). The past explains the present: Emotional adaptations and the structure of ancestral environments. *Ethology and Sociobiology, 11,* 375–424.

TOPPING, K., HOLMES, E. A., & BREMNER, W. (2000). The effectiveness of school-based programs for the promotion of social competence. In R. Bar-On & J. D. A. Parker (Eds.), *The Handbook of Emotional Intelligence,* San Francisco: Jossey-Bass.

TORGERSEN, S. (1986). Genetic factors in moderately severe and mild affective disorders. *Archives of General Psychiatry, 49,* 690–694.

TORREY, E. F. (1995). *Surviving schizophrenia: A manual for families, consumers and providers* (3rd ed.). New York: Harper Perennial.

TORREY, E. F. (1997). *Out of the shadows: Confronting America's mental illness crisis.* New York: Wiley.

TOWNSHEND, B., COTTER, N., VAN COMPERNOLLE, D., & WHITE, R. L. (1987). Pitch perception by cochlear implant subjects. *Journal of the Acoustical Society of America, 82,* 106–115.

TRAFIMOW, D., TRIANDIS, H. C., & GOTO, S. G. (1991). Some tests of the distinction between the private self and the collective self. *Journal of Personality and Social Psychology, 60,* 649–655.

TRANEL, D., BECHARA, A., & DAMASIO, A. R. (2000). Decision making and the somatic marker hypothesis. In: M. S. Gazzaniga (Ed.), *The new cognitive neurosciences* (pp. 1047–1061). Cambridge, MA: MIT Press.

TREISMAN, A. (1969). Strategies and models of selective attention. *Psychological Review, 76,* 282–299.

TREISMAN, A. (1986). Features and objects in visual processing, *Scientific American, 254,* 114–125.

TREISMAN, A., & GELADE, G. (1980). A feature integration theory of attention. *Cognitive Psychology, 12,* 97–136.

TREISMAN, A. M. (1986). Features and objects in visual processing. *Scientific American, 255,* 114B–125.

TRIANDIS, H. C. (1989). The self and social behavior in different cultures. *Psychological Review, 96,* 506–520.

TRINDER, J. (1988). Subjective insomnia without objective findings: A pseudodiagnostic classification. *Psychological Bulletin, 103,* 87–94.

TRIPP, C. A. (1987). *The homosexual matrix* (2nd ed.). New York: New American Library.

TRIVERS, R. L. (1972). Parental investment and sexual selection. In B. Campbell (Ed.), *Sexual selection and the descent of man: 1871–1971* (pp. 136–179). Chicago: Aldine.

TROPE, T., & GAUNT, R. (1999). A dual-process model of overconfident attributional inferences. In S. Chaiken & Y. Trope (Eds.), *Dual-process theories in social psychology* (pp. 161–178). New York: Guilford.

TRUAX, K., WOOD, A., WRIGHT, E., CORDOVA, D. I., & CROSBY, F. J. (1998). Undermined: Affirmative action from the targets' point of view. In J. K. Swim & C. Stagnor (Eds.), *Prejudice: The target's perspective* (pp. 171–188). New York: Academic Press.

TSIEN J. Z. (2000). Building a brainier mouse. *Scientific American, 282,* 62–68.

TSUANG, M. T. (1983). Suicide in the relatives of schizophrenics, manics, depressives and controls. *Journal of Clinical Psychiatry, 44,* 396–400.

TULVING, E. (1974). Cue-dependent forgetting. *American Scientist, 62,* 74–82.

TULVING, E. (1983). *The elements of episodic memory.* New York: Oxford University Press.

TULVING, E. (1985). How many memory systems are there? *American Psychologist, 40,* 385–398.

TULVING, E., KAPUR, S., CRAIK, F. I. M., MOSCOVITCH, M., & HOULE, S. (1994). Hemispheric encoding/retrieval asymmetry in episodic memory: Positron emission tomography findings. *Proceedings of the National Academy of Science of the United States of America, 91,* 2016–2020.

TULVING, E., KAPUR, S., MARKOWITSCH, H. J., CRAIK, F. I. M., HABIB, R., & HOULE, S. (1994). Neuroanatomical correlates of retrieval in episodic memory: Auditory sentence recognition. *Proceedings of the National Academy of Science of the United States of America, 91,* 2012–2015.

TULVING, E., & PEARLSTONE, Z. (1966). Availability versus accessibility of information in memory for words. *Journal of Verbal Learning and Verbal Behavior, 5,* 381–391.

TUMA, J. M. (1989). Mental health services for children: The state of the art. *American Psychologist, 44,* 188–199.

TUNNELL, G. (1981). Sex role and cognitive schemata: Person perception in feminine and androgynous women. *Journal of Personality and Social Psychology, 40,* 1126–1136.

TURIEL, E. (1983). *The development of social knowledge: Morality and convention.* Cambridge, England: Cambridge University Press.

TURK, D. C. (1996). Clinician attitudes about prolonged use of opioids and the issue of patient heterogeneity. *Journal of Pain and Symptom Management, 11,* 218–230.

TURK, D. C., & OKIFUJI, A. (1997). What factors affect physicians' decisions to prescribe opioids for chronic non-cancer pain patients? *Clinical Journal of Pain, 13,* 330–336.

TURKHEIMER, E. (1998). Heritability and biological explanation. *Psychological Review, 105,* 782–791.

TURNER, M. E., & PRATKANIS, A. R. (1998a). A social identity model of groupthink. *Organizational Behavior and Human Decision Processes, 73,* 210–235.

TURNER, M. E., & PRATKANIS, A. R. (1998b). Twenty-five years of groupthink theory and research: Lessons from the evaluation of a theory. *Organizational Behavior and Human Decision Processes, 73,* 105–115.

TURNER, M. E., & PRATKANIS, A. R. (1994). Affirmative action as help: A review of recipient reactions to preferential selection and affirmative action. *Basic and Applied Social Psychology, 15,* 43–69.

TURNER, M. E., PRATKANIS, A. R., PROBASCO, P., & LEVER, C. (1992). Threat, cohesion, and group effectiveness: Testing a social identity maintenance perspective in groupthink. *Journal of Personality and Social Psychology, 63,* 781–796.

TVERSKY, A., & KAHNEMAN, D. (1973). On the psychology of prediction. *Psychological Review, 80,* 237–251.

TVERSKY, A., & KAHNEMAN, D. (1983). Extensional versus intuitive reasoning: The conjunction fallacy in probability judgment. *Psychological Review, 90,* 293–315.

TYE-MURRAY, N., SPENCER, L., & WOODWORTH, G. G. (1995). Acquisition of speech by children who have prolonged cochlear implant experience. *Journal of Speech and Hearing Research, 38,* 327–337.

TYLER, H. (1977). The unsinkable Jeane Dixon. *Humanist, 37,* 6–9.

UCHINO, B. N., UNO, D., & HOLT-LUNSTAD, J. (1999). Social support, physiological processes, and health. *Current Directions in Psychological Science, 8,* 145–148.

ULLMAN, M. T., CORKIN, S., COPPOLA, M., HICKOK, G., GROWDON, J. H., KOROSHETZ, W. J., & PINKER, S. (1997). A neural dissociation within language: Evidence that the mental dictionary is part of declarative memory, and that grammatical rules are processed by the procedural system. *Journal of Cognitive Neuroscience, 9,* 266–276.

URSIN, H. (1978). Activation, coping, and psychosomatics. In H. Ursin, E. Baade, & S. Levine (Eds.), *Psychobiology of stress: A study of coping men.* New York: Academic Press.

UTTS, J. (1986). The gansfeld debate: A statistician's perspective. *Journal of Parapsychology, 50,* 393–402.

VAKOCH, D. A., & STRUPP, H. H. (2000). Psychodynamic approaches to psychotherapy: Philosophical and theoretical foundations of effective practice. In C. R. Snyder & R. Ingram (Eds.), *Handbook of psychological change* (pp. 200–216) New York: Wiley.

VAN DEN HEUVEL, O. A., VAN DE WETERING, B. J. M., VELTMAN, D. J., & PAULS, D. L. (2000). Genetic studies of panic disorder: A review. *Journal of Clinical Psychiatry, 61,* 756–766.

VAN PRAAG, H., KEMPERMANN, G., & GAGE, F. H. (1999). Running increases cell proliferation and neurogenesis in the adult mouse dentate gyrus. *Nature Neuroscience, 2,* 266–270.

VAN PRAAG, H., SCHINDER, A. F., CHRISTIE, B. R., TONI, N., PALMER, T. D., & GAGE, F. H. (2002). Functional neurogenesis in the adult hippocampus. *Nature, 415,* 1030–1034.

VAN VORT, W., & SMITH, G. P. (1987). Sham feeding experience produces a conditioned increase of meal size. *Appetite, 9,* 21–29.

VANCE, A. L., VELAKOULIS, D., MARUFF, P., WOOD, S. J., DESMOND, P., & PANTELIS, C. (2000). Magnetic resonance spectroscopy and schizophrenia: What have we learnt? *Australian and New Zealand Journal of Psychiatry, 34,* 14–25.

VAUGHN, B. E., LEFEVRE, G. B., SEIFER, R., & BARGLOW, P. (1989). Attachment behavior, attachment security, and temperament during infancy. *Child Development, 60,* 728–737.

VAUGHN, C. E., & LEFF, J. P. (1976). The influence of family and social factors on the course of psychiatric illness: A comparison of schizophrenic and depressed neurotic patients. *British Journal of Psychiatry, 129,* 125–137.

VELMANS, M. (1991). Is human information processing conscious? *Behavioral and Brain Sciences, 14,* 651–726.

VISINTAINER, M. A., VOLPICELLI, J. R., & SELIGMAN, M. E. P. (1982). Tumor rejection in rats after inescapable or escapable shock. *Science, 216,* 437–439.

VOGT, T., & BELLUSCIO, D. (1987). Controversies in plastic surgery: Suction-assisted lipectomy (SAL) and the HCG (human chorionic gonadotropin) protocol for obesity treatment. *Aesthetic Plastic Surgery, 11,* 131–156.

VON LANG, J., & SIBYLL, C. (Eds.). (1983). *Eichmann interrogated* (R. Manheim, Trans.). New York: Farrar, Straus & Giroux.

VYGOTSKY, L. S. (1986). *Thought and language* (A. Kozulin, Trans.). Cambridge, MA: MIT Press. (originally published 1934)

WADDEN, T. A., BERKOWITZ, R. I., VOGT, R. A., STEEN, S. N., STUNKARD, A. J., & FOSTER, G. D. (1997). Lifestyle modification in the pharmacological treatment of obesity: A pilot investigation of a potential primary care approach. *Obesity Research, 5,* 218–226.

WAGNER, W. M., & MONNET, M. (1979). Attitudes of college professors toward extrasensory perception. *Zetetic Scholar, 5,* 7–17.

WAHLBERG, D. (1999, October 21). Binge drinking remains problem. *Ann Arbor News,* A1.

WALKER, C. E., HEDBERG, A., CLEMENT, P. W., & WRIGHT, L. (1981). *Clinical procedures for behavior therapy.* Englewood Cliffs, NJ: Prentice-Hall.

WALKER, E. (1978). *Explorations in the biology of language.* Montgomery, VT: Bradford.

WALLACE, SCHNEIDER, MCGRIFFIN (2002). Genetics of depression. In I. H. Gotlib & C. L. Hammen (Eds.), *Handbook of depression.* New York: Guilford.

WALLACH, M. A., KOGAN, N., & BEM, D. J. (1962). Group influence on individual risk taking. *Journal of Abnormal and Social Psychology, 65,* 75–86.

WALLACH, M. A., KOGAN, N., & BEM, D. J. (1964). Diffusion of responsibility and level of risk taking in groups. *Journal of Abnormal and Social Psychology, 68,* 263–274. WALLACH, M. A., & WALLACH, L. (1983). *Psychology's sanction for selfishness.* San Francisco: Freeman.

WALLER, S. J., LYONS, J. S., & CONSTANTINI-FERRANDO, M. F. (1999). Impact of comorbid affective and alcohol use disorders on suicide ideation and attempts. *Journal of Clinical Psychology, 55,* 585–595.

WALSTER, E., ARONSON, E., ABRAHAMS, D., & ROTTMAN, L. (1966). Importance of physical attractiveness in dating behavior. *Journal of Personality and Social Psychology, 4,* 508–516.

WALTERS, J., & GARDNER, H. (1985). The development and education of intelligences. In F. Link (Ed.), *Essays on the intellect.* Washington, DC:

Curriculum Development Associates/Association for Supervision and Curriculum Development.

WALZER, M. (1970). *Obligations.* Cambridge, MA: Harvard University Press.

WAMPOLD, B. E., MONDIN, G. W., MOODY, M., STICH, F., BENSON, K., & AHN, H. (1997). A meta-analysis of outcome studies comparing bona fide psychotherapies: Empirically, "all must have prizes." *Psychological Bulletin, 122,* 203–215.

WANDELL, B. A. (1995). *Foundations of Vision.* Sunderland, MA: Sindaur Associates.

WANDELL, B. A., & Maloney, L. T. (1986). Color constancy: A method for recovering surface spectral reflectance. *Journal of the Optical Society of America, 3,* 29–33.

WARD, I. L. (1992). Sexual behavior: The products of perinatal hormonal and prepubertal social factors. In A. A. Gerall, H. Motz, & I. L. Ward (Eds.), *Sexual differentiation* (pp. 157–179). New York: Plenum.

WARRINGTON, E. K., & SHALLICE, T. (1984). Category specific semantic impairments. *Brain, 107,* 829–853.

WARRINGTON, E. K., & WEISKRANTZ, L. (1978). Further analysis of the prior learning effect in amnesic patients. *Neuropsychologica, 16,* 169–177.

WASON, P. C., & JOHNSON-LAIRD, P. N. (1972). *Psychology of reasoning: Structure and content.* London: Batsford.

WASSERMAN, E. A. (1990). Detecting response-outcome relations: Toward an understanding of the causal texture of the environment. *Psychology of Learning and Motivation, 26,* 27–82.

WATERMAN, A. S. (1985). Identity in the context of adolescent psychology. In A. S. Waterman (Ed.), *Identity in adolescence: Progress and contents.* San Francisco: Jossey-Bass.

WATSON, J. B. (1930). *Behaviorism* (rev. ed.). New York: Norton.

WATSON, J. B., & RAYNER, R. (1920). Conditioned emotional reactions. *Journal of Experimental Psychology, 3,* 1–14.

WATSON, M., HAYILAND, J. S., GREER, S., DAVIDSON, J., & BLISS, J. M. (1999). Influence of psychological response on survival in breast cancer: A population-based cohort study. *Lancet, 354,* 1331–1336.

WEAVER, E. G. (1949). *Theory of hearing.* New York: Wiley.

WECHSLER, D. (1958). *The measurement and appraisal of adult intelligence.* Baltimore: Williams.

WECHSLER, H., DAVENPORT, A., DOWDALL, G., MOEYKENS, B., & CASTILLO, S. (1994). Health and behavioral consequences of binge drinking in college, a national survey of students at 140 campuses. *Journal of the American Medical Association, 272,* 1672–1677.

WECHSLER, H., DOWDALL, G. W., MAENNER, G., GLEDHILL-HOYT, J., & LEE, H. (1998). Changes in binge drinking and related problems among American college students between 1993 and 1997. *Journal of American College Health, 47,* 57–68.

WEGNER, D. M., SCHNEIDER, D. J., CARTER, S., III, & WHITE, L. (1987). Paradoxical consequences of thought suppression. *Journal of Personality and Social Psychology, 53,* 1–9.

WEIGLE, D. S. (1994). Appetite and the regulation of body composition. *FASEB Journal, 8,* 302–310.

WEINBERG, M. S., SCHWARTZ, G. E., & DAVIDSON, R. E. (1979). Low-anxious, high-anxious, and repressive coping styles: Psychometric patterns and behavioral and physiological responses to stress. *Journal of Abnormal Psychology, 88,* 369–380.

WEINBERGER, D. (1990). The construct validity of the repressive coping style. In J. L. Singer (Ed.), *Repression and dissociation: Implications for personality theory, psychopathology, and health* (pp. 337–385). Chicago: University of Chicago Press.

WEINBERGER, J. (1996). Common factors aren't so common: The common factors dilemma. *Clinical Psychology: Science and Practice, 2,* 45–69.

WEINBERGER, J., & MCCLELLAND, D. C. (1990). Cognitive vs. traditional motivational models: Irreconcilable or complementary? In R. Sorrentino & E. T. Higgins (Eds.), *Handbook of motivation and cognition* (pp. 562–597). New York: Guilford.

WEINE, S. M., BECKER, D. F., MCGLASHAN, T. H., LAUB, D., LAZROVE, S., VOJVODA, D., & HYMAN, L. (1995). Psychiatric consequences of "ethnic cleansing": Clinical assessments and trauma testimonies of newly resettled Bosnian refugees. *American Journal of Psychiatry, 152,* 536–542.

WEINE, S. M., VOJVODA, D., BECKER, D. F., MCGLASHAN, T. H., HODZIC, E., LAUB, D., HYMAN, L., SAWYER, M., & LAZROVE, S. (1998). PTSD symptoms in Bosnian refugees 1 year after resettlement in the United States. *American Journal of Psychiatry, 155,* 562–564.

WEINSTEIN, N. D. (1980). Unrealistic optimism about future events. *Journal of Personality and Social Psychology, 39,* 806–820.

WEINSTEIN, N. D. (1987). Unrealistic optimism about susceptibility to health problems. Conclusions from a community-wide sample. *Journal of Behavioral Medicine, 10,* 481–500.

WEINSTEIN, N. D. (1989). Optimistic biases about personal risks. *Science, 246,* 1232–1233.

WEINSTEIN, N. D. (1998). Accuracy of smokers' risk perceptions. *Annals of Behavioral Medicine, 20,* 135–140.

WEIR, C., & SEACREST, M. (2000). Developmental differences in understanding of balance scales in the United States and Zimbabwe. *Journal of Genetic Psychology. 2000, 161,* 5–22.

WEISS, D. D., & LAST, C. G. (2001). *The developmental psychopathology of anxiety.* New York: Oxford University Press.

WEISS, J. M., GLAZER, H. I., POHORECKY, L. A., BRICK, J., & MILLER, N. E. (1975). Effects of chronic exposure to stressors on avoidance-escape behavior and on brain norepinephrine. *Psychosomatic Medicine, 37,* 522–534.

WEISS, R. D., MIRIN, S. M., & BARTEL, R. L. (1994). *Cocaine* (2nd ed.). Washington, DC: American Psychiatric Press.

WEISSMAN, M. M. (1993). Family genetic studies of panic disorder. Conference on panic and anxiety: A decade of progress. *Journal of Psychiatric Research, 27* (suppl.), 69–78.

WEISSTEIN, N. A., & WONG, E. (1986). Figure-ground organization and the spatial and temporal responses of the visual system. In E. C. Schwab & H. C. Nusbaum (Eds.), *Pattern recognition by humans and machines. Vol. 2. Visual perception* (pp. 31–64). Orlando, FL: Academic Press.

WEISZ, J. R., DONENBERG. G., HAN, S., & KAUNECKIS, D. (1995). Child and adolescent psychotherapy outcomes in experiments versus clinics: Why the disparity? *Journal of Abnormal Child Psychology, 23,* 83–106.

WELLER, L., & WELLER, A. (1993). Human menstrual synchrony: A critical assessment. *Neuroscience and Behavioral Reviews, 17,* 427–439.

WELLINGTON, S., & GISCOMBE, K. (2001). Women and leadership in corporate America. In C. Costello & A. Stone (Eds.), *The American woman, 2001–02* (pp. 87–106). New York: Norton.

WELLMAN, H. M. (1994). Early understanding of the mind: The normal case. In S. Baron-Cohen (Ed.), *Understanding other minds: Perspectives from autism.* (pp. 10–39). New York: Oxford University Press.

WELLS, G. L., FERGUSON, T. J., & LINDSAY, R. C. L. (1981). The tractability of eyewitness confidence and its implication for triers of fact. *Journal of Applied Psychology, 66,* 688–696.

WERTHEIMER, M. (1912/1932). Experimentelle studien uber das sehen von beuegung. *Zeitschrift Für Psychologie, 61,* 161–265.

WERTHEIMER, M. (2000). *A brief history of psychology* (6th ed.). Fort Worth: Harcourt.

WEST, C., & ZIMMERMAN, D. H. (1983). Small insults: A study of interruptions in cross-sex conversations between unacquainted persons. In B. Thorne, C. Kramarae, & N. Henley (Eds.), *Language, gender, and society.* Rowley, MA: Newbury House.

WESTBROOK, G. L. (1994). Glutamate receptor update. *Current Opinion in Neurobiology, 4,* 337–346.

WESTEN, D. (1998). The scientific legacy of Sigmund Freud: Toward a psychodynamically informed psychological science. *Psychological Bulletin, 124,* 333–371.

WESTERMEYER, J. (1993). Cross-cultural psychiatric assessment. In A. C. Gaw (Ed.), *Culture, ethnicity, and mental illness* (pp. 125–144). Washington, DC: American Psychiatric Press.

WHALEN, P. J., RAUCH, S. L., ETCOFF, N. L., MCINERNEY, S. C., LEE, M. B., & JENIKE, M. A. (1998). Masked presentation of emotional facial expressions modulate amygdala activity without explicit knowledge. *Journal of Neuroscience, 18,* 411–418.

WHEEDEN, A., SCAFIDI, F. A., FIELD, T., IRONSON, G., BANDSTRA, E., SCHANBERG, S., & VALDEON, C. (1993). Massage effects on cocaine-exposed preterm neonates. *Journal of Developmental and Behavioral Pediatrics, 14,* 318–322.

WHEELER, S. C., & PETTY, R. E. (2001). The effects of stereotype activation on behavior: A review of possible mechanisms. *Psychological Bulletin, 127,* 797–826.

WHEELER, S. C., JARVIS, W. B. G., & PETTY, R. E. (2001). Think unto others: The self-destructive impact of negative racial stereotypes. *Journal of Experimental Social Psychology, 37,* 173–180.

WHITAM, F. L., & MATHY, R. M. (1986). *Male Homosexuality in Four Societies: Brazil, Guatemala, the Philippines, and the United States. Vol. Special Studies.* New York: Praeger.

WHITAM, F. L., & MATHY, R. M. (1991). Childhood cross-gender behavior of homosexual females in Brazil, Peru, the Philippines, and the United States. *Archives of Sexual Behavior, 20,* 151–170.

WHITE, C. (1977). Unpublished Ph.D. dissertation, Catholic University, Washington, DC.

WHITE, G. L., FISHBEIN, S., & RUTSTEIN, J. (1981). Passionate love and the misattribution of arousal. *Journal of Personality and Social Psychology, 41,* 56–62.

WHITE, G. L., & KIGHT, T. D. (1984). Misattribution of arousal and attraction: Effects of salience of explanations for arousal. *Journal of Experimental Social Psychology, 20,* 55–64.

WHORF, B. L. (1956). *Language, thought, and reality: Selected writings of Benjamin Lee Whorf* (edited by T. B. Carroll). Cambridge, MA: MIT Press; New York: Wiley

WHYTE, W. H. (1956). *The organization man*. New York: Simon & Schuster.

WICKER, A. W. (1969). Attitudes versus actions: The relationship between verbal and overt behavioral responses to attitude objects. *Journal of Social Issues, 25*, 41–78.

WIEBE, D. J., & MCCALLUM, D. M. (1986). Health practices and hardiness as mediators in the stress-illness relationship. *Health Psychology, 5*, 425–438.

WIENS, S., MEZZACAPPA, E. S., & KATKIN, E. S. (2000). Heartbeat detection and the experience of emotions. *Cognition and Emotion, 14*, 417–427.

WILCOXIN, H. C., DRAGOIN, W. B., & KRAL, P. A. (1971). Illness-induced aversions in rat and quail: Relative salience of visual and gustatory cues. *Science, 171*, 823–828.

WILKES, A. L., & KENNEDY, R. A. (1969). Relationship between pausing and retrieval latency in sentences of varying grammatical form. *Journal of Experimental Psychology, 79*, 241–245.

WILKINS, W. (1984). Psychotherapy: The powerful placebo. *Journal of Consulting and Clinical Psychology, 52*, 570–573.

WILLIAMS, D. C. (1959). The elimination of tantrum behavior by extinction procedures. *Journal of Abnormal and Social Psychology, 59*, 269.

WILLIAMS, G. C. (1996). *Plan and purpose in nature*. London: Weidenfeld and Nicholson.

WILLIAMS, J. M., & DUNLOP, L. C. (1999). Pubertal timing and self-reported delinquency among male adolescents. *Journal of Adolescence, 22*, 157–171.

WILLIAMS, M. D., & HOLLAN, J. D. (1981). The process of retrieval from very long-term memory. *Cognitive Science, 5*, 87–119.

WILLIAMS, R. B. (1995). Somatic consequences of stress. In M. J. Friedman (Ed.), *Neurobiological and clinical consequences of stress: From normal adaptation to post-traumatic stress disorder*. Philadelphia: Lippincott-Raven.

WILLIAMS, R. B., JR., BAREFOOT, J. C., HANEY, T. L., HARRELL, F. E., BLUMENTHAL, J. A., PRYOR, D. B., & PETERSON, B. (1988). Type A behavior and angiographically documented coronary atherosclerosis in a sample of 2,289 patients. *Psychosomatic Medicine, 50*, 139–152.

WILSON, E. O. (1963). *Pheromones. Scientific American, 208*, 100–114.

WILSON, E. O. (1975). *Sociobiology: The new synthesis*. Cambridge, MA: Harvard University Press.

WILSON, E. O. (1978). *On human nature*. Cambridge, MA: Harvard University Press.

WILSON, M. A., & MCNAUGHTON, B. L. (1994). Reactivation of hippocampal ensemble memories during sleep. *Science, 265*, 676–679.

WILSON, M. I., & DALY, M. (1985). Competitiveness, risk-taking and violence: The young male syndrome. *Ethology and Sociobiology, 6*, 59–73.

WILSON, P. (1995). *Instant calm*. New York: Plume.

WILSON, T. D., DUNN, D. S., KRAFT, D., & LISLE, D. J. (1989). Introspection, attitude change, and attitude-behavior consistency: The disruptive effects of explaining why we feel the way we do. In L. Berkowitz (Ed.), *Advances in experimental social psychology* (Vol. 22). San Diego: Academic Press.

WILSON, T. D., LASER, P. S., & STONE, J. I. (1982). Judging the predictors of one's mood: Accuracy and the use of shared theories. *Journal of Experimental Social Psychology, 18*, 537–556.

WILSON, W. H., & CLAUSEN, A. M. (1995). 18-month outcome of clozapine treatment for 100 patients in a state psychiatric hospital. *Psychiatric Services, 46*, 386–389.

WILSON, W. R. (1979). Feeling more than we can know: Exposure effects without learning. *Journal of Personality and Social Psychology, 37*, 811–821.

WINCH, R. F., KTSANES, T., & KTSANES, V. (1954). The theory of complementary needs in mate selection: An analytic and descriptive study. *American Sociological Review, 29*, 241–249.

WINDHOLZ, M. J., MARMAR, C. R., & HOROWITZ, M. J. (1985). A review of the research on conjugal bereavement: Impact on health and efficacy of intervention. *Comprehensive Psychiatry, 26*, 433–447.

WINGER, G., HOFFMAN, F. G., & WOODS, J. H. (1992). *A handbook on drug and alcohol abuse* (3rd ed.). New York: Oxford University Press.

WINSON, J. (1990). The meaning of dreams. *Scientific American, 262*, 86–96.

WINTER, D. G. (1973). *The power motive*. New York: Free Press.

WINTER, D. G., STEWART, A. J., JOHN, O. P., KLOHNEN, E. C., & DUNCAN, L. E. (1998). Traits and motives: Toward an integration of two traditions in personality research. *Psychological Review, 105*, 230–250.

WISE, R. A. (1982). Neuroleptics and operant behavior: The anhedonia hypothesis. *Behavioral and Brain Sciences, 5*, 39–87.

WISNIEWSKI, E. J., & MEDIN, D. L. (1991). Harpoons and longsticks: The interaction of theory and similarity in rule induction. In D. Fisher, M. Pazzani, & P. Langley (Eds.), *Concept formation: Knowledge and experience in unsupervised learning*. San Mateo, CA: Morgan-Kaufman.

WOELK, H., BURKARD, G., & GRUNWALD, J. (1994). Benefits and risks of the hypericum extract LI 160: Drug monitoring study with 3,250 patients. *Journal of Geriatric Psychiatry and Neurology, 7* (suppl. 1), 34–38.

WOLCHIK, S. A., BEGGS, V. E., WINCZE, P. P., SAKHEIM, D. K., BARLOW, D. H., & MAVIS-SAKALIAN, M. (1980). The effect of emotional arousal on subsequent sexual arousal in men. *Journal of Abnormal Psychology, 89*, 595–598.

WOLMAN, B. B., DALE, L. A., SCHMEIDLER, G. R., & ULLMAN, M. (Eds.). (1986). *Handbook of parapsychology*. New York: Van Nostrand & Reinhold.

WOLPE, J. (1958). *Psychotherapy by reciprocal inhibition*. Stanford, CA: Stanford University Press.

WOLRAICH, M., HANNAH, J., BAUMGAERTEL, A., & FEUER, I. (1998). Examination of DSM-IV criteria for attention deficit hyperactivity in a county-wide sample. *Journal of Developmental and Behavioral Pediatrics, 19*, 162–168.

WOOD, G. (1986). *Fundamentals of psychological research* (3rd ed.). Boston: Little, Brown.

WOOD, W., LUNDGREN, S., OUELLETTE, J. A., BUSCEME, S., & BLACKSTONE, T. (1994). Minority influence: A meta-analytic review of social influence processes. *Psychological Bulletin, 115*, 323–345.

WOOD, W., WONG, F. Y., & CHACHERE, J. G. (1991). Effects of media violence on viewers' aggression in unconstrained social situations. *Psychological Bulletin, 109*, 371–383.

WOODY, R. H., & ROBERTSON, M. (1988). *Becoming a clinical psychologist*. Madison, CT: International Universities Press.

WORD, C. O., ZANNA, M. P., & COOPER, J. (1974). The nonverbal mediation of self-fulfilling prophecies in interracial interaction. *Journal of Experimental Social Psychology, 10*, 109–120.

WORTMAN, C. B., & BREHM, J. W. (1975). Responses to uncontrollable outcomes: An integration of reactance theory and the learned helplessness model. *Advances in Experimental and Social Psychology, 8*, 277–236.

WRIGHT, L. (1988). The type A behavior pattern and coronary artery disease, quest for the active ingredients and the elusive mechanism. *American Psychologist, 43*, 2–14.

WURTZ, R. H., GOLDBERG, M. E., & ROBINSON, D. L. (1980). Behavioral modulation of visual responses in monkeys. *Progress in Psychobiology and Physiological Psychology, 9*, 42–83.

WURTZEL, E. (1995). *Prozac nation*. New York: Berkley.

YAGER, T., LAUFER, R., & GALLOPS, M. (1984). Some problems associated with war experience in men of the Vietnam generation. *Archives of General Psychiatry, 41*, 327–333.

YARBUS, D. L. (1967). *Eye movements and vision*. New York: Plenum.

YEHUDA, R. (2000). Biology of posttraumatic stress disorder. *Journal of Clinical Psychiatry, 61*, 14–21.

YEHUDA, R., MCFARLANE, A. C., & SHALEY, A. Y. (1998). Predicting the development of posttraumatic stress disorder from the acute response to a traumatic event. *Biological Psychiatry, 44*, 1305–1313.

YESAVAGE, J. A., LEIER, V. O., DENARI, M., & HOLLISTER, L. E. (1985). Carry-over effect of marijuana intoxication on aircraft pilot performance: A preliminary report. *American Journal of Psychiatry, 142*, 1325–1330.

YOST, W. A., & NIELSON, D. W. (1985). *Fundamentals of hearing* (2nd ed.). New York: Holt, Rinehart & Winston.

YOUNGER, J., ADRIANCE, W., & BERGER, R. J. (1975). Sleep during transcendental meditation. *Perceptual and Motor Skills, 40*, 953–954.

YU, B., ZHANG, W., JING, Q., PENG, R., ZHANG, G., & SIMON, H. A. (1985). STM capacity for Chinese and English language materials. *Memory and Cognition, 13*, 202–207.

ZAHN-WAXLER, C., KLIMES-DOUGAN, B., & SLATTERY, M. J. (2000). Internalizing problems of childhood and adolescence: Prospects, pitfalls, and progress in understanding the development of anxiety and depression. *Development and Psychopathology, 12*, 443–466.

ZAJONC, R. B. (1965). Social facilitation. *Science, 149*, 269–274.

ZAJONC, R. B. (1968). Attitudinal effects of mere exposure. *Journal of Personality and Social Psychology, Monograph Supplement, 9*, 1–29.

ZAJONC, R. B. (1980). Compresence. In P. B. Paulus (Ed.), *Psychology of group influence*. Hillsdale, NJ: Erlbaum.

ZAJONC, R. B. (1984). On the primacy of affect. *American Psychologist, 39*, 117–123.

ZAJONC, R. B., HEINGARTNER, A., & HERMAN, E. M. (1969). Social enhancement and impairment of performance in the cockroach. *Journal of Personality and Social Psychology, 13*, 83–92.

ZAJONC, R. B., MURPHY, S. T., & INGLEHART, M. (1989). Feeling and facial efference: Implications of the vascular theory of emotion. *Psychological Review, 96*, 394–416.

ZALUTSKY, R. A., & NICOLL, R. A. (1990). Comparison of two forms of longterm potentiation in single hippocampal neurons. *Science, 248*, 1619–1624.

ZAMANSKY, H. S., & BARTIS, S. P. (1985). The dissociation of an experience: The hidden observer observed. *Journal of Abnormal Psychology, 94,* 243–248.

ZEKI, S. (1993). *A vision of the brain.* Boston: Blackwell Scientific Publications.

ZELAZO, P. R., ZELAZO, N. A., & KOLB, S. (1972). Walking in the newborn. *Science, 176,* 314–315.

ZHANG, Y., PROENCA, R., MAFFEI, M., BARONE, M., LEOPOLD, L., & FRIEDMAN, J. M. (1994). Positional cloning of the mouse obese gene and its human homologue. *Nature, 372,* 425–431.

ZILLMANN, D. (1984). *Connections between sex and aggression.* Hillsdale, NJ: Erlbaum.

ZILLMANN, D., & BRYANT, J. (1974). Effect of residual excitation on the emotional response to provocation and delayed aggressive behavior. *Journal of Personality and Social Psychology, 30,* 782–791.

ZIMBARDO, P. G. (1969). The human choice: Individuation, reason and order vs. deindividuation, impulse, and chaos. In W. J. Arnold & D. Levine (Eds.), *Nebraska symposium on motivation* (pp. 237–307). Lincoln: University of Nebraska Press.

ZIMBARDO, P. G. (1970). The human choice: Individuation, reason and order versus deindividuation, impulse and chaos. In W. J. Arnold & D. Levine (Eds.), *Nebraska symposium on motivation* (Vol. 16). Lincoln: University of Nebraska Press.

ZIMBARDO, P. G. (1972). Pathology of imprisonment. *Society, 9,* 4–8.

ZLOTNICK, C., ELKIN, I., & SHEA, M. T. (1998). Does the gender of a patient or the gender of a therapist affect the treatment of patients with major depression? *Journal of Consulting and Clinical Psychology, 66,* 655–659.

ZOLA-MORGAN, S., & SQUIRE, L. R. (1985). Medial-temporal lesions in monkeys impair memory on a variety of tasks sensitive to human amnesia. *Behavioral Neuroscience, 99,* 22–34.

ZOLA-MORGAN, S. M., & SQUIRE, L. R. (1990). The primate hippocampal formation: Evidence for a time-limited role in memory storage. *Science, 250,* 228–290.

ZOLA-MORGAN, S. M., SQUIRE, L. R., & AMARAL, D. G. (1989). Lesions of the hippocampal formation but not lesions of the fornix or the mamalary nuclei produce long-lasting memory impairments in monkeys. *Journal of Neuroscience, 9,* 898–913.

ZUBER, J. A., CROTT, H. W., & WERNER, J. (1992). Choice shift and group polarization: An analysis of the status of arguments and social decision schemes. *Journal of Personality and Social Psychology, 62,* 50–61.

ZUCKER, K. J. (1990). Gender identity disorders in children: Clinical description and natural history. In R. Blanchard (Ed.) *Clinical management of gender identity disorders in children and adults* (pp. 3–23). Washington DC: American Psychiatric Press.

ZUCKER, K. J., & BRADLEY, S. J. (1995). *Gender identity disorder and psychosexual problems in children and adolescents.* New York: Guilford.

ZUCKERMAN, M. (1979). *Sensation seeking: Beyond the optimal level of arousal.* Hillsdale, NJ: Erlbaum.

ZUCKERMAN, M. (1991). *Psychobiology of personality.* Cambridge, England: Cambridge University Press.

ZUCKERMAN, M. (1995). Good and bad humors: Biochemical bases of personality and its disorders. *Psychological Science, 6,* 325–332.

ZURIF, E. B. (1990). Language and the brain. In D. N. Osherson & H. Lasnik (Eds.), *An invitation to cognitive science: Language* (Vol. 1). Cambridge, MA: MIT Press.

ZURIF, E. B. (1995). Brain regions of relevance to syntactic processing. In: D. N. Osherson, L. R. Gleitman, & M. Liberman (Eds.) *An invitation to cognitive science, second edition: Language* (Vol. 1), pp. 381–397. Cambridge, MA: MIT Press.

ZURIF, E. B., CARAMAZZA, A., MYERSON, R., & GALVIN, J. (1974). Semantic feature representations for normal and aphasic language. *Brain and Language, 1,* 167–187.

CREDITS

Photographs

Chapter 1
1: © Artville/Getty Images; 2: © Laura Dwight; 4: (left) © Jonathan Nourok/Photo Edit; 4: © Bill Aron/Photo Edit; 5: © Bettmann/CORBIS; 6: Archives of the History of American Psychology, the University of Akron; 7: (bottom left) © CORBIS; (bottom center, right) © Bettmann/CORBIS; 10: © Volker Steoer/Peter Arnold, Inc.; 11: (left) © Mary Kate Denny/Photo Edit; (right) © David Young-Wolff/Photo Edit; 12: Kactus Foto/SuperStock; 13: © John Eastcott/Yva Momatiuk/Stock Boston; 23: © Michael Newman/Photo Edit/PictureQuest

Chapter 2
30: © Digital Art/CORBIS; 36: © Omicron/Science Source/Photo Researchers; 43: F2-9: © Martin Rotker/Phototake; 47: (above) © Le Duc/Monkmeyer; (below) Courtesy of Marcus E. Raichle; 50: © Bertrand Rieger/Getty/Stone; 56: F2-18: © CNRI/SPL/Photo Researchers; 57: © The Everett Collection; 58: (left) © Laura Doss/CORBIS; (right) © Margaret Ross/Stock Boston

Chapter 3
64: © Marco Cauz/CORBIS; 66: (both) © Corbis/Bettmann; 68: (all) © Laura Dwight; 70: F3-2: © Creatas/PictureQuest; 71: © Michael Newman/Photo Edit; 72: F3-3 (above): Courtesy of Carolyn Rovee-Collier; F3-4 (below): © Rick Malkames; 75: © Laura Dwight; 76: F3-5 (both): © Laura Dwight; 77: (all) © Laura Dwight; 80: © Monika Graff/The Image Works; 81: F3-9 (top left): © Bios (Michael Gunther)/Peter Arnold, Inc.; (top right) © IFA/Peter Arnold, Inc.; (bottom left) © Hans Pfletschinger/Peter Arnold, Inc.; (bottom right) © Fred Bruemmer/Peter Arnold, Inc.; 83: © Michelle Bridwell/Photo Edit; 84: (left) © Lawrence Migdale/Stock Boston; (right) © David Young-Wolff/Photo Edit; 87: © Michael Newman/Photo Edit; 88: © Laura Dwight; 90: F3-11: © Martin Rogers/Stock Boston; 91: © Will & Deni McIntyre/Photo Researchers; 93: © Elizabeth Crews; 94: (left)

© Sylvie Villeger/Explorer/Photo Researchers; (right) © Kathy Sloane/Photo Researchers; 95: © Mark Richards/Photo Edit; 98: © Joel Gordon; 99: © Ariel Skelley/CORBIS

Chapter 4
106: © Jerry Tobias/CORBIS; 109: © Ake Lindau IBL, Rex Instock/Stock Connection/PictureQuest; 112: F4-5: Courtesy of Geoffrey Loftus; 121: © David Sutherland/Getty Images/Stone; 122: F4-18: Courtesy of Macbeth/Munsell Color, New Windsor, NY; 127: © Charles & Josette Lenars/CORBIS; 128: © Ralf-Finn Hestoft/Index Stock Imagery/PictureQuest; 134: Courtesy of Geoffrey Loftus; 135: © Porter Gifford/Stock Boston; 136: © Joel Gordon; 137: © Peter Vandermark/Stock Boston

Chapter 5
146: © Renee Lynn/CORBIS; 147: © The McNeil River State Game Sanctuary, photo by Jon C. Pascal; 150: F5-2: D. L. Yarbuss (1967) "Eye Movements and Vision," *Plenum Publishing Corporation*. Reproduced by permission of the publisher; 151: © Norbert vonder Groeben/The Image Works; 154: F5-4: Salvador Dali, *Slave Market with Disappearing Bust of Voltaire*, 1950, The Salvador Dali Museum, St. Petersburg, Florida; 157: F5-7: © Macduff Everton/CORBIS; 159: California Museum of Photography, University of California, Riverside; 160: © Tim Davis/Getty Images/Stone; 161: © Tim Davis/Getty Images/Stone; 170: © Najlah Feanny/Stock Boston; 174: © David Frazier/The Image Works; 177: © Hiroyuki Matsumoto/Getty Images/Stone; 178: © Baron Wolman/Woodfin Camp; 180: M. Corbetta, F.M. Miezen, S. Dobmeyer, D.L. Shulman, S.E. Persen, "Attentional modulation of neural processing of shape, color and velocity in humans, *Science* V. 248, p. 1558 1990, Reprinted by permission of the American Association for the Advancement of Science; 184: F5-34 (above): © Lawrence Migdale/Photo Researchers; F5-35 (below): From *Sensations and Perception* by E. Bruce Goldstein, © 1989, 1984, 1980 Wadsworth Publishing Co.; 185: F5-36: © Martin Rogers/Stock Boston

Chapter 6
194: © Peter Holst/The Image Bank/Getty Images; 196: © Bonnie Kamin/Photo Edit; 202: © Chuck Savage/Corbis Stock Market; 204: (both) © Louis Psihoyos/Matrix International; 205: © Christian Blackman/CORBIS; 207: © Joel Gordon; 209: © Oscar Burriel/Latin Stock/SPL/Photo

Researchers; 211: © H. Arneson; 212: © Paul A. Souders/CORBIS; 215: © James Shaffer/Photo Edit; 219: © Mark Antman/The Image Works; 225: (left) © Jeremy Walker/SPL/Photo Researchers; (right) Courtesy of Dr. Charles Honorton

Chapter 7
232: © Taxi/Getty Images; 235: © Corbis/Bettmann; 240: © Tom & Dee Ann McCarthy/CORBIS; 243: F7-6: © Richard Wood/Index Stock; (right) Nina Leen, © Life Magazine/TimePix; 245: F7-7: Courtesy of Naval Oceans System Center; 246: © Jose Luis Pelaez Inc./Corbisstockmarket.com; 248: © Jeff Greenberg/Peter Arnold, Inc.; 249: © William Johnston/Stock Boston; 250: © Jerry McCormick-Ray/Photo Researchers; 252: © R. Malmares, WNET/Thirteen; 253: F7-10: Yerkes Primate Research Center, Emory University; F7-11 (all): © SuperStock; 254: © Najlah Feanny/CORBIS SABA

Chapter 8
266: © Firefly Productions/CORBIS; 268: © Tom Stewart/CORBIS; 269: © Corbis/Hulton Deutsch Collection; 275: (right) © Jose Luis Pelaez Inc./Corbisstockmarket.com; F8-5 (left): © Michael Newman/Photo Edit; From *Alice in Wonderland*, Abridged by Josette Frank, Random House, 1955; 282: © Shackman/Monkmeyer Press; 287: © Patrick Durand/Corbis Sygma; 289: © Mary Kate Denny/Photo Edit; 296: © Jeff Greenberg/Photo Edit; 297: © David G. Curran/Rainbow; 299: © Gaitano/CORBIS

Chapter 9
312: © Mug Shots/CORBIS; 317: © Owen Franken/CORBIS; 320: © Laura Dwight; 323: © David Young-Wolff/Photo Edit; 325: (left) © Michael Nichols/Magnum Photos; (right) © Paul Fusco/Magnum Photos; 327: (left) © Russell Hansen/Peter Arnold, Inc.; (right) © Art Wolfe/Photo Researchers; 330: © James Shaffer/Photo Edit; 343: © Bob Daemmrich/The Image Works; 344: F9-13: © Susan Holtz; 345: © David Young-Wolff/Stone/Getty Images; 348: © Susan Holtz

Chapter 10
352: © R.W. Jones/CORBIS; 354: (left) © Amy C. Etra/Photo Edit; (right) © Topham/The Image Works; 356: Courtesy of K.C. Berridge; 358: © Joel Gordon; 360: © Michael Newman/Photo Edit; 361: © Bryce Flynn/Stock Boston; 364: © Richard Howard; 370: (left) © Corbis/Bettmann; (right): © AFP/CORBIS; 373: © Camera

M.D. Studios, 1973, all rights reserved;
377: © David C. Fritts/Animals, Animals

Chapter 11
388: © Eyewire/Getty Images; 396: F11-3: From Whalen, Rauch, Etcoff, McInerney, Lee & Jenike, Masked presentation of emotional facial expressions modulate amygdala activity without explicit knowledge; *Journal of Neuroscience* 1998, 18: 411-418; 399: (left) © D. Lowe/Stock Boston; (right) © Paula Lerner/Woodfin Camp; 404: © Syracuse Newspapers/The Image Works; 407: (top, all) New Guinea faces from *Face of Man*, New York, Garland, 1980, Paul Ekman/Pergamon; (bottom, all) © Paul Ekman; 412: Courtesy of Ashby Plant; 413: © Bob Daemmrich/Stock Boston; 415: © Catherine Ursillo/Photo Researchers; 416: F11-8 (both): Courtesy of Dr. Jose M.R. Delgado; 417: F11-10: © Albert Bandura; 422: (left) © Byron/Monkmeyer Press; (right) © Michael Newman/Photo Edit

Chapter 12
426: © Getty Images/Stone; 428: © Gary Wagner/Stock Boston; 430: © 1986, Reproduced with permission of The Riverside Publishing Company, Chicago, Illinois; 434: AP/Wide World Photos; 437: (top) © Bob Daemmrich/Stock Boston; (middle) © Jeff Greenberg/Rainbow; (bottom) © Jack Grove/Photo Edit; 441: © Ellen B. Senisis/The Image Works; 444: © Mary Kate Denny/Photo Edit; 448: (left) © Michael Newman/Photo Edit; (right) © Sidney/Monkmeyer Press

Chapter 13
452: © Jon Feingersh/CORBIS; 453: © Peter Byron; 455: © Arnold Gold/The Image Works; 462: © ER Productions/CORBIS; 463: © Bettmann/Corbis; 464: © Tony Freeman/Photo Edit; 465: © Laura Dwight; 466: F13-3: © Spencer Grant/Stock Boston; 467: AP/Wide World Photos; 470: © Cindy Roesinger/Photo Researchers; 472: © Albert Bandura; 473: © Laima Druskis/Stock Boston; 475: © Mary Steinbacher/Photo Edit; 477: Carl Rogers Memorial Library; 480: (left) AP/Wide World; (right) © Bettmann/Corbis; 481: © AFP/CORBIS; 485: © Myrleen Ferguson Cate/Photo Edit; 488: © Alison Wright/Stock Boston

Chapter 14
492: © PhotoDisc/Getty Images; 494: (left) © Laima Druskis/Stock Boston; (right) © David Young-Wolff/Photo Edit; 495: © Ilkkla Uimonen/Corbis Sygma; 497: © Larry L. Miller/Photo Researchers; 500: © Kindra Clineff/Getty Images/Stone; 501: © Vincent DeWitt/Stock Boston; 505: F14-05: Courtesy of Dr. Lisa Shin, from Shin, Kosslyn, Alpert, Rauch, Macklin, & Pittman (1997), "Visual imagery and Perception in Posttraumatic Stress Disorder: A Positron Emission Tomographic Investigation." *Archives of General Psychiatry* 54: 233-241; F14-06: Courtesy of J. Douglas Bremner, MD; 509: © Bob Daemmrich/Stock Boston; 511: AP/Wide World Photos; 513: © AFP/CORBIS; 515: © Gerard Vandystadt/Photo Researchers; 516: © Amy C. Etra/Photo Edit; 519: © Dan McCoy/Rainbow

Chapter 15
526: © Artville/Getty Images; 528: (left) © Bettmann/Corbis; (right) © Wartenberg/Picture Press/Corbis; 529: © Steven Peters/Getty Images/Stone; 537: © John Cancalosi/Peter Arnold; 540: F15-5 (left): © Dr. Lewis Baxter/Peter Arnold, Inc.; F15-6

(right): UCLA School of Medicine, from Schwartz, Stoessel, Baxter, Martin & Phelps (1996) Systematic change in cerebral glucose metabolic rate after successful behavior modification treatment of obsessive-compulsive disorder, *Archives of General Psychiatry* 53: 109-113; 543: AP Wide World Photos; 545: F15-9 (above): Courtesy of Monte S. Buchsbaum, MD; F15-10 (below): Courtesy of Dr. Wayne Drevets, NIMH, from Drevets, WC, Todd, RD, Depression, mania and related disorders, in: *Adult Psychiatry*, Guze, SB (ed), Mosby Year Book 1997: 99-141, St. Louis, MO; 550: Privizhorn Collection, Ruprecht-Karls-Universitat Heidelberg Klinikum; 552: Laboratory of Psychology and Psychopathology, National Institute of Mental Health; 553: F15-14: © Photo Researchers; 554: F15-15 (above): Courtesy of S. Galderisi, from Galderisi, Vita, Rossi, Stratta, Leonardi & Invernizzi. (2000) Qualitative MRI findings in patients with schizophrenia. *Psychiatry Research: Neuroimaging Section*, 98: 117-126; F15-16 (below): Courtesy of David A. Lewis, MD, University of Pittsburgh School of Medicine

Chapter 16
568: © CORBIS; 571: (above) © Stock Montage; (below) © Corbis/Bettmann; 577: © Michael Newman/Photo Researchers; 584: © Frank Pedrick/The Image Works; 585: © Peter Tumley/Corbis; 595: © Najlah Feanny/Stock Boston; 597: © Michael Newman/Photo Edit

Chapter 17
604: AP/Wide World Photos; 605: (all) AP/Wide World Photos; 606: © Getty Images/Stone; 608: © Mark E. Gibson; 609: (above) © Peter Tumley/CORBIS; F17-2 (below): Philip G. Zimbardo, Inc.; 610: © David M. Grossman/Photo Researchers; 611: www.crimelibrary.com; 614: (all) The Asch Study of the Resistance of Majority Opinion from *Scientific American*, November, 1995, Vol. 193, No. 5, by Solomon E. Asch; 615: (left) © Bill Lai/Rainbow; (right) © Sandy Felsenthal/CORBIS; 617: © Chuck Savage/CORBIS; 618: © Jon Jones/Corbis Sygma; 619: (all) From the film *Obedience*, distributed by the New York University Film Library; © 1965 by Stanley Milgram, Reprinted by permission of Alexandra Milgram; 622: © Steve Kaufman/CORBIS; 624: © Bossu Regis/Corbis Sygma; 630: © Bettmann/Corbis; 633: (all) © Philip Zimbardo; 634: © John Neubauer/Photo Edit; 637: © Gary Conner/Photo Edit

Chapter 18
644: © Taxi/Getty Images; 647: © Bonnie Kamin/Photo Edit; 648: (both) © Joel Gordon; 650: © Jose Luis Pelaez, Inc./CORBIS; 655: © Don Smetzer/Getty Images/Stone; 659: (left) © Michael Newman/Photo Edit; (right) © David Young-Wolff/Photo Edit; 662: © Susan Van Etten/Photo Edit; 665: © Cleo/Photo Edit; 667: (left) © Ronnie Kaufman/CORBIS; (right) © Zigy Kaluzny/Getty Images/Stone; 670: © Comstock

Tables, Boxes, Illustrations
Chapter 1
3: K. Sheingold and Y. J. Tenney (1982) "Recall of An Early Memory," adapted from "Memory for a Salient Childhood Event," from U. Neisser (ed.) Memory Observed: Remembering in Natural Context, copyright © 1982 by W. H. Freeman & Company. Adapted by permission of the publisher.

4: L. Eron, et al. (1972) "Does Television Violence Cause Aggression?" American Psychologist, 27:253-262. Copyright © 1972 by The American Psychological Association. Adapted by permission.

Chapter 2
32: Adapted from Human Anatomy by Anthony J. Gaudin and Kenneth C. Jones. Copyright © 1988 by Anthony J. Gaudin and Kenneth C. Jones. Reprinted by permission of the authors. 32: Adapted from Human Anatomy by Anthony J. Gaudin and Kenneth C. Jones. Copyright © 1988 by Anthony J. Gaudin and Kenneth C. Jones. Reprinted by permission of the authors. 36: Adapted from Search for the Human Mind by Robert Sternberg. Copyright © 1994 by Harcourt Brace & Company, reproduced by permission of the publisher. 43: Adapted from Human Anatomy by Anthony J. Gaudin and Kenneth C. Jones. Copyright © 1988 by Anthony J. Gaudin and Kenneth C. Jones. Reprinted by permission of the authors. 45: Adapted from Human Anatomy by Anthony J. Gaudin and Kenneth C. Jones. Copyright © 1988 by Anthony J. Gaudin and Kenneth C. Jones. Reprinted by permission of the authors. 48: Reprinted from Neuropsychologia, Volume 9, by R. D. Nebes and W. Sperry, p. 247. Copyright © 1971, with kind permission of Elsevier Science, Ltd., The Boulevard, Langford Lane, Kiddington, Oxford, OX5 1DX, UK. 58: Reprinted from Proceedings of the Association for Research in Nervous and Mental Diseases, Volume 33, by R. W. Thompson, p. 209-231. Copyright © 1954.

Chapter 3
73: T. Field, "Massage Therapy Facilitates Weight Gain in Preterm Infants," Current Directions in Psychological Science, 10, p. 51-53. © 1986 Blackwell Publishers. Reprinted by permission. 75: From Review of Child Development Research, Vol. 1, edited by M. L. Hoffman & L. W. Hoffman. Copyright © 1964 by the Russell Sage Foundation. Reprinted by permission of Russell Sage Foundation. 79: Adapted from Baillargeon, R., "Object Performance in 3½ and 4½ Month Old Infants," from Developmental Psychology, 23:655-664. Copyright © 1987. Reprinted with permission of the Academic Press. 85: Kohlberg, L. (1969) "Stages of Moral Reasoning," from "Stages and Sequence: The Cognitive Developmental Approach to Socialization" in Handbook of Socialization Theory and Research, D. A. Goslin (ed.) Reprinted by permission of Rand McNally. 89: Reprinted by permission of the publisher from Infancy: Its Place in Human Development by Jerome Kagan, R. B. Kearsley and P. R. Zelazo, p. 107, Cambridge, Mass.: Harvard University Press, Copyright © 1978 by the President and Fellows of Harvard College.

Chapter 4
108: Galanter, E. (1962) "Contemporary Psychophysics," from Roger Brown & collaborators (eds.), New Directions in Psychology, Vol. 1. Reprinted by permission of Roger Brown. 115: From Sensation and Perception by E. Bruce Goldstein. Copyright © 1989, 1984, 1980 by Wadsworth Publishing Company. Reprinted by permission of Wadsworth, a division of Thomson Learning. 116: Adapted from Human Color Vision by Robert M. Boynton, copyright © 1979 by Holt, Rinehart & Winston. Reprinted by permission of Harcourt Brace & Company. 117: Adapted from Human Color Vision by Robert M. Boynton, copyright © 1979 by

Holt, Rinehart & Winston. Reprinted by permission of Harcourt Brace & Company. **117:** J. E. Dowling and B. B. Boycott (1969) "Organization of the Primate Retina" from Proceedings of the Royal Society of London, Series B, Vol. 166, p. 80-111. Adapted by permission of the Royal Society of London. **124:** Reprinted from "Spectral Sensitivity of the Foveal Cone Photopigments Between 400 and 500 nm," in Vision Search, 15, p. 161-171. © 1975, with permission from Elsevier Science. **129:** From Sensation and Perception, 3/e, by S. Coren and L. Ward, © 1989. Used by permission of John Wiley & Sons, Inc. **136:** E. H. Erickson, "Sensory Neural Patterns in Gustation," from Zotterman (ed.), Olfaction and Taste, Vol. 2, p. 205-213. Copyright © 1963, with kind permission of Elsevier Science. **138:** D. D. Kosambi (1967) "Living Prehistory in India," from Scientific American 215:105. Copyright 1967 by D. D. Kosambi. Reprinted by permission of Dr. Meera Kosambi and Mr. Jijoy B. Surka.

Chapter 5
165: Based on G. M. Reicher (1969) "Perception of Letters & Words" from "Perceptual Recognition as a Function of the Meaningfulness of the Material," in Journal of Experimental Psychology, 81:275-280. **166:** From L. Biederman, Computer Vision, Graphics, and Image Processing, 32, p. 29-73, © 1985 Academic Press. Used with permission. **167:** From L. Biederman, Computer Vision, Graphics, and Image Processing, 32, p. 29-73, © 1985 Academic Press. Used with permission. **168:** From E. G. Boring (1930) "A New Ambiguous Figure," from American Journal of Psychology, 42:444-445. **168:** From G. H. Fisher (1967) "Perception of Ambiguous Stimulus Materials," from Perception & Psychophysics, 2:421-422. Reprinted by permission of the Psychonomic Society. **181:** After Mortimer Mishkin, Leslie G. Ungerleider, & Kathleen A. Macko (1983), "Object vision and spatial vision: two cortical pathways," Trends in Neuroscience, 6(10):414-417. **187:** R. Held and A. Held (1963) "Movement Produced in the Development of Visually Guided Behavior," from Journal of Comparative and Physiological Psychology, 56:872-876. Copyright © 1963 by the American Psychological Association. Adapted with permission.

Chapter 6
198: © The New Yorker Collection 1979, Dana Fradon from cartoonbank.com. All Rights Reserved. **203:** G. M. Pion (1991) "Psychologists Wanted: Employment Trends Over the Past Decade," in R. R. Kilbur (ed.) How to Manage Your Career in Psychology, copyright © 1991 by the American Psychological Association. Reprinted by permission. **213:** From L. A. Warner, R. C. Kessler, M. Hughes, J. C. Anthony, & C. B. Nelson (1995). Prevalence and correlates of drug use and dependence in the United States. Archives of General Psychiatry, 52, 219-229. **224:** © Bill Yates. Reprinted with special permission of King Features Syndicate.

Chapter 7
236: Adapted from Conditioned Reflexes by E. P. Pavlov. Copyright © 1927 by Oxford University Press. Reprinted by permission of Oxford University Press. **237:** "The Sensory Generalization of Conditioned Responses With Varying Frequencies of Tone," from Journal of General Psychology, Vol. 17, p. 125-148, 1937. Reprinted by permission of the Helen Dwight Reid Educational Foundation.

238: Adapted from "Differential Classical Conditioning: Verbalization of Stimulus Contingencies," by M. J. Fuhrer & P. E. Baer, reprinted by permission from Science, Vol. 150, December 10, 1965, p. 1479-1481. Copyright © 1965 by American Association for the Advancement of Science. **239:** R. A. Rescorla (1967) "Pavlovian Conditioning & Its Proper Control Procedures," from Psychological Review, Vol. 74:71-80. Copyright © 1967 by the American Psychological Association. **241:** J. Garcia and R. A. Koelling (1966) 'The Relation of Cue to Consequence in Avoidance Learning," from Psychonomic Science, 4:123-124. Reprinted by permission of the Psychonomic Society. **247:** Adapted from Barry Schwartz, Psychology of Learning and Behavior, 3/e, with the permission of W. W. Norton & Co., Inc. **252:** From Mind, Brain and Behavior by Bloom and Lazerton. Copyright © 1988 by Educational Broadcasting Corporation. Used with permission of W. H. Freeman and Company.

Chapter 8
268: A. W. Melton (1963) "Implication of Short-Term Memory for a General Theory of Memory," from Journal of Verbal Learning and Verbal Behavior, 2:1-21. Adapted by permission of the Academic Press. **274:** DOONESBURY © Garry B. Trudeau. Reprinted with permission of UNIVERSAL PRESS SYNDICATE. All rights reserved. **277:** Adapted from "High Speed Scanning in Human Memory," reprinted with permission from Science, Vol. 153, August 5, 1966, p. 652-654 by S. Sternberg. Copyright © 1966 by the American Association for the Advancement of Science. **278:** © 1985, reprinted courtesy of Bill Hoest and Parade Magazine. **278:** P. A. Carpenter, M. A. Just, and P. Shell (1990), "What one intelligence test measures: A theoretical account of the Processing in the Raven Progressive Matrices Test," Psychological Review, 97(3): 404-431. Adapted by permission of the American Psychological Association. **279:** B. B. Murdock (1962) 'The Serial Position Effect in Free Recall," from Journal of Experimental Psychology, 64:482-488. Copyright © 1962 by the American Psychological Association. Adapted by permission. **283:** E. Tulving and Z. Pearlstone (1976) "Availability and Accessibility," from Journal of Memory and Language, 5:381-391. Reprinted by permission of Academic Press. **286:** D. Godden and A. D. Baddeley (1975) "Context-Dependent Memory in Two Natural Environments: On Land & Under Water," from British Journal of Psychology, 66:325-331. **290:** Reprinted from Neuropsychologia, Vol. 16, p. 169 172, by W. K. Warrington and L. Weiskrantz, "Further Analysis of the Proper Learning Effect in Amnesiac Patients." Copyright © 1978, with permission from Elsevier Science, Ltd. **302:** Adapted from "Acquisition of a Memory Skill," reprinted by permission from Science, Vol. 208, 1980, p. 1181-1182 by I. A. Ericsson, et al. Copyright © 1980 by American Association for the Advancement of Science.

Chapter 9
322: Dan I. Slobin (1971) from "Developmental Psycholinguistic," in A Survey of Linguistic Science, edited by W. O. Dingwall, p. 298-400. **331:** F. J. Wesniewski and D. L. Medin (1991) "Harpoons & Logisticks: The Interaction of Theory & Similarity in Rule Induction," in Concept Formation: Knowledge & Experience in Unsupervised Learning, ed. by D. Fisher, M. Pazzani, & P. Langley. Copyright © 1991 by Morgan Kaufman Publishers,

Inc. Reprinted by permission of the publisher. **340:** L. A. Cooper & R. N. Shepard (1973) "Chronometric Studies of the Rotation of Mental Images," in Visual Information Processing, ed. by W. G. Chase. Adapted by permission of Academic Press. **340:** L. A. Cooper & R. N. Shepard (1973) "Chronometric Studies of the Rotation of Mental Images," in Visual Information Processing, ed. by W. G. Chase. Adapted by permission of Academic Press. **340:** S. M. Kosslyn, et al. (1978) "Scanning Mental Images," from "Visual Images Preserve Metric Spatial Information: Evidence from Studies of Image Scanning," in Journal of Experimental Psychology, 4:47-60. Copyright © 1978 by the American Psychological Association. Adapted by permission of the American Psychological Association. **341:** From Robert J. Sternberg, Beyond IQ: A Triarchic Theory of Human Intelligence, © 1985 by Robert J. Sternberg. Reprinted by permission of Cambridge University Press.

Chapter 10
365: B. G. Hoeble and P. Teitelbaum (1970) "Effects of Force Feeding and Starvation, Food Intake and Body Weight of a Rat With Ventromedial Hypothalamic Lesions," in Journal of Comparative & Physiological Psychology, 61:189-193. Copyright © 1966 by the American Psychological Association. Adapted by permission. **369:** L. M. Craighead, A. J. Stunkard, & R. M. O'Brien (1981) "Behavior Therapy and Pharmacotherapy for Obesity," in Archives of General Psychiatry, 38:763-768. Copyright © 1981 by the American Medical Association. **378:** J. R. Hopkins (1977) "Sexual Behaviors in Adolescence," in Journal of Social Issues, Vol. 33(2):67-85. Adapted with permission of the Society for the Psychological Study of Social Issues. **380:** A. P. Bell, M. A. Weinberg, & S. K. Hammerstein, Sexual Preference: Its Development in Men & Women.

Chapter 11
398: From D. D. Daner, D. A. Snowden, W. V. Friesen (2001). Positive emotions in early life and longevity: Findings from the nun study. Journal of Personality and Social Psychology, 80, 804-813. Copyright © 2001 by the American Psychological Association. Reprinted by permission of the American Psychological Association. **400:** From J. S. Lerner and D. Keltner (2001). "Fear, anger, and risk" in Journal of Personality and Social Psychology, 81, 146-159. Copyright © 2001 by the American Psychological Association. Reprinted by permission of the American Psychological Association. **401:** From L. F. Shafer (1947), "Symptoms of Fear in Combat Flying," in Journal of Consulting Psychology, 11:137-143. **402:** Adapted with permission from B. L. Frederickson, R. A. Mancuso, C. Branigan, & M. M. Tugade (2000), "The Undoing Effect of Positive Emotions, in Motivation and Emotion, 24:237-258. © 2000 Kluwer Academic/Plenum Publishers. **403:** Adapted from G. W. Hohmann, "The effect of dysfunctions of the autonomic nervous system on experienced feelings and emotions," Paper read at the New School for Social Research, New York, October 1962. **405:** Adapted from article by P. Ekman, et al., "Autonomic Nervous System Activity Distinguishes Among Emotions," from Science, Vol. 221, p. 1208-1210, September 16, 1983. Copyright © 1983 American Association for the Advancement of Science. **418:** Adapted from A. Bandura, et al., "Imitation of Film-Mediated Aggressive

Models," in Journal of Abnormal Psychology, 66:8. Copyright © 1963 by the American Psychological Association. Adapted by permission. **419:** After Eron, Huesmann, Lefkowitz, & Walder, 1972.

Chapter 12
431: From A. Anastasia and S. Urbina, Psychological Testing, 7/e, © 1997 Prentice-Hall. **433:** Copyright © 1949, 1974, 1991 by the Psychological Corporation. **435:** From The dynamic assessment of retarded performers by Reuven Feuerstein, © 1979 University Park Press. Used with permission. **441:** Adapted from A. Sameroff, et al. (1993), "Stability of intelligence from preschool to adolescence: The influence of social and family risk factors," in Child Development, 64, p. 80-94. Adapted by permission of the Society for Research in Child Development. **445:** From "Familiar Studies of Intelligence: A Review," T. Bouchard, et al., Science, Vol. 212, #4498, p. 1055-1059, 29 May 1981. Copyright © 1981 American Association for the Advancement of Science. Used by permission of Thomas Bouchard.

Chapter 13
454: From H. J. Eysenck and S. Rachman (1965), The Causes and Cures of Neurosis, by H. J. Eysenck. Copyright © 1965 by H. J. Eysenck and S. Rachman. Reprinted by permission of EdiTS. **460:** © 2002 by Sidney Harris. **478:** After Abraham H. Maslow, "Hierarchy of Needs," from Motivation and Personality. Copyright © 1954 by Harper and Row Publishers, Inc. Reprinted by permission of Pearson Education, Inc., Upper Saddle River, NJ. **479:** A. H. Maslow (1967), "Self-actualization and beyond." In Challenges of Humanistic Psychology, J. F. T. Bugenthal (ed.). Copyright © 1967 by Abraham H. Maslow. Used with permission of McGraw-Hill Publishers.

Chapter 14
497: Reprinted with permission from T. H. Holmes & R. H. Rahe (1967) "The Social Readjustment Rating Scale," in the Journal of Psychosomatic Research, Vol. 11, No. 2, p. 213-218. Copyright © 1967 Elsevier Science. **500:** Adapted from W. E. Schlenger, R. A. Kolka, J. A. Fairbank, & R. L. Hough (1992), "The Prevalence of Post-Traumatic Stress Disorder in the Vietnam Generation: A Multi-Method, Multi-Source Assessment of Psychiatric Disorders," from Journal of Traumatic Stress, 5, 333-363. **507:** After S. Cohen, D. A. J. Tyrrell, and A. P. Smith (1991) "Psychological stress and susceptibility to the common cold," The New England Journal of Medicine, 325:606-612. Used with permission from S. Cohen. **514:** From Type A Behavior and Your Heart by Meyer Friedman and R. N. Rosenman, copyright © 1974 by Meyer Friedman. Used by permission of Alfred A. Knopf, a division of Random House, Inc. **517:** From S. W. Cole, M. E. Kemeny, S. E. Taylor, and B. R. Visscher (1996), "Elevated Physical Health Risk Among Gay Men Who Conceal Their Homosexual Identity," Health Psychology, 15, p. 243-251.

Copyright © 1996 by the American Psychological Association. Reprinted with permission. **520:** G. E. Schwartz (1975) "Biofeedback, Self-Regulation, & the Patterning of Physiological Processes," in American Scientist 63:316. Reprinted by permission of The Scientific Research Association.

Chapter 15
530: From Diagnostic and Statistical Manual of Mental Disorders, Fourth Edition, Washington, DC: American Psychiatric Association, 1994. **531:** From R. C. Kessler, K. A. McGonagle, S. Zhao, and C. B. Nelson (1994), "Lifetime and 12-month prevalence of DSM-III-R psychiatric disorders in the United States: Results from the National Comorbidity Study," Archives of General Psychiatry, 51(1):8-19. Copyright © 1994 by the American Medical Association. **534:** From Abnormal Psychology: The Problem of Maladaptive Behavior, 7/e, by I. G. Sarason and B. R. Sarason. Copyright © 1993 by I. G. Sarason and B. R. Sarason. Adapted by permission of Prentice-Hall, Upper Saddle River, NJ. **535:** Adapted from R. M. Rapee, T. A. Brown, M. M. Anthony, & D. H. Barlow (1992), "Response to hyperventilation and inhalation of 5.5% carbon dioxide–enriched air across the DSM-III-R anxiety disorders," Journal of Abnormal Psychology, 101, 538-552. Copyright © 1992 by the American Psychological Association. Adapted with permission. **552:** A. Jablensky (1989). "Epidemiology and cross-cultural aspects of schizophrenia," in Psychiatric Annals, 19, 516-524. Reprinted by permission of SLACK, Inc. **553:** Schizophrenia: The Epigenetic Puzzle, by I. I. Gottesman & J. Shields. Copyright © 1992 Cambridge University Press. Reprinted by permission of the publisher. **555:** M. Karno & J. H. Jenkins (1993). Cross-cultural issues in the course and treatment of schizophrenia. Psychiatric Clinics of North America, 16, 339-350. Reprinted by permission of W. B. Saunders. **561:** A. M. Ludwig, J. M. Brandsma, C. B. Wilbur, F. Benfeldt, & D. H. Jameson (1972), "The Objective Study of a Multiple Personality," in Archives of General Psychiatry, 26:298-310. Copyright © 1972 by the American Medical Association.

Chapter 16
573: H. J. Steadman, E. P. Mulvey, J. Monahan, P. C. Robbins, P. S. Applebaum, T. Grisso, L. Roth, & E. Silver (1998). Violence by people discharged from acute psychiatric inpatient facilities and by others in the same neighborhoods. Archives of General Psychiatry, 55, 393-401. © 1998 American Medical Association. **575:** © 2002 by Sidney Harris. **581:** Reprinted with permission from The Coping with Depression Course: Psychoeducational Intervention for Unipolar Depression, by P. M. Lewinsohn, D. O. Antonucio, J. L. Skinmetz, & L. Teri. Copyright © 1984 by Castalia Publishing Company. All rights reserved. **587:** © 2002 by Sidney Harris. **588:** M. E. P. Seligman (1995). The effectiveness of psychotherapy: The Consumer Reports study. American Psychologist, 50, 965-974. Copyright © 1995 by

the American Psychological Association. Reprinted with permission.

Chapter 17
612: Adapted from M. M. Darley & B. Latane (1968), "Bystander Intervention in Emergencies: Diffusion of Responsibility," in Journal of Personality and Social Psychology, 8:377-383. Copyright © 1968 by the American Psychological Association. Adapted with permission. **620:** From Obedience to Authority: An Experimental View by Stanley Milgram. Copyright © 1974 by Stanley Milgram. Reprinted by permission of Alexandra Milgram. **621:** From Obedience to Authority: An Experimental View by Stanley Milgram. Copyright © 1974 by Stanley Milgram. Reprinted by permission of Alexandra Milgram. **637:** Adapted from Fig. 1 on p. 923 in T. Postmes, R. Spears, & S. Cihangir (2001), "Quality of decision making and group norms," in Journal of Personality and Social Psychology, 80, 918-930. Copyright © 2001 by the American Psychological Association. Adapted with permission.

Chapter 18
649: Adaptation of Fig. 1 on p. 1018 from R. H. Fazio, J. R. Jackson, B. C. Dunton, & C. J. Williams (1995), "Variability in automatic activation as an unobtrusive measure of racial attitudes: A bona fide pipelines?" in Journal of Personality and Social Psychology, 69, 1313-1027. Copyright © 1995 by the American Psychological Association. Adapted with permission. **650:** A. Luchens (1957) "Primary Recovery in Impression Formation, in The Order of Presentation Persuasion, edited by C. I. Hovland, p. 34-35. Yale University Press. **653:** From S. T. Friske, M. Lin, & S. L. Neuberg (1999). "The continuum model: Ten years later," in S. Chaiken & Y. Trope (eds.), Dual-process Theories in Social Psychology, p.231-254. New York: Guilford Press. **661:** R. E. Petty & J. T. Cacioppo (1984), "The effects of involvement on response to arguments quantity and quality, central and peripheral routes to persuasion," in Journal of Personality & Social Psychology, 46:6-81. Copyright © 1984 by the American Psychological Association. Adapted with permission. **668:** From S. Chen & S. M. Andersen (1999), "Relationships from the past in the present: Significant-other representation and transference in interpersonal life," in Advances in Experimental Social Psychology, 31, 123-190. Copyright 1999, Elsevier Science (USA), reproduced by permission of the publisher. **669:** Fig. 1, p. 597 from A. Aron, E. N. Aron, & D. Smollan (1992), "Inclusion of other in the self scale and the structure of interpersonal closeness," in Journal of Personality and Social Psychology, 63, 596-612. Copyright © 1992 by the American Psychological Association. Reprinted with permission. **670:** R. Sternberg (1986), "Triangular Theory of Love," in Psychological Review, 93:119-135. Copyright © 1986 by the American Psychological Association. Adapted with permission.

NAME INDEX

SUBJECT INDEX

Page numbers followed by f indicate figures; t, tables; b, boxes.

Brain, 256
  anterior system of, 179
  appraisals in, 395–396, 396f
  asymmetries in, 47–50
  blood flow in, post-traumatic stress
      disorder and, 505f
  decision making and, 338
  depression and, 545, 545f
  divisions of labor in
      perception and, 179–183
      between working memory and
          long-term memory, 280
  functional organization of, 40f–41f
  language and, 50–51
  living, pictures of, 45–47
  locational organization of, 40f–41f
  normal, versus schizophrenic brain,
      553, 553f
  obsessive-compulsive disorder and,
      540, 540f
  posterior system of, 179
  schizophrenia and, 554f
  smarter, building, research and, 256
  stimulation of, aggression and, 416f
  systems of, attention and,
      179–180
Brain damage, face recognition and, 3
Brain imaging, 179
Brainstem, 40
BRDU, neurogenesis and, 46
Breakdown of conscious restraints,
    obesity and, 367–368
Breast cancer, pessimism and, 508
Breathalyzer, 215
Breeding, selective, 57–58, 58f
Brightness, 121
Brightness constancy, 174–175
Broaden and build theory, 399
Broca's aphasia, 318–319
Broca's area, 48, 51, 318
Buffers
  acoustic, 276f
  obedience to authority and,
      621–622, 623t
  visual, 276f
Bugs, cocaine and, 220
Bulimia, 369–372
Burn patients, distraction via virtual
    reality in diminishment of
    severe pain in, 152–153
Busyness, cognitive, 656
Bystander effect, 610–613

C
Caenorhabditis elegans, 236
Caffeine, 136, 212, 213, 361
California Psychological Inventory
    (CPI), 457–458
Cancer, lung, correlation between
    smoking and, 21
Candle problem, 344, 344f, 348f
Cannabinoid receptors, 222
Cannabis, 213t, 222–223, 223t
Capacities of newborn, 69–74
Carbon dioxide, fight-or-flight
    response and, 535, 535f, 536
Caricatures, 171
Caring tendencies, selfishness and, 25
Carousel, kitten, 186, 187f
Case histories, 22
Cast shadow, 157–158
Castration, 376
Castration anxiety, 463
CAT. See Computerized axial
    tomography (CAT; CT).
Categorization, 326, 332, 333
  in amnesiac patients, dot patterns
      and, 332, 332f
  as building block of thought,
      326–333
  initial, stereotypes and, 653

neural basis of behavior and,
    331–333, 332f
processes of, 329–330
Catharsis, 418–423, 419f
Cathartic effect of violence, 4
Caudate nucleus, obsessive-compulsive
    disorder and, 540
Causal attribution, 656
Causality heuristic, 336–337
Causation, correlation and, 20–21
CCK. See Cholecystokinin (CCK).
CD-ROM links, 29
  consciousness, 231
  emotion, 425
  evolution, genes, and behavior, 63
  intelligence, 451
  language and thought, 351
  learning and conditioning, 264
  memory, 311
  motivation, 387
  perception and, 193
  personality, 491
  psychological development, 105
  psychological disorders, 567
  psychology, 29
  sensory processes, 145
  social cognition, 677
  social influence, 643
  stress, health and coping, 525
Cell membrane, semipermeable, 33
Cells
  complex, response of, 163
  glial, 33
  hypercomplex, response of, 163
  simple, response of, 163, 163f
Cellular basis of learning,
    261, 262f
Central nervous system, 38–39
Central route to persuasion, 660,
    661–662, 661f
Central sulcus, 44
Central tendency, measures of,
    A2–A4, A3f
Cerebellum, 39–42
Cerebral cortex, 41, 43
Cerebrum, 40, 43–45, 43f
Chance distribution, A6, A6f
Change, detection of, 110f
CHD. See Coronary heart disease
    (CHD).
Checking, obsessive-compulsive
    behavior and, 539
Chemicals, endogenous, 313
Chemotherapy, 236–237
Chess, 80f, 254f, 344–345, 345f
Chiasm, optic, 44
Child rearing, instrumental
    conditioning and, 244
Childhood
  cognitive development in, 74–84
  gender nonconformity in, 380, 380t
Childhood amnesia, 3–4, 10, 16–17,
    290–291, 291f
Childhood memory, Piaget's, 294
Childhood viewing of violent television,
    adult aggression and, 4, 4f
Children
  aggression in, effects of media
      violence on, 4
  development of, influence of parents
      on, 100–101
  imitation of adult aggression by,
      417, 417f, 418f
  memories of, constructive memory
      and legal system and, 299–300
  with psychological disorders, 587
  stress of, at mother's departure, 89f
Chimpanzees
  aggression and, 414–415
  language experiments and,
      324–325, 325f

Chlordiazepoxide, 593
Chlorpromazine, 37–38, 591
Cholecystokinin (CCK), 363
Chromosomes and genes, 55–57, 56f
Chronic pain, opioids in treatment of,
    140–141
Chronological age (CA), 430
Chunking
  knowledge acquisition and, 80–81
  and memory span, 301–302, 302f
  working memory and, 276
Cigarette smoking, 212, 212f, 509
  correlation between lung cancer
      and, 21
  gene for, 214
Circadian rhythm, 202
Clairvoyance, 224
Clang associations, schizophrenia and,
    549–550
Class interval, frequency distributions
    and, A2
Classical conditioning, 234, 235–241,
    260–261
  constraints on, 240–241, 241t
  diagram of, 236f
  personality development and, 470
  stimuli and responses in, 235t
Cleansing, ethnic, 500
Client-centered therapy, 582
Cliff, visual, 185, 185f, 406
Clinical psychologists, 15, 573–574
Clinical psychology, 17
Clock-dependent alerting process,
    sleep theory and, 202
Closure, grouping and, 155
Clozapine, 37–38, 592
Coaction, 606
Coca-Cola, 220
Cocaine, 219f, 220, 221f, 223t
Cocaine bugs, 220
Cochlea, 128–129, 129f
Cochlear implant, 132, 133
Codeine, 218
Coding
  of intensity and quality, 114–115,
      114f, 115f
  phonological, 273
  sensory, 113–115
  visual, 273–274, 275f
Coefficient, validity, 429
Coefficient correlation, 20, 430,
    A9–A12, A11f
Cognition
  culture and, 657
  social. See Social cognition.
Cognitive appraisal and emotion, 390,
    392–396
Cognitive approach to personality
    development, 471–476
Cognitive behavior therapy, 521
Cognitive busyness, 656
Cognitive development
  Anderson's Theory of Intelligence
      and, 437–439
  in childhood, 74–84
Cognitive dissonance theory, 626–628,
    627f, 629
Cognitive factors
  classical conditioning and, 238–240
  instrumental conditioning and,
      249–250
Cognitive impairment as reaction to
    stress, 502
Cognitive map, 251–252, 252f
Cognitive neuroscience, 16
Cognitive perspective, 11–12
  mental disorders and, 532
  psychological disorders and,
      545–548, 547t
Cognitive potentials, multiple, Ceci's
    biological theory and, 440

Cognitive social-learning person
    variables, 473
Cognitive techniques in management
    of stress, 521
Cognitive theory, stress and, 511–513
Cognitive triad, 545–546
Cognitive-behavior therapies in
    treatment of psychological
    disorders, 580–581, 581f, 581t
Cognitive-developmental theory,
    gender identity and sex typing
    and, 95–96
Coitus, premarital, 378, 378f
Coke, 220
Colds, stress and, 507f
Collective unconscious, 464
Collectivism, 412–414
College drinking, pluralistic ignorance
    and, 616–617
College students
  alcohol usage by, 216
  hazings and, 628
Color
  and brightness constancy,
      perception and, 174–175
  seeing, 121–126, 121f
Color appearance, 121–122, 122f
Color blindness, 57, 124, 124f
Color circle, 123, 123f
Color constancy, 121
Color mixture, 122–123
Color solid, 122, 122f
Color vision, 124–126, 124f, 125f, 126f
Color-matching experiment, 122
Combat fatigue, 499
Commitment, triangular theory of
    love and, 670, 670t
Common herbs in treatment of mental
    disorders, 594
Communication
  of emotion through facial
      expressions, 406–408
  language and, 314–319
  persuasive, 659–662
Community Mental Health Centers
    Act of 1963, 572
Community-based programs in
    treatment of psychological
    disorders, 583–584
Companionate love versus passionate
    love, 669–670
Competencies, social learning theory
    and, 473
Competition, cooperation versus, 498
Complementary aft3rimages, 125, 125f
Complex cell, response of, 163
Complex learning, 234, 251–256
Complex sentences, development of
    language and, 321
Compliance
  induced, 627, 627f
  social influence and, 613–625
Componential subtheory, 439, 442
Compound conditioned stimulus
    presentation, 238
Comprehension
  effects of context on, 316–317, 316f
  of language, 314
Compulsive behavior, 539
Compulsive use of drugs, 213
Computer dance, interpersonal
    attraction and, 664
Computerized axial tomography
    (CAT; CT), 45
Computers
  drawing program on, 171, 171f
  psychological processes and, 8–9
Con artists, antisocial personality
    and, 557
Concentration, 196f
Concentrative meditation, 208

Oral stage of psychosexual
development, 463–464
Organization
dimensional, of emotion, 420
long-term memory and, 285
memory and, 304, 304f, 305f
Organizational psychologists, 15
Orientation, sexual. *See* Sexual
orientation.
Osmotic thirst, 360, 360f
Outer ear, 128–129, 129f
Outline of Psychoanalysis, An, 460
Oval window, 129
Overdose, heroin, 218
Overeating, 4f, 367
Overextension of words, 320
Overgeneralization, depression
and, 547t
Overjustification effect, 2, 3f, 629

P
Pain, 137–139
chronic, opioids in treatment of,
140–141
congenital insensitivity to, 137
distraction via virtual reality
in diminishment of,
152–153
gate control theory of, 138
nonstimulus determinants of,
138–139, 138f, 139f
phasic, 138
system of, 138
tonic, 138
Pain behaviors, 141
Pair bonding and mating strategies,
670–674
Panic, vulnerability-stress model of,
537, 537f
Panic attack, 534
Panic disorders, 534–537, 535f, 536f,
537f, 581, 581f
Paradigm, temporal-integration,
271, 272f
Parallax, motion, 158
Parallel play, 84, 84f
Paranoid, definition of, 550
Paranoid schizophrenia, 569
Paraprofessionals, 585
Parapsychology, 224–229
Parasympathetic nervous system,
51, 402
Parenting styles, 91–92
Parents
influence of, on development of
children, 100–101
influence of, on personality or
intelligence of their children,
100–101
Paresis, general, 571
Paroxetine, 592
Partial genetic identity, 24
Partial reinforcement, 246–247
Partial-report experiment,
270–271, 270f, 271f,
272–273, 272f
Passion, triangular theory of love and,
670, 670t
Passionate love versus companionate
love, 669–670
Patterns
seeing, 120, 120f
temporal, 115
Pavlov's experiments, 235–236, 236f
Paxil, 38, 484, 592
PCP, 222, 223t
Peak experiences, 479
Peg-turning study, 627–628
Penicillin, 571
Penis envy, 468
People's Temple, 623, 629–630

Perception, 146–193, 148f
abstraction and, 170–173
active, perceptual development and,
186–187, 187f
attention and, 150–153
categories of, 149
CD-ROM links, 193
constructive, 294–295
of depth, perceptual development
and, 185, 185f
of distance, 156–157
disturbances of, schizophrenia and,
550–551
divisions of labor in brain and,
179–183
of forms, perceptual development
and, 184–185, 184f
localization and, 154–160
of motion, 158–160
perceptual development, 183–189
perceptual constancies and,
173–179
pitch, theories of, 130–131
recognition and, 160–170
use of, 148–149
visceral, 403
web resources, 193
Perceptual constancies, 173–179,
174f, 185
Perceptual development, 183–189
Perceptual interference, 295
Performance components, 439
Performance scale, Wechsler Adult
Intelligence Scale and, 432
Performance-contingent rewards, 3
Perfume, 134, 134f
Periaqueductal gray, 138–139
Peripheral attention, 197
Peripheral nervous system, 38–39, 51
Peripheral route to persuasion, 660,
661–662, 661f
Peripheral signals, physiological
hunger cues and, 363
Persistence, visible, sensory memory
and, 271, 272–273, 272f
Personal Construct Theory,
473–474, 474f
Personal constructs, 473–474, 473f
Personal distress, psychological
disorders and, 528–529
Personal involvement, persuasion and,
661, 661f
Personality, 452–491
antisocial, 557–558
assessment of, 454–459
behaviorist approach to, 469–471
CD-ROM links, 491
of children, influence of parents on,
100–101
cognitive approach to, 471–476
definition of, 454
development of, 463–464
effect of medications on, 484
evolutionary approach to, 481–483
genetics of, 483–489
humanistic approach to, 476–481
interactions between environment
and, 483–489
medication and, 484
oral, 463–464
personality inventories, 456–459
psychoanalytic approach to,
459–469
psychopathic, 556
and social development, 86–97
structure of, 460
web resources, 491
Personality disorders, 556–560
biological factors of, 557–558
borderline, 558–560
personality factors of, 558

social factors of, 558
types of, 556t
Personality dynamics, 460–463
Personality factors of personality
disorders, 558
Personality inventories, 456–459
Personality psychologists, 15
Personality traits, 454–459
Personalization, depression and, 547t
Person-environment relationship, 392
Perspective, perception of distance
and, 157
Persuasion, central and peripheral
route to, 660, 661–662, 661f
Persuasive communication, 659–662
Pessimism
breast cancer and, 508
illness and, 511–512, 511f
PET. *See* Positron emission
tomography (PET).
Phallic stage of psychosexual
development, 463
Phasic pain, 138
Ph.D degree, psychologists and,
573–574
Phenomena
classical conditioning and,
236–238, 236f
instrumental conditioning and,
245–248
Phenothiazines, 591
Phenylketonuria (PKU), 56–57
Pheromones, 134
Phobias, 537–538
conditioned, 258–259
innate, 258–259
simple, 537–538
snake, 537f
social, 538
systematic desensitization and in
vivo exposure and, 576
Phobic disorders, 533–541
Phonemes, 314–315
combinations of, development of
language and, 320
development of language and, 320
Phonological buffer, 275
Phonological coding, working memory
and, 273
Photographic albums, long-term
memory and, 282
Photon, 109
Physical attractiveness, interpersonal
attraction and, 664–665
Physical characteristics, behavior
genetics and, 54
Physical description, abstraction
and, 170
Physiological hunger cues, 362–363
Physiological psychologists, 15
Physiological reactions to stress,
502–510
Physiology, 5
Piaget's childhood memory, 294
Piaget's stages of cognitive
development, 74–79
Piaget's theory
alternatives to, 79–82
critique of, 78–79, 79f
Picrotoxin, 38
Piecemeal integration, 654
Pitch, 127, 130–131
Pitch perception, theories of, 130–131
Pituitary gland, 54, 364f
PK. *See* Psychokinesis (PK).
PKU. *See* Phenylketonuria (PKU).
Place theory of pitch perception, 130
Plaque, coronary heart disease and, 505
Plasticity, synaptic, 261
Platform, chimpanzee constructing, 253f
Play, parallel, 84, 84f

Pluralistic ignorance, 610, 611–612
college drinking and, 616–617
Polarization, group, group decision
making and, 634–635
Polygenic, 57
Polygon, frequency, A2
Populations, statistical inference and,
A5–A6
Positive correlation, 20, 21f
Positive emotions, 398–399, 402
Positive hallucinations, hypnosis and,
210–211
Positive psychology, 17
Positive regard, unconditional,
477–478
Positive reinforcement, learning curves
and, 243, 244t
Positron emission tomography (PET),
46–47, 47f, 179–180, 180f,
182, 268, 341, 504, 545, 545f
Postconventional morality, 85
Posterior association areas, 45
Posterior system of brain, 179
Post-event memory reconstruction,
295–296
Posthypnotic amnesia, 209, 210, 210f
Posthypnotic response, 210
Posthypnotic suggestion, 462
Post-traumatic stress disorder (PTSD),
498–501, 499f, 500f, 501f,
504–505, 505f
Potassium, 370
Potentiation, long-term, 260–261
Power function of physical
magnitude, 111
Practical abilities, componential theory
and, 439
Pragmatic rules, 335
Preattentive processes, recognition
and, 161–162, 161f
Precognition, 224
Precognitive dreams, 227
Preconscious, 459, 459f
Preconscious memories, 197
Preconventional morality, 85
Predicate, 315, 316f
Predictability
classical conditioning and, 238–240
contiguity versus, 238–239, 239f
and emotion, 239–240
stress and, 496
Preferential looking method of
studying infants, 183
Prefrontal cortex, schizophrenia
and, 554f
Prefrontal lobes, memory and, 280
Pregnancy, alcohol use and, 216
Premarital coitus, 378, 378f
Preoperational stage
of cognitive development, 76–77
Piaget's, 76–78, 77f, 78f
Presence of others, social influence
and, 606–613
Pressure, sense of, 137
Primacy effect, schematic processing
and, 650, 650t
Primary appraisal dimensions,
394, 394t
Primary auditory area, 45
Primary conditioned reinforcers,
245–246
Primary motor area, 44, 44f
Primary reinforcers, 354
Primary somatosensory area, 44
Primary visual area, 44, 45f
Primary visual cortex (V1), 180–181,
181f
Priming, 290
memory in amnesia and,
289–290, 290t
stereotypes and, 647

Sensory processes—cont'd
taste, 136–137
temperature, 137
vision, 116–126
web resources, 144
Sensory response magnitude, 272, 272f
Sensory store, memory and, 269
Sentence units, language units and processes and, 315–316, 316f
Sentences
complex, development of language and, 321
primitive, development of language and, 321
production of, 316, 316f
Separation anxiety, 89
Separation of objects, localization and, 154–155
September 11th bombing, 135f, 640, 645
Serial search, 277
Serotonin, 38, 55, 536, 592
antisocial personality and, 557
bipolar disorder and, 592
eating disorders and, 372
mood disorders and, 544
obsessive-compulsive disorder and, 540
personality and, 484
schizophrenia and, 553
seizures and, 595
Serotonin reuptake inhibitors, 592, 593
Sertraline, 592
Set point, 359, 367
Severe pain, distraction via virtual reality in diminishment of, 152–153
Sex, hormonal system involved in, 375, 375f
Sex differences
in mate preferences, evolutionary origins of, 672
sexuality and, 379
Sex hormones, 375–376
Sex typing, 93–97
Sex-linked disorders, 57
Sex-linked genes, 57
Sex-linked traits, 57
Sexual abuse, 496
Sexual Behavior
in the Human Female, 22
in the Human Male, 22
Sexual development
in adolescents, 97
early, 373–374
Sexual dysfunction, 586–587
Sexual objectification, 370–371
Sexual orientation, 379–384
causes of, 380–384, 380t
different, frequency of, 379–380
innateness of, 382–383
social determination of, 382–383
Sexual selection, 55
Sexuality
adult, 375–379, 375f
gender and, 373–384
human, 22
Shading, perception of distance and, 157–158
Shadow(s)
attached, 157–158
cast, 157–158
perception of distance and, 157–158
Shadowing, 151–152
Sham feeding, 362
Shape constancy, perception and, 175, 175f
Shaping
contextual subtheory and, 440
instrumental conditioning and, 244–245, 245f

Shared environments versus nonshared environments, effect of, on personality, 488–489
Shell shock, 499
Shermans, 222
Shock, shell, 499
Shock generator, 619–624, 619f, 620f, 621f, 623t, 626, 627
Short-term store, memory and, 269
Signal-detection theory, 111–113, 112f
Signals, 112–113
embedded in noise, 112, 112f
hunger, integration of, 363–365, 364f, 365f
peripheral, physiological hunger cues and, 363
Significance
of difference, A8–A9, A9t
statistical, A8
Silence of the Lambs, The, 557
Similarity, 336
grouping and, 155
interpersonal attraction and, 666–667
Simple cell, 163, 163f
Simple networks, 164–165, 164f, 165f
Simple phobias, 537–538
Single-cell recording, 114, 114f
Situation, defining, bystander effects and, 610–611
Situational attribution, 655
Situational correction, 656
Six Years With God, 630
Size, relative, perception of distance and, 157
Size constancy, 175–176, 176f, 185
Size-distance principle, 177
Skeletal muscles, 51
Skepticism, psi phenomena and, 228–229
Skewed distribution, A3, A3f
Skewness, A3–A4
Skills, memory in amnesia and, 289–290, 290t
Skin popping, heroin and, 218
Skinner box, 243, 243f, 252
Skinner's experiments, instrumental conditioning and, 242–245
Sleep
avoidance of problems in, 203, 203t
and dreams, 199–207
electrophysiological activity during, 201f
non-REM (NREM), 200–202, 204
opponent-process model of, 202
REM versus NREM, 200–202, 204
stages of, 199–207, 200f, 201f
succession of stages of, 200, 201f
Sleep apnea, 204
Sleep debt, 203
Sleep deprivation, 202–203, 202f, 203f, 509–510
Sleep disorders, 202–204
Sleep drive, homeostatic, 202
Sleep theory, 202
Sleeping pills, 204
Slow to warm up temperament, 87
Smarter brain, building, research and, 256
Smell, 132–135
of death in insects, 134
minimum stimuli for, 108t
in newborn, 71
system of, 134–135, 135f
Smoking, 212, 212f, 509
correlation between lung cancer and, 21
gene for, 214
Smooth muscles, 51
Snake phobia, 537f
Snellen acuity, 120

Sniffing, heroin and, 218
Snorting cocaine, 220
Snow lights, cocaine and, 220
Social behavior, early, 88–89, 89f
Social change, 618f
Social cognition, 644–677
attitudes, 658–664
CD-ROM links, 677
definition of, 646
impression formation and, 646–658
interpersonal attraction, 664–674
modes of, 674
web resources, 676
Social cognitive neuroscience, 16
Social desirability effects, 22
Social development, personality and, 86–97
Social facilitation, 606–608, 606f, 607f
Social factors of personality disorders, 558
Social influence, 604–643
CD-ROM links, 643
compliance and obedience, 613–625
group interactions, 632–640
informational, 616
internalization, 626–632
normative, 616
presence of others and, 606–613
social psychological views of inexplicable happenings, 640–641
web resources, 643
Social inhibition, 606–608, 607f
Social learning
gender differences in mate selection and, 672–673
personality development and, 469–471
Social learning theory, 414, 415–417, 416f
gender identity and sex typing and, 94–95
personality development and, 472–473
Social norms, 609, 632
Social perspective to schizophrenia, 555, 555f
Social phobias, 538
Social psychology, 606
Social roles, influence of, on mate selection, 673
Social stereotype, 296
Social workers, psychiatric, 573–574
Social-cognitive theory, 472–473
Socially acquired process, perceptual development as, 188–189
Sociobiology, 481
Sociocultural approaches
to development as alternative to Piaget's theory, 82
to therapy in treatment of psychological disorders, 582–586
Sociocultural causes of anorexia and bulimia, 370–372
Sociological perspective, mental disorders and, 532
Sociopaths, 389, 557
Solar spectrum, 121, 121f
Somatic system, 38–39, 51
Somatosensory area, primary, 44
Sound
physics and psychology of, 122
timbre of, 127–128, 127f
Sound intensity, 129–130, 129f
Sound waves, 127–128, 127f
Sounds, preference for, in newborns, 72, 72f
Source wavelengths, color and brightness constancy and, 174

Span of apprehension, 270
Spatial intelligence, 437f, 437t
Special factors (s), intelligence tests and, 434
Specialization, hemispheric, 10, 50
Species
animal, ability of, to learn human language, 324–325
conditioning in varieties of, 236–237
Specific abilities, intelligence and, 439
Specific processors, intelligence and, 439
Specificity, coding and, 115
Spectrum, solar, 121, 121f
Speech
development of, 68
egocentric, 82
private, 82
Speech sounds, language units and processes and, 314–315
Speed, 220
Speed freak, 220
Sperling's experiments, sensory memory and, 270–271
Spinal cord, 40
Spinal cord lesions, relationship between emotionality and, 403, 403f
Spindles, sleep and, 200
Split-brain research, 48–50, 48f, 49f
Spoken words as symbols, 148–149
Spontaneous recovery, 236
Spontaneous remission, psychotherapy and, 587–588
Spurious associations, 255
St. John's wort, 594
Stage theory of development, Erikson's, 465
Standard, stimulus intensity and, 109
Standard deviation, A4, A5
Standard scores, statistical inference and, A7–A8
Stanford Prison Experiment, 632–634, 633f
Stanford-Binet Intelligence Scale, 430–431, 430f, 431f, 431t, 432
Stapes, 129
Starvation, effects on, on rats with VMH lesions, 365, 365f
Statistical inference, A5–A9
Statistical methods and measurement, A1–A12
coefficient of correlation, A9–A12
descriptive statistics, A2–A5
statistical inference, A5–A9
Statistical norms, deviation from, psychological disorders and, 528–529
Statistical significance, 19, A8
Statistics, 18, 19
definition of, A1
descriptive, A2–A5
Stepping reflex, 68
Stereoscope, Holmes-Bates, 159f
Stereotype activation, automatic, 648, 649f
Stereotype threat, 652
Stereotypes, 646–647
automatic, 647–649, 649f
behavioral effects of, 652t
cognitive effects of, 652t
controlling, 654
effects of, 652t
impression formation and, 646–652, 653, 653f
and information processing, 649–651, 650t
self-fulfilling, 651–652
social, 296
Sternberg memory-scanning task, 277

Valproate, 593
Variable, 18
Variable interval (VI), 247f, 247t, 248
Variable ratio (VR), 247, 247f, 247t, 248f
Variance, 443, A4, A5t
Variation, distribution differing in, A4
Ventromedial hypothalamic syndrome, 363–364
Verb phrase, 316, 316f
Verbal labels and abstraction, 172f
Verbal scale, Wechsler Adult Intelligence Scale and, 432
Vesicles, synaptic, 35–36
VI. *See* Variable interval (VI).
Vicarious learning, 415–416
Vicarious reinforcement, 470
View-Master toys, binocular disparity and, 156
Violence
 likelihood of, mental disorders and, 573, 573f
 media, effects of, on children's aggression, 4, 4f, 419, 419f, 422f
Virtual reality, distraction via, in diminishment of severe pain, 152–153
Virtuosos, hypnotic, 210
Visceral perception, 403
Visible persistence, sensory memory and, 271, 272–273, 272f
Vision, 116–126
 color, theories of, 124–126, 124f, 125f, 126f
 light and, 116
 minimum stimuli for, 108t, 109f
 in newborn, 69–70, 70f
Visual acuity, 70f, 120
 contrast sensitivity and, 184
 decrease in, in periphery, 118, 118f
 tests of, 120, 120f
Visual area, primary, 44, 45f
Visual buffers, 276f

Visual cliff, 185, 185f, 406
Visual coding, working memory and, 273–274, 275f
Visual cortex
 perception and, 180–182, 181f
 primary, 180–181, 181f
Visual field, 69–70
Visual hallucinations, schizophrenia and, 551
Visual neglect, 341
Visual pathways, 45f
Visual search task, 162, 162f
Visual system, 116–118, 116f, 117f, 118f
Visual-spatial sketchpad, 275
Vital air, Chinese view of emotions and, 570
VR. *See* Variable ratio (VR).
Vulnerabilities, knowledge of, mental health and, 600
Vulnerability-stress model
 mental disorders and, 532–533
 of panic and agoraphobia, 537, 537f

W
WAIS. *See* Wechsler Adult Intelligence Scale (WAIS).
Wakefulness, opponent-process model of, 202
Waking zombies, 202–203
Wanting versus liking, 355, 356
Warmth
 client-centered therapy and, 582
 interpersonal relationship of, psychotherapy and, 589
Washing, obsessive-compulsive behavior and, 539
Water pipe, cannabis and, 222
Wave, sound, 127
Wavelengths
 available, 174
 of color, 121, 121f
 light, 116, 121f, 130

 of sound, 130
 source, 174
Weapon focus, selective attention and, 151
Web resources
 consciousness, 231
 emotion, 424–425
 evolution, genes, and behavior, 63
 intelligence, 450
 language and thought, 351
 learning and conditioning, 264
 memory, 310
 motivation, 386–387
 perception and, 193
 personality, 491
 psychological development, 105
 psychological disorders, 567
 for psychology, 29
 sensory processes, 144
 social cognition, 676
 social influence, 643
 stress, health and coping, 525
Weber fraction, 110
Weber-Fechner law, 109–111
Wechsler Adult Intelligence Scale (WAIS), 432, 432t, 433f
Wechsler Intelligence Scale for Children (WISC), 432, 432t, 433f
Weight control
 dieting and, 368
 programs of, 368–369, 369t
Wernicke-Geschwind model, 51
Wernicke's aphasia, 318–319
Wernicke's area, 50–51, 318
White matter, 43
White Nights, Jim Jones and, 630, 630f
White noise, 224
Who, 130
Whole-report condition, 270
Window, oval, 129
Withdrawal, 213, 357, 551
Women's liberation movement, 480

Word associations, idiosyncratic, schizophrenia and, 549
Word salad, schizophrenia and, 549
Word units, language units and processes and, 315
Words, 315
 development of language and, 320–321
 perception of, 165, 165f
Working backward from goal, 343
Working memory, 273–280
 division of brain labor between long-term memory and, 280
 systems of, 275–276, 276f
 transfer from, to long-term memory, 279, 279f
World Health Organization, 529
World Trade Center bombing, 135f, 640, 645
Written words as symbols, 148–149

X
X chromosomes, 57
Xanax, 593
Xylocaine, 34

Y
Y chromosome, 57
Y intersection, 164
Yoga, 208
Yoked controls in stress experiment, 507–508, 508f
Young-Helmholtz theory, 124–125

Z
Zen, 208
Zoloft, 38, 592
Zombies, waking, 202–203